COLLECTED WORKS OF A.M. KLEIN

COMPLETE POEMS

PART 2

A.M. KLEIN

Complete Poems

PART 2
ORIGINAL POEMS, 1937–1955
AND POETRY TRANSLATIONS

EDITED BY
ZAILIG POLLOCK

UNIVERSITY OF TORONTO PRESS
Toronto   Buffalo   London

© University of Toronto Press 1990
Toronto   Buffalo   London
Printed in the United States of America

ISBN 0-8020-5802-7

Printed on acid-free paper

Canadian Cataloguing in Publication Data

Klein, A. M. (Abraham Moses), 1909-1972.
   Complete poems

   (Collected works of A.M. Klein)
   ISBN 0-8020-5802-7 (set)

   I. Pollock, Zailig. II. Title. III. Series:
   Klein, A. M. (Abraham Moses), 1909-1972. Collected
   works of A.M. Klein.

   PS8521.L45A17   1990   C811'.52   C90-094506-0
   PR9199.3.K588A17 1990

FRONTISPIECE: Klein in the early 1940s
National Archives Canada, 58346
Photo by Associated Screen News Limited, Montreal

This book has been published with the help of grants from the Canadian Federation for the Humanities, using funds provided by the Social Sciences and Humanities Research Council of Canada, and from the Canada Council and the Ontario Arts Council under their block grant programs.

Contents

Preface xvii

ORIGINAL POEMS, 1937–1955

c. 1937/1937

Blueprint for a Monument of War 453
Of Daumiers a Portfolio 458

c. 1938/1938

Barricade Smith: His Speeches 463
Of Castles in Spain 473
Childe Harold's Pilgrimage [Version 1] 475
Childe Harold's Pilgrimage [Version 2 (c. 1953/c. 1955)] 480

c. 1938/1940

To the Chief Musician, a Psalm of the Bratzlaver, a Parable 486
To the Chief Musician, a Psalm of the Bratzlaver, When He Considered How the Pious Are Overwhelmed 487
Of Remembrance 488
To the Chief Musician: A Psalm of the Bratzlaver, Touching a Good Gardener 489
To the Chief Musician, a Psalm of the Bratzlaver, Which He Wrote Down As the Stammerer Spoke 491

c. 1940/1940

In Re Solomon Warshawer [Version 1] 493
In Re Solomon Warshawer [Version 2 (c. 1953/1955)] 498
For the Chief Physician 505
Grace before Poison 505
Maschil of Abraham: A Prayer When He Was in the Cave 506
A Prayer of Abraham That He Be Forgiven for Blasphemy 508
A Prayer of the Afflicted, When He Is Overwhelmed 508
A Psalm for Five Holy Pilgrims, Yea, Six on the King's Highway 509
A Psalm of Abraham concerning the Arrogance of the Son of Man 510
A Psalm of Abraham of That Which Was Visited upon Him 510
A Psalm of Abraham, Praying a Green Old Age 511
A Psalm of Abraham, to Be Written Down and Left on the Tomb of Rashi 512
A Psalm of Abraham, Touching His Green Pastures 513
A Psalm of Abraham, When He Was Sore Pressed 514
A Psalm of Abraham, Which He Made Because of Fear in the Night 515
A Psalm of Justice, and Its Scales 516
A Psalm of Resignation 517
A Psalm, to Be Preserved against Two Wicked Words 517
A Psalm to Teach Humility 518
Shiggaion of Abraham Which He Sang unto the Lord 519
A Song of Degrees 520
To the Chief Bailiff, a Psalm of the King's Writ 521
To the Chief Musician, Al-Taschith, Michtam of Abraham; When One Sent, and They Watched the House to Kill Him 521
To the Chief Musician, a Psalm of Israel, to Bring to Remembrance 522
To the Chief Musician, Who Played for the Dancers 523
To the Prophets, Minor and Major, a Psalm or Song 524

c. 1940/1941

A Benediction for the New Moon 525
A Prayer of Abraham, against Madness 526
A Psalm of Abraham, When He Hearkened to a Voice, and There Was None 527
A Psalm of Time and the Firmament 528
A Song for Wanderers 528

vii / Contents

c. 1941/1941

A Psalm of Abraham, concerning That Which He Beheld upon the Heavenly Scarp 530
A Psalm or Prayer – Praying His Portion with Beasts 531
Ballad of Quislings 532
Ballad of the Days of the Messiah 533
Ballad of the Dream That Was Not Dreamed 534
Ballad of the Evil Eye 536
Ballad of the Nuremberg Tower Clock 537
Ballad of the Nursery Rhymes 538
Ballad of the Thwarted Axe 539
Ballad of the Werewolves 541
Of the Friendly Silence of the Moon 542
Polish Village 542
Sennet from Gheel 543
Yehuda Halevi, His Pilgrimage 544

1941

In Memoriam: Arthur Ellis [Version 1] 557
In Memoriam: Arthur Ellis [Version 2 (c. 1946/1946)] 559
In Memoriam: Arthur Ellis [Version 3 (1954)] 561

c. 1942/1942

Autobiographical 564
Come Two, like Shadows 567
Dentist 568
Desideratum 569
Et j'ai lu tous les livres 570
Girlie Show 571
The Golem 572
Love 573
My Dear Plutophilanthropist 574
Pawnshop 575
Penultimate Chapter 577
That Legendary Eagle, Death 578
Variation of a Theme 579

c. 1942/1943

The Hitleriad 581

c. 1943/1943

Actuarial Report 607
And in That Drowning Instant 608
Not All the Perfumes of Arabia [Version 1] 610
Not All the Perfumes of Arabia [Version 2 (c. 1952/1952)] 611

c. 1944/1944

Address to the Choirboys 613
Basic English 615
Bread 617
Commercial Bank 618
The Green Old Age 619
The Library 620
Montreal 621
Ni la mort ni le soleil 623
A Psalm Touching Genealogy 624
Spring Exhibit 624

c. 1942/c. 1944

Epitaph 626
Les Vespasiennes 627
Of Tradition 628
Post-War Planning 629
Saga the First 629
Song without Music 630
Tailpiece to an Anthology 631
Tribute to the Ballet Master [Version 1] 631
Tribute to the Ballet Master [Version 2] 632

c. 1944/1945

Portrait of the Poet as Landscape 634
Portrait of the Poet as Landscape [Deleted Section] 640

ix / Contents

c. 1945/1945

Indian Reservation: Caughnawaga 641
The Provinces 642
The Rocking Chair 644
Sonnet Unrhymed 645

c. 1945/1946

Air-Map 646
The Break-up 646
The Cripples 647
For the Sisters of the Hotel Dieu 648
Frigidaire 649
Grain Elevator 650
M. Bertrand 651
The Snowshoers 652
The Sugaring 653

c. 1946/1946

Doctor Drummond 655
The Notary 656
Political Meeting 657
Quebec Liquor Commission Store 659
The Spinning Wheel 660
The White Old Lady 661
Sestina on the Dialectic 662
Meditation upon Survival 663

1946

At Home 665
Lowell Levi [Version 1] 666
Portrait, and Commentary [Version 2 of 'Lowell Levi'] 666
To the Lady Who Wrote about Herzl 668
Wishing to Embarrass Me, but Politely 669
Wrestling Ring 669

x / Contents

c. 1945/1947

Beaver 671
Dominion Square 672

c. 1947/1947

Elegy 673
Song of Innocence 678
Annual Banquet: Chambre de Commerce 678
Dress Manufacturer: Fisherman 679
Filling Station 680
Hormisdas Arcand 681
Krieghoff: Calligrammes 682
Les Filles majeures 683
Librairie Delorme 684
Lone Bather 685
Lookout: Mount Royal 686
M. le juge Dupré 687
Monsieur Gaston 688
The Mountain 689
Parade of St. Jean Baptiste 691
Pastoral of the City Streets 694
Sire Alexandre Grandmaison 696
Université de Montréal 697
Winter Night: Mount Royal 698

1947

O God! O Montreal! 700

1948

Cantabile 701

c. 1950/1950

Benedictions 704
Stance of the Amidah 704
Who Hast Fashioned 706
Of the Making of Gragers 707

xi / Contents

1952/1954
    Epigrams [1] 708

c. 1953/1955
    Spinoza: On Man, on the Rainbow 714

1955
    Epigrams [2] 715

POETRY TRANSLATIONS

ARAMAIC

    The Kaddish [Version 1] 721
    The Kaddish [Version 2] 722

HEBREW

Solomon ben Moses ha-Levi Alkabeẓ
    O Site Most Kingly, O Royal Sanctum 724

Chaim Nachman Bialik
    Beneath the Burden ... 725
    The Chastisement of God 726
    Come, Gird Ye Your Loins, and in Might Robe Yourselves 727
    God Grant My Part and Portion Be ... 728
    The Lord Has Not Revealed 730
    On My Returning 732
    The City of Slaughter [Version 1] 733
    In the City of Slaughter [Version 2 of 'The City of Slaughter'] 744
    The Dance of Despair [Version 1] 749
    Dance of Despair [Version 2 of 'The Dance of Despair'] 752
    Seer, Begone [Version 1] 755
    O Thou Seer, Go Flee Thee – Away [Version 2 of 'Seer, Begone'] 756
    When the Days Shall Grow Long 757
    The Word 759

xii / Contents

    Thy Breath, O Lord, Passed Over and Enkindled Me [Version 1] 760
    A Spirit Passed before Me [Version 2 of 'Thy Breath, O Lord, Passed
        Over and Enkindled Me'] 761
    Upon the Slaughter 763
    Stars Flicker and Fall in the Sky 764

Immanuel (ben Solomon) of Rome
    The Prescription 765

Micah Joseph Lebensohn
    Wine 766

Yehuda Halevi
    To Jerusalem the Holy 768
    Bear Thou, O Wind, My Love 768
    Lord, Hele Me, Y-wis I Shal Be Heled 769
    Ode to Zion 769
    O Dove beside the Water Brook 771
    O Heighte Sovereign, O Worldes Prys 772
    Rubaiyat of Yehuda Halevi 773

Poets of the Yishuv

Abraham Broides
    Upon the Highway 776

Uri Zvi Greenberg
    Kings of the Emek 777
    Mother Jerusalem 778

Judah Karni (Valovelski)
    Be There No Altar 780
    Make Blind, O Sun of Jerusalem 780
    With Every Stone 781

David Shimoni (Shimonovitz)
    The Glory of the Homeland 782

Abraham Shlonsky
    Behold 784
    Sabbath 785

Mordecai Temkin
    Unfavoured 786

Rachel (Rachel Bluwstein)
    Now Such Am I ... 787
    Rachel 787
    Kinnereth 788
    Dawn 789
    The Childless One 789

YIDDISH

Mordecai Etziony
    The Prayer of a Physician 790

Jacob Glatstein
    The Eleventh: In Memory of Isaac, Son of the Tailor 792
    The Gifted One 793
    Smoke 794

Moyshe Leib Halpern
    Portrait of the Artist 795
    Canticum Canticorum 796
    The Last Song 797
    Ki-Ki 797
    The Golden Parrot 798
    Conceit Curious 799
    Last Will and Testament 799

Leib Jaffe
    We Are a Generation, Heaven-Doomed 800
    You Walk upon Your Sunlit Roads 801

H. Leivick (Leivick Halpern)
    No More Tears 802
    The Windows Are Grated 803

Mani-Leib (Mani-Leib Brahinsky)
    Sunset 804

Jacob Isaac Segal
    And This I Know 804
    Autobiographical 805
    Goats 806
    A King 807
    King Rufus 808

Confession 809
Old Gold 811
Reb Zorach 812
Song 813
War 814
Speak to Your People, Therefore, in This Wise 815

Jewish Folk-Songs
    Shall I Be a Rabbi? 816
    Come You Here, Philosopher 817
    Charm 818
    Tear Not Your Hair, My Sweetheart 818
    And When One Burns – One Burns Brandy 819
    On the Attic Sleeps a Roof 819
    Yoma, Yoma, Play Me a Ditty 820
    Hush! Hush! 821
    We Ask Our Boarding-Mistress 822
    Song of Wine 822
    The Golden Parrakeet 824
    When I Knead the Dough 825
    I Go upon the Balcony 825
    Once upon a Time; This 826
    Better a Hebrew Teacher 827
    O My Mother Sent Me 828
    On the Hill, over the Hill 829
    Gone Is the Yesterday 829
    And at My Prayers I Will Quiver 830
    Asks the World an Old, Old Question 831
    And When Messiah Will Come 831
    O What Do You Wish, My Dearest Child 832
    Tell Me, Pretty Maiden, O Hearken Pretty Maiden 833
    What Is Loftier than a House? 833
    When He Has Frolicked for a Little 834
    Lovely Am I, O Lovely, and Lovely Is My Name 834
    I Sit Me Down upon a Stone 835

Chassidic Folk-Songs
    L'chayim, Rebbe! 835
    Oy, Our Rebbenu 836

God Willing, at the Rebbe's 836
Myerka, My Son 838
A Thou Song 839
Levi Yitschok's Kaddish 840
M'laveh Malkeh 841
Thou Hast Chosen Us 842
O There, O There, Where Is Our Holy Rebbe [Version 1] 842
Where Our Good Rebbe Is to Be Found [Version 2 of 'O There, O There, Where Is Our Holy Rebbe'] 843
The Rebbe, He Wanted [Version 1] 844
The Rebbe, He Wanted [Version 2] 845
In God's Good Time 847
A Burglary 848
Tell Us, Rebbenu 849
Yoshka, Yoshka 850
Oy, Vey, Rebbenu 850
Our Rebbe, the Miracle-Worker, Once 851
And When Our Rebbe Walks 852
Our Rebbe [Version 1] 853
Our Rebbe [Version 2] 854
My Noddle It Is Humming 854
The Train 855
How Fares the King? 856
The Rebbele, the Gabbai'le, the Cantor'l, the Shamash'l 857
Tsig, Tsigitsapel 858
Miracles and Wonders 859
Akavyah ben M'halallel 860
Omar Adoishem l'Ya-akoiv! 860
Bar Yochai 862
The Rebbe Elimelech 862
Yonder! Yonder! 864
Vesomachto 865

LATIN

Horace
    Of the Ancient House of the Clinii [Version 1] 866
    Of the Ancient House of the Clinii [Version 2] 868
    To Lydia 869
    To Leuconoe 870
    To L. Munatius Plancus 871

Abbreviations 875

Textual Notes
    Original Poems, 1937–1955 879
    Poetry Translations 924

Explanatory Notes
    Original Poems, 1937–1955 953
    Poetry Translations 1029

Appendix A: Contents of Published and Unpublished Collections 1061

Appendix B: Poems Revised in the Early Fifties 1075

Appendix C: Pages Which End with the Last Line of a Stanza or Verse Paragraph 1079

Index of Titles 1081

Index of First Lines 1099

Preface

This is Part 2 of an edition of A.M. Klein's *Complete Poems*. Part 1 contains the Introduction, Textual Chronology, Editorial Procedures, Acknowledgments, Biographical Chronology, original poems arranged chronologically up to 1934, and textual and explanatory notes for those poems. Part 2 contains the remainder of Klein's original poems, his poetry translations, textual and explanatory notes for those original poems and poetry translations, and appendices listing (1) the contents of the published and unpublished collections, (2) the poems revised in the early fifties, and (3) pages which end with the last line of a stanza or verse paragraph.

ORIGINAL POEMS, 1937–1955

c. 1937/1937

Blueprint for a Monument of War

Instructions to the stenographer:
Address: The Board for Monuments of War
The thirteenth residence, Rue de la Mort;
If within five days not delivered on the chairman's desk,
5 Return to My Self, Esq.

Copy for Mr. Algernon B. Brown –
Look up the who's who for the alphabet,
Trailing his name, like the train of milady's gown.
(This is the man who sold the soldiers shoes –
10 Aye, what a host of feet there marched then, wet!
Now is he rated pillar of the town,
Sits with his footwear – first-class – on the desk,
Puffs at his pipe, is sad about the war,
And plans great honour for the boots that walk no more ...)

15 Also a copy for Sir Alfred Poyns.
(General of the Army – *he* survived!
Great man! The hour struck. He girded his loins.
And with the arrival of slaughter, he arrived.
His ghost now pens his memoirs, to narrate
20 His epic of indomitable will
His saga, both of destiny and fate,

How he was bravely timid, shrewdly rash,
And how he bought – attend the bargain, and thrill!
The salient for ten thousand lives, cold cash ...)

25 Omit not, please, Rev. Smith and Rabbi Cohen,
The one in his temple, t'other in his church,
Twin footstools, burnished, of the heavenly throne.
These men know monuments; it is their perch.
They also know, as they have always known
30 Infallibly what side the Lord was on.

Address him – lest we forget – the editor:
Mustering infantry in pica;
                                   zooming in paragraphs;
Throwing his word-grenades;
                                   featly bombarding
Big Bertha headlines on the metropolis.
35 Advancing the slogans;
                                retreating with epigrams;
Fighting courageously;
                                bugling the call; –
All
On the map that hangs upon his office-wall!

(His essays did prelude obituaries.
40 *Hinc illae lachrymae*, this blueprint packet:
The editorial we; the obit; the *hic jacet*.)

Epistle and Enclosure:
The blueprint's clear, and all who skip may see:
Gathered the unseamed flesh, the jagged bone
45 Of the eclectic anonymity,
The valiant alias, the brave unknown.
Dig, then, the grave, as deep as spade will go –
Who lived in a trench, may in a trench lie dead.
Lift up the hero, minus nose, thumb, toe,
50 And crypt the treaty underneath his head.
So is it wiser. Parchment will preserve

Mortality from the immortal worm.
The monument? 'Tis simple, but 'twill serve:
To wit: a stone, a cairn, cemented, firm.
55 The corpse, perforce such sure impedimentum
Never to rise. *Exegi monumentum!*

Memorials need mnemonics. Surely, then,
Our pawn, the unknown soldierman, y-clept
Andrew Angelo François Xavier Sam
60 Stanislaus Thomas Abraham
Jones
(God rest his bones)
Deserves some chiselling, grandiloquent and apt!

So be it.
65 Who shall gainsay that on a tombstone, Latin
Is for the great departed
A winding sheet of satin?
Wherefore, Horatius Flaccus, who fought and ran away
And therefore lived to fashion many a martial lay,
70 Be with us now.

Dvlce et decorvm est pro patria mori

(What is more beautiful than dying? Think,
More beautiful than flowering into flesh,
Than gaining glory in indelible ink
75 Upon an archive page, and what more noble
Than being consumed by scientific stink?

Nothing; unless for some wild slogan's sake
To hang in barbed wire i' the light o' the moon.
And hear the thunder roll, the thunder break,
80 And watch the issuing guts until you swoon ...)

Mors et fvgacem perseqvitvr virvm

And if, among the number of men, there be
Some men whom Death has skipped –
Why, gentlemen, your duty is most clear:
85 Conscript, conscript.

Virtvs reclvdens immeritis mori
Coelvm, negata temptat iter via

(Behold my brother, sans both legs
A military loss
90 However, now he ambulates
On a Victoria Cross.)
P.S.
If you desire English text, then go
To Rupert Brooke whose bugles always blow;
95 Or Mr. Tennyson
Who will tell any son
Of battle's benison!
P.P.S.
Appendix for the Pious – Isaiah, chapter sixty-seven.
100   And it shall come to pass that the king's high counsellor,
desiring honourable mention in a footnote of the chronicles,
shall stand up upon a balcony and he shall shout: They hold
me in derision.
The alien three oceans beyond us holds me in derision.
105 Wherefore you shall be amazed, you shall stand confused, you
shall not know when or how. It shall be a thing you have
not heard.
But the emissaries of the whetted tongue shall go forth to the
market-places, and shall stand them up upon a chariot, and
110 shall pound upon their chests, groaning: Honour, honour.
Until you too shall rise, shaking your fists, and crying with a
loud voice: We shall not be held in derision.
You shall journey long distances to lands in a picture-book.
Your farewells shall be full of glory; paid speakers will laud
115 you.

The manufactories of bunting shall do much trade; the writers of martial musick shall win them renown.
The speeches shall be uttered, the bugles shall be blown, and the kisses wafted
120 And you shall go the long way over many seas.
This also I know, that the high-counsellor and his brother the swordsmith will rub their hands, warm at the prospect of seven fat years
And will hasten to their secret chambers, there to calculate
125 calculations.
And you shall journey great distances to lands in a picture-book,
And shall discover yourselves in the midst of a strange people, who have not ever lifted a little finger against you, or said
130 a short word ill of you
And you shall array yourselves, each against the other
And the voice of the captain shall thunder, and it shall rain brimstone.
For many days you shall rest in the watery pit
135 Until your feet shall be swollen, and you shall remember with great longing a pair of slippers and a chair.
Vermin shall crawl about you, the louse shall move in on you
And you shall curse your fingers because they are few.
Worse than the great noise of the instruments of war shall be
140 the terrible silence
When you shall bethink yourself of kith and kin, and of the king's counsellor
Causing himself to be regarded full-face and in profile.
The generals shall be bathed in lotions, the captains shall be
145 perfumed with myrrh
And you, son of man, shall own mud as your breastplate, and mire as your armour.
The battle shall rage, and men with strange devices shall signal to one another
150 Signals of victory, honour, and inches of land.
Until both you and the alien shall be weary, and the counsellors weary of profit.
    Peace shall be heard in the land, but who shall hear it?

Truce shall be called in the land, who shall hearken unto it?
155 For your brothers shall lie in foreign fields, where the crow
may bring them the tiding, and the worm whisper the
news.

c. 1937/1937   1937

Of Daumiers a Portfolio

I

His Lordship

Who remembers not this eminently capable man,
Magician of costumes; factotum: changer of roles?
How, in his youth, he gowned himself: a lawyer:
And with cold logic proved contiguous the poles ...
5 How, later, having wedded a legal fiction,
His wife: the Corporation: endowed him, debtor;
Whereat he stayed, in gratitude, for all time faithful,
Except when other corporations endowed him better ...
Again, having eloquently defended on the hustings
10 The chastity of three deflowered regimes –
Behold him in overalls, among the paupers!
I am the toiler's friend! He smiles; he beams.
On to the bench he goes now, gifted maestro;
Before him walks a crier, and he cries:
15 Silence! The Honourable Mr. Justice Hogarth,
Arriving in robes judicial, his new disguise!

II

Sentence

These robbers filched electricity:
This is a crime to property!
In jail for one month let them be,
20 To privately own – their privacy.

III

A Song of Three Degrees

The prisoner confessed most willingly.
Of his own free will he confessed, my Lord.
There were no threats, no, nor cajolery.
I say this on my good policeman's word.
25 The bruises on his face? The bruises? They're
The sure stigmata of a contrite course:
Behold you, too, how penitence doth stare
Out of a black eye, coloured with remorse.
I swear there was no use of physical force.

IV

Prosecutor

30 Holy, holy, holy,
Consider the prosecutor;
Who failing arguments acute
Finds arguments acuter.

V

Public Utility

    The pimp, he pays his fine and costs,
35 Which monies go to stock
    The Treasury which builds more streets
    For streetwalkers to walk.

    The wench, alas, must earn her fine.
    So back to her tenement,
40 This civil servant toils and spins;
    She keeps the Government.

VI

La Glorieuse Incertitude

    The law is certain; and the law is clear.
    Having invoked Justinian, exorcised
    That Pothier of the tomes where s is f,
45 The five good judges of the higher court,
    Each conning the same gospel, toothlessly
    Splutter their wisdom on the fleur-de-lys.
    Two greybeards, cutting syllogistic dolls,
    Issue their answer: unambiguous *Yea*.
50 Two others, scissoring a similar script,
    With many curlecued wherefores, shape their *Nay*.
    The fifth, a younger sage, and nimbler, skips
    Trippingly on his hypothetic way
    To halt him, cutely, pendent in mid-air.
55 The law is certain; and the law is clear.

VII

Sleuth

Dizzy amidst a whorl of fingerprints;
Playing ballistics; learned; nobody's fool;
Reading from unseen ink invisible hints;
Look! A detective of the modern school.
60 By sniffing, he could trace a noxious wind.
He solved *The Mystery of the Door Ajar;*
In pride, he framed his cases, – even pinned
A rap of arson on a falling star.
So trained, and so instructed, no surprise
65 Startled his rapt admirers when he found –
Because in Hull, tears shone in a servant's eyes,
And at Quebec, a swabbing sailor groaned,
A man on relief at Hochelaga wept –
The province by sedition swept.

VIII

Guardian of the Law

70 How have you become not that which once you were,
Brass-buttoned blue-serged hero of my youth!
I laid me down, when six, to sleep untroubled
By dreams of ogres, fearsome and uncouth,
Or sound of robbers whispering in the dark;
75 And this, because you walked the street and park.
A prober of door-knobs, peerer into glass-fronts,
From curb to curb escorter of the blind,
Friendly your smile to me that day I wandered
Around the corner, and wept, and could not find
80 The way back to the apron of my home.
You held me, dried my tears, and wiped my nose –
(Your uniform smelled like my own father's clothes) –
You led me, and I followed, like a mouse,

Until I suddenly ran, to recognize my house!
85 And now have I seen you in your colour, slave,
Paid hater of your kin!
Against the unarmed and helpless, mightily brave
Mightily noble – for a fin!
For I have seen you grin
90 Outside the factory where my father is
A spool for a spool of thread
Yes, seen you grin, and strike my father's friend
With baton on the head!
So do you earn your bread,
95 And butter,
And good red jam well-bled!

IX

Corrigendum

Now finally, by way of corrigendum:
Judges there be, not only solemn, but wise
To whom their justice is no thing of trade.
100 The law requests I make this fair addendum.
It is made.

c. 1937/1937   1937

c. 1938/1938

Barricade Smith: His Speeches

I

Of Violence

What does the word mean: *Violence?*
                                              Are we not content?
Do not our coupons fall, like manna, from the bonds?
Are we not all well-fed?
                                   Save for twelve months of Lent?
Is it not slander to aver the Boss absconds
5 With all the embezzled dollars in his delicate hand?
Is there not heard a sound
Of belching in the land?

Who, then, would speak of violence, uncouth and impolite?
Surely not we, the meek, the docile, the none-too-bright!
10 The askers with cap-in-hand, the rebels, à Emily Post
Who know too well our place, our manners,
                                                and our host!

Wherefore, though wages slither, and upward soar the rates,
Not we will be the churls rudely to doubt that boast
Of Labor and Capital, that Siamese twin alright,

15 One of whom eats, the other defecates.

The Board of Directors sits
And cudgels its salaried wits: —
At cost of life and limb
Show profits, and still be
20 Unviolent as a hymn.

They syncopate your groans
                        on gramaphones;
Your muscles throb in their Rolls-Royce;
They triturate your sweat in cocktail-shakers.

But they are not violent, for violence is wicked;
25 And worse than that — I shudder to say the word,
That fell indictment —
It simply is not cricket!

Go therefore, tell your wives that the breadbox must stay breadless,
The rent unpaid, the stove unheated, you enslaved;
30 Because you *must* be above *all* things, well-behaved.
And having uttered these heroic words, slink hence
Into some unleased corner, and there vanish —
But not with any violence.

II

Of Dawn and Its Breaking

Where will you be
35 When the password is said and the news is extra'd abroad,
And the placard is raised, and the billboard lifted on high,
And the radio network announces its improvised decree:
You are free?
Where will it find you, that great genesis?
40 Preparing your lips for a kiss?

Waiting the call of next in a barbershop?
Rapt with the ticker's euphony?
Or practising some negroid hop?
Where will you be
45 When the news is bruited by the auto horn?
Holding a pair of aces back to back?
Paring a toe-nail, cutting out a corn?
Or reading, with de-trousered back,
Hearst's tabloid, previously torn?

50 Or will you be – O would that you should be! –
Among those valiant ones returning to their homes
                              To tell
Their daughters and their sons to tell posterity
How they did on that day,
55 If not create new heaven, at least abolish hell.

III

Of the Clients of Barnum

Clients of Barnum, yours no even break!
The maestros have you, have you on the hip!
They gloat: they hold you ready for the take:
And you, O rube, fall smacko for the gyp!

60 Sucker, you stand no chance; the cards are nicked,
The factory, believe you me, is one clip joint;
The sadness is you know not you are licked
Come from the cleaners, you have missed the point.

Buffalo'd, taken for a ride, you gape;
65 Say dirty work at the cross-roads, but can not
Articulate its manner, form or shape.

For deadheads, here where X proclaims the spot,
Enters Politico, and p.d.q. —
To tell you what a lovely land is ours;
70 With him, Kid Pedagogue, the champ who slew
All challenging low wages and long hours;
Also Don Pulpiteer, to promise you,
Not earthly dwellings, — no — celestial bowers!
Is it not time
75 Before they shove you on an unemployment shelf,
Or freeze you in a pension-frigidaire,
That you do get
Wise to yourself?

IV

Of Psalmody in the Temple

They do lie heavily upon me, these
80 Sores of the spirit, failings of the flesh!
Wherefore, O triply-purgatoried soul,
Scram;
And chastened O my body,
Take it on the lam —
85 To the colossal, suprasuper hideout, blow,
To the lotiferous movie-show!

There I do sit me down in thick upholstery;
I do not want.
A tale is prepared before me: heroine enters,
90 Slim; and a villain, gaunt:
Also a well-groomed esquire saying *I love you* —
Fade out, fade in;
Shots of a lot of legs, and a couple of stooges,
Close-up, a grin.
95 The decent, the fair, win prizes; the wicked
Their just deserts.

The prince weds Cinderella, and virtue triumphs
Until it hurts.

O these felicitous endings, sweet finales,
100 They comfort me –
O bodies' beatitude, O soul's salvation,
Where this can be!
Most surely I shall dwell in this great temple
And take my bliss
105 Forever out of scenes which end forever
In an eight-foot kiss.

V

Of Faith, Hope and Charity

Beware, – spiritual humankind, –
Faith, contraceptive of the mind;
And hope, cheap aphrodisiac,
110 Supplying potency its lack;
And also that smug lechery
Barren and sterile charity.

VI

Of Beauty

Seeing that planets move by dynamos,
And even the sun's a burnished well-oiled spring,
115 What glory is there, say, in being a rose
And why should skylarks still desire to sing,
Singing, and no men hear, men standing close
Over some sleek, mechanic and vociferous thing?

For these there is one beauty; put it on a table:
120 A loaf of bread, some salt, a vegetable.

VII

Of Poesy

    Bard, paying your rental of the ivory tower,
    With the old coin of hoarded metaphor,
    Abandon now the turret where you cower;
    Descend the winding staircase; and let your
125 Speech be, not of the thrush's note, long sour,
    But of the Real, alive upon a floor.

    Let Keats forget his father's stables, smelling
    The mythical odour of the asphodel;
    Let Wordsworth clutch his sensitive bosom, leaping
130 When he beholds a rainbow he can sell;
    Let butler Tennyson pour out old vintage
    For the good knights of Arthur's King Hotel.

    But you, O streamlined laureate,
    What's Hecuba to you?
135 How long will you yet bind your fate
    With stars archaic and with obsolete dew?

    Go out upon a roof, and laud the moon!
    Your words are sweet and flattering, as if
    The moon were a good corpse, a threnodied stiff!
140 O idiot bard, O frenzied loon,
    Such words to blow
    Upon that smooth hydraulic dynamo!

    For soon, O sooner than the laurel grows –
    Will come to you, superior of the mass,
145 The foreman Death,
    To push you into one of many rows
    And bodily have you manufacture grass, –
    Of your sweet immortality, true token,
    Wage of the foreman Death
150 His time-clock, broken.

VIII

Of Soporifics

These be repasts lethean of your kind:
the tabloid whispering, the penny sheet
shouting the scoop that even the richest meet
with mésalliance, murder, maddened mind;
155 the sermon showing corpses wined and dined;
the radio hour and its jovial bleat;
the circus come to town, a breadless feat;
two weeks of grace for fifty weeks of grind.
These are the brews that are allowed to mull
160 in crucibles of bone one would call sane;
these are concoctions patented to dull
the too-keen edge of the too-querulous brain,
persuading the cockerel dung is beautiful,
and the bespatted, spit is only rain.

IX

Of Shirts and Policies of State

165 A shirt! a shirt! a kingdom for a shirt!
Open your paper; bargains, if you please!
A principality goes for less than dirt,
The palmiest state for any pied chemise.
A red blouse buys the franchise of the czar;
170 The brown habergeon claims an Arian realm;
Where once were candid togas, blackshirts are;
Shirtless is but mahatma at his helm.

Wherefore, O Machiavel,
Get you a rag, a shoulder-strap or a brassiere,
175 And be it but of the right proper hue
And kings will come in trembling and in fear
And peoples, hoarsely obedient, will come to you!

Make haste; and use dispatch!
The shirts of the spectrum governance the world!
180 Get yourself, therefore, while you can, a patch
Of rainbow silk, of motley linen, and
Declare another philosophic shirt unfurled!

X

Of the Lily Which Toils Not

You, Tillie the Toiler and Winnie the Worker, consider
This fabulous lily – and her milk-fed pride, –
185 She toils not, no, and neither does she spin!
O not like yours her most egregious skin,
Her epidermis gilt-edged, bonded hide!

For she has been a child most delicate,
Bathed in milk, filched from the wild goat's haunt;
190 She has thrived, has grown, has come to man's estate, –
She is the season's worthiest debutante!

Her grandfather sold cheap gawds in quantity;
Non-lilies in their hundreds toiled for them.
Now dough is no consideration, see, –
195 The girl must have her court and diadem.

Call the reporters, call the photographers!
Here, for The Sportsman, a snap of Lilia
Patting the groomed posterior of a horse;
And for The Social Star,
200 Lily and jaguar.
And please, good fellow, print this one apart, –
(It goes to show our hot-house Lily has
Not only a big bosom, but a heart.)

Photo of limousine, and background-slums,
205 Lily dispensing to the poor unmentioned sums,
Already titled for the typesetter:
Deb and debtor.
Isn't that cute?
Also do not forget to comment on the style of her spring-suit.
210 Have a drink; drink hearty;
Here are passes to the party.

And what a party! Outré, à l'outrance!
Strawberries from the Himalayas, and
Fowl hatched somewhere in some uncharted land
215 And other tidbits, costly all, and all
Prepared by (trumpets!) Oscar Cinq of France.

The wine, the flowers, the music, and the guests!
The liquor gurgled of Napoleon's wars,
The hired jester made financial jests,
220 The slick musicians juggled their music scores,
While dignified doormen guarded all the doors
Permitting only the distingué who
Could swear he never laced up his own shoe.

Tillie, it was a glorious sight to see!
225 Tails and white ties, and gowns, and naked backs;
Chrysanthemums, pink, brought from beyond the sea,
Tinted, by artists, with bright blues and blacks, –
And brooding, like a spirit,
Over the champagne flood that never once did ebb,
230 Lily the Deb!

Of course, I did not see it all myself;
Sadly, I lacked, what millionaires call pelf,
And so I must, in honesty, relate,
That Barry Cade-Smythe did not crash the gate.

235 But Barricade Smith did love her from afar,
    Watched her, in due time, go upon a cruise
    And come back, headlined in the nation's news,
    As wife of the tenth cousin of the Czar.

    Whom, in due time, she buried. No one needs
240 To be reminded of that tragic cut
    Of her Paris widow's weeds.

    That season over, with the coming of the spring
    And dividends blossoming on many a bank,
    She wedded, being now a lady of rank,
245 A closer relative of a deposed king.
    Whom, in due course,
    She did divorce,
    And sent him packing, with a little tip,
    Two million dollars, and a discarded ship.

250 And still to-day, Tillie, if you have the time,
    And Winnie, if you care, you may,
    Ahunting go to Africa, or climb
    Some hills Helvetian, yodelling, and find
    Lily at play;
255 Or on the Riviera, or shooting birds of clay, –

    Perhaps, however, you cannot get away.

    c. 1938/1938   1938

Of Castles in Spain

To One Gone to the Wars

For S.H.A.

Unworthiest crony of my grammar days,
   Expectorator in learning's cuspidor,
Forsaking the scholar's for the gamin's ways,
   The gates of knowledge for the cubicular door,

5 How you have shamed me, me the noble talker,
   The polisher of phrases, stainer of verbs,
Who daily for a price serve hind and hawker,
   Earning my Sabbath meat, my daily herbs.

'Tis you who do confound the lupine jaw
10   And stand protective of my days and works,
As in the street-fight you maintain the law
   And I in an armchair – weigh and measure Marx.

Alas, that fettered and bound by virtues long since rusty,
I must, for spouse and son,
15 Withhold, as is befitting any prison trusty,
My personal succour and my uniformed aid,
And from the barracks watch the barricade –
Offering you, meek sacrifice, unvaliant gift,
My non-liturgic prayer:
20 For that your aim be sure,
Your bullet swift
Unperilous your air, your trenches dry,
Your courage unattainted by defeat,
Your courage high.

Toreador

25 Unfurl the scarlet banner, Toreador,
Take up your stance;
Let, then, the bull bicornate for the gore,
Snorting, advance,
To meet your clean thrust, bringing to his knees
30 The taurine beast.
Let banner upon blood proclaim the peace
Of bull, deceased.

Sonnet without Music

Upon the piazza, haemophilic dons
delicately lift their sherry in the sun.

35 Having recovered confiscated land,
and his expropriated smile redeemed,
the magnate, too, has doff'd his socialized face.
He beams a jocund aftermath to bombs.

Also, the priest, – alas, for so much bloodshed! –
40 cups plumpish hand to catch uncatechized belch.

The iron heel grows rusty in the nape
of peasant feeding with the earthworm – but
beware aristocrat, Don Pelph, beware!
The peon soon will stir, will rise, will stand,
45 breathe Hunger's foetid breath, lift arm, clench fist,
and heil you to the fascist realm of death!

c. 1938/1938   1938

Childe Harold's Pilgrimage [Version 1]

Of yore yclept in old Judaea Zvi;
Cognomen'd Cerf where Latin speech is carolled;
Dubbed Hirsch, a transient, in wild Allmany;
For sweet conformity now appellated Harold, –
5 Always and ever,
Whether in caftan robed, or in tuxedo slicked,
Whether of bearded chin, or of the jowls shaved blue,
Always and ever have I been the Jew
Bewildered, and a man who has been tricked,
10 Examining
A passport of a polyglot decision –
To Esperanto from the earliest rune –
Where cancellation frowns away permission,
And turning in despair
15 To seek an audience with the consul of the moon.

For they have all been shut, and barred, and triple-locked,
The gates of refuge, the asylum doors;
And in no place beneath the sun may I –
On pilgrimage towards my own wide tomb –
20 Sit down to rest my bones, and count my sores;
Save near thy shimmering horizon, Madagascar!
Where in the sickly heat of noon I may
Bloom tropical, and rot, and happily melt away.

Aye, but thy fell is somewhat safe in Muscovy!
25 Quoth Kamenev to me.
And truth it is, as all the world avows:
Provided
I cast off my divine impedimenta,
And leave my household gods in the customs house.

30 And there is also Palestine, my own,
   Land of my fathers, cradle of my birth,
   Whither I may return, king to his throne,
   By showing the doorman, Mr. Harold's worth
   Several thousand pounds (and not by loan!)
35 Redemption for the pawned and promised earth!

   O mummied Pharaoh in thy pyramid,
   Consider now the schemes thy wizards schemed
   Against those shrewd proliferous Israelites!
   Son of Hamdatha, though the witless Mede
40 Did gibbet thee, behold thy inventions deemed
   Wisdom itself by many worthy wights.
   Rejoice, Judaeophobes,
   The brew you brewed and cellared is not flat!
   See, in the air, mad Antiochus, the
45 Inimitate image of thy frenzy, and
   Lean Torquemada, look about thee, and grow fat.

      Sieg heil!
   Behold, against the sun, familiar blot:
   A cross with claws!
50 Hearken
   The mustached homily, the megaphoned hymn:
   Attila's laws!
   He likes me not.
   He does not like my blood in state unspilled;
55 Pronounces me begotten of canaille
   Talmudic, biblic riff-raff, and polluted
   Blood of the prophets, and their Marxian guild.
   The sage has elocuted.
   Not blue my eyes, ergo, I am ill-bred;
60 My head is short, wherefore, I am too long
   By a head!
   Tow hair on Teuton skull – this is the token
   By which to take the measure of the strong.
   The seer has spoken.

65 So sound the trumpet!
   And join, ye burghers, in the ditty that the pimp Horst Wessel
   Wrote for his strumpet!

   O fellowman — forgive the archaic word! —
   Break now your sullen silence, and expound
70 Wherefore you deem me that foul mote in your eye,
   That bone in your throat, that ugly scab, that plague,
   That in your gospels you so character
   Me and my kin, consanguine and allied?
   Is it my wealth you envy, my wine-goblet,
75 My candlesticks, my spattered gaberdine?
   Why, take them; all my goods and chattels — yours.
   Take them, I shall not so much as say O,
   And let there be an end. The scowl persists.
   It is my thoughts, then, that you do begrudge me?
80 Good; I'll expunge them! I will bid my brain
   Henceforth to cease, go dry, be petrified,
   And as it was in my mother's womb, remain.
   Cousin, will that be pleasing to you? No?
   You are not pleased at all. Pray do not tell me,
85 I will myself unfathom the dark reason —
   My father's heresy, his obstinate creed?
   That is the sword between us? Bring it down.
   I pledge you, for the sake of peace, that I
   Will be your most observing true marrano
90 That ever bent the knee to several gods.
   Not so, you say, for being a generous mind
   You will forgive the false. What is it, then,
   That ghostly thing that stalks between us, and
   Confounds our discourse into babel speech?
95 I am too forward; wherever you seek me not
   There you do find me, always, big in your sight.
   That, too, good brother, is no difficult matter —
   For I will dwarf myself, and live in a hut
   Upon the outskirts of nowhere, receive no mail,
100 And speak so low that only God shall hear me!
   So, surely shall we be as bosom-friends.

I stray; I grope; I have not read your mind.
Perhaps I am a man of surly manners,
Lacking in grace, aloof, impolitic,
105 To wit, an alien? And *that* is false.
For on occasion and in divers lands
I have sojourned, set up abode with you,
Drank the same drinks, partook of the same food,
Applauded the same music, uttered the
110 Very same language, thought a similar thought, –
And still you have sneered *foreigner*, and still
Your hate was great, as reasonless hatred is.

Stranger and foeman, I know well your wish!
My blood, my blood! Shall I, then, sever a vein,
115 Drain off an artery, open the valves
Of my much too-Semitic heart, and be
That blond cadaver pleasing to your eye?
Have I not well conjectured? Is not your mind
Now laid on the table, pointed, like a dagger?

120 In such sad plight, in such sore case,
My sire would turn his bearded face
Upwards, and, fast or festive day,
Would don his prayershawl, and pray.
To him in converse with his God,
125 The wicked king was less than sod,
And all his machinations were
Less than the yelpings of a cur.
For as my father prayed, he heard
The promise of the holy word,
130 And felt them watching over him,
The furious fiery seraphim.

My father is gathered to his fathers, God rest his wraith!
And his son
Is a pauper in spirit, a beggar in piety,
135 Cut off without a penny's worth of faith.

Esau, my kinsman, would, in like event,
Devise a different answer for the foe;
And let the argumentative bullet dent
The heart of the tyrant, let the steel blade show
140 The poor mortality of the heaven-sent,
And let the assassin's bomb, vociferous, throw
Defiance to the oppressor,
Booming *No!*

Alas, for me that in my ears there sounds
145 Always the sixth thunder of Sinai.

What, now, for me to do?
Gulp down some poisoned brew?
Or from some twentieth story take
My ignominious exit? Make,
150 Above this disappearing Jew,
Three bubbles burst upon the lake?
Or dance from a rope upon the air
Over an overturnèd chair?

No, not for such ignoble end
155 From Ur of the Chaldees have I the long way come;
Not for such purpose low
Have I endured cruel Time, its pandemonium,
Its lunatic changes, its capricious play;
And surely not that I might at long last
160 Vanish
Have my feet crossed these many frontiers, and
My brain devised its thoughts.

'Tis not in me to unsheathe an avenging sword;
I cannot don phylactery to pray;
165 Weaponless, blessed with no works, and much abhorred,
This only is mine wherewith to face the horde:
The frozen patience waiting for its day,
The stance long-suffering, the stoic word,
The bright empirics that knows well that the

170 Night of the cauchemar comes and goes away, –
A baleful wind, a baneful nebula, over
A saecular imperturbability.

c. 1938/1938   1940

Childe Harold's Pilgrimage [Version 2]

Of yore yclept in old Judaea *Zvi*;
Cognomen'd *Cerf* where Latin speech is carolled;
Dubbed *Hirsch*, a transient, in wild Allmany;
For sweet conformity now appellated *Harold*,
5 Always and everywhere,
Whether in caftan robed, or in tuxedo slicked,
Whether of bearded chin, or of the jowls shaved blue,
Always and at all frontiers have I been the Jew
Shunted and shuttled, been the Hebrew tricked
10 Examining
A passport of a polyglot decision
(To esperanto from the earliest rune)
Where cancellation frowned away permission,
Man turning in despair
15 To seek him his visa from the consul of the moon.

For they have all been shut, and barred, and triple-locked,
The gates of refuge, the asylum doors;
And in no place beneath the sun may I,
Who've tugged at the latch of all the longitudes,
20 Sit down to rest my bones, and count my sores, –
Save at your shimmering horizons, Madagascar!
Where in the sickly heat of noon I may
Bloom tropical, and rot, and happily melt away.
No home nor haven is for us;
25 All doors are exodus.

O mummied Pharaoh in your pyramid,
Consider now the schemes your wizards schemed
Against those shrewd proliferous Israelites!
Son of Hamdatha, though the witless Mede
30 Did gibbet you, see your inventions deemed
Now of *realpolitik*'s highest flights.
Rejoice, Judaeophobes,
The brew you brewed and cellared is not flat!
See, in the air, mad Antiochus, the
35 Inimitate image of your frenzy, and,
Lean Torquemada, look about you, and grow fat.

Sieg heil!
Behold, against the sun, familiar blot:
A cross with claws!
40 Hearken
The mustached homily, the megaphoned hymn:
Attila's laws!
He likes me not.
He does not like my blood in state unspilled;
45 Pronounces me begotten of canaille
Talmudic, biblic riff-raff, the polluted
Blood of the prophets, an ignoble melt.
The sage has elocuted.
Not blue my eyes, ergo, I am ill-bred;
50 My head is short, wherefore, I am too long
By a head!
Tow hair on Teuton skull – this is the token
By which to take the measure of the strong.
The seer has spoken.

55 O fellowman – forgive the obsolete word! –
Break now your sullen silence, and expound
Why you consider me that mote in your eye,
That bone in your throat, that abscess on your flesh,
That in your choler you so character
60 Me and my kin, consanguine and allied?
Is it my wealth you envy, my wine-goblet,

My candlesticks, my spattered gaberdine?
Why, take them; all my goods and chattels – yours.
Take them, I shall not so much as say *Oh!*
65 And let there be an end.
                          Your scowl persists.
They are my thoughts, then, that you do begrudge me?
Good; I'll expunge them! I will bid my brain
Henceforth to cease, go dry, be petrified,
And as it was in my mother's womb, remain.
70 Cousin, will that be pleasing to you?
You are not pleased at all. No, do not tell me,
I will myself illumine the dark reason –
My father's heresy, his obstinate creed?
That is the sword between us!
                              Bring it down.
75 I pledge you, for the sake of peace, that I
Will be your most observing true marrano
That ever bent the knee to several gods.
Ah, you protest. Yours is a generous heart.
Error you can forgive. What is it, then,
80 That hops between us, mischievous familiar,
And with a spell brings outrage to your eyes?
I am too forward; wherever you seek me not
There you do find me, always, big in your sight.
That too, good brother, is no difficult matter –
85 For I will dwarf myself, and live in a hut
Upon the outskirts of nowhere, receive no mail,
And speak so low that only God shall hear me!
Then, surely must we be as bosom friends.
The spot's not touched. I have not read your mind.
90 Is it, perhaps, – I whisper this – my manners,
That now are much too loud, – and now too hushed –
Now ultra-demonstrative, an instant later
All of self-effacement and punctiliousness,
The alien's typical alternations?
                                  False!
95 For on occasion and in divers lands
Sojourning, I've set up abode with you,

Drank the same drinks, partook of the same food,
Applauded the same music, uttered the
Very same language, thought a similar thought, —
And still you have sneered *Foreigner!* and still
Your hate was great, as reasonless hatred is.

Stranger and enemy, I have read your wish!
My blood! Shall I, then, sever a vein,
Drain off an artery, open the valves
Of my much too-Semitic heart, and be
That blond cadaver pleasing to your eye?
Have I now well conjectured? Is not your mind
Now laid on the table, pointed, like a dagger?

In such sad plight, in such sore case,
My father would turn his bearded face
Upwards, and, fast or festive day,
Would don his prayershawl, and pray.
To him in converse with his God,
Tsar Nicholas was less than sod,
And all his machinations were
Less than the bark of his borzoi.
For as my father prayed, he heard
The promise of the holy word,
And felt them watching over him,
The furious fiery seraphim.

My father is gathered to his fathers, God rest his wraith!
And his son
Is a pauper in spirit, a beggar in piety,
Cut off without a penny's worth of faith.

Esau, my kinsman, would, in like event,
Devise a different answer for the foe;
Would let the argumentative bullet dent
The heart of the despot, let the steel blade show
His poor mortality how effluent,
Would let the apoplectic bomb assert

In the scattering square its rage
And the tyrant's hemorrhage.

Alas for me, that in my ears there sounds
Always the sixth thunder of Sinai.

135 What, now, for me to do?
Gulp down some poisoned brew?
Or from some twentieth story take
My ignominious exit? Make,
Above this disappearing Jew,
140 Three bubbles burst upon the lake?
Or dance from a rope upon the air
Over an overturnèd chair?

No, not for such ignoble end
From Ur of the Chaldees have I the long way come;
145 Not for such purpose low
Have suffered Time, its pandemonium,
Its lunatic changes, its capricious play;
And surely not that the ethic and the lights eternal
Kindled upon the wick of the renewing brain
150 Should gutter at the last, and be obscured,
Outsnuffed, and my own self snuffed out
Have I endured all that I have endured
As evil whirled about me and about.

'Tis not in me to unsheathe an avenging sword.
155 I cannot don phylactery to pray.
Weaponless, blessed with no works, and much abhorred,
This only is mine wherewith to face the horde:
The frozen patience waiting for its day,
The stance long-suffering, the stoic word,
160 The bright empirics that knows well that the
Night of the cauchemar comes but goes away, –

485 / c.1938/1938

A baleful wind, a baneful nebula, over
A saecular imperturbability.

c. 1953/c. 1955

c. 1938/1940

To the Chief Musician, a Psalm of the Bratzlaver, a Parable

An aged king, his brittle shins in hose,
Spoonfed, dribbling over a purple bib,
Upon a time and at a banquet board
Raised bony palm, and stayed the resined bows,
5 And hushed the drums, and stilled the cornet's chord.
Then caused to issue from his seventh rib
These toothless words:
                        Thane of four graveyard ells,
Soon shall you mark me, vassal of the worm.
The eager belfry waits to cluck its bells;
10 The royal sexton, palsied and infirm,
Lets rust grow on his spade, moss on my tomb.
Wherefore, my son, my immortality,
Ascend my throne; don crown; let cannon boom!
For though from my high tower in the sky
15 My rheumy eyes have seen your star and doom,
Be of good cheer, of noble temper be;
And never let a baneful wind blow dust
Between yourself and your felicity ...

c. 1938/1940   1944

To the Chief Musician, a Psalm of the Bratzlaver, When He Considered How the Pious Are Overwhelmed

Guerdon for wit is lavished in the realm;
About the young prince hover old wise men,
Chewing the tips of their beards, lean sages pen
Theses with long Greek words. Astrologers
5 Fall into ditches gazing at the stars.
The prince eats doctrine, while his scholars cram
The pinnacled platters of the daily feast –
So in a land where no direction is
Each simpleton's a wise man of the East.

10 Only the prince's cracked pate wants a stitch.
He talks in riddles, he moans in heavy sleep,
His brain is troubled with the wizard's itch;
Sometimes he laughs, and sometimes he doth weep.
He stalks through the lonely halls and sighs and sighs;
15 Of woman's womb and from snipped navelcord,
Released to wander beneath blank blue skies,
Wherefore, and to what end? My father's end?
The king who wears a diadem of roots?
The sages speak of God, the First, but what
20 The seed of which he is the Fruit of Fruits?
And what am I, the king, my majesty
Pedigreed bone, blue blood, anointed skin?

Alas, the marble pillars have no tongues
No sound without replies to sound within.

25 Meantime, the prince's generals have gout
Philosophers, discoursing happiness
Have put the bannered myrmidons to rout
Soldiers read books, and captains play at chess.

>   There is no citadel above the port,
> 30   The spider-web hangs from the cannon's mouth,
>   The mortar drops from every frontier fort.

c. 1938/1940

Of Remembrance

> Go catch the echoes of the ticks of time;
> Spy the interstices between its sands;
> Uncover the shadow of the dial; fish
> Out of the waters of the water-clock
> 5 The shape and image of first memory.
>
> Recall:
> The apple fallen from the apple-tree:
> O child remembering maternity!
>
> The candle flickering in a mysterious room:
> 10 O foetus stirring in the luminous womb!
>
> One said he did remember, he did know
> What time the fruit did first begin to grow:
> O memory of limbs in embryo!
>
> Another did recall the primal seed –
> 15 Conceiver of conception of the breed!
>
> A third, the sage who did the seed invent –
> O distant memory of mere intent!
>
> Recall the fruit's taste, ere the fruit was fruit –
> Hail memory of essence absolute!

20 Recall the odour of fruit, when no fruit was,
    O Spirit untainted by corporeal flaws!

    Recall the fruit's shape, ere the fruit was seen!
    O soul immortal that has always been!

    Said one, and he the keenest of them all:
25 No thing is what I vividly recall –
    O happy man who could remember, thus,
    The Mystery beyond the mysterious.

    c. 1938/1940   1951

To the Chief Musician: A Psalm of the Bratzlaver, Touching a Good Gardener

I

It was a green, a many-meadowed county!
Orchards there were, heavy with fruitage; and
Blossom and bud and benison and bounty

Filled with good odour that luxurious land.
5 Stained with crushed grass, an old and earthy yeoman
Sceptred that green demesne with pruning wand.

II

Suddenly came the chariots of the foeman;
Suddenly vanished that good gardener, –
Ruled in the land, three companies of bowmen.

10 One company polluted its sweet air,
   Another rendered its ripe fruitage bitter;
   A third made foul its beauty which was fair.

   People of starving sparrows, loud their twitter!
   Wherefore I did bespeak a neighboring folk:
15 Behold your kin devoured by a wolf's litter,

   Release their land, unburden them their yoke
   Or similar evil may transgress your borders!

   III

   Now, though they made them ready, as I spoke,
   In tippling and in gluttonish disorders
20 They tarried on their march, until one day
   As they descried the invaders' spectral warders,

   Their flagons soured, their viands did decay,
   And odor and taste did utterly forsake them.
   Then in their sore distress, they sought to pray.

25 O but my ungraped water did so slake them!
   My poor dry crust did such rich taste afford!
   They ate, they drank, they slept, and none could wake them.

   IV

   Wherefore, alone, I mingled with the horde,
   And unknown walked in many public places.
30 God save me from the ugly filth I heard!

   And from those gates, beset by wrothful faces
   Where Bribery stretched its hand, and turned its head!
   And from quick Lust, and his two-score grimaces!

Salute them, now, three companies of dread:
35 Filth, in its dun array, the clean taste killing;
Embattled Bribery, with stealthy tread

Advancing on the vanquished, all too-willing
To barter visions for a piece of gold;
And legioned Lust, at its foul buckets swilling ...

V

40 They did salute them, did my henchmen bold,
With many a sword, and many an eager arrow,
And driven was the foe from wood and wold.

Then did we come upon him, in a narrow
Streetyard, followed by children, and a cur, –
45 We brought him fruit, high-pilèd in a barrow,
Gift for a king, – for that good gardener.

c. 1938/1940   1944

To the Chief Musician, a Psalm of the Bratzlaver, Which He Wrote Down As the Stammerer Spoke

At unprehensile Time, all fingers clutch.
Can it be counted on an abacus?
Or weighed on scales, most delicate to the touch?
Or measured with rods? What Mathematicus
5 Can speak thereof, save as a net on the brain,
A web some much-afflated spider weaves
On which hang chronicles, like drops of rain?
That, and no more, the quarry he retrieves.

But, truly, in what smithy is it forged?
10 In what alembic brewed? By what bird hatched?
I, but a stammerer, by the spirit urged,
Having approached that Door, found it unlatched,
Say Time is vacuum, save it be compact
Of men's deeds imitating godly act.

c. 1938/1940   1944

c. 1940/1940

In Re Solomon Warshawer [Version 1]

On Wodin's day, sixth of December, thirty-nine,
I, Friedrich Vercingetorix, attached
to the vııth Eavesdroppers-behind-the-Line,
did cover my beat, when suddenly the crowd I watched
5 surrounded, in a cobbled lane one can't pass through,
a bearded man, disguised in rags, a Jew.

In the said crowd there were a number of Poles.
Mainly, however, there were Germans there;
blood-brothers of our Reich, true Aryan souls,
10 breathing at last – in Warsaw – Nordic air.

These were the words the Jew was shouting:
I took them down verbatim:

Whom have I hurt? Against whose silk have I brushed?
On which of your women looked too long?
15 *I tell you I have done no wrong!*
Send home your children, lifting hardened dung,
And let your curs be hushed!
For I am beard and breathlessness, and chased enough.
Leave me in peace, and let me go my way.

20 At this the good folk laughed. The Jew continued to say
   he was no thief, he was a man for hire,
   worked for his bread, artist or artisan,
   a scribe, if you wished, a vendor or a buyer,
   work of all kinds, and anything at all:
25 paint a mural, scour a latrine,
   indite an ode, repair an old machine,
   anything, to repeat,
   anything at all,
   so that he might eat
30 and have his straw couch in his abandoned stall.

   Asked for his papers, he made a great to-do
   of going through the holes in his rags, whence he withdrew
   a Hebrew pamphlet and a signet ring,
   herewith produced, Exhibits 1 and 2.

35 I said: No documents in a civilized tongue?
   He replied:

   Produce, O Lord, my wretched fingerprint,
   Bring forth, O angel in the heavenly court,
   My dossier, full, detailed, both fact and hint,
40 *Felony, misdemeanor, tort!*

   I refused to be impressed by talk of that sort.

   From further cross-examination, it appeared,
   immediate history: a beggar in Berlin,
   chased as a vagrant from the streets of Prague,
45 kept as a leper in forced quarantine,
   shunned as the pest, avoided like a plague,
   he had escaped, mysteriously come
   by devious routes, and stolen frontiers, to
   the *nalewkas* of Warsaw's sheenydom.

50 Pressed to reveal his foul identity,
he lied:

One of the anthropophagi was he,
or, if we wished, a denizen of Mars,
the ghost of my father, Conscience – aye,
55 the spectre of Reason, naked, and with scars;
even became insulting, said he was
Aesop the slave among the animals ...
Sir Incognito – Rabbi Alias ...
The eldest elder of Zion ... said we knew
60 his numerous varied oriental shapes,
even as we ought to know his present guise –
the man in the jungle, and beset by apes.

It was at this point the S.S. man arrived.
The Jew was interrupted; when he was revived,
65 he deposed as follows:

At low estate, a beggar, and in flight,
Still do I wear my pride like purple. I
Am undismayed by frenzy or by fright,
And you are those mirrored in my pitying eye.
70 *For you are not the first that I have met –*
O I have known them all,
The dwarf dictators, the diminutive dukes,
The heads of straw, the hearts of gall,
Th' imperial plumes of eagles covering rooks!

75 *It is not necessary to name names,*
But it may serve anon,
Now to evoke from darkness some dark fames,
Evoke,
Armada'd Spain, that gilded jettison;
80 *And Russia's last descended Romanov,*
Descending a dark staircase
To a dank cellar at Ekaterinoslov;
Evoke

> The glory that was Babylon that now is gloom;
85 And Egypt, Egypt, scarcely now recalled
> By that lone star that sentries Pharaoh's tomb;
> And Carthage, sounded on sand, by water walled;
> And Greece – O broken marble! –
> And disinterred unresurrected Rome.

90 These several dominions hunted me;
> They all have wished, and more than wished, me dead;
> And now, although I do walk raggedly,
> I walk, and they are echoes to my tread!

> Is it by your devices I shall be undone?

95 Ah, but you are philosophers, and know
> That what has been need not continue so;
> The sun has risen; and the sun has set;
> Risen again, again descended, yet
> To-morrow no bright sun may rise to throw
100 Rays of inductive reason on Judaeophobic foe.

> Is there great turmoil in the sparrow's nest
> When that bright bird, the Sun, descends the west?
> There is no fear, there is no twittering;
> At dawn they will again behold his juvenescent wing!

105 Such is the very pattern of the world,
> Even the sparrows understand;
> And in that scheme of things I am enfurled,
> Am part thereof, the whole as it was planned,
> With increase and abatement rife,
110 Subject to sorrow, joined to joy –
> Earth, its relenting and recurring life!

> Yes, but the signet ring, the signet ring!
> Since you must know, barbarian, know you shall!
> I who now stand before you, a hunted thing,
115 Pressed and pursued and harried hither and yon,

I was, I am the Emperor Solomon!
O, to and fro upon the face of the earth,
I wandered, crying: Ani Shlomo, *but —*
But no one believed my birth.

120 *For he now governs in my place and stead,*
He who did fling me from Jerusalem
Four hundred parasangs;
Who stole the crown from off my head,
And robed him in my robes, beneath whose hem
125 *The feet of the cock extend, the tail of the demon hangs!*
Asmodeus!

Mistake me not: I am no virtuous saint;
Only a man, and like all men, not godly,
Damned by desire —
130 *But I at least waged war, for holy booty,*
Against my human taint;
At least sought wisdom, to discern the good;
Whether of men, or birds, or beasts of the wood;
Spread song, spread justice, ever did aspire —
135 *Howbeit, man among men, I failed —*
To lay the plan, and work upon the plan
To build the temple of the more-than-man!

But he, the unspeakable prince of malice!
Usurper of my throne, pretender to the Lord's!
140 *Wicked, demoniac, lycanthropous,*
Leader of hosts horrific, barbarous hordes,
Master of the worm, pernicious, that cleaves rocks,
The beast that talks,
Asmodeus! —

145 *Who has not heard the plight of his domain?*
Learning is banished to the hidden cave;
Wisdom decried, a virtue of the slave;
And justice, both eyes seared, goes tapping with a cane.
His counseler is the wolf. He counsels hate.

150   *His sceptre is a claw.*
      And love is a high crime against the state.
      The fury of the forest
      Is the law.

      Upon his charnel-throne, in bloodied purple,
155   *Hearkening to that music where the sigh*
      Pauses to greet the groan, the groan the anguished cry,
      Asmodeus sits;
      And I –

      At this point the S.S. men departed.
160   The Jew was not revived. He was carried and carted,
      and to his present gaoler brought;
      awaiting higher pleasure.
                          And further deponent saith not.

c. 1940/1940   1944

In Re Solomon Warshawer [Version 2]

      On Wodin's day, sixth of December, thirty-nine,
      I, Friedrich Vercingetorix, attached
      to the viith Eavesdroppers-behind-the-Line,
      did cover my beat, when, suddenly, the crowd I watched
5   surrounded, in a cobbled lane one can't pass through,
      a bearded man, in rags disguised, a Jew.

      In the said crowd there were a number of Poles.
      Mainly, however, there were Germans there:
      blood-brothers of our Reich, true Aryan souls,
10   breathing at last – in Warsaw – Nordic air.

These were the words the Jew was shouting:
I took them down verbatim:

Whom have I hurt? Against whose silk have I brushed?
On which of your women looked too long?
15 *I tell you I have done no wrong!*
Send home your children, lifting hardened dung,
And let your curs be hushed!
For I am but beard and breathlessness, and chased enough.
Leave me in peace, and let me go my way.

20 At this the good folk laughed. The Jew continued to say
he was no thief; he was a man for hire;
worked for his bread, artist or artisan;
a scribe, if you wished; a vendor; even buyer;
work of all kinds, and anything at all:
25 paint a mural, scour a latrine,
indite an ode, repair an old machine,
anything, to repeat,
anything at all,
so that he might eat
30 and have his pallet in his abandoned stall.

Asked for his papers, he made a great to-do
of going through the holes in his rags, whence he withdrew
a Hebrew pamphlet and a signet ring,
herewith produced, Exhibits 1 and 2.

35 I said: No documents in a civilized tongue?
He replied:

Produce, O Lord, my wretched fingerprint,
Bring forth, O angel in the heavenly court,
My dossier, full, detailed, both fact and hint,
40 *Felony, misdemeanor, tort!*

I refused to be impressed by talk of that sort.

From further cross-examination, it appeared,
immediate history: a beggar in Berlin;
chased, as a vagrant, from the streets of Prague;
45 kept, as a leper, in forced quarantine;
shunned as the pest, avoided like the plague;
then had escaped, mysteriously come
by devious routes and stolen frontiers to
the *nalewkas* of Warsaw's sheenydom.

50 Pressed to reveal his true identity,
he lied:

One of the anthropophagi was he,
or, if we wished, a denizen of Mars,
the ghost of *my* father, Conscience – aye,
55 the anatomy of Reason, naked, and with scars;
even became insulting, said he was
Aesop the slave among the animals ...
Sir Incognito ... Rabbi Alias ...
The eldest elder of Zion ... said we knew
60 his numerous varied oriental shapes,
even as we ought to know his present guise –
the man in the jungle, and beset by apes.

It was at this point the S.S. man arrived.
The Jew was interrupted. When he was revived,
65 he deposed as follows:

At low estate, a beggar, and in flight,
Still do I wear my pride like purple. I
Do fear you, yes, but founder not from fright.
Already I breathe your unfuturity.
70 *For you are not the first whom I have met –*
O I have known them all,
The dwarf dictators, the diminutive dukes,

501 / c.1940/1940

The heads of straw, the hearts of gall,
Th' imperial plumes of eagles covering rooks!

75 *It is not necessary to name names,*
But it may serve anon,
Now to evoke from darkness some dark fames,
Evoke,
Armada'd Spain, that gilded jettison;
80 *And Russia's last descended Romanov,*
Descending a dark staircase
To a dank cellar at Ekaterinoslov;
Evoke
The peacock moulted from the Persian loom ...
85 *Babylon tumbled from its terraces ...*
Decrescent and debased Mizraim, remembered only
By that one star that sentries Pharaoh's tomb ...
Evoke
O Greece! O broken marble! ...
90 *And disinterred unresurrected Rome ...*

They would have harried me extinct, these thrones!
Set me, archaic, in their heraldries,
Blazon antique! ... For they were Powers ... Once! ...
But I, though still exilian, rest extant,
95 *And on my cicatrices tally off*
Their undone dynasties!
Shall I dread you – who overlived all these?

Here impudence was duly rebuked, and the Jew confronted with Exhibit 2.

100 *Yes, but that signet ring! ... Freiherr, that seal*
Once flashed the pleasure majestatical!
For I, who in tatters stand investitured,
Who, to these knightly men, am dislodged pawn,
Abdicate and abjured,
105 *I was, I am, the Emperor Solomon!*
O, to and fro upon the face of the earth,

I wandered, crying: Ani Shlomo, *but —*
But no one believed my birth.

For he now governs in my place and stead,
110 *He who did fling me from Jerusalem*
Four hundred parasangs!
Who stole the crown from off my head!
Who robed him in my robes! Beneath whose hem
The feet of the cock extend, the tail of the demon hangs!
115 *Asmodeus!*

Mistake me not; I am no virtuous saint;
Only a man, and like all men, not god-like ...
From birth beset by his own heart's constraint,
Its brimstone pride, the cinders of its greed,
120 *(Brazier behind the ribs that will not faint!)*
Beset, inflamed, besooted, charred, indeed, —
Only a man, and like all men, not god-like,
Damned by desire —
But I at least fought down that bellows'd gleed,
125 *Tried to put out the sulphurs of that fire! ...*
At least craved wisdom, how to snuff the blaze,
Sought knowledge, to unravel good from evil,
Sought guidance from the Author of my Days.

The understanding heart, and its enthymemes,
130 *Being granted me, I learned from beast ... bird ... man;*
Would know; and eavesdropped nest ... and house ... and lair.
The wild beasts spoke to me, told me their dreams,
Which, always biped, towards the human ran ...
O, how that flesh did long to doff its fur!
135 *The fluttering birds, the twittering birds of the air:*
'Would you cast off from your feet,' they said, 'earth's mass,
That weighted globe of brass,
And soar into your own?
With azure fill your heart! ... Be hollow of bone!'
140 *And from my self, and from the breed of Adam,*
I fathom'd that heart's depths, how it may sink

Down to the deep and ink of genesis,
And lie there, that once could the heavens explore,
A sponge and pulse of hunger on the ocean-floor ...
Saw also, and praised, for then knew possible,
The heart's saltations! ...
That always – vanitatum vanitas! –
That always after back to grossness fell.

Thus taught, thus prompted, upward I essay'd, –
Some not mean triumphs scored,
Spread truth, spread song, spread justice, which prevailed,
Builded that famous footstool for the Lord, –
Yet human, human among mortals, failed!
Was thwarted the greater yearning, the jubilee
Wherein the race might at the last be hailed
Transcendent of its own humanity!
For I Qoheleth, King in Jerusalem,
Ecclesiast of the troubled apothegm,
Concluding the matter, must affirm mankind
Still undivined.

However, though worsted, I had wrestled, but he –

Our royal Jew, now questioned *in camera*,
was not, this time, molested. It was thought
some enemy intelligence might come through
from his distractions, some inkling of the plot
now being pursued by his ten losing tribes.
Therefore the record, as ordered, here gives the whole Jew, –
for which the subscribing officer subscribes
apology.

But he, unspeakable prince of malice!
Usurper of my throne, pretender to the Lord's!
Wicked, demoniac, lycanthropous,
Goad of the succubi, horrific hordes!
Master of the worm, pernicious, that cleaves rocks,

175 *The beast that talks,*
Asmodeus! –

Who has not felt his statutes? ... His scientists,
Mastering for him the lethal mysteries;
His surgeons of doctrine, cutting, like vile cysts
180 *From off the heart, all pities and sympathies;*
His judges, trembling over their decrees,
Lest insufficient injustice displease;
And his psychiaters, guarding against relapse,
For fear the beast, within the man, collapse.

185 *His statecraft, and its modes and offices?*
Here motive is appetite; and oestric hate
The force that freaks and fathers all device.
All love's venereal; or excess; or bait.
Ambush all policy, and artifice;
190 *And all reward conferred, all honour*
Hierarchical to the degrees of Hate.

Upon his lych-throne, robed in bloodied purple,
Listening to those harmonies where the sigh
Exhaling greets the groan, the groan is pitched to the cry,
195 *Asmodeus sits;*
And I –

At this point the S.S. men departed.
The Jew was not revived. He was carried and carted,
and to his present gaoler brought;
200 awaiting higher pleasure.
                        And further deponent saith not.

c. 1953/1955   1957

For the Chief Physician

A song for hunters: In that wood,
That whispering jungle of the blood
Where the carnivorous midge seeks meat,
And yawns the sinuous spirochete,
5 And roars the small fierce unicorn,
The white-robed hunters sound the horn.
May they have goodly hunting. May
Their quarry soon be brought to bay.

c. 1940/1940   1944

Grace before Poison

Well may they thank thee, Lord, for drink and food:
For daily benison of meat,
For fish or fowl,
For spices of the subtle cook,
5 For fruit of the orchard, root of the meadow, berry of the wood;
For all things good,
And for the grace of water of the running brook!
And in the hallelujah of these joys
Not least is my uplifted voice.

10 But this day into thy great temple have I come
To praise thee for the poisons thou has brayed,
To thank thee for pollens venomous, the fatal gum,
The banes that bless, the multifarious herbs arrayed
In all the potency of that first week
15 Thou didst compose the sextet of Earth spoken, made!

Behold them everywhere, the unuttered syllables of thy breath,
Heavy with life, and big with death!
The flowering codicils to thy great fiat!

The hemp of India – and paradise!
20 The monk's hood, cooling against fever;
And nightshade: death unpetalled before widened eyes;
And blossom of the heart, the purple foxglove!
The spotted hemlock, punishment and prize,
And those exhilarators of the brain:
25 Cocaine;
Blood of the grape; and marrow of the grain!

And sweet white flower of thy breath, O Lord,
Juice of the poppy, conjuror of timeless twilights,
Eternities of peace in which the fretful world
30 Like a tame tiger at the feet lies curled.

c. 1940/1940   1951

Maschil of Abraham: A Prayer When He Was in the Cave

How is he changed, the scoffers say,
This hero of an earlier day,
Who in his youth did battle with
The wicked theologic myth;
5 Who daily from his pocket drew
(*Aetat.* sixteen) a writing, true,
Attested, sealed, and signed, its gist:
God swearing He did not exist;
Who in his Zion lay at ease
10 Concocting learned blasphemies
To hate, contemn, and ridicule
The godly reign, the godly rule.

How is he now become as one
Trembling with age before the Throne, –
15 This xxth century scientist,
A writer of psalms, a liturgist;
A babbling pious woman, he
Who boasted that his thoughts were free,
And who at worst did nullify
20 By ignorance the deity.

O Lord, in this my thirtieth year
What clever answer shall I bear
To those slick persons amongst whom
I sat, but was not in their room?
25 How shall I make apocalypse
Of that which rises to my lips,
And on my lips is smitten dumb: –
Elusive word, forgotten sum.

O could I for a moment spare
30 My eyes to them, or let them hear
The music that about me sings,
Then might they cease their twitterings.

Then might they also know, as I,
The undebatable verity,
35 The truth unsoiled by epigram,
The simple *I am that I am*.
But failing these powers in me, Lord,
Do Thou the deed, say Thou the word,
And with Thy sacred stratagem
40 Do justify my ways to them.

c. 1940/1940   1944

A Prayer of Abraham That He Be Forgiven for Blasphemy

Consider my speech, O Lord, not too severely;
It does not mean what it does seem to say.
With strangers I must see my tongue says merely
The hollow nought, the vacuous cliché!
5 For You I need not choose my language; surely
Need not measure the words with which I pray;
Surely, Lord, You would have it this way rather.
I speak to you this day
Even as once I spoke to my sire, now with You.
10 And I never loved one more than I did my father.

c. 1940/1940   1941

A Prayer of the Afflicted, When He Is Overwhelmed

I would not tell this to the man met on the street,
The casual acquaintance, even the intimate friend,
Stopping to speak of the news, complain about the heat:
Him would I tell my triumphs mount, and have no end,
5 And tricks are fine, thank you, and never were they better.
But to tell you, O Lord, it is a different matter –
I would not have you pity my cheap lies.
You know the truth, the ache I have and had,
The blind alleys, the frustrations, and the sighs.
10 O Lord, the times they are not good at all,
And one might even say that they are bad.

c. 1940/1940   1941

A Psalm for Five Holy Pilgrims, Yea, Six on the King's Highway

One comes: – he is a very blossoming tree –
With frankincense and perfumery:
Sweet savour for his nostril'd deity.

Another bears God trinkets, smooth and rich,
5 And little idols polished overmuch –
All holy objects pleasant to the touch.

And still another seeks the mystic word
With all the rainbows of his jewelled hoard –
His goodly proffer to the sight of the Lord.

10 With delicates and sweetmeats and with fruit,
Food of the blossom, eating of the root,
Comes one to flatter the taste of the Absolute.

And the fifth pilgrim trips upon the sod,
Blowing sweet music from a hollow rod:
15 Sounds gratifying to the ear of God.

Not sight, sound, smell, taste, touch, his freight,
One brings his heart for pawning with his fate:
He, surely, he shall come within the Gate!

c. 1940/1940   1944

A Psalm of Abraham concerning the Arrogance of the Son of Man

Consider this creature, its peculiar pride,
This braggart loud in his invented brag!
Is he not weaker than the ant, and than the dog
Duller, and than the ape but little better bred?

5 Yet is he arrogant: the orbit of the stars,
The wandering planets, the most marvellous sky,
Nor yet this weird earth, this terrible sea,
Induce humility in his orgulous course.

However, not all souls are violins
10 Evocative of music at the touch.
Indeed, there be some that no sage could teach
Nor any subtlety break through their chalky bones.

But Man, Man, Man, who perforce daily
Must in the privy take your humble seat,
15 A bencher of the jakes, slave to a gut,
How do you still esteem yourself, grand, noble, holy?

c. 1940/1940   1941

A Psalm of Abraham of That Which Was Visited upon Him

A prowler in the mansion of my blood!
I have not seen him, but I know his signs.
Sometimes I hear him meddling with my food,
Or in the cellar, poisoning my wines, –

5 Yet face to face with him I never come;
But by a foot print, by a book misplaced,
Or by the imprint of an inky thumb,
Or by the next day's meal, a strange new taste,

I know that he has breached my household peace,
10 I know that somehow he has let him in.
Shall I fling open a window, and shout *Police!*
I dare not. He is of my kith and kin.

c. 1940/1940   1952

A Psalm of Abraham, Praying a Green Old Age

I who have expiated life in cities,
Whose lungs have inhaled dust and noisome oils,
Whose ears have heard no bird's or cricket's ditties,
Whose eyes have only surmised fruitful soils,

5 I who have merely guessed the birds' existence
By sparrow-droppings on the brim of a hat,
I am that one who now, with meek persistence
Pray humbly to the Lord of Eden, that

I may in such green sunny places pass
10 The ultimate years that when at last I leave,
My shoes be smooth with unguent of crushed grass
And green be on the elbow of my sleeve.

c. 1940/1940   1941

A Psalm of Abraham, to Be Written Down and Left on the Tomb of Rashi

Now, in this terrible tumultuous night,
When roars the metal beast, the steel bird screams,
And images of God, for fraud or fright,
Cannot discern what is from that which seems, –
5 I, in bewilderment, remember you,
Mild pedagogue, who took me, young and raw,
And led me, verse by verse, and clue by clue,
Mounting the spiral splendid staircase of the Law, –
You, Rabbi Solomon bar Isaac, known
10 Rashi, incomparable exegete,
Who did sustain my body and my bone
With drink talmudic and with biblic meat, –
Simple, and for a child were they, your words,
Bringing into the silent wooded script,
15 Texts that came twittering, like learned birds,
Describing mightily the nondescript.
Not these can I forget, nor him ignore,
That old archaic Frank expounding lore
From his Hebraic crypt.

20 Nothing was difficult, O Master, then,
No query but it had an answer, clear, –
But now though I am grown, a man of men,
The books all read, the places seen, the dear
Too personal heart endured all things, there is
25 Much that I cannot grasp, and much that goes amiss,
And much that is a mystery that even the old Gaul,
Nor Onkelus, nor Jonathan, can lucidate at all.

Yours were such days, great rabbi, like these days,
When blood was spilled upon the public ways,
30 And lives were stifled, for mere glut of gore,
As they marched on, those murderous four,

Hunger and hate and pestilence and war!
    Wherefore, O Parshandatha of the law,
Unriddle me the chapter of the week:
35 Show me the wing, the hand, behind the claw,
The human mouth behind the vulture beak;
Reveal, I pray you, do reveal to me
Behind the veil the vital verity;
Show me again, as you did in my youth,
40 Behind the equivocal text the unequivocal truth!

O vintner of Troyes,
Consider the cluster of my time, its form and shape,
And say what wine will issue from this bitter grape!

I wait your answer; in the interim
45 I do, for you who left no son to read
The prayer before the sacred cherubim,
Intone, as one who is of your male seed,
A Kaddish:
            May it reach eternity
And grace your soul, and even bring some grace
50 To most unworthy, doubt-divided me.

c. 1940/1940   1953

A Psalm of Abraham, Touching His Green Pastures

From pastures green, whereon I lie,
Beside still waters, far from crowds,
I lift hosannahs to the sky
And hallelujahs to the clouds,

5 Only to see where clouds should sit,
And in that space the sky should fill,
The fierce carnivorous Messerschmidt,
The Heinkel on the kill.

They'll not be green for very long,
10 Those pastures of my peace, nor will
The heavens be a place for song,
Nor the still waters still.

c. 1940/1940   1944

A Psalm of Abraham, When He Was Sore Pressed

Would that the Lord had made me, in place of man-child, beast!
Even an ox of the field, content on grass,
On clover and cud content, had made me, made me the least
Of his creatures, one of a herd, to pass
5 As cattle, pastured and driven and sold and bought
To toil on ploughland or before a cart!
For easier is the yoke than the weight of thought,
Lighter the harness than the harnessed heart!

c. 1940/1940   1944

A Psalm of Abraham, Which He Made Because of Fear in the Night

Thou settest them about my bed,
The four good angels of the night,
Invisible wings on left and right,
An holy watch at foot and head:

5 Gabriel, Uriel, Raphael,
And Michael, of the angelic host
Who guard my sleep-entrusted ghost
Until day break, and break the spell.

Until day break, and shadows pass
10 My bones lie in a sack of flesh,
My blood lies caught in carmined mesh,
And I am wholly trodden grass.

But those the warders of life and limb
Escort my soul to distant shores,
15 My soul that in its dreaming soars
With seraphim and cherubim,

To lands unrecognized, to shores
Bright with great sunlight, musical
With singing of such scope and skill,
20 It is too much for human ears.

I see the angel's drinking-cup,
That flower that so scents the air!
The golden domes! The towers there!
My mind could never think them up!

25 Yet when the shadows flee away,
And fly the four good angels, and

I fare forth, exiled from that land,
Back to my blood, my bone, my day,

Untowered, unflowered, unscented banks,
30 Back to the lumpy sack of skin,
The head, the torso, and the shin,
I offer up, to Thee, my thanks.

c. 1940/1940   1944

A Psalm of Justice, and Its Scales

One day the signal shall be given me;
I shall break in and enter heaven, and,
Remembering who, below, held upper hand,
And who was trodden into misery, –
5 I shall seek out the abominable scales
On which the heavenly justice is mis-weighed.
I know I am no master of the trade,
Can neither mend nor make, clumsy with nails,
No artisan, – yet am I so forespoken,
10 Determined so against the automaton,
That I must tamper with it, tree and token,
Break bolts, undo its markings, one by one,
And leave those scales so gloriously broken,
That ever thereafter justice shall be done!

c. 1940/1940   1944

A Psalm of Resignation

I shall no more complain; I shall not ask
The question that betrays the doubting soul.
Tactful my words, my face shall be a mask.
I shall but say the flaws are part of the perfect whole.
5 Can it be otherwise?
For I am weary of the quarrel with my God,
Weary of cavilling at the works of the Lord;
For who indeed can keep his quarrel hot
And vigorous his cries,
10 When He who is blasphemed, He answers not,
Replies no word, not even a small sharp word?

c. 1940/1940   1953

A Psalm, to Be Preserved against Two Wicked Words

I am not of the saints, O Lord, to wear
The broken shoes of poverty, and dance.
For I am made sick at heart with terrible fear
Seeing the poor man spurned, looked at askance,
5 Standing, his cap in hand, and speaking low,
And never getting his fellow's heart or ear.
O may I never beg my daily bread,
Never efface my pride, like a dirty word;
And never grovel that my little chick be fed.
10 Preserve me from poverty, O Lord.

Preserve me, too, and Thou who knowest hearts,
Know'st this prayer does from the heart arise,
Preserve me from possessions, from the marts,
The mints, the mansions, all the worldly goods,
15 Debasing even the man of noblest parts.

From too much wealth that warps the very saints,
From power that ambushes the soul by stealth,
From suzerainty that fevers, and then faints:
Preserve me, Lord, from wealth.

20 But in Thy wisdom Thou canst so ordain
That wealth and poverty be known no more.
Then hadst Thou answered me, again and again,
Answered Thy servant, neither rich nor poor.

c. 1940/1940   1944

A Psalm to Teach Humility

O sign and wonder of the barnyard, more
beautiful than the pheasant, more melodious
than nightingale! O creature marvellous!

Prophet of sunrise, and foreteller of times!
5 Vizier of the constellations! Sage,
red-bearded, scarlet-turbaned, in whose brain
the stars lie scattered like well-scattered grain!

Calligraphist upon the barnyard page!
Five-noted balladist! Crower of rhymes!

10 O morning-glory mouth, O throat of dew,
announcing the out-faring of the blue,
the greying and the going of the night,
the coming on,
the imminent coming of the dawn,
15 the coming of the kinsman, the brightly-plumaged sun!

O creature marvellous – and O blessed Creator,
Who givest to the rooster wit
to know the movements of the turning day,
to understand, to herald it,
20 better than I, who neither sing nor crow
and of the sun's goings and comings nothing know.

c. 1940/1940   1944

Shiggaion of Abraham Which He Sang unto the Lord

O incognito god, anonymous lord,
with what name shall I call you? Where shall I
discover the syllable, the mystic word
that shall evoke you from eternity?
5 Is that sweet sound a heart makes, clocking life,
Your appellation? Is the noise of thunder, it?
Is it the hush of peace, the sound of strife?

I have no title for your glorious throne,
and for your presence not a golden word, –
10 only that wanting you, by that alone
I do evoke you, knowing I am heard.

c. 1940/1940   1944

A Song of Degrees

Consider the son of man, how he doth get him knowledge and
   wisdom!
Not to the sorcerer does he go, nor yet to the maker of books;
   not from the gait of angels does he take example; he
5   mimics not the antics of the cherubim.
The beasts of the field are his teachers; feather and fur his
   instructors, instructing him the way that he shall go
   therein.
Before their hooves, he sits, a disciple; to the eyrie, he climbs,
10   crying, *Master, Master.*
To the ape he bows down, the ape, flinging the cocoafruit,
   devising slings.
He worships the elephant for that he has an ivory sword.
He sees the bow of the porcupine, and the arrows of his quills;
15   a parable in shell the tortoise brings to him.
Even the noisome beast, whose spikenard sendeth forth the
   smell thereof, instructs him how that the enemy may
   be abashed.
How wonderful, therefore, is this son of man, who lets no
20   pride between him and his doctors, –
Yea, at this very instant, he gapes at the eagle's talons dropping
   volcanic rock.

c. 1940/1940   1944

To the Chief Bailiff, a Psalm of the King's Writ

Death, the peddler, came to my door this day.
Sold me his merchandise, old wares under a new name.
Forever and forever, piecemeal, must I pay.
Defaulting, he revendicates the same.

5 I shall not have peace any more.
But, every day, I shall arise,
And find him spying at my door, –
The agent with the estimating eyes:
Watching the parcels brought to me,
10 My mode of life, my personal mail,
And hoping most malignantly
That shortly shall those payments fail:
Whereat the bailiffs at his side
Unseen, like unseen creditor Death,
15 Shall claim their writ, hearth, home, and hide,
In lieu of merchandise, my breath.

c. 1940/1940   1941

To the Chief Musician, Al-Taschith, Michtam of Abraham; When One Sent, and They Watched the House to Kill Him

When I in prayer beseech thy benison,
Many are they thy favours I could seek:
A long and worthy life for my only son,
A happy hearth for my wife, and for my mother
5 Health, and untroubled waiting in the sun,

(A golden crown in Eden for my father!)
And for my several kin, I could also speak,
Of this one's need, desire of that one,
And ask for each of thy abundant grace: –
10 Save that today I ask no blessings, no,
I am but one of many almoners
Who ask for him thy devastating curse.

May his flesh fall from him, and may he living rot
Until he is not sure he is, or he is not.
15 May he be flung from fever into an icy cold
And may his days be long for him, but he not old.
May strange diseases take him, doctors come
From far-off lands to twitter over him,
Matter-of-factly, without pity,
20 As over a strange new scum.
O may his brain be peopled by grim ghosts
And may he wake from sleep, in sweaty fear,
Fearing four murderers at the four bed posts!

And after a fortnight of convulsions may he finally die,
25 And be remembered, if remembered at all,
In the name of some newly found, particularly disgusting fly,
Or in the writing on a privy wall.

c. 1940/1940   1944

To the Chief Musician, a Psalm of Israel, to Bring to Remembrance

By the rivers of Babylon, there we sat down, we wept
When we remembered Zion, –
O they are many that have had our tears!
The alluvium of Nilus is still fat
5 With the tender little bones of our firstborn,

And Tiber is still yellow like our badge.
Shall one forget the bears, and the Jews like bears
That danced on the shores of the savage Vistula?
Forget the crystal streams of castled Spain
10 So many fires failed to boil to salt?
Forget the Rhine? O Rhenish wines are sharp.
The subtle salt of blood gives them their sharpness.

Gather them up, O Lord, these many rivers,
And dry them in the furnace of Thy wrath!
15 Let them not be remembered! Let them be
So many soon-to-be forgotten clouds
Dropping their rain
Upon the waters of Thy favorite Jordan!

c. 1940/1940   1944

To the Chief Musician, Who Played for the Dancers

These were the ones who thanked their God
With dancing jubilant shins:
The beggar, who for figleaf pride
Sold shoelaces and pins;
5 The blindman for his brotherly dog;
The cripple for his chair;
The mauled one for the blessed gasp
Of the cone of sweet kind air.
I did not see this dance, but men
10 Have praised its grace; yet I
Still cannot fathom how they danced,
Or why.

c. 1940/1940   1944

To the Prophets, Minor and Major, a Psalm or Song

They are upon us, the prophets, minor and major!
Madame Yolanda rubs the foggy crystal.
She peers, she ponders, the future does engage her;
She sees the *Fuehrer* purged by Nazi pistol.

5 Sir Aries Virgo, astrology-professor,
Regards the stars, and prophesies five truces.
Herr Otto Shprinzen, of the same guild, a guesser,
From the same stars the contrary deduces.

They too have thoughts, those scriptural inspectors;
10 They count the verses, the hapaxlegomena,
By means of esoterical detectors
Foretell next year's right-guaranteed phenomena.

Ides is foretold, and doomsday, and God's thunders.
January greets the unseen with a seer.
15 Augurs prognosticate, from signs and wonders,
Many a cradle, yea, and many a bier.

These, then, the soothsayers, and this their season:
But where, O where is that inspired peasant,
That prophet, not of the remote occasion,
20 But who will explicate the folded present?

c. 1940/1940   1944

c. 1940/1941

A Benediction for the New Moon

Elder, behold the Shunamite, the rumour of her face,
And young man, know, the mirror of thy love!

Praise ye, therefore, the moon: each after his own fashion!
Sing ye a song:
5 The warrior for the brass buckler of David;
The learned man in his tent
For the bright candle smiling on his book.
Before that newly-minted coin
Rub, O little merchantman, thy joyous palms!

10 For the weaver of your tides,
Sing, O mariners, shuttlers of ships!
Praise it, O hunters, the hind you cannot stalk!

Lift up your heels; lift up your eyes to see,
Each after his own fashion, the seal of God
15 Impressed upon His open writ!

c. 1940/1941					1944

A Prayer of Abraham, against Madness

Lord, for the days allotted me,
Preserve me whole, preserve me hale!
Spare me the scourge of surgery.
Let not my blood nor members fail.

5 But if Thy will is otherwise,
And I am chosen such an one
For maiming and for maladies –
So be it; and Thy will be done.

Palsy the keepers of the house;
10 And of the strongmen take Thy toll.
Break down the twigs; break down the boughs.
But touch not, Lord, the golden bowl!

O, I have seen these touched ones –
Their fallow looks, their barren eyes –
15 For whom have perished all the suns
And vanished all fertilities;

Who, docile, sit within their cells
Like weeds, within a stagnant pool.
I have seen also their fierce hells,
20 Their flight from echo, their fight with ghoul.

Behold him scrabbling on the door!
His spittle falls upon his beard,
As, cowering, he whines before
The voices and the visions, feared.

25 Not these can serve Thee. Lord, if such
The stumbling that awaits my path –

Grant me Thy grace, Thy mortal touch,
The full death-quiver of Thy wrath!

c. 1940/1941   1944

A Psalm of Abraham, When He Hearkened to a Voice, and There Was None

Since prophecy has vanished out of Israel,
And since the open vision is no more,
Neither a word on the high places, nor the Urim and
    Thummim,
Nor even a witch, foretelling, at En-dor, –
5 Where in these dubious days shall I take counsel?
Who is there to resolve the dark, the doubt?

    O, these are the days of scorpions and of whips
    When all the seers have had their eyes put out,
    And all the prophets burned upon the lips!

10 There is noise only in the groves of Baal.
Only the painted heathen dance and sing,
With frenzied clamouring.
Among the holy ones, however, is no sound at all.

c. 1940/1941   1944

A Psalm of Time and the Firmament

Was it not kindled a million years ago
The starlight that now falls upon my brow?
Was it not uttered ages long ago,
The singing of that distant star, heard now?

5 That star is a dead coal these many years,
Fallen, perhaps, from the starry firmament,
And dead as are its ancient worshippers.
Its voice has long been still; its fire spent.

Yet on this night, I hear its voice, long mute,
10 And see its flame that has not been at all
Since days when David played upon his flute,
Even the days of the towering babel-wall.

c. 1940/1941

A Song for Wanderers

What was the song the gypsy sang
Singing to his fiddle?
The open road, and the pleasant place,
The sun that shines with a gypsy face,
5 The two halves of the beautiful world,
And O, himself in the middle!

What was the song the sailor sang
To the wind's soughing?
The silver on the moonlit sea,

10 The stars for jolly company,
   The harbor pub, and the girl in port,
   And O, a good wind blowing!

   What was the song the weary Jew
   Sang to his sorrow?
15 No song at all made sweet his lips,
   Not of travelled roads nor travelling ships.
   No song today wells from the heart
   That has no morrow!

   c. 1940/1941   1944

c. 1941/1941

A Psalm of Abraham, concerning That Which
He Beheld upon the Heavenly Scarp

1
And on that day, upon the heavenly scarp,
The hosannahs ceased, the hallelujahs died,
And music trembled on the silenced harp.
An angel, doffing his seraphic pride,
5 Wept; and his tears so bitter were, and sharp,
That where they fell, the blossoms shrivelled and died.

2
Another with such voice intoned his psalm
It sang forth blasphemy against the Lord.
Oh, that was a very imp in angeldom,
10 Who, thinking evil, said no evil word –
But only pointed, at each *Te Deum*
Down to the earth, and its abhorrèd horde.

3
The Lord looked down, and saw the cattle-cars:
Men ululating to a frozen land.
15 He saw a man tear at his flogged scars,
And saw a babe look for its blown-off hand.
Scholars, he saw, sniffing their bottled wars,
And doctors who had geniuses unmanned.

4
The gentle violinist whose fingers played
20 Such godly music, washing a gutter, with lye,
He saw. He heard the priest who called His aid.
He heard the agnostic's undirected cry.
Unto Him came the odour Hunger made,
And the odour of blood before it is quite dry.

5
25 The angel who wept looked into the eyes of God.
The angel who sang ceased pointing to the earth.
A little cherub, now glimpsing God's work flaw'd,
Went mad, and flapped his wings in crazy mirth.
And the good Lord said nothing, but with a nod
30 Summoned the angels of Sodom down to earth.

c. 1941/1941   1955

A Psalm or Prayer – Praying His Portion with Beasts

The better to understand Thy ways,
Divinity I would divine,
Let me companion all my days
The more-than-human beasts of Thine;

5 The sheep whose little woolly throat
Taught the child Isaac sacrifice;
The dove returning to Noah's boat,
Sprigless, and with tearful eyes;

The ass instructing Balaam
10 The discourse of inspired minds;
And David's lost and bleating lamb,
And Solomon's fleet lovely hinds;

Enfold me in their fold, and let
Me learn their mystic parables –
15 Of food that desert ravens set,
And of the lion's honeyed fells.

Above all, teach me blessedness
Of him, Azazel, that dear goat,
Sent forth into the wilderness
20 To hallow it with one sad note.

c. 1941/1941   1944

Ballad of Quislings

Poltroons may fear the foeman, for such are less than cattle,
But men will fear no other man who can be met in battle,
Where courage and the claymore cut apart the bitter quarrel,
Awarding one the willow, and the other one the laurel.

5 For the enemy who marches to the beating of his drum,
Men take their several stances: *Let him come! Let him come!*
But where shall men take counsel that they be not beblitzed
By the renegade, the falseface, the traitor in our midst?

O not from stranger hostile, but from that cordial native
10 Who rattles for a pleasant noise the shackles of the caitiff,
Preserve us, and protect us, and from our congregation
Uproot him, mask and members, and fling him to damnation!

O from the subtle traitor and double-damnèd knave,
Inhaling breath of freeman, exhaling speech of slave,
15 Protect us, and Lord, save us, for we are weak before
The enemy, with roses, whose shadow's at our door!

For how shall men of goodwill discern his parrot-screech?
And how discern the weasel wrapt in his weasel-speech?
Is not his loud toast proffered? His hand in friendship up?
20 And how surmise the dagger, or poison in the cup?

God grant he be found out, and *be* found soon thereafter
A-hanging, a fifth column, from taut rope and broad rafter,
His soul go up in sulphur, and he go out a-sizzling,
To that place where no horses are, nor any unsinged quisling!

c. 1941/1941   1953

Ballad of the Days of the Messiah

1
O the days of the Messiah are at hand, are at hand!
    The days of the Messiah are at hand!
I can hear the air-raid siren, blow away the age of iron,
    Blast away the age of iron
5 That was builded on the soft quick-sand.
    O the days of the Messiah are at hand!

2
O Leviathan is ready for the feed, for the feed!
    Leviathan is ready for the feed!
And I hold firm to the credo that both powder and torpedo
10   Have so fried that good piscedo
He is ready for the eating, scale and seed!
    Leviathan is ready for the feed!

3
Yea, the sacred wine is ready for the good, for the good,
    The wine of yore intended for the good –

15 Only all that ruddy water has now turned to blood and
      slaughter
    Has fermented into slaughter,
  Aged for so long, as it has been, in the wood –
    That wine of yore intended for the good!

  4
  O I see him falling! Will he shoot? Will he shoot?
20   Will Messiah's falling herald aim and shoot?
  'Tis Elijah, he announces, as he falls from sky, and bounces
    Out of all those silken flounces
  Of the heaven-sent and colored parachute:
    Messiah, he is coming, and won't shoot!

  5
25 Don't you hear Messiah coming in his tank, in his tank?
    Messiah in an armor-metalled tank?
  I can see the pillared fire, speeding on the metal tire
    Over muck and out of mire
  And the seraphim a-shooting from its flank!
30   O Messiah, he stands grimy in his tank!

  c. 1941/1941   1944

Ballad of the Dream That Was Not Dreamed

Manikin, manikin, in your chair,
Pantalooned, slippered, dreaming there,

What is the dream your evening weaves
Out of the journal between your sleeves?

5 I do not know your dreaming lore.
   I never dreamed this dream before.

   Manikin, manikin, what do you see
   Upon the screen of your revery?

   I see a dagger's shadow track
10 A shadow, and hide in its back!

   Manikin, manikin, what do you hear
   As music of your daily sphere?

   I hear the silver pieces fall,
   Thirty silver pieces in all.

15 Manikin, manikin, who do you smell
   That is like brimstone out of hell?

   It seems that they are odours three:
   Ink poisoned, blood, and t.n.t.

   Manikin, manikin, is there a name
20 Writ on the journal of your dream?

   I see no name; but a mark instead
   A double double cross, in red.

   Poor little manikin, 'tis no dream
   The images are as they seem.

25 Poor little manikin, wake to find
   This was no dream bred in your mind.

   c. 1941/1941

Ballad of the Evil Eye

    Booted and armed, the frontier guard
    Looks at the humble Jew,
    Begging for exit. His face is hard,
    His heart is iron, too.

5 'A passport to the devil,
    A visa plumb to hell
    Is all that I will grant to-day
    To the sons of Israel!'

    O weep not, weep not, broken Jew,
10 Nor lie you down to die.
    Not lonely are you in your plight,
    Nor sole in misery.

    This churl he hath an evil look
    He hath an evil eye.
15 He sees the bird upon the wing:
    It falleth from the sky.

    He looketh at the peasant man
    So hale of lith and limb.
    The peasant man, he cannot stir
20 For that he looked at him.

    His look it is a wicked look
    Beyond imagining.
    For it doth cripple, it doth maim
    God's every living thing.

25 God grant that it may come to pass
    That this knave may espy

537 / c.1941/1941

Himself in water or in glass
Staring with evil eye!

c. 1941/1941

Ballad of the Nuremberg Tower Clock

Nuremberg tower-clock struck one:
The swastika clawed at the sun.

Ring wrong! Ring wrong! The clock struck two:
Behind a curtain trembled a Jew.

5 Nuremberg tower-clock struck three:
Storm-troopers shouted blasphemy,

And as the public square did roar
The clock-hands heiled, and they heiled four!

The herald, as the clock struck five,
10 Read out the purged from the old archive.

The Fuehrer's words, vulpine, prolix,
Drowned out the song of the hour of six.

Indeed, they blared and shouted, even
As Nuremberg clock heckled: seven.

15 Somewhere, as Nuremberg clock showed eight
With crumbs a burgher wiped his plate.

A poet, at the hour of nine,
Thought, in his cell, of the beautiful Rhine.

O, in their sleep the clock struck ten:
20 Men stirred in a dream of murdered men.

Gestapo music rose to heaven:
The clock, delirious, struck eleven.

And O in that eleventh chime
Expired, as did human time.

c. 1941/1941   1944

Ballad of the Nursery Rhymes

Upon a day, and after the roar had died,
And the dust had settled, and the cities were no more,
He sat him down, alone, in a world that was wide,
As wide as is to a child his nursery floor.

5 And he sang all alone remembered snatches of song,
He wandered with the wandering of his mind:
Hey-diddle-diddle, and the music all gone wrong,
And the old clock turned by three mice that were blind.

His small voice cracked as he sang Cock Robin dead,
10 And twenty-four birds who mourned him from a pie,
And Simple Simon, begging his rationed bread,
And the poor dame whose ducks did always die.

O sad was his song when he sang Jack's tumbled crown,
And Jill who fell in channel from frying-pan,
15 And all the bridges that were broken down,
And fee-fi-fum, the bloods of the race of man.

539 / c.1941/1941

    And when night fell, night found him singing still:
    The sheep's in the meadow, the wolf is in the corn,
    And Humpty-Dumpty on a bombed window-sill,
20 Watching the moon, and the hornets on its horn.

c. 1941/1941   1952

Ballad of the Thwarted Axe

(*Coram* the German People's Court)

The judges sat in their blood-red robes,
The victim in the dock was stood,
The clerk read a number on a writ,
And the room smelled blood.

5   *Headsman, headsman, whet your axe,*
      Against the sparking stone,
      The blade that's eaten by the flint,
      The better eats the bone!

    The perjurers recite their rote,
10 The body, manacled, stands mute;
    It cannot be they speak of him,
    If they do speak the truth.

      Headsman, headsman, take their words,
      Each of a whetstone shape,
15   *And sharpen that good axe of yours,*
      To meet a stubborn nape!

    The prosecutor weaves his phrase,
    With withes of lust, and warpèd lore,
    Accused regards his shadow, now

20 Lying on the floor.

> *Headsman, headsman, that skilled man,*
> *He weaves a beautiful*
> *Red basket, firm and large enough*
> *To hold a severed skull!*

25 The chief judge in his blood-red robe,
Opens his red-lined book,
And blows therefrom a poisoned breath,
That pales the poor man's look.

> *Headsman, headsman, catch that breath,*
30 > *That is as sharp as lime!*
> *O, it will eat away the limbs*
> *Of any judge's crime.*

The court is done with its assize
Of overt acts and dead intents;
35 Now sawdust blots the red ink of
The bleeding documents.

> *Headsman, headsman, – cheated man!*
> *Whom thorough judges mock.*
> *You shall have no use for your axe,*
40 > *A ghost stands in the dock!*

c. 1941/1941   1944

Ballad of the Werewolves

Three werewolves on a deadman's chest!
Yo-ho-ho, and a bottle of blood!
(Hairlip, Ratface, and Medal-on-the-Chest
Quaff their liquor.) After us the flood!

5 Yo-ho-ho, and a bottle of life
For to batten the werewolves three!
Break it, uncork it, pry it with a knife!
'Tis good strong rum for Our trinity!

What if the corpse, he has been bled
10 To give us this swig of the tasty drink?
Look on the blood when it is red!
Skoal! and lose not the fortieth wink!

O wash us in the blood of the lambs
That once stood fleeced in the shivering fold!
15 Our guts crave blood, even Abraham's,
Quaffed from the heads that have been rolled!

A bottle of blood, and the moon on high,
And the werewolves crying, bold and clever:
Yo-ho-ho, here's blood in your eye!
20 The full moon doesn't last forever!

c. 1941/1941

Of the Friendly Silence of the Moon

Loosen the tangles of the dark,
Slip the moon in a sheath;
Let all be blackness, pitch and stark,
Rain darkness on the heath.

5 For every time the moon is out,
Death boards a bombing-plane!
His skull grins down upon his route,
The metric trickle of his brain.

Back to your sulphurous cocoon,
10 That hangs on the still night's breath!
Back to the caves of the poisoned moon!
Back to your hangar, Death!

Fool, that I wished for moonlight once,
To lay me down to sleep,
15 It is the moon brings evil ones,
Who make that slumber creep.

c. 1941/1941

Polish Village

At length, the peasant, plodding from the woods,
Came on his village, emptied of its folk,
Save for his sisters, weeping behind their hoods,
And his father's broken body, hanging from the oak.

543 / c.1941/1941

5 In his sisters' weeping, he heard no Polish phrase.
   They did not name the murderers, nor sob: *Why*.
   They showed him geese walking their arrogant ways
   And wheelmarks following the road to a broken sky.

   He wept, and to his holy church he ran,
10 And stood before the figure of Christ, and saw
   O those dear wrists re-broken! the newly-bleeding man!
   Jesus recrucified into a swastika!

   c. 1941/1941   1942

Sennet from Gheel

   And these touched thunders, this delyredrum
   Outbrasting boom from shekels of cracked steel
   Arrave the whirled goon dapht, as zany in Gheel!
   Mad as a hater, come, Nick knows warfrom!
5 Bedlam, Bicetre, and hundemonium
   Are compos and sain compared to the unweal
   Of these wildbats that frap in belfrydom!
   Or are these horrorbingers we are guerred
   And hale in Gheel, and lucid like the rest,
10 As good and woad as other humus merde?
   If so, sweet Lord of Hosts, kind exorcist,
   Fling us, un-levined, back to whence we erred,
   Zuruck to our lunasylum of the blest.

   c. 1941/1941   1944

Yehuda Halevi, His Pilgrimage

1

Liveth the tale, nor ever shall it die!
Upon his scroll the scribe has lettered it.
The learned rabbin, in his homily,
Its telling gilds with verse of holy writ.
5 O many a darkened Jewerie is lit
By its mere memory. It doth not fail.
Yet, in this latter day, who shall have wit,
Whose cunning of words shall in this day avail
For speech too grieving even for throat of nightingale?

2

10 Only the fingers of the wind may play
The harp of David on the willow tree;
And Solomon his song, none durst essay.
The sons of Asaph eke have ceased to be;
Dust are their temple throats; and also, he,
15 The chief musician is now stifled mould.
In Israel is no song save threnodie;
Shall then, for want of singer, stay untold
The tale of the pale princess and the jongleur bold?

3

Bard – and no Levite of degrees, no sweet
20 Singer in Israel, but a humble wight,
A process-server, a pleader at the leet,
Born, yea, miscarried to a pagan night, –
Sing thou the song that any other might,
Singing for supper; tell the tale as one
25 Who for a penny sobs his sorry plight,
And let thy words for her be orison
Of saddening evening, and dark midnight, and bright dawn.

4
Whilom in Toledoth, that ancient town,
Founded by Hebrews, built by the conquering Moor,
30 And governed now by that great Christian Don,
There dwelt the incomparable troubadour –
Bird on the lintel of the ghetto-door!
Brightest of feather of those plumaged throats, –
Melodious ibns of the golden lore,
35 Who sang the bubbling wine, the riddle's coats,
The ditty, merry or sad, and Love's so difficult notes!

5
Albeit he could joust with the wittiest,
Even with Ezra's sons, their courtesie, –
Apt at the wassail-word, the wedding jest,
40 The Saracen or Frankish measure, he –
Ermined in *tallith*, crown'd with phylactery,
Halevi, minnesinger of the Lord,
Liege to the manor of divinity,
Has utterly foresworn the profane word.
45 Homage he gives to God, and carols only at His board.

6
His was the ballad of the fluttering heart:
The hooded falcon on the wrist of God.
He sang its flights, its venery, its art,
Its moulting, and its final resting sod.
50 The jewell'd rhyming he devised to laud
The King in whose courts he carolled and was glad,
Were such as never issued from mere clod,
Or from the sage or the divinely mad,
Whether from Mantua or Lesbos or Baghdad.

7
55 Did he not also in that wondrous script
Of Al-Kazari chronicle that king,
The heathen begging of the godly-lipped
Some wisdom for his pious hearkening, –

A candle for the dark, – a signet ring
60 To make the impress of the soul, – that prince
Who covenanted with the mightiest King,
Abjured false testaments and alcorans,
Accepting only Torah and its puissance.

8
Scorn not the largess lavished on the bard
65 By Seigneur hearkening the bard's refrain:
The minted moon no merchant ever marr'd;
The sun, the silver currency of Spain;
The mountain flower, the flower of the plain;
And from the beaker of the soul, that wine
70 Which sours not; and from the bowled brain
Grape clusters torn from paradisal vine;
Honey of Samson's bees; and milk from Pharaoh's kine!

9
Thus, in that crowded town Castilian,
Where crypted is that psalter, writ on gold
75 In ink of molten ruby, th' inspired man,
Halevi, served God, luminously-souled.
Aye, and the learned glossators of old
Tell also of his leechcraft, subtil, wise,
For chills and fevers, humors hot and cold,
80 Simples for all who craved his remedies, –
Nazarite, Moslem, Hebrew – God's ailing entities.

10
Still is there aught which troubles him; it hath
No name nor appellation, yet it is.
Sometimes, it is a shadow on his path,
85 But thrown by whom he doth not know, y-wis!
Sometimes upon his brow, it is a kiss, –
Was it the wind or feather in the air?
He knoweth not; but there is aught amiss.
Daughter of sound? A footstep on a stair?
90 And in the synagogue, song heard, and no one there?

11

The stars are manna in the sky; the moon,
Fleshpot of Egypt. By its light he cons
Old parchment to a Babylonian tune.
He nods, he drowses. Sleep, the Cushite, fawns
95 Upon Halevi, and he dreams. O once
There were those wizards who could rede these things,
Make clear the dreaming to the dreaming ones –
Baker or cupbearer or young princelings –
But who shall now interpret these imaginings?

12

100 Behold in his dream, a castle on a hill,
Moated and massive, ominously-walled!
Of all its towers, one to a pinnacle
Rises, as if by constellations called
To keep all masonry abased, enthralled.
105 And from that tower is heard a voice, a sigh,
Bitter with Sorrow, sorrow that doth scald
Its hearer as it doth its votary,
At the barred casement of that doleful tower on high.

13

O beautiful beyond compare is she,
110 That lady in the tower of her gaol!
She is the very rose for mystery,
And like the lily is she lily-pale.
She speaketh, and it is as if a tale
Of the sharp thorn were told by the white rose,
115 Of fragrance that for agony doth fail,
And beauty stabbèd of her dagger'd foes,
Unpetall'd, plundered, and left lying in her throes.

14

'I was a princess in my father's hall,
Of all his daughters, his sweet favorite!
120 Was there a wish, a word my lips let fall, –
The King, my father, not fulfilling it?

O did I wish — as young girls without wit
Might wish — the golden platter of the moon,
Forthwith, I swear, the chamberlain would flit
125 Hither and yon, send messengers, — 'tis done!
So long ago that was — a dream, remembered, gone!

15
'Peace in the realm, my father on his throne!
The vintner, swarth, sits drinking underneath
The shadow of his grapes; the hay, new-mown,
130 Gladdens the peasant on the yellow heath.
And in the garden, I, the King's daughter, wreathe,
Many a flower for the King's delight,
Beauty the late summer doth bequeath, —
Peace in the realm! the generals, old, now fight
135 Only with bloodless chessmen throughout the noiseless night.

16
'Suddenly came the foe barbaric, slew,
Plundered and slaughter'd our poor scythe-arm'd youth:
They were a flame that through our hamlets flew
And left not standing palace, nor hut, nor booth.
140 Utterly without pity, without ruth,
Their sword proclaimed to widow and maid our shame;
The orphan, all affrighted by the uncouth
Stranger, remembered not his own pet name,
Remembering only, as I, the war-cry, flight, and flame.

17
145 'My father! O my father! I know not
Even to this day of his fate. I faint,
I shudder at the dark, the horrible thought.
Perhaps he fled the conqueror's constraint,
A beggar, and unrecognized, a saint,
150 In some far land of alien wont and word!
It may be — on his shield what blot, what taint! —
He picks the morsels flung beneath the board
By the loud drunken captains feasting with their lord!

18

'And me – alas! – be blotted out that day
155 Of ribald jest and ruffianish leer
When the barbarian spied me for his prey!
Again I see him, and again I hear
His frightening gutturals. Now, in this drear
Tower am I immured, and to be shown
160 Neighboring princes entertainèd here,
I am their caged bird, their unwitting clown,
Their most ungracious guest, their tarnished trophied crown.

19

'Who shall release me from this bondage? What
Warrior, mounted and plumed, shall some great day
165 Gallop the highway, jump the noisome moat,
Dismount, draw sword, and leap his clanging way
Up the long staircase, bloodied with affray,
And at long last, break down this studded door?
It shall not ever be – alack-a-day! –
170 Ransom shall not be mine, not ever more,
And perish I shall surely on this stony floor.

20

'O, if no prince shall ever bring release,
Nor any soothsayer use wizardry
Encompassing my freedom, then, God please
175 That soon – or I will surely cease to be –
One little precious gift be granted me!
May I soon hear my good folk speech again!
May I once more, before pale memory
Whitens the mind, hear talk that is like rain
180 Unto parched fields, like sunshine on the ripening grain!

21

'Hast thou some potion that will render me
A bird to flutter from these bars abhorr'd,
Halevi, bring it me; hast thou some plea
To melt the iron of this mailèd horde,

185　Place it before the Throne; hast thou a sword,
　　　Lift it against my gaolers; at the least,
　　　Bring me thy ringing, winging, singing word.'
　　　The shadow lifted, and the dreaming ceased.
　　　The moon had vanished, and the sun smiled from the east.

　　　22
190　What fumes within the alembic of his brain
　　　Conjured this dream? What pollen wafted from
　　　Blossoming orchards beyond the turbulent main
　　　Quickens the memory? What mountain drum
　　　Beating beyond the horizon, sends its hum
195　Echoing softly in Halevi's ear?
　　　In sooth, he knoweth not whence these things come;
　　　But he hath seen a far-off princess, near,
　　　A dark thing happening, and the Lord would make it clear!

　　　23
　　　He will no more of herbaries, nor drugs,
200　Nor physic that is arrogant; he will
　　　Give, as a gift, his phials and his jugs,
　　　And all the script of sage Aristotele.
　　　Begone, Toledo, incense-scented gaol!
　　　He will take staff in hand, and fare him forth
205　To unknown shores, across the perilous swell
　　　Of seas uncharted, whether south or north;
　　　And he will seek her out, that princess of great worth.

　　　24
　　　Cordova, diadem of Andaluse!
　　　Not from thy robed scholars, splitting hairs,
210　Nor from thy merchants of bright silk, came news
　　　Of her he sought, nor from the market-fairs
　　　Loud with the gossip of strange pilgrimers.
　　　They had not heard her fame. They knew her not.
　　　Each lifted dinars from his stringed purse
215　Stamped with some royal head; alas, this wrought
　　　Gold was not precious with the face of her he sought!

25
It is a ship, a full white beautiful swan,
Gliding to Africa on the Great Sea!
Alnath, alphered, alferoz, ald'baran, –
Loveliest blossoms on the heavenly tree
Guiding the slowly-moving argosy.
The mariners sing chanties of sea-folk;
Halevi marvels at the calm blue sea
Whose little waves salaam to the oak,
Breaking the glassy waters. And then the tempest broke!

26
The wind plucked out the stars from heaven; and
The sea, a furious serpent, leaped at the sky,
The ship, a pebble in a tall djinn's hand,
The little men, less than homunculi.
Quoth now the Berber captain, wrathfully:
'There is in our midst an unbelieving cur,
Faring to Egypt with his heathenry!
Into the sea with him, young mariner!
In fish's belly, let him reach Iskandahar!'

27
Answered Halevi: 'Pray unto your God!'
'Aye, that we have!' 'Then let me pray to mine!'
Then was Halevi's prayer like a rod
Smiting the wild uplifted wave supine.
To liturgy heart-rending came divine
Answer unto the sea-swept wind-swept dove!
The mariners gape now at the calm brine
And now stare at the kindly sky above
Where ald'baran, alnath, alphered, alferoz rove!

28
Are they not written in the annal books
The places of his perilous journeying:
The bright saharas, shimmering, with no brooks;
The deserts wild; the mountains harboring

Assassins; and the sweet oases spring
Where tribes fanatic curl in the scimitar?
250 And is not, too, recorded the welcoming
That Cairo, Demieyet, Iskandahar,
Made for the learned minstrel coming from afar?

29
But nowhere did he find the face he sought.
The silent pyramids, the ancient Nile
255 Knowing so many secrets, knew her not.
Shereef and scarrèd cid and rabbin smile
At this his search, and bid him tarry awhile
In new Mizraim where no pharaoh is;
In vain: the shadow grows upon the dial;
260 Time flies; and in the dungeon of distress
Waits, pale, her hair hung loose, the beautiful princess.

30
What Asian cities did his sandals shun?
He sought them all; the cities of great bazars;
The Gates where justice triumphs in the sun,
265 The village of the clanging armourers.
He sought them all; there where the gardener mars
The rose to attar, and the too-sweet air
Silences birds, and makes to swoon the stars!
He was to the fief of the crippled conjuror.
270 Ever he chased a shadow in a vision of nowhere.

31
Weary, and footsore, and in spirit low,
At length, at long last, after many days,
He is upon the dusty roads that go
Bowing to Palestine. O offer praise
275 Halevi, to thy Lord, for thine eyes gaze
Now upon land that is that holy stem
Whose flower, in heaven, blossoms forth ablaze
A flower, a flame, a talismanic gem –
Lift up thine eyes – the glorious Hierusalem!

32

280 O wondrous miracle that came to pass!
The blindfold of the dream is dropped away.
It is no vision, seen as through a glass, –
It is the brightness of the high noon-day.
Behold the princess in her sad array!
285 Certes 'tis she, and no vain stratagem!
It is she whom the vision did soothsay!
The princess of the fallen diadem!
Jerusalem, the princess! Fair Jerusalem!

33

Aye, but that dark dreaming is now bright.
290 The princess Zion is that princess fair
Gaoled by the cross-marked arrogant Frankish knight!
Still is she beautiful, though full of care;
Still is the jasmine fragrant from her hair
And still within her eyes is, shining, kept
295 Remembered sunshine. But despair, despair
Like a hot wind of the desert, overswept
Halevi, and he sang what was not song. He wept.

34

'Grieving for them, thy captive sons who are
The last sheep of thy flock, O Zion, take,
300 Accept from them their greeting from afar,
Their greeting and their longing and their ache.
Receive the homage of thy vassal, whose
Tears, like the dew of Hermon, seek thy hills,
Where he would be a jackal, all night long
305   Wailing thy bitter news,
Where he would dream away thy manacles,
And be the harp melodious for thy song!

35

'Peniel! Bethel! Mahanayim! sod
Where walked thy saints, where rests the Immanence,
310 Whose gates are open to the gates of God,

Whose light is not the light of firmaments
But the illumination of the Lord!
Shrines holy! where I would pour out my soul
As was the spirit of the sacred One
315   Upon you once out-poured,
How have you fallen to an evil dole,
Where slaves now lord it from your sullied throne!

36

'Thy ruins, thy waste places, and thy void,
Thy dwellings rendered rubble and small rock,
320 The chambers of thy cherubim destroyed –
Yea, there, though bleeding, barefoot, would I walk.
I will cut off my hair, and that day curse
That flung thy crowned ones among heathen foes;
I'll fast, for food and drink must surely reek
325   When I behold the curs,
Tearing the lion's litter, and day shows
The eagle bleeding from the raven's beak!

37

'O Zion, altogether beautiful!
Thy sons rejoice them in thy time of peace,
330 And in thy sorrow, their cup, too, is full.
They weep thy ruins, yet they never cease
From striving towards thee from captivity.
They bend the knee unto thy gates, thy sons,
Scattered on mountains, driven over seas,
335   Remembering, Zion, thee,
Yearning to touch the plinth of thy shattered stones
O but to touch the boughs of thy palm-trees!

38

'Can Shinar and Pathros equal thee for glory?
Can Urim and Thummim be surpassed by spells?
340 With whom compare thy kings, thy prophets hoary,
Thy Levites and thy singers? All things else
Will pass away – idol, idolater –

Only thy crown is for eternity!
Thou art God's dwelling place, His goodly booth!
345   O none is happier
Than he who with thee waits thy dawn to see
Thee once again as thou wast in thy youth!

39
'God granted that I might go wandering
Where He to seer and prophet was revealed.
350 God gave me wings that I might fly; and fling
My broken heart upon thy broken field.
O, I will fall upon my face, and kiss
Thy very stones, so blessed in thine earth;
I will take hold of thee, thy clods, thy soil,
355   Thy very dustiness,
And hold it as a thing of extreme worth –
Prized above rubies, and the richest spoil.'

40
Would that with these his tears this tale might end,
Even with this sad guerdon, this poor meed!
360 Zion abased by the irreverend,
Yet Zion, seen; Zion beheld, in deed!
But so 'twas not ordained, not so decreed;
Lo, from afar, and shouting a wild oath
Rideth an Arab on his thundering steed.
365 Nameless that rider, save for war-name, Death.
Zion, O Princess, receive thy minstrel's trampled breath!

41
Murdered, the minnesinger of the Lord!
Where rest his bones? None knows. Surely he dwells
In the third temple of the hallowed word,
370 Where Zion, even now, still hears the bells
Of high-priest moving at his rituals,
Where the fair princess still hears prophecy,
And joyful music, and the oracles
Consolatory of her misery,

375 Saying: The daughter of the king will yet be free.

42
Liveth the tale, nor ever shall it die!
The princess in her tower grows not old.
For that she heard his charmèd minstrelsy,
She is forever young. Her crown of gold,
380 Bartered and customed, auctioned, hawked and sold,
Is still for no head but her lovely head.
What if the couch be hard, the cell be cold,
The warder's keys unrusted, stale the bread?
Halevi sang her song, and she is comforted!

c. 1941/1941   1944

1941

In Memoriam: Arthur Ellis, 1870–1938
Executioner [Version 1]

1
No man is there but walks his long last mile;
All time is clocked to an electric switch.
Through months of fatal Fridays, no reprieves
Upon our verdicts smile,
5 Not for the doomed, nor those that doom, reprieves:
All mount the gallows; all descend the ditch.
Therefore have hempen days evoked your ghost
My dubious friend, recalled our tavern-talks,
And that young lawyer was again your host
10 Who heard you drop your deeds in pinewood box,
Tell of your skilful knots, and of that post
Where Death stood vertical, unorthodox.

2
Who'd boast a hangman of his social set?
Citizens stood facetious at your name.
15 The Man with the Rope, they said, The Lark at Dawn
Frock-coated Mister Death
And saying, tightened their ties in sombre fun.
Even your juries polled their twelve-fold shame
Upon your head, and black-capped judges whose
20 Justiciary fingertips you were

Despised you looping their man with your noose,
Despised you giving their deed sepulture.
And from all relatives, of course, abuse,
And from your country, only so much per.

3

25 Myself was not more kindliness; I deemed
You, thought unspoken, of a freakish breed
As man repulsive, charming, if a snake.
Your python knowledge gleamed
In crime and clue, and in confession's ache.
30 Your talk of hanged men, shocked, expelling seed,
Of the men docile, of those loud with rage,
Of eavesdropping upon eternity,
Your talk of final menus and of the
Terrible fright of the most frightening stage
35 Truly entranced me, as with speech of sage.
At the same time, your talk disgusted me.

4

But I recall you now with pity, ghost,
Recall your incognito life, your name
Kept out of phone-books, all your mail addressed
40 To some provincial post,
And neighbours told you never were at home,
You travelled in the public interest.
Always you bore an alias; you went
Friendless and childless your own long last mile.
45 Giving, you took the piecemeal punishment
Forever baffled by the civic guile
Which damned the servant of its orders, while
It hailed the courtroom's murderous intent.

5

My pity is the pity for my like.
50 All generation follows your red trade.
We eat our bread with blood; our rationed meat
Is cannibal, and decayed.

Invoking a great word, like you, we strike.
Like you, we prosper only on defeat.
55 Murder it is, and all men live by it,
Executors, or executioners.
The deed is noble, out of Holy Writ –
Kill off the evil, ere it will do worse –
Yet we performing this hard task, admit
60 Ourselves accursèd with your special curse.

1941

In Memoriam: Arthur Ellis 1867–1937 Executioner in Canada [Version 2]

1

No man is there but walks his long last mile;
all time is clocked to an electric switch.
Through months of fatal Fridays, no reprieves
upon our verdicts smile, –
5 not for the doomed, nor those that doom, reprieves:
both climb the gallows, both slide down the ditch –
Wherefore have hempen days evoked your ghost, –
shall I call you friend? – evoked our tavern-talks,
and that young lawyer was again your host,
10 with whom you bandied Crippen and Guy Fawkes,
with whom you quaffed the swift embarrassed toast
to Death the vertical, the unorthodox.

2

Who'd boast a hangman as of his social set?
Citizens stood facetious at your name:
15 *The Man with the Rope*, they said, *The Lark at Dawn*,
Frock-coated Mister Death;
and tightened their ties in unconvicted fun.
Even your juries polled their twelve-fold shame

upon your head, and black-capped judges whose
20 justiciary fingertips you were,
despised you even as you looped the noose,
the noose they wove, that they must answer for.
And from all relatives, of course, abuse;
and from your country, only so much per.

3
25 Myself was not more kindliness; I deemed
you — thought unspoken — of a hell of a breed,
as man, miscarried; charming, if a snake.
Your python knowledge gleamed
with clues, crimes, and not-guiltys always fake.
30 Your talk of hanged men, shocked, expelling seed —
O Love and Death upon the frightening stage! —
of trite confession, last gastronomy,
of the men docile, of those loud with rage,
all curiosa of the fatal tree,
35 the bitter apples of your pilgrimage,
tempted; and, now I say it — jaundiced me.

4
Still, I recall you now with pity, Ghost,
recall your incognito life, your name
kept out of phone-books, all your mail addressed
40 to some provincial post,
and neighbours told — suspicious of your game —
you travelled in the public interest.
O, baffled were you by the civic guile
which praising the courtroom's murderous intent
45 scorned you its servant, as if *you* stood trial!
Like crime, you bore an alias; you went
friendless and childless your own long last mile.
And each death, piecemeal, marked your own descent.

5
My pity is the pity for my like.
50 All generation's of your calling. All
are carnivorous, almost all men's meat
is cannibal.
Invoking a great word, like you, we strike.
Like you, we prosper only on defeat.
55 The deed is noble, out of Holy Writ,
and reasoned, *Kill off evil or see worse;*
yet this just murder, we performing it,
unmasks us, the masked executioners,
who at our fatal function must admit
60 ourselves accursèd with your special curse.

c. 1946/1946   1946

In Memoriam: Arthur Ellis 1867–1937 Executioner in Canada [Version 3]

1
There's not a man but must at last go up
towards the zero dangling for his breath!
There's not a one but is the strapped pendulum
that must his own time stop!
5 To each, to all, those shortened Fridays come,
braiding, both judged and judge, in one twined death ...
Wherefore have hempen days evoked your ghost,
macabre friend, evoked our tavern-talks,
and that young lawyer was again your host
10 with whom you bandied Crippen and Guy Fawkes,
with whom you quaffed the quick embarrassed toast
to Death the vertical, the unorthodox.

2

Who'd boast a hangman as of his social set?
Citizens stood facetious at your name:
15 *The Man with the Rope*, they said, *The Lark at Dawn*,
Frock-coated Mister Death ...
and tightened their ties in unconvicted fun.
Even your juries polled their twelve-fold shame
upon your head, and black-capped judges, whose
20 justiciary fingertips you were,
despised you at the looping of the noose
that made the flourish to *their* signature.
And from all relatives, of course, abuse,
and from your country, only so much per.

3
25 Myself was not more kindliness; I thought
you – thought unspoken – of a freakish breed:
as man, miscarried; charming, if a snake ...
Your python knowledge fraught
with *causes celebres*, not-guiltys (always fake) ...
30 your talk of hanged men, shocked, expelling seed –
O Love and Death upon that frightening stage! –
of trite confession, last gastronomy,
of the men docile, of those loud with rage, –
all curiosa of the fatal tree,
35 the bitter apples of your pilgrimage,
tempted, and, bitten into, jaundiced me.

4
Still, I recall you now with pity, Ghost!
recall your incognito life, your name
kept out of phone-books, all your mail addressed
40 to some provincial post;
and neighbours told – suspicious of your game –
you travelled in the public interest.
Oh baffled were you by the civic guile
which, praising the courtroom's murderous intent,
45 still scorned in you its own name, deed, and style ...

compelled you to an alias ... Thus you went
friendless and childless your own long last mile.
And each death, piecemeal, marked your own descent.

5
My pity is the pity for my like.
50 All generation's of your calling. All
are carnivorous, almost all men's meat
is cannibal.
Invoking a great word, like you, we strike.
Like you, we prosper only on defeat.
55 The deed is noble, out of Holy Writ,
and reasoned, *Such death's evil, but kills worse;*
yet this just murder, we performing it,
unmasks us, the masked executioners,
who at our lethal function must admit
60 ourselves accursèd with your special curse.

1954

c. 1942/1942

Autobiographical

1
Out of the ghetto streets where a Jewboy
Dreamed pavement into pleasant bible-land,
Out of the Yiddish slums where childhood met
The friendly beard, the loutish Sabbath-goy,
5 Or followed, proud, the Torah-escorting band,
Out of the jargoning city I regret,
Rise memories, like sparrows rising from
The gutter-scattered oats,
Like sadness sweet of synagogal hum,
10 Like Hebrew violins
Sobbing delight upon their eastern notes.

2
Again they ring their little bells, those doors
Deemed by the tender-year'd, magnificent:
Old Ashkenazi's cellar, sharp with spice;
15 The widows' double-parloured candy-stores
And nuggets sweet bought for one sweaty cent;
The warm fresh-smelling bakery, its pies,
Its cakes, its navel'd bellies of black bread;
The lintels candy-poled
20 Of barber-shop, bright-bottled, green, blue, red;

And fruit-stall piled, exotic,
And the big synagogue door, with letters of gold.

3
Again my kindergarten home is full –
Saturday night – with kin and compatriot:
25 My brothers playing Russian card-games; my
Mirroring sisters looking beautiful,
Humming the evening's imminent fox-trot;
My uncle Mayer, of blessed memory,
Still murmuring Maariv, counting holy words;
30 And the two strangers, come
Fiery from Volhynia's murderous hordes –
The cards and humming stop.
And I too swear revenge for that pogrom.

4
Occasions dear: the four-legged aleph named
35 And angel pennies dropping on my book;
The rabbi patting a coming scholar-head;
My mother, blessing candles, Sabbath-flamed,
Queenly in her Warsovian perruque;
My father pickabacking me to bed
40 To tell tall tales about the Baal Shem Tov, –
Letting me curl his beard.
O memory of unsurpassing love,
Love leading a brave child
Through childhood's ogred corridors, unfear'd!

5
45 The week in the country at my brother's – (May
He own fat cattle in the fields of heaven!)
Its picking of strawberries from grassy ditch,
Its odour of dogrose and of yellowing hay, –
Dusty, adventurous, sunny days, all seven! –
50 Still follow me, still warm me, still are rich
With the cow-tinkling peace of pastureland.
The meadow'd memory

Is sodded with its clover, and is spanned
By that same pillow'd sky
55 A boy on his back one day watched enviously.

6
And paved again the street: the shouting boys
Oblivious of mothers on the stoops
Playing the robust robbers and police,
The corn-cob battle, – all high-spirited noise
60 Competitive among the lot-drawn groups.
Another day, of shaken apple-trees
In the rich suburbs, and a furious dog,
And guilty boys in flight;
Hazelnut games, and games in the synagogue, –
65 The burrs, the Haman rattle,
The Torah-dance on Simchas-Torah night.

7
Immortal days of the picture-calendar
Dear to me always with the virgin joy
Of the first flowering of senses five,
70 Discovering birds, or textures, or a star,
Or tastes sweet, sour, acid, those that cloy;
And perfumes. Never was I more alive.
All days thereafter are a dying-off,
A wandering away
75 From home and the familiar. The years doff
Their innocence.
No other day is ever like that day.

8
I am no old man fatuously intent
On memoirs, but in memory I seek
80 The strength and vividness of nonage days,
Not tranquil recollection of event.
It is a fabled city that I seek;
It stands in Space's vapours and Time's haze;
Thence comes my sadness in remembered joy

85 Constrictive of the throat;
   Thence do I hear, as heard by a Jewboy
   The Hebrew violins,
   Delighting in the sobbed oriental note.

   c. 1942/1942   1951

Come Two, like Shadows

   Out of the yesterday, and ages gone
   Come two, like shadows on a bedroom wall,
   To haggle for the psychic jettison.
   It is a mighty wrestling, by my soul,
5 And which shall garner, at the very last,
   The paltry winnings, I can not foretell,
   Nor which of the shadows shall give up the ghost.

   Plato is one whose shadow I surmise
   As one surmises the man behind a screen.
10 His words, however, phosphoric, to my eyes –
   From whom, to whom, and what they nobly mean, –
   Love that is fleshless, passion that is dry –
   Betray the spirit come to keep me clean,
   Clean, – tropical only in philosophy.

15 That other shadow has a bedside manner.
   He holds my wrist; he bids me speak out *Ah*;
   Tell him about the dream of the crimson banner
   And of the carnivorous ladies that dream saw.
   – O, they are two in a surrealist void
20 Who haunt me: Plato and his shaven jaw,
   And the pudendal face of Doctor Freud.

   c. 1942/1942   1943

Dentist

The planetary motion of the blood,
Also the peregrinations of routine,
And the bright pendulum of dialectic,
      All go awry,
5 Lose their direction and their polarhood
      Before the keen
Weltschmerz residing in a cavity!

Sometimes, in such a dire case, this man –
He of the aloe'd pellets against pain –
10 Has been to my anguish – antiseptic Hero!
      But now, to-day,
I know him different, clumsy Caliban,
      Narcoticized brain,
Gloating with pincers over my dismay!

15 The panic of his nightmare's still with me:
This ogre of the hypodermic claws,
Smelling of novocaine and drugged mayhem,
      Knee on my chest,
Still runs amok among the ivory,
20   Distorts my jaws,
Still keeps my gurgled havoc unexpressed!

May thirty-two curses blight that torturer!
May his gums soften! May he lose his friends
Turning in silence from his exhalations!
25   His tinsel wreath
Fall from his mouth, abscessed, with clotted gore
      At its forked ends!
Thirty-two curses on his thirty-two teeth!

Pity he cries? May only thirty-one
30 Of those foul nibs slip from their gummy curves,
Leaving his food in lumps, uncut, unmolar'd
      For belly's sake –
And may one canine, comic and alone,
      And quick with nerves,
35 Remain – his weltschmerz and his livelong ache!

c. 1942/1942   1944

Desideratum

I am no contradictor of Cabbala:
that there are nerves two hundred forty-eight –
couriers through the forest of the flesh –
is sure arithmetic, and sacred; that
5 organs and limbs three hundred sixty-five
give motion to this Adam's also granted;
and that these two corporeal sums add up –
gematria inspired and symbolic –
to number the six hundred and thirteen
10 edicts of Holy Writ, is truth most glorious!

                                    Yet
I would these limbs were separable, these
members divisible from their heap o' bones:
a realm compact of sovereign entities,
15 the body's Powers, Dominations, Thrones,
all regnant for themselves, not galley-slaves
fettered unto the simultaneous oars.
Aye, where there stood one lonely worshipper,
six hundred thirteen would run godly chores!
20 And this were immortality man craves!

Instance this much-desired case: the skull
though severed from unbleeding shoulders, lives.
Severed, it ambulates to some green knoll,
its eyes upon the blessed sunshine thrive,
25 its ears, they are two beings all of sound,
its mouth, though throatless, speaks; its sheathed brain,
a watch whose tickings were in heaven wound,
unwinding Time ...
     The severed body? Let
that body, headless, go about its business,
30 its grosser tasks, ejaculate, excrete,
digest, perspire, micturate. The head
knows no dependence, lives!

c. 1942/1942   1944

Et j'ai lu tous les livres

From library to library I go –
The brothels of the mind – to seek the thrill
Exotic I shall, it seems, never know.
The condom novels, the journalonanist spill,
5 The cyclopedia's two score and twelve ways
And the minette of sapphic tongue, do not
Silence the strange desires of my days
Nor still the lechery of erected thought.
Houses of fame, farewell! I go again
10 To walk the bookless alleys of ascetic rain.

c. 1942/1942

Girlie Show

1
... What men or gods are these? What maidens loth?
    What mad pursuit? What feigning to escape? ...
Who are these satyrs, ribald and uncouth?
    What vestals, these, in pantomime of rape?
5 Does Pan still live? And is his rite still kept?
    I thought his flutes were silenced long ago,
        Himself remembered only on a vase;
Hellas, I thought, all hornèd Hellas slept.
    Who are these dancers, then, and these fauns, who
10   With beard of fingers, whistle lewd applause?

2
With quivering breasts, and ever-parted lips,
    Their navels bold, and violent their loins,
The dancing girlies thrill all fingertips,
    As music titillates the assembled groins.
15 O, in their crypts, there roar the little beasts
    Ready for sacrifice! ... The footlights blaze,
        Like altar-flames, where meeting comics cross
Waving their wands: two largely trousered priests
    Doing the ritual of oblique praise
20   In worship of the un-named omphalos.

3
This is the temple! Here the crippled come
    To throw away the crutches of their sex!
Who ails of sluggish blood, or members numb,
    Glows here again; who, of the dead reflex,
25 Stays clod at sight of the mere public parts,
    Here finds his blood, goat-footed, capering.
        Here, as the strip-tease queen struts on the stage,
To music pizzicato on g-string,

Her satin'd buttocks, smooth or quick, by starts,
30   The spent renew, the old forget, their age.

4
The son of Hermes lives! Not in bright glades
    Nor in dark forests, seek his votaries,
But enter here through marbled colonnades
    (Where smile, from feathers, photo'd goddesses)
35 The city sanctuary of the shaggy one.
    The ushers cry their aphrodisiac toys.
        The flutists set their reeds. The curtains soar.
At once, the legs and music are begun.
    The inflamed devotees make joyful noise.
40   And once more Pan is god, as he was god of yore.

c. 1942/1942

The Golem

This is the golem.
He is wooden, and he is painted brown.
In walking, he carefully lifts each foot
As if to kick it out of muck.
5 The mechanism in his throat goes cluck-cluck-cluck.
His dexter, at the hailed word, goes up and down.
Upon his upper lip, six hairs are stuck.

This is the golem.
The rabbi Nubal and his holy vessels
10 With pious incantation gave this clod
The strength wherewith he wrestles.
He was to serve none other but their god,
And save them from the bear of the human walk:

A hewer of wood – to keep their Sabbath hot;
15 A drawer of water – to fill his master's crock.

The incantation, alas, was too well wrought.
The golem ran amok!
                    He ran amok,
And all Bohemia's forests did not suffice
For his mad hewing; before his drawing of water
20 The rivers trembled. Had they turned to ice –

Mortified rabbi, how will you now undo
Your doing? How revoke your invocation,
Saving you call again the abjured spell:
The horns of iron, the bladed chariot, the
25 *Satanic chemical?*

c. 1942/1942   1945

Love

Love, love, love,
O lyric-love, half angel and half slut!
Uncleanest of the four-saxon-littered herd!
Foul euphemism of the apes in rut!
5 Laundered obscenity, the figleaf word
To hide the ambush of the treacherous gut!

It moves the sun and all the stars, this love.
Much pullulation goes on in its name.
Even reserved men wear it, with a glove.
10 All flatter the wench to believe herself grand dame.

The lady evangelist cries *Love*: the poet, too,
Passionate that his name be writ in water;
The playboy, likewise; and the salesman-crew
Roaming the country for the farmer's daughter.

15 All, all, testiculate their urgent throes:
June bridal cars sounding priapic horns,
The Ripper Jack whose luve's a red red rose,
And the monorchid, valiant among thorns.

O, oyster-swallowing gents and oat-ripe boys,
20 Always the jubilee turns jeremiad,
For after the long planning, brief the joys,
And after, always, every man is sad.

c. 1942/1942   1944

My Dear Plutophilanthropist

My dear plutophilanthropist,
Unclench your tight white-knuckled fist,
And give, as others of the tribe,
The annual philanthropic bribe:
5 From ancien and from nouveau-riche
The unimpeachable baksheesh!
It shuts the big mouth of the poor
From seeking and from getting more,
Narcoticizing with crumb'd bread
10 Rebellion in the pauper-head
And it costs nothing; for returned
Is merely part the pauper earned –
The sweetest saw-off to be had:
Two cents the dollar – Is that bad? –
15 And even these two paltry cents

Being tax-exempt, are Government's.
For us the cake, — the poor a maka —
Great is the Hebrew ideal: zdaka!
Can better business deal be made
20 Than this most double-dealing trade
Which here below, preserves your own
And up above, takes to the Throne
The blessing of the synagogue:
This overlord helped underdog.
25 Can better profit come to you —
All this, all this, and heaven, too?

c. 1942/1942

Pawnshop

1
May none be called to visit this grim house,
all cup-boards, and each cup-board skeleton'd
with ghost of gambler, spook of shiftless souse,
with rattling relict of the over-dunned!
5 Disaster haunts it. Scandals, once-renowned,
speak from its chattels. In its darkness glow
the phosphor-poor who stalk its rooms at night.
One should have razed it to the salted ground
antitheses ago,
10 and put its spectres long ago to flight!

2
Near waterfront, a stone's throw from the slums,
it lifts, above its wreckage, three gold buoys;
yet to its reefage tattoo'd flotsam comes
unsnaring bag and baedeker of toys.
15 Also those stranded on their own dear shores, —

the evicted tenant, the genteel with false name,
the girl in trouble, the no-good sons and heirs,
waver, and pause before its brass-bound doors,
look right and left, in shame,
20 enter, and price, and ticket their despairs.

3
Oh, for a coloured cardboard, wave out of sight
the dear, the engraved, the boasted inventory:
(a) family plate – hocked for the widow's mite;
(b) birthday gifts; the cups marked *champion* (c);
25 (d) tools; (e) special, vase picked up in Crete;
en bloc: watch; ring, endowing bride;
camera; medal; crushed accordion; –
rich votives of penultimate defeat,
weighed, measured, counted, eyed
30 by the estimating clerk, himself in pawn.

4
Whose lombard schemes, whose plotting kapital
thrusts from this lintel its three burnished bombs
set for a time, which ticks for almost all
whether from fertile suburbs or parched slums?
35 The architect is rusted from his plaque.
Was his name Adam? Was his trade a smith
who thought a mansion to erect of wealth
that houses now the bankrupt bricabrac,
his pleasure-dome made myth,
40 his let-do hospitality made stealth?

5
This is our era's state-fair parthenon,
the pyramid of a pharaonic time,
our little cathedral, our platonic cave,
our childhood's house that Jack built. Synonym
45 of all building, our house, it owns us; even
when free from it, our dialectic grave.
Shall one not curse it, therefore, as the cause,

type, and exemplar of our social guilt?
Our own gomorrah house,
50 the sodom that merely to look at makes one salt?

c. 1942/1942   1948

Penultimate Chapter

The carefully-evolved and cultured tribes
   Moved blithely in their habitats and keels,
Superior in the scripture of their scribes,
   And safe in discovered fire, invented wheels.

5 Foretold by neither seer nor seismograph,
   The imminent earthquake of ancestral mires
Stilled not their boast, nor falsified their laugh.

   Closeted were the skeletons of their sires!

Buried; but, in the frightening-fauna'd rock,
10   The dry bones quickened, in the nether plain
Stirred, and grew scales, and yearned once more to stalk
   The lesser prey. The strata burst!

                      Again
The wingèd reptiles in their slimy hosts,
   Their beaks saw-toothed, and their wingspread claw'd,
15 Swooped on the men who fled them, crying:
                            Ghosts!
Our wild progenitors have left their sod!

They fled to their coasts. Out of the wallowing sea
   The ichthyosaurus! The pigmies stood unmanned
Before the horrific stare of ancestry.

20   They scurried back upon the higher land, –
     Only to meet hooves' thunder, lightning tusks:
         Titanothere and tetrabelodon!

Terror unkerneled the dry human husks.

The mammoths (circa 1951) ...

c. 1942/1942   1953

That Legendary Eagle, Death

Somewhere above the innocent clouds there flies
The legendary eagle. Never yet
Have I beheld him. I have heard his cries.
And once his shadow and my shadow met.

5 I fear the vengeful king who sent him up!
Those claws are curled about the stones of our feud!
When will those stones fall, and that king eavesdrop
Upon the echoings of my splattered blood?

Often I hoped to make my enemy sad,
10 Impatient in his windy turret for
News of the eagle, and none to be had –
Lost in the skies, dead on the ocean floor.

I therefore aimed, by shadow and by call,
My arrows at what I thought his wings of jet.
15 The arrows rose. The eagle did not fall.
That wrathful king will have his vengeance yet.

c. 1942/1942   1953

Variation of a Theme

1
Enamort have I been of bleaseful Death,
Knelled him soft names in manes a muted rhyme;
Or, vault-face, trumpeted my herald breath
Into Gold Gotha echoes of his fame:
5 *The Lord of Ghosts; the Imperor of Bearse;*
Rex Tumulus; great Sherasod the Prince;
Menhir von Wrinklemop; Barow de Hearse;
Le Comte de Funct; von Waggoner, C.G.; Sire Mintz.

2
Mr. O. Topsy-Turf, of Cher Noel House;
10 *The Mausolem, Sir Koph-Ag, L.A.G.;*
That mandarin chap Suo Seid; the Russ
Undone Checkofsky; Ripper R.I.P.;
Sven Swansong; Harry Carey, Samurai;
Nick Ropoulos; Regratter Abie Taff;
15 *The Cryptic Patriark; Chief Wenanwei;*
Allover Cromlech; Rotter Doestenasher, graph.

3
O I have skald his eili-aces rite,
And conjoured him in alles shapes and garbs, –
As heirold in black ossuary dight,
20 As Abbot Ware, as Coopèd haeming barbs,
As Myster Wynken brinken nods; I've seen
Hymn in his cere-monies and costumes, yea
As houriental djinn, of yestern mien,
As mielancholy Dane, and aye as Francheman gai.

4

25 His gags, his joker-knots, his escapades,
His bower, his mite, they monsternate me not.
I know his tryx, the way-pence of his trades, –
He has been sybilled blacker than he wrot.
I do not fear him, and it may well be
30 That I aspyre his embrass, would cry:
'Acain my brooder, comes to call for me,
And more than ever, mortal, it seems rich to die!'

c. 1942/1942   1944

c. 1942/1943

The Hitleriad

I

Heil heavenly muse, since also thou must be
Like my song's theme, a sieg-heil'd deity,
Be with me now, but not as once, for song:
Not odes do I indite, indicting Wrong!
5 Be with me, for I fall from grace to sin,
Spurning this day thy proffered hippocrene,
To taste the poison'd lager of Berlin!

Happier would I be with other themes –
(Who rallies nightmares when he could have dreams?)
10 With other themes, and subjects more august –
Adolf I sing but only since I must.
I must! Shall I continue the sweet words
That praise the blossoming flowers, the blossoming birds,
While, afar off, I hear the stamping herds?
15 Shall I, within my ivory tower, sit
And play the solitaire of rhyme and wit,
While Indignation pounds upon the door,
And Pity sobs, until she sobs no more,
And, in the woods, there yelp the hounds of war?

20 I am the grandson of the prophets! I
    Shall not seal lips against iniquity.
    Let anger take me in its grasp; let hate,
    Hatred of evil prompt me, and dictate!
    And let the world see that swastika-stain,
25 That heart, where no blood is, but high octane,
    That little brain —
    So that once seen the freak be known again!

    Oh, even as his truncheon'd crimes are wrought,
    And while the spilt blood is still body-hot,
30 And even as his doom still seems in doubt,
    Let deeds unspeakable be spoken out.
    Wherefore, O Muse, I do invoke thy aid,
    Not for the light and sweetness of the trade,
    But seeing I draw a true bill of the Goth,
35 For the full fire of thy heavenly wrath!
    Aid me, and in good time, for as I talk
    The knave goes one step nearer to the dock;
    And even as triumphant cannon boom
    He marches on his victories — to doom!

    II

40 See him, at last, the culprit twelve men damn.
    Is this the face that launched the master-race
    And burned the topless towers of Rotterdam?
    Why, it's a face like any other face
    Among a sea of faces in a mob, —
45 A peasant's face, an agent's face, no face
    At all, no face but vegetarian blob!
    The skin's a skin on eggs and turnips fed,
    The forehead villainous low, the eyes deepset —
    The pervert big eyes of the thwarted bed —
50 And that mustache, the symbol of the clown
    Made emperor, and playing imperial pranks —

Is this the mustache that brought Europe down,
And rolled it flat beneath a thousand tanks?

III

Judge not the man for his face
Out of Neanderthal!
'Tis true 'tis commonplace,
Mediocral,
But the evil of the race
Informs that skull!

You ask, is paragon'd
The Nordic in this thrall?
Why, chivalry's not found
In him at all!
And he's the beast not blond,
Nor is he tall.

His strength is as the strength
Of ten, and ten times ten;
For through him, magnified
Smallness comes to our ken –
The total bigness of
All little men.

IV

The dossier, then; the facts, the untampered text:
Let *this* world know him, ere he goes to the next!
Where was he born? (Born is the word that I
Use, seeing *littered* is not poesy.)
Where was he born? In Braunau at the Inn –
And Austria paid for that original sin! –
Born to a father, old and over-wined
Who had he slept one night, had saved mankind!

80 At first hight Schicklgruber – 'what a name
    To herald through the mighty trump of fame' –
    Heil Schicklgruber! Schicklgruber, heil!
    Methinks this lacks the true imperial style,
    And certainly no poet's nor mob's tongue
85 Could shake from shekel-shackle-gruber – song!
    The gods are kind. His father changed his name,
    And saved, at least the Schicklgrubers' shame.
    Soon he removed to Linz. Now, note this well,
    This was the town where Rilke wove his spell,
90 Where Rilke dreamed the beautiful and good –
    And on this *boden*, Hitler dreamed of *blut*!
    His teachers have since died; and fortunate they
    Who else had died ten deaths to see the day
    The dunce of the corner corner better men,
95 And great wealth his who could not count to ten!
    Doctrine he spurned, and scholarship despised:
    Let others win the palms so meanly prized –
    The teacher's apple and the fiat lux –
    Sheepskin for sheep, and for the bookworm books.
100 Let others learn to love their fellowmen;
    He had no fellow, neither now, nor then.
    Let others learn to love their neighbours. He
    Hated his father and all Linz-ery.
    (Forgive the young: he'd see his hate untwined
105 To take in, generously, all humankind.)
    Wherefore, uncouth, untutored, unconcerned,
    He left his school most thoroughly unlearned,
    Fit for the plough – before it, not behind! –
    And as time proved, the premier German mind!

V

110 But did he not in art show promise, such
    As to forgive, if not all ignorance, much?
    He did; the first of many promises
    Still unfulfilled, most tolerable, this:

He drew a line, it was not crooked, so
115 He thought that he was Michelangelo!
Yet is it true that in due time, he would
Incarnadine him murals with much blood;
To Europe's marbled treasures adding his
Ruins out-ruining Acropolis;
120 Yes, with a continent for easel, he
Would yet show vicious virtuosity,
Would yet achieve the opus of his dream,
The classic painting, masterpiece supreme:
The Reich's *Last Supper* (out of stolen pots)
125 With quislings six, and six iscariots!

Meanwhile he dreamed, and dreaming saw himself
Rich and esteemed on many a library shelf,
In many paintings hanging from a wall,
(This hanging theme, is it prophetical?)
130 And *Hitler fecit, pinxit Hitler* was
The only Latin of his final class.
He comes before his betters to stand test:
Is this an artist, for he is ill-dressed?
Is he to paint, because he cannot write?
135 *We believe his linens would look better – white!*
And for the first time Adolf's judged aright.

VI

Here stutters biography. The scribes conflict
In qualifying Vienna's derelict:
Was he a bricklayer, as some aver,
140 A paperhanger, or a carpenter?
The witnesses ignore.
It seems, in any case, – symbolic thing! –
He always worked on scaffolding.
Some others say – on oath – he had no trade,
145 Blame his survival on the public aid.
He slept, they say, in flophouses; he wore

Castoff; he ate handouts at the door;
('Tis no disgrace. Disgraceful only is
Ignoring in others one's own miseries.)
150 He fed on alms, these say. 'Twas Jewish food.
Hate knows no firmer ground than gratitude.

VII

And then there came – blow, trumpets; drummers, drum! –
The apocalypse, the pandemonium,
The war the Kaiser from his shrivelled hand
155 Let fall upon the European land.
Mark well, O men, the manner of our man:
He who not once in his entire life-span
Was either by sympathy or sorrow swept,
Heard of the carnage imminent – and wept!
160 He wept – but let us his own words employ:
'I fell on my knees, I wept, I wept for joy!'

Now this was the stuff of which a soldier's made!
But after four years, where is Adolf's braid?
Where are his medals? His promotions, where?
165 He had none; could it be he'd failed to dare?
Or could it be the brave of the front-line
Too often showed the salient his spine,
And chose too often duties, unsung, drear –
But safe – 'to bring dispatches to the rear'?
170 O could it be that this was, after all,
How Adolf humbly stayed a corporal?
Alas, that then the untaught General Staff
Knew *intuition* as an epitaph,
And did not, as in later times, bestow
175 On this non-sense its generalissimo!

VIII

    Why, even in his private little war,
    His march on Munich, when for the first time
    This painter showed his phobia of red,
    It was old Ludendorff, the warrior,
180 Still battling Foch, but now in pantomime,
    Who marched breast forward, while – while Adolf fled,
    Fled, with the fleeing of his own brave words,
    Fled, fell on his face, and not upon his spear,
    Got up, and fled, a rabbit to its hutch.
185 Such was the hero, flashing others' swords!
    Such was the leader, leading bouts with beer!
    Such was the puttering-out of the Great Putsch!

IX

    Let it be said of Hitler, then, that he
    Had courage, when he had a guarantee;
190 He risked, when primed assurance smiled; he dared
    When the positions had been well-prepared.
    He sought the German power, – but no haste:
    The dotard Hindenburg would see him placed.
    He marched across the Rhine; yet it was plain
195 A bullet would have marched him back again.
    He coveted the Czech-land; yet he waited
    Until that prize was generously donated.
    Circumspect, cautious, of an humble air –
    Until he found he could afford to dare.
200 Then, summoning the pensioned warriors,
    Then, even then, he followed his true course,
    Mounting no charger, but a Trojan horse!

X

So, you may say, he was a miracle
Of bold persuasion and of iron will, –
205 And sure he needs no courage who has skill!
What skill? And what persuasion? Skill to use
Hatred as bomb, and rhetoric as fuse?
Persuasion to persuade the Swabian mind
It was the unwhipped cream of humankind?
210 A bag of tricks, a mountebank's recipes,
Fit only for the half-mentalities
By birth and training sedulously bred
To swap, for circuses, their daily bread.
Consider with what petty bribes these were
215 Perverted from both Kant's and Goethe's lore,
Pure Reason bartering for Force impure,
And their Faust-soul betraying for a whore!
Consider for what baubles they sold out:
The shoddy uniform; the chorus'd shout;
220 The bonfired books; the robot-like salutes;
The ever-marching military boots!
These, such as these, no genius, but mere quack
Could soon reduce from people to a claque,
And bid them be, enamoured and enticed,
225 Of crooked cross re-crucifying Christ!

XI

Go to *Mein Kampf* if you would know his trade,
And there learn how a people is unmade,
And how, with mocking pantomime,
The tyrants on its ruins climb.
230 There learn the rules,
(Transparent unto all, save fools)
There take the lessons from the literate boors
And learn to lead the lofty-destined Reich –
Or Barnum-Bailey tours!

235 Learn it from Adolf's very prosiness,
Indited by his fellow-convict, Hess,
(Though adept at the demagogic yell,
It is averred that Adolf could not spell)
Learn it from him, who, east, west, north and south,
240 Excelled in the loud bigness of his Mouth!

Learn
How with the double-jointed rhetoric
He turned men's minds – (and stomachs) – and the trick;
Hear him reveal the charlatan's technique:
245 The prearranged ad-libs, the advisèd shriek,
The spontaneities prepared, the stance
Best suited for prophetic eloquence,
The iterated and ecstatic prose,
And above all, the pose, the Wagnerian pose!
250 And hear him brief his wisdom, brashly smooth:
'The lie, if oft repeated, is the truth!'

Read, marvelling, the slogans that did foil
The Hun intelligence: Blood, Honour, Soil:
The worship of the blood, in Arians veined,
255 And in all others preferably uncontained;
The practice of an Honour, modified
By the dear temperature of one's own hide;
And as for Soil, a simple ratio:
Nazis above, all others deep below!

260 Add then, the insured craft with which he chose
The chosen people for his choicest prose:
Here was a scapegoat to his measure made,
Big enough to inform his wild tirade
And too small to return its foe his due:
265 The strange ubiquitous Jew!

When could one find a better scapegoat than
The bearded Hebrew cosmopolitan,
Than this the Israelite, not far to seek,

Who was at once an alien, and weak?
270 Is it the rich who rouse the tribune's ire?
Some Jews are rich, and can well feed his fire.
Is it the poor, the indigent radical?
Judaea's destitution is not small.
The Jew's unsocial – he will not join in
275 The civic hubbub, the political din,
And also he's too forward; everywhere
Smell his ambitious presence in the air!
Pietist, he pollutes with his old creed
The pagan vigour of the German breed;
280 And at the same time lifts the mystic mist
From off the German mind – the atheist!
All evil from this Marxian plutocrat:
The Weimar laws, and the Versailles diktat,
The lowered standards and the rising costs,
285 Inflation and heat-waves, taxes and sharp frosts,
All, all achieved by the Semitic hosts.
The theorem did not matter, nor its flaws, –
Sufficient to sneer 'Jew' to win applause,
Yelp 'Jude,' and await the frenzied jeers –
290 And thus assure the Reich its thousand years!

So did he still the German hunger with
The ever-novel but right ancient myth,
And taught his people first to heil and hoot,
Then legislate, then doom, then persecute,
295 Visiting even on the blondest Jew
The crime his great-great-great-grandmother knew!

Such his persuasion, and – the authentic curse –
Such the too-soon persuaded Berliners.
(Observe the method in this madness, since
300 The Jew being beaten, the world did not wince,
The vogue was shown, by flesh-barometer,
He could persist, yet no great risk incur.)

XII

Yet not alone
Did Hitler do the deeds for which he must atone!
305 Henchmen he had,
    Spirits and genii whom he did evoke
    Out of the bottled Herren-volk,
    Frustrated men, who'd tried all things, and failed,
    And then determined to be jailed, or hailed!
310 *Herr Goebbels such a one –*
    Club-footed, rat-faced, halitotic, the
    Brave Nordic ideal, a contrario!
    A kept man; eloquent, a Ph.D;
    Carried no gun, forsooth; a radio
315 Lethal enough for him, shouting its lies,
    Exploding lebensraum and libido;
    Subtle in puncturing all human foibles
    Saving his own, prolific in alibis, –
    Goebbels.

320 *And such that other, Rosenberg,*
    The penman of the mob; had written books;
    Corrected Adolf's grammar; could devise
    Seventy reasons for atrocities;
    Scorned pity; credited with stabbing hooks
325 Into the too-compassionate Christian crux;
    Concocted, weekly, blood-philosophies,
    To genuflect non-Arians to their knees;
    Was daft about his twentieth-century spooks;
    Herr Rosenberg, burdened with double shame:
330 A Baltic birth, and a Semitic name.

    Nor was he absent, that ubiquity,
    Goering, the arsonist, who loved disguise –
    A uniform for every pantomime,
    Including asbestos for the Reichstag crime –
335 Goering distinguished, mainly, by his size,
    By the great girth's unrationed symmetries,

Ridiculous, in ersatz-land, sublime!
There was geheimrat who was not geheim!
Big in his own, and other people's eyes!
340 Loved hunting, pref'rably biped quarry;
Loved art, if stolen; loved imported grub;
Addicted to the narcotic and the gory;
Bore weapons (daggers); led a lion-cub;
And thought that full-face photos spread his glory.
345 (There is, of course, no profile to a tub.)

Nor yet was overlooked the fashion-plate:
Be not deceived by the manners of this fop,
His hat and gloves, his apathetic heils.
This was no dandy, but a man of wiles,
350 The double-swasticrossing Ribbentrop.
Think him not milksop, no, nor champagne-sop.
His morning coat was cut to the latest styles
Of armour-plate; he was the villain who smiles,
And pours the cocktails with the poison-drop.
355 He was the fingerman who spied the job;
The Cliveden layout was his tour-de-force,
And it was he contacted the Vichy mob,
And he who fed oats to the Trojan horse,
'Twas he, the master of the slick hobnob,
360 Who put in protocol the Nazi curse!

XIII

And other lesser fry there were
Who joined the Nazi exchequer,
Careerists who sought living-space
Upon the body of their race,
365 Each coming forward, for a price,
To sell his own especial vice:
Von Papen, spy and diplomat,
Hiding low cunning in high hat,
Giving his masters fealty

370 As long as they held mastery,
    Reliable, whate'er might happen
    To serve the good of Herr Von Papen!

    And Himmler, Heinrich, mild and meek,
    Most studious of the human shriek,
375 Inquisitive about the extent
    To which men could take punishment,
    Already planning for the foe
    The order of the Gestapo,
    Already practising to bowl
380 With all the heads that needs must roll,
    Already forging chains and gyves
    For the long night of the long knives,
    Himmler, most self-effacing, and
    Effacing others with Kultur's impartial hand.

385 Oily, obscene, fat as a hog,
    The thick scourge of the synagogue,
    The loutish uncouth pedagogue,
    Streicher, brings up his hefty rear,
    Among his bandit peers, a peer –
390 Meet now, the brothel-keeper for
    The votaries of racial lore,
    Who procured, by his journal's traffic
    The titillation pornographic,
    The lewd urge, the concupiscent thrill
395 By which he proved him human still.

    He also stood, with beckoning claw
    Holding uncandid camera –
    The fawning Hoffman, who dared give
    The Fuehrer his sole negative;
400 And he, hook-nosed, was also there,
    The learnèd doctor Haushofer,
    Expanding Hitler's empery
    By dint of pure cartography:
    The soldiers pluck what his school picks –

405 The art is geopolitics.
　　Nor should one fail to speak to-day
　　Of the besotted Robert Ley
　　Since drunken underneath a table
　　To speak himself he is unable;
410 Nor yet forget – alack-a-day,
　　Volatile Hess who flew away.

　　O what a crew unto their leader like!
　　As master mongrel, so each crawling tike,
　　And all the saviours of the German Reich!

XIV

415 Aye, were not others at that honeymoon,
　　Herr Strasser and his strange gregorian tune,
　　And Captain Roehm, ever in love with youth,
　　Best man among the paladins of truth?
　　Where are they now?
420 These knights reproachable but without fear?
　　O where is Schleicher's intellectual brow?
　　Why does not Heines, stalwart, reappear?
　　Where are the crows of yesteryear?

　　Departed, gentlemen, but without dirge.
425 The gallant Fuehrer had to have his purge;
　　These worthies, therefore, came to bitter ends:
　　They'd sinned the supreme sin – they were his friends!

XV

　　Yet not by their sole aid did Adolf rise,
　　His greatest help came from his enemies:
430 The eye-glass'd Junker looking down
　　Upon the upstart corporal clown;
　　The simple Social Democrat;

The Catholic, and concordat;
The too-shrewd plutocratic vons
435 Thyssen, Hugenberg and sons;
The dialectic theorist who saw the ever-thickening mist
And cheered, in hope that soon therefrom
The light, hegelian, would come;
And even Hindenburg, who in alarm,
440 Sold a republic for a private farm!

Each in his fashion, and for personal sake
Led Germany to Hitler's stake.
Yes, let it be told, let it be written down
How even from afar
445 There came the aid that burned the Republic brown;
Let it be told
How gold tycoon, how monied czar,
Reaction black, and Interest, dirty-grey
Trembled before the rumour of that plot
450 Plotting for Europe its Muscovian day,
And trembling, dropped more coin into the Nazi pot!

Let us not name the names, but let us speak
Only about munition'd dividends,
Of markets rising to an envied peak,
455 Of rubber's conscienceless elastic ends,
Of timely trains by fascists always mann'd,
And of umbrellas, which, alas, did leak.
Those who have memory will understand.

XVI

Who are those thousands in the goose-step march?
460 *Athletes*, said Papen, sly and arch.
Whose are those planes that through the ether race?
Commerce, said Goering, with cherubic face.
The tanks that still keep coming, on and on?
Said innocent Ley: *The Volkswagon.*

465 And all those lovely gases, what are they?
Said Goebbels: *Cure-alls for a better day.*

Within the chancelleries, the diplomats
Chuckled and winked behind their polished hats;
And Downing Street announced from Number Ten
470 The balance of power balanced once again.

XVII

There were – the decade's grace – who saw
This moulting of the moral law,
Who cried against the knaveries
Designed to please and to appease,
475 And such an one was he who stood
Late and alone against the flood,
The man who hated sham and cant,
Unfortunately brilliant,
Churchill, who kept our world extant!

480 Across the seas, still doomed to wait,
Man's conscience-made-articulate,
Roosevelt sent forth his biblic words
As he would yet send forth, for vengeance
The steel leviathans, the flaming swords,
485 The swift seraphic engines!

Ah, he who might have led great France
Against the brazen countenance,
Was gone from twilight into night, –
The Tiger, ever-burning bright!

XVIII

490 But was there not, to cope with this intrigue –
To keep the peace – the wise Wilsonian league?
The League of Nations – what a hope was there,
Fled with the years, vanished in spoken air!
It could have had no other fate. Alas,
495 Who looked, could long have seen it in the glass:
The kisses blown with weak asthmatic breath
By old men gesturing themselves to death.
Were these the men to put teeth in the law,
Who had no tooth in their collective jaw?
500 Were these the men that would the peace maintain
Themselves upholding only with a cane?
Could these look in the future, who could not
See without specs, and those, at home, forgot?
Most miserable world which had to lean
505 Upon the dotards of this dying scene!

While such as these, then, guard the public weal
And safety totters, and security
Goes palsied, doddering and down-at-heel,
While Senex drones, and all Geneva snores,
510 He'd be no burglar, who in such event
Did not bethink him of his burglary,
To try his key in all the tempting doors!

And Hitler read his opportunity!

XIX

How blind these were, he thought, who did not see
515 The new excalibur that rose in air
That certain weapon of short victory,
Which using, even the unrash might dare
The great assault, the sudden lightning thrust!
Before this thing, defenses could not score,

520 And pacts were sand, and maginot were dust –
     This Stuka of the fourth-dimensional war!
     Let then, the old men, therefore, rack their wits,
     Magniloquizing their paralysis
     As if it were a tactic of Clausewitz.
525 From hidden hangars and fake factories
     Would soon emerge the weapons of the blitz!
     Then would there be, old men, a peace, the peace
     That passeth boundaries!

XX

     Now, the career he built on such foundations
530 With allies, passive, active, such as these
     Is black and public on the garb of nations.
     It has no secrecies.
     Is there a wickedness this wicked man
     Did not accomplish? An iniquity
535 That he did not decree?
     A crime that was not indexed in his plan?
     He did encompass all
     The high crimes and the misdemeanours low,
     Enormous, diabolical,
540 Lavish of suffering, and of woe
     Beyond recall.

     I shall not here complain that he did not
     Know decency, or love, or honour, or
     The other virtues surplus to the codes:
545 They were beyond his thought,
     Here was a land his spies did not explore –
     Uncharted were these roads.

XXI

But Law, uncommentaried and unburden'd Law,
The child-eye choosing between right and wrong,
550 The manly option made against the beast,
That, by the man so high above the throng,
That might have been expected,
That, at least!
At least! That little least was more
555 Than he could suffer, who despised
The norms that only weak men prized –
Not Pity, cloth by cripple spun,
Not Justice – blind – he put out both her eyes,
Nor Culture, here he cocked his gun,
560 Nor Worth, nor yet Humanity effete,
The weakling's meat!

Wherefore, in lieu of the illumined law
He ushered in, the better for his deeds,
The burglar's darkness and the murderer's fog.
565 He tore the statutes; he abjured the creeds;
He stamped on the Decalogue!

He coveted.
O what did this much-shrivelled little soul
Not covet, not lust after? Everything
570 That was not his:
The painter's brush, a purer genesis,
The fame of letters not won by himself,
Bismarckian role,
Power and place and pelf.

575 But had he merely coveted, merely bayed
At the unreachable reaches of the distant moon,
Out of his thwarting, out of hope delayed
He would have perished soon,
Heart-broken, foiled, his wrist-veins cut –
580 But

He also stole. He was a thief. He stole.
Even the credos of his sloganry
He piecemeal filched to make a patchwork whole.
(Forgiveable – a petty larceny!)
585 His depredations rose.
He robbed the rich; impartial, robbed the dole.
The folk he loved, he taxed; and those he hated
He confiscated.
The poor man for his pension-pennies sobbed.
590 The church he also held up for its toll.
The house of God was robbed.

Fed thus with native quarry, flesh and gore
He licked his whiskers, crouched, then stalked for more.

XXII

See, on historic film his crimes deployed,
595 Felonies flickering from celluloid!
And through the planes' sharp retina, behold
His victims, and their plight,
The beaten, and the ambushed, and the sold!

Austria, gay and bright and musical
600 Receiving in the silenced hall
The mud-bespattered guest;
And brave Bohemia, – Honour's epitaph –
Broken in half,
Half blackmailed, plundered of the rest.

605 (Watch for the montage of accomplished guile:
As Skoda skids, the four smug men will smile.)

The scenes now change, but madness knows no halt.
Norway is sacked, and Poland's sown with salt
Explosive! Holland also visited,
610 Whose dykes and Dutchmen bled.

(Montage again: the camera goes berserk
With vertical flame and towers diagonal;
Then rests to show the generals; they smirk.)

Closeup. The fascist and his rods
615 Flogging the Jugoslavian fading out
To Greece, her freemen broken, like her gods.

Roofs; and the Eiffel Tower's prominence –
France!
Bereft of Buonaparte
620 Her sated mirrors shattered, and her heart.
France, that too soon, too humble, did descend
From brightness to the dark,
Bereft of Joan of Arc,
Upon an evil day on evil hours come.
625 Within her conquered hall
Domrémy voice is dumb.
The lesser corporal
Over prostrated France
Mimics with carpet-fretting feet
630 Napoleonic stance!

Look west, and see the towers of London-town
Declining, battered, but not battered down –
The burglar mounted, but he came too late:
He broke, but did not enter.
635 Look east, the Russian lifts avenging hands,
Waylaid, assaulted, wounded – he still stands
By dint of that unthawed triumvirate:
Cold steel, and Stalin cool, and icy Winter!

XXIII

As footnote to the headlined Terror, know
640 His ally fared no better than his foe.
War was a science; treaties were an art.

Wherefore, with artful pacts, he pushed the free
Contracting the parties of the second part
Through slow contraction to nihility.
645 Met, plenipotent – farewelled, impotent,
They came as sovereigns, and as servants went.
He made of Magyarland a state in fee,
A German province out of Italy,
A dairy out of Denmark, and
650 An oil-well of Roumanian land.

And are these methods banned?
Where treaties could avail, why use the rod?
Why seek by force, what could be got by fraud?
He'd even make a ten-year truce with God!
655 To bear false witness was no crime. Wherefore
Upon his blood-and-soiled honour swore
He longed for peace. Was believed. And then prepared for war.

XXIV

Nor did he merely wage his war on Man.
Against the Lord he raised his brazen brow,
660 Blasphemed His name, His works, contemned His plan,

Himself a god announced, and bade men bow
Down to his image, and its feet of clay!
God's places of true worship were laid low,

And idols on the high places held their sway;
665 Astrologers were prophets in the land,
And mad philosophers rose to inveigh

Against the diktat of the Lord's command.
Iniquity espoused, and evil wived,
Kindliness, pity, brother-love, were banned.

670 The creed of the Black Forest was revived,
And ceased the ancient pieties for men.
Of manliness and godliness deprived,

The pagan, named for beasts, was born again.
The holy days were gone. The Sabbath creed
675 Unfit for slaves, superfluous to his reign,

Stood unobserved. The nine-month-littered breed
Traduced their parents to the Gestapo;
Adulterous, the stud-men spawned their seed.

The Madman named the Lord his personal foe,
680 And chained the bearers of His sacred word.
This is the sign, he shrilled: *In hoc vinco!*

He raised aloft the blood-stained sword;
Upon the square the heathen horde
Roared.

XXV

685 But not with human arrogance come I
To plead our Maker's cause, and make His cause
The mighty measure of my feeble words.
Himself, in His good time, the Lord of Hosts,
The slowness of His anger moved at last,
690 And His longsuffering at last forespent
Will rise, will shine, will stretch forth His right hand
And smite them down, the open impious mouth,
The tongue blaspheming, silenced, in the dust!

I come now rather as a man to men,
695 Seeking the justice for that voice which cries
Out of the ground, the voice of our brothers' blood!
That blood will not be still again,
Those bones unblessed will still arise,

Yes, and those living spectres, of the mind unhinged,
700 Will still beat at our padded memory, until
Their fate has been avenged!

XXVI

Let them come forth, those witnesses who stand
Beyond the taunt of perjury, those ghosts
In wagons sealed in a forgotten land,
705 Murdered; those phantoms the war-tidings boast,
Those skeletons still charred with the gestapo brand!

Let them come forth and speak, who lost their speech
Before the midnight gun-butt on the door,
The men made dumb with their last voiceless screech
710 In ghetto-yard, and on the Dachau floor, –
Let them accuse now, who did once in vain beseech!

Summon them, bailiff of the dead, the ghosts
Who once were brave men stood against a wall,
Summon them, all the exsanguinated hosts,
715 Hero and martyr, liquidated; call,
Call forth the witnesses, the uninterrèd ghosts,

And let them speak. And let the dead attest
Their murder and its manner and its cause, –
From shattered jaw, from perforated breast
720 Speak out their mauling at the bestial claws.
Speak out, or neither we, nor they, again know rest.

Let them in all their thousands speak the shame
Visited on them, and the ignoble death,
The nameless ones, and those of a great fame:
725 With wounded whisper and with broken breath
Speaking the things unspeakable, and the unspeakable name!

605 / c.1942/1943

    Then from such evidence, such witnessing,
    Surely the anger of the world will burst,
    Surely the wrath of nations will outfling
730 Against this culprit, multitude-accursed
    Doom indexed by the black gloves of their reckoning!

    Thief, perjurer, blasphemer, murderer,
    Let him be blotted out, and all his crew.
    Efface the evil; let it be no more.
735 Let the abomination cease; and through
    Implacable Justice let emerge the world, clean, new!

    Bold malefaction brought at last to bay!
    Avenged the martyrs! Mankind truly purged!
    Returned at last the spectres to their clay!
740 And over the green earth, at last emerged,
    After the cock-crow of the guns, the cloudless day!

XXVII

    And on that day as the unrighteous pass,
    Unrighteousness will pass away, and men
    Will see once more, as when their vision was
745 Illumined by the lightning strokes the ten, –
    Gesturing Truth ungagged will speak again,
    And Man will don his godliness once more –
    Then from four corners of the earth will sing
    The sons of heaven, the bright freedoms four;
750 The field will glow again with harvesting,
    And glow with argosies the deep; again
    Will frolic in the ether, sunlight-blue'd –
    Not the grim vulture of the brood
    Its talons dripping blood,
755 But the bright friendly somersaulting plane
    Writing against the sky
    So all may read on high

Man loyal to his human brotherhood,
To human brotherhood, and to the godly reign!

c. 1942/1943   1944

c. 1943/1943

Actuarial Report

We, the undersigned
Magi of your actuarial staff
Having examined the data of the year
And drawn therefrom the hereto-appended graph
5 (The hanging gardens of Death, shown tier by tier)
Regretfully prognosticate a rising trend:
They will increase, our policy-holders,
Doomed to an untimely end.

We have seen the medical certificates
10 Guessing the cause of death; we have examined
The corpses slabbed in our filing cabinets;
We have deduced the necessary deductions.
The incidence of earthquake has been studied,
Not overlooked are pestilence and dangerous intersections.
15 The act of God is equated;
And the will-to-self-destruction (two premiums paid)
Is also calculated.
      Had there, however, been only these
Funereal figures on our adding-machines
20 It would have been easy; to wit, the status quo.
There was to be considered, unfortunately,
A state of hostilities.

It is true, of course, we have the saving war-clause.
Nonetheless, there are risks, perils, and bad luck
25 Remote from the battlefields, but laying
The dead hand on our deeds.
Such are anxiety, trouble at home, measured rations,
The abnormalities of separation; in fine,
General absence from felicity.
30 Accordingly, we have taken the measurements, and we know
The steps of death are hastened. He comes with bodyguard:
Famine, disease, and other motley personages.
His ingenuities are increased. He moves with up-to-date motion,
Certainly he gets about more than he has of recent years.
35   Our contracts begin to have his personal smell. And we
Have become the keepers of his diary.

Sirs, we had much rather come back from our spying
To say, like magi of old,
A son is born.
40 Regrettably, all that we can see for the present fiscal year
Is many a father dying.

c. 1943/1943   1953

And in That Drowning Instant

And in that drowning instant as
the water heightened over me
it suddenly did come to pass
my preterite eternity

5 the image of myself intent
on several freedoms

609 / c.1943/1943

          fading to
myself in yellowed Basle-print
vanishing

        into ghetto-Jew
a face among the faces of
the rapt disciples hearkening
the raptures of the Baal Shem Tov
explaining Torah

          vanishing
amidst the water's flickering green

to show me in old Amsterdam
which topples

        into a new scene
Cordova where an Abraham
faces inquisitors

        the face
is suddenly beneath an arch
whose Latin-script the waves erase

and flashes now the backward march
of many

     I among them

          to
Jerusalem-gate and Temple-door!

For the third time my body rises
and finds the good, the lasting shore!

c. 1943/1943   1951

Not All the Perfumes of Arabia [Version 1]

Undoubtedly terror may through the widened eyes
Enter the heart, as image enters mirror;
As poison into the ears of royal Denmark
Through portals of the ears may enter Terror; –
5 But the real horror, the truly shuddering nefas
Is surely particled on the scented dust,
Is surely through the nostrils made to pass
Through the duct whispering, through the stealthy vein
Meandering, at length to thrust
10 Its cry of havoc into the haunted brain!

Even now, as the broadcaster at the regular hour
Announces his name, the place of his gadgets, and
His historic theme:
The evil currencies of the bloodied land –
15 It is not words I hear,
Nor are they sights I see,
I smell the smell of fear.

        Sevastopol: and fee-fi-fum
        Cordite and lilac odours fill
20   This powder-pollinated room;
        And from each sailor-syllable
        Rises upon the spindrift foam
        The large green ocean-water smell.

        The stukas of his speech dive down –
25   The dust of rubble stifles! Doom
        That slinks in nether Paris-town
        Evokes the stench of sewer scum;
        And Hellas of the white renown
        The starving mouth's effluvium!

30 　　　　　The little panic smell of sweat
　　　　　　Of men who stand against a wall
　　　　　　Awaiting the twelve-muzzled threat –
　　　　　　Is that fetor judaical?
　　　　　　The fragrance herrenvolk beget?
35 　　　　　Or is this musk dispersed from hell?

The voice of the announcer, like Mephisto's in the play
Crackles and dies. – Within the vibrating room, –
Fear, and the brimstone fume.

c. 1943/1943　　　　　　　　　　　　　　1943

Not All the Perfumes of Arabia [Version 2]

Undoubtedly terror may through the widened eyes
enter the heart, as image enters mirror;
as poison into the ears of royal Denmark
through portals of the ears may enter Terror; –
5 but the real horror, the truly shuddering *nefas*
surely is through the nostrils made to pass,
is inhaled, surely, and as an odour – pulver of pain! –
whirls havoc in the brain!

Even now, as the broadcaster at the regular hour
10 announces his name, the place of his gadgets, and
his historic theme:
they are not words I hear
nor are they sights I see,
I smell the smell of fear.

15 See where the mushroom
curls corruption on the air!

Shall scents and attars
avail there?

c. 1952/1952   1952

c. 1944/1944

Address to the Choirboys

Another moon, and the penitential days
Will be upon us.
                There are many signs:
My mother following her mother's ways,
Keeping two fasts the week; the ram's horn blown
5 Each morning, pastoral, on the city air;
The tombstone maker dusty with his stone;
And every evening, from the practising choir,
The song of the Cantor, teaching downy boys
The cantillation of the sacred prayer.

10   *O Lord, thou art my Judge and Prosecutor!*
    The Keeper of the Book which reads itself,
    Witness who has seen all, remembering.

The sorrow of Rabbi Amnon made that song!
A sad and bitter day it was
15 That day they bore him to the House of God,
His legs cut off, that were so fleet, so strong
To serve their Maker, lopped those holy arms
That wound and wore phylacteries, – cut off:
The corners of his world, outpouring blood!

20 'Abjure thy faith, and there's an end to strife!'
And Rabbi Amnon –
(O but this flesh, this stalk, these leaves and petals
Do so desire life!)
The Rabbi stayed in hesitation
25 Between the pity of children, and his fathers' pride,
And hesitated.
And only, at length, defied!

> Let us give strength to holiness this day,
> This day being terror-full, and full of doom,
30 > And therein raise Thy mighty Majesty.

Therefore, these stumps, they were the Lord's dictate –
Not any that small arrogant man could utter –
Punishment for unfaith which hesitates.

Like the white petals of an eastern bloom
35 His limbs torn off, and he that flower, dying
The rabbi hears above him flutter
The wings of angels, angels sighing
Softly his doom.

O they are at the year's beginning written
40 *And on the fast day of atonement sealed:*
Who pass away, and who shall come to pass,
Who at his time, and who before his time;
Who through the death by water, who through the death
By sword, by fire, by ferocious beast.

45 Sing on, ye innocent choirboys, this song
The sorrow of Rabbi Amnon made
Against a day like ours, like ours a wrong!
Sing, in your innocence, O milk-sweet voices
Smooth like your cheeks your song,
50 Your cherry lips know nothing yet of sorrow
And only music in your throat rejoices
Nor are the tragic phrases tragic on your tongue.

615 / c.1944/1944

O let no lips dare tell you of their meaning –
Their burden of sorrow, their weight of suffering –
55 But in your innocence warble, lean white throats,
And in your young unknowing jubilations, sing.

c. 1944/1944   1944

Basic English

(To Winston Churchill)

1
Of trope of testament and Caesar's wars
    Grand rhetor, voice
    Of warrior-days,
Not you, I thought, would give the lion's nod
5 To these eight hundred laboratory mice
Scrawny with fasting, certainly not you
    Of the armada'd phrase!

2
Exporters' argot, small talk of small trade,
    The agent's slang
10   Bartering beads,
This is the very speech of nursery blocks,
Pidgin palaver, grunt of Caliban,
By no means the awaited syllables
    For even lesser breeds.

3
15 Reducing motion to mere come and go,
    Narrowing act
    To give and get,
Flowers no longer flower in the mind;

Fades from the eyes nuance; and eloquence
Sticks in the throat. The dumb are merely raised
  To the inarticulate.

4
Exhausted well of English, and defiled –
  Is it with this
  Semantic spray
You would baptize the cultured continents?
Shall Europe judge and Asia esteem
The wassail liquor of our English speech
  From this, the don's weak tea?

5
In jargoning ports, perhaps, in jungle-river,
  One may make use
  Of such boned gauds:
The drummer, bringing flag and bargain, may
So dragoman himself, perhaps, and thus
Close his shrewd deal, – but only after many
  Gestures, head-shakes, nods.

6
For lettered nations this desesperanto?
  For races that
  Boast alphabet,
And song and synonym and subtlety?
Amused, but polite, the city-dwellers smile;
And that good-will these mumbos were to breed
  We neither – give nor get.

7
For where among the vocables, castrate
  Of Saxon strength,
  O Sponsor, where
The Hellenic music or the Latin storm?
Where are the thunders of our choric voice?

And where is Shakespeare's scope and Milton's reach?
    Your words triphibian, where?

8

50 Basic as bread, and English as all water –
    These bread-and-water
    Calories
Are not for men unpainted and in clothes!
O, rather for loincloths on some fronded isle,
55 Trading at beach, or at the mission chanting –
    These skimmed simplicities!

9

Orator, organist of history, –
    Much mightier tones
    Have we to sound
60 Than these flat octaves, playing sad or glad.
Ours is a sweeping measure, resonant,
And destined, for its splendors, not its strictures,
    To be renowned!

c. 1944/1944   1944

Bread

Creation's crust and crumb, breaking of bread,
Seedstaff and wheatwand of all miracles,
By your white fiat, at the feast-times said,
World moves, and is revived the shrouded pulse!

5 Rising, as daily rises the quickening east,
O kneading of knowledge, leaven of happiness,
History yearns upon your yearning yeast!
No house is home without your wifeliness.

No city stands up from its rock-bound knees
10 Without your rustic aid. None are elect
Save you be common. All philosophies
Betray them with your yokel dialect.

O black-bread hemisphere, oblong of rye,
Crescent and circle of the seeded bun,
15 All art is builded on your geometry,
All science explosive from your captured sun.

    Bakers most priestly, in your robes of flour,
    White Levites at your altar'd ovens, bind,
    Bind me forever in your ritual, your
20   Worship and prayer, me, and all mankind!

c. 1944/1944   1948

Commercial Bank

Flowering jungle, where all fauna meet
crossing the marbled pool to thickets whence
the prompted parrots, alien-voiced, entreat
the kernel'd hoard, the efflorescent pence, –

5 wondrous your caves, whose big doors must be rolled
for entrance, and whose flora none can seek
against the armed unicorn, furred blue and gold,
against the vines fatal, or the berries, that touched, shriek.

How quiet is your shade with broad green leaves!
10 Yet is it jungle-quiet which deceives:

toothless, with drawn nails, the beasts paw your ground –
O, the fierce deaths expiring with no sound!

c. 1944/1944   1948

The Green Old Age

     Pity who wear the castoffs of the years,
     dressing in clown's clothes the unclownish ones,
     with baldness on head, and hairiness in ears,
     and cellophane upon the chalky bones,
5   and in concealed sacking, stones!

     Sweet flakes in the blood, the mouth exhaling acid;
     the bowels becalmed, and the loud bile in rage;
     the artery hardened, and the member flaccid;
     nor ever at normal the pulsating gauge –
10   metathesis of age

     which strives again toward its babyhood
     where neither the shanks nor sphincters will behave,
     nor syntax stand, and where, as if it would
     be joined again, the spinal cord does crave
15   the navel of the grave.

     Be blessed the doctors who with toxic ease, –
     coned odour, marrowed needle, candid pill, –
     the waxing of these mooned monstrosities
     forestall; and give into the hand and will
20   the proleptic miracle.

c. 1944/1944   1948

The Library

On leather, beneath rafters, beside oak,
we sat and talked only of *amor intellectualis*.
The books, at their stances, on the mounting wall,
gold-lettered, crested, red,
5 like seventh-generation lackeys stood:
dumb, high-blood-pressured, seen and not heard. Progress
was air in that room, refinement, and soft manners:
the original robber baron bred down to
sweetness and tungsten.

10 His opinions were sensitive, his gestures fine,
fine, and like his cigarettes were monogrammed.
The culture of the best schools, to wit, morals and sport,
worn neatly, like his clothes.
He sighed, – from the world's lung. He had *weltschmerz*,
15 like a painless disease. Thinkers he quoted,
and was pure reason; poets, and was kind.
Even the blood moving his vocal cords
seemed an intrusion.

Yet suddenly, and for no reason at all,
20 his temper changed, and all his breeding sloughed,
Swiss governess and English tutor dead,
– or more than ever alive? –
it was a cinema-change. As if the books were boards,
and, at a button, had slid away, revealing
25 bars, and behind, cement – his secret – where wild beasts
yawned, and waved paw, circled, ran forward, roared
for the week's meat.

c. 1944/1944   1952

Montreal

1
O city metropole, isle riverain!
Your ancient pavages and sainted routs
Traverse my spirit's conjured avenues!
Splendor erablic of your promenades
5 Foliates there, and there your maisonry
Of pendent balcon and escalier'd march,
Unique midst English habitat,
Is vivid Normandy!

2
You populate the pupils of my eyes:
10 Thus, does the Indian, plumèd, furtivate
Still through your painted autumns, Ville-Marie!
Though palisades have passed, though calumet
With tabac of your peace enfumes the air,
Still do I spy the phantom, aquiline,
15 Genuflect, moccasin'd, behind
His statue in the square!

3
Thus, costumed images before me pass,
Haunting your archives architectural:
Coureur de bois, in posts where pelts were portaged;
20 Seigneur within his candled manoir; Scot
Ambulant through his bank, pillar'd and vast.
Within your chapels, voyaged mariners
Still pray, and personage departed,
All present from your past!

4

25 Grand port of navigations, multiple
The lexicons uncargo'd at your quays,
Sonnant though strange to me; but chiefest, I,
Auditor of your music, cherish the
Joined double-melodied vocabulaire
30 Where English vocable and roll Ecossic,
Mollified by the parle of French
Bilinguefact your air!

5

Such your suaver voice, hushed Hochelaga!
But for me also sound your potencies,
35 Fortissimos of sirens fluvial,
Bruit of manufactory, and thunder
From foundry issuant, all puissant tone
Implenishing your hebdomad; and then
Sanct silence, and your argent belfries
40 Clamant in orison!

6

You are a part of me, O all your quartiers –
And of dire pauvreté and of richesse –
To finished time my homage loyal claim;
You are locale of infancy, milieu
45 Vital of insitutes that formed my fate;
And you above the city, scintillant,
Mount Royal, are my spirit's mother,
Almative, poitrinate!

7

Never do I sojourn in alien place
50 But I do languish for your scenes and sounds,
City of reverie, nostalgic isle,
Pendant most brilliant on Laurentian cord!
The coigns of your boulevards – my signiory –
Your suburbs are my exile's verdure fresh,

55 Your parks, your fountain'd parks —
　　Pasture of memory!

　　8
　　City, O city, you are vision'd as
　　A parchemin roll of saecular exploit
　　Inked with the script of eterne souvenir!
60 You are in sound, chanson and instrument!
　　Mental, you rest forever edified
　　With tower and dome; and in these beating valves,
　　Here in these beating valves, you will
　　For all my mortal time reside!

　　c. 1944/1944　　　　　　　　　　　　　　1948

Ni la mort ni le soleil

(On a maxim of de la Rochefoucauld)

　　Neither on death, nor at the blazing sun
　　Can mortal gaze
　　Without being blinded by the one
　　As by the other's rays:
5 They are two fascinations eyes reject,
　　Looking, yet loath
　　To fix themselves upon the sight elect —
　　Bright worlds both.

　　c. 1944/1944　　　　　　　　　　　　　　1952

A Psalm Touching Genealogy

Not sole was I born, but entire genesis:
For to the fathers that begat me, this
Body is residence. Corpuscular,
They dwell in my veins, they eavesdrop at my ear,
5 They circle, as with Torahs, round my skull,
In exit and in entrance all day pull
The latches of my heart, descend, and rise –
And there look generations through my eyes.

c. 1944/1944   1945

Spring Exhibit

How pleasant are the times and their cezannes,
But pleasanter than all, the thyme of spring!
Blooms dilly-tanty fresco through God's manse,
And through its galaries, birds on the wing!
5 Van-terre is gone, white fogey criticans;
The paintillest buds at last are burgeoning.

Manet from heaven falls upon the plane
Where little fauns go fralipping the grass.
Again the babbling breukels flow, again
10 Riveros mighty move where marble was.
Gone is the glassic ice; the root-men reign;
The whorled is new, in fern, and furze, and grass.

Herald the vangogh of the year, its colour, flash!
O are these trees or but a dream of trees?
15 These flowers, of vermeils bold, chrome yellows brash, –
The world's sweet sistine day! the field's louvrese!
Youth in plenair, with all things green and fresh,
Unchagalled days in primotif release!

c. 1944/1944   1944

Epitaph

    Good friend, for Jesu's sake, forbear
    Upon this shriven dust to tread,
    Nor move these blessèd stones.
    Here, he who left the middling air,
5 His passable life, his secondbest bed,
    Upon his best now rests his bones.

    * * *

    The curtain falls, and the stage-traffic ends.
    Silenced the herald's sennets, the murderers' knocks:
    Howbeit, Shakespeare, unaware, still sends
10 The Globe his whispers from his prompter's box.

    c. 1942/c. 1944

Les Vespasiennes

Dropped privily below the crotch of squares –
its architecture is like the sets in dreams:
the wide slow staircase ... the unknown loiterers ...
the floor that would be counted ... the mirrors' gleams
5 dancing with daffodils ... and before their white niches
all effigies reversed:
precisely that mise-en-scene, that whiteness which
is seen as having been in dreams seen first:

an anxiety dream where fallen seraphims,
10 maimed by metabolism, like children of men,
do get their leeching, and rise above their limbs,
and think themselves the angels once again:
and thus, standing in that dream, I and its persons
know at the chemical core,
15 at the bubbling self, that which was built on and known
even by Vespasian the Emperor,

namely: that we are not God. Not God. Why, not,
not even angels, but something less than men,
creatures, sicknesses, whose pornoglot
20 identities swim up within our ken
from the *graffiti* behind the amputate door, –
(the wishful drawing and rhyme!)
creatures – the homo, the pervert, the voyeur,
all who grasp love and catch at pantomime.

25 See how they linger here, while the normal (Who?)
climb up from the subterranean dantesque
into the public square, the shine, the blue,
and don again their feathers and the mask
angelic, and are 'valiant again to cope
30 with all high enterprise

of true pure love and sweet spiritual hope,'
as if no privies were and only Paradise!

c. 1942/c. 1944

Of Tradition

With my own eyes I saw it, I who loved my father
And cherish now my father's memory, I saw
My friend spilling his father to the ground:
The scene that walked with symbols round the room
5 Scattered in shards, the shards glazed in corners,
The plinth of the vase, delicate little coffin,
Broken, and ashes, ashes that begot him, grey on ground.
Do not, he said, speak to me of my father,
I have had enough, and more than enough
10 Of parables, comparisons, examples.
His impotence blubbered, remorse bit its lip,
And whisky-breath lay mourning in the air.
Inverted rite of Onan, seed spilling sire!
I turned away, and only his father's portrait
15 Looked on himself in ashes,
Lying with cigarette-ash, with carpet-dust, with dried invisible phlegm.

c. 1942/c. 1944

Post-War Planning

Shall he be sat on a wired electrical seat
So he burn till the sinews orate with his siblilant sound?
Or dangled from gallows, a sheeny with gesturing feet?
Or coffined alive in an artfully-breathable ground?

5 Or led out to pasture, and pastured on thistles and grass?
Or stood to his neck in vile coprophagous earth?
Or shall he be doomed to the choking chamber of gas
Catching his breath in a concave copy of mirth?

Or stoned like a dog? Or drowned like a whiskered cat?
10 Or bubbled with air till his veins, till his heart be stopped?
Or chopped with an axe, a carcass at both ends flat?
Or lifted on high in a plane over water, and dropped?

c. 1942/c. 1944

Saga the First

From the fjord faring, striding the stream,
By the wind winnowed, flailed by the flood,
Lo, Lief the lusty, Red Eric's son!

That safe strand seeking which to his wit
5 Gave greensward guerdon for waters wan,
Lief wandered, wending ships to new shore!

Vinland, the Viking named it in Norse!

Kneeling the Norseman gave God his thanks
For bounty better than gold-hoard got:
10 Wheat unsown waving, wineberries wild,
Birches of blossoming bark, in a land
Hoarded by Him since the work of His word!

c. 1942/c. 1944

Song without Music

My suite is like a violin, so full
Of mewsick begging to be played.
                                    Rise up
O Love, and pass thy resin'd resonant beau
Over that dear amati bawdy. Call
5 Her the names of love, thy straddle-various,
Thy hoyden, thy tartini, thy
Viola da gamba.
                       Loosen the g-string. Play
Fidelio, play the movement of thy song.
Cajole with kisses that cithara; let
10 Her breasts be utters at creamona shaped –
On alto and in tuffenbruck thy notes!

What fluent melodies may thence issue,
What pizzicato trills, what muted chords
Throbbing beneath the hair of Pegasus?

c. 1942/c. 1944

Tailpiece to an Anthology

Is this your Canadian poet, with the foreign name?
What does he know of fir trees? Can he get along
With matters of old French or Indian fame?
Has ever a local flower sprouted in his song?
5 And this the man to sing Canadian weather
Confederated vegetation, Canuck dew?
O, he and the maple do not go together.
A guide he needs to paddle his canoe.

A Canadian poet! Why,
10 He has not stolen even a single line
From British poesy!

c. 1942/c. 1944

Tribute to the Ballet Master [Version 1]

Since motion was, there has been no such dance!
You have excelled yourself, cher maitre. Who
Else would have thought to take all reels at once
Into the single one-step. Only you!
5 The tango of the slithering plane,
The general's strategic waltz;
The rumba of the tank; the hospital shuffle;
The ante-mortem minuet of the slain
One weaving into the other, and out again
10 Broken by distracting somersaults –
A masterpiece, eccentric and eclectic,
Distinguished in that all feet foot it spry,

The hob-nailed boot, cothurnus, diplomat's gaiter,
All join in the dance, well-drummed and hectic,
15 All dancers, and no spectator!
All dancers, elephant and elf,
All dancing high.
Cher maitre you have excelled yourself.
You have reason to be proud; and I applaud.
20 I would, of course, if I were you –
Sensitive about the paralysed polonaise,
Touchy about the gout-smitten gavottes,
Ignore that critic who speaks of
The Tautentanz of Hottentots.

c. 1942/c. 1944

Tribute to the Ballet Master [Version 2]

You have excelled yourself, cher maitre!
   Your hollow-boned steps enhance
The lethal science of saltation
   To the supremest dance!

5 The rumba of the panzer-buttocks
   The slither of the tango-ing plane
The hospital shuffle; the ante-mortem
   Minuet of the slain;

The fox-hole flop; the waltz strategic;
10   And the slow South Pacific crawl,
Cher maitre in your magnum opus
   Are all of these steps, all.

And all do foot it, whether shod
    Or barefoot, or in diplomat gaiter
15 A folk-dance, on my word! And you
    Are sole spectator.

c. 1942/c. 1944

c. 1944/1945

Portrait of the Poet as Landscape

I

Not an editorial-writer, bereaved with bartlett,
mourns him, the shelved Lycidas.
No actress squeezes a glycerine tear for him.
The radio broadcast lets his passing pass.
5 And with the police, no record. Nobody, it appears,
either under his real name or his alias,
missed him enough to report.

It is possible that he is dead, and not discovered.
It is possible that he can be found some place
10 in a narrow closet, like the corpse in a detective story,
standing, his eyes staring, and ready to fall on his face.
It is also possible that he is alive
and amnesiac, or mad, or in retired disgrace,
or beyond recognition lost in love.

15 We are sure only that from our real society
he has disappeared; he simply does not count,
except in the pullulation of vital statistics –
somebody's vote, perhaps, an anonymous taunt
of the Gallup poll, a dot in a government table –

20 but not felt, and certainly far from eminent –
    in a shouting mob, somebody's sigh.

    O, he who unrolled our culture from his scroll –
    the prince's quote, the rostrum-rounding roar –
    who under one name made articulate
25 heaven, and under another the seven-circled air,
    is, if he is at all, a number, an x,
    a Mr. Smith in a hotel register, –
    incognito, lost, lacunal.

    II

    The truth is he's not dead, but only ignored –
30 like the mirroring lenses forgotten on a brow
    that shine with the guilt of their unnoticed world.
    The truth is he lives among neighbours, who, though they will allow
    him a passable fellow, think him eccentric, not solid,
    a type that one can forgive, and for that matter, forego.

35 Himself he has his moods, just like a poet.
    Sometimes, depressed to nadir, he will think all lost,
    will see himself as throwback, relict, freak,
    his mother's miscarriage, his great-grandfather's ghost,
    and he will curse his quintuplet senses, and their tutors
40 in whom he put, as he should not have put, his trust.

    Then he will remember his travels over that body –
    the torso verb, the beautiful face of the noun,
    and all those shaped and warm auxiliaries!
    A first love it was, the recognition of his own.
45 Dear limbs adverbial, complexion of adjective,
    dimple and dip of conjugation!

And then remember how this made a change in him
affecting for always the glow and growth of his being;
how suddenly was aware of the air, like shaken tinfoil,
50 of the patents of nature, the shock of belated seeing,
the lonelinesses peering from the eyes of crowds;
the integers of thought; the cube-roots of feeling.

Thus, zoomed to zenith, sometimes he hopes again,
and sees himself as a character, with a rehearsed role:
55 the Count of Monte Cristo, come for his revenges;
the unsuspected heir, with papers; the risen soul;
or the chloroformed prince awaking from his flowers;
or – deflated again – the convict on parole.

III

He is alone; yet not completely alone.
60 Pins on a map of a colour similar to his,
each city has one, sometimes more than one:
here, caretakers of art, in colleges;
in offices, there, with arm-bands, and green-shaded;
and there, pounding their catalogued beats in libraries, –

65 everywhere menial, a shadow's shadow.
And always for their egos – their outmoded art.
Thus, having lost the bevel in the ear,
they know neither up nor down, mistake the part
for the whole, curl themselves in a comma,
70 talk technics, make a colon their eyes. They distort –

such is the pain of their frustration – truth
to something convolute and cerebral.
How they do fear the slap of the flat of the platitude!
Now Pavlov's victims, their mouths water at bell,
75 the platter empty.
               See they set twenty-one jewels
into their watches; the time they do not tell!

Some, patagonian in their own esteem,
and longing for the multiplying word,
join party and wear pins, now have a message,
80 an ear, and the convention-hall's regard.
Upon the knees of ventriloquists, they own,
of their dandled brightness, only the paint and board.

And some go mystical, and some go mad.
One stares at a mirror all day long, as if
85 to recognize himself; another courts
angels, – for here he does not fear rebuff;
and a third, alone, and sick with sex, and rapt,
doodles him symbols convex and concave.

O schizoid solitudes! O purities
90 curdling upon themselves! Who live for themselves,
or for each other, but for nobody else;
desire affection, private and public loves;
are friendly, and then quarrel and surmise
the secret perversions of each other's lives.

IV

95 He suspects that something has happened, a law
been passed, a nightmare ordered. Set apart,
he finds himself, with special haircut and dress,
as on a reservation. Introvert.
He does not understand this; sad conjecture
100 muscles and palls thrombotic on his heart.

He thinks an impostor, having studied his personal biography,
his gestures, his moods, now has come forward to pose
in the shivering vacuums his absence leaves.
Wigged with his laurel, that other, and faked with his face,
105 he pats the heads of his children, pecks his wife,
and is at home, and slippered, in his house.

So he guesses at the impertinent silhouette
that talks to his phone-piece and slits open his mail.
Is it the local tycoon who for a hobby
110 plays poet, he so epical in steel?
The orator, making a pause? Or is that man
he who blows his flash of brass in the jittering hall?

Or is he cuckolded by the troubadour
rich and successful out of celluloid?
115 Or by the don who unrhymes atoms? Or
the chemist death built up? Pride, lost impostor'd pride,
it is another, another, whoever he is,
who rides where he should ride.

V

Fame, the adrenalin: to be talked about;
120 to be a verb; to be introduced as *The*;
to smile with endorsement from slick paper; make
caprices anecdotal; to nod to the world; to see
one's name like a song upon the marquees played;
to be forgotten with embarrassment; to be –
125 to be.

It has its attractions, but is not the thing;
nor is it the ape mimesis who speaks from the tree
ancestral; nor the merkin joy ...
Rather it is stark infelicity
130 which stirs him from his sleep, undressed, asleep
to walk upon roofs and window-sills and defy
the gape of gravity.

VI

Therefore he seeds illusions. Look, he is
the nth Adam taking a green inventory

135 in world but scarcely uttered, naming, praising,
     the flowering fiats in the meadow, the
     syllabled fur, stars aspirate, the pollen
     whose sweet collision sounds eternally.
     For to praise

140 the world – he, solitary man – is breath
     to him. Until it has been praised, that part
     has not been. Item by exciting item –
     air to his lungs, and pressured blood to his heart. –
     they are pulsated, and breathed, until they map,
145 not the world's, but his own body's chart!

     And now in imagination he has climbed
     another planet, the better to look
     with single camera view upon this earth –
     its total scope, and each afflated tick,
150 its talk, its trick its tracklessness – and this,
     this he would like to write down in a book!

     To find a new function for the déclassé craft
     archaic like the fletcher's; to make a new thing;
     to say the word that will become sixth sense;
155 perhaps by necessity and indirection bring
     new forms to life, anonymously, new creeds –
     O, somehow pay back the daily larcenies of the lung!

     These are not mean ambitions. It is already something
     merely to entertain them. Meanwhile, he
160 makes of his status as zero a rich garland,
     a halo of his anonymity,
     and lives alone, and in his secret shines
     like phosphorus. At the bottom of the sea.

c. 1944/1945   1948

Portrait of the Poet as Landscape
[Deleted Section]

However, for bread and the occasional show,
he finds him, kindler of copy, daily at desk.
For mongers and martmen he swinks it, writing
their war-whoops, hailing their heroes, thrust to his task:
5 *Pirouette, pica; triumph, O twelve-point!*
Throw the sword in the scales, proud asterisk!

Skop of the sales-force, bard of their booty, he offers
to shoddy his shrilling, his gusto for gussets, to zippers his zest.
With housewives he's homey, and pally with paters, a kinsman,
10 a con man, he butters his bosses, he jumps at their jests.
A fighter with fables he is, and a queller with questions,
chapman of chattels, hawker at hest.

c. 1944/1945   1945

c. 1945/1945

Indian Reservation: Caughnawaga

Where are the braves, the faces like autumn fruit,
who stared at the child from the coloured frontispiece?
And the monosyllabic chief who spoke with his throat?
Where are the tribes, the feathered bestiaries? –
5 Rank Aesop's animals erect and red,
with fur on their names to make all live things kin! –
Chief Running Deer, Black Bear, Old Buffalo Head?

Childhood, that wished me Indian, hoped that
one afterschool I'd leave the classroom chalk,
10 the varnish smell, the watered dust of the street,
to join the clean outdoors and the Iroquois track.
Childhood; but always, – as on a calendar, –
there stood that chief, with arms akimbo, waiting
the runaway mascot paddling to his shore.

15 With what strange moccasin stealth that scene is changed!
With French names, without paint, in overalls,
their bronze, like their nobility expunged, –
the men. Beneath their alimentary shawls
sit like black tents their squaws; while for the tourist's
20 brown pennies scattered at the old church door,
the ragged papooses jump, and bite the dust.

Their past is sold in a shop: the beaded shoes,
the sweetgrass basket, the curio Indian,
burnt wood and gaudy cloth and inch-canoes –
25 trophies and scalpings for a traveller's den.
Sometimes, it's true, they dance, but for a bribe;
after a deal don the bedraggled feather
and welcome a white mayor to the tribe.

This is a grassy ghetto, and no home.
30 And these are fauna in a museum kept.
The better hunters have prevailed. The game,
losing its blood, now makes these grounds its crypt.
The animals pale, the shine of the fur is lost,
bleached are their living bones. About them watch
35 as through a mist, the pious prosperous ghosts.

c. 1945/1945   1948

The Provinces

First, the two older ones, the bunkhouse brawnymen,
biceps and chest, lumbering over their legend:
scooping a river up in the palm of the hand,
a dangling fish, alive; kicking open a mine;
5 bashing a forest bald; spitting a country to crop;
for exercise before their boar breakfast,
building a city; racing, to keep in shape,
against the white-sweatered wind; and always
bragging comparisons, and reminiscing
10 about their fathers' even more mythic prowess,
arguing always, like puffing champions rising
from wrestling on the green.

Then, the three flat-faced blond-haired husky ones.

And the little girl, so beautiful she was named –
15 to avert the evil of the evil eye –
after a prince, not princess. In crossed arms cradling her,
her brothers, tanned and long-limbed.
(Great fishermen, hauling out of Atlantic
their catch and their coal
20 and netting with appleblossom the shoals of their sky.)

And, last, as if of another birth,
the hunchback with the poet's face; and eyes
blue as the glass he looks upon; and fruit
his fragrant knuckles and joints; of iron marrow; –
25 affecting always a green habit, touched with white.

Nine of them; not counting
the adopted boy of the golden complex, nor
the proud collateral albino, – nine,
a sorcery of numbers, a game's stances.

30 But the heart seeks one, the heart, and also the mind
seeks single the thing that makes them one, if one.
      Yet where shall one find it? In their history –
the cairn of cannonball on the public square?
Their talk, their jealous double-talk? Or in
35 the whim and weather of a geography
curling in drifts about the forty-ninth?
Or find it in the repute of character:
romantic as mounties? Or discover it
in beliefs that say:
40 this is a country of Christmas trees?
      Or hear it sing
from the house with towers, from whose towers ring
bells, and the carillon of laws?
Where shall one find it? What
45 to name it, that is sought?
The ladder the nine brothers hold by rungs?

The birds that shine on each other? The white water
   that foams from the ivy entering their eaves?

   Or find it, find it, find it commonplace
50 but effective, valid, real, the unity
   in the family feature, the not unsimilar face?

   c. 1945/1945   1948

The Rocking Chair

   It seconds the crickets of the province. Heard
   in the clean lamplit farmhouses of Quebec, –
   wooden, – it is no less a national bird;
   and rivals, in its cage, the mere stuttering clock.
5 To its time, the evenings are rolled away;
   and in its peace the pensive mother knits
   contentment to be worn by her family,
   grown-up, but still cradled by the chair in which she sits.

   It is also the old man's pet, pair to his pipe,
10 the two aids of his arithmetic and plans,
   plans rocking and puffing into market-shape;
   and it is the toddler's game and dangerous dance.
   Moved to the verandah, on summer Sundays, it is,
   among the hanging plants, the girls, the boy-friends,
15 sabbatical and clumsy, like the white haloes
   dangling above the blue serge suits of the young men.

   It has a personality of its own;
   is a character (like that old drunk Lacoste,
   exhaling amber, and toppling on his pins);
20 it is alive; individual; and no less
   an identity than those about it. And

it is tradition. Centuries have been flicked
from its arcs, alternately flicked and pinned.
It rolls with the gait of St. Malo. It is act
25 and symbol, symbol of this static folk
which moves in segments, and returns to base, —
a sunken pendulum: *invoke, revoke;*
loosed yon, leashed hither, motion on no space.
O, like some Anjou ballad, all refrain,
30 which turns about its longing, and seems to move
to make a pleasure out of repeated pain,
its music moves, as if always back to a first love.

 c. 1945/1945   1948

Sonnet Unrhymed

When, on the frustral summit of *extase,*
— the leaven of my loins to no life spent,
yet vision, as all senses, sharper, — I
peer the vague forward and flawed prism of Time,
5 many the bodies, my own birthmark bearing,
and many the faces, like my face, I see:
shadows of generation looking backward
and crying *Abba* in the muffled night.

  They beg creation. From the far centuries
10 they move against the vacuum of their murder,
yes, and their eyes are full of such reproach
that although tired, I do wake, and watch
upon the entangled branches of the dark
my sons, my sons, my hanging Absaloms.

 c. 1945/1945   1945

c. 1945/1946

Air-Map

How private and comfortable it once was,
our white mansard beneath the continent's gables!
But now, evicted, and still there –
a wind blew off the roof? –
5 we see our fears and our featherbeds plumped white
on the world's crossroads.

c. 1945/1946   1948

The Break-up

They suck and whisper it in mercury,
the thermometers. It is shouted red
from all the Aprils hanging on the walls.
In the dockyard stalls
5 the stevedores, their hooks rusty, wonder; the
wintering sailors in the taverns bet.

A week, and it will crack! Here's money that
a fortnight sees the floes, the smokestacks red!
Outside *The Anchor's* glass, St. Lawrence lies
10   rigid and white and wise,
    nor ripple and dip, but fathom-frozen flat.
  There are no hammers will break that granite lid.

But it will come! Some dead of night with boom
to wake the wagering city, it will break,
15 will crack, will melt its muscle-bound tides
  and raise from their iced tomb
  the pyramided fish, the unlockered ships,
  and last year's blue and bloated suicides.

c. 1945/1946   1948

The Cripples

(Oratoire de St. Joseph)

Bundled their bones, upon the ninetynine stairs –
St. Joseph's ladder – the knobs of penance come;
the folded cripples counting up their prayers.

How rich, how plumped with blessing is that dome!
5 The gourd of Brother André! His sweet days
rounded! Fulfilled! Honeyed to honeycomb!

Whither the heads, upon the ninetynine trays,
the palsied, who double their aspen selves, the lame,
the unsymmetrical, the dead-limbed, raise

10 their look, their hope, and the *idée fixe* of their maim, –
knowing the surgery's in the heart. Are not
the ransomed crutches worshippers? And the fame

of the brother sanatorial to this plot? –
God mindful of the sparrows on the stairs?
15 Yes, to their faith this mountain of stairs, is not!

They know, they know, that suddenly their cares
and orthopedics will fall from them, and they
stand whole again.

        Roll empty away, wheelchairs,
and crutches, without armpits, hop away!

20 And I who in my own faith once had faith like this,
but have not now, am crippled more than they.

c. 1945/1946   1948

For the Sisters of the Hotel Dieu

In pairs,
as if to illustrate their sisterhood,
the sisters pace the hospital garden walks.
In their robes black and white immaculate hoods
5 they are like birds,
the safe domestic fowl of the House of God.

O biblic birds,
who fluttered to me in my childhood illnesses
– me little, afraid, ill, not of your race, –
10 the cool wing for my fever, the hovering solace,

the sense of angels –
be thanked, O plumage of paradise, be praised.

c. 1945/1946   1948

Frigidaire

Even in July it is our winter corner,
hill 70 of our kitchen, rising white
and cool to the eye, cool to the alpenfinger.
The shadows and wind of snowfall fall from its sides.

5 And when the door swings away, like a cloud blown,
the village is Laurentian, tiered and bright,
with thresholds of red, white roofs, and scattered greens;
and it has a sky, and clouds, and a northern light.

Is peopled. On its vallied streets there stands
10 a bevy of milk, coifed like the sisters of snow;
and beaded bosoms of butter; and red farmhands;
all poised, as if to hear from the distant meadow,

there on the heights, with its little flowers of white,
the cubes that seem to sound like pasture bells.
15 Fixed to that far-off tingle they don't quite
hear, they stand, frozen with eavesdropping, like icicles.

And there on the heights, the storm's electric, thriving
with muffled thunder, and lightning slow and white!
It is a private sky, a weather exclusive,
20 a slow, sensational, and secret sight.

c. 1945/1946   1948

Grain Elevator

Up from the low-roofed dockyard warehouses
it rises blind and babylonian
like something out of legend. Something seen
in a children's coloured book. Leviathan
5 swamped on our shore? The cliffs of some other river?
The blind ark lost and petrified? A cave
built to look innocent, by pirates? Or
some eastern tomb a travelled patron here makes local?

But even when known, it's more than what it is:
10 for here, as in a Josephdream, bow down
the sheaves, the grains, the scruples of the sun
garnered for darkness; and Saskatchewan
is rolled like a rug of a thick and golden thread.
O prison of prairies, ship in whose galleys roll
15 sunshines like so many shaven heads,
waiting the bushel-burst out of the beached bastille!

Sometimes, it makes me think Arabian,
the grain picked up, like tic-tacs out of time:
first one; an other; singly; one by one; –
20 to save life. Sometimes, some other races claim
the twinship of my thought, – as the river stirs
restless in a white Caucasian sleep,
or, as in the steerage of the elevators,
the grains, Mongolian and crowded, dream.

25 A box: cement, hugeness, and rightangles –
merely the sight of it leaning in my eyes
mixes up continents and makes a montage
of inconsequent time and uncontiguous space.
It's because it's bread. It's because
30 bread is its theme, an absolute. Because

always this great box flowers over us
with all the coloured faces of mankind ...

c. 1945/1946   1948

M. Bertrand

Oh, but in France they arrange these things much better!
M. Bertrand who always, before kissing the female wrist
rolls the r in *charmante*
admits he owes everything to those golden Sorbonne years.
5 Returned now to our forest, he is sad and nostalgic;
indeed, pained; he winces when his brother says *icitte*.
O, he can never forget fair Paris, its culture and cuisine,
particularly as he stalks deaf and hungry
among the barbarians who never were seasick.
10   Still, he has one consolation – the visitor from abroad,
the old classmate, the *conférencier*, perhaps, even
a bearded *maître* of the Academy.
Then is he revived, like a dotard by the *Folies Bergères*,
revived, stimulated, made loquacious with *argot*,
15 and can't do enough for his guest, but would lavish on him
jowl-kiss, hand-kiss, and other kisses Parisian.

c. 1945/1946   1948

The Snowshoers

The jolly icicles ringing in their throats,
their mouths meerschaums of vapour,
from the saints' parishes they come, like snowmen
spangled, with spectrum colour
5 patching the scarf green, sash red, sky-blue the coat –
come to the crystal course. Their airy hooves
unslung from their backs are ready
to stamp their goodlucks on the solid foam.
Till then, the saints all heralded,
10 they snowball their banter below the angular eaves.

O gala garb, bright with assomption, flags
on limb and torso curled –
furling of white, blue zigzags, rondures red!
A candy-coloured world!
15 And moods as primary as their tuques and togs, –
of tingling cold, and the air rubbed down with snow
and winter well-being!
Like a slapdash backdrop, the street moves with colours,
the zones and rhomboids moving
20 toward the enhancing whiteness of the snow.

And now, clomping the packed-down snow of the street
they walk on sinews
gingerly, as if their feet were really swollen,
eager for release
25 from the blinders of buildings; suddenly they cut
a corner, and – the water they will walk!
Surf of the sun!
World of white wealth! Wind's tilth! Waves

of dazzling dominion
30 on which their coloured sails will billow and rock!

c. 1945/1946   1948

The Sugaring

For Guy Sylvestre

Starved, scarred, lenten, amidst ash of air,
roped and rough-shirted, the maples in the unsheltered grove
after their fasts and freezings stir.
Ah, winter for each one,
5 each gospel tree, each saint of the calendar,
has been a penance, a purchase: the nails of ice!
wind's scourge! the rooted cross!
Nor are they done with the still stances of love,
the fiery subzeros of sacrifice.

10 For standing amidst the thorns of their own bones,
eased by the tombs' coolth of resurrection time, –
the pardon, the purgatorial groans
almost at bitter end,
but not at end – the carving auger runs
15 spiral the round stigmata through each limb!
The saints bleed down their sides!
And look! men catch this juice of their agonized prime
to boil in kettles the sap of seraphim!

O, out of this calvary Canadian comes bliss,
20 savour and saving images of holy things,
a sugared metamorphosis!
Ichor of dulcitude
shaping sweet relics, crystalled spotlessness!

And the pious pour into the honeyed dies
25 the sacred hearts, the crowns,
thanking those saints for syrops of their dying
and blessing the sweetness of their sacrifice.

c. 1945/1946   1948

c. 1946/1946

Doctor Drummond

It is to be wondered whether he ever really
saw them, whether he knew them more than type,
whether, in fact, his occupational fun –
the doctor hearty over his opened grip –
5 did not confuse him into deducing
his patients' health and Irish from his own.

Certainly from his gay case-histories
that now
for two-tongued get-togethers are elocutional,
10 one would never have recognized his clientele.

Consider this patrician patronizing the *patois*,
consider his *habitants*, the homespun of their minds and
   motives,
and you will see them as he saw them – as *white* natives,
characters out of comical Quebec,
15 of speech neither Briton nor Breton, a fable folk,
a second class of aborigines,
docile, domesticate, very good employees,
so meek that even their sadness
made dialect for a joke.

20 One can well imagine the doctor,
    in club, in parlour, or in smoking car,
    building out of his practise a reputation
    as raconteur.
    But the true pulsing of their blood
25 his beat ignores,
    and of the temperature of their days, the chills
    of their despairs, the fevers of their faith,
    his mercury is silent.

    c. 1946/1946   1946

The Notary

    Next to the *curé*, he is hierarch,
    the true poet functional of this place,
    laureate of its lands.
    O, as longing's redacted, hope given witnesses,
5   its scarlet seal ambition, through him work
    the larger myths and motives, and the heart
    counts its beats on the margin, and our county lies
    cadastral on his hands!

    Formal in black, gold watch, and lyric collar,
10 he's ceremonial, a priest, a bard;
    money and love are his themes.
    He speaks, for all, the imprescriptible word;
    and with his name, sacred upon the roll,
    makes rich a date, and permanent a wish,
15 giving desire its deed, and the blessing of the hands
    to the English-measured dreams.

And with a flourish moves the immoveable,
gratifies the unborn of the unborn!
The certainties are his!
20 Yes, so to our custom dedicate and sworn,
he it is makes all getting honourable, –
truly our poet, coining the bride her song,
and making even out of the last will
our cherished elegies!

c. 1946/1946   1948

Political Meeting

(For Camillien Houde)

On the school platform, draping the folding seats,
they wait the chairman's praise and glass of water.
Upon the wall the agonized Y initials their faith.

Here all are laic; the skirted brothers have gone.
5 Still, their equivocal absence is felt, like a breeze
that gives curtains the sounds of surplices.

The hall is yellow with light, and jocular;
suddenly some one lets loose upon the air
the ritual bird which the crowd in snares of singing

10 catches and plucks, throat, wings, and little limbs.
Fall the feathers of sound, like *alouette's*.
The chairman, now, is charming, full of asides and wit,

building his orators, and chipping off
the heckling gargoyles popping in the hall.
15 (Outside, in the dark, the street is body-tall,

flowered with faces intent on the scarecrow thing
that shouts to thousands the echoing
of their own wishes.) The Orator has risen!

Worshipped and loved, their favourite visitor,
20 a country uncle with sunflower seeds in his pockets,
full of wonderful moods, tricks, imitative talk,

he is their idol: like themselves, not handsome,
not snobbish, not of the *Grande Allée! Un homme!*
Intimate, informal, he makes bear's compliments

25 to the ladies; is gallant; and grins;
goes for the balloon, his opposition, with pins;
jokes also on himself, speaks of himself

in the third person, slings slang, and winks with folklore;
and knows now that he has them, kith and kin.
30 Calmly, therefore, he begins to speak of war,

praises the virtue of being *Canadien*,
of being at peace, of faith, of family,
and suddenly his other voice: *Where are your sons?*

He is tearful, choking tears; but not he
35 would blame the clever English; in their place
he'd do the same; maybe.

Where *are* your sons?
                       The whole street wears one face,
shadowed and grim; and in the darkness rises
the body-odour of race.

c. 1946/1946   1948

Quebec Liquor Commission Store

Nonetheless Ali Baba had no richer cave,
nor lamps more sensitive Aladdin's thumb
than this cave, and these lamps which, at the touch,
evoke the growing slave,
5 and change the rag-poor world to purple-rich.
'O Vizier, wrapped in all knowledge and experience,
bring me, bring me in a flower of air,
the scent of the world's motion, the pollen, the fire,
the fumes, of magnificence!'
10 'Your servant, my Lord, has done according to your desire!

'And brought you also the pleasures of the skin about the round,
the sycophancy of glass, the palm's cool courtier,
and the feel of straw, all rough and rustical,
by some king's daughter donned;
15 and for your royal eyes, your Ishmael
with rub and abracadabra and obeisance brings
those forms and shapes, that harem opulence
that my Lord dotes on; and, of the same scope
their voices, like happenings
20 on cushions behind curtains, like whispers at the thrilled ear's lobe.'

'Well done! thou gurgling knave, and above all, well done,
in the conjuring of those mischievous genii
who nip at the paps of palate, hop on the tongue,
in the throat make merry and fun!
25 Lithe, they go tumbling in the paunch's nets! And rung
by rung, disporting, they climb into the brain's bazaar!
Wonderful are their tricks and somersaults,
such ingenuities as do make a king forget

the troubles that there are
30 even for kings, the rag-poor past, the purple that may set.'

c. 1946/1946   1948

The Spinning Wheel

You can find it only in attics or in ads,
heirloom a grandmother explains, woodcut
to show them native, quaint, and to be had
at the fee feudal; but
5 as object it does not exist, is aftermath
of *autre temps* when at this circle sat
domesticity,
and girls wearing the black and high-necked blouse
at its spokes played house.

10 Now it is antique, like the *fleur de lys*,
a wooden fable out of the olden time, –
as if the epileptic loom and mad factory
that make a pantomime
out of this wheel do so for picturesqueness
15 only, and to achieve a fine excess,
not for the dividend
surely. No. Just to preserve romance,
the rites, the wage-rates of old France.

Symbol, it still exists; the seigneur still,
20 though now drab and incorporate, holds domain
pre-eminent; still, to his power-foaming mill
the farmer brings his grain
his golden daughters made banality;
and still, still do they pay the seigneury
25 the hourly corvée,

the stolen quotient of the unnatural yields
of their woven acres and their linen fields.

c. 1946/1946   1948

The White Old Lady

The panic jangles repeated themselves every year.
The neighbours, clutching the black cup, whispered *Police!*
The Cote des Neiges place again! Lights come on, lights go off!
   She is here!

5 And every evening the sergeant, wearily: Police.
And heard: She is standing at all of the windows at once.
She is pulling down white blinds, but we see her shadow.
   Monstrosities

go on in that house. The sergeant takes evidence.
10 Report: Someone anaemic is going whitely mad.
Ditto: That dwelling is a smuggling place for lepers,
   a cache for diamonds.

A smoke-filled den. Seek there your missing and dead –
muffled by linens, cased in the white plaster wall.
15 Visitors, we know, have come unseen, and there's vice
   that can't be said.

But every time the police came, stepped into the hall,
there was only a white old lady, frail, like powder,
with a pleasant smile, living alone, and no one
20   else at all.

c. 1946/1946   1946

Sestina on the Dialectic

   Yes yeasts to No, and No is numinous with Yes. All is
a hap, a haze, a hazard, a do-doubtful, a flight from, a travel to.
Nothing will keep, but eases essence, – out! – outplots its
plight. So westers east, and so each teaches an opposite: a
5 nonce-thing still.

   A law? Fact or flaw of the fiat, still – a law. It binds us,
braided, wicker and withe. It stirs the seasons, it treads the
tides, it so rests in our life there's nothing, there's not a sole
thing that from its workings will not out.

10   The antics of the antonyms! From, to; stress, slack, and
stress, – a rhythm running to a reason, a double dance, a
shivering still.

   Even the heart's blood, bursting in, bales out, an ebb and
flow; and even the circuit within which its pulsebeat's
15 beam – man's morse – is a something that grows, that
grounds, – treks, totters. So.

   O dynasties and dominions downfall so! Flourish to flag
and fail, are potent to a pause, a panic precipice, to a picked
pit, and thence – rubble rebuilding, – still rise resurrective, –
20 and now see them, with new doers in dominion!

   They, too, dim out.

   World's sudden with somersault, updown, inout,
overandunder. And, note well: also that other world, the
two-chambered mind, goes with it, ever kaleidoscopic, one
25 scape to another, suffering change that changes still, that
focusses and fissions *the* to *a*.

When will there be arrest? Consensus? A marriage of
the antipathies, and out of the vibrant deaths and rattles
the life still? O just as the racked one hopes his ransom, so I
30 hope it, name it, image it, the together-living, the together-
with, the final synthesis. A stop.

But so it never will turn out, returning to the rack within,
without. And no thing's still.

c. 1946/1946

Meditation upon Survival

At times, sensing that the golgotha'd dead
run plasma through my veins, and that I must live
their unexpired six million circuits, giving
to each of their nightmares my body for a bed –
5 inspirited, dispirited –
those times that I feel their death-wish bubbling the
channels of my blood –
I grow bitter at my false felicity –
the spared one – and would almost add my wish
10 for the centigrade furnace and the cyanide flood.

However, one continues to live, though mortally.
O, like some frightened, tattered, hysterical man
run to a place of safety – the whole way run –
whose lips, now frenzy-foamed, now delirium-dry,
15 cry out the tenses of the verb to die,
cry love, cry loss, being asked: *And yet unspilled
your own blood?* weeps, and makes
his stuttering innocence a kind of guilt –
O, like that man am I, bereaved and suspect,
20 convicted with the news my mourning breaks.

Us they have made the monster, made that thing
that lives though cut in three: the severed head
which breathes, looks on, hears, thinks, weeps, and is bled
continuously with a drop by drop longing
25 for its members' re-membering!
And, the torn torso, spilling heart and lights
and the cathartic dregs!
These, for the pit! Upon the roads, the flights –
– O how are you reduced, my people, cut down to a limb! –
30 upon the roads the flights of the bodiless legs.

Myself to recognize: a curio;
the atavism of some old coin's face;
one who, though watched and isolate, does go –
the last point of a diminished race –
35 the way of the fletched buffalo.
Gerundive of extinct. An original.
What else, therefore, to do
but leave these bones that are not ash to fill –
O not my father's vault – but the glass-case
40 some proud museum catalogues *Last Jew*.

c. 1946/1946   1950

1946

At Home

    Orchids of music flutter from the keys.
    This air, it is a very spiritual air.
    The Doktor Hjalmar Schacht,
    Squarehead, cravatted, wingcollared, obese,
5 Murmurs *Divine! Divine!* and shifts, like ledgers,
    His buttocks overflowing in his chair.

    The pastor beside him swoons his eyelids down.
    It speaks of the very soul! O beautiful!
    In smiles the music ends.
10 The guests rise. Striped pants, gallant, stalk towards gowns,
    And cultured compliments float past the marble
    Of Goethe in the hall.

    O blond and bland, not a whit more innocent
    Is a sieve!
15 *Cemented in the cellar It rots in lime ...*
    And even That will nothing be in time ...
    How decorous and sweet the murderers live!

    1946

Lowell Levi [Version 1]

Mr. Lowell Levy, finds it difficult to distinguish
between an aleph and a swastika.
Nonetheless, he undertakes to edit a journal devoted to Judaica.
Que faire?
5 He runs a series of articles, urbane and learned,
on the Jewish delicatessen, the Jewish dairy.
O Sinai and Pumbeditha and the Bronx
and the Bronx.

1946

Portrait, and Commentary
[Version 2 of 'Lowell Levi']

Rich and remote in panelled offices
Or paunchy on the sands of Florida
The absentee lords of Jewry, both
Alien among their own, and alien
5 Among their Christian sons-in-law,
Consider their status:
Between the goy and the kike we are undone.

Wherefore, a cunning one
Said: Fiat! Let there be
10 Forthwith established for to teach the one
A Jewish speech pianissimo, and t'other
The credos of that great prestige-theology
That ours has been –
A magazine!

15 Thus Lowell Levi, who finds it hard to distinguish
   The four-shanked aleph from the swastika
   Is, for the roosters of bnai-Adam, made
   An editor:
   Eunuch maieutic of Judaica.
20 (But Lowell really doesn't give
   The kosher bristle of a swine
   For either what his sponsors believe,
   Or Zionist, or shaved divine:
   The love that Lowell has to give
25 Is, Trotsky, – only thine!)

   Within his sanctum, partisans polyglot
   Shake, to the sotto of their angst's refrain,
   Dialectic palmleaves over the citron brought
   Out of marrano Spain.
30 And slyly winding phylacteries
   About his slick Engelic notes
   Lowell sells Torah, sells it plain:
   Commodity of skins of goats.

   (The bosses in the Bermoothes,
35 Unvexed of Zion, lie at ease,
   While Lowell sets their Jewry straight
   To the undegenerate workers' state)

   The Western Union wire wails
   But where's the credo; its details:
40 What Judaism means to me?
   The monthly verity?

   So Lowell Levi prepares the authentic Jewish
   Series: and, first lesson,
   Leads with a tractate –
45 O sages of Sura and Pumbeditha's wise!
   A tractate on the Brooklyn delicatessen.

Upon their sanded laps in Florida,
Nostalgic barons read pastramic law,
While from New York the next month's issue leaves.
50 *Laughter ripples sleeves.*

1946

To the Lady Who Wrote about Herzl

Impudent female! salvaged none knows whence;
Bighearted one, forgiving, loving again
The poor duped Swabians; O learned hen
Posteriorizing the eggs of existenz, –
5 Until but yesterday thy dowdy lore,
Hegelian bosom, waddling mental gait,
Thy fatidical pose and tones inflate
Amused; but now they do amuse no more.
Mine honoured Herzl's tomb thou didst assoil!
10 Riding thy freudian broomstick, raptured witch,
Thou didst with droppings of thy hatred soil
Our dead king's marble.   Daughter of Belial,
Thou didst survive! Thou, and thine owlish screech!
While all our doves lie silent in that hell.

1946

Wishing to Embarrass Me, but Politely

Wishing to embarrass me, but politely,
they compliment my mystique.
They
who see neither the shark in the glass of water
5 nor the tiger springing from the mote in the air,
they are the realists!

1946

Wrestling Ring

The inverted funnel pouring its light like alcohol
upon the Roman arch of the wheeling torsos:
stance, grapple, and grip; under their leather
muscles as big as mice: about the square,
5 like the sex of stallions the round taut rope:
all is vigor, mansmell, and potence.

Now, look:
See, as the favorite has the villain on the hip,
spreadeagled,
10 luminous with sweat, light, and pain –
the little runt in the sixth row back – a sibling? –
hop on his seat.
His small arms fill the arena; his anaemia

flows through the blue veins of the cigarette smoke;
15 the tatooer's needle his voice:
    Donnes-y-là! Donnes-y!
Into his seat, he drops back
exhausted.

1946

c. 1945/1947

Beaver

He lifts his middle-aged cabby-face from roots,
hears the far ferment of the fall. *The time!*
Soon drunk with juice of timber, he smiles logs:
the joy of habitat.

5 Twigs, branches, bitten bole – they teeth him and tusk him;
mud webs his feet, he shines as if with sweat;
now in deep water builds his forest, fruited
with fish, by currents breezed, by quivering quiet.

Come frost, and ice his mud!
                              Come flakeful fall
10 his herbage hibernate!
                       Come flurrying months
and whitely roof him over his crystal plinths:
he waits the spring – a merman animal.

c. 1945/1947   1952

Dominion Square

    Here in a sudden meadow dropped amongst brick
    our culture pauses to gather up the clues
    that shape dominion in its miniature,
    that show, in little more than a city block
5 the composite land: its loved indigenous trees;
    lettered on lawn, some petals of its flora;
    and in its criss-cross paths the shape of a flag.
    Our values smile in this square, our [...], our modes:
    the thirty-storied limestone wedding-cake
10 the Sun Life baked to sanctify its seed;
    the roofed apostles who bless in green their flock,
    and the men on benches who only rise to beg.
    Our dialects: the bronze of Bobby Burns
    beloved of the businessman his once a year,
15 the calèche at the curb, rolled from old France
    and the hotel-door's foreign eloquence
    converge, as in a radio sound-room, here.
    But do not linger; but are bruited hence
    by streetcar through the angular city, by
20 tunnel through mountain to the suburbs, by
    the trains that whistle from this terminus
    into the flat, the high, the dark, the sunlit distances.

    c. 1945/1947

c. 1947/1947

Elegy

    Named for my father's father, cousin, whose cry
    Might have been my cry lost in that dark land –
    Where shall I seek you? On what wind shall I
    Reach out to touch the ash that was your hand?
5 The Atlantic gale and the turning of the sky
    Unto the cubits of my ambience
    Scatter the martyr-motes. Flotsam-of-flame!
    God's image made the iotas of God's name!
    O through a powder of ghosts I walk; through dust
10 Seraphical upon the dark winds borne;
    Daily I pass among the sieved white hosts,
    Through clouds of cousinry transgress,
    Maculate with the ashes that I mourn.
        Where shall I seek you? There's not anywhere
15 A tomb, a mound, a sod, a broken stick,
    Marking the sepulchres of those sainted ones
    The dogfaced hid in tumuli of air.
    O cousin, cousin, you are everywhere!
    And in your death, in your ubiquity,
20 Bespeak them all, our sundered cindered kin:
    David, whose cinctured bone –
    Young branch once wreathed in phylactery! –
    Now hafts the peasant's bladed kitchenware;

And the dark Miriam murdered for her hair;
25 And the dark Miriam murdered for her hair;
The relicts nameless; and the tattoo'd skin
Fevering from lampshade in a cultured home, —
All, all our gaunt skull-shaven family —
The faces are my face! that lie in lime,
30 You bring them, jot of horror, here to me,
Them, and the slow eternity of despair
That tore them, and did tear them out of time.

Death may be beautiful, when full of years,
Ripe with good works, a man, among his sons,
35 Says his last word, and turns him to the wall.
But not these deaths! O not these weighted tears!
The flesh of thy sages, Lord, flung prodigal
To the robed fauna with their tubes and shears;
Thy chosen for a gold tooth chosen; for
40 The pervert's wetness, flesh beneath the rod; —
Death multitudinous as their frustrate spore! —
This has been done to us, Lord, thought-lost God;
And things still hidden, and unspeakable more.
   A world is emptied. Marked is that world's map
45 The forest color. There where thy people praised
In angular ecstasy thy name, thy Torah
Is less than a whisper of its thunderclap.
Thy synagogues, rubble. Thy academies,
Bright once with talmud brow and musical
50 With song alternative in exegesis,
Are silent, dark. They are laid waste, thy cities,
Once festive with thy fruit-full calendar,
And where thy curled and caftan'd congregations
Danced to the first days and the second star,
55 Or made the marketplaces loud and green
To welcome in the Sabbath Queen;
Or through the nights sat sweet polemical
With Rav and Shmuail (also of the slain), —
O there where dwelt the thirty-six, — world's pillars! —
60 And tenfold Egypt's generation, there

Is nothing, nothing ... only the million echoes
Calling thy name still trembling on the air.

Look down, O Lord, from thy abstracted throne!
Look down! Find out this Sodom to the sky
65 Rearing and solid on a world atilt
The architecture by its pillars known.
This circle breathed hundreds; that round, thousands, –
And from among the lesser domes descry
The style renascent of Gomorrah built.
70 See where the pyramids
Preserve our ache between their angled tons:
Pass over, they have been excelled. Look down
On the Greek marble that our torture spurned –
The white forgivable stone.
75 The arch and triumph of subjection, pass;
The victor, too, has passed; and all these spires
At whose foundations, dungeoned, the screw turned
Inquisitorial, now overlook –
They were delirium and sick desires.
80 But do not overlook, O pass not over
The hollow monoliths. The vengeful eye
Fix on these pylons of the sinister sigh,
The well-kept chimneys daring towards the sky!
From them, now innocent, no fumes do rise.
85 They yawn to heaven. It is their ennui:
Too much the slabs and ovens, and too many
The manshaped loaves of sacrifice!
   As thou didst do to Sodom, do to them!
But not, O Lord, in one destruction. Slow,
90 Fever by fever, limb by withering limb,
Destroy! Send through the marrow of their bones
The pale treponeme burrowing. Let there grow
Over their eyes a film that they may see
Always a carbon sky! Feed them on ash!
95 Condemn them double deuteronomy!
All in one day pustule their speech with groans,
Their bodies with the scripture of a rash,

With boils and buboes their suddenly-breaking flesh!
When their dams litter, monsters be their whelp,
100 Unviable! Themselves, may each one dread,
The touch of his fellow, and the infected help
Of the robed fauna with their tubes and shears!
Fill up their days with funerals and fears!
Let madness shake them, – rooted down – like kelp.
105 And as their land is emptying, and instructed,
The nations cordon the huge lazaret, –
The paring of thy little fingernail
Drop down: the just circuitings of flame,
And as Gomorrah's name, be their cursed name!

110 Not for the judgment sole, but for a sign
Effect, O Lord, example and decree,
A sign, the final shade and witness joined
To the shadowy witnesses who once made free
With that elected folk thou didst call thine.
115 Before my mind, still unconsoled, there pass
The pharaohs risen from the Red Sea sedge,
Profiled; in alien blood and peonage
Hidalgos lost; shadows of Shushan; and
The Assyrian uncurling into sand; –
120 Most untriumphant frieze! and darkly pass
The shades Seleucid; dark against blank white
The bearded ikon-bearing royalties –
All who did waste us, insubstantial now,
A motion of the mind. O unto these
125 Let there be added, soon, as on a screen,
The shadowy houndface, barking, never heard,
But for all time a lore and lesson, seen,
And heeded; and thence, of thy will our peace.
   Vengeance is thine, O Lord, and unto us
130 In a world, wandering, amidst raised spears
Between wild waters, and against barred doors,
There are no weapons left. Where now but force
Prevails, and over the once-blest lagoons
Mushroom new Sinais, sole defensive is

135 The face turned east, and the uncompassed prayer.
Not prayer for the murdered myriads who
Themselves white liturgy before thy Throne
Are of my prayer; but for the scattered bone
Stirring in Europe's camps, next kin of death,
140 My supplication climbs the carboniferous air.
Grant them Ezekiel's prophesying breath!
Isaiah's cry of solacing allow!
O thou who from Mizraim once didst draw
Us free, and from the Babylonian lair;
145 From bondages, plots, ruins imminent
Preserving, didst keep Covenant and Law,
Creator, King whose banishments are not
Forever, – for thy Law and Covenant,
O for thy promise and thy pity, now
150 At last this people to its lowest brought
Preserve! Only in thee our faith. The word
Of eagle-quartering kings ever intends
Their own bright eyrie; rote of parakeet
The laboring noise among the fabians heard;
155 Thou only art responseful.
                    Hear me, who stand
Circled and winged in vortex of my kin:
Forego the complete doom! The winnowed, spare!
Annul the scattering, and end! And end
Our habitats on water and on air!
160 Gather the flames up to light orient
Over the land; and that funest eclipse,
Diaspora-dark, revolve from off our ways!
Towered Jerusalem and Jacob's tent
Set up again; again renew our days
165 As when near Carmel's mount we harbored ships,
And went and came, and knew our home; and song
From all the vineyards raised its sweet degrees,
And thou didst visit us, didst shield from wrong,
And all our sorrows salve with prophecies;
170   Again renew them as they were of old,

And for all time cancel that ashen orbit
In which our days, and hopes, and kin, are rolled.

c. 1947/1947   1951

Song of Innocence

About the Crematorium where the Jews
Burn, the Nations sit in their pews,
Watching the heavenly Carbonic Bands
Cast shadows over the Bibles in their hands.

5 It shocks their Piety, this Altar, and they look
Away, and into the good Book.
Devotion done, they lift their eyes to see
The sky clear, full of Grace again, smoke-free;
And on the smoke-stack score-board – dots:
10 A Six and one-two-three-four-five-six Noughts.

c. 1947/1947

Annual Banquet: Chambre de Commerce

And as the orators, rewarded roars, scored, soared, bored –
The man of capital:
You certainly have a wonderful country. Why don't you
Exploit it?

5 To which his neighbour and host
   Seeking in pocket and pouch
   Bosom and hip and thigh
   At last produced it, bold and double-column.

   Quebec: The place for industry
10   *Cheap power. Cheap labour.*
      No taxes (first three years).
      No isms (forever).

   Verso, the guest beheld; and smiled:
      Photograph of Mr. & Mrs. Damase Laberge
15   on the occasion of their 25th wedding anniversary,
      surrounded by their children and grandchildren
      to the number of thirty-two; from left to right ...

   O love which moves the stars and factories ...

   c. 1947/1947   1948

Dress Manufacturer: Fisherman

In his wandered wharf on the brake side of the lake;
in boots bucolic;
thatched and eaved with brim and circle of straw,
he'll sit for hours, himself his boat's prow
5 dangling the thread of his preoccupation.

Far from the lint and swatches, among lilies
chinned upon glass,
among the bulrushes his childhood only read, –
over cool corridors
10 pearled with bubbles, speckled with trout,
beneath the little songs, the little wings,

his city ardours all go out
into the stipple and smooth of natural things.

And he becomes, at the end of his filament,
15 a correspondent of water and of fish,
one who casts line and riches –
the glittering foolish spoon the rainbow fly –
to hide within the wish
that for so many years beat from the heat
20 of his enterprise and city sky
the simmering emphasis of his summer loss.

Here he would sink the curbstones!
And on the granite of his effort
grow a moss!

25 Back to the hotel, tanned, percer-proud
with the ransom of his youth –
a hero with private trout –
he's familiar in the kitchen, a fisherman
all evening in the lobby kidded and praised;
30 is modest, but encourages talk; and knows
with every compliment and trout
his childhood summers from the water raised.

c. 1947/1947   1948

Filling Station

With snakes of rubber and glass thorax,
like dragons rampant,
statistical, red with ambush,
they ambuscade the highway.

5 Only in the hinterland, and for neighbours,
the extant blacksmith drives
archaic nails into the three-legged horse.

But on Route 7
the monsters coil and spit from iron mouths
10 potent saliva.

(Beyond the hills, of course;
the oxen, lyric with horns, still draw
the cart and the limping wheels.)

c. 1947/1947   1948

Hormisdas Arcand

Hormisdas Arcand, about to found a new party
manufactures him historic manifesto.
Alas, he can not get
beyond the principal
5 first blast.
It keeps repeating itself, like a youpin meal.
Et, pour vrai dire, what more political
is there to say after you have said:
A bas les maudits Juifs!

c. 1947/1947   1948

Krieghoff: Calligrammes

Let the blank whiteness of this page be snow
and majuscule the make of Cornelius:
    then tented A's inverted V's
may circumflex and shade the paysage page
5   with French-Canadian trees;
or equal the arrows of the frozen flow
    by the last minus of degrees
stopped in their flight; or show
the wigwams and the gables –
10 of Krieghoff the pat petted verities.

And any signs will do:
the ladder H that prongs above the chimney;
prone J's on which the gay sleighs run;
the Q and her papoose;
15 crucifix Y; or bosomed farmwife B –
wanting an easel and the painter's flourish
with alphabet make free,
make squares, make curlecues
of his simplicity.

20 But colours? Ah, the two colours!

These must be spun, these must be bled
out of the iris of the intent sight:
red rufous roseate crimson russet red
    blank   candid   white.

c. 1947/1947   1948

Les Filles majeures

Evenings, they walk arm in arm, in pairs, —
as if to emphasize their incompleteness, —
and friendly together make an ambiguous form,
like a folded loneliness,
or like mirrors that reflect only each other.

And in the daytime, they are aunts; they pet,
they censor their sisters' children, take them for walks,
help them with privacies, and buy them presents.
It is baby talk
and precocity that is their topic, their event.

Their life is like a diary, to be filled.
Therefore they'll sit at concerts where music invents
them love-affairs; or lectures – for the mind's eye;
or, almost male, will tend
their gardens; or social service. Thus, the days hold.

Sometimes, having found another grey hair
they will put on the uniform of conventional dress
with the single item florid, the single feather
for the elusive one. Alas
always they return, and sighs the sisterly mirror.

Thereafter they shield themselves, brood on, avoid,
hate the entire vocabulary of love.
The shine of left-handed rings makes them feel odd,
and certain small words grieve
them, insult their spinsterhood.

For them, for them the world lacks symmetry!
And they themselves seem to themselves
like vases, broken in half, the halves perversely

    stood upon shelves
30 unfinished, and rich with flowers never to be.

c. 1947/1947   1948

Librairie Delorme

    Among the penny arcades and the dime shows,
attic above the dark racked secondhand stores
its number; neighbour to cubicles in heat,
hashjoints, vodvils, poolrooms – the scruffed doors
5 the derelict swings, the cop on the corner knows –
Far from the pomp epopic of its themes,
far from the pemmican West, out of the storm
confederate, upon a city street:
Canadiana: Librairie Delorme:
10 door grated: wooden stairs: the incunabulate dreams

    stacked: shadows catalogued. The runted past
grows only the thickness of dust and greys frustrate
the Intendants' enterprises, and Laval's –
in brochures bandied. Though Jesuits relate,
15 and explorers claim, and statesmen think they last
none come to listen, save the bibliophile;
or Hollywood for manners; or the bright
young candidate who'd show *de facto* false;
an abbé, perhaps, beatified with sight
20 of green Laurentia kneeling to church-bell.

    Monsieur Delorme ... Stooped and with doctoral beard
he is all anecdote and courtesy,
one who loves bindings and the old regime
that in his mind is gobelin'd fleur de lys
25 and in the chapel of his speech revered.

Nonetheless seems at peace with the conqueror's state,
is casual, diffident, a-political;
and from his manner you would never dream
he was a man was putting up for sale
30 his family heirlooms and his family plate.

c. 1947/1947   1948

Lone Bather

Upon the ecstatic diving board the diver,
poised for parabolas, lets go
lets go his manshape to become a bird.
Is bird, and topsy-turvy
5 the pool floats overhead, and the white tiles snow
their crazy hexagons. Is dolphin. Then
is plant with lilies bursting from his heels.

Himself, suddenly mysterious and marine,
bobs up a merman leaning on his hills.

10 Plashes and plays alone the deserted pool;
as those, is free, who think themselves unseen.
He rolls in his heap of fruit,
he slides his belly over
the melonrinds of water, curved and smooth and green.
15 Feels good: and trains, like little acrobats
his echoes dropping from the galleries;
circles himself over a rung of water;
swims fancy and gay; taking a notion, hides
under the satins of his great big bed, –
20 and then comes up to float until he thinks
the ceiling at his brow, and nowhere any sides.

His thighs are a shoal of fishes: scattered: he
turns with many gloves of greeting
towards the sunnier water and the tiles.

25 Upon the tiles he dangles from his toes
lazily the eight reins of his ponies.

An afternoon, far from the world
a street sound throws like a stone, with paper, through the
    glass.
Up, he is chipped enamel, grained with hair.
30 The gloss of his footsteps follows him to the showers,
the showers, and the male room, and the towel
which rubs the bird, the plant, the dolphin back again
personable plain.

c. 1947/1947   1948

Lookout: Mount Royal

Remembering boyhood, it is always here
the boy in blouse and kneepants on the road
trailing his stick over the hopscotched sun;
or here, upon the suddenly moving hill;
5 or at the turned tap its cold white mandarin mustaches;
or at the lookout, finally,
breathing easy, standing still

to click the eye on motion forever stopped:
the photographer's tripod and his sudden faces
10 buoyed up by water on his magnet caught
still smiling as if under water still;
the exclamatory tourists descending the caleches;
the maids in starch; the ladies in white gloves;

other kids of other slums and races;
15 and on the bridle-paths
the horsemen on their horses like the tops of f's:

or from the parapet make out
beneath the green marine
the discovered road, the hospital's romantic
20 gables and roofs, and all the civic Euclid
running through sunken parallels and lolling
in diamond and square, then proud-pedantical
with spire and dome
making its way to the sought point, his home.

25 home recognized: there: to be returned to –

lets the full birdseye circle to the river,
its singsong bridges, its mapmaker curves, its
island with the two shades of green, meadow and wood;
and circles round that water-tower'd coast;
30 then, to the remote rhapsodic mountains; then,
– and to be lost –
to clouds like white slow friendly animals
which all the afternoon across his eyes
will move their paced spaced footfalls.

c. 1947/1947   1948

M. le juge Dupré

M. le juge Dupré has all the qualities.
Especially gratitude.

Exempli gratia:
There are in Dupré's court –

5 since Mtre. Hamelin of the law firm of
   Hamelin, Hamelin, Couillard & Foy
   got him and gave him his seat upon the bench –
   there are in Dupré's court
   no cases ever lost
10 not ever, ever lost
   by Hamelin, Hamelin, Couillard & Foy.

c. 1947/1947

Monsieur Gaston

   You remember the big Gaston, for whom everyone predicted
   a bad end? –
   Gaston, the neighbour's gossip and his mother's cross?
   You remember him *vaurien*, always out of a job,
5 with just enough clinking coinage
   for pool, bright neckties, and blondes, –
   the scented Gaston in the poolroom lolling
   in meadows of green baize?
   In clover now. Through politics. *Monsieur* Gaston.

10 They say the Minister of a certain department does not move
   without him; and they say, to make it innocent, –
   chauffeur.
   But everyone understands. Why, wherever our Gaston smiles
   a nightclub rises and the neons flash.
15 To his slightest whisper
   the bottled rye, like a fawning pet-dog, gurgles.
   The burlesque queen will not undress
   unless Monsieur Gaston says yes.
   And the Madame will shake her head behind the curtain-rods
20 unless he nods.

A changed man, Gaston; almost a civil servant,
keeps records, appointments, women; speaks tough English;
is very much respected.
You should hear with what greetings his distinguished
    approach is greeted;
25 you should see the gifts he gets,
with compliments for his season.

c. 1947/1947   1948

The Mountain

Who knows it only by the famous cross which bleeds
into the fifty miles of night its light
knows a night-scene;
and who upon a postcard knows its shape –
5 the buffalo straggled of the laurentian herd, –
holds in his hand a postcard.

In layers of mountains the history of mankind,
and in Mount Royal
which daily in a streetcar I surround
10 my youth, my childhood –
the pissabed dandelion, the coolie acorn,
green prickly husk of chestnut beneath mat of grass –
O all the amber afternoons
are still to be found.

15 There is a meadow, near the pebbly brook,
where buttercups, like once on the under of my chin
upon my heart still throw their rounds of yellow.

And Cartier's monument, based with nude figures
still stands where playing hookey
20 Lefty and I tested our gravel aim
(with occupation flinging away our guilt)
against the bronze tits of Justice.

And all my Aprils there are marked and spotted
upon the adder's tongue, darting in light,
25 upon the easy threes of trilliums, dark green, green, and white,
threaded with earth, and rooted
beside the bloodroots near the leaning fence –
corms and corollas of childhood,
a teacher's presents.

30 And chokecherry summer clowning black on my teeth!

The birchtree stripped by the golden zigzag still
stands at the mouth of the dry cave where I
one suppertime in August watched the sky
grow dark, the wood quiet, and then suddenly spill
35 from barrels of thunder and broken staves of lightning –
terror and holiday!

One of these days I shall go up to the second terrace
to see if it still is there –
the uncomfortable sentimental bench
40 where, – as we listened to the brass of the band concerts
made soft and to our mood by dark and distance –
I told the girl I loved
I loved her.

c. 1947/1947   1948

Parade of St. Jean Baptiste

Bannered, and ranked, and at its stances fixed
the enfilade with vestment colours the air.
Roll now the batons of the tambours round
ruminant with commencement, and now sound
5 annunciative, ultramontane, the
fanfares of jubilee!
It moves: festive and puissant the chivalry
advances chief, law crouped and curvetting –
finish and force, undulant muscle and braid –
10 O centaurs en gambade!

They move as through a garden, moving between
gay altitudes of flowers, populous
of all the wards and counties burgeoning here:
ribbons and countenances, joys and colours –
15 nuances of meridian, the blue,
the rose, the vert, the blond, all lambencies
to this rich spectacle turned heliotropic,
graceful and levitant: Quebec, its people:
flotation of faces; badinage of petals:
20 profound from suburbs surfaced on
the Real to spy Imagination.

Applause! Ovation of hourras! There pass
before the flowering faces, imaged, the
animal fables, myths of the crayon'd class,
25 the nursery's voyage and discovery:
redeemed and painted is the Indian;
lake sirens chant again; and sorcery
again makes princess out of Cendrillon,
(by Massicotte, research; and courtesy
30 of Simpson's and of Eaton T. and Son)
last! last! the coachmen of *chasse-galerie*.

Oh, all, – parents, their infant epaulettes –
Here all are dauphins of a vanished empery.

The grand progenitor! Hébert! Salute
35 as acted en tableau revivified
the pioneer fiat, the patrimonial geste
deracinating forest into prairie!
Surge, visions of farms the river parcelled out!
Conjured, the parish parallelograms,
40 the chapel's verdant foyer! (Does not this scene,
habitants of the fumed and pulverous city
immured in granite canyons and constrict,
does it not veil the eyes with memories
sylvan, campestral? Does it not palpitate pain
45 current nostalgic away from the factory
to the mountain liberties and large champaign?)

Now, into their vision, from the parishes
with gonfalons emergent juvenal
the schools and seminaries, potent with race:
50 name after name, catena of grand fame,
tradition-orgulous. Martyr and saint
chrysostomate their standards. Aspiration
surrounds them, and the future dowers with power –
regenerate, augmentative: the nation.
55 The berceuses are its anthems; thus survives
philoprogenitive Quebec; thus grants survival
unto the spired culture elsewhere tomb'd.
Yes, here with students and their cassock'd doctors,
the angels of Aquinas dance their dances,
60 and march the pious mascots of St. Francis.

Quebec, Quebec, which for the long blanched age –
infidelium partes – multiplied
pagan its beasts and painted savages –
(while Rome was rounded with St. Peter's dome
65 and Europe vertical with tower and cross
supported constellations) – is still rich

of realms spiritual the Jesuits founded,
and Sabbaths of the monks of Yamachiche.
Crosses of clergy, luxe armorial,
70 still vivify with their insignia
the evangelical air, and benedictions
douce-digital from priest and eminence
still quadrilate the inhospitable tense.

And sudden! camaraderie and jokes.
75 Ablute and pompous, staid, the rotund mayor
(remember in Maisonneuve his gestured discourse –
Cyrano, né p'tit gars de Ste. Marie?)
with chain of office now, and magistral,
promenades, flanked by seniors of the city.
80 These are not allegorical; the people
familiar, still, as if with candidates,
cry out allusions, scandals; parodize
the clichés and the rhetoric suave.
But unconcerned and bland, the marked elect
85 march recognitions through the colonnade –
ineffably correct.

Patronial, of recent heraldry:
the piston sinistral, the scutcheon coin,
blazon and bar of bank, – the seigneurie
90 of capital, new masters of domain.
See, this is he, the pulp magnifico,
and this the nabob of the northern mine;
this man is pelts, and this man men allow
factotum. To the servants of their wage,
95 *le peup'*, the docile, the incognito
paupers, they do offer the day's homage,
but know their seasons appertain to them,
they being loyal, inexpensive, liege.

O who can measure the potency of symbols?
100 The hieratic gesture murdering grief?
The gloss on suffering? The jewelled toy

    that sports away quotidian the anguish?
    For the grey seasons and the frustrate heart,
    therefore, these rituals, which are therapy,
105 a ceremonial appeasement. O
    single and sole upon the calendar
    the baptist's day with rite and rapture tints
    dolor that for its annuair of days
    will dance, refract, this one day's images.

110 Departed is the enfilade; the people
    in groups chromatic through the boulevards
    disperse; spectators benched and poled, descend;
    the traffic gauntlets gesture; klaxons sound;
    all motion is pastelled; gala and gay
115 the picnic-loud tramway.
    It is a prelude for the pleiades
    that pyrotechnic will this night illume
    pères de famille idyllic and content,
    and in the dense boskage the ancient intimate experiment.

    c. 1947/1947   1948

Pastoral of the City Streets

I

Between distorted forests, clapped into geometry,
in meadows of macadam,
heat-fluff-a-host-of-dandelions dances on the air.
Everywhere glares the sun's glare,
 5 the asphalt shows hooves.

                    In meadows of macadam
grazes the dray horse, nozzles his bag of pasture,
is peaceful. Now and then flicks through farmer straw
his ears, like pulpit-flowers; quivers
10 his hide; swishes his tempest tail
a black and sudden nightmare for the fly.
The sun shines, sun shines down
new harness on his withers, saddle, and rump.

On curbrock and on stairstump the clustered kids
15 resting let slide some afternoon: then restless
hop to the game of the sprung haunches; skid
to the safe place; jump up: stir a wind in the heats:
laugh, puffed and sweat-streaked.

O for the crystal stream!

20 Comes a friend's father
with his pet of a hose,
and plays the sidewalk black
cavelike and cool.

O crisscross beneath the spray, those pelting petals and peas
25 those white soft whisks
brushing off heat!
O underneath these acrobatic fountains
among the crystal,
like raindrops a sunshower of youngsters dance:
30 small-nippled self-hugged boys
and girls with water sheer, going *Ah* and *Ah*.

II

And at twilight,
the sun like a strayed neighbourhood creature
having been chased
35 back to its cover

the children count a last game, or talk, or rest,
beneath the bole of the tree of the single fruit of glass
now ripening,
a last game, talk, or rest,
40 until mothers like evening birds call from the stoops.

c. 1947/1947   1948

Sire Alexandre Grandmaison

When Sire Alexandre Grandmaison, Seigneur of Biche,
read the final draft of the bill, placed by his secretary,
(who watched such things,) upon his heirloom desk,
he was desolate.
5 That day was a lost day, and Sire Alexandre
outraged, forgot those lesser domains and fiefs:
    Quebec Paper Products, Ltd.
    Champlain Industries, Inc.
    Laurentian Cold Storage, Ltd.
10   La Société de Fiducie, and subsidiaries
of all of which he had been duly elected president.

To think of it!
The ancient rights attaching now commuted!
King Louis' honour, which not even the English would touch
15 paid off at six per cent:
pious ceremony reduced
to legal tender at a banker's wicket!

Mais, que voulez-vous? It was a parliament
of grocers, notaries, farmers' sons who would

20 crate custom, barter the fleur de lys for leeks.
    It was a too commercial age.

    c. 1947/1947   1948

Université de Montréal

Faculté de Droit

   Flaunting their canes, their jaunty berets, the students throng
   slick serpentine the street and streamer the air
   with ribbons of ribaldry and bunting song.
   Their faces, shadowed seminary-pale,
5 open, flash red, announce their epaulettes,
   escape from Xenophon and old Virgile.
   Gaily they wind and stagger towards their own
   and through the maze already see themselves
   silken and serious, a gownèd guild
10 a portrait painter will one day make traditional
   beneath the Sign of the *Code Napoléon*.

   This, then, their last permitted juvenal mood
   kicked up by adolescence before it dons
   the crown and dignity of adulthood.
15 Today, the grinning circle on the *Place d'Armes*,
   mock trial, thumbdown'd verdict, and, singsong,
   the joyous sentence of death; tomorrow, the
   good of the state, the law, the dean
   parting deliberate his beard
20 silvered and sabled with rampant right and wrong.

   Thus will they note in notebooks, and will con
   the numbers and their truths, and from green raw
   celebrants of the Latin Quarter, duly

warp and wrinkle into *avocats*.
25 The solid men. Now innocence and fun.
O let them have their day, it soon will go!
Soon are begun
for haggler and schemer and electioneer –
the wizened one who is a library key,
30 the fat one plumped upon the *status quo* –
the fees and fetters of career.
Soon they enter
their twenty diaries, clocked and elaborate,
and soon, too soon, begin to live to leave
35 *en bon père de famille*, – a sound estate.

c. 1947/1947   1948

Winter Night: Mount Royal

Slowly, and flake by flake ... At the drifted frond
of the terraces and ski-runs over me
there falls a snow of sound:
tinkle of frost   minims of mercury
5   campanile cold

Horseman and horse among the chandeliers
parting the crystal twigs? Some belfry burst
frozen, and fractured into chips of sound?
The air itself
10 made little globes,
their rounds ringing in Fahrenheit descant?

White innocence the mountainside is mist,
its bells as secret as the bells of its flowers.

Now nearer, and jollier, and fourtimed, canters
15 the bend of the road this jingle of this silver!
Big-eyed, equestrian, trotting
the nickle blossoms,
the bells and hellos of his yoke and harness!

Heraldic, guled, the sleigh in a flurry of sound –
20 hooves upon snow the falsettos of water
and bells cavalier –
passes before me, is festive, and passes beyond
the curve of the road, the heels of its runners
scrolling it into the mist.

25 They are now fainter, have no direction, lost.
One would say the hidden stars were bells
dangling between the shafts of the Zodiac.
One would say
the snowflakes falling clinked together their sparkles
30 to make these soft, these satin-muffled
tintinnabulations.

c. 1947/1947   1948

1947

O God! O Montreal!

These were but innuendo:
Louis Fréchette, poet, assigning in bankruptcy,
and Butler in the Gallery of Art
(discoboli jockstrapped and brassiered nymphs)

5 *Our* century's explicit.
The scale of wages
of the municipal employees of the City of Montreal
      Concordia Salus
ranks the librarian (assistant) just below
10 the first-class stableman.

Whoa, Pegasus!

1947   1947

1948

Cantabile

De litteris, et de armis, praestantibusque ingeniis

And when they brought him back
the fibbiest fabricator of them all
      il miglior fabbro
they didn't know what to do with him
5   at the customs he had had nothing to declare
saving and except a number of synonyms, to wit:
zhid, sheeny, jewboy, youpin, kike, yitt, shweef.
                          and the ballad
    But bye and rade the Black Douglas
10   And wow but he was rough!
    For he pulled up the bonny brier
    And flang't in St. Mary's Lough.

didn't know what to do with him ... hang him?
old, *exhaussé*, a poet, there was a question of ethics, moreover
15   one kuddent make a martyr of him, cood one?
               St. Ezra Benedict

So the seven psychiatrists feigned insanity
committed him.

USURA: that his offence
20 that he sought to extract an exorbitant interest
                              from a limited talent.
speculated in the culture exchanges
passed off   χρύσω   χρυσοτέρα
25 the Dante coinage, Provençal, Chinese yen
not as his own, but his for increment.

It must be admitted, however, that as a pawnbroker
he was distinguished.
He invented a new way to ring a coin on the table
30 was expert in the bite for counterfeit,
trafficked only in the best mdse. and to his friends gave discounts
for the rest was fierce, bearded like the pard, like his Jew.
            Pound   Libra   £

USURA

35 The cantos? 'The art of conversation' said Tate (Allen) meaning
small talk shouted.
80 of them 80
anecdote, persiflage, ideogram, traduction
                    traductore – tradittore
40 all to the same if any effect – the syphilisation of our gonorera
                    and Pound its thunder clap,
a good role but the wrong actor.

Don't you think said the lady from Idaho on tour at Rapallo
that he will be remembered?   Yes
45 As the author of a Gradus ad parnassum
   "   a compiler of several don'ts
   "   a perpetrator of ditto
   "   a dropper-down of learning's crumbs
and as the stoic of the empty portals.

50 Otherwise, as Jimmy, quoting himself and poor Mr. Breen
        E.P.: EP
        'EP.   Est Perditus.

1948   1948

c. 1950/1950

Benedictions

For that he gave to a stone understanding to understand
   direction.
For that he made no slave for me.
For that he clothes the naked with the nudities of beasts.
For that he erects the contracted.
5 For that he smites me each dawn with a planet.

c. 1950/1950   1951

Stance of the Amidah

O Lord, open thou my lips; and my mouth shall declare thy praise:

God of Abraham, God of Isaac, God of Jacob, who hast
   bound to the patriarchs their posterity and hast made
5 thyself manifest in the longings of men and hast condescended
   to bestow upon history a shadow of the shadows of thy
   radiance;

Who with the single word hast made the world, hanging before us the heavens like an unrolled scroll, and the earth old manuscript, and the murmurous sea, each, all-allusive to thy glory, so that from them we might conjecture and surmise and almost know thee;

> *Whom only angels know*
> *Who in thy burning courts*
> *Cry: Holy! Holy! Holy!*
> *While mortal voice below*
> *With seraphim consorts*
> *To murmur: Holy! Holy!*
> *Yet holiness not know.*

Favour us, O Lord, with understanding, who hast given to the bee its knowledge and to the ant its foresight, to the sleeping bear Joseph's prudence, and even to the dead lodestone its instinct for the star, favour us with understanding of what in the inscrutable design is for our doomsday-good;

O give us such understanding as makes superfluous second thought; and at thy least, give us to understand to repent.

At the beginning of our days thou dost give – O! at the end, forgive!

Deem our affliction worthy of thy care, and now with a last redeeming, Redeemer of Israel, redeem!

Over our fevers pass the wind of thy hand; against our chills, thy warmth. O great Physician, heal us! and shall we ailing be healed.

From want deliver us. Yield the earth fruitful. Let rain a delicate stalk, let dew in the bright seed, sprout ever abundance. Shelter us behind the four walls of thy seasons, roof us with justice, O Lord, who settest the sun to labour for our evening dish!

Thyself do utter the Shma! Sound the great horn of our freedom, raise up the ensign of freedom, and gather from

the four corners of the earth, as we do gather the four fringes
to kiss them, thy people, thy folk, rejected thine elect.
      Restore our judges as in former times restore our Judge.
Blessed art thou, O Lord, King, who lovest righteousness
and judgement.
      Favour them, O Lord, thy saints thy paupers, who do
forgo all other thy benedictions for the benediction of
thy name.
      O build Jerusalem!
      Anoint thy people David!
      Our prayers accept, but judge us not through our
prayers: grant them with mercy.
      Make us of thy love a sanctuary, an altar where the heart
may cease from fear, and evil a burnt offering is consumed
away, and good, like the fine dust of spices, an adulation of
incense, rises up.
      O accept, accept, accept our thanks for the day's three
miracles, of dusk, of dawn, of noon, and of the years which
with thy presence are made felicitous.
      Grant us – our last petition – peace, thine especial
blessing, which is of thy grace and of the shining and the
turning of thy Face.

c. 1950/1950   1951

Who Hast Fashioned

      Blessed art thou, O Lord,
      Who in Thy wisdom has fashioned man as Thou hast
fashioned him: hollowed and antrious, grottoed and gutted,
channelled; for mercy's sake gifted with orifice, exit, and vent!
      Did one of these only suffer obstruction, survives not
the hour that man!
      Thy will according, there drops the baneful excess: the

scruff falls; from the pores surreptitious the sweat; and the
nails of the fingers are cut; the demons are houseless.
     Be blessed for the judgment of the eight great gates who
dost diminish us to make us whole; for the piecemeal deaths
that save; for wax and cerumen, which preserve all music, and
for flux of the sinus, which gives the brain coolness, its
space, and for spittle prized above the condiments of Asia; even
for tears.

c. 1950/1950   1951

Of the Making of Gragers

     The following are the proper instruments wherewith
Haman and all of that ilk may best be confounded:

clappers   utterants   &   mutterants
racketrakers   funaphores   hullabellows
filippics   titus-taps   sonorosnorers
fracasators   clangabangs &   clackacousticons
drums and bimbamboomicores   vociferators
nazinoisicans   palmapats   gourds
ratatats   cymbals   &   stridors
knuckleknacks & castanets   brekekex
ton' o' thunders   datadiscords
panpandemonia   torquemadatumps borborigmi
brontobronks   chmelnizzicatos   pharophonics
hellodeons   whistles & fee-fi-fo-fifers
          etceterows

c. 1950/1950   1950

1952/1954

Epigrams [1]

1. To Forgive Divine

Even if in the gutter you were lying dying of thirst
mouth open, tongue parched,
I would want to, but wouldn't
spit in your face.

2. As to Quantum

5 Seeing three on the left side, and on the right three,
is it illegal to whisper
six?

3. Caesar's Plagiarist

The noble Antony
issues from Cleopatra's chambers, says:
10 *Vidi, vici, veni.*
Poor Caesar! now left with only
alea est jacta – conquest.

4. 'Farcie de Comme'

O poet of the removeable glass eye –
Cyclops! –
What a companion you might have been
to Ulysses of the brand,
Poet of new directions!

5. Snowfall ... Eiderdown ... Cumulus ...

Defeated
the laureate's now ensconced in the cubicle
of an advertising agency where he invents
beautiful appellations and suave epithets
            for toilet-paper.
His fame runs from world's end to world's end.

6. Initiation

I remember the old Coltoon, circumciser, in action.
The blood of his Judaisms still cries out.
      He is dead now.
In his time he cut a wide swath.

7. Babe in the Woods

The idealist
is smitten humble and dumb
as suddenly he stumbles
into a murmur of mumbled numbers
of which he can not make out the sum.

8. *Beatific Vision*

Avrohom, Yitzchok, and Yaacov, patriarchs;
Chief of the prophets, Moses;
35 prophetaeque majores minoresque –
all at the golden board reclining
their crowns atilt, their beards awry,
all singing
Yo-ho-ho and ho-ho-ho
40 sanna!

9. *Aye, but a Man's Reach*

To the perfume that the rose dreams of,
its own perfume
is but a body-odour.

10. *?*

This spinster neither spins
45 nor toils,
yet is her thumb callous'd
also.

11. *Déjà Vu*

Throwback and atavism of Mizraim:
          Nilotic Jew
50 I hear the hieratic on the air
      see shadows of embalmers, breathe
flowers of sarcophagi.

The landscape, however, is as it was:
            of pyramids, none.

12. Cui Bono?

55 Who can fail to admire the
     self-mastery of X
 to whom, he says, it is a matter of indifference
 whether his poems are
     or are not taken up?
60 The gods, he says, eavesdrop.

13. The More's the Pity

 Smile never on the ugly ones;
 they will mistake your compassion for
 passion.

14. From the Beyond

 Privy to the Eleusinian mysteries
65 Euphorias reports
 that its priests were so cleansed of the world
    they called themselves the dead.
 Euphorias also details their menus.

15. Canine Felicity

 The music of what sphere?
70 What does the dog hear that I can't hear?

16. Technique

 'What wit, what wonder, winged words work!'
 He is troubled only to know
    is it alliteration or assonance?

17.

All worship is doomed to schisms, heresies,
                    disillusions.
The reverend Reverend, therefore, called it luck
When he found that his idol had had only
one foot of clay.

18. *Unveiling*

And now the smiles fall to the floor
                 like dentures,
And the smiling eyes are removed from their sockets
The face is poker-face.

19.

Hard to be a Jew?
Not for the Jew, said the gentile –
But to be circumcised at forty! ...

20.

They smote us hip and thigh;
They razed our cities to the ground;
Our fields they sowed with salt.
We flourished.

21. *Counsel*

That man is too good: suspect his motives;
That other is too evil: search out his impulses;
Is simply good and evil:
                        that is the norm.

22. Inarticulate

The man said nothing, nothing at all, but sat
As in a brown study making interior noises. One moment
was nasal, the next cleared his throat of its r's; but
said nothing. Was still.
He pursed his lips to a letter: no sound.
He sighed.
O, the sorrow that susurrus spelled!

23. Recollection

Strolling the Champs Elysée
I have remembered you
Jean Valjean, and your life in the sewers of Paris:
not without envy.

24. From the Japanese

The birds twitter, excited, behind their copper wires.
A horse has passed.

25. On Examining a Bill of Fare

Quails before manna?

26.

You fear me; and with good reason.
Did I have the power
I would carve your hearts out, and stuff the hollows
With testicles, yours.

1952/1954

c. 1953/1955

Spinoza: On Man, on the Rainbow

All flowers that in seven ways bright
Make gay the common earth,
All jewels that in their tunnelled night
Enkindle and flash forth

5 All these, now in the sky up-thrust,
To dazzle human sight
Do hang but on a speck of dust,
But dust suffused by light.

c. 1953/1955

1955

Epigrams [2]

Dial B and L

All honour to the memory of Alexander Graham Bell!
                                             Old Noah, he
may have first planted the vine, but Alexander
seeded a jungle!

5   Trellis and creeper and curling of wire,
          Boskage of copper and tendril of roof

And, what fruit!
Did the grapes of old Noah tintinabulate?
Not so those of Alexander Graham Bell
10   May they ring for him in hell!
        May they ring for him in hell's darkness and umber
                            forever a wrong number!

Mâ Aleyk – No Evil Befall You

His greeting is of the faith, like the muezzin's.
        The bazaars and the souks, they are as nothing
15   to his interest in your health. Wellah!

His smile is the hamzin for warmth, the simum for cordiality.
And already I feel the sand in my eyes!

Mais, c'est pas de mes oignons, ça!

This globe, this world, this onion of humanity!
Unsheathe it, sheath by sheath
20   mask after mask –
even the core is unsheathable! –
pungency, bitterness, tears!

Hommage

Madame, I see that you have indeed considered the ant,
and its antennae.
25 Why else should your clitoris be so apparent on your forehead?

Apologia

How was I to know, those months in my mother's womb,
that exit meant ambush?

Ritual

The great tycoon is dead.
The eulogies have been said.
30 And, look! they put pennies on his eyes.
– To speed a resurrection?

Palmam Qui Meruit

O tribune, tribune manqué, passed over in favour
of an unworthier one,
bear up, hold fast, political success
is a course in the callousing of disappointments.

1955

POETRY TRANSLATIONS

ARAMAIC

The Kaddish [Version 1]

Sanct and exaltate
in the world which to His will He wrought
be the great Name!
May his reign come regnant
5 during your lifetime and during your days and during the life
    of all the House of Israel,
right round speedily
and at a near time
and say ye
Amen.

10 *Cong.* Be the name great
        blessed for all time, eterne, sempiternal, forever.

Blessed, makarized, glorified, extolled and exalted, eulogized,
    lauded, most hallelujah'd
be the Name of the Holy One
blessed be He.
15 Yea, though He be above and beyond and worlds past the
    compass
of all hymns and benedictions, all paean and praise and uttered
    solatium
that here below we articulate,

and say ye
Amen.

20 *Cong.* May the name of the Lord be blessed from now to all time.

May peace full-measured descend from heaven, bringing, preserving, life to us all, and to all of Israel
and say ye
Amen.

Cong. My help is from the Lord who heaven and earth did make.

25 He who maketh peace in his altitudes
may he make peace for us here below
and for all Israel
and say ye
Amen.

c. 1951/1952

The Kaddish [Version 2]

(An experiment in translation)

Sanct and exaltate in the world which to his will he wrought be the great Name! May his reign come regnant during your lifetime and during your days and during the life of all the House of Israel, right round speedily and at a near
5 time, and say ye, Amen.
Be the great Name forever blessed, eterne, sempiternal, world upon world.

Blessed be, and glorified, and honoured high, and held aloft and much extolled, exalted, magnified, and
10 hallelujah'd
the name of the Holy One, blessed be He:
though he be high above all benedictions, hymns, doxologies, glorifications that are anywhere in the world uttered; and say ye, Amen.
15 O, acceptable to their Father who is in heaven be the prayers and supplications of the whole House of Israel; and say ye, Amen.
May great peace descend from heaven; and life; for us, and all of Israel; and say ye, Amen.
20 Who maketh peace in his high places, peace may He bring, for us and for all of Israel; and say ye, Amen.

c. 1951/1952   1952

HEBREW

SOLOMON BEN MOSES HA-LEVI ALKABEZ

O Site Most Kingly, O Royal Sanctum

    O site most kingly, O royal sanctum,
    Arise, go forth from among your ruins!
    Enough your sitting in the vale of sorrow!
        The Lord has readied His compassion.

5 Bestir you from your dust. Array you
    By grace of David, son of Jesse
    In this my people's beauteous garment!
        My soul, it knows redemption nearing!

    Arise! Arouse! Arise and waken!
10 For it has come at last, the dawning!
    Lift up your voice your song to utter;
        For on you is revealed God's glory.

c. 1949/1949   1951

CHAIM NACHMAN BIALIK

Beneath the Burden ...

Beneath the burden of your love,
Bowed down, I cannot lift me up!
Ah, woe is me! I am become
A penny shaken in your cup!

5 Why do you so besiege my hearth?
What evil have I done? What good?
I am no prophet, no, nor bard,
I am a humble hewer of wood.

A hewer of wood, a man of the axe,
10 Doing my day's work to the full:
Dusk falls, my arm is weary, and
The edge of my much-used axe is dull.

Of a short day a journeyman,
A labourer on your estates,
15 No time have I for jubilee,
And no time now for your debates.

How shall we show our countenance,
And how the morrow greet? Depart!
Each to summation of his life!
20 Each to the burdens of his heart!

c. 1936/1936					1943

The Chastisement of God

The chastisement of God, is this His curse:
That you shall your own very hearts deny
To cast your hallowed tears on foreign waters,
Your tears on luminous false threads to thread,
5 To breathe your breath in marble alien,
And in the heathen stone to sink your soul.

The teeth of the gluttons of your flesh drips blood —
But you shall feed them also your own souls:
And Pithom and Rameses for those that hate you
10 Shall you erect, your children used as brick.
Yea, and their cry, from wood and stone arising,
Within the portal of your ear shall die.

If one of these shall grow on eaglet's wings
For ever from his eyrie shall you fling him;
15 And should he, mighty, thirsting the sun, soar upwards
Not, not for you shall sunlight be revealed,
And not on you effulgence glow, when his
Pinions divide the clouds, a path for sun.
For high upon crags, shall he lift up his scream;
20 The echo thereof shall not your ears attain.

So shall you, one by one, the noblest spurn
And so shall you at last remain bereaved,
Your tent laid waste, and glory fled from your hearth,
Calamity and terror shall be yours.
25 The foot of God shall spurn your threshold, and
Joy shall not tap upon your windowpane.
Seek you your ruins for prayer — you cannot pray;
Summon consolatory tears — in vain;
Withered shall be your heart, a cluster of grapes,
30 Shrunken, flung in a corner of the vat,

Wherefrom the heart-rejoicing sap shall never rise
Nor ever shall restore the soul that pines.

Yea, you shall stir the hearth to find cold stones
Where in the chilled ashes mews the cat.
35 In grief and sorrow shall you sit. Without
The melancholy world; within you, dust.
Dead flies in your windows you shall then behold.
And in the desolate cracks, the spider's web:
And you shall hear the shaking of the wall,
40 And in the chimney, wailing Penury.

c. 1936/1936   1945

Come, Gird Ye Your Loins, and in Might Robe Yourselves

Come, gird ye your loins, and in might robe yourselves!

In the thick of the woods, in the caves of the rocks,
There gathered the remnant of stout Maccabees.
The singing of psalms, and the sword's ringing shocks
5 Woke forest and crag from their silence and peace.
In the camp of the woods, in the dark of the cave
Came succour and aid to the brave!
And we, much enfeebled and ground in the dust,
Let us beat on the hearts of our sons with our clamour!
10 Let the word of our God be our pillar and trust,
And our God be our thundering hammer.
Not yet have we squandered all strength in the fight –
The Lord is our might!

Arise! to the aid of the people, arise!

15 With what? Do not waver! With what comes to hand!
   With whom? Do not pause, for the man who doth grieve
   For the sake of his brother's pain, him let the band
   Gather up and recruit; to his kin let him cleave!
   Each sacrifice worthy, in all gifts rejoice!
20 The hour of peril permits of no choice!
   The salvage of good, and the remnant of light
   Which God in our hearts has still left, let us raise
   Let us gather together, to glow, brave and bright –
   A banner, an ensign, for troublesome days!
25 They will rise, then, and join us, from east and from west –
   A legion prepared, at its people's behest!

   c. 1936/1936   1941

God Grant My Part and Portion Be ...

   Meek of the earth, humble in wit and works,
   Unknown and unseen dreamers, mute of soul,
   Stinted in speech, of beauty most abundant,
   Privily embroidering your lives –
5 God grant my part and portion be with you!

   Like coral of the reaches of the sea,
   The pleasant savour of your minds lies hidden;
   And blooms your nobleness like berries wild
   Burgeoning in the shadow of a wood!

10 Unbidden, you are bountiful; and lavish
   Without a knowledge of munificence.
   O poets of most lovely silence, priests
   Amidst the hush and quiet of the Lord,
   No alien eye beholds your festivals
15 No, nor the days of mourning that are yours.

The mighty and the mean, the saint and sinner
You greet without knee-crooking, with the same
Compassionate and comprehending smile.

Tiptoeing slowly through the paths of life,
20 The heart awake, the ear alert, the eye
Most watchful, for its very touch you shudder
For beauty's least caress, you quake and tremble.
You pass, and without pose or effort, sow
That faith and purity that from you flows
25 Like azure from the dome of heaven, like
Numberless shadows from the pleasant wood.

Yea, skilled in silence, voiceless, without speech,
Utters your mouth no arrogance, your hand
Fashions no masterpieces, works of pride.
30 Desire and longing do within you fail.
Your place is not with the array of seers,
Nor in museums is your share and lot.
Lonely and echoless your footstep dies.
Howbeit, your life, the simple days of your life –
35 Behold the vision superb, the work of art,
Ye keepers of God's image upon earth!

Daily, and in the brilliance of your eyes,
Yea, in the wrinkles of your countenance
The beauty of your lives does drop by drop
40 Flow into the hollow of the world
As flows into the river's brimming heart
The waters of a secret spring, unknown.

As the Lord liveth, they will not be lost;
Not the mere flutter of your eyelash, nor
45 The least accounted stirrings in your heart!
But like the music of the spheres, they will
Forever tremble in the vaulted sky
And even at the end of days, when no
Echo will be of Haiman and Jeduthun,

50 Nor memory of the wisdom of those two:
   Cholcol and Darda, sages of the east,
   Even then these will still live and be revealed
   In the light and brilliance of some unknown's gaze,
   Or in the wrinkles of his countenance.

   c. 1936/1936   1943

The Lord Has Not Revealed

   Neither in the dreams of my nights has the Lord revealed
   Nor in oracles for me has He divined,
   In what place my last day will lay hold of me,
   And what the form and likeness of my end:
5 Whether within my tent, upon my couch I shall expire,
   My much-beloved children at my hand,
   Beside me in silence, come unto me, even to the last one,
   A guard of love and halidom at my bed,
   Counting, like treasures beyond price,
10 My final breathings, into the lap of God;

   Or whether, despised and reviled, cursed of God and of man,
   Spurned by my fellows, and from family fled,
   I shall in some forsaken sheepfold and on a heap of straw
   Where none shall witness the going of my soul
15 And no hand quiver over my quenched eyes,
   Breathe out my life, profaned and defiled;

   Or, whether, beset by hunger and thirst
   For life and all its pleasant ways,
   The contempt of my soul shall rise against the wrath of God,
20 And spurning the gift of His hand
   I shall fling, as one flings a dirty shoe
   From off the foot, my soul before His foot.

May it not be that from long suffering I shall grow stale
And from much silent waiting
25 My soul in bitterness shall be spilled out?

Perhaps, like a pearl of an eternal glow
With my last tear, my life shall also fall,
Trembling,
And after many generations shine
30 For eyes that never did behold me.

It may be, like a moth about a flame
Fluttering, shall my life depart,
Or like that very flame before its oil is spent
Convulsed in the agony of its death
35 For many days its sacrificial incense rising
A blandishment for the eyes,
Until of a sudden into the dark abyss,
It falls forever quenched.

Or will my death be like a sun before its setting:
40 Suddenly its own illumined pyre,
Its flames in the clouds, its beacons on the mountaintops,
And its dying rays
A thing of wonder for a thousand eyes.

Who knows but God may harden His heart against me
45 And in my very lifetime, I shall die:
O, they will bind my soul in winding sheets of writing-paper,
Inter me in the coffin of a bookcase,
Where the mole will nightly nibble at my bones,
And the rat out of the hole at my corpse gnaw.
50 Upon my own grave I shall place my foot
And with my own mouth utter my own Kaddish.

And it may also happen that my death shall come,
Unsavory, insipid, in a manner not awaited,
When like a hungry dog in a wintry night of storm
55 Behind some wall, the bitter cold shall take me,

The soft snow cover me, a sombre stain,
Efface a Man's shame, and the shame of his life,
And the wind bear away, the tempest snatch
The last gritting of my teeth, the curse of death.

c. 1936/1936   1942

On My Returning

    A ghost of stubble, a leaf that flutters
        On holy books from page to page:
    Again I see the graybeard's features —
        Anguish-shrivelled, wizened age.

5 Again I see the dry old woman,
        Plying needle, darning socks,
    Lips forever twitching, omen
        Oaths will issue when she talks.

    And as of yore, beside the oven
10   Still unmoved there sleeps the cat
    Dreaming, in his purring heaven,
        He strikes treaties with the rat.

    And as of yore, the spider spreading
        Webs within his darkened track
15 Where swollen flies find their last bedding,
        There in the same old western crack.

    You have not changed, by jot or tittle
        Ancient, old, of yesterday —

O let me join you, big and little,
20   Together let us rot away!

c. 1936/1936   1937

The City of Slaughter [Version 1]

Arise and go now to the city of slaughter;
Into its courtyards wend thy way;
There with thine own hand touch, and with the eyes of thine head,
Behold on tree, on stone, on fence, on mural clay,
5 The spattered blood and dried brains of the dead.
Proceed thence to the ruins, the split walls reach,
Where wider grows the hollow, and greater grows the breach;
Pass over the shattered hearth, attain the broken wall
Whose burnt and barren brick, whose charred stones reveal
10 The open mouths of such wounds, that no mending
Shall ever mend, nor healing ever heal.

There will thy feet in feathers sink, and stumble
On wreckage doubly wrecked, scroll heaped on manuscript,
Fragments again fragmented –

15 Pause not upon this havoc; go thy way.
The perfumes will be wafted from the acacia bud
And half its blossoms will be feathers,
Whose smell is the smell of blood!

And, spiting thee, strange incense they will bring –
20 Banish thy loathing – all the beauty of the spring,
The thousand golden arrows of the sun
Will flash upon thy malison;
The sevenfold rays of broken glass

Over thy sorrow joyously will pass,
25 For God called up the slaughter and the spring together, —
The slayer slew, the blossom burst, and it was sunny weather!

Then wilt thou flee to a yard, observe its mound.
Upon the mound lie two, and both are headless —
A Jew and his hound.
30 The self-same axe struck both, and both were flung
Unto the self-same heap where swine seek dung;
Tomorrow the rain will wash their mingled blood
Into the runnels, and it will be lost
In rubbish heap, in stagnant pool, in mud.
35 Its cry will not be heard.
It will descend into the deep, or water the cockle-burr.
And all things will be as they ever were.

Unto the attic mount, upon thy feet and hands;
Behold the shadow of death among the shadows stands.
40 There in the dismal corner, there in the shadowy nook,
Multitudinous eyes will look
Upon thee from the sombre silences —
The spirits of the martyrs are these souls,
Gathered together, at long last,
45 Beneath these rafters and in these ignoble holes.
The hatchet found them here, and hither do they come
To seal with a last look, as with their final breath,
The agony of their lives, the terror of their death.
Tumbling and stumbling wraiths, they come, and cower there.
50 Their silence whimpers, and it is their eyes which cry
Wherefore, O Lord, and why?
It is a silence only God can bear.

Lift then thine eyes to the roof; there's nothing there,
Save silences that hang from rafters
55 And brood upon the air:
Question the spider in his lair!
His eyes beheld these things; and with his web he can
A tale unfold horrific to the ear of man:

A tale of cloven belly, feather-filled;
60 Of nostrils nailed, of skull-bones bashed and spilled;
Of murdered men who from the beams were hung,
And of a babe beside its mother flung,
Its mother speared, the poor chick finding rest
Upon its mother's cold and milkless breast;
65 Of how a dagger halved an infant's word,
Its *ma* was heard, its *mama* never heard.

O, even now its eyes from me demand accounting,
For these the tales the spider is recounting,
Tales that do puncture the brain, such tales that sever
70 Thy body, spirit, soul, from life, forever!
Then wilt thou bid thy spirit – Hold, enough!
Stifle the wrath that mounts within thy throat,
Bury these things accursed,
Within the depth of thy heart, before thy heart will burst!
75 Then wilt thou leave that place, and go thy way –
And lo –
The earth is as it was, the sun still shines:
It is a day like any other day.

Descend then, to the cellars of the town,
80 There where the virginal daughters of thy folk were fouled,
Where seven heathen flung a woman down,
The daughter in the presence of her mother,
The mother in the presence of her daughter,
Before slaughter, during slaughter, and after slaughter!
85 Touch with thy hand the cushion stained; touch
The pillow incarnadined:
This is the place the wild ones of the wood, the beasts of the field
With bloody axes in their paws compelled thy daughters yield:
Beasted and swined!

90 Note also, do not fail to note,
In that dark corner, and behind that cask

Crouched husbands, bridegrooms, brothers, peering from the
    cracks,
Watching the sacred bodies struggling underneath
The bestial breath,
95 Stifled in filth, and swallowing their blood!
Watching from the darkness and its mesh
The lecherous rabble portioning for booty
Their kindred and their flesh!
Crushed in their shame, they saw it all;
100 They did not stir nor move;
They did not pluck their eyes out; they
Beat not their brains against the wall!
Perhaps, perhaps, each watcher had it in his heart to pray:
A miracle, O Lord, – and spare my skin this day!

105 Those who survived this foulness, who from their blood awoke,
Beheld their life polluted, the light of their world gone out –
How did their menfolk bear it, how did they bear this yoke?
They crawled forth from their holes, they fled to the house of
    the Lord,
They offered thanks to Him, the sweet benedictory word.
110 The *Cohanim* sallied forth, to the Rabbi's house they flitted:
Tell me, O Rabbi, tell, is my own wife permitted?
The matter ends; and nothing more.
And all is as it was before.

Come, now, and I will bring thee to their lairs,
115 The privies, jakes and pigpens where the heirs
Of Hasmoneans lay, with trembling knees,
Concealed and cowering, – the sons of the Maccabees!
The seed of saints, the scions of the lions!
Who, crammed by scores in all the sanctuaries of their shame,
120 So sanctified My name!

It was the flight of mice they fled,
The scurrying of roaches was their flight;
They died like dogs, and they were dead!
And on the next morn, after the terrible night

125 The son who was not murdered found
     The spurned cadaver of his father on the ground.
     Now wherefore dost thou weep, O son of man?

     Descend into the valley; verdant, there
     A garden flourishes, and in the garden
130 A barn, a shed, – it was their abbatoir;
     There, like a host of vampires, puffed and bloated,
     Besotted with blood, swilled from the scattered dead,
     The tumbril wheels lie spread –
     Their open spokes, like fingers stretched for murder,
135 Like vampire-mouths their hubs still clotted red.

     Enter not now, but when the sun descends
     Wrapt in bleeding clouds and girt with flame,
     Then open the gate and stealthily do set
     Thy foot within the ambient of horror:
140 Terror floating near the rafters, terror
     Against the walls in darkness hiding,
     Terror through the silence sliding.
     Didst thou not hear beneath the heap of wheels
     A stirring of crushed limbs? Broken and racked
145 Their bodies move a hub, a spoke
     Of the circular yoke;
     In death-throes they contort;
     In blood disport;
     And their last groaning, inarticulate
150 Rises above thy head,
     And it would seem some speechless sorrow,
     Sorrow infinite,
     Is prisoned in this shed.
     It is, it is the Spirit of Anguish!
155 Much-suffering and tribulation-tried
     Which in this house of bondage binds itself.
     It will not ever from its pain be pried.
     Brief-weary and forespent, a dark Shekinah
     Runs to each nook and cannot find its rest;
160 Wishes to weep, but weeping does not come;

Would roar; is dumb.
Its head beneath its wing, its wing outspread
Over the shadows of the martyr'd dead,
Its tears in dimness and in silence shed.

165 And thou, too, son of man, close now the gate behind thee;
Be closed in darkness now, now thine that charnel space;
So tarrying there thou wilt be one with pain and anguish
And wilt fill up with sorrow thine heart for all its days.
Then on the day of thine own desolation
170 A refuge will it seem, —
Lying in thee like a curse, a demon's ambush,
The haunting of an evil dream.
O, carrying it in thy heart, across the world's expanse
Thou wouldst proclaim it, speak it out, —
175 But thy lips shall not find its utterance.

Beyond the suburbs go, and reach the burial ground.
Let no man see thy going; attain that place alone,
A place of sainted graves and martyr-stone.
Stand on the fresh-turned soil.
180 Such silence will take hold of thee, thy heart will fail
With pain and shame, yet I
Will let no tear fall from thine eye.
Though thou wilt long to bellow like the driven ox
That bellows, and before the altar balks,
185 I will make hard thy heart, yea, I
Will not permit a sigh.

See, see, the slaughtered calves, so smitten and so laid;
Is there a price for their death? How shall that price be paid?

Forgive, ye shamed of the earth, yours is a pauper-Lord!
190 Poor was He during your life, and poorer still of late.
When to my door you come to ask for your reward,
I'll open wide: See, I am fallen from My high estate.

I grieve for you, my children. My heart is sad for you.
Your dead were vainly dead; and neither I nor you
195 Know why you died or wherefore, for whom, nor by what laws;
Your deaths are without reason; your lives are without cause.

What says the Shekinah? In the clouds it hides
In shame, in agony alone abides;
I, too, at night, will venture on the tombs,
200 Regard the dead and weigh their secret shame,
But never shed a tear, I swear it in My name.
For great is the anguish, great the shame on the brow;
But which of these is greater, son of man, say thou —
Or liefer keep thy silence, bear witness in My name
205 To the hour of My sorrow, the moment of My shame.

And when thou dost return
Bring thou the blot of My disgrace upon thy people's head,
And from My suffering do not part,
But set it like a stone within their heart!

210 Turn, then, to leave the cemetery ground,
And for a moment thy swift eye will pass
Upon the verdant carpet of the grass —
A lovely thing! Fragrant and moist, as it is always at the coming of the Spring!
The stubble of death, the growth of tombstones!
215 Take thou a fistful, fling it on the plain
Saying,
'The people is plucked grass; can plucked grass grow again?'

Turn, then, thy gaze from the dead, and I will lead
Thee from the graveyard to thy living brothers,
220 And thou wilt come, with those of thine own breed,
Into the synagogue, and on a day of fasting,
To hear the cry of their agony,
Their weeping everlasting.
Thy skin will grow cold, the hair on thy skin stand up,

225 And thou wilt be by fear and trembling tossed;
Thus groans a people which is lost.

Look in their hearts – behold a dreary waste,
Where even vengeance can revive no growth,
And yet upon their lips no mighty malediction
230 Rises, no blasphemous oath.

Are they not real, their bruises?
Why is their prayer false?
Why, in the day of their trials
Approach me with pious ruses,
235 Afflict me with denials?

Regard them now, in these their woes:
Ululating, lachrymose,
Crying from their throes,
We have sinned! and *Sinned have we!* –
240 Self-flagellative with confession's whips.
Their hearts, however, do not believe their lips.
Is it, then, possible for shattered limbs to sin?
Wherefore their cries imploring, their supplicating din?
Speak to them, bid them rage!
245 Let them against me raise the outraged hand, –
Let them demand!
Demand the retribution for the shamed
Of all the centuries and every age!
Let fists be flung like stone
250 Against the heavens and the heavenly Throne!

And thou, too, son of man, be part of these:
Believe the pangs of their heart, believe not their litanies:
And when the cantor lifts his voice to cry:
Remember the martyrs, Lord,
255 *Remember the cloven infants, Lord,*
Consider the sucklings, Lord,
And when the pillars of the synagogue shall crack
At this his piteous word

And terror shall take thee, fling thee in its deep,
260 Then I will harden My heart; I will not let thee weep!

Should then a cry escape from thee,
I'll stifle it within thy throat.
Let them assoil their tragedy, –
Not thou, – let it remain unmourned
265 For distant ages, times remote,
But thy tear, son of man, remain unshed!
Build thou about it, with thy deadly hate
Thy fury and thy rage, unuttered,
A wall of copper, the bronze triple plate!
270 So in thy heart it shall remain confined
A serpent in its nest – O terrible tear! –
Until by thirst and hunger it shall find
A breaking of its bond. Then shall it rear
Its venomous head, its poisoned fangs, and wait
275 To strike the people of thy love and hate!

Leave now this place at twilight to return
And to behold these creatures who arose
In terror at dawn, at dusk now, drowsing, worn
With weeping, broken in spirit, in darkness shut.
280 Their lips still move with words unspoken.
Their hearts are broken.

No lustre in the eye, no hoping in the mind,
They grope to seek support they shall not find:
Thus when the oil is gone,
285 The wick still sends its smoke;
Thus does the beast of burden,
Broken and old, still bear his yoke.

Would that misfortune had left them some small solace
Sustaining the soul, consoling their gray hairs!
290 Behold the fast is ended; the final prayers are said.
But why do they tarry now, these mournful congregations?

Shall it be also read,
The Book of Lamentations?

It is a preacher mounts the pulpit now.
295 He opens his mouth, he stutters, stammers. Hark
The empty verses from his speaking flow.
And not a single mighty word is heard
To kindle in the hearts a single spark.
The old attend his doctrine, and they nod.
300 The young ones hearken to his speech; they yawn.
The mark of death is on their brows; their God
Has utterly forsaken every one.

And thou, too, pity them not, nor touch their wound;
Within their cup no further measure pour.
305 Wherever thou wilt touch, a bruise is found.
Their flesh is wholly sore.
For since they have met pain with resignation
And have made peace with shame,
What shall avail thy consolation?

310 They are too wretched to evoke thy scorn.
They are too lost thy pity to evoke,
So let them go, then, men to sorrow born,
Mournful and slinking, crushed beneath their yoke.
Go to their homes, and to their hearth depart –
315 Rot in the bones, corruption in the heart.

And when thou shalt arise upon the morrow
And go upon the highway,
Thou shalt then meet these men destroyed by sorrow,
Sighing and groaning, at the doors of the wealthy
320 Proclaiming their sores, like so much peddler's wares,
The one his battered head, t'other limbs unhealthy,
One shows a wounded arm, and one a fracture bares.
And all have eyes that are the eyes of slaves,
Slaves flogged before their masters;
325 And each one begs, and each one craves:

Reward me, Master, for that my skull is broken
Reward me for my father who was martyred!
The rich ones, all compassion, for the pleas so bartered
Extend them staff and bandage, say *good riddance*, and
330 The tale is told:
The paupers are consoled.

Avaunt ye, beggars, to the charnel-house!
The bones of your fathers disinter!
Cram them within your knapsacks, bear
335 Them on your shoulders, and go forth
To do your business with these precious wares
At all the country fairs!

Stop on the highway, near some populous city,
And spread on your filthy rags
340 Those martyred bones that issue from your bags,
And sing, with raucous voice, your pauper's ditty!
So will you conjure up the pity of the nations,
And so *their* sympathy implore.
For you are now as you have been of yore
345 And as you stretched your hand
So will you stretch it,
And as you have been wretched
So are you wretched!

What is thy business here, O son of man?
350 *Rise, to the desert flee!*
Thy cup of affliction thither bear with thee!
Take thou thy soul, rend it in many a shred!
With impotent rage, thy heart deform!
Thy tear upon the barren boulders shed!
355 *And send thy bitter cry into the storm!*

c. 1936/1937   1948

In the City of Slaughter [Version 2]

(In memoriam: The Martyrs of the Kishineff pogrom)

Arise, and go now – go to the city of slaughter!
Into its inner courtyards make your way.
There, with your own hands, touch, with your own eyes see –
    splashed red! –
On brick, on tree, on fence, on stone, on clay,
5 The clotted blood and spilled brains of the dead!

Proceed thence through the sacked city, the split walls reach,
Where wider grows the hollow and greater grows the breach:
Pass over the shattered hearths ... these broken walls ...
    Burnt brick ... and stripped foundations ... O, these
        reveal
10 The open mouths of such wounds as no mending
Shall ever mend, nor healing ever heal!

Litter of feathers ... bed-clothes ... rubble ... shards ...
Wrecked household ware ... torn parchment ... trodden
    tome ...
(What hopes lie tattered here! Scattered what garnered
    hoards!)
15 Breakage and fracture ... fragments again fragmented ...

Pause not upon this havoc. Go your way.
    Though half their blossoms will be bloodied feathers,
    Though all their fragrance be the smell of blood,
Still will the trees about you stand bright with sprig and
    spray ...
20   Their scents will stink in your nostrils, but
    Put down disgust, for, surely, not
    All things here are polluted ... still
    Do the golden shafts of sunlight spill

            Their sunshine on whatever's ill.
25   The prisms of the broken glass
            Still gaily bid your anguish pass –
For God called up the slaughter and the spring together:
The slayer slew, the blossom burst, and it was sunny weather!

        You will fly this scene: you will come to a yard: observe
            its mound.
30 Upon the mound lie (headless) 2:
A dog, a Jew.
        The one axe struck both down, and both were cast
On to this common midden.
To-night the pigs will root here at their strange new mast!
35 To-morrow the rains into the runnels will
Dissolve this mingled flux to make one flood
            With feculence and swill.
Not ever will be heard the voice of that blood!
It will descend into the earth, will water the cockle-burr.
40   And all things will be as they were before ...
            As though they never were.

You stumble up to an attic, stair by stair ...
Over its shadows Death's still greater shadow broods.
Here, from a darkened nook, from a covert corner, there,
45   A thousand eyes, from their murky quietudes,
            Pair and pair,
Upon you fix their endless stare.

The spirits of the martyrs are these souls,
Made small with fear ... huddled together ...
50 Beneath these eaves ... in their ignoble holes!
        The hatchet found them here, and to this place they come
            To seal with a last look
        Their death, its shame; their life, its odium!
Tumbling and stumbling ghosts, they cower here.
55 Their eyes beg, and their silence is worse than cry:
            Wherefore, O Lord, and why?

This is a silence only God can bear.

Survey this sanctum. Your eyes at the rafters stop.
Nothing ... Even the damp has dripped its last cold drop.
60   But the spider – there!
His eyes saw all these things! Let *him* weave witness
And the tales bear:
A tale of cloven belly, feather-stuffed ...
Of nostrils skewered ... skulls smashed ... lives out-snuffed ...
65 Of slit throats dangling from the beams ...
Of the spared babe, found warm at its mother's teat,
The mother, speared, still feeding it ...
Of how a dagger halved a child's last word:
Its *ma* – was heard, its *mama* never heard.

70 O, even now his eyes from me demand accounting
For these the tales the spider is recounting,
Tales that do puncture the brain, such tales as sever
        Spirit from body and both from life forever!
Here you will say to your heart: *Enough!*
75 Here you will stifle your anger, here you will try
To sink down deep these things accursed,
To make them small in your heart – lest your heart burst!
You will leave that place. You will go your way.
But see –
80 The world is as it was, the sun still shines,
        It is a day like any other day.

Into the dark, then, into the cellars of the town!
There where the virginal daughters of our folk were fouled,
Where seven heathen flung each woman down,
85 And fought to pre-possess, possessed them, and bespawled:
The daughter in the presence of her mother,
The mother in the presence of her daughter,
Before slaughter, during slaughter, and after slaughter!

                Touch with your hands these sheets defiled, and touch
90   These pillows incarnadined:
                Here did the stallions ramp it! This was the wild boars'
                    couch!
                Here did your daughters swoon as the rabble
                Feasted here, and swined!

                But the cream of the spectacle! ... In that dark corner,
95   Beneath that empty mortar, and from behind
                The broken staves of that cask, there crouched and watched
                        Husbands ... bridegrooms ... brothers ...
                                Watching
                        Sister ... sweetheart ... wife ...
100   Each struggling, fighting, fluttering ... debauch'd!
                        These – men – were – not – struck – blind!
                Saw shame, reaped rape, but, cautious, held their cry,
                        Safe-silent, whimpered not, nor whined ...
                        Debased, dishonor'd, they saw it all;
105   Self-hushed they lay, though racked;
                        They did not move, nor stir, but stared
                        Unseeing at the fact;
                        They did not pluck their eyes out; they
                        Preserved their minds intact.
110   Why, each one found it in his heart to pray:
                Work miracle, O Lord! – and spare my skin this day!

                Each dam who lived on, though ravished, who from this
                    violence rose,
                Knew that within and without, from lappet and head to the
                    toes,
                Pollution was hers, and smutching, and the light of her day at
                    its close.
115   As for the men –
                They crawled forth from their holes, they fled to the house of
                    the Lord,
                They offered their thanks to Him, who was their Saviour and
                    Sword.
                Their Cohanim sallied forth, to the Rabbi's house they flitted:

> *Tell me, O Rabbi, say: Is my own wife still permitted? ...*
120   The episode ends. All things return to course.
Things are not better than they were before, nor worse.

Come, now, and I will show you their hide-aways and lairs
The privies, jakes, and pigpens where the heirs
Of the Hasmoneans hid, and trembled at the knees –
125 The scions of the lions! The sons of the Maccabees!
And show you the dark refuge where the grandsons of the saints
By twenties and by thirties did, cowering, abide,
Declaring God's name sanctified, His glory magnified!

A scuttering of rats – such was their scutter,
130 A scurrying of pismires was their flight.
Like dogs, they lay dead in the gutter ...
And, the next morning, after the dread night,
The son who was not murdered found
The cadaver of his father on the ground.

135 You weep? You cannot suffer this, nor stay?
Gnash with your teeth, O son of man, and melt away!

The city falls to a trough, and in that trough
There is a park, and amidst that park's sweet green,
A barn-like strange erection – a shed? – a stable? –
140 Still stands – it was their abattoir – serene.
    Here like a coil of lizards, puffed and swollen,
    Like a cycle of vampires, still enlarged with suck,
    Involved and cogged, a wreckage of wild wheels
    Lies sunk in muck.
145   The hubs are bloodied, their felloes bent and buckled,
    Their spokes, like menace, stuck.
Enter not yet. At sundown ... when the sun
In blood and fire down the sky is rolled.
Then enter – You will find yourself at terror's
150 Centre and heart; its circle will enfold
You round about, terror

749 / Hebrew

>Against the walls in darkness hiding
>Hovering from the rafters, horror,
>Terror through the silence sliding.
>155 Did you not hear, from beneath the rutted wheels
>A stirring of crushed limbs? Broken and maimed
>Their bodies move a hub, a spoke
>Of the circular yoke [...]

c. 1953/1953   1953

The Dance of Despair [Version 1]

>*Muppim and Huppim! Strike blows on your drums!*
>*Milalai, Gilalai — and set the fifes level!*
>*And pluck ye the catgut, the fiddle that strums!*
>*And be ye of good cheer! — and go to the devil!*

>5 There's no fish and no flesh, there's no bread and no cake!
>Shall we then eat our hearts out? O dancers, awake!

>For God's in His heaven, and He can do all;
>For His sake let's trip it in loud madrigal!

>Let the wrath of our souls and our heart's burning flame
>10 Set all legs a-dancing, both lusty and lame,

>The dance that will be like to thunder and levin
>To shudder man's earth, and to startle God's heaven!
>   *Muppim and Huppim ...*

>There's no milk and no honey; of wine, not a drop:
>Console you, console you, green gall fills the cup!

15 So toast it *To Life*, and then quaff to the dregs
Like men, and not palsied; then toss ye your legs,

Go to, to the dance, to the dance with a will,
The thrill on your faces, your voices a-thrill,

So none will be wiser, nor friends, neither foe
20 Of your heart's final throb and your heart's last throe!
            Muppim and Huppim ...

Without shirt, without shoe, without raiment or gown –
It is a small matter; for clothes wear you down!

Wherefore, plumeless and plucked, let us – eagles – aspire
And rise ever higher and higher and higher,

25 In the teeth of ill-luck and bad omen to fly
Through the fury of tempest, the storm's raging cry!

For shoeless or shod, you will go to your doom:
Shod or shoeless, the dance always ends at the tomb.
            Muppim and Huppim ...

Kith and kin, flesh and friends – woe, alas, there are none!
30 Who, then, is that body that you will lean on?

So join you your fellow, and dancing aright,
You will know strength and power, and glory and might.

In one hurly-burly let all be enrolled,
The dark hair of young men, the white of the old, –

35 And let the dance whirl and the circle go
Hither and yon, back and forth, to and fro.
            Muppim and Huppim ...

No land nor estate, and no rafter nor roof:
But keep you from fear, and from terror aloof.

For wide is the world, and far-flung; wherefore, blessed
40 Who found for His people this much-scattered rest;

And blessed He who roofed the wide world with His sky,
Stuck the sun on a nail for a candle on high.

And bless Him for every small favour and grace
O praise Him with trumpets! With madrigals, praise!
                              Muppim and Huppim ...

45 No glory, no splendour, foundation, nor truth!
Has a cork stopped the welkin? Forfend it, forsooth!

Our guardian, He sleeps not, forgets not our woes:
He'll feed us, as He feeds His dogs and His crows!

With leaping and hopping we will overcome
50 The errors we made in the mystical sum.

And our paean of plagues and our dance of death
Will shrive us of sin and of profane breath. –
                              Muppim and Huppim ...

No pity, no right, no revenge, no reward,
Must silence ensue then? The dumb have the word.

55 Give speech to the ankle; let leg and shank pour
Their eloquent wrath on the stones of the floor.

And let your dance circle, enkindling a fire
Each footstep a faggot, the dance a great pyre!

And thus, as the dance swells, and rises and falls,
60 You will shatter your skulls on the stones of the walls.

Muppim and Huppim! Strike blows on your drums!
Milalai, Gilalai — and set the fifes level!
And pluck ye the catgut, the fiddle that strums!
And be ye of good cheer! — and go to the devil!

c. 1936/1937   1948

Dance of Despair [Version 2]

Cry, Muppim and Huppim! Strike blows on your drums!
Milalai! Gilalai! — to lips set the fife!
Pluck wild at the catgut, with fingers, with thumbs!
A wedding! ... Your father takes Lilith to wife!

I

5 A wedding? No fish? Nor no meat? Neither bread nor yet cake?
    Shall we feast on our hearts, then? ... No. Dancers, awake!

    There's a God still in heaven, omnipotent there —
    For His sake let's kick them, our feet in the air!

    Let the wrath of our souls and our heart's burning flame
10 Set all legs a-dancing, both lusty and lame,

    A dance that will be like as thunder and levin
    To shudder man's earth and to startle God's heaven!

II

There's no milk and no honey, of wine not a drop!
But still there is liquor — there's gall in the cup!

15 Now, steady the hand, and drink down to the dregs!
L'chaim! L'chaim! ... And again to your legs,

To your legs, to the dance, to the dance with a will,
The thrill on your faces, your voices a-thrill,

So none will be wiser, nor friend, nor yet foe,
20 Of your heart's final throb and your heart's last throe!

III

Without shirt, without shoe, without raiment or gown —
This is a small matter: for clothes wear you down!

Wherefore, plumeless and plucked, let us — eagles — aspire
And rise ever higher and higher and higher

25 In the teeth of ill-luck, of bad omen to fly
Through the fury of tempest, the storm's raging cry!

For shoeless or shod, we go towards the same doom:
The very last step of the dance is ... the tomb.

IV

Kith and kin, comrades, friends, — they are gone, there are none.
30 Whose, then, is the body that one may lean on?

Your partner's – who partners your dance for this hour
And brings you new strength and new might and new power!

In one hurlyburly, then, let be enrolled
The dark hair of young men, the white of the old,

35 And let the dance whirl and the circle go
About and reverse, back and forth, to and fro!

V

Neither lot nor yet plot, neither rafter nor beam!
But fear not! Things are not as ill as they seem!

For wide is the world, and far-flung; wherefore, blessed
40 Who found for His people this much-scattered rest;

And blessèd is He who nailed sun up on high
And gave us for shelter the sheltering sky!

O bless Him for every small favour and grace!
O praise Him with trumpets! With madrigals, praise!

VI

45 No glory! No splendour! The truth, too, is hid!
Has a cork sealed the fountains of grace? ... God forbid!

Our guardian, He sleeps not, forgets not our woes:
He'll feed us, as He feeds – His dogs and His crows!

So, leaping and hopping, let us overcome
50 The errors we made in the mystical sum,

755 / Hebrew

As our paean of plagues, as our jubilant shins
Ablute us, acquit us, absolve us our sins!

VII

No justice! No mercy! Reproof, nor reward!
Must silence ensue then? ... The dumb have the word.

55 Give speech to the ankle; let leg and shank pour
Their eloquent wrath on the stones of the floor;

And let the dance circle, on legs or on crutches,
To kindle, inflame whatsover it touches;

And thus, as the dance swells, and rises, and falls, –
60 Go shatter your skulls on the stones of the walls!

Cry, Muppim and Huppim! Strike blows on your drums!
Milalai! Gilalai! – to lips set the fife!
Pluck wild at the catgut, with fingers, with thumbs!
A wedding! ... Your father takes Lilith to wife!

c. 1953/1953   1953

Seer, Begone [Version 1]

'Seer, begone!' One of my kind flees not!
Slowly to walk, this I have learned from my herds.
Nor has my tongue learned phrases finely wrought:
Like the heavy blows of an axe, so fall my words.

5   And if my strength is spent – 'tis not mine the fault!
    Yours is the guilt and you must bear the sin.
    My hammer found no anvil to cry halt;
    Wood that was rotten took my sharp axe in.

    'Tis nothing. I make peace with this my fate.
10 I gird in my belt the rude tools of my art,
    A day-labourer, unpaid his wage and rate,
    Quietly as I came, I now depart.

    Unto my valley and my tent I go.
    I make a covenant with trees this day.
15 And as for you, who are corruption, know
    To-morrow the storm carries you away.

    c. 1936/1937

O Thou Seer, Go Flee Thee – Away
[Version 2 of 'Seer, Begone']

'Fly! Run away!' Not such as I do run.
I followed cattle, they taught me to walk slow.
Slow comes my speech, my words come one by one
The strokes of an axe they come down, blow by blow.

5   The strokes fell false? ... Not mine, not mine the blunder.
    Yours was the fault the strokes were falsely sunk:
    My hammer struck, and found no anvil under;
    My axe struck punk.

    No matter; I accept my fate, retire,
10 And gird my gear about my loins once more:
    A hired man, but cheated of his hire
    I will return – at my pace – to my door;

And there, in the deep forest, will strike root
With the great sycamore, and there hold firm;
15 But unto you, – rot, fungus, trodden fruit –
I prophesy – the whirlwind and the storm!

c. 1953/c. 1955

When the Days Shall Grow Long

And it shall come to pass when the days shall grow long
And every day shall be like yesterday, and like the day before,
Days that are merely days, little in profit and great in trouble,
Then shall weariness lay hold of man and beast alike.
5 At twilight a man shall go forth, meditating, to the sea's edge,
And behold, the waters shall not turn back,
Wherefore he shall yawn and be wearied.
He shall fare forth to the Jordan; lo, it shall not be driven back;
He shall yawn, he shall be bored.
10 Orion and the Pleiades he shall behold; but they shall not stir from their places,
Boredom shall encompass him,
Wherefore they shall sit them down, man and beast, and grow mouldy together,
And the burden of their lives shall be heavy upon them;
Out of great desolation, a man shall pluck the hairs from his head,
15 And the cat shall lose its whiskers.

Then lonesomeness shall rise up,
Of its own self rise, like stale mushrooms in the bole of a rotted tree.
Lonesomeness shall fill up hollow and crack,
Like vermin snuggling in rags.
20 And it shall come to pass that when a man

Shall repair to his tent at dusk to break his bread
And shall dip his crumb and his herring in vinegar,
Then shall lonesomeness take hold of him;
When he shall drink his cup, lukewarm, stagnant,
25 Longing shall suddenly be his;
And when he shall fling his shoe and sock into a corner near the bedpost,
He shall be sick with longing.
They shall sit, then, man and beast together; longing shall consume them;
From great longing a man shall moan in his dreams,
30 The cat shall lament, and a scratching upon the tin roof shall be heard.

Then hunger shall appear;
A hunger mighty and great, unlike any before,
Not hunger for bread or bard, but hunger for the Messiah!

Every morning, with the blossoming of the sun, shall rise
35 Man from his bed, from the privacy of his tent,
Broken by the sleepless tossings of the night, sated with dreams, empty-souled,
The web of troubled sleep still upon his lashes, terror of the night still in his bones,
And still the ululating of the cat in his ears, and the tattoo of his claws digging in his brains and entrails,
And he shall hasten to the windowpane; he shall wipe off its vapour;
40 He shall hurry to his threshold; he shall roof his eyes with the palm of his hand;
He shall lift his unwashed eyes, fevered, and hungry for salvation,
Regarding the lane beyond the wall, the heap of rubbish near his house,
And he shall seek his Messiah!
His wife shall wake from beneath the sheets,
45 Unkempt of hair, low-spirited, scrawny and peaked,

And shall remove her shrivelled breast from the mouth of her sucking child,
And she shall mightily hearken:
Is that the sound of the Messiah's tread?
Did you not hear the braying of his ass?
50 Yea, even a child from the cradle shall lift up its head,
And a rat from his hole shall peep:
Is that the sound of the Messiah's tread?
Did not the bells upon his ass's harness jingle?
And the maidservant panting at the kettle in the scullery
55 Shall poke out her besmirched face:
Is that the sound of the Messiah's tread?
Did you not hear the blast upon his ram's horn? ...

c. 1936/1937   1948

The Word

Fling, O prophet, the coal of fire from thine altar;
Cast it before the crass, the lewd;
Upon it let them roast their meats, and heat their kettles,
And warm the palms of their hands!
5 Fling also unto them, the spark of thy heart; and let it kindle
The cigarette between their teeth, and light
The crafty smile that lies in ambush underneath mustache,
The snare that lies in waiting in their eyes.
Behold them strut, these gentlefolk, behold them go
10 Twittering the prayers that you taught them.
They suffer your anguish, yea, they hope your hope – they long
For the destruction of your very altars:
Whereupon they will make haste to the ruins, snout among the ruins,
Carry away the broken stones,

15 To sink them in the floor of their hearths, place them in the garden-wall,
   Set them, monuments on cemeteries!
   And if among the shards they will discover
   Your charrèd heart –
   Why, to the kennels they will fling it!

c. 1936/1937

Thy Breath, O Lord, Passed Over and Enkindled Me [Version 1]

Thy breath, O Lord, passed over and enkindled me.
Thy fingertips did briefly pluck my heart-strings.
I held me back; the storm in my heart I spoke not.
My heart on itself enfolded, my song not flowing from my throat.

5 Wherewith shall I enter thy temple, how shall my prayer be clean?
For my speech, O Lord is unworthy, and is profanity's self.
There is no word unbefouled, and that to the very root,
No phrase which besmirched lips have left unuttered and clean.
No syllable left unsaid in the very house of shame.
10 I have seen them, the white doves, at dawn, soar heavenwards,
And then at dusk return, dark ravens schooled in dirt,
An ugly caw in their throats, and carrion in their beaks.
Loud drumming words have beset me, harlots surrounding me –
They glitter with false jewels, pretty themselves with [...]
15 The paint is thick on their eyes, and rottenness in their bones
They fondle the children of lust, the bastards of thought and pen.
Impudent, false they all are, proud-tongued and empty of heart

Like thorn and like wildgrass they grow; there is no fleeing
   from them.
And daily with spilling of slops, with pouring of cesspool –
20 Their odour assaileth the nose of him who pours out his heart
Alone in his room, and who seeks to cleanse the breath of [...]
Whither to flee from their stench, and where from the horde
   to hide
Where is the seraph to cleanse my lips with a coal of fire.
I shall go to the birds of the field, that twitter the coming of
   dawn
25 I shall rise, I shall go to the tots, the children that play in the
   gates
[...] go in their midst I shall learn, their [...], their laughter,
   I
Shall wash my speech in their purity, be clean with the breath
   of their mouths

c. 1936/c. 1937

A Spirit Passed before Me [Version 2 of 'Thy Breath, O Lord, Passed Over and Enkindled Me']

   A spirit passed before my face, it dazzled me; for an
instant your fingertip, O Lord, quivered the strings of my
heart.
   I stood there humbled, hushed, all ardor quelled. My
5 heart curled within me; my mouth could not muster a
psalm.
   And, in truth, with what was I to come into the Temple?
And how could my prayer ever be pure?

   For my speech, O Lord, is altogether abhorrent, has
10 become a broth of abomination.
   There is not a word in it that has not been infected to

the root; not a phrase but heard and it is mocked, not a locution but it has boarded in a house of shame.

My doves, my pure doves, that I had sent forth at dawn towards the sky, at dusk they came back, and, behold, they were crows!
From their throats there issued the rook's cawing; their beaks stank of carcasses; naturalized of the dungheaps, my doves!

It encompasses me, this cluttering rampage of language, it surrounds me, like a wreathing of harlots gone out on the town.
They glitter their gewgaws and gauds, they preen themselves, their eyes are fucus'd red, rot is in their bones.
This is their grace.

And at their skirts there trail the imps of incest, bastards of the pen, the get of fancy, words monstrous, arrogant, loathsome, a flux from empty-cockled hearts.
As the wildgrass they grow, they multiply like the thistle, there is no escape from them.

Daily, as the gutters are swept and the urinals emptied, their fetor, too, rises and corrupts the air, penetrates even to the man shut solitary in his room, unsabbaths his peace.

Where shall I run from this stench? Where shall I hide from this jangle?
Where is the seraph and his gleed shall cauterize my lips?

Only in the twittering of the birds, twittering at sunrise, or in the company of little children, playing in the street their simple games, only there may I be cleansed.
I will go, therefore, I will mingle with them, I will join

in the *aleph-bais* of their talk and their lessons: and in that
clean breath feel clean again.

c. 1953/c. 1955

Upon the Slaughter

    Heavenly spheres, beg mercy for me!
    If truly God dwells in your orbit and round,
    And in your space is His pathway that I have not found, –
    Then you pray for me!
5 For my own heart is dead; no prayer on my tongue;
    And strength has failed, and hope has passed:
    O until when? For how much more? How long?

    Ho, headsman, bared the neck – come, cleave it through!
    Nape me this cur's nape! Yours is the axe unbaffled!
10 The whole wide world – my scaffold!
    And rest you easy: we are weak and few.
    My blood is outlaw. Strike, then; the skull dissever!
    Let blood of babe and graybeard stain your garb –
    Stain to endure forever!

15 If Right there be, – why, let it shine forth now!
    For if when I have perished from the earth
    The Right shine forth,
    Then let its Throne be shattered, and laid low!
    Then let the heavens, wrong-racked, be no more!
20 – While you, O murderers, on your murder thrive,
    Live on your blood, regurgitate this gore!

    Who cries *Revenge! Revenge!* – accursed be he!
    Fit vengeance for the spilt blood of a child
    The devil has not yet compiled ...

25 No, let that blood pierce world's profundity,
Through the great deep pursue its mordications,
There eat its way in darkness, there undo,
Undo the rotted earth's foundations!

    c. 1936/c. 1937   1948

Stars Flicker and Fall in the Sky

Stars flicker and fall in the sky,
All melts in the gloom, part to part.
Darkness falls on the world, and falls
The shadow across my heart.

5 Dreams flicker and wane and fall;
Hearts blossom, and burst, and fade:
O, look in my heart and see
The ruin time has made!

All pray for the light, the light!
10 All pray for the rising sun.
But weary and dark are these prayers
Each ending as it was begun!

O, how the long nights drag on!
O even the moon cannot keep
15 Awake, but weary, must yawn,
Waiting for day and for sleep.

    c. 1953/c. 1955

IMMANUEL (BEN SOLOMON) OF ROME

The Prescription

Summoned to attend this beautiful lady, eight days ailing,
I found the subject couched on a bed of ivory, clothed in fine
    linen, reclining on purple.
I was proceeding – courteously and in my best bedside
    manner –
To take her pulse when in a great access of modesty this lady
    ups
5 And claps cloth to wrist!
I was not a little annoyed; I would even the score; wherefore
Upon her swathed wrist I further placed a brick, and having
    called for fire-tongs,
Went through a pantomime of probing with them
The brick that held the cloth that hid the wrist.

10   Then I cried out:
O this lady is most seriously ill! Treatment delayed too long,
There is no time to be lost now! I prescribe
For immediate preparation – but immediate!

    Wolf's horn; tincture of marble; three scruples of
    moonlight;
15   Hen's milk (the hen a year old); one mob's eye;
    the gall of a pigeon; the plume
Of a red raven, and
To be added thereto, shadow, and of galbanum the
    mere odour.
Do not forget, moreover, the frog's tail, the dash
    of ostrich-milk, the murmuration of a dove.

    The above
20   Mollified with the oil of two cloves of pomegranate,
    and

> Boiled in a vessel of wax, then
> Sprinkled upon the skins of flayed ants
> Is to be applied at sunset to the abdominal region.

Should the ailment resist such medication,
25 Make use of the following:
  The plucked beard of an infant, so scorched in the waters of the Mare Rubrum
  That the fumes thereof rise to the lady's delicate nostrils.
  It is important that with the hairs – black – of the palm of her hand
  You degratinate her tongue.

30   Such is my diagnosis, and such my prescription,
      Remedy drawn from the pharmacopoeias of experts:
      My authors are Hippocrates, Razzi, Avenzohar, and other
                          eminences of science.

c. 1953/c. 1955

MICAH JOSEPH LEBENSOHN

Wine

'And wine maketh glad the life ...' Ecclesiastes 10.19

Like an arrow shot
To Death from Birth:
Such is your lot,
Your day upon earth.

5 Each moment is
   A graveyard board
   For moments that
   Come afterward.

   Now Death and Life
10 Like brethren act:
   Beneath the sky
   They made their pact.

   So Void and Vita
   Destroy, create;
15 Now swallow up,
   Regurgitate.

   The past is past;
   The future lies
   Still overcast;
20 The present flies.

   Who shall rejoice
   Us, scatter woe,
   Make sweet our life
   And bring Death low!

25 My hearties, wine!
   Wine scatters woe,
   Makes glad the life,
   And brings Death low!

   c. 1937/1937   1937

YEHUDA HALEVI

To Jerusalem the Holy

In sooth, what savoure hath now food for me?
How can I hie me to the sote feste
The while that I in western londe be,
And my forweped herte is in the east?
5 In what wyse, eek, shall I my vow express,
Zion, mine oath to thee, how shall I show
Sith thou art bound in bond of heathenesse
And I in Maurish fetters am laid low?
– The splendour and richesse of alle Spain,
10 Y-wis it is a smal thing in mine eyn
Whan that I long for to behold agayn
Even the pore duste of thy shende shrine!

c. 1936/1936   1948

Bear Thou, O Wind, My Love

Bear thou, O wind, my love
    Upon thy wing
And bring it at the cool
    Of evening
5 To him of whom I ask
    Remembering
The days before we went
    Awandering
And swore our love forever
10   Convenanting

Beside the apple-tree
   That blossoming spring.

c. 1936/c. 1938

Lord, Hele Me, Y-wis I Shal Be Heled

Lord, hele me, y-wis I shal be heled!
Lat not thine anger brennen, nor me y-brent,
My medecin, or stronge or weak, been thine
My lechecraft, or good or ill,
5 Thine is the choice, and no physician's
And of thy lore is if fair or foul.
Certes it is not on mine lechecraft that I lean,
But only on thine healing, O my lord.

c. 1936/c. 1938

Ode to Zion

1
Grieving for them, thy captive sons who are
The last sheep of thy flock, O Zion, take,
Accept from them their greeting from afar,
Their greeting and their longing and their ache.
5 Receive the homage of thy vassal, whose
Tears, like the dew of Hermon, seek thy hills,
Where he would be a jackal, all night long
   Wailing thy bitter news,

Where he would dream away thy manacles,
10 And be the harp melodious for thy song!

2
Peniel! Bethel! Manhanayim! sod
Where walked thy saints, where rests the Immanence,
Whose gates are open to the gates of God,
Whose light is not the light of firmaments
15 But the illumination of the Lord!
Shrines holy! Where I would pour out my soul
As was the spirit of the Sacred One
     Upon you once out-poured,
How have you fallen to an evil dole,
20 Where slaves now lord it from your sullied throne!

3
Thy ruins, thy waste places, and thy void,
Thy dwellings rendered rubble and small rock,
The chambers of thy cherubim destroyed –
Yea, there, though bleeding, barefoot, would I walk,
25 I will cut off my hair, and that day curse
That flung thy crowned ones among heathen foes;
I'll fast, for food and drink must surely reek
     When I behold the curs,
Tearing the lion's litter, and day shows
30 The eagle bleeding from the raven's beak!

4
O Zion, altogether beautiful!
Thy sons rejoice them in thy time of peace.
And in thy sorrow, their cup, too, is full.
They weep thy ruins, yet they never cease
35 From striving towards thee from captivity.
They bend the knee unto thy gates, thy sons,
Scattered on mountains, driven over seas,
     Remembering, Zion, thee,
Yearning to touch the plinth of thy shattered stones
40 O but to touch the boughs of thy palm-trees!!

5
Can Shinar and Pathros equal thee for glory?
Can Urim and Thummim be surpassed by spells?
With whom compare thy kings, thy prophets hoary,
Thy Levites and thy singers? All things else
45 Will pass away – idol, idolater –
Only thy crown is for eternity!
Thou art God's dwelling place, His goodly booth!
    O none is happier
Than he who with thee waits thy dawn to see
50 Thee once again as Thou wast in thy youth!

6
God granted that I might go wandering
Where He to seer and prophet was revealed.
God gave me wings that I might fly; and fling
My broken heart upon thy broken field.
55 O, I will fall upon my face, and kiss
The very stones, so blessed in thine earth;
I will take hold of thee, thy clods, thy soil,
    Thy very dustiness,
And hold it as a thing of extreme worth –
60 Prized above rubies, and the richest spoil.

c. 1936/c. 1938   1948

O Dove beside the Water Brook

O dove beside the water brook
On whom my eyes delight to look!

Lo, silver may be found and mined
The like o' my dove one cannot find

5 So fair, so beautiful a gem
   Like Tirzah, like Jerusalem.

   Why fareth she upon the way
   To rest in different tents each day
   When in my heart a dwelling is
   [...]

10 Her breasts which wrought on me such spell
   The wizards of Mizraim well
   Might learn therefrom new magic duty
   Have tricked me, kept my heart for booty.

   Consider the precious gem how that
15 It pales, it blushes, shades, goes bright
   And wonder that from this one heaven
   There flash illuminations seven.

   Convert the adder's bane to honey
   Though many a wight does wed for money
20 I do not take, but give to thee
   My heart a double dowerie.

   c. 1936/c. 1938

O Heighte Sovereign, O Worldes Prys

O heighte sovereign, O worldes prys
Of the greete King most wonder fair citee
My soul y-bannyshed by weste, flies
The mappemounde for to seken thee!

5 Whan I remembre me thy whilom glorie
Thine honour gone, thy wonnyngen to-broke
Swich pitee and swich routhe been in that storie
My tonge y-parched is, my throte achoke.

God yif me egle's wings for to flee!
10 Than wolde I soore, ever onward thrust
To raughten the plot of thy sanctitee
And water with my teeres they sacred dust.

Al be thy King is gon, and in the plas
Of Gilead's bawme, is serpent's baneful rage
15 And snak and scorpioun on public ways
Yet have I longed for this pilgrimage.

Swich pilgrimage is certes stoniness.
O then wolde I thy very stones kiss
Then sweeter than honey that fro the flowers drips
20 Shal be the taste of this erth upon my lips!

c. 1936/c. 1938

Rubaiyat of Yehuda Halevi

1
From him whom Love's sweet anguish now destroys,
Wherefore withold the heralds of thy choice,
O lovely one? Dost thou not know that he
Desires but the greeting of thy voice?

2
5 Since parting, parting now divides our days
Stay yet a while; let me regard thy face;

I know not if my heart remains with me,
Or with thee wanders forth upon thy ways.

3
O may my dreams into thy dreams take flight!
10 I charge thee, by the life of love, keep bright,
As I have kept, the nights of our desire,
The memory of the days of our delight.

4
A sea of tears between us, O dear heart!
I seek to cross; I fail. Do thou but start
15 Towards it, and I swear the waters would
Before the falling of thy footsteps, part.

5
Surely I shall, even from the grave's distress,
Inquire of my darling's happiness.
O grant it me that in that tomb I hear
20 The tingling of the bells upon her dress!

6
Wherefore deniest thou my blood is shed?
Thy hands have shed my heart's blood; I have bled.
And this my word two witnesses confirm:
Thy cheeks of scarlet, and thy lips of red.

7
25 A smile upon thy lips: the ruby glows
Over the row of pearls! The sun's light grows
Upon thy face, but when thy raven hair
Thereon is spread, night comes, and daylight goes!

8
Some do adorn themselves with charms, man-made;
30 But thou in glory and splendour art arrayed;
Beauty and grace the raiment of thine eyes,
Than silk which clothes thee finer, than brocade.

9

Between the honey of thy kisses, and
The gall of parting, it doth take its stand,
35 My heart which thou hast made into thin plate,
And torn to shreds, and cut in many a strand!

10

My spikenard and my myrrh upon thy breast
My honey on thy lips, I do request
From fate but these two gifts: the scarlet thread
40 Upon thy lips, the girdle of thy waist.

11

Thy voice I cannot hear, but hear I do
Upon my heart thy footsteps passing through –
O from those footsteps may I gather up
The blossoms so besprent with my heart's dew!

12

45 Daughters and sons wish freedom's sweet release
To be thy slaves, thy handmaidens; and these,
These much desire to be thy kith and kin:
The Sun and Moon, the Plough, the Pleiades!

c. 1936/1938   1946

Poets of the Yishuv

ABRAHAM BROIDES

Upon the Highway

I

I know the path of camels in the sand;
The burden of the heavy hump of woe;
The tryst with the Messiah.

I know the labour in the quarries, the
5 Cleaving of ancient boulders, and I know
The tryst with the Messiah.

II

Good is the sanctuary of mine eastern sun,
To wed my lips unto the lips of wells,
To bless the Creator.

10 And good to hunger among friends, and eat
The green tomato and the sooted bun,
And bless the Creator.

c. 1931/1931   1931

URI ZVI GREENBERG

Kings of the Emek

What is the crown of kings, and what the glory
That troubadours have sung in seventy tongues
To royalty ensconced in palaces?
What is the marvel of blue blood in kings?
5 The time has come for men to stand erect,
Though shoeless, in a tattered gaberdine,
And know the benison of fingers ten,
The worth of native soil to simple men:

By heart let young men con this Hebrew epic;
10 The splendour of the barefoot pilgrimage
Of this most modern age;

For we have seen the red of Hebrew blood
Streaming through fields and making soft the glebe
Gentiles who sowed in joy, in gladness reaped ...
15 Now do we know fertility of a desert
Now do we know why monarchs of the Emek
Are not arrayed in purple ...

c. 1931/1931   1946

Mother Jerusalem

I have left my comrades, and the four ells of my youth I have
    abandoned.
I kissed the parched lips of no mother, and the hand of a father
    I pressed not.
5 My way lay before me upon the sea, for dawn had risen on the
    waters, and the Lord beckoned to the sailor from the
    sea towards Jerusalem.
Jerusalem – the Holy City! Suzerain of the soul's domain!
    Source of red blood in the veins! Shrine of prayer for
10   the forsaken! City of Splendour and the vision of the
    dying!
The Shekina looks down from a casement. The Shekina weeps
    upon crags.
Yet to me, O Jerusalem, thou art the body of my mother,
15   lacerated; every stone a limb lopped off, and its blood,
    ever flowing, never seen – the soul's blood!
Thy head was, and is not; the skull is shattered.
Upon thy neck they have yoked a mosque, House of Glory for
    the Moslems, even as a winding sheet over a dead body, a
20   winding sheet in which the blood below has been
    sponged.
Upon thy shoulders, Ephraim died, the minion in his purple,
    and Benjamin, in his silk, he who made choice of the
    moon.
25 And the sunsets in Gischala were bloody with thy blood.
A wall, terrible it is, encircles thy poverty, it has the darkness
    of stones, and thy silence was a great crying, heard
    of the lunatic and the saint in his agony.
As of yore the sun still stands in its strength, as in the days of
30   the Temple.
In no wise shall you make her small; her day is long for thy
    torture. Behold we stand in the furnace, and are burnt
    so that thou may'st live.

I stood upon the ramparts; the last legion of Beth-David,
35   children of Europe, a riddle most maddening.
And as I saw in the waste of the fields no vineyards, but thy
       shame, and the abomination that is on thy hem, and
       the terror that cometh with night.
And the anguish whispering in the blood of thine hands – for
40   the prophecies of thy prophets were fulfilled – alas, the
       woe!
Then was the desire in me to bellow like a bull: Jerusalem,
       how dost thou suffer this terror and this shame, and
       dost not tumble down into the valley of Jehoshaphat, as
45   into a grave?

       * * *

If I regard the city with closed eyes, a marvel let it be. Would
       that I could stand here until the end of time and
       regard it with closed eyes, yea, and be silent; would that
       I could bring my lips to hers, parched as the lips of
50   my mother who is one.
One wall of the Temple is there for me: quietly I murmur to
       its stones, city and mother Jerusalem!
At night – a shuddering ... On strange ladders they mount to
       you, thy moon-sick ones – yea they are sick with
55   love. They clamber up this wall; they walk on its stones
       as on coals! Is this indeed Jerusalem? And they fall
       into the darkness between the chasm of cold rocks.
It irks me that I entered thy gates in no golden *tallis* even as
       the High Priest entered towards dusk, when the stars
60   went forth upon the roofs to sing of love.
And it irks me when Jews walk within thy gates, no psalms
       upon their lips, and their arms not raised like
       menorahs.

c. 1931/1931   1940

JUDAH KARNI (VALOVELSKI)

Be There No Altar

Be there no altar, then upon high places
I offer up my humble sacrifice;
And be the city asleep with a thousand faces
I sound the loud alarum of my sighs.

5 Be there no temple, I will mightily shatter
The remnant of this much-demolished wall;
Be there no holy water, I will spatter
Upon this city the swift blood of my skull.

Nor priest, nor prophet — assuredly I shall
10 Lay hands on leper, perjurer, pariah,
Saying: Art thou the one whom men do call
Messiah?

c. 1931/1931   1932

Make Blind, O Sun of Jerusalem

Make blind, O Sun of Jerusalem, and shrivel
The pupils of mine eyes; for I desire
Never to see these barren crags, the evil
Fallen upon the heritage of my sire.

5 Smite me, O Sun of Jerusalem, with fever!
Like a dead fondling let me roll upon

The refuse of the Lord, and of his cities.
With wildernesses I shall not be one.

Slay me at mid of day before the vision
10 Of mine own people; with my ultimate breath
Let me undo Jerusalem's sad derision,
If not in my life, at least upon my death.

c. 1931/1931   1932

With Every Stone

Set me in breaches of the wall, with stone;
Establish me with mallets; let me be
A hostage for my folk; let me atone
The sin of them who let this ruin be.

5 How good to know I am a stone with stones
Of Jerusalem; how good to bind my soul
Unto this wall! Should humbler be my bones
Than this my spirit, kin to my people's goal?

With stone of Jerusalem take me and fling
10 All in this rampart; set your lime thereon.
Then, from the crumbled walls let my bones sing
        To the anointed one.

c. 1931/1931   1934

DAVID SHIMONI (SHIMONOVITZ)

The Glory of the Homeland

    The moon set; the sky darkened; and the stars
    Gained splendour as if pumiced once again.
    It was, as if this while, the moon gone down,
    Their usurped realm was vindicated; and
5 The conflagration of their beauty rose.
    Quick was their lustre; all about was silence,
    Save for the murmur, when the ear inclined
    To hearken to the music of the spheres.
    They wove their golden lace on pale-blue samite ...
10 The wondrous scripture of their blaze they writ
    In such wise that eternity revealed
    Its secrets ...
    The youth regarded them, these festive heavens,
    In silence sucked their beauty, drank their light
15 And sought to make them in his soul, a soul ...
    Quoth the poet.

    My soul most greatly humbled in this land:
    Nature unwound its scroll – I could not read,
    Strange alphabet! and syntax esoteric!
20 Truly was I ensorceled by this beauty,
    Yet hardly had my bird-heart quivered, hardly
    Had glory filled me, but I knew my soul
    To be sojourning still in lands of exile ...
    The palm-tree I beheld; the poplar-tree
25 Drew me with its sad beauty. Winter cast
    A spell on me; I dreamed of wastes of snow.

    My self most greatly humbled, it knew not
    That nature makes no haste to drop the veil,
    Showing her face to strangers.

30 My labours I began. In Galilee
    We paved roads. I crushed stones. The sun
    Glowed down upon me on my quarried rocks.
    The sun glowed, but the sun dried not my sweat ...

    Upon my right, the hills; upon my left
35 The thundering of waves; I heeded neither.
    Weary, forespent was I; a very infant
    At this hard labour, yet withal no laggard.

    No time to raise my eyes to heaven, and
    No time to marvel at my green environs ...
40 Only of nights in dreams there shone before me
    The hills of Galilee, its skies; I heard
    The sound of many waters, and in waking
    My heart rejoiced at dawn, and it was glad.

    I passed on to Judaea, planted trees
45 In Kiriath Ya'arim, in Rehoboth herded,
    In Bair Tobia I broke soil; in Gederah
    I was a watcher, and in Petach Tikvah
    I led clear water to the golden groves.
    Mine the first fruits. And then a teamster, I!
50 I ceased to brood on nature and her beauty.
    When suddenly one night while I was sitting
    Before the stable-door, I felt I knew,
    The cataract had fallen from my eyes,
    The magic of the night grew kin to me,
55 It stood revealed, most lofty and most near,
    After a long estrangement, known to me.

    I now regard the sky, though lofty, near,
    The pangs of exile I recall; recall
    The ecstasy of revelation; and
60 My heart brims over, I am spent with joy,
    Drunken with glory ...

c. 1931/1931   1935

ABRAHAM SHLONSKY

Behold

Behold my country – the carcass of a savage,
Its hide is parchment – parchment for a Torah
Upon which the eternal quill
Has writ the word of God.
Where is the aborigine who may read
This scroll of Genesis?
Where is he, worthy to don tallis
In answer to the summoning of the Torah?

Perhaps these are the camels
That wandered in the wilderness
Out of the paths, well-trodden of the Lord ...
That now do scratch their humps
Against the feet of the Heavenly throne ...
Behold the camels of Gilboa lying down!

Strike well, O sun of Tammuz, upon my scaly land!
We will draw from the udders of the night
The milk of dew.

c. 1931/1931   1946

Sabbath

The funnels of the ship have ceased to smoke.
No more the mermaid weeps upon the ocean.
The Sabbath skies descend on earth which broods,
Like an old beldam at her long devotion.

5 For they are seven, the days within the week,
And seven the branches of the tall menorah.
And he who lights the candelabra, he
Will pour the oil that spreads its golden aura.

O pour the oil; regard what joy, what song
10 From this thy golden goblet has been poured
On roofs, on pleasaunces, on desert sands!
Behold thy hand has spilled this thing, O Lord!

Do you recall our singing, in strange ships
When, for thy name's sake, we sailed to thy shore:
15   'When Jews will come to Palestine
    Joy will try each man's door.'

Have you forgotten? Behold your hand stretched out.
Stretched out to welcome us upon our way.
O, surely we will take the highest seat
20 At the great feast of thy great Sabbath-day.

c. 1931/1931   1931

MORDECAI TEMKIN

Unfavoured

    I am not favoured with the arms
    Of conquerors and homeland pioneers,
    Yet at a distance I do take my place,
    My arms outstretched,
5 These my white arms.
    Humbled indeed am I when these arms rest,
    These delicately-veined arms rest upon my knees,
    And when before me,
    A forest of bruised arms bear gifts:
10 The pale wounds of the land.

    Yet none will know. My ear attends.
    A faithful steed,
    I snort at every sound
    Heard from the farthest parasangs
15 The sound of bright staves driven into land
    Forsaken.
    Such is the covenant of the land.

    Yea, and at the blows of hammers
    Upon thy gates, Jerusalem,
20 I tremble, I arise,
    I rise from off my couch to greet the guests.

    No man can know that lowliness of love
    When empty are the lover's hands.
    So, even as a beggar at a garden-fence
25 In the fields of Jezreel, I stand forlorn.

    c. 1931/1931   1931

RACHEL (RACHEL BLUWSTEIN)

Now Such Am I ...

Now such am I; as quiet
    As waters in a pool, as calm;
Loving unfestive peace, the eyes of little children,
    And the poems of Francis Jammes.

5 Once long ago, my soul arrayed in purple,
    I stood on mountain peaks,
And was as one with the great winds
    And with the eagle's shrieks!

Once long ago – ah, that was long ago!
10   Times change; times pass away.
And now –
    Behold me, me today!

c. 1937/1937   1946

Rachel

Her blood flows in my blood;
    Her voice in mine is heard,
Rachel, great ancestress,
    Keeper of Laban's herd.

5 My house is small for me,
    The city strange, since her

Wide robes were fluttered in
    The desert air.

Wherefore I shall keep fast
10   Unto my chosen ways
Knowing my very limbs
    Hold memories of those days!

c. 1937/1937   1946

Kinnereth

It may be these things never did occur.
Perhaps, somehow,
I never did arise at break of day
To do labour in the garden
5 With the sweat of my brow;

Did never, in the long and fiery days
Of harvest time,
High on the wagon laden with its sheaves,
Lift up my voice in rhyme;

10 Did never bathe within the blue
And quiet of your stream,
O my Kinnereth, O Kinnereth mine!
Were you, indeed? Or did I dream a dream?

c. 1937/1937   1951

Dawn

A jug of water in the hand, and on
My shoulder – basket, spade, and rake.
To distant fields, – to toil – my path I make.

Upon my right, the great hills fling
5 Protecting arms; before me – the wide fields!
And in my heart, my twenty Aprils sing ...

Be this my lot, until I be undone:
Dust of thy road, my land, and thy
Grain waving golden in the sun!

c. 1937/1937   1946

The Childless One

Would that I had a little boy,
    A wise lad, and with raven locks,
To take him by the hand, and walk
    Slowly upon the garden-walks.

5 And 'Uri' would I call my son,
    A delicate name, and full of joy,
A name that is a sunbeam – such
    The name of my small winsome boy.

Yet shall I grow bitter, like Mother Rachel ...
10 Yet shall I pray, like Hannah in Shiloh ...
Yet shall I wait
For him.

c. 1937/1937   1946

YIDDISH

MORDECAI ETZIONY

The Prayer of a Physician

(Dedicated to the memory of Rabbeinu Moses-ben-Maimon)

To Thee, O great Arcane,
Creation's Force and Source,
Of nature Fons et Origo,
Prime Mover! –
5 – O be-Thou-what-Thou-be! –
To Thee, in my dire helplessness,
I make my prayer.

Not for the sake of fame desired,
Nor yet for fortune's sake,
10 But for the sake of those who in delirium cry,
And those who in their agony lie broken,
I do address myself to Thee.

O, not – forfend it! – that I envy Thy might
And of Thy wisdom am jealous,
15 I plead, but for the sake of flesh that is wounded,

And limbs that move not
I send my prayer to Thee.

Thou who hast poured of Thy wisdom
Upon the heads of Pasteur, Hippocrates,
20 And on Maimonides,
Fount of philosophy,
Accept my plea!

Do make sharp my senses
That without error or confusion
25 They may perceive.
Make clear to my sight
The body's eloquent flaws, its diagnostic rash,
And from my hearing
Let not the least stutter of the pulse
30 Escape.

Make them strong and hale,
The twelve-score-and-eight members of my frame!
Teach them to serve me
Altogether and in harmony:
35 When I fare forth to the sick-bed,
Let them not tremble, my hands;
Nor my feet, stumble.

So that I choose, straightway, and without doubt,
The remedy to follow the disease,
40 Make straight my judgement,
Make straight my judgement that I may know,
And keen my perception that I may recognize
Each illness in its particularity.
Let no invalid by my error be undone.

45 To others' pain, make sensitive my soul,
And to another's anguish open my heart.
And O – if the healing of mine enemy is in my hand,
Cleanse me of hatred.

Preserve me, Thou great Healer,
50 From envying my fellow his leechcraft,
His scope and reach.
May his insight and inventions bring
Joy and well-being
Also to me.

55 Source of all Truth!
Aid me against stiff-neckedness and pride.
Teach me humility to know
The angle of my own shortsightedness.
And never let – O never let
60 An ill man through my error be undone,
Nor through that error, Thy holy name be soiled.

And grant, grant that the courage and self-sacrifice,
Which shone up through the lives
Of Koch, Ricketts, and Noguchi,
65 Illumine also my dark path.

c. 1947/1947   1947

JACOB GLATSTEIN

The Eleventh: In Memory of Isaac, Son of the Tailor

Not Abraham did this altar build;
Not his own father his death willed.
It was that knave, that *Rasha*, who
Out of the prayerbook led this Jew.
5 O God, for that he was to a pious mother born
His flesh by combs of iron will be torn.

A humble tradesman it was the Teuton-Tartar
Elected to make saint and martyr.

How good it is that from the holy script he never strayed:
10 For now he is himself into the prayerbook prayed,
Himself a part of the *machzor* made!
The son of a tailor, he
Is now himself intoned into our sacred liturgy!
Of him all future generations will make encomium.
15 Open, ye, therefore, a way:
To the ten martyrs, the eleventh is come!

c. 1947/1947   1947

The Gifted One

The Lord, He endowed him with herds and with flocks,
And children, bright and yet orthodox, –
Capacious trousers, a vest armorial,
And all for himself a privy marmoreal.
5 Also He gave him, munificently
A largess of talent, from cap-a-pie
So shaking the palmleaf and citron, God's praise he intones.
For he has, and possesses, and has, and owns.

The palms, like rhymes, about his mansion grow.
10 It is with sadness, smug and satisfied,
This poet lathers his muzzle to and fro.
With him on Sabbaths visiting critics are at ease,
Caressing his well-bred vulgarities.
O, his cows are Jewish!
15 And they read Holy Writ, his roosters solemn!
With a defunctive myrtle-branch he tickles his spinal column.

Hosannahs, therefore, and praises! A plague the envious ones!
For he has, and possesses, and has, and owns.

An ogre, he marches over the world, valleys and hills.
20 His pockets jingle with coinage, and crepitate with bills.
He grows fatter and grosser, and slobbers and slavers,
And with fondling rhymes
Commiserates all the poor not-havers,
Winking the while to the God he enthrones,
25 For he has, and possesses, and has, and owns.

   c. 1947/1947   1947

Smoke

Up from the chimney of the crematory
Spirals a Jew towards the Lord of Glory;
And as his smoke is volatiled
Upward there curl his wife and child.

5 O there in the skyey cenotaphiums
There weep and wander their sacred fumes.
       Lord God, where Thou art sought
       All of us also there are – not.

   c. 1947/1947   1947

MOYSHE LEIB HALPERN

Portrait of the Artist

    Small freckles constellate my face;
    Among my black hairs, white ones run;
    I am not handsome; I am not
    An Adonis, lovely one.

5 Platyrhine nose and devil's brow.
    My lips are lupine in intent;
    Howbeit those my eyes are blue,
    Are blue and most benevolent.

    My feet are motionless before
10 The dancers in their madrigal,
    To music both my big ears are
    Appreciative as a wall ...

    But with a heart that hammers out
    My song, I sing me as I please,
15 While to its tempo the world hops,
    The world hops to my liturgies ...

    The eagle has his mighty wings,
    Behold I have my mighty arms!
    And life is struggle? I have blood
20 That answers to its loud alarms ...

c. 1932/1932   1932

Canticum Canticorum

This song is greater than all others:
In the beginning there were three brothers.
One of the dreamy eyes,
One sturdy as an oak,
5 And one who stalked about, his head bent by a yoke.
He of the dreamy eyes
Unto himself did take the moon;
The sturdy one
Mortgaged the sun;
10 For the yoked head remained the darkness without noon.
Therefore he wept with a great weeping.
    It roused from his eternal snore
    Kalibabi, the philosopher,
Who lit his lantern, and
15 Went groping for such time among the starry band
That on his magic stone of wisdom he engraved
To wit: that somewhere, and not far from any place
Upon the road which neither curves nor straight lines trace,
Doth someone sit who is not wholly there ...
20 Who weeps, the wherefore he is not aware ...
Yea, from that day – even as numberless the hairs upon the head,
    So are those years unreckon'd –
The yoked head wanders in the darkness, and
    With weeping fills the land.
25 Now we, the sages of the world, who hear him weep,
Do turn the flame about the sigil, and about,
Deciphering, in haste before the illiterate sleep,
That somewhere, and not far from any place
Upon a road which neither curves nor straight lines trace,
30 Doth someone sit, who is not wholly there,
Who weeps, the wherefore he is not aware ...

c. 1932/1932   1932

The Last Song

Since men ceased to put their faith in God,
Love, too, kept from them her ecstasies:
Wherefore they flung themselves in water,
Hung themselves upon the limbs of trees.

5 So the sky now spurned the blue of river;
In the woods the lone bird sang no song;
In the field those things now lay abandoned:
Ploughshare and pastoral-flute and harvest-prong.

Thus the sweet earth wasted into desert.
10 And the roads which once were, now were not.
So the prophet sat on a stone, lonely.
Till the prophet into stone was wrought.

c. 1932/1932   1945

Ki-Ki

Flying he comes, the little dwarf Ki-Ki
Upon the wings of the bird, Flutter-flea.
Then hearing of the poet and his weeping,
He brings him a small letter in his keeping ...

5 This letter coming from the Morning Land,
Writ in the very Empress's own hand,
Sends to the poet from her royal heaven,
Love and regards, and love, and kisses seven ...

Then dreaming of his luck, this bard doth sigh
10 And wakes to pen his queen a sweet reply,
Ordering that his letter should be given
To the good empress in her royal heaven ...

Wherefore he nods, the little dwarf Ki-Ki
Unto his bird of dawn, fleet Flutter-flea;
15 And they both fly, through air and cloud full-riven,
Into the red dawn, into the royal heaven.

c. 1932/1932   1932

The Golden Parrot

The sun will climb over and under the hill,
Then Love will come peacefully unto her own.
Then Love will come peacefully unto her own,
To Loneliness sitting upon a gold stone,
5   Weeping, and weeping alone.

The sun will go over and under the hill.
Then the Gold Parrot will fly through the air,
Then the Gold Parrot will fly through the air,
And on her bright wings will bear us there,
10   Where Longing bids us fare ...

The sun will go over and under the hill,
Then Night will appear and will sing lu-lu,
Then Night will appear and will sing lu-lu,
To eyes that are weary, to eyes that sue
15   For sleep and for naught to do.

c. 1932/1932   1932

Conceit Curious

A curious thought: As I gaze on my pen,
And stare at my hand, and watch it write,
It seems that I have died to-night ...

Died in the house of this heathen dame,
5 And left as the ruin of my defeat –
A pen and a song on a written sheet.

The song, perhaps, is not complete.
Where is it? Upon the threshold it lies,
Flown through the window, as the wind flies.

10 To-morrow, perhaps, you will come to me,
And wait for my greeting-cry to you,
And step on my song with your waiting shoe ...

You will be wrathful, and curse, perhaps,
And leave me a note beneath my door,
15 Saying: I shall not come any more ...

c. 1932/1932   1932

Last Will and Testament

When I will die, then let my hearse
Be the bound body of a horse,
And let my corpse ride on its way
Escorted neither night nor day,
5 Until my flesh, until my bone,

Will fall in shreds on grass and stone.
   And you who at my side, for naught,
   Your days as sacrifices brought,
   Destroy the things I need no more.
10 I have left your roof and door.
   Imagine only that there was
   An evil dream which soon did pass.
   Nobody here beheld me go;
   And I was never here below ...

c. 1932/1932   1932

LEIB JAFFE

We Are a Generation, Heaven-Doomed

   We are a generation, heaven-doomed,
   To seek, to burn, to bow, to bend –
   Yet never reach our end.

   Ours is a land in which the very stones
 5 Are moistened with the marrow of our bones,
   Where youth and nature hold eternal feud,
   And where the rocks are with rich blood bedewed.

   For he who dwelt here, and who breathed here
   Never thereafter, with satiety
10 Was happy, nor with the smug placid mood.

   Here hearts are laden with tempestuous ache,
   Here strength is of a sacrificial worth,
   So that both soul and body a firm union make
   With our parched earth.

15 Ours is a land where all who long and seek
   Do raise aloft their arms in faith and pride,
   And they are crucified.

   We are the sons of heroes and of leaders
   Who never reach the goal, who watch from heights
20 Forlorn and distant, at the last ray of living,
   Our land of struggle, and its Pisgah sights!

   Yes, we shall climb, and ever climb again
   Happy, yet sad; in doubt, yet full of faith,
   And though we fall, we shall forever rise,
25 Still higher climbing, the sun's splendour in our eyes ...

   c. 1933/1933   1933

You Walk upon Your Sunlit Roads

   You walk upon your sunlit roads
      Contented and most happy; yet
   Who knows that I have made these stones
      Moist with my blood and sweat?

5 You walk upon your sunlit roads,
      Youth jubilant, in dancing bands;
   You walk beneath the shade of trees
      Planted with mine own hands.

   Who knows the names of those who burned
10   Their lives upon these fevered lands?
   Who on sharp thorns and briars pierced
      Their hands, their hearts and hands?

Who knows them? 'Tis of little point,
    My life is given, my very blood
15 That it be radiant for you,
    For you that it be good.

    c. 1933/1933   1933

H. LEIVICK (LEIVICK HALPERN)

No More Tears

There are no more tears,
No more mirth. They are weak.
Weak are the righteous,
The wicked are weak.

5 Their bodies are whipped,
Welted and barred.
So who fears flogging
Flatters the guard.

We are all of us shadows
10 The cell-mates of pain.
Do you fear the silence?
Rattle your chain!

    c. 1945/1945   1945

The Windows Are Grated

The windows are grated,
And frozen the walls.
At the door hangs a lantern;
Its light lifts and falls.

5 And under cheap sack-cloth
Is warm blood and bone.
I stare at a single
Dot on cold stone.

So all is forgotten,
10 In far reveries –
Who knows but that maybe
I earned my release.

Or maybe I died, and
This lamp at the door
15 Is burning to show that –
What I am no more?

c. 1945/1945   1945

MANI-LEIB (MANI-LEIB BRAHINSKY)

Sunset

The sun goes down.
Put on your white robe,
Loosen your tresses, and
Bind your brow with a band.
5 Let not dust stain your sweet soul any more,
And step three steps beyond your dusty door.

In sorrow look at the west; in silence twine
Your aching fingers into a suppliant sign;
And curve your lips into a smile that cries:
10 This day dies ...
The sun will sleep. The sun will sleep. For sleep
It must! and if you long to weep, why, weep.
The sun will sleep.

c. 1944/1944   1944

JACOB ISAAC SEGAL

And This I Know

And this I know: It is a devil's play,
And a pursuit of wether by fierce whelp,
Where far more terrible than an army of words,
Is that wild syllable, the keen one: Help!

5 For he who comes with aid and comfort, comes
   Attired in festal robes, and neatly says
   The most heroic words, the finest thoughts,
   The most compassionate of sentences.

   Pity is taught in all the copy-books;
10 All children know what thanks a good deed bodes;
   Wherefore devoutly children will do right
   By beggars crawling on the public-roads ...

   They throw to them their mother's daily pennies,
   And forthwith they are proud of what they've done;
15 There gleam before the blind eyes of the beggars
   Coins that are golden, chiselled from the sun ...

   So in good children's dreams Elijah comes,
   The prophet comes to watch them in their sleep:
   A hoary-bearded shepherd shepherding
20 A flock of stock-blind sheep ...

   c. 1931/1931   1941

Autobiographical

   At last I tore me from their fetters;
   Again to you my steps I turned:
   A very pauper, and in tatters,
   From the last threshold spurned.

5 Assuredly you come on my way,
   I hear the echo of your tread;
   There is no soul upon the highway;
   And Summer nods her weary head ...

The grass is silent, dead all things are;
10 The feeble wind lies where it must;
A sparrow of a sickly colour
Breathes from earth a sickly dust ...

I too – no more that soaring eagle –
In the bright splendour of this trance –
15 No more the daily I.J. Segal –
Stand still before your countenance ...

No dazzlement afflicts my vision;
No trembling takes hold of my knees;
Here I can make but one decision:
20 I fall in silence on my knees.

   c. 1931/1931   1941

Goats

There lie two goats
   On grass in the sun.
From behind a tree
   A hare doth run

5 Towards them; it stops,
   That sly little hare.
The comrade goats
   Sit and stare.

They twist their beards
10   This way and that:
What creature is this?
   Mouse or cat?

Their goatees quiver,
   Shake without halt –
15 The hare makes an artful
   Somersault

And lo! a wonder!
   Mystery!
The hare is now
20   Behind the tree!

c. 1931/1931

A King

Beyond the farthest oceans
There lives a king most holy,
Who bears himself towards all men
Humble, meek, and lowly ...

5 From hearth to hearth he wanders,
In villages and cities,
And rocks the children's cradles,
And sings them his own ditties ...

And when they fall asleep from
10 The telling of his fables,
He drives into the pasture
The goats from their stables.

He sits upon a knoll. He
Watches the goats chewing,
15 And broods on metaphysic
Of his own brewing ...

Oh, it is an honour,
And a joy most subtle
To be a folk's monarch
20 And tender of its cattle!

O, but these are glories,
And not unseemly trucklings,
To be a folk's monarch
And guardian of its sucklings!

c. 1931/1931   1939

King Rufus

To a king who had
A red little beard,
A red little horse
Was most endeared.

5 And also red
Were his jerkin and hose;
The monarch loved
A red, red rose.

And crimson apples
10 The monarch sought
For cooking in
His scarlet pot.

In fine, a royal
Person warm in
15 Vestments that were
Wholly carmine.

When one beheld him
Journey his course
Upon his fleet little
20 Russet horse

He seemed to crackle
He seemed to be
An ever burning
Granary ...

25 Scarlet, rufous,
Roseate,
What a fiery
Potentate!

c. 1931/1931   1939

Confession

For whom am I these things recounting?
For my most welcome guest, Reb Death,
Who comes to ask of me accounting
For my exhaled and squandered breath;

5 For all my doubts and hesitations,
And all my foolish fears and sighs,
And for those sorrowful collations
Over the which I spent my eyes.

I never did become a scholar,
10 And no doubt never grew more smart,
While all the wise ones and the learned
Came riding from the public mart,

Each boasting profit-making cinches,
And at the inn caroused all night
With wine and unspiritual wenches.
Even God's warden shut lips tight

When he, with optics very pious
Beheld, and winked right over it
And sat him down, in cunning silence
To ponder over Holy Writ.

These things I know, for I have seen them.
But do not count me among those
Who cavil at their bitter portion,
And grumble of their throes and woes.

Of course, I have been hurt by these things
By seeing the sated rich men kick
Good folk about, while they go pompous
Behind silk stomach, and golden stick.

But I, I certainly have gathered
The little that to my way came
And with my measured days, allotted,
Played the right proper bitter game.

And now the little period passes:
What is the change that I owe you?
O write it down among the grasses,
Hard by the wall, and writ in dew.

My son will grow up, the pauper-dauphin,
And he will pay my debt, no fear,
Pay for the skimpy scantling coffin,
And for the final glass of beer.

c. 1940/1940   1940

Old Gold

Even as a great country withers, and goes to rot,
A peaceful folk is broken, falls at last –
Such was the falling of that poor small hut,
My grandfather's. His memory be blessed!

5 Seven the generations beneath that roof,
And the roof was bent, and let in rain and day.
Baggage and bag I took, and warp and woof,
And, the lost exile, fared forth on my way.

The cat with the silver spotting sensed and knew
10 And followed me to every broken pane;
And the last guest, a Lithuanian Jew
And my grandfather's gnarled and crooked cane;

And the sweet morning psalmody of yore
That dozed upon the balcony; and the
15 Old Vienna shawl my old grandmother wore,
Grey silk, with blue and scarlet blossomry;

And wonderful tales about the Baal Shem Tov,
And wisdom out of pious books, the whole
Residuum which once so richly throve, –
20 Its song, its melody, its secret soul.

And the dear folksong ambled after me
Riding upon that little golden goat
Which shook its beard in the golden lullaby
And shook the crib in the marvellous anecdote.

25 The ship in the harbour waited, and did brood;
Upon the masts hung seagulls, timorous;

And on the shore the silent twilight stood;
It entered in that waiting ship with us.

c. 1940/1940   1940

Reb Zorach

Rabbi Joshua ben Chananya polishes needles,
Benedict de Spinoza grinds in glass,
And Rabbi Jochanan the Cobbler cobbles.
Also Reb Zorach of Chutarl, Koretz,
5 Opens his little shop of Torah-ware.
Somehow he is afraid to pass the public street,
Afraid of the posts, the stones upon the bridge
And even of the first encountered dogs,
Huddling behind a wall, conspirators.

10 His hand shivers.
Into the keyhole he pushes the icy key,
Reb Zorach, merchant of Torah, retail only:
  A little alphabet wisdom;
  Scrap-bags of suckling *pilpul*;
15   Also a few nursery verses
  To be taken by dead-tired Cabbalists
  Prior to sleeping.

Reb Zorach complains: 'The rich Gamaliel
Before the Sanhedrin poked small fun at me,
20 And at my merchandise, my Torah-stock,
My extra-special, so he bandied, stock ...'
'But Hillel, that good man, spoke up for me:
"God's light shines on the threshold of his door;
His honest hand is the holy scales of God!" '

25 Nevertheless, Reb Zorach will close shop
   And take the seventeen knapsacks of the poor
   And go upon the highways of the world.

   Only that good man Hillel will ask for him
   Naming his name in piety, and even
30 Making a golden parable for his grace.
   For otherwise than others saw his life
   In the copper ringing of the scholar's penny,
   Will Hillel perceive the matter ...

   c. 1940/1940   1940

Song

   World, I would take and lift thee up –
      A sheep lost in the dell,
   And bear thee to the high hill-top,
      To the golden well!

5 Surely I know thy tiredness,
      Thy tongue, a parched and thirsty thing;
   I, too, am weary and athirst,
      And can find no spring.

   O, high upon the sunlit hill
10   The well is cool and deep.
   The sun laves her bright face in it,
      Before she goes to sleep.

   But from the hills there always fall
      The cold and mournful shadows,
15 The dying rays of spotted red
      Upon the valley's meadows.

World, I would take and lift thee up –
   A sheep lost in the dell,
And bear thee to the high hill-top,
20   To the golden well!

   c. 1940/1940   1940

War

They are still full of wrath, the many gods,
Wrathful the one against the other god.
The God of Water against the God of Flame,
The God of Language against the God of Wisdom,
5 The God of Yesterday against To-morrow's
And He, the Lord of Truth against the One of Falsehood!

The God of Lies shows two sharp oxen-horns,
But the horns of the God of Truth are small and sorry.
The God of Beauty, with the antlers of a deer
10 Stands in a quiet wood, as in a dream,
And wonders at the light of the young day.
He drinks the dew in with his mild brown eyes.
But the God of Death, that sable haggard hunter,
Hidden behind a tree, has drawn his bow.
15 O, all the trees and saplings hold their breath!

My good, my much-beloved brothers, tell me,
What shall one do, what shall one think of doing,
To calm the bitter quarrel of the gods?
How shall one bring these enemies together
20 That they may see each other, and perhaps,
Find love and favour in each other's eyes?

Have we not many books, all cramm'd with wisdom,
And scrolls replete with phrase and talisman?
Are they not still extant, the testaments
25 Of those great sages who did keep them clean
Within the precincts of Thy holy Law?

May we not, therefore, in this field of wisdom
Discover some sign, some omen that may bring
Some little peace, and halt the bloody quarrel
30 Of these, the greater and the lesser gods?

c. 1940/1940   1940

Speak to Your People, Therefore, in This Wise

Speak to your people, therefore, in this wise:
To bear your burden, and to share your grief;
Make parables in your twilit synagogues;
Weave there your legends of most pure belief.

5 To ignore your tatters – the shoes polished –
Intent only upon your brilliancies;
In your humblest see Akiva, and in
Your loneliest a saint to recognize;

To reconcile myself to your low estate;
10 To follow your footsteps, seek your alley-ways,
And there to rent myself, a teacher of children,
And teach your children the sung 'aleph-bais';

To leave to the lofty brows their pompous tomes,
Research to the proud, the birth-proud smug patrician;
15 To be preserved from silken wealth; to go
In humble raiment on a humble mission.

A simple follower of the Baal Shem Tov,
Mere murmurer of the verses of his Psalms
And for the sake of his great love of a Jew
20 To bring to the faint and hurt, their salves and balms.

c. 1945/1945   1945

JEWISH FOLK-SONGS

Shall I Be a Rabbi?

Shall I be a rabbi?
Here I cannot meddle.
Shall I be a merchant –
What have I to peddle?
5 Now the fodder has run out
Oats and hay I am without;
And the wife's a nasty lip
And I want a brandy-nip;
I behold a stone
10 Sit me down, and moan ...

Shall I be a shochet?
That is for my betters ...
Shall I be a teacher?
I know not my letters ...
15 And the horse a stubborn beast,
And the wheels they are not greased
And the wife's a nasty lip
And I want a brandy-nip;

817 / Yiddish

I behold a stone
20 Sit me down, and moan ...

   c. 1929/1929   1936

Come You Here, Philosopher

Come you here, philosopher,
You kitten-brained wise-acre,
Sit down near the Rebbe's desk,
And catch some wisdom, fakir.

5 A steamboat you devised for us,
And boast about the notion;
The Rebbe spreads his kerchief out
And spans the sea and ocean ...

A railway you have fashioned, and
10 You brag and use your odd words ...
The Rebbe smoothes his gartel down,
And makes a voyage Godwards ...

A telephone invented, you
Grow proud in what you've given –
15 The Rebbe shakes the myrtle branch,
The sound is heard in heaven ...

Do you know what the Rebbe does
Alone within his study?
He soars above, and there says grace
20 Before the heavenly body ...

   c. 1929/1929   1930

Charm

Little goat, little colt, pussy-cat,
Charmed words most entrancing –
Father beats up mother; and
The children set a-dancing ...
5 Father on his tours has gone;
Mother sleeps in bed alone;
Father comes back from his travel;
Mother cries in pain of travail ...

c. 1929/1929   1946

Tear Not Your Hair, My Sweetheart

Tear not your hair, my sweetheart,
Weep not your bitter tears,
The Czar takes me away now
Only for three short years ...

c. 1929/1929

And When One Burns – One Burns Brandy

And when one burns – one burns brandy,
And when one bakes – one bakes bread,
And when one dies,
One lies dead …

5 Waxen candles
Drop their grime;
And when one dies, one
Dies in time …

c. 1929/1929   1946

On the Attic Sleeps a Roof

On the attic sleeps a roof,
Decked with shingles, split and small;
In the cradle dreams a child
Naked with no clothes at all …

5   Hop, hop, even so,
       From the thatch the goat pulls straw,
       Hop, hop, even so …

In the attic stands a crib,
Where a spider makes his bed,
10 O, he suckles on my blood,
And my life hangs on his thread …

>   Hop, hop, even so,
>   From the thatch the goat pulls straw,
>   Hop, hop, even so ...

15 On the roof the rooster crows,
    And his comb is fiery-red –
    Let my wife go borrow, and
    Let her buy the children bread ...

>   Hop, hop, even so,
20   From the thatch the goat pulls straw,
>   Hop, hop, even so ...

c. 1929/1929   1946

Yoma, Yoma, Play Me a Ditty

    Yoma, Yoma, play me a ditty,
    What does our young girl crave?
    'This young girl wants new shoes that won't hobble her,
    We must go and tell the cobbler.'
5   No, mother, no
        My will it is not so,
        You know not what I know ...

    Yoma, Yoma, play me a ditty,
    What does our young girl crave?
10 'The little girl wants a brand-new bonnet,
    We will buy, and she will don it.'
        No, mother, no
        My will it is not so,
        You know not what I know ...

15 Yoma, Yoma, play me a ditty
   What does our young girl crave?
   'This young girl craves for a handsome sweetheart;
   Let the Shadchan ply his neat art ...'
       Yes, mother, yes,
20   You now make the right guess.
       You know what I confess ...

   c. 1929/1929   1946

Hush! Hush!

   Hush! Hush! let a silence fall
   Rebbe will dance God's madrigal ...
   Hush! Hush! be, Chassidim, quiet,
   Rebbe knows a dance, and he will try it ...

5 And when the Rebbe hops,
   The four walls hop in rhyme.
   Let us all clap hands in right good time ...

   And with the Rebbe's legs
   The table-legs dance too ...
10 Stamping, let us keep the measure true ...

   And when the Rebbe sings
   His holy benediction,
   Satan becomes an empty fiction ...

   c. 1929/1929   1932

We Ask Our Boarding-Mistress

We ask our boarding-mistress —
When will you set the table?
She strolls here, she strolls there,
We might as well talk Babel ...

5 We tell our boarding-mistress
The dinner hour's nearing —
She strolls here, she strolls there,
She is most hard of hearing ...

Our boarding-mistress tells us
10 *Eat children, eat in plenty ...*
And to herself she murmurs —
Each glutton crams for twenty ...

c. 1929/1929   1946

Song of Wine

Good liquor, prized and ever unshent,
I bow to you as to an ancient,
O you, full bumper, I will cherish.
Without you, I am doomed to perish.
5   Tra-la-la, la-la, la-la
    Tra-la-la, la-la, la-la
    Tra-la-la, la-la, la-la
    Tra-la, la-la, la-la

For when the Shadchan met my grandad,
10 His purpose almost went unended.
They chaffered dowry for my mother –
In vain the argument and pother
Until a goblet interposed –
The happy match was made and closed.

15 Indeed, forthright, there was the bridal,
We guzzled all night long wine, mead, ale.
From our deep glasses we did cozen
Loud healths for bridegroom and for his chosen,
Through liquor mother was made wife,
20 And it was liquor gave me life.

I still recall my circumcision –
The wine-glass then served its odd mission.
The guests cried 'Good luck. May his holler
Become the speech of Rabbi-scholar.'
25 And that is why it pleases me
To quaff these goblets lustily.

At my Bar-Mitzvah I orated,
And spoke of wine, and highly rated
It, I told that 'twas not just we
30 Who drank it, His Russian Majesty
Did likewise. Brethren, rich and poor,
Right here is wine, there glasses, pour.

And I recall at my espousals
There were most heathenish carousals;
35 And when they broke the destined platter,
We all bibbed wine, and none drank water,
And though I was the bridegroom, I
Permitted not my throat to dry.

When I was wedded, I remember
40 Wine made blood fire, and bone an ember,
The Rabbi said his benediction, –

The contents of the cup was fiction,
And I stood by, and licked my cup,
I licked it down, I licked it up.

c. 1929/1929   1944

The Golden Parrakeet

From a foreign land has fluttered hither
    The golden parrakeet
    The golden parrakeet
She has lost in her flight a golden feather
5   Alas, for sore deceit.

'Tis not for sorrow of the feather
    As for the parrakeet
    As for the parrakeet
'Tis not my son-in-law [...]

10 As bitter as 'tis – O mother love,
    A bird upon the sea
    A bird upon the sea
So in my husband's house, O mother,
    Bitterer me.

15 As bitter as 'tis, O mother dear,
    A bird without a nest
    A bird without a nest
So bitter it is to be, O mother,
    A mother-in-law's guest.

c. 1929/1929

When I Knead the Dough

When I knead the dough
She cries – too much water!

When I chop the fish
She screams – it is bitter.

5 When I make the bed
She yells – far too high!

When I heat the oven
There is smoke in her eye.

When I walk slowly:
10 'Look, how she rolls!'

When I walk quickly:
'She ruins her soles.'

c. 1929/1929   1944

I Go upon the Balcony

I go upon the balcony
To look upon the town.
There lights a little featherling
Hopping up and down.

5 Beautiful the little bird,
More beautiful its flight.
It drops a letter from its beak.
I read, to left from right.

    I scan the first small line; I read
10 My true love is to bed;
I scan the second line; I read
My true love, he is dead.

    O gather together the lasses,
O maidens fair arise,
15 Let every sweetheart help me
To weep out my eyes ...

    c. 1929/1929   1946

Once upon a Time; This

Once upon a time; this
Story is sad and blue-ish
For it beginneth with a
Monarch who was Jewish.
5   Lulunka, my bride
   Lulunka, my chick
      I lost so great a love, my
      Heart is sore and sick.

Upon a time there was a
10 King who had a queen; the
Queen possessed a vineyard
Lulunka, my child.

A tree stood in the vineyard
A branch hung from the tree,
And in the nest between the branches
A bird lived happily.

Alas, the king died ere his day,
The queen, she pined and peaked away;
The branch fell down to earth, at last,
The bird forsook the nest.

O where is there that ladder
Of a thousand rungs and spars?
And where is there that wise man
To count me the stars ...

O where is there that wise man
Who shall count my wounds for me
And where that sure physician
To heal my heart for me?

c. 1929/1929

Better a Hebrew Teacher

Better a Hebrew teacher
Though he be a hothead,
Than a college student
With his pants half-rotted.

Better a bible-tutor
With half-a-dozen tots,
Than a medical doctor,
His hat split in nine spots.

Better a Talmud student
10 Though not of the first water,
Than an apothecary
Who fries his meat in butter.

c. 1929/1929   1946

O My Mother Sent Me

O my mother sent me
To have a hen undone;
Whereupon I fell in love
With the Shochet's son.
5 But O, is that a Shochet's son, a handsome and a brave,
May I perish for his bones; I am his very slave ...

O my mother sent me
To ask a Kosher-query,
The Rabbi fell in love with me,
10 While expounding theory.
But O was that a Rebbele, a handsome and a brave,
I perish for his skull-cap's point; I am his very slave ...

c. 1929/1929   1932

On the Hill, over the Hill

On the hill, over the hill
The pairs of doves have flown
And hardly have I caught my breath
My youthful years are gone.

5 O harness me, goodfellows,
My sable horses, haste
And we will ride in hot pursuit
And maybe overtake in rout
The fugitive years of youth.

10 I overtook them on the bridge
After many a mile –
O years, my years, return to me
Sojourn with me awhile.

Assuredly we shall not stay,
15 You are a churlish host,
For in your days of youth you should
Have made of us the most.

c. 1929/1929

Gone Is the Yesterday

Gone is the yesterday
Nor yet has dawned the morrow.
Left is a tidbit of to-day,
Betray it not with sorrow.

5 Quaff a thimble brandy
　While living and while dancing
　For with God's will, in heaven,
　There is no drink-dispensing.

　c. 1929/1929

And at My Prayers I Will Quiver

　And at my prayers I will quiver,
　And make fantastic motions
　For love of the Rebbe and his worthies
　　My heart is all emotions.

5 Oh, oh, Rebbenu, I stand and I shiver
　While in my heart there burns a flame.
　I will be a Chassid, pious and ecstatic
　　And worthy of the name.

　In the mikva I will dip me,
10 In wintry twenty below zero,
　And conquer planets for the Rebbe.
　　I will be a hero.

　And in the hottest heats of summer
　Will wear a shawl of silken spangles,
15 A caftan I will buy, and wear it,
　　A cap of seventeen angles.

　c. 1929/1929

Asks the World an Old, Old Question

    Asks the world an old, old question:
    Tra-la-tra-ri-di-di-dam
    Comes the answer
    Tra-di-ri-di-lai-lum
5 But if you will, why twist the logic?
    Trai-dam
    Still remains the old, old question
    Tra-la-tra-ri-di-di-dam
    Comes the answer
10 Tra-di-ri

c. 1929/1929

And When Messiah Will Come

    And when Messiah will come
    Our life will trip in carols;
    And wine and brandy will be
    Guzzled from the barrels!

5 And when Messiah will come
    We will not be conscripted,
    And all our foes will perish,
    Apostates not excepted!

    And when Messiah will come
10 On holy land we'll pray,

And all our foes, their tails between
Their legs, will slink away.

c. 1929/1929   1939

O What Do You Wish, My Dearest Child

O what do you wish, my dearest child,
That I find you a cobbler's apprentice?
No, father, it is not becoming.
A cobbler's apprentice now hammers his leather,
5 And now beats his wife, in fair or foul weather.
No, father, it is not becoming!

A tailor's apprentice sews one to the other
His patches and curses his wife's father's father.

A journeyman-carpenter hammers his casket,
10 And if his wife hungers for food, she must ask it.

A baker's apprentice bakes bread upon bread;
Thrice daily his wife must declare herself dead.

A scholar-lad sits all day long, and he squeezes
His benches; his wife dines and sups on diseases.

15 A merchant makes money from fauna and flora,
And kisses his wife, like a holy Torah.

c. 1929/1929   1944

Tell Me, Pretty Maiden, O Hearken Pretty Maiden

'Tell me, pretty maiden, O hearken pretty maiden
In that far country what will you do?'
'Through the village I will wander, gather linen I will launder,
Just to be with you.'

c. 1929/1929

What Is Loftier than a House?

What is loftier than a house?
What is nimbler than a mouse?

You addle-pate, you dolt, you fool,
You have no brains behind your skull
5 For smoke goes loftier than a house
And a cat is nimbler than a mouse.

What is deeper than a well?
What is bitterer than gall?

You addle-pate, you dolt, you fool,
10 You have no brains behind your skull
For Torah is deeper than a well
And Death is bitterer than gall.

c. 1929/1929

When He Has Frolicked for a Little

When he has frolicked for a little
He will learn Torah, jot and tittle;
The child will con his daily verses,
And we will hear the town rehearse his
5 Sweet merits; and at his own wedding
Acute *Responsa* he'll be threading.
The whole world will eke out a pleasure
From bridegroom, bride, and dowry-treasure.
A dowry-purse of worth exceeding,
10 And such a family of breeding!
The groom will dwell there, without payment,
For three good years, in food and raiment.

    c. 1929/1929   1944

Lovely Am I, O Lovely, and Lovely Is My Name

Lovely am I, O lovely, and lovely is my name;
Matchmakers seek to wed me to rabbis of great fame;
How much a rabbi knows, 'tis true, no other knows,
But I am to my mother her dearly-cherished rose.

5 Water in the chamber, and sticks in the shed,
If I do not like a lad, he'll have these on his head.

    c. 1929/1929   1944

I Sit Me Down upon a Stone

I sit me down upon a stone;
I weep; I sorrow; I make moan;
For all the virgins get them spouses
But only I remain alone.
5 Alackaday! O star of sorrow,
When shall I become a bride,
On this day? or on the morrow?
Surely I am not so funny;
And all the world knows, we have money!

c. 1929/1929   1944

CHASSIDIC FOLK-SONGS

L'chayim, Rebbe!

L'chayim, Rebbe! A happy week to you!
And every Chassid echoes it: You! You!
With liquor we're not niggardly,
Let us drink anew!
5 Through prayer we have won ourselves a right good week and new,
Through prayer we have won ourselves a right good week and new,
A right good week and new!

c. 1946/1946

Oy, Our Rebbenu

Oy, our Rebbenu! *Gewald*, our Rebbenu!
The good Lord giving
Health and living
For his dwelling we'll be leaving
5 Oy, our Rebbenu! *Gewald*, our Rebbenu! Oy, our Rebbe
Oy, Oy, Oy, Oy, Oy, Oy, Oy, Oy, Oy, Oy
Then, *gewald*, our Rebbenu! Oy, our Rebbenu!
Oy, our Rebbe! *Gewald*, our Rebbe
Oy, our Rebbe! *Gewald*, our Rebbe
10 Oy, our Rebbenu! *Gewald*, our Rebbenu!
Oy, our Rebbenu! *Gewald*, our Rebbenu!

c. 1946/1946

God Willing, at the Rebbe's

Gewald! Gewald! Gewald! Gewald! Gewald!
My good brother, my dear brother,
My good brother, my dear brother,
When – when – will we see each other?
5 When – when – will we see each other?

    O, if health and living
    Be of God's giving,
    At the Rebbe's court, we will
    See us again

10   O, if health and living
        Be of God's giving,
        At the Rebbe's court, we will
        See us again

Gewald! Gewald! Gewald! Gewald! Gewald!
15 My good brother, my dear brother,
My good brother, my dear brother,
When – when – will we drink together?
When – when – will we drink together?

        O, if health and living
20   Be of God's giving,
        At the Rebbe's court, we will
        Quaff it again

        O, if health and living
        Be of God's giving,
25   At the Rebbe's court, we will
        Quaff it again

Gewald! Gewald! Gewald! Gewald! Gewald!
My good brother, my dear brother,
My good brother, my dear brother,
30 When – when – will we dance together?
When – when – will we dance together?

        O, if health and living
        Be of God's giving,
        At the Rebbe's court, we will
35   Hop it again.

        O, if health and living
        Be of God's giving,
        At the Rebbe's court, we will
        Hop it again.

c. 1946/1946

Myerka, My Son

    Myerka, my son, Myerka, my son, O Myerka, my son –
    Do you realize before whom you stand?
    Do you realize before whom you stand?
    Lifnei melech malchei hamlochim!
5 Dear Father!
    Before the King of the kings of all kingdoms!
    Dear Father!
    Lifnei melech malchei hamlochim!
    Dear Father!

10 Myerka, my son, Myerka, my son, O Myerka, my son,
    What will you petition from Him?
    What will you petition from Him?
    Bonai, chaye mezonay –
    Dear Father,
15 For the daily bread of my house, and for children!
    Dear Father!
    Bonai, chaye mezonay –
    Dear Father!

    Myerka, my son, Myerka, my son, O Myerka, my son –
20 Do you know, then, in truth, who you are?
    Do you know, then, in truth, who you are?
    Hineni he-oni mi-ma-as ...
    Dear Father!
    A pauper in deeds, so behold me,
25 Dear Father!
    Hineni he-oni mi-ma-as.

c. 1946/1946

A Thou Song

Reboinoi shel Olam
O Lord of the World,
Reboinoi shel Olam, Reboinoi shel Olam, Reboinoi shel Olam,
'Tis a thou-song I'll sing thee ... Thou ... Thou ... Thou ...
  Thou ...
5 *Ayeh emtzoeko, v'ayeh lo emtzoeko?*
  O, where shall I find Thee? And where, where art Thou not to
  be found?
  Thou ... Thou ... Thou ... Thou ...
  For where I fare – Thou!
  Or here or there – Thou!
10 Only Thou! None but Thou! Again, Thou! Ever Thou!
  Thou ... Thou ... Thou ... Thou ...
  Do things go well – Thou!
  Forfend it, ill – Thou!
  Ay, Thou, Thou, Thou, etc.
15 Eastward, Thou! Westward, Thou! Northward, Thou!
    Southward, Thou!
  Thou! Thou! Thou! Thou! Thou!
  The heavens, Thou! And earth, Thou!
  Skyscape, Thou! Landscape, Thou!
  Thou, Thou, etc.
20 Whither I turn me,
  Where I tarry – Thou!
  Thou!

c. 1946/1946

Levi Yitschok's Kaddish

Good morning to you, Reboinoi shel Olam!
I, Levi Yitschok ben Soreh of Berditchev
Come to you with a lawsuit brought by Yisroel, your people.
What grudge do you hold against your people Israel?
5 Why do you always pick on Yisroel your people?
For is aught ado, then: Speak to the Children of Israel!
For is something up, then: Bid thou the Children of Israel!
A thing to be done, then: Address thou the Children of Israel!
Dear Father, sweet Father in heaven –
10 How many nations does the world boast?
The Persians! Babylonians! The Edomites!
The Muscovites maintain that only their monarch is monarch!
The Germans do maintain that only their kingdom is kingdom!
And the Englishmen do hold that only their empire is empire!
15 And I, Levi Yitschok ben Soreh of Berditchev, say:
Yisgadal, v'yiskadash, shmai rabah!
And I, Levi Yitschok ben Soreh of Berditchev, say:
Lo ozuz mimkomi – I will not abandon my plea
Ere an end is decreed
20 An end to our wandering fate!
Yisgadal, v'yiskadash, shmai rabah!

c. 1946/1946

M'laveh Malkeh

O, brother, say,
What is that day
We love, and do enjoy all,
   When humble Jew, and good Jew,
5   The pious one, the true Jew
Deems himself right royal!
   O humble Jew and good Jew
   Thinks himself right royal!

The Sabbath day
10 Is that day –
Be you, therefore, jolly!
   Dance you, therefore, brother,
   Alone, and altogether
For Sabbath day is holy!

15 For it is clear –
'Tis crystal-clear –
The bride is Sabbath, surely!
   The bridegroom, brother,
   Is none other
20 Than all of sacred Jewry!

c. 1946/1946

Thou Hast Chosen Us

Thou hast chosen us from among all nations,
And Thou hast loved us, and lavished favour on us
        Oy, gewald! Oy, gewald!
Hast loved us, and lavished favour on us, lavished favour on us
5   Oy, gewald! Oy, gewald!

And Thou hast raised us above all nations,
And with Thy laws hast blessed and hallowed us
        Oy, gewald! Oy, gewald!
Hast raised us above all peoples; and with Thy precepts
sanctified us, with Thy Holy Law!
10   Oy, gewald! Oy, gewald!

c. 1946/1946

O There, O There, Where Is Our Holy Rebbe [Version 1]

O there, O there, where is our holy Rebbe
  Where is our holy Rebbe
O there great faith is found
O there great faith is found
5   The glory and the faith enduring ever!

O there, O there, where is our holy Rebbe
  Where is our holy Rebbe
O there are blessings to be found
O there are blessings to be found
10   The blessings and the wisdom enduring ever!

O there, O there, where is our holy Rebbe
   Where is our holy Rebbe
O there is greatness found
O there is greatness found
15   The grandeur and greatness enduring ever!

O there, O there, where is our holy Rebbe
   Where is our holy Rebbe
There is eloquence found
There is eloquence found
20   Knowledge and eloquence enduring ever!

c. 1946/1946

Where Our Good Rebbe Is to Be Found
[Version 2 of 'O There, O There, Where Is Our Holy Rebbe']

O there, O there, where our good Rebbe is to be found,
   O there great faith, great faith is found!
There is the glory, and there the faith beyond compare!

O there, O there, where our good Rebbe is to be found,
5   O benedictions there abound!
There is all wisdom, and benedictions blessing all!

O there, O there, where our good Rebbe is to be found,
   O there is exaltation found!
Mightiness there, and exaltation to great heights!

10 O there, O there, where our good Rebbe is to be found,
   Great eloquence, its sacred sound!
There is the Judgment, and the speech that does endure!

1951/1955

The Rebbe, He Wanted [Version 1]

The Rebbe, he wanted to go to the city
Alas, he had no horse.
So he issued an order to all his Chassidim
And soon he had horses, of course.

5   And when our Rebbe rides, our Rebbe rides, there ride
       Chassidim, the whole of his lot
       Who from this favour get a pleasure that as yet
       Mithnagdim certainly have not
                  Certainly have not.

10 The Rebbe, he wanted some beef for his dinner,
Alas, of beef there was none.
So he issued an order to all the town's cattle –
In an hour his steak was well done.

       And when our Rebbe eats, our Rebbe eats, there eat
15   Chassidim, the whole of his lot
       Who from this favour get a pleasure that as yet
       Mithnagdim certainly have not
                  Certainly have not.

The Rebbe, he wanted some honey for licking
20 But honey, alas, there was not.
So he issued an order to all the bees buzzing
In an hour, his honey was brought.

       And when our Rebbe licks, our Rebbe licks, there lick
       Chassidim, the whole of his lot
25   Who from this favour get a pleasure that as yet
       Mithnagdim certainly have not
                  Certainly have not.

Our Rebbe, he wanted some snuff for to sniff at
But no one, it seems, had the stuff.
30 So he issued an order to all the Turk fezzes
In a trice, there was snuff – and enough!

And when our Rebbe sniffs, our Rebbe sniffs, there sniff
Chassidim, the whole of his lot
Who from this favour get a pleasure that as yet
35 Mithnagdim certainly have not
                      Certainly have not.

c. 1946/1946

The Rebbe, He Wanted [Version 2]

The Rebbe wished to journey up to the city,
But he didn't own a horse,
So he issued a decree to all his Chassidim
The horses appeared, in due course!

5 And when our Rebbe rides, our Rebbe rides, there ride
With him our Chassidim, ho!
Who from this favour get that kind of pleasure that
Mithnagdim surely cannot ever know.
                Cannot ever know!

10 The Rebbe wanted beefsteak for his next dinner –
In the kitchen, there was none,
So he issued a decree to all the town's cattle –
In one hour, his steak was well done!

And when our Rebbe eats, our Rebbe eats, there eat
15   With him our Chassidim, ho!
Who from this favour get that kind of pleasure that
Mithnagdim surely cannot ever know.
    Cannot ever know!

The Rebbe wanted honey for his sweet licking –
20 But such honey, he had not,
So he issued a decree to all the bees buzzing,
In one hour, his honey was brought!

And when our Rebbe licks, our Rebbe licks, there lick
With him our Chassidim, ho!
25   Who from this favour get that kind of pleasure that
Mithnagdim surely cannot ever know.
    Cannot ever know!

The Rebbe wished for Turkish tobacco for sniffing,
But it seems, none had the stuff!
30 So he issued a decree to all the Turk fezzes
In one hour, there was snuff – and enough!

And when our Rebbe sniffs, our Rebbe sniffs, there sniff
With him our Chassidim, ho!
Who from this favour get that kind of pleasure that
35   Mithnagdim surely cannot ever know.
    Cannot ever know!

1951/1955

In God's Good Time

In God's good time, and the Messiah appearing
What will happen to our Rebbe, God-fearing?
Of wine and brandy, there will be great showers
To be guzzled by those Chassidim of ours!
5   Oy, vay!
       God grant we see that day!

The trees, they will blossom with cakes in bunches!
Meerschaums and pipes one will break from their branches,
And from their leafage, one will snip and cut
10 Good Turkish tobacco for the saintly lot!
       Oy, vay!
       God grant we see that day!

And a cow one will take, not any whichever,
But one descended from the Red Heifer
15 And harness her neat for the Rebbe's driving –
In God's good time, and the Messiah arriving!
       Oy, vay!
       God grant we see that day!

His coach upholstered with parchment, not leather,
20 And its wheels well built out of right good cedar
And the axle made of the wood called gopher,
And the whip – eight tzitzis dangled from a shofar.
       Oy, vay!
       God grant we see that day!

25 Not bricked and mortared is the Rebbe's regal
House but built out of *tsholent* and *kigel*
And his chair adorned with parchmentry
Oy, vay, God grant that we see that day!

Oy, vay!
God grant we see that day!

1951/1955

A Burglary

At my Rebbe's, there did happen, there did happen
    At my Rebbe's, at my Rebbe's, there did happen
        A burglary.

Seven shirts as big as swatches –
Oi, oi!
Four in tatters,
Three with patches –
        A burglary!

At my Rebbe's, there did happen, there did happen
    At my Rebbe's, at my Rebbe's, there did happen
        A burglary.

Seven candelabra taken,
Oi, oi!
Three were legless,
Four were broken –
        A burglary!

c. 1946/1946

Tell Us, Rebbenu

Tell us, Rebbenu!
What will happen when the Messiah comes?
When the Messiah comes, we will banquet and feast it!
And what will we eat upon this festival day?
5 The Wild Ox and Leviathan!
The Wild Ox and Leviathan!
The Wild Ox and Leviathan!
Will we eat upon this festival day.

Now tell us, Rebbenu,
10 What will we drink upon this festival day?
Wine Preserved from of Yore
Wine Preserved from of Yore
Yes, wine preserved from of yore, will we drink
And the Wild Ox and Leviathan
15 Will we eat upon this festival day.

Now tell us, Rebbenu,
Who'll teach us Torah on this festival-day?
Moishe Rebenu
Moishe Rebenu
20 Moishe Rebenu
He will instruct us
And the Wild Ox and Leviathan
Will we eat upon this festival-day.

1951/1955

Yoshka, Yoshka

Yoshka, Yoshka, harness the horse, and
Let us rush right over
To the fair; for if the nag halts
We'll not get rid of him, not ever ...

5 The Rebbe he bade us drink and dine
Drinking brandy, and not wine.
          La, la, etc.

Repeat.
Yoshka, Yoshka.

1951/1955

Oy, Vey, Rebbenu

Oy, vey, Rebbenu
I stand here, and shiver!
I stand here, and shiver!
Before the Rebbe, and his Chassidim –
5 I am all a-quiver!
I am all a-quiver!

And at my prayers, I will shake me
And make all kinds of motions –
And make all kinds of motions –
10 Before the Rebbe and his Chassidim
I am all emotion!
I am all emotion!

O, to the *mikveh*, I will hurry
Even in the coldest weather –
15 Even in the coldest weather –
O for the Rebbe and his Chassidim,
I perish altogether …
I perish altogether …

1951/1955

Our Rebbe, the Miracle-Worker, Once

Our Rebbe, the Miracle-Worker, once
Fared forth on the ocean wide
The voyage should have taken seasons
Rebbe, he made it in a single night!

5 For when our Rebbe sails
   For when our Rebbe sails
   All his Chassidim, they sail, too.
   And what did then their eyes behold?
   What no one else did ever view!

10 The ship fell in great peril, but
Rebbe prayed and blessed her out –
And scoffers who disbelieve this truth,
Be their names rubbed and blotted out.

   For when our Rebbe sails
15 For when our Rebbe sails
   All his Chassidim, they sail, too.
   And what did then their eyes behold?
   What no one else did ever view!

The Rebbe waved with his sleeve, and with
20 Holy look about him looked –
And lo! from the sea there sprang a fish –
Already boiled-and-cooked!

    That fish that was not hooked,
    O boiled it was, and cooked,
25   Spiced with horseradish, rich and red!
    It leapt upon the Rebbe's plate,
    And thence into his gullet fled!

Although the atheists who scoff,
In their disbelief persist –
30 Do you, still ask for further proof
That our Rebbe is involved in this?

    For when our Rebbe sails
    For when our Rebbe sails
    All his Chassidim, they sail, too.
35   And what did then their eyes behold?
    What no one else did ever view!

c. 1946/1946

And When Our Rebbe Walks

And when our Rebbe walks,
And when our Rebbe walks
All the Chassidim, they walk, too

And when our Rebbe eats,
5 And when our Rebbe eats
All the Chassidim, they eat, too

And when our Rebbe drinks,
And when our Rebbe drinks
All the Chassidim, they drink, too

10 And when our Rebbe sleeps,
And when our Rebbe sleeps
All the Chassidim, they sleep, too

c. 1946/1946

Our Rebbe [Version 1]

Our Rebbe went into the desert
    Oi, our Rebbe, our Rebbe
And caught him a fish there, the wizard,
    Oi, our Rebbe, our Rebbe

5 And he took the fish home to his lady
    Oi, our Rebbe, our Rebbe
And the Rebbitzin, she made it ready,
    Oi, our Rebbe, our Rebbe

Ready, and very digestible
10   Oi, our Rebbe, our Rebbe
For the Chassidim who sat at his table,
    Oi, our Rebbe, our Rebbe

But suddenly one heard a loud screaming –
    Oi, our Rebbe, our Rebbe
15 And the Rebbe awoke from his dreaming,
    Oi, our Rebbe, our Rebbe.

c. 1946/1946

Our Rebbe [Version 2]

Our Rebbe, he went forth into the desert
    Oi, our Rebbe, our Rebbe,
And caught him a fish there, the marvellous wizard,
    Oi, our Rebbe, our Rebbe.

5 So he took that fish back home to his lady,
    Oi, our Rebbe, our Rebbe,
She scaled it, and cleaned it, and made it all ready,
    Oi, our Rebbe, our Rebbe.

All ready, and seasoned, and palatable
10   Oi, our Rebbe, our Rebbe,
To all the Chassidim who sat at his table,
    Oi, our Rebbe, our Rebbe.

But suddenly there was heard a loud screaming, –
    Oi, our Rebbe, our Rebbe –
15 And the Rebbe he woke from his glorious dreaming,
    Oi, our Rebbe, our Rebbe!

1951/1955

My Noddle It Is Humming

My noddle it is humming
With my Rebbe's din and drumming –
I heard such subtleties and such rare lore.
Patiently, every tenet

5 Of his, I will explain it
And miracles and marvels and much more.

O, you'll marvel and you'll wonder
At each tale that I will render,
Marvel, Jews, so favoured and so blessed.

10 Metatron, prince in heaven, there
There at my Zaddik's parks his luggage!
Doubt it at your peril if you dare!
          Oy vey!

Oy, vey, blessed who saw these wonders spread
15 For only our Chassidim's eyes,
Who saw our Rebbe's happy face,
Shining forth its godly grace!
The doubter doubts, it is above his head.

1951/1955

The Train

God willing, after Sabbath
I'll to the Rebbe again,
And there will picture and tell him
About the iron train.

5   O but it has a whistle,
        Loud, and past all choking!
        Below, it pours out water,
        Above, it flies out smoking!
        S ...

10 Coals – bright – burning
    It deems a food delicious,
    And right hot boiling water
    The soupiest of dishes!

    A German, he must be who
15 Conducts this kind of trip
    A coachman, a strange coachman
    Who doesn't have a whip!

    Rebono shel Olam,
    His schedule do confound
20 So that never on the Sabbath
    Will his wheels go round!

    c. 1946/1946

How Fares the King?

Rabosai, Rabosai, scholars for this task:
Here's a query, here's a query.
Ask it, ask!

Answer, then, my query; answer:
5 How does the King drink tea?

    One takes a loaf of sugar, and one bores a little hole in it, and one pours hot water into it, and one stirs, and one stirs ...
        O, in this wise, in this wise, in this wise, does the King drink tea!

10 Rabosai, Rabosai, scholars for this task:
Here's a query, here's a query.
Ask it, ask!

Answer, then, my query; answer:
How eats the King potatoes?

15   One builds a bulwark of butter, and a soldier-boy with
his shooting-toy, shoots through the butter a hot potato,
– which strikes the King *plum* in his open mouth!
        O, in this wise, in this wise, in this wise, eats the King
            potatoes!

Rabosai, Rabosai, scholars for this task:
20 Here's a query, here's a query.
Ask it, ask!

Answer, then, my query; answer:
How sleeps the King at night?

        One fills a bedroom with feathers, one flings therein His
25 Majesty, and three battalions stand and shout: Sha!

1951/1955

The Rebbele, the Gabbai'le, the Cantor'l, the Shamash'l

The Rebbele, the Gabbai'le, the Cantor'l, the Shamash'l –
Every holy vessel will be hopping!

Shout, then, shout again,
All, with might and main:
5 The Rebbele himself soon will hop it!

The Rebbele, the Gabbai'le, the Cantor'l, the Shamash'l –
Every holy vessel will be hopping!
The Rebbele, the Gabbai'le, the Cantor'l, the Shamash'l –
Every holy vessel will be hopping!

1951/1955

Tsig, Tsigitsapel

Who maketh a statement, he, he must prove it!
A miracle happened, and I'll tell you of it.
                              Tsig, tsigitsapel, etc.

This miracle happened on Hoshana Rabah:
5 A goat, it was foaled, in the barn of the Gabbai;

And the Rebbe he ordered it cleaned and well curried,
And then, without questions, to the mikveh hurried.

Chassidim behind him, the Rebbe before –
When lo! the goat leaped, and it was no more!

10 Chassidim did hunt it in seven directions –
And even Cohanim left their benedictions,

And after them Doba the merchantess jumped it
Behind her the Rebbe's plump helpmate plumped it.

At last, to the goat's tail, the Shochet traced him,
15 Who – saving your grace – there soundly disgraced him!

1951/1955

Miracles and Wonders

The Rebbe comes,
The Rebbe comes,
The Rebbe has arrived now!

Ay, ay, ay, ay
5 Ay, ay, ay, ay
Miracles and wonders ... Ay.

Our Rebbe he does wonders
Even in the water –
He enters it a dry man
10 And he comes out much wetter,

Ay, ay, ay, ay
Ay, ay, ay, ay
Miracles and wonders ... Ay.

The Rebbe, he does wonders –
15 And I'm not merely talking:
There comes to him a blindman,
And he sets him a-walking,

Ay, ay, ay, ay
Ay, ay, ay, ay
20 Miracles and wonders ... Ay.

c. 1946/1946

Akavyah ben M'halallel

Akavyah ben M'halallel sayeth:
Consider thou, therefore, three things,
And thou wilt be saved from error and sinning.

Consider and know
5 Whence didst thou come into being, being and life?

And whither, and whither, and whither
Thou art destined to go, thou art destined to go.

To a place of dust, of dust and worms, of worms and death –
    corruption!

And before whom thou art destined to give account and
    reckoning –
10   Before the King of the kings of all earth's kingdoms –
    Blessed be He!

Akavyah, Akavyah ben M'halallel says this:
ben M'halallel sayeth.

1951/1955

Omar Adoishem l'Ya-akoiv!

Said the Lord, the Lord, to Jacob –
Yes, father, yes,
Hast thou not promised us:

Fear not, my loyal Jacob!
5 Yes, father, yes.

Why, then, are we driven so, Father mine,
Why, then, are we harried so, Father mine,
    When will it end, end, O when?

Chose the Lord, the Lord, his Jacob –
10 Yes, father, yes,
Hast thou not promised us:
Fear not, my loyal Jacob!
Yes, father, yes.

Why, then, are we driven so, Father mine,
15 Why, then, are we harried so, Father mine,
    When will it end, end, O when?

Raised the Lord, the Lord, his Jacob –
Yes, father, yes,
Hast thou not promised us:
20 *Fear not, my loyal Jacob!*
Yes, father, yes.

Why, then, are we driven so, Father mine,
Why, then, are we harried so, Father mine,
    When will it end, end, O when?

1951/1955

Bar Yochai

    Bar Yochai, Bar Yochai, Bar Yochai,
        blessed art thou.
        With blessed oil, with oil of rejoicing,
        did thy comrades well anoint thee
5   Bar Yochai, Bar Yochai, Bar Yochai,
        blessed art thou.

                (repeat)

c. 1946/1946

The Rebbe Elimelech

    When our Rebbe Elimelech
    Wished to have himself a frolic
    Wished to have himself a frolic
        Elimelech
5 He did doff his robes of prayer
    And did don – what he did wear
    And he sent for his fiddlers, for both.

        When the fiddle-fiddling fiddlers did fiddle-fiddling fiddle
            They fiddle-fiddling fiddled it, did they.
10   When the fiddle-fiddling fiddlers did fiddle-fiddling fiddle
            They fiddle-fiddling fiddled it, did they.

    When our Rebbe Elimelech
    Wished to have himself a frolic
    Wished to have himself a frolic

15   Elimelech
   He did duly say Havdala
   With his shamash Reb Naphthali
   And he sent for his string-men, for both.

           And the catgut-plucking string-men, they did pluck the
               catgut, string-men,
20   They most pluckingly did shiver it, did they.
           And the catgut-plucking string-men, they did pluck the
               catgut, string-men,
               They most pluckingly did shiver it, did they.

   When our Rebbe Elimelech
   Wished to have himself a frolic
25 Wished to have himself a frolic
       Elimelech
   His phylacteries, he wound them;
   And his spectacles – he found them,
   And he sent for his drummers, for both.

30   And the drumming-thumping drummers, they most
               thumpingly did drum it,
               They most thumpingly did boom-boom it, did
                   they!
           And the drumming-thumping drummers, they most
               thumpingly did drum it,
               They most thumpingly did boom-boom it, did
                   they!

1951/1955

Yonder! Yonder!

I

O do you know the land where the citron's growing
Where the goats nibble *bokser* like grass, like grass,
Where wine like water is ever flowing,
And roasted ducks and goslings through the bright air pass?

5 And with those palmleaves
And with those palmleaves
Roofs are covered gaily
And almonds, and almonds
On dry sticks blossom daily.

10   O thither, thither, there, Oy, Rebenu,
     Gewald, gewald,
     There I would fare, would fare, would fare,
     O, even now
     Fare, would fare,
15   O even now!

II

O do you know the land where our own Messiah
Will come to us riding upon his white steed
And where he will blow on his mighty ram's horn
And wake the dead and have them, them and the living freed?

20 And he will lead us,
And he will lead us,
Lead his loved Yisroel

865 / Yiddish

Into the land
Into the land
25 Now held by Yishmoel.

c. 1946/1946

Vesomachto

And do you rejoice upon your feast-day,
And be you but rejoicing ever
      La-la-la-la-la

And do you rejoice upon your feast-day
5 And be you but rejoicing ever
      La-la-la-la-la

et seq.

c. 1946/1946

LATIN

HORACE

Of the Ancient House of the Clinii [Version 1]

    Of the ancient house of the Clinii, prince,
    patron through whom alone my name
    has currency, myself status, Maecenas,
    to-day,
5 to-day vocation is my theme.

    Now, some there are for whom the chariots are the obsession
    they know all about the Olympics, including the records of
        dust raised:
    the turning wheels, the turn of the track accomplished,
    the King's Plate won – this, this sets them high, ichor in their
        veins,
10 gods.

    Others go for the trophies of politics,
        the honorary degree, the dignified sinecure, and even,
            perhaps
                    the freedom of a city.

There's also the wheat-king — him only his granary
15 bursting with cornucopia
will satisfy (of — the bushel in a wet year, and in a drought — ah ...)
As for the farmer — try and get him away from his muds and manures
to cleave in a Cyprian bottom the clear Myrtoan water.
Why not all the gold of Attalus will tear him away from his hoe!

20 The landlubber merchant, seasick, by the sou'wester
has no eyes for the beauty of the Icarian sea —
he dreams the city, can't get back to it fast enough
things maritime are much too green.

Then there's the connoisseur — give him his Massic
25 a proper milieu (a sacred stream)
a convenient shade (branches of arbutus)
and he'll lie there all day long with limbs outstretched — felicity!

The camp, music of wind-instruments, drums,
30 and war, that great frustrator of maternity —
is there anything else the soldier thinks about?

Well may his wife wait for him, but the huntsman
under the cold sky has other game in mind — a hind
the dogs are baying at,
35 a wild-pig, aye, of the breed of Lake Fucinus
snorting its net.

And I, too, O Prince, must confess my weakness.
It is the ivy-chaplet, that's what is in me mania,
the laurels raising me to the gods, granting me the company
of nymphs and satyrs
40 away from the masses,

that is, of course, as long as Euterpe grants me the freedom of
   the flute
as long as Polyhymnia continues to extend me my barbitos.

Yes, mania is the word, and if you, O Maecenas, would also
   deign to count me
as of the elect
45 surely I shall rise, I shall grow, head among the stars
I shall pluck me constellations for my laurels!

1955

Of the Ancient House of the Clinii [Version 2]

Of the ancient house of the Clinii, prince,
    O Maecenas,
patron through whom alone my name has currency
                        and myself status, to-day
5 my theme's vocation.

Now some there are for whom the chariot is the *ideé fixe;*
these know all about the Olympics,
                including the record of dusts raised,
the turn of the wheel, the turn of the track accomplished
10 the King's Plate won – this, this sends them high, ichor in the
   veins,
gods.

Others go for the trophies of politics:
    the honorary degree, the dignified sinecure, perhaps,
        even
                the freedom of a city.

15   And there's the
                                      regratteur —
   him only his granary, crammed with all Africa, will somewhat
      appease.
   Obsession, possession, cornucopia bursting his barns!

   But, one will ask, how about the farmer, sweating on his soil?
   Well, try to part him from his muds and manures!
20 Give him a choice,
   Yes, even to cleave in a Cyprian bottom the clear Myrtoan
      water!
   I say, not all the gold of Pergamus will tear him away from his
      hoe! ...

   Sea-sickness, that's what he fears, just like the landlubber
      merchant
   caught with his chattels on the Icarian sea. (Sou'wester!)
25 who groans for his city, his beautiful city, and bending over
      the rail
   avers things maritime as much too green.

   O various is man and his tastes various!

   1955

To Lydia

What have you done to the man, Lydia? What kind of love is it
That has turned our Sybaris into a wreck, a changeling?

I, I knew him when.
There wasn't a finer-looking man-about-town on the Campus
   Martius!

5 In the field there wasn't a man could sit in the saddle like he!
  The horses of Gaul – those wild ones! – they brooked him master!
  And who doesn't remember him on the beach by the Tiber?
  Or exercising in the palestra – what a body, what a stance!

                              But look at him now.
10 He's more scared of the wrestler's oils than of snake-blood;
  and he won't put his hand to a weapon – he! –
  who could throw his discus, and his javelin, right up with the champions,
                                    and farther!

  You've made him a claustrophobe, that's what you've made him, an introvert!
15 You have turned him, who once was like Achilles in his glory,
  into that earlier Achilles, you know, whom his mother, the sea-goddess Thetis
  dressed up like a woman, skirt, ribbons and all,
  fearing the slaughter of Troy, and the fate that awaited her son.
                              That's what you've done!

20 O Lydia, by all the gods!

  1955

To Leuconoe

This is the one taboo – to think of to-morrow!
            O Leuconoe
Life expectancy is for agents of insurance to dope out, not us.
Olympus is a gate one cannot crash.

5   As for going to the astrologers out of
                    Babylon –
that's the numbers racket all over again.

Take it as it comes, then, and as the day goes –
that's it!
Is this winter our last? Will Jupiter give us another?
10 The winds blow, the breakers break against the Tyrrhenian
   rocks.
It's all as uncertain as the weather.

Be wise, girl, and mix yourself another drink –
           but not with hope, not as much as a jigger of hope.
And do it now. Time, as they say, flies. Grab what you can
   to-day.
15 To-morrow – that's the original gyp.

1955

To L. Munatius Plancus

Let the Bureaux de Tourisme and Chambers of Commerce
                    proclaim the attractions
   of each their metropolises.
Let the public relations council of the city of Rhodes
5   super-colossolize its Colossus;
Mytilene, cash in on the credit of Sappho.
Let the same functionaries have their word, too,
       about the hotels of Corinth (with exposures on two
          seas!)
       about the vintage of Thebes (cellared by Bacchus
          himself!)

10 about the Temple of the Ephesian Diana, that great specific for
   the troubled mind!
                              also
Delphos and Apollo!
                              The vales of Thessaly!

I hear that the publicity man for the city of Athens
15   (Urbs Palladis Athenae)
   is composing, in terms at once erudite and lyrical,
   its baedeker in fourteen volumes!
                              That should get him remission of
                              taxes!

There is also a versatile one who is writing about both Argos
   and Mycenae:
20 it is said that he brings to his labours two incomparable
   qualities:
                   an admiration for its nouveaux-riches,
                   a love of horses.

Nonetheless I, I'm staying put.
Of course Lacedaemon has its lovely resorts,
25 beyond doubt the plains of rich Larissa are delectable country,
   but me, I'm happy where I am,
   here
   by the waters of the resounding Albunae
   by the romantic cataracts of Anis, in the beautiful groves of
      Tiburnus
30 (by the gods! they've got me doing it)
   here in the orchards of the thousand streams ...

1955

ABBREVIATIONS

TEXTUAL NOTES

EXPLANATORY NOTES

APPENDICES

INDEX OF TITLES

INDEX OF FIRST LINES

Abbreviations

The following abbreviations in the textual and explanatory notes conform to Usher Caplan's 'Bibliography and Index to Manuscripts,' in *The A.M. Klein Symposium*, ed. Seymour Mayne (Ottawa: University of Ottawa Press 1975), p. 89, with some additions.

WORKS BY KLEIN

Books and Pamphlets

H	*The Hitleriad*. New York: New Directions 1944
HNJ	*Hath Not a Jew ....* New York: Behrman's Jewish Book House 1940
HPC	*Huit poèmes canadiens (en anglais)*. Montreal: [Canadian Jewish Congress 1948]
P	*Poems*. Philadephia: The Jewish Publication Society of America 1944
PFC	*Poems of French Canada*. [Montreal: Canadian Jewish Congress 1947]
RC	*The Rocking Chair and Other Poems*. Toronto: The Ryerson Press 1948
SS	*The Second Scroll*. New York: Alfred A. Knopf 1951
SVP	*Seven Poems*. [Montreal: Canadian Jewish Congress 1948]

Volumes in the *Collected Works*

BS	*Beyond Sambation: Selected Essays and Editorials 1928–1955*. Ed. M.W. Steinberg and Usher Caplan. Toronto: University of Toronto Press 1982
LER	*Literary Essays and Reviews*. Ed. Usher Caplan and M.W. Steinberg. Toronto: University of Toronto Press 1987

876 / Abbreviations

Stories   Short Stories. Ed. M.W. Steinberg. Toronto: University of Toronto Press 1983

Published Volumes Containing Klein's Handwritten Revisions

HNJrev   revised copy of *Hath Not a Jew* ... [MS 2744]
Prev1   revised copy of *Poems* [MS 2745]
Prev2   revised copy of *Poems* [MS 2746]

Bound Typescript Volumes

22S   *XXII Sonnets* (1931) [MS 1464–89]
GH   *Gestures Hebraic* (1932) [MS 1490–1592]
GHP   *Gestures Hebraic and Poems* (1932) [MS 1733–1953]
P32   *Poems* (1932) [MS 1593–1732]
P34   *Poems* (1934) [MS 1954–2040]
SP   *Selected Poems* (1955) [MS 2041–116]

Periodicals

CF   *Canadian Forum*
CJC   *Canadian Jewish Chronicle*
MJ   *Menorah Journal*

Anthologies

Efros   Israel Isaac Efros. *Selected Poems of H.N. Bialik*. New York: Histadruth Ivrith of America 1948
Klinck and Watters   Carl F. Klinck and R.E. Watters. *Canadian Anthology*. Toronto: Gage Press 1955
Leftwich   Joseph Leftwich. *The Golden Peacock*. Cambridge, Mass.: Sci-art Publishers 1939
Schwarz   Leo W. Schwarz. *A Golden Treasury of Jewish Literature*. New York: Farrar and Rinehart Inc. 1937
Smith   A.J.M. Smith. *The Book of Canadian Poetry*. Chicago: University of Chicago Press 1943

REFERENCE WORKS

Caplan   Usher Caplan. 'A.M. Klein: An Introduction.' Dissertation. State University of New York at Stony Brook 1976

JE	*The Jewish Encyclopedia.* New York and London: Funk and Wagnalls Co. 1906
LOTD	Usher Caplan. *Like One That Dreamed: A Portrait of A.M. Klein.* Toronto: McGraw Hill Ryerson Ltd. 1982
OED	*The Oxford English Dictionary.* Oxford: Oxford University Press 1928.
S	Solomon Spiro. *Tapestry for Designs: Judaic Allusions in 'The Second Scroll' and 'The Collected Poems of A.M. Klein.'* Vancouver: University of British Columbia Press 1984

Textual Notes

ORIGINAL POEMS, 1937–1955

BLUEPRINT FOR A MONUMENT OF WAR. CF 17 (Sept. 1937), 208–9.
15 for] *ed.*; of CF
70/71 *line space supplied by ed.*
71/72 *line space supplied by ed.*

OF DAUMIERS A PORTFOLIO. 1. *New Frontier* 2, 4 (Sept. 1937), 10–11 (NF)*;
   2. MS 24643–4, revised tearsheets of NF (NFrev).
98 there] NFrev; they NF

BARRICADE SMITH: HIS SPEECHES. 1. MS 2498–9, a typescript [section X] (MS1);
   2. MS 2195–206, a typescript [sections I–IX] (MS2); 3. MS 2207–12, a typescript [sections VIII–X] (MS3); 4. CF 18 (Aug. 1938), 147–8 [sections I–II]*; (Sept. 1938), 173 [sections III–IV]*; (Oct. 1938), 210 [sections V–VII]*; (Nov. 1938), 242–3 [sections VIII–X]*.
Submitted to *Canadian Forum*, 25 June 1938 [letter of acknowledgment, 30 June 1938, MS 58].
MS2 groups together three sets of typescripts which differ slightly from one another in format: MS 2195–200 [sections I–IV]; MS 2201–4 [sections V–VII]; MS 2205–6 [sections VIII–IX]. The typescripts contain numerous minor revisions to accidentals, which are incorporated into CF.
10 à Emily] MS2; Emily CF
41 next] the next MS2
44 be] *ed.*; be? MS2, CF
73 dwellings, –] MS2; dwellings – CF
74/75 *no line space in* MS2; *line space in* CF
151 of] for MS2, MS3
160 crucibles] crucible MS2, MS3
194 Now] MS1, MS3; Now, CF

203/04 *line space in* MS1; *page break in* MS3; *no line space in* CF
206 typesetter] typesetters MS1
213 from] for MS1, MS3
245 king.] MS1, MS3; king, CF

OF CASTLES IN SPAIN. 1. CF 18 (June 1938), 79*; 2. a typescript in the Joseph N. Frank papers, Public Archives of Canada (F).

F was sent by Klein to Joseph Frank in a letter dated 5 Aug. 1938, in which he explains that, since he has only one copy of the poem, he is sending Frank a 'transcript' of CF.

In a letter to Sam Abramson, dated 4 June 1938, Klein says that the poem was composed 'several months ago.' In the same letter he says that all three poems in the sequence are dedicated to Abramson (not just the first, as in CF). In F the dedication is written in immediately after the main title.

CHILDE HAROLD'S PILGRIMAGE. 1. *Opinion* 8, 8 (Sept. 1938), 15–16 (O); 2. CJC, 18 Nov. 1938, p. 6; 3. *Judaean Annual* 10, 8 (June 1939), 7–10 (J); 4. HNJ, pp. 6–13* [version 1]; 5. HNJrev* [version 2, 90–163]; 6. MS 2248–51 (MS)* [version 2, 1–89].

The reading 'sick' [66] occurs only in HNJ. The other versions of the poem which contain the relevant passage, O and CJC, have 'pimp.' On the assumption that this change, which adversely affects the sense, was forced on Klein by his publisher, I have restored 'pimp' in version 1.

MS, which breaks off partway through line 90, is based on HNJrev. Version 2 follows MS for 1–89 and HNJrev for the rest. HNJrev retains 24–35 and 65–7, which are omitted in MS.

The two sets of notes which follow list variants from HNJ in O, CJC and J, and variants from MS in HNJrev for the section [1–89] where the two texts overlap.

Version 1
20 sores;] O, CJC, J; sores. HNJ
33 doorman] Briton O, J; agent CJC
65–8 *not in* J
66 pimp] O, CJC; sick HNJ
77 so much as say] say so much as CJC
88 you,] O, CJC, J; you HNJ
156 Not] Nor CJC

Version 2
1 Of yore yclept] 'Yclept of yore HNJrev
9 Shunted ... Hebrew] Bewildered, and a man who has been HNJrev
24–5 *not in* HNJrev

47 an ignoble] of the Marxian *HNJrev*
59 choler] gospels *HNJrev*
90 Is it, perhaps, – I ⟨seek⟩ [...] *MS*
93 punctiliousness] punct[?] *HNJrev*

TO THE CHIEF MUSICIAN, A PSALM OF THE BRATZLAVER, A PARABLE. 1. MS 2677, a typescript (MS1); 2. *New Directions* 8 (1944), 198; 3. MS 2678, a typescript (MS2); 4. *P*, p. 35*.
In a letter to Joseph Frank, 5 Aug. 1938, Klein reports that he is 'at work on a poetic rendition of Rabbi Nachman Bratzlaver's "Tale of the Seven Beggars" '; lines 9–14 of TO THE CHIEF MUSICIAN, A PSALM OF THE BRATZLAVER, WHICH HE WROTE DOWN AS THE STAMMERER SPOKE are quoted in 'Lillian Freiman: a Tribute,' *CJC*, 8 Nov. 1940, p. 3. Hence the assigned date of composition, c. 1938/1940, for all the 'Bratzlaver' poems.
Heading preceded by 'Psalm XLI' *in MS2, and by* 'Psalm XXIX' *in P*

TO THE CHIEF MUSICIAN, A PSALM OF THE BRATZLAVER, WHEN HE CONSIDERED HOW THE PIOUS ARE OVERWHELMED. 1. the unrevised typescript for MS1rev (MS1); 2. MS 2685–6 (MS1rev); 3. MS 2688–9, a typescript (MS2)*; 4. MS 2687, a revised copy of the first page of MS2 [1–18] (MS2rev)*.
For the date of composition see note to TO THE CHIEF MUSICIAN, A PSALM OF THE BRATZLAVER, A PARABLE.
Since the second page of MS2rev, containing 19–31, is missing, MS2 is the copy-text for these lines.
Heading 'Guerdon of Wit' *MS1; preceded by* 'Psalm 178' *in MS1rev, and by* 'Psalm XXXVI' *in MS2, MS2rev*
the Bratzlaver] Rabbi Nachman *altered to* the Bratzlaver *MS1rev*
Pious] Learned *altered to* Pious *MS1rev*
14 sighs and sighs] sighs and sighs and sighs *all other versions*

OF REMEMBRANCE. 1. MS 2679–80 (MS1); 2. the unrevised typescript for MS2rev (MS2); 3. MS 2681–2 (MS2rev); 4. *CJC*, 24 Oct. 1947, p. 6; 5. *SS*, pp. 191–3*.
For the date of composition see note to TO THE CHIEF MUSICIAN, A PSALM OF THE BRATZLAVER, A PARABLE.
Heading preceded by 'VII' *and by* 'Psalm 181' *in MS1, and by* 'Psalm XLIII' *in MS2, MS2rev*
Heading successively (a) 'To the Chief Musician, a Psalm of the Bratzlaver, to Bring to Remembrance' *(b)* 'To the Chief Musician, a Psalm of the Bratzlaver, a Psalm of the Beginning of Things' *MS1; same as (b) in MS2, MS2rev, CJC*
10 O infant swaddled in its tomb! *CJC*
15 conception of the breed] conception, bard of breed *CJC*
17 O distant memory] Sweet recollection *CJC*

20 odour of fruit] fruit's smell *altered to* odour of fruit MS1
21 O] Pure CJC
25 No thing] Nothing *all other versions*

TO THE CHIEF MUSICIAN: A PSALM OF THE BRATZLAVER, TOUCHING A GOOD
    GARDENER. 1. MS 2683–4, a typescript (MS); 2. P, pp. 37–9*.
Klein defended the reading 'filth' in 30 [1 July 1943], but the Jewish Publication
    Society insisted it be changed [3 Dec. 1943] and he was forced to comply
    [15 Dec. 1943]. The original reading has been restored.
For the date of composition see note to TO THE CHIEF MUSICIAN, A PSALM OF THE
    BRATZLAVER, A PARABLE.
Heading preceded by 'Psalm XLIV' *in* MS, *and by* 'Psalm XXXI' *in* P
18 Now] Yea MS
30 filth] MS; words P

TO THE CHIEF MUSICIAN, A PSALM OF THE BRATZLAVER, WHICH HE WROTE DOWN
    AS THE STAMMERER SPOKE. 1. MS 2690, a typescript (MS); 2. CJC, 8 Nov.
    1940, p. 3 [9–4]; 3. P, p. 36*.
For the date of composition see note to TO THE CHIEF MUSICIAN, A PSALM OF THE
    BRATZLAVER, A PARABLE.
Heading preceded by 'Psalm XLII' *in* MS, *and by* 'Psalm XXX' *in* P
9 truly] soothly MS, CJC
12 found] find CJC
14 Of worthy deed and meritorious act. MS, CJC

IN RE SOLOMON WARSHAWER. 1–2. CJC, 19 Apr. 1940, p. 3 [75–104] (CJC1);
    galleys for MJ, given by Klein to Leo Kennedy (LK); 3. MJ 28, 2 (Summer
    1940), 138–42; 4. *Smith*, pp. 391–5 (S1); 5. P, pp. 49–55* [version 1]; 6. CJC,
    27 Feb. 1953, p. 4 [75–89] (CJC2); 7. Prev1; 8. Prev2; 9. MS 2345–52 (MS);
    10. the unrevised typescript for SPrev (SP); 11–12. *Klinck and Watters*, pp. 385–9
    (KW); *Smith*, 3rd ed. (1957), pp. 352–6 (S2)* [version 2]; 13. SP 2082–9
    (SPrev).
The texts can be divided into two distinct groups: (1) CJC1, LK, MJ, S1, P, and CJC2;
    (2) Prev1, Prev2, MS, SP, KW, S2, SPrev. The texts in the second group probably
    date from 1953 at the earliest, since CJC2, which appeared in that year, reproduces
    the earlier unrevised version. P was revised in 3 closely related stages. Prev1
    contains numerous revisions to 1–93 [pp. 49–52]. The rest of Prev1 is unrevised,
    with a few minor exceptions. Prev2 follows the revisions in Prev1 very closely,
    and adds many new ones to the second half of the poem. However, at some point
    Klein decided to make additions to the poem which were too extensive to be
    written into the margins. MS contains complete drafts of three passages,
    which become 83–104, 116–69, and 177–96 in version 2; MS also contains

preliminary sketches for 166–9 and 184–91. The three drafts are numbered, and corresponding numbers in PREV2 indicate the passages they are to replace: 83–115, 127–38, and 145–8. Once Klein had decided to replace these passages entirely, he erased the initial revisions he had made to them in PREV2. The conflation of PREV2 and MS is the basis of SP. SPREV contains nine revisions, of which six appear in KW and not in S2; two appear in S2 and not in KW; and one appears in neither. KW and S2 are probably based on separate carbon copies of SP, which Klein revised on different occasions, without including revisions from the earlier version (whichever one it was) in the later. He did, however, in both cases, copy the revisions into the master copy of SP, as well as adding one more revision at a later date. All nine revisions in SPREV – substantives and, as far as can be determined, accidentals – occur in Klein's 1955 McGill reading, which must, therefore, be based on a later revision of SP than are KW and S2 (despite the 1957 publication date of S2). The reading itself contains a number of variants from SPREV, but they are all of the kind that could easily arise at a public reading, and Klein is almost certainly reading from SPREV as we have it.

Line spacing in version 2 follows SP, rather than S2, which is erratic; in several cases, when errors in S2 result in impossible readings, the correct readings have been silently restored from the earlier versions.

The two sets of notes that follow list variants from P in the first group of texts, and from S2 in the second. Not noted in the second set are: passages left unrevised in PREV1; the initial revisions in PREV2 to the passages later replaced from MS; the preliminary sketches in MS. All the texts contain an inconsistency which has been allowed to stand: in 63 'the S.S. *man* arrived'; in 159 (version 1)/197 (version 2) 'the S.S. *men* departed.' 'Men' is altered to 'man' in the McGill reading.

Version 1
30/31 *page break in* MJ; *line space in all other versions except* P
69 those mirrored in] the objects of *all other versions*
87 sounded] founded S1
92 although I do] albeit I *all other versions*
97 risen;] *all versions except* P; risen: P
103 twittering;] *all versions except* P; twittering: P
104 juvenescent] brightly plumaged *all other versions*
112 Yes] Aye *all other versions*
140–1 lycanthropous, / Leader] lycanthropous / Leader *all other versions*

Version 2
6 in rags disguised] SPREV, McGill reading; disguised in rags PREV1, PREV2, SP, KW; in rags, disguised S2
37 fingerprint,] *all versions except* S2; fingerprint! S2
54 my] our *altered to* his PREV1

84–8 The gardens, that were Babylon, that terrace is gloom; / And Egypt, Egypt, scarcely now recalled / By that lone star that sentries Pharaoh's tomb ... / Sounded on sand, Karthago, by water walled ... prev1
93 Pride of old triumph. Powers ... they were ... once! prev1
124 gleed] *all versions except s2*; greed s2
128 Sought out the king my father's God, His words, His ways. sprev, kw, McGill *reading*
134 fur!] *all versions except s2*; fur! ... s2
145 possible,] possible ms, sp, kw
185–91 Who does not know the modes of his statecraft? / Here motive is appetite; and oestric hate / Pregnator of its every imp and graft. / All love here is venereal ... Banned ... Or bait ... / The skulk and pounce of the forest / Here are norm, / Whence love's the aberration, love the treason, / Overt and covert, fact, style, form! *deleted in ms*
194 greets the] clots to sprev, McGill *reading*

FOR THE CHIEF PHYSICIAN. 1. *Opinion* 11, 12 (Oct. 1941), 28 (o); 2. p, p. 9*.
Accepted for publication by *Opinion*, 18 Nov. 1940 [ms 115].
Heading preceded by 'Psalm 161' *in* o, *and by* 'Psalm vii' *in* p

GRACE BEFORE POISON. 1. the unrevised typescript for *PoMs* (ms1); 2. *Poetry* archives (PoMs); 3. *Poetry* 58 (Apr. 1941), 6–7 (Po); 4. the unrevised typescript for ms2rev (ms2); 5. ms 2691–2 (ms2rev); 6. *New Directions* 8 (1944), 197; 7. cjc, 24 Oct. 1947, p. 6; 8. ss, pp. 190–1*.
Receipt acknowledged by E.K. Brown, 12 Nov. 1940 [ms 113]. PoMs is part of a group of typescripts stamped 'Jan 22 1941.'
Heading preceded by 'Psalm 154' *in* ms1, PoMs, Po, *and by* 'Psalm x' *in* ms2, ms2rev
Heading 'To the Chief Musician upon Shoshannim. A Song of Loves' *all other versions*
8 And] *illegible in* ms1; Yea, PoMs, Po

MASCHIL OF ABRAHAM: A PRAYER WHEN HE WAS IN THE CAVE.
1. *Reconstructionist* 6, 18 (10 Jan. 1941), 12 (r); 2. p, pp. 2–3*; 3. prev2; 4. prev1.
Submitted to *Reconstructionist*, 21 Nov. 1940 [ms 117].
Heading preceded by 'Psalm 152' *in* r, *and by* 'Psalm ii' *in* p, prev1, prev2
11–12 That proved, by minus and by plus, / The vacuum ubiquitous. prev1
14 age] fear prev1
15 scientist] sciolist prev2, prev1
19–20 *not in* prev1
24/25 Surely I cannot, nor desire / To speak, as rabbi or as friar. r

25 How shall I] How else, then, R
29–32 *not in* PREV1
33 For I would that they knew, as I, PREV1
34 undebatable] first and final R
36 simple] *not in* PREV1
39–40 And ... / Do] That will complete the theorem, / And R

A PRAYER OF ABRAHAM THAT HE BE FORGIVEN FOR BLASPHEMY. 1. MS 2566 (MS); 2. MJ 29 (Autumn 1941), 280*.
Submitted to *Menorah Journal*, 5 Dec. 1940 [MS 119].
Heading preceded by 'Psalm 166' *in* MS, MJ

A PRAYER OF THE AFFLICTED, WHEN HE IS OVERWHELMED. 1. the unrevised typescript for MSrev (MS); 2. *Opinion* 11, 12 (Oct. 1941), 28*; 3. MS 2567 (MSrev).
Accepted for publication by *Opinion*, 18 Nov. 1940 [MS 115]. MSrev appears to date from the early fifties.
Heading preceded by 'Psalm 160' *in all versions*
5 And ... fine] The times are good MSrev

A PSALM FOR FIVE HOLY PILGRIMS, YEA, SIX ON THE KING'S HIGHWAY. 1. MJ 29 (Autumn 1941), 280–1; 2. P, p. 19*.
Submitted to *Menorah Journal*, 5 Dec. 1940 [MS 119].
Heading preceded by 'Psalm 167' *in* MJ, *and by* 'Psalm XIV' *in* P
8 rainbows] rainbow MJ
16 Not taste, touch, smell, sound, sight, his bait, MJ

A PSALM OF ABRAHAM CONCERNING THE ARROGANCE OF THE SON OF MAN.
1. MS 2592, a typescript (MS1); 2. MJ 29 (Autumn 1941), 283*; 3. MS 2593, a typescript (MS2).
Submitted to *Menorah Journal*, 5 Dec. 1940 [MS 119].
Heading preceded by 'Psalm 171' *in* MS1, MJ, *and by* 'Psalm XXXV' *in* MS2
16 grand,] MS1, MS2; grand MJ

A PSALM OF ABRAHAM OF THAT WHICH WAS VISITED UPON HIM. 1. the unrevised typescript for MS1rev (MS1); 2. MJ 29 (Autumn 1941), 284; 3. MS 2594 (MS1rev); 4. MS 2595, a typescript (MS2); 5. CJC, 21 Nov. 1952, p. 4*; 6. MS 2596, a revised copy of MS2 (MS2rev); 7. MS 2571 (MS3); 8. SP 2092.
Submitted to *Menorah Journal*, 5 Dec. 1940 [MS 119].
CJC has 'know' in 3, but this has been emended to 'hear,' the reading in all other versions. 'Hear' makes better sense; the typesetter probably misread 'I hear him' in 3 as 'I know him,' through confusion with 'I know his' in 2.

Heading preceded by 'Psalm 173' *in* MS1, MJ, *and by* 'Psalm xxxv' *in* MS1rev, MS2; 'The Prowler' MS3, SP
Was Visited] Is Visited MS1, MJ, MS1rev, MS2, MS2rev
3 hear] *all versions except* CJC; know CJC
7 *successively (a)* Or by the whorling of an inky thumb, *(b)* Or by the whorlèd impress of a thumb, MS2rev; *same as (b) in* MS3, SP
8 a strange new] its sombre MS1, MJ, MS1rev, MS2; its metal MS2rev, MS3, SP
11–12 *successively (a)* Shall I fling open a window, and shout *Police!* / I do not dare. He's of my very own kin. *(b)* But still I dare not cry out, shout *Police!..* / I know him. He's my very own flesh and blood. *(c)* But still I dare not cry out, shout *Police!..* / Because I know him. *And* he's my own kin. MS2rev; *(c) altered to (d)* Should I then run to a window, and shout *Police!?* / I dare not. For I know him. My own kin. MS3; *same as (d) in* SP

A PSALM OF ABRAHAM, PRAYING A GREEN OLD AGE. 1. the unrevised typescript for MSrev (MS); 2. MJ 29 (Autumn 1941), 283–4*; 3. MS 2597 (MSrev). Submitted to *Menorah Journal*, 5 Dec. 1940 [MS 119].
Heading preceded by 'Psalm 172' *in* MS, MSrev, *and by* 'Psalm 171' *in* MJ
5 birds'] MSrev; birds MS; bird's MJ

A PSALM OF ABRAHAM, TO BE WRITTEN DOWN AND LEFT ON THE TOMB OF RASHI. 1. *Opinion* 10, 7 (May 1940), 10 (O); 2. P, pp. 42–3; 3. CJC, 10 Apr. 1953, p. 10*; 4. PrevI; 5. SP 2110–11.
Heading 'Epistle to Be Left on the Tomb of Rashi' O; *preceded by* 'Psalm xxxiv' *in* P, PrevI
8 Law] *all versions except* CJC; law CJC
17–19 *not in* PrevI, SP
26–32 Much that is dim, / Inscrutable past all the targumim. / Ours is a time, great rabbi, like your time, / A time of murder and despising of life. / It is a flood age. Giant wickedness, / Constrict in dearth – the world is not enough – / Makes room with slaughter of lives deemed excess. / It is the age that evildom begat. / The cry of blood goes up, but no one hears. / O we do long for rest and Ararat / As all our arks are floated out on tears. PrevI, SP
28 these days,] P; these days O, CJC
30 mere glut] the glut O, P
39 youth,] O, SP; youth P, CJC, PrevI
43/44 *line space in all versions except* CJC
47 seed,] P, PrevI, SP; seed O, CJC

A PSALM OF ABRAHAM, TOUCHING HIS GREEN PASTURES. 1. *Poetry* archives (PoMS); 2. a typescript in the Ralph Gustafson papers, University of Saskatchewan Library; 3. *Poetry* 58 (Apr. 1941), 6 (Po); 4. P, p. 5*.

Receipt acknowledged by E.K. Brown, 12 Nov. 1940 [MS 113]. *PoMS* is stamped 'Jan 22 1941.'
Heading 'Psalm 151' *PoMS, Po; preceded by* 'Psalm IV' *in P*

A PSALM OF ABRAHAM, WHEN HE WAS SORE PRESSED. 1. *Opinion* 11, 12 (Oct. 1941), 28 (O); 2. *P*, p. 4*.
Accepted for publication by *Opinion*, 18 Nov. 1940 [MS 115].
Heading preceded by 'Psalm 159' *in O, and by* 'Psalm III' *in P*

A PSALM OF ABRAHAM, WHICH HE MADE BECAUSE OF FEAR IN THE NIGHT. 1. *MJ* 29 (Autumn 1941), 281–2; 2. *First Statement* 1, 14 (1943), 1 (FS); 3. *P*, pp. 44–5*; 4. Prev1.
Submitted to *Menorah Journal*, 5 Dec. 1940 [MS 119].
Heading preceded by 'Psalm 168' *in MJ, and by* 'Psalm XXXV' *in P, Prev1*
4 An] A *Prev1*
11 carmined] its carmined *MJ, FS*
21 angel's drinking-cup] angels' drinking-cups *FS*

A PSALM OF JUSTICE, AND ITS SCALES. 1. *MJ* 29 (Autumn 1941), 282; 2. *P*, p. 29*; 3. Prev1; 4–5. SP 2091; MS 2599, a copy of SP (MS).
Submitted to *Menorah Journal*, 5 Dec. 1940 [MS 119].
Heading preceded by 'Psalm 169' *in MJ, and by* 'Psalm XXIII' *in P, Prev1;* 'Psalm of Justice' *SP, MS, McGill reading*
3–4 Armed with a sky-blue blueprint in my hand, / Safe combination in my memory, *MJ*
6 is mis-weighed] was mis-weighed *Prev1, SP, MS, McGill reading*

A PSALM OF RESIGNATION. 1. *MJ* 29 (Autumn 1941), 285; 2. *CJC*, 10 Apr. 1953, p. 10*.
Submitted to *Menorah Journal*, 5 Dec. 1940 [MS 119].
Heading preceded by 'Psalm 175' *in MJ*
4 but say] say *MJ*

A PSALM, TO BE PRESERVED AGAINST TWO WICKED WORDS. 1. MS 2603, a typescript (MS1); 2. MS 2604, a revised copy of MS1 (MS1rev); 3. *P*, pp. 12–13*; 4. Prev1; 5. Prev2.
Submitted to *Jewish Frontier*, 4 Dec. 1940 [MS 118].
Heading preceded by 'Psalm 163' *in MS1, and by* 'Psalm IX' *in P, Prev1, Prev2*
3 at … terrible] with a vicarious *Prev1*
4 When I behold the beggar, looked askance, *MS1, MS1rev*
spurned] humbled *Prev1*
6 his fellow's] that great man's *Prev1*

7 beg my daily] come to beg my PREV1
11 Thou who know'st] You who know men's PREV1
12 Know'st] Know that PREV1
14–15 all ... parts] all that must debase PREV1
15 even ... noblest] were I even of noble PREV2
20 Lord] O Lord MS1, MS1rev

A PSALM TO TEACH HUMILITY. 1. *MJ* 29 (Autumn 1941), 284–5; 2. *P*, p. 33*; 3. SP 2056.
Submitted to *Menorah Journal*, 5 Dec. 1940 [MS 119].
Heading preceded by 'Psalm 174' *in* MJ, *by* 'Psalm XXVII' *in* P, *and by* 'Psalm XXXIX' *in* SP

SHIGGAION OF ABRAHAM WHICH HE SANG UNTO THE LORD. 1. *Opinion* 11, 12 (Oct. 1941), 28 (O); 2. *P*, p. 30*.
Accepted for publication by *Opinion*, 18 Nov. 1940 [MS 115].
Heading preceded by 'Psalm 158' *in* O, *and by* 'Psalm XXIV' *in* P

A SONG OF DEGREES. 1. *Reconstructionist* 7, 3 (21 Mar. 1941), 6; 2. *P*, p. 6*; 3. PREV1.
Submitted to *Reconstructionist*, 21 Nov. 1940 [MS 117].
1 doth get] gets PREV1
6–8 His teachers – the beasts of the field! PREV1

TO THE CHIEF BAILIFF, A PSALM OF THE KING'S WRIT. 1. MS 2673, a typescript (MS1); 2. *MJ* 29 (Autumn 1941), 282–3*; 3. MS 2674, a typescript (MS2).
Submitted to *Menorah Journal*, 5 Dec. 1940 [MS 119].
Heading preceded by 'Psalm 170' *in* MS1, MJ, *and by* 'Psalm XXXVII' *in* MS2

TO THE CHIEF MUSICIAN, AL-TASCHITH, MICHTAM OF ABRAHAM; WHEN ONE SENT, AND THEY WATCHED THE HOUSE TO KILL HIM. 1. *Poetry* archives (POMS); 2. *Poetry* 58 (Apr. 1941), 7–8; 3. MS 2675–6 (MS); 4. *New Directions* 8 (1944), 198–9 (ND)*.
Receipt acknowledged by E.K. Brown, 12 Nov. 1940 [MS 113]. POMS is part of a group of typescripts stamped 'Jan 22 1941.'
Heading preceded by 'Psalm 155' *in* POMS, P, *and by* 'Psalm LX' *in* MS
6/7 *line space in* ND, *but in no other versions*

TO THE CHIEF MUSICIAN, A PSALM OF ISRAEL, TO BRING TO REMEMBRANCE.
1. *Opinion* 11, 12 (Oct. 1941), 26 (O); 2. *P*, p. 32*.
Accepted for publication by *Opinion*, 18 Nov. 1940 [MS 115].
Heading preceded by 'Psalm 157' *in* O, *and by* 'Psalm XXVI' *in* P

TO THE CHIEF MUSICIAN, WHO PLAYED FOR THE DANCERS. 1. MS 2693, a typescript (MS1); 2. P, p. 17*.
Submitted to *Jewish Frontier*, 4 Dec. 1940 [MS 118].
Heading preceded by 'Psalm 165' *in* MS1
10–11 praised ... fathom] told its wonder; aye, / But no man has told MS1

TO THE PROPHETS, MINOR AND MAJOR, A PSALM OR SONG. 1. *Opinion* 11, 12 (Oct. 1941), 28 (O); 2. P, p. 31*.
Accepted for publication by *Opinion*, 18 Nov. 1940 [MS 115].
Heading preceded by 'Psalm 162' *in* O, *and by* 'Psalm xxv' *in* P

A BENEDICTION FOR THE NEW MOON. 1. MS 2233–4 (MS); 2. P, p. 26*.
Heading preceded by 'Psalm xxviii' *in* MS, *and by* 'Psalm xxi' *in* P
2/3 The moon glows in the sky, / And for the sons of men, there glows the circle in the brain! *before line space in* MS
11 mariners ... of] men who go down to the sea in MS
12 *precedes line 10 in* MS
12/13 *no line space in* MS

A PRAYER OF ABRAHAM, AGAINST MADNESS. 1. *Jewish Frontier* 9, 4 (Mar. 1942), 8 (JF); 2. P, pp. 27–8*; 3. Prev1.
Heading 'A Psalm of Abraham on Madness' JF; *preceded by* 'Psalm xxii' *in* P, Prev1
17–20 Who sit, each docile in his cell / When yet a narrower cubicle, / The nightmare brain, the daydream skull / Constrict them new degrees of hell. Prev1
23–4 He knows his wife and child no more. / He is unclean, and fearsome, weird! JF
27 grace, Thy] Prev1; grace, thy JF, P
mortal] fatal Prev1

A PSALM OF ABRAHAM, WHEN HE HEARKENED TO A VOICE, AND THERE WAS NONE. 1. MS 2572 (MS1); 2. the unrevised typescript for SP (MS2); 3. *First Statement* 1, 14 (1943), 2 (FS); 4. MS 2598 (MS3); 5. P, p. 1*; 6. Prev2; 7. Prev1; 8. SP 2112.
Heading 'Psalm' MS1, MS2, SP; *preceded by* 'Psalm 182' *in* MS3, *and by* 'Psalm I' *in* P, Prev2, Prev1
5 these] the MS2, FS, SP
I] one MS1, MS2, FS, SP
6 to ... doubt] to resolve the involved doubt Prev2; will resolve the blotted doubt Prev1, SP
8 When] And MS1, MS2, FS, SP

A PSALM OF TIME AND THE FIRMAMENT. MS 2602.
Heading preceded by 'Psalm 176'

A SONG FOR WANDERERS. P, p. 18.
Included among the psalms in the original MS of *Poems*.
Klein altered 'Nor of travelled roads' to 'Not of travelled roads' in 16 at the suggestion of the Jewish Publication Society [letter to JPS, 15 Sept. 1943].

A PSALM OF ABRAHAM, CONCERNING THAT WHICH HE BEHELD UPON THE HEAVENLY SCARP. 1. MS 2587–8 (MS1); 2–3. MS 2589–90, a typescript (MS2); a typescript in the Klein papers, Canadian Jewish Congress Archives (MS3); 4. a typescript in the Ralph Gustafson papers, University of Saskatchewan Library (MS4); 5. *Poetry* archives (PoMS); 6. *Poetry* 59 (Mar. 1942), 315–16 (Po); 7. Smith, p. 396 (S); 8. *New Directions* 8 (1944), 196 (ND); 9. P, pp. 7–8; 10. PrevI; 11. Prev2; 12. SP 2080–1; 13. *Klinck and Watters*, p. 384 (KW)*.
Submitted to *Poetry*, 13 Aug. 1941. MS3 is included in a set of lecture notes dated 28 Oct. 1941.
The reading 'gutter' [20] occurs in all versions of the poem before P. For P, Klein was forced to change 'gutter' to the innocuous 'pavement,' by his publishers, the Jewish Publication Society, despite his strenuous objections. Although Klein let the new reading stand in later versions of the poem based on P, the original has been restored for the reasons given by Klein in his letter to the JPS defending 'gutter,' dated 1 July 1943: 'In stanza 4, the word "gutter" is underlined, and your reader suggests "wall or street," – but no; the correct word is "gutter" which is more picturesque and which emphasizes the humiliation of the "gentle violinist." '
No heading in MS1; heading preceded by 'Psalm VIII' *in MS2, MS3, and by* 'Psalm VI' *in P, PrevI, Prev2;* 'Upon the Heavenly Scarp' *PoMS, Po, S, ND*
1 that] the eighth MS1
4 seraphic] angelic *altered to* seraphic MS1
6 where] when MS1, MS2, MS3, MS4, PoMS
7 his] the MS1, MS2, MS3, MS4, PoMS, Po, S, ND, P
9 imp] saint MS1
10 thinking] if he thought MS1
11 *successively (a)* But singing, jubilant, pointed a quivering wing *(b)* But pointing to the earth and its [...] *(c)* Only he psalmodied, and mischievously *(d)* Only with every ⟨paean and every⟩ Te Deum MS1
12 He pointed to the earth, its unspeakable horde. MS1
abhorrèd] unspeakable MS1, MS2, MS3, MS4, PoMS, Po, S, ND, P; abhorred PrevI, Prev2, SP
14/15 ⟨He saw the violinist whose frenzied bars / Beat on the gates of heaven, with such wild [...]⟩ MS1

15 He saw a pious man tear at his scars. *altered to* He saw a man tear at his flogged scars. MS1
16 And] He MS1
20 Such] That MS1
gutter] MS1, MS2, MS3, MS4, PoMS, Po, S, ND; pavement P, Prev1, Prev2, SP, KW
24 before ... dry] spilt, before it is yet dry *altered to* before it is quite dry MS1
26 ceased ... earth] *successively (a)* he sang no more *(b)* sang no more *(c)* ceased pointing to the earth MS1
27 now ... flaw'd] who'd spied the earthly sod MS1, MS2, MS3, MS4, PoMS, Po, S, ND, P
29 And the good] And then the *altered to* And the good MS1
30 Sent the two Sodom angels down back to earth. *altered to* Sent the two angels of Sodom down to earth. MS1

A PSALM OR PRAYER – PRAYING HIS PORTION WITH BEASTS. 1. MS 2573–4 (MS1); 2. MS 2575 [17–20] (MS2); 2. *Hebrew Union College Monthly* 29, 4 (Apr. 1942), 15 (HUC); 3. *First Statement* 1, 14 (1943), 2; 4. P, p. 34*.
Submitted to *Hebrew Union College Monthly*, 5 Aug. 1941 [MS 147].
Heading 'Psalm' MS1, HUC; *preceded by* 'Psalm XXVIII' *in* P
6 the child Isaac] Isaac *altered to* the child Isaac MS1
17 *successively (a)* And teach me, [...] *(b)* And dearer than all these friends I bless [...] *(c)* O let me befriend [...] *(d)* Above all teach me the blessedness MS1
18 dear] ⟨that⟩ saintly MS1
20 hallow it] break its silence MS1

BALLAD OF QUISLINGS. 1. MS 2156–7 (MS1); 2. MS 2158–9, a typescript (MS2); 3. *Saturday Night* 56 (30 Aug. 1941), 25 (SN); 4. CJC, 17 Apr. 1953, p. 4*.
Receipt acknowledged by *Saturday Night*, 22 Aug. 1941 [MS 148].
7 be not] may not be *all other versions*
13 damnèd] SN; damned *all other versions*
16 with] who brings us *altered to* with MS1
whose shadow's] a-standing *all other versions*
21 and be] and he be *all other versions*

BALLAD OF THE DAYS OF THE MESSIAH. 1. MS 2161–2 (MS1); 2. MS 2163–4 (MS2); 3. MS 2165–6, a typescript (MS3); 4. *Hebrew Union College Monthly* 29, 1 (Nov. 1941), 13 (HUC); 5. CJC, 5 Dec. 1941, p. 12; 6. P, pp. 61–2*.
7 O Leviathan] Leviathan MS1
10 good] fish *altered to* good MS1
13 Yea] MS2, MS3, HUC, CJC; And MS1; Yes P
good ... good] saints, for the saints *altered to* good, for the good MS1
15 ruddy] sacred MS1

blood] gas MS1
17 Aged ... been] *successively (a)* Kept and aged for so long *(b)* [?] and aged for so long *(c)* aged for so long, as it has been MS1
20 Messiah's falling herald] the good Messiah's herald MS1; Messiah's herald MS2, MS3, HUC, CJC
21 'Tis] HUC, CJC; Hear, MS1; 'Tis, MS2, MS3, P
25–30 *altered from stanza 2 to stanza 5 in* MS1

BALLAD OF THE DREAM THAT WAS NOT DREAMED. MS 2167–8.
17 It seems] Methinks *altered to* It seems
22 A] The *altered to* A

BALLAD OF THE EVIL EYE. 1. MS 2169–70 (MS1); 2. MS 2171–2, a typescript (MS2)*.

BALLAD OF THE NUREMBERG TOWER CLOCK. 1. MS 2173–4 (MS1); 2–3. MS 2175, a typescript (MS2); the unrevised typescript for MS3rev1 and MS3rev2 (MS3); 4. MS 2178–9 (MS3rev1); 5. MS 2180–1 (MS3rev2); 6. MS 2176–7 (MS4); 7. *Saturday Night* 57 (8 Nov. 1941), 10 (SN); 8. CJC, 24 Mar. 1944, p. 4*.
Receipt acknowledged by *Saturday Night*, 22 Aug. 1941 [MS 148].
8 heiled ... heiled] hailed, and they hailed MS2, MS3, MS3rev1
10 from] MS1, SN; for *all other versions*
11 words] voice *altered to* words MS1
12 Drowned out] Annulled SN
13 they] it *altered to* they MS1
shouted, even] defying heaven *in margin in* MS3rev1
14 clock] ⟨tower⟩ clock MS1
23 O in that] in that last SN

BALLAD OF THE NURSERY RHYMES. 1. MS 2182 (MS1); 2. MS 2183, a typescript (MS2); 3. CF 21 (Nov. 1941), 244; 4. CJC, 24 Mar. 1944, p. 4 (CJC1); 5. MS 2184, a revised tearsheet of CF (CFrev); 6. CJC, 24 Oct. 1952, p. 4*.
Submitted to *Poetry*, 13 Aug. 1941.
2 the cities] cities MS1, MS2, CF, CJC1
4 his] its CFrev
6 He wandered] Wandering *all other versions*
11 his] for *all other versions*
14 in] from *altered to* in MS1
15 all the bridges that were] London bridge that was all *all other versions*
16 bloods of the race of man] blood of an Englishman *all other versions*
19 bombed] cracked *altered to* bombed MS1
20 moon ... its] hornets of the moon's honeyed *altered to* moon, and the hornets on its MS1

BALLAD OF THE THWARTED AXE. 1. MS 2185–6 (MS1); 2. MS 2187–8 (MS2); 3. MS 2189–90, a typescript (MS3); 4. CF 21 (Oct. 1941), 244; 5. CJC, 24 Mar. 1944, p. 4; 6. P, pp. 59–60*.
Submitted to *Poetry*, 13 Aug. 1941.
Heading Ballad] The Ballad MS1
Subheading not in MS1, MS2, MS3
German] German's CJC
3 on a writ] in a book *altered to* on a writ MS1
6 sparking] hardy MS1
10 The body, manacled,] The corpse in the dock MS1
18 lust, and warpèd lore] lust and lore MS1
22 He weaves] Has woven you *altered to* He weaves MS1
25 robe] robes MS1, MS2
26 red-lined] *successively (a)* little *(b)* fatal *(c)* red-lined MS1; red-lined *altered to* little red-lined MS2; little red-lined MS3, CF, CJC
27 blows] reads *altered to* blows MS1
32 any judge's] the most terrible MS1
33–6 MS1 *has two versions of this stanza. The first is:* The business of the court is done. / The motions have been made. / And justice reigns, according to / The set rules of the trade. *The second, incomplete version, added to the right of the first, is:* The business of the court is done / The pantomime [...] / And sawdust blots the red ink of / The ⟨still⟩ bleeding documents.
33 The business of the court is done *altered to* The court is done ⟨now⟩ with its assize MS2
38 thorough] the *altered to* the lean MS1

BALLAD OF THE WEREWOLVES. 1. MS 2191 (MS1); 2. MS 2192 (MS2); 3. MS 2193, a typescript (MS3); 4. MS 2194, a revised copy of MS3 (MS3rev)*.
Receipt acknowledged by *Canadian Forum*, 1 Oct. 1941 [MS 148-A].
3 Chest] Breast MS1
8 It is the ichor of the Trinity! MS1; It is champagne [...] *altered to* Tis good strong rum for Our trinity! MS2
10 swig] taste *altered to* swig MS2
12 Skoal] Drink MS1; Drink *altered to* Skoal MS2
the] sleep's MS1
19 here's] here is MS1

OF THE FRIENDLY SILENCE OF THE MOON. 1. MS 2493 (MS1); 2. MS 2494 (MS2); 3. the unrevised typescript for MS3rev (MS3); 4. MS 2496, a typescript (MS4); 5. MS 2497, a revised version of MS4 (MS4rev); 6. MS 2495 (MS3rev)*.
Submitted to *Poetry*, 13 Aug. 1941.

Heading 'The Ballad of the Mortal Moon' MS1; 'Ballad of the Mortal Moon' *altered to* 'Of the Friendly Silence of the Moon' MS2
2 Slip] Sheathe *all other versions*
8 His cross-bones are seen plain *altered to* As the metre ticks in his brain. MS1; The metre ticks in his brain. MS2, MS3, MS4, MS4rev
9–10 *follow* 11–12 *in* MS1 *and originally in* MS2
9 your sulphurous] that poisonous MS1; that sulphurous *altered to* your sulphurous MS2
15 It is the moon] Tis moonlight that MS1
16 creep] deep *all other versions*

POLISH VILLAGE. 1. MS 2534 (MS1); 2. MS 2535 (MS2); 3. *Saturday Night* 58 (31 Jan. 1942), 3 (SN)*.
Receipt acknowledged by *Saturday Night*, 22 Aug. 1941 [MS 148].
6 Why] MS1; why MS2, SN
11 man] MS1, MS2; Man SN

SENNET FROM GHEEL. 1. MS 2613 (MS1); 2–3. MS 2614, a typescript; MS 2616, a typescript; 4. *Poetry* archives; 5. *Poetry* 59 (Mar. 1942), 316–17; 6. MS 2615, a typescript; 7. *New Directions* 8 (1944), 195*.
Submitted to *Poetry*, 13 Aug. 1941.
13 Zuruck] Back *altered to* Zuruck MS1
our] the *altered to* our MS1

YEHUDA HALEVI, HIS PILGRIMAGE. 1. MS 5408–13 [298–357] (MS1); 2. MS 5411–13, a typescript [298–357] (MS2); 3. *CJC*, 19 Sept. 1941, pp. 9–12 (CJC1); 4. the unrevised typescript for MS3rev (MS3); 5. MS 2727–37 (MS3rev); 6. MS 2712–26, a typescript (MS4); 7. *CJC*, 9 May 1941, p. 3 [338–47] (CJC2); 8. *P*, pp. 65–82*; 9. *CJC*, 12 Dec. 1947, p. 4 [298–357] (CJC3); 10. *CJC*, 20 Aug. 1948, p. 4 [298–357] (CJC4).
MS1, MS2, CJC3, and CJC4 consist of Klein's translation of Yehuda Halevi's ODE TO ZION, which was probably completed earlier than the rest of the poem.
In the title, the spelling 'Halevi' of CJC1, rather than 'Ha-Levi,' has been followed, since the former is used throughout the body of the poem in all versions.
Klein altered 'her' to 'she' in 286 of *P*, at the suggestion of the Jewish Publication Society, but he commented that it was a 'somewhat pedantic correction, since popular usage justifies the other' [letter to JPS, 1 July 1943].
Heading Halevi] CJC1; Ha-Levi *all other versions*
2 his] the CJC1
6 By mere remembrance of that wondrous tale! CJC1
18 the pale ... bold] jongleur and the princess he consoled CJC1; the pale princess and jongleur bold MS3, MS3rev

stanza 8 not in CJC1, MS3, MS3rev
82 Still] Yet *all other versions*
126 Alas, that that was long ago, so many years agone! *all other versions*
149 beggar, ... a] beggar in tatters, yea, an unknown *all other versions*
170 I am forsaken in this den, forlore, *all other versions*
191 Conjured] Conjure CJC1
205 across the perilous] yea, and across the *all other versions*
266 there] yea, *all other versions*
270 T'was [sic] vain to seek a dream in the illumined air CJC1
286 she] her *all other versions*
297 song] a song CJC1
303 thy hills] the hills CJC3
304 he] I *altered to* he MS1
306 Where he] Or I *altered to* Or he MS1; Or he MS2
313 where] MS1, MS2, MS3, MS3rev; Where CJC1, MS4, P, CJC3, CJC4
321 there,] MS1, MS2; there *all other versions*
bleeding] naked MS1, MS2
331 They ... they] Weeping thy ruins, they do MS1; Weeping thy wine, they do MS2
332 striving towards] longing for *altered to* striving toward MS1; striving toward MS2
captivity.] MS1, MS2; captivity, *all other versions*
333 bend the knee] genuflect MS1, MS2
335 Remembering,] MS1, MS2; Remembering *all other versions*
347 thou] MS1, MS2, CJC1, MS3, MS3rev, MS4, CJC2; Thou P, CJC3, CJC4
348–57 *follow 317 in* MS1, MS2
348 granted] grant me MS1, MS2
might] may MS1, MS2
350 gave] give MS1, MS2
might] may MS1, MS2
354 thee] them MS1, MS2
362 But ... not] Alas, not so was it *all other versions*
368 knows] know *all other versions*
378 charmèd] MS3, MS3rev; charmed CJC1, MS4, P

IN MEMORIAM: ARTHUR ELLIS. 1. MS 2317–21 (MS1)* [version 1]; 2. MS 2326–8 (MS2); 3. MS 2322–5 (MS3); 4. MS 2330–2 (MS4); 5. the unrevised typescript for MS5rev (MS5); 6. MS 2339–41 (MS5rev); 7. the unrevised typescript for MS6rev1 and MS6rev2 (MS6); 8. MS 2333–5 (MS6rev1); 9. the unrevised typescript for MS7rev (MS7); 10. *Circle* 7–8 (1946), 59–60 (C)* [version 2]; 11. MS 2336–8 (MS6rev2); 12. MS 2342–4 (MS7rev); 13. MS 2308–12 (MS8); 14. MS 2313–6 (MS9); 15. SP 2100–2* [version 3].

The texts can be divided into four distinct groups, largely on the basis of variants in stanzas 1, 3, and 5: (1) MS1, MS2, and MS3. The date 1941 has been assigned to this group, since SP, a much later version, is dated 1941, which probably refers to the original date of composition as Klein recalled it many years later. 'Early draft' has been pencilled into MS3 in what appears to be a later hand. (2) MS4, MS5, MS5rev, MS6, MS6rev1, MS7, and C. (3) MS6rev2, a typescript with numerous minor revisions not adopted in later versions. (4) MS7rev, MS8, MS9, and SP. MS8 consists of a number of preliminary sketches for 1–6. MS9 is a complete draft, with two versions of stanza 1, the second marked 'June 15/54 draft.'

Version 1 has been emended in a few instances, since punctuation in MS1 is incomplete and 59 is missing one word: 'task' has been supplied from MS2–MS4. The following list includes important variants from C [version 2] which do not occur in either MS1 [version 1] or SP [version 3].

10 with ... bandied] Hearkening lore of MS4, MS5, MS5rev, MS6
11 swift embarrassed] horizontal MS4, MS5
16 Death;] MS3, MS4, MS5, MS5rev, MS6, MS6rev1, MS7, MS6rev2; Death MS1, MS2; Death: C; Death ... MS7rev, MS9, SP
17 And loosened their ties for comfort and for fun. MS2
21–2 noose, / the] ed.; noose / the MS6rev1, MS7, C; *not in other versions*
22 That was to give *their* victims sepulture; MS2; That was to bring *their* victims sepulture; MS3; That hastened *their* deeds to their sepulture; MS4, MS5, MS5rev, MS6, MS6rev2
28 Your] *all versions except* C; You C
29 In crime and clue, – and Innocence was fake. MS2, MS3, MS4, MS5, MS5rev, MS6
32 trite ... gastronomy] secrets eavesdropped near eternity, MS3; trite confession, dawn's eternity MS4, MS5, MS5rev, MS6
35 I drank the *listen* of your pilgrimage. MS2
36 Tempted and charmed and simply sickened me. MS3; Tempted; and now I say it, – sickened me. MS4, MS5, MS5rev, MS6; intrigued, and at the same time, sickened me. MS6rev2
48 Each death was, piecemeal, your death-punishment. MS3; And each death, piecemeal was your punishment. MS4, MS5
50–2 *successively* (a) All generation follows your red trade. / We eat our bread with blood. Our portioned meat / Is cannibal. (b) All generation is of your calling. We / In blood devour[?] our bread. Our portioned meat / Is cannibal. (c) All generation is of your calling. We / Are cannibal again. Our portioned meat / Is our enormity. MS3

AUTOBIOGRAPHICAL. 1. MS 2131–4 (MS1); 2. *Smith*, pp. 398–400; 3. MS 2135–7, a typescript (MS2); 4. *CF* 23 (Aug. 1943), 106; 5. *Chicago Jewish Forum* 3 (Winter 1944–5), 102–3; 6. SS, pp. 123–6*; 7. MS 2138–40 (MS2rev); 8. MS 2141–4, a typescript (MS3); 9. SP 2113–6.

In a letter dated 12 Jan. 1943, A.J.M. Smith reports that he has received back the manuscript of his anthology, including AUTOBIOGRAPHICAL, for correction; hence the assigned date of composition, c. 1942/1942.

Stanzas 2 and 3 were originally reversed in MS1. MS1 contains the marginal notation 'Copy for Smith.'

Heading 'Autobiography' CF
4 loutish] lumbering MS2rev, MS3, SP
31 From [...] *altered to* Fiery from Volhynia's murderous hordes – MS1
35 dropping on] falling upon *altered to* dropping on MS1
41–4 Beard in my fingers curled. / O memory of unsurpassed love, / Love leading sleepy child / Past the slain ogres to a wingèd world MS2rev, MS3, SP
53 with its clover, and] still with clover, still MS2rev, MS3, SP
54 pillow'd] sail-blown MS2rev, MS3, SP
55 *successively (a)* A small boy thought the couch of jubilee. *(b)* On which my land-locked dreams put out to sea. MS2rev; *same as (b) in* MS3, SP
76 innocence] early innocence MS1
81 Childhood's first chalks and pastels of event MS2rev, MS3, SP

COME TWO, LIKE SHADOWS. 1. MS 2252 (MS1); 2–4. the unrevised typescript for MS2rev (MS2); MS 2254 (MS3); *Poetry* archives (POMS); 5. *Poetry* 61 (Feb. 1943), 595*; 6. MS 2253 (MS2rev); 7. MS 3473–4 (MS4); 8. MS 2255, a revised copy of MS3 (MS3rev); 9. SP 2093.

Submitted to *Poetry*, 31 Aug. 1942.

1 yesterday] yesterdays MS3rev, SP
5 last,] MS2rev, MS3rev, SP; last *all other versions*
9 man] shadow MS4
12 fleshless] all soul MS3rev, SP
14 *successively (a)* Agapic of doctrine, and of praxis high. *(b)* Decent in doctrine, and in praxis high. MS3rev; *same as (b) in* SP
20 shaven] razor'd MS3rev, SP

DENTIST. 1. MS 2259–60 (MS1); 2. MS 3486–9 (MS2); 3. MS 2261–2 (MS3); 4. the unrevised typescript for MS4rev1 and MS4rev2 (MS4); 5. MS 2263–4 (MS4rev1); 6. MS 2267–8, a typescript (MS5); 7. *Preview* 20 (May 1944), 12 (Pr)*; 8. MS 2265–6 (MS4rev2).

MS2 occurs in a semi-fictionalized diary entry dated Oct. 1942.
MS4rev2 appears to date from the early fifties.

12 I see him clear, as in meridian, *altered to* I see it clear, as in meridian, MS4rev2
13 *successively (a)* Unfogged and plain, *(b)* His might and main, MS4rev2; *same as (b) in* McGill reading
15 his] the MS1, MS2; his *altered to* that MS4rev2; that McGill reading
16 This] The MS1, MS2, MS3, MS4, MS4rev1, MS4rev2, McGill reading

17 drugged] sterile MS1, MS2
19 among the ivory] within that toothery MS4rev2
20 Distorts] Still twists MS1, MS2, MS3, MS4, MS4rev1, MS4rev2, McGill reading
21 keeps ... unexpressed] deems my groan a scientific jest MS1, MS2; keeps my wrath in gurgles, unexpressed MS3, MS4; keeps my gargled havoc unexpressed MS5
24 exhalations] pyorrhea MS1, MS2; pyorrhea *altered to* exhalations MS3
25 tinsel] joggling MS4rev2, McGill reading
28 on his] for my *altered to* on his MS1
29 Pity ... cries] But no! But no! MS1, MS2; But no! Too good MS3, MS4
31 in ... unmolar'd] unmolar'd, and uncrumbled MS1; unmolar'd and uncrumbled *altered to* in lumps, uncut, unmolar'd MS2

DESIDERATUM. 1. MS 2269–70 (MS1); 2. MS 2273, a typescript (MS2); 3. *Contemporary Verse* 8 (June 1943), 3; 4. *New Directions* 8 (1944), 194–5*; 5. MS 2274 (MS2rev); 6. MS 2271–2 (MS3); 7. SP 2063–4.
Submitted to *New Directions*, 3 Nov. 1942 [MS 194].
10 edicts] prescripts MS3, SP
18 Then, then where stood but one sole worshipper MS3; *altered to* Then, there where stood but one sole worshipper SP
19–20 thirteen ... craves] thirteen, singing of their staves, / would run their thirteen and six hundred chores MS3, SP
20 immortality] an ubiety MS2rev
24 thrive] MS3, SP; thrives *all other versions*
30–1 ejaculate ... micturate] ingest ... digest MS2rev, MS3, SP
32 is king and served by vassals! MS1, MS2; *successively (a)* knows no dependence, lives! *(b)* knows no dependence, living liege to none, / is paramount, suzerain, sole! *(c)* no-meek dependence knows, is liege to none, / is paramount, suzerain, sole! MS2rev; *same as (c) in* SP

ET J'AI LU TOUS LES LIVRES. 1. MS 3464 (MS1); 2. MS 2287 (MS2)*.
MS1 occurs in a semi-fictionalized diary entry dated 26 Sept. 1942.
6 And] Nor the *altered to* Even MS1
10 To] Into *altered to* to MS1

GIRLIE SHOW. 1. MS 2294–5 (MS1); 2. MS 3489, 3491–2 (MS2); 3. the unrevised typescript for MS3rev (MS3); 4. MS 2296–7 (MS3rev)*.
MS2 occurs in a semi-fictionalized diary entry dated Oct. 1942.
7 Himself] And he *all other versions*
9–10 Who are these fleeing dancers, then, and who / These fauns with beard of fingers, whistling lewd applause? *altered to* Who are these dancers, then, and these fauns who / With beard of fingers, whistle lewd applause? MS1

11 breasts] bubs *all other versions*
14 As] And *altered to* As MS2
20 un-named] nameless MS1, MS2
28 pizzicato on] played upon a sole MS1; played upon a sole *altered to* pizzicato for MS2
30 renew] renew ⟨again⟩ MS1
34 feathers] ⟨furs or⟩ feathers MS1
35 city] urban MS1
38 The chorus-girls about their queen are spun MS1
40 And once more] And *all other versions*

THE GOLEM. 1. MS 2298 (MS); 2. *Opinion* 15, 7 (June 1945), 8 (O); 3. *CJC*, 13 July 1945, p. 9*.
Submitted to *Poetry*, 31 Aug. 1942.
4 muck.] MS; muck O, CJC
18 Bohemia's] of Europe's *altered to* Bohemia's MS
22 doing? How] doing, and *altered to* doing? How MS
24–5 O and CJC *combine what are two lines in* MS; CJC *does not have italics.*

LOVE. 1. MS 2405 (MS1); 2. the typescript for MS2rev1, MS2rev2 (MS2); 3. MS 2409 (MS2rev1); 4. MS 2408 (MS2rev2); 5. MS 2406, a typescript (MS3); 6. *New Directions*, 8 (1944), 199 (ND)*; 7. MS 2407, a revised copy of MS3 (MS3rev); 8. MS 2126 (MS4).
Submitted to *New Directions*, 3 Nov. 1942. MS3rev and MS4 appear to date from the early fifties.
Heading ⟨'Post-Coitus'⟩ MS1; *untitled in* MS2, MS2rev1, MS2rev2, MS3; ⟨'Homo'⟩ MS3rev; 'Amo ... Amas ... Et Cetera' MS4
1–2 Love ... / O] Love! MS4
2 half angel] MS1, MS2, MS2rev1, MS2rev2, MS4; halfangel MS3, MS3rev; half-angel ND
3 Uncleanest of] Uncleanest, MS1, MS2
four-saxon-littered] four-littered saxon MS4
4 Foul euphemism] A sudden singing *altered to* Love! sudden singing MS4
6 To hide] That hides MS3rev, MS4
10 Saith the Canticum: it hath a most vehement flame. MS3rev; It hath, saith the many-wived one, a most vehement flame. *altered to* It hath, saith Solomon, a most vehement flame. MS4
15 testiculate] testiculate *altered to* attest the call of MS4
20–2 What is the profit that is to be had? / The word is glibly said, and done the joys: / After coitus, every man is sad. MS1, MS2; *same in* MS2rev1 *except for 22*
22 And after, always,] And always after MS2rev1

900 / Textual Notes pp 574–6

MY DEAR PLUTOPHILANTHROPIST. MS 3475–6.
Occurs in a semi-fictionalized diary entry dated Sept. 1942.
Heading supplied by ed.
17–18 *originally followed* 26

PAWNSHOP. 1. MS 3492–4 [1–40] (MS1); 2. MS 2513–14 [1–40] (MS2); 3. *First Statement* 2, 12 (Apr.–May 1945), 26–8 (FS); 4. *Accent* 5, 4 (Summer 1945), 195–6 (A); 5. RC, pp. 22–3*; 6. MS 2515–16, revised tearsheets of A (Arev).
MS1 *occurs in a semi-fictionalized diary entry dated Oct. 1942.*
Arev *appears to date from the early fifties.*
1 this] the FS
4 relict] relicts MS1
6 chattels ... glow] chattels, both their shame and woe. MS1; chattels, both their thrill and throe. MS2
7 phosphor ... stalk] fleshless poor stalk through MS1, MS2; minds of the poor who stalk FS, A
9 antitheses] O many a year MS1, MS2
12 above] upon *altered to* above MS2
14 dropping their snared bag of exotic toys. MS1; dropping the snared bags of exotic toys. MS2, FS, A, Arev
21 Trinkets of wanhope, salvage of their plight, MS1; *altered to* Frustration's trinkets, salvage of their plight, MS2
Oh] So FS, A; Thus *altered to* And Arev
22 laid on the counter, sorry inventory; MS1; laid on the counter, final invent'ry: MS2
23 (a) family] the family *all other versions*
the widow's] a widow's MS1
24 the birthday gifts – those jewels of memory – MS1; the birthday gifts; the cups of victory; MS2, FS, A, Arev
25 (d) ... special,] the workman's tools; the MS1, MS2; the unpensioned tools; the FS, A, Arev
26 *en bloc*: watch] old hero's medal *altered to* the hero's medal MS1; the hero's medal MS2, FS, A, Arev
27 medal] watch; lens *all other versions*
28 rich] O *all other versions*
31–2 Whose ... this] This is the house built by das Kapital: / it thrusts from MS1, MS2
35–7 Monument unintended, on its plaque / decipher still the name of architect, / one Adam Smith whose world of wondrous wealth MS1, MS2; That entrepreneur is rusted from his plaque. / Was his name Adam? Was his trade a smith / who thought a mansion to erect of wealth FS; The architect is

rusted from his plaque / anonymous, but stands his monolith, / the mansion he erected to house wealth *A rev*
38–40 breaks bankrupt into pawnshop bricabrac. / This is the house elect, / shrine of the let-do liberty of stealth. MS1, MS2
39 myth,] FS; myth *all other versions*
40 stealth?] stealth. *A rev*
41 parthenon] pantheon *A rev*

PENULTIMATE CHAPTER. 1. MS 2517 (MS1); 2. the unrevised typescript for MS2rev (MS2); 3. MS 2520 (MS2rev); 4. MS 2519, a typescript (MS3); 5. CF 23 (May 1943), 36; 6. MS 2518, a revised copy of MS3 (MS3rev); 7. MS 2521, a revised tearsheet of CF (CFrev); 8. CJC, 17 Apr. 1953, p. 4*; 9. SP 2098–9.
Submitted to *Poetry*, 31 Aug. 1942.
2 blithely] gaily MS1, MS2
9 fauna'd] fauna's SP
10 quickened,] quickening MS1, MS2
13 wingèd] MS1, MS2, MS2rev, MS3, MS3rev; winged CF, CFrev, CJC, SP
19 horrific stare of] gape of the *altered to* horrific stare of MS1
20 land, –] MS1, MS2, MS2rev, MS3, MS3rev; land – CF, CFrev, CJC, SP
24 The mammoths had inherited their own! MS1, MS2; *successively (a)* (The mammoths, circa 1941) *(b)* The mammoths, circa nineteen forty one *(c)* The mammoths (circa 1941) ... MS2rev; *same as (c) in* MS3, CF, MS3rev, SP; *6 written above the* 4 *of* 1941 *in* CFrev

THAT LEGENDARY EAGLE, DEATH. 1. MS 2669, a typescript (MS1); 2. CF 23 (Sept. 1943), 127; 3. CJC, 17 Apr. 1953, p. 4*; 4. MS 2668 (MS2).
Submitted to *Poetry*, 31 Aug. 1942.
CF *and* CJC *have no line spaces.*
Heading 'That Legendary Eagle' MS2
8 My last gasp, and last whisper of my blood?.. MS2
11 the eagle] his eagle MS2
12 (Lost in the skies? Dead on the ocean floor?) MS2
13 I therefore aimed] And therefore aimed MS1, CF; And aimed, therefore MS2

VARIATION OF A THEME. 1. the unrevised typescript for MS1rev (MS1); 2. *Preview* 5 (July 1942), 1–2 (Pr); 3. *New Directions* 8 (1944), 193–4*; 4. MS 2705 (MS1rev); 5. MS 2704 [1–15] (MS2).
MS1rev *and* MS2 *appear to date from the early fifties.*
Heading 'Finger Exercises' *written in above in* MS1rev
of] on *all other versions*
1 bleaseful] blissful *altered to* bliss-ful MS1rev; bliss-ful MS2
2 him ... a] his soft names and manes in MS1rev, MS2

rhyme] rhymn *all other versions*
3 And trumpeted, vault-face, his quietus breath MS2
7 Barow] Barrow *all other versions*
9 Cher Noel] Hatchment MS2
11 *marked for deletion in* MS1rev; Mr. X. Hume, the P.M.; that palled Russ MS2
Suo] Suey MS1, Pr
12 Undone Checkofsky] Ne-colei Hell-ytch Pr
Ripper] Spector MS2
13 Harry Carey] Hari Kari MS1rev; Harry Kari MS2
16 *marked for deletion in* MS1rev; *not in* MS2
28 wrot] rot MS1rev
30 embrass] homebrass MS1rev
31 Acain] O Cain MS1rev
32 it seems] seems it MS1rev

THE HITLERIAD. 1. a typescript in the Lavy Becker papers, Public Archives of Canada (B); 2. *First Statement* 2, 1 (Aug. 1943), ii–3 [1–109] (FS1); 3. *First Statement* 2, 3 (Oct. 1943), 4–7 [303–451] (FS2); 4. *The Hitleriad* (1944) (H)*; 5. MS 6017–25, a typescript [40–8, 50–3, 152–61, 258–9, 412–27, 529–66, 594–630, 685–end] (MS); 6. *CJC*, 4 Oct. 1946, pp. 6–7 ['The Dock at Nuernberg': 'The Testimony' (702–31), 'Goering' (332–45), 'Ribbentrop' (347–60), 'Rosenberg' (321–30), 'The Lesser Fry' (361–95), 'The Little Man Who Was Not There' (54–71, 226–90, 297–302)].
B was sent by Klein to Joe Dainow on 27 Aug. 1943; Dainow sent it to Lavy Becker on 3 Sept. 1959. B contains a few minor revisions which are mostly incorporated into FS1, FS2, and H. Neither B nor FS1 is divided into numbered sections. MS was used for a reading at the Jewish Public Library of Montreal soon after the publication of H. One page is missing from MS, between MS 6017 (p. 4 in the typescript) and MS 6018 (p. 6); MS 6017 ends with 161, and MS 6018 begins with 258.
In a letter to Ralph Gustafson, dated 1 Apr. 1942, Klein writes that he has 'got about four hundred lines of [THE HITLERIAD] done'; hence the assigned date of composition, c. 1942/1943.
4 indicting] I indict B, FS1
5 for ... to] as I perpetrate the B, FS1
6 Spurning ... proferred] Forsaking freshness of thy B, FS1
18 until ... more] and all hell's Terrors roar B, FS1
22–3 hate, / ... prompt] hate / Of wickedness sit in B, FS1
50 mustache, the] mustache, with spittle ever wet, / O that mustache, the B, FS1
92 died; and] died. How B, FS1
96 Doctrine ... and] For he spurned doctrine, B, FS1
99 bookworm] bookworms B

103 Linz-ery.] B; Linz-ery FS1, H
106 Wherefore] A boor B, FS1
116 Yet is it] And it is B
126 Meanwhile] As yet B
129 (The hanging picture was prophetical) B
137–8 At this point the bright light becomes obscure. / Some say he worked; but they won't say for sure. B
142–3 case ... scaffolding] case, his work was on / A scaffold, and may end as 'twas begun! B
145 Blame ... survival] And blame his long age B
146–7 He slept together with the flophouse poor; / He ate the handouts at the kitchen-door; B
153 apocalypse] great event B
172 then ... untaught] in that war, the B
173 as an] a good B
175/76 It's true that Hitler wears an Iron Cross, / The spoils of war. / He never had it, Sirs, until he had / All Germany's iron ore. B
178 This] The B
190 primed] kind B
217 their] its B
237 Though] For although B
245 advisèd] B; advised H, CJC
253 intelligence:] B; intelligence; H, CJC
260 Add] Note B
261 choicest] ugliest B
266 When] Where B
266–7 scapegoat ... cosmopolitan,] whipping-boy / To win the plaudits of the hoi polloi B
285 Inflation ... sharp] Inflation, reparation, heat-waves, B
287 theorem] reasons B
its] their B
288 sneer] cry B
289 Yelp] Cry B
293 heil] jeer B
297 – the authentic curse –] what was much worse B
301 The ... shown] Showing the knave B
315 him, shouting its] him, to shoot his B; him. Shooting its FS2
340 pref'rably] B, FS2; preferably H
343 (daggers)] not in FS2
384 Kultur's] the kultur'd altered to kultùr'd B; kultur'd FS2
402 empery] Holy See altered to empery B
425 The ... had] Hitler, it seems, did have B, FS2

436–8 *not in* B, FS2
450 Plotting for] To bring to B, FS2
452 us ... let] these remain anonymous. Let B
472 moulting ... the] breaking down of B
482 biblic] mighty B
483–4 for ... leviathans] avenging, / The dreadnaughts grim B
485 engines] birds B
503 those] these B
508 palsied] senile B
512 To try] Trying B
516 That] The B
521 This] The B
531 Is ... of] Are known to sorrowing *altered to* Is known to sorrowing B
536 was ... in] had no place within B
547 were these] *not in* B
547/48 Not this his sin. The Hottentot / Is not expected to be polyglot, / Nor yet the Hun / A paragon – B
557 cloth ... spun] much too overdone B
573 Bismarckian] A corporal's napoleonic B
574/75 He mounted to his Berchtesgaden height / And looked on Austria, – and coveted. / Peaceful the little lands lay there – for spite / To see him frustrated. B
582 the ... his] his creeds, his evil B
584 a petty] petty *altered to* a petty B
587–8 *follow 591 in* B
592 quarry ... and] booty, sauced with B
593 whiskers ... stalked] chops, and looked about B
more.] more: / Plunder and spoils! B
594–8 Behold the continent, and there behold / His battered victims binding up their wounds, – / The once-free men, in slavery now sold: B
605–7 *not in* B
608–9 Norway ... / Explosive!] And Poland plundered, and Norway despoiled / And B
611–30 His whip in Jugoslavia was coiled, / And Hellas he new-ordered into hell, / And France – / Here was a prize, and also sweet revenge! / Prostrated France, that too soon fell, / Her head beneath the victor's arrogant stance! B
626 Domrémy] *ed.*; Domremy H, MS
637 triumvirate:] *ed.*; triumvirate; B, H
639–46 Count up his prey, attempted and achieved, / The lands he crushed, the continents bereaved, / Nor yet forget that he could also stoop / To cheat his partners, and his friends to dupe, B
647 He ... Magyarland] Making of Hungary B

649–51 And why not stoop? B
656 blood ... honour] honour – overtaxed – he B
671 ceased] closed *altered to* ceased B
673 named for beasts] chanting Spring B
678 Honoured were sires of adulterous seed. B
679 Madman ... personal] Fuehrer – speak it not – named God a B
foe,] B; foe. H
692 open] *not in* B
698 bones] ghosts B
700 beat ... padded] haunt human B
705 phantoms] spectres B
716 uninterrèd] B; uninterred H, MS
725 wounded ... broken] ghostly whisper and with spectral B
730 multitude] multiple CJC
730–1 Its doom against this culprit, thrice-accursed: / An end, an end forever to this sordid thing! B
737 Bold] Foul B
746 Gesturing ... ungagged] And so-long-silent Truth B
759 To human brotherhood,] *not in* B

ACTUARIAL REPORT. 1. MS 2117–18 (MS); 2. *Preview* 12 (Mar. 1943), 7–8 (Pr); 3. CF 23 (June 1943), 60; 4. CJC, 17 Apr. 1953, p. 4*; 5. MS 2119, a revised tearsheet of CF (CFrev); 6. SP 2103–4.
Line spacing follows CFrev and SP. These agree with MS and Pr, with the exception of 17/18, which is ambiguous in both cases, and 29/30, which is a page break in MS and a line space in Pr. Line spacing in CJC is erratic, and CF has no line spaces.
19 Funereal] Tabulate CFrev, SP
23 we] that we CFrev, SP
24–5 and bad luck / Remote] and / Bad luck remote CFrev, SP
25 battlefields] battlefield MS, Pr
27 rations,] MS, CFrev, SP; rations Pr, CF, CJC
28 in fine,] Pr; ⟨and⟩ in fine MS; in fine CF, CJC; in brief, CFrev, SP
31 death are] Death to have been CFrev, SP
bodyguard] bodyguards MS
32 motley] assisting CFrev, SP
38 magi] the magi MS, Pr

AND IN THAT DROWNING INSTANT. 1. MS 2127–8 (MS1); 2. the unrevised typescript for MS2rev (MS2); 3. MS 2600 (MS2rev); 4. *Opinion* 13, 12 (Oct. 1943), 17; 5. SS, pp. 195–7*.

Heading 'A Psalm of That Which Is Remembered at the Moment of Drowning'
   MS2; 'Psalm VIII' *added in* MS2rev
16 an] this *all other versions*

NOT ALL THE PERFUMES OF ARABIA. 1. MS 2487 (MS1); 2. the unrevised typescript for MS2rev (MS2); 3. MS 2489 (MS2rev); 4. *Contemporary Verse* 8 (June 1943), 4–5; 5. *Opinion* 14, 2 (Dec. 1943), 13* [version 1]; 6. CJC, 21 Nov. 1952, p. 4* [version 2].

Version 1
5 truly shuddering] shuddering *altered to* truly shuddering MS1
8 vein] brain MS1, MS2

ADDRESS TO THE CHOIRBOYS. 1. MS 2353–5 (MS1); 2. MS 2120–1, a typescript (MS2); 3. *Opinion* 14, 7 (May 1944), 5 (O); 4. CJC, 18 Aug. 1944, p. 9*; 5. MS 2122–3 (MS2rev).
MS2rev appears to date from the early fifties.
Line spacing follows O rather than CJC, which is erratic.
Heading Address to] Instruction for MS1
24 stayed] stayed too long MS2rev
26 *not in* MS2rev
27 defied] at wavering length defied MS2rev
28 day,] *all versions except* CJC; day. CJC
33 unfaith] the unfaith MS1
36 hears] lies, and hears MS1
40 sealed:] *all versions except* CJC; sealed; CJC
43 water ... death] water, or death by beast of the field, MS1
44 ferocious beast] other ends untimely MS1
52/53 *page break in* MS1; *line space in* MS2, MS2rev; *no line space in* O, CJC
54 sorrow ... suffering] anguish – pain, majestic *altered to* tumulous sharp suffering MS1

BASIC ENGLISH. 1. MS 2213–15 (MS1); 2. MS 2215a (MS1a); 3. the unrevised typescript for MS2rev1 and MS2rev2 (MS2); 4. MS 2219–21 (MS2rev1); 5. the unrevised typescript for MS3rev (MS3); 6. MS 2216–18 (MS3rev); 7. CF 24 (Sept. 1944), 138*; 8. MS 2228 (CFrev); 9. MS 2222–4 (MS2rev2); 10. SP 2065–7; 11. MS 2225–7 (SPrev).
MS1a consists of an incomplete variant of stanza 8 on the verso of MS 2215.
Subheading not in MS1, MS2, MS2rev1, MS3, MS3rev; For Winston Churchill MS2rev2, SP, SPrev
20 Sticks] Blobs MS3rev
31 such] these MS1, MS2, MS2rev2, SP, SPrev, McGill reading

33-4 So ... deal] With these poor counters dragoman himself / Closing his deal *MS1, MS2, MS2rev2, SP, SPrev, McGill reading; successively (a)* With such poor counters dragoman himself / Closing his deal *(b)* Possibly with such-like shrewdly [...] *(c)* Perhaps, in this voice, dragoman himself / Closing his deal *(d)* So dragoman himself, perhaps, and thus / Close his shrewd deal *MS2rev1*
34-5 but ... / Gestures,] and this rest certain, only / After *deleted alternative in MS2rev1*
35 head-shakes] ⟨and⟩ head-shakes *MS1*
46-7 The Latin music, Greek perception, French / Finesse? Where are the thunders of our voice? *MS1, MS2; successively (a)* The basso of the Latin, or the tone / Hellenic? Where, the thunders of our voice? *(b)* The storm of Latin, lightning [...] *(c)* The Hellenic music or the Latin storm? / Where are the thunders of our choric voice? *MS2rev1*
50 water] waters *MS1a*
51-3 These ... / Are] No compliment. / Is bread and water / Diet *MS1a*
54 fronded] painted *altered to* fronded *MS1*
56 skimmed] loud *altered to* skimmed *MS1*
62 splendors] splendor *MS1, MS2*
strictures] dullness *MS1, MS2*

BREAD. 1. MS 2240 (MS1); 2. *Preview* 19 (Mar. 1944), 1 (Pr); 3. *Contemporary Poetry* 5, 1 (Spring 1945), 3 (CP); 4. RC, p. 14*; 5. MS 2241, a typescript (MS2); 6. SP 2051, a copy of MS2.
SP contains a number of markings indicating phrasing and emphasis, probably intended for Klein's McGill reading.
Heading 'A Psalm for the Breaking of Bread' *CP*
1 breaking] bounty *altered to* breaking *MS1*; bounty *CP*
3 at the feast-times] thrice at mealtimes *altered to* at the feast-times *MS1*
4/5 *no line space in MS1, Pr, CP*
5 daily rises] rises *altered to* daily rises *MS1*
7/8 *line space in MS1, Pr, CP*
17 Bakers most priestly] Most priestly bakers *altered to* Bakers most priestly *MS1*; Bakers, white, priestly *CP*
18 White ... ovens] O Levites at your altar'd ovens *MS1, Pr*; Serving the altar'd ovens, Levites *CP*

COMMERCIAL BANK. 1. the unrevised manuscript for MSrev (MS); 2. *Preview* 19 (Mar. 1944), 1; 3. MS 2256 (MSrev); 4. RC, p. 26*.
8 berries,] *all versions except RC*; berries *RC*

THE GREEN OLD AGE. 1. the unrevised typescript for MS1rev (MS1); 2. MS 2299

(MS1rev); 3. MS 2300, a typescript (MS2); 4. *Preview* 22 (Dec. 1944), 10–11;
5. *Accent* 5, 4 (Summer 1945), 197; 6. RC, p. 24*.
1 years,] *all versions except* RC; years RC

THE LIBRARY. 1. MS 2387–9 (MS1); 2. MS 2396–7, a typescript (MS2); 3. the
unrevised typescript for MS3rev1 (MS3); 4. *Preview* 22 (Dec. 1944), 10 (Pr);
5. CJC, 21 Nov. 1952, p. 4*; 6. MS 2398–9, a revised copy of MS2 (MS2rev);
7. MS 2394–5 (MS3rev1); 8. MS 2392–3, a revised copy of MS3 (MS3rev2);
9. MS 2390–1 (MS4); 10–11. SP 2096–7; MS 2400–1, a carbon copy of SP (MS5).
Pr is based on MS3; CJC, though published later, is based on the earlier MS2.
1 beside] *all versions except* CJC; besides CJC
2 amor intellectualis] deathless things *altered to* amor intellectualis MS1
4 red] ⟨tinted⟩ red MS1
5–6 seventh-generation ... / dumb] seventh-generational lackeys stood / dumb
    MS1, MS2, MS3, Pr, MS2rev, MS3rev1; butlers of the seventh generation
    stood / dumb MS3rev2; butlers of the seventh generation / stood dumb MS4, SP,
    MS5
7 was air in] was in MS1
8 *not in* MS3rev2, MS4, SP, MS5
9 sweetness and light. MS1; pursuit of the perfect, / and sweetness and light, /
    saccharine, tungsten. MS4, SP, MS5
10 sensitive] very sensitive MS3rev2; most sensitive MS4, SP, MS5
his gestures fine] his gestures very fine MS3rev2; delicate his gestures MS4,
    SP, MS5
11–13 fine ... neatly] monogrammed. He wore / the culture of the best schools,
    the latest in ethics, / neatly MS4, SP, MS5
12 to wit,] *not in* MS1
14–15 had ... disease] caressed his forehead, / and soothed weltschmerz MS4, SP,
    MS5
16 pure reason] progressive *altered to* pure reason MS1
19 at all,] 'in the premises,' MS4, SP, MS5
20 His sweetness [?], his light had picked up thunder *rejected revision in* MS1
23 it was] *not in* MS3rev2, MS4, SP, MS5
As ... boards] *indented half-line in* MS3rev2, MS4, SP, MS5
25 cement] the cage MS3rev2, MS4, SP, MS5
26 roared] *all versions except* MS2, CJC; reared MS2, CJC

MONTREAL. 1. *Preview* 21 (Sept. 1944), 3–5 (Pr); 2. RC, pp. 29–31*; 3–4. MS
2439–41, a typescript (MS); SP 2071–3, a carbon copy of MS.
33 hushed] O Pr
36–7 and ... issuant] tonnerre / Frappant from foundry Pr
42 pauvreté] Pr; pauvrete *all other versions*

44 infancy] enfancy *Pr*

NI LA MORT NI LE SOLEIL. 1. a typescript in the A.J.M. Smith papers, University of Toronto Library (s); 2. *Contemporary Poetry* 5, 1 (Spring 1945), 3; 3. *CJC*, 24 Oct. 1952, p. 4*; 4. MS 2486 (MS); 5. SP 2095.
s was included in a letter from Klein to A.J.M. Smith, dated 14 Jan. 1944.
Heading On] After *SP*
de] de *altered to* le duc de *MS*; le duc de *SP*
8 Bright worlds] *all versions except CJC*; Brightworlds *CJC*

A PSALM TOUCHING GENEALOGY. 1. MS 2293 (MS1); 2. MS 2293 (MS2); 3. *Pr*, p. 46; 4. MS 2605, a typescript (MS3); 5. *Chicago Jewish Forum* 3 (Spring 1945), 162* (c).
Although MS1 and MS2 are on the same sheet [MS 2293], some time probably intervened between them since they are written in different ink.
The typescript of *Pr* was submitted later than the other typescripts for the *Poems* volume, on 11 July 1944; hence the assigned date of composition, c. 1944/1944. The reading 'begat' has been restored in 2. It is the form used in Klein's source [Jeremiah 16.3], as well as the form he uses in his commentary on the poem (see explanatory note to 2).
Heading 'Genesis' *MS1*; *no heading in MS2*; *preceded by* 'Psalm XXXVI' *in Pr*
2 begat] *MS1, MS2, Pr*; begot *MS3, C*
6 All day, in exit and in entrance, pull *altered to* In exit and in entrance they do pull *MS1*

SPRING EXHIBIT. 1–2. MS 2654, a typescript; MS 2655, a typescript; 3. *New Directions* 8 (1944), 195*.

EPITAPH. 1. MS 2285 (MS1); 2. MS 2286 (MS2)*.
Handwriting, style, and subject matter link EPITAPH and a number of other poems to Klein's 'Raw Material' file [MS 3454–558], which dates from c. 1942/c. 1944.
3 blessèd] sheltering blessèd *MS1*; ⟨sheltering⟩ blessèd *MS2*
4 the] his *MS1*; his *altered to* the *MS2*
8 herald's ... murderers'] *successively (a)* speech, the sennets, and the *(b)* herald's sennets, and ruffians' *(c)* herald's sennets, and murderers' *MS1*

LES VESPASIENNES. 1. MS 2381–2 (MS1); 2. the unrevised typescript for MS2rev1 (MS2); 3. MS 2383–4 (MS2rev1); 4. MS 2385–6, a revised copy of MS2 (MS2rev2); 5. SP 2107–8*.
For the date of composition see note to EPITAPH [c. 1942/c. 1944].
6 effigies] the saints *MS1, MS2, MS2rev1*
21 amputate] skirted *MS1, MS2*

22 those wishful drawings and rhymes – MS1, MS2, MS2rev1
27 public square] square, the little winds MS1, MS2, MS2rev1

OF TRADITION. MS 2501.
For the date of composition see note to EPITAPH [c. 1942/c. 1944].

POST-WAR PLANNING. 1. MS 2562 (MS1); 2. MS 2563 (MS2); 3. MS 2564, a typescript (MS3)*.
For the date of composition see note to EPITAPH [c. 1942/c. 1944].
5–6 and 7–8 reversed in MS1; originally reversed in MS2
6 Stitched open with bullets, with knives, or with acid, his girth? MS1

SAGA THE FIRST. MS 2612.
For the date of composition see note to EPITAPH [c. 1942/c. 1944].

SONG WITHOUT MUSIC. 1. MS 2644 (MS1); 2. MS 2645 (MS2)*.
For the date of composition see note to EPITAPH [c. 1942/c. 1944].
2 mewsick] miosic MS1; miosic altered to mewsick MS2
10 utters] unclear; could be letters

TAILPIECE TO AN ANTHOLOGY. MS 2660.
For the date of composition see note to EPITAPH [c. 1942/c. 1944].

TRIBUTE TO THE BALLET MASTER. 1. MS 2698–9* [version 1]; 2. MS 2700* [version 2].
For the date of composition see note to EPITAPH [c. 1942/c. 1944].

PORTRAIT OF THE POET AS LANDSCAPE. 1. the unrevised typescript for MSrev (MS); 2. *First Statement* 3, 1 (June–July 1945), 3–8 (FS); 3. MS 2556–61, revised tearsheets of FS (FSrev); 4. RC, pp. 50–6*; 5. MS 2546–55 (MSrev); 6. SP 2044–50.
MS and FS contain seven sections, the third of which is deleted in later versions. It is printed separately in this edition.
An outline of the poem [MS 7594] contains a reference to Hans Natonek, whose *In Search of Myself* (1943) Klein comments on in a note dated 5 Dec. 1943 [MS 3557]; hence the assigned date of composition, c. 1944/1945.
Heading Landscape] a Nobody MS, FS
22 culture] cultures FS, FSrev, MSrev, SP
24 one] our MS
28 the witness missing from the courthouse roll. MS; a being incognito and lacunal. FS; a being incognito, lost, lacunal. FSrev; *successively (a)* a vanished

bystander, a nothing at all. *(b)* incognito, vacuate, lacunal. *(c)* incognito, lost, lacunal. msrev

31 world] worlds fs, fsrev, msrev, sp
33 think] do think fs, fsrev
35 just like a poet] and shifts euphoric msrev, sp
45 Dear] O *all other versions*
49 like shaken tinfoil] the vowels of heaven sp
61 one:] *all versions except* rc; one; rc
67 Thus] O *all other versions*
88 symbols ... concave] shadows out of Plato's cave msrev, sp
98 upon the reservation introvert. ms, fs
99–100 He ... on] And he does not understand it, and is full / of a sad conjecture, muscling in ms, fs; He does not understand this, and is full / of pains and frowns and muscles in fsrev
104 Wigged] O wigged *all other versions*
113–14 cuckolded ... successful] betrayed by the cinema troubadour / making his plagiary msrev, sp
116 Pride,] O *all other versions*
120 The;] ms, msrev, sp; The: fs, fsrev, rc
128 merkin] ego's msrev, sp
134 nth] ms, fs, fsrev, msrev; nth rc, sp
142 been. Item] been lived. O item *all other versions*
148 this] the *all other versions*
149 its total scope, its synthesis olympic, ms, fs; of its total scope, saturnine focus, fsrev
150 its ... tracklessness] fields where no negatives can live ms, fs, fsrev
152 déclassé] *ed.*; declassé *all versions*
156 forms] form fs, fsrev
163 sea.] sea .... msrev; sea ... sp

INDIAN RESERVATION: CAUGHNAWAGA. 1. MS 2306–7, a typescript (ms1); 2. the unrevised typescript for Poms (ms2); 3. *Poetry* archives (Poms); 4. *Poetry* 66 (Sept. 1945), 318–19 (Po); 4. rc, pp. 11–12*.
In a letter dated 12 July 1945, Marion Stobel of *Poetry* asked Klein to change 'alimentary' in 18. Klein suggested replacing the line with 'Beneath the sufferance of their shawls.' See explanatory note to 18.
5 Rank] O *all versions except* rc
6 kin! –] ms1, Poms, Po; *punctuation illegible in* ms2; kin' – rc
18 alimentary] elementary ms2
19 sit ... squaws] Their squaws, sit like black tents ms1
24 burnt ... and] The burnt wood, ms1
25 trophies ... traveller's] History scalped as trophies for a ms1

28 a] the *MS1*
32 now] *not in MS1*

THE PROVINCES. 1. MS 2568–70 (MS); 2. *Northern Review* 1, 1 (Dec. 1945–Jan. 1946), 27–8 (NR); 3. RC, pp. 2–3*.
13 Then] And, then *MS, NR*
32 Yet] O *MS, NR*
44–5 What ... sought?] Fixed in their faith? / Heaped in their hopes? Wrought in their [...] works? *MS*; Fixed in their faith? / Heaped in their hopes? Wrought in their wit and works? *NR*
47 that] they *MS, NR*

THE ROCKING CHAIR. 1. MS 2606–7 before the addition of MS3 (MS1); 2. MS 2608 [29–32] (MS2); 3. a revised version of 29–32 added to MS 2607 (MS3); 4. MS 2609 [25–32] (MS4); 5. *Nation* 161 (6 Oct. 1945), 341; 6. RC, p. 1*; 7–8. SP 2068–9; MS 2610–11, a copy of SP (MS5).
MS1 and MS2 are on a single folded sheet. After writing out the complete poem (MS1), beginning on the outside fold (MS 2606) and finishing on the right half of the inside fold (MS 2607), Klein circled 29–32 as unsatisfactory and tried out a number of versions of the passage on the left side of the inside fold (MS2). He then copied a new version of the passage (MS3) back into the original MS1; crossed out the whole of the final stanza, including the added passage; and, finally, rewrote the whole stanza, in its present form, on a separate sheet (MS4).
16 dangling above] *successively (a)* about the *(b)* dangling about *(c)* dangling above *MS1*
29–32 It is the poor man's Louis Quatorze, his seat / in the trough of time, it moves, and does not move; / O, it is like an old ballad which does always repeat / the same refrain, something about an unforgettable first love! *MS1*; *successively (a)* O, in the trough of time a dreamer's seat / which seems to move, and does not move, yet moves [...] *(b)* O, it is like an old ballad [...] *(c)* O it is music; like an old French ballad / which [...] *(d)* Truly, it is like a ballad, all refrain / which from its [...] *(e)* O, like some antique ballad, all refrain / which turns about its longing, and always moves / from longing back to longing a [...] *(f)* O, like some antique ballad, all refrain / which turns about its longing, and moves / to make a pleasure out of repeated pain / it seems to go back, again and again, to a first love *MS2*; O like some antique ballad, all refrain / which turns about its longing, and seems to move / to make a pleasure out of repeated pain / it moves, as if always back to a first love. *MS3*

SONNET UNRHYMED. 1. MS 2647 (MS1); 2. MS 2648 (MS2); 3. MS 2649, a typescript

(MS3); 4. *Accent* 5, 4 (Summer 1945), 197*; 5. MS 2650, a revised copy of MS3 (MS3rev); 6. SP 2094.
1 frustral ... extase] height of barren ecstasy *altered to* frustrate height of ecstasy MS1
2 life] growth MS1
10 murder] age MS1
12 although tired] although wearied MS1; though sleep-laden MS3rev, SP
13 dark] darkness MS3rev, SP

AIR-MAP. 1. *Poetry* archives; 2. *Poetry* 70 (July 1947), 178; 3. PFC, p. 5; 4. SVP, p. 5; 5. HPC, p. 10; 6. RC, p. 19*.

THE BREAK-UP. 1. *Poetry* archives; 2. *Poetry* 70 (July 1947), 179; 3. PFC, p. 6; 4. SVP, p. 6; 5. HPC, p. 11; 6. RC, p. 25*.

THE CRIPPLES. 1. *Poetry* archives (PoMS); 2. *Poetry* 70 (July 1947), 177–8; 3. PFC, p. 3; 4. SVP, p. 4; 5. HPC, p. 9; 6. RC, p. 4*.
Klein insisted on the spelling 'ninetynine' in a letter to Frank Flemington, his editor at Ryerson Press, 6 Mar. 1948. See explanatory note to 1.
1 ninetynine] PoMS; ninety-nine *all other versions*
7 Whither] *all versions except* RC; whither RC
ninetynine] PoMS; ninety-nine *all other versions*
11 the surgery's] their surgery's *all other versions*
15 Yes] O *all other versions*

FOR THE SISTERS OF THE HOTEL DIEU. 1. *Poetry* archives; 2. *Poetry* 70 (July 1947), 178; 3. PFC, p. 4; 4. SVP, p. 5; 5. HPC, p. 10; 6. RC, p. 6*; 7. MS 2291 (MS); 8. SP 2070, a carbon copy of MS.
SP contains a number of markings indicating phrasing and emphasis, probably intended for Klein's McGill reading.
8 fluttered to me] over me fluttered MS, SP, *McGill reading*

FRIGIDAIRE. 1. *Poetry* archives (PoMS); 2. *Poetry* 70 (July 1947), 180–1 (Po); 3. PFC, p. 8; 4. SVP, p. 8; 5. HPC, p. 13; 6. RC, p. 18*; 7. SP 2074; 8. MS 2292, a carbon copy of SP.
17 And there] O, there PoMS, Po, PFC, SVP, HPC

GRAIN ELEVATOR. 1. *Poetry* archives; 2. *Poetry* 70 (July 1947), 175–6; 3. PFC, p. 2; 4. SVP, p. 3; 5. HPC, p. 8; 6. RC, p. 7*.

M. BERTRAND. 1. MS 2436 (MS); 2. *Poetry* archives; 3. *Poetry* 70 (July 1947), 179–80; 4. PFC, p. 7; 5. SVP, p. 7; 6. HPC, p. 12; 7. RC, p. 41*.

No heading in MS
5 Returned now] Now, returned *all other versions*
16 hand-kiss] *all versions except* RC; hand kiss RC

THE SNOWSHOERS. 1. MS 2639; 2. *Queen's Quarterly* 54 (Winter 1947–8), 412; 3. RC, p. 5*; 4. SP 2076–7.
Mentioned in the draft of a letter, 30 July 1946 [MS 313].

THE SUGARING. 1. MS 2658–9, a typescript; 2. RC, p. 10*.

DOCTOR DRUMMOND. 1. MS 2280–1, a typescript (MS1); 2. MS 2278–9, a typescript (MS2); 3. CF 26 (Sept. 1946), 136*.
11 patrician patronizing the] patrician, his MS1
19 made] makes MS2

THE NOTARY. 1. MS 2490–1, a typescript; 2. RC, p. 42*.
Mentioned in the draft of a letter, dated 30 July 1946 [MS 313].
10 ceremonial, a priest,] *ed.*; ceremonial a priest, MS; ceremonial a priest RC
17 And ... flourish] A wonder-worker! MS
18 gratifies] and gratifies MS
19 His, his are the certainties! MS
22 truly] he is MS

POLITICAL MEETING. 1. CF 26 (Sept. 1946), 136; 2. RC, pp. 15–16*; 3. SP 2078–9.
Heading (For Camillien Houde)] *not in* CF
23 Allée] *ed.*; Allee *all versions*
27 on himself] at himself SP
31 Canadien] Canadian CF
38 shadowed and] grave, wordless, CF

QUEBEC LIQUOR COMMISSION STORE. 1. a typescript in the Earle Birney papers, University of Toronto Library (CPMS); 2. *Canadian Poetry Magazine* 10, 2 (Dec. 1946), 19–20 (CP); 3. RC, pp. 27–8*.
Mentioned in the draft of a letter, 30 July 1946 [MS 313]. CPMS was submitted to *Canadian Poetry Magazine* on 16 Oct. 1946.
Heading 'Quebec Liquor Commission' CPMS, CP
17 those] CPMS, CP; these RC
21 thou gurgling knave] my sudden and slick man CPMS, CP
25 Lithe] O CPMS, CP
And] O CPMS, CP

THE SPINNING WHEEL. 1. a typescript in the Earle Birney papers, University of

Toronto Library (CPMS); 2. *Canadian Poetry Magazine* 10, 2 (Dec. 1946), 20–1; 3. *RC*, p. 17*.
CPMS was submitted to *Canadian Poetry Magazine* on 24 Oct. 1946.

THE WHITE OLD LADY. 1. MS 2706; 2. CF 26 (Sept. 1946), 136*.

SESTINA ON THE DIALECTIC. 1. MS 2619 (MS1); 2. MS 2617–18 (MS2); 3. MS 2626–7, a typescript (MS3); 4. MS 2628–9, a revised copy of MS3 (MS3rev1); 5. MS 2630–1, a second revised copy of MS3 (MS3rev2); 6. the unrevised typescript for MS4rev1 and MS4rev2 (MS4); 7. MS 2622–3 (MS4rev1); 8. MS 2620–1 (MS5); 9. MS 2624–5 (MS4rev2); 10. MS 2632–3 (MS6); 11. SP 2632–3, a revised copy of MS6*.
Mentioned in the draft of a letter, 30 July 1946 [MS 313].
MS1 consists of rough sketches for 29–33. In MS3rev1 the end words ('with,' 'to,' 'out,' 'so,' 'still') are listed at the bottom of the page and marked in the text. MS2 is laid out in sestina format.

3 eases] ease its *MS2, MS3, MS3rev1, MS3rev2, MS4, MS4rev1, MS5*

outplots] outplot *MS2, MS3, MS3rev1, MS3rev2, MS4, MS4rev1, MS5*

6–7 binds ... withe] binds us length and breadth and width *MS2, MS3; queried in MS3rev1;* braids us in wicker and withe *altered to* binds us braided wicker and withe *MS3rev2*

10 slack,] *MS2, MS3, MS3rev1, MS3rev2, MS4, MS4rev1, MS4rev2;* slack *MS5, MS6, SP*

13 heart's blood, bursting] *MS5, MS4rev2;* blood in the bay bursts *MS2, MS3, MS3rev1, MS3rev2, MS4, MS4rev1;* heart's blood bursting *MS6, SP*

14 circuit] bower *MS2, MS3, MS3rev2, MS4, MS4rev1, MS5; queried in MS3rev1*

pulsebeat's] pulsebeats *MS2, MS3, MS3rev1, MS3rev2, MS4, MS4rev1*

16 grounds, –] *MS2, MS5;* grounds – *all other versions*

19–20 rise ... them] resurrective, rise! See them, now *MS2, MS3, MS3rev1, MS3rev2, MS4, MS4rev1;* above *altered to* rise resurrective, – and now see them *MS5*

22–3 updown ... well] inout, overandunder, updown. Note *MS2, MS3, MS3rev1;* inout, updown, overandunder. Note *MS3rev2, MS4, MS4rev1;* updown, inout, overandunder. Note *altered to* updown, inout, overandunder. And note well *MS5*

24–5 ever ... another] ding-dong, crazy carol, Hegel to Hyde *MS2, MS3, MS4, MS4rev1;* Hegel to Hyde *queried in MS3rev1;* ding-dong, crazy carol, Heckyll to Hyde *MS3rev2;* ding-dong, crazy carol, Hegel to Hyde *altered to* ever kaleidoscopic, one scape to [...] *MS5*

27 Consensus] Accord *MS2, MS3, MS3rev1, MS3rev2, MS4, MS4rev1;* Accord *altered to* Consensus *MS5*

30 hope it, name it] hope and, name and *altered to* hope it, name it *MS2*

30–1 image ... stop] *successively (a)* together living the golden hyphen: with. / At last [...] *(b)* together of the golden hyphen: with. At last [...] *(c)* exorcise it, the shimmering of the golden hyphen: with. / At last O lyric synthesis! *(d)* exorcise it, the shimmering synthesis, expanse and vistas[?] to lyric heights upraised. Love's last. *(e)* exorcise it, the lyric synthesis, the uplands within which all flaws are overshone! MS3rev2; *same as (e) in* MS4, MS4rev1

MEDITATION UPON SURVIVAL. 1. MS 2423–4 (MS1); 2. MS 2427–8, a typescript (MS2); 3. MS 2431–2, a revised version of MS2 (MS2rev1); 4. MS 2429–30, a second revised version of MS2 (MS2rev2); 5. MS 2425–6, a typescript (MS3); 6. *Contemporary Verse* 32 (Summer 1950), 9–10 (CV)*; 7. MS 2433–4, a revised tearsheet of CV (CVrev).
Mentioned in the draft of a letter, 30 July 1946 [MS 313].
CVrev appears to date from the early fifties.
2 run plasma] plasmic run MS2rev1
3 unexpired] unachieved MS2rev1
six] five MS1, MS2, MS2rev1
8 *successively (a)* I do grow bitter at my false felicity – *(b)* I cannot help but curse my false felicity – *(c)* I do besmear my luck with irony – MS2rev1
11 However, one continues] But, of course, one continues MS1, MS2; But one continues, of course, MS2rev1
14 dry,] MS1, MS2, MS2rev1, MS2rev2, MS3; dry CV, CVrev
15 cry out] cry MS1, MS2, MS2rev1
die,] *all versions except* CV; die. CV
16 cry love] MS1, MS2, MS2rev1, MS2rev2, CVrev; cry, love MS3, CV
20 my mournings taken for secret merrimakes! MS1, MS2, MS2rev1; *successively (a)* my heart convicted by the pulse it takes *(b)* convicted in the news my sobbing breaks *(c)* convicted with the news my mourning breaks. MS2rev2
22 the severed] First, severed MS1, MS2
26 And] Then MS1, MS2
27 and the] *not in* MS2rev1
28 Upon] While – MS2rev1
33–4 *originally reversed in* MS1
37–8 else ... ash] else but to depute / my bones that are not ash – and wire – MS1, MS2, MS2rev1; else but to depute / my bones that strangely are not ash MS2rev2
39 the glass-case] the case of glass MS1, MS2, MS2rev1, MS2rev2; a glass-case CVrev
40 *successively (a)* that waits me in some anthropological institute? *(b)* that waits them in some anthropological institute? *(c)* – tagged JEW – in some anthropological institute? MS1; *same as (c) in* MS2, MS2rev1, MS2rev2; lit up in some museum, and marked: Jew CVrev

AT HOME. 1. MS 2129 (MS1); 2. MS 2130, a typescript (MS2)*.
Closely related to an article by Klein on the Nuremberg Trials, 'The Herrenvolk,'

published 3 May 1946 [BS, pp. 257–8]; hence the assigned date of composition, 1946.
3 The] Herr *altered to* The MS1
7 The ... him] The pastor at [...] *altered to* The pastor beside him MS1
8 It ... O] Beautiful! Beautiful! O too *altered to* It speaks of the very soul! O MS1
10 Striped pants] Frock-coat *altered to* Striped pants MS1
towards] to *altered to* towards MS1
13 not a whit] and aryan, not *altered to* not a whit MS1

LOWELL LEVI. 1. MS 2410 (MS1)* [version 1]; 2. MS 2536 (MS2); 3. MS 2537–9 (MS3); 4. MS 2540–2 (MS4); 5. MS 2543–5, a typescript (MS5)* [version 2]. MS2 consists of a sheet of rough sketches. These are not noted among the variants. The 'tractate on the Brooklyn delicatessen' referred to in 46 appeared in the Mar. 1946 issue of *Commentary*; hence the assigned date of composition, 1946.

Version 1
1 finds ... to] cannot *altered to* finds it difficult to MS1
5–6 of ... dairy.] on delicatessens in the Bronx. *altered to* of articles, urbane and learned, / on the Jewish delicatessen, the Jewish dairy. MS1

Version 2
3–5 both / ... their] alien / Among their own, and alien among / Their *altered to* both / Alien among their own, and alien / Among their MS3
7 we] we *altered to* they MS3
9 Fiat!] *not in* MS3
12 credos ... prestige-] splendour of the pure *altered to* prestige of pure MS3
16 the swastika] the swastika *altered to* a swastika MS3
17 the] these *altered to* the MS3
29/30 And Lowell winds phylacteries *altered to* ⟨And Lowell sells the Torah as / Commodity of skins of goats / Winding,⟩ MS3
31 slick Engelic] editorial MS3
32 plain:] as MS3
38 But, says Western Union, the promised faith? MS3
39 *not in* MS3
41 *not in* MS3
47 laps] thighs *altered to* laps MS3

TO THE LADY WHO WROTE ABOUT HERZL. 1. MS 2694 (MS1); 2. MS 2695; 3. MS 2696, a typescript*.
For the date of composition see explanatory note.
Heading Lady] Dame MS1
1 salvaged none] come from God *altered to* salvaged none MS1
2–3 Bighearted ... Swabians] *successively (a)* Declaring thy love for all the sons of

men / Including the humbled fritz *(b)* Bighearted one, forgiving, loving
again / The German masses (duped) *(c)* Bighearted one, forgiving, loving again /
The poor duped Swabians MS1
4 Posteriorizing the] Cackling the fragile *altered to* Posteriorizing the MS1
6 waddling mental] the waddling of thy *altered to* waddling mental MS1
7 pose and] pose, thy *altered to* pose and MS1
8 they do] it does *altered to* they do MS1
11–12 with ... marble] the droppings of thy hate uncoil / Over our glory MS1
13 thine owlish] thy eldritch *altered to* thine owlish MS1

WISHING TO EMBARRASS ME, BUT POLITELY. MS 2410.
On the same sheet as LOWELL LEVI; hence the assigned date of composition, 1946.
Heading supplied by ed.

WRESTLING RING. 1. MS 2411 (MS1); 2. the unrevised typescript for MS2rev (MS2);
3. MS 2711 (MS2rev)*.
MS1 is on the verso of LOWELL LEVI [MS 2410]; hence the assigned date of
composition, 1946.
4 about] and about MS1
5 rope] ropes MS1
11 sixth] seventh MS1
15 and his voice is a needle *altered to* the tatooer's needle his voice MS1
16 Donnes-y-la! Break him a leg! Make him a cripple! MS1

BEAVER. 1. MS 2229, a typescript (MS1); 2. MS 2230, a revised copy of MS1 (MS1rev);
3. CJC, 21 Nov. 1952, p. 4*.
MS1 contains the address of Klein's law office from 1941 to 1949, 276 St James W.
The poem was therefore composed considerably earlier than its 1952 date of
publication, and in its style and theme it is close to the poems included in RC;
hence the assigned date of composition, c. 1945/1947.
3 juice] the juice MS1, MS1rev
5 bole] MS1, MS1rev; hole CJC
7 now in deep] and in MS1, MS1rev
forest] small forest MS1, MS1rev
9 *not split in* MS1, MS1rev
10 *not split in* MS1, MS1rev
11 and] will MS1, MS1rev
over] at MS1, MS1rev
12 he waits] waiting MS1, MS1rev

DOMINION SQUARE. MS 2282.

DOMINION SQUARE is closely related to the poems included in RC; hence the assigned date of composition, c. 1945/1947.
11 the] ⟨and⟩ the
13 bronze] bust *altered to* bronze
15 calèche] *ed.;* caleche

ELEGY. 1. *New Palestine*, 4 Apr. 1947, pp. 106–7 (NP); 2. CJC, 25 Apr. 1947, pp. 8–9; 3. MS 2283–4, a revised tearsheet of NP (NPrev); 4. SS, pp. 127–34*.
11 Daily I] And daily NP, CJC
12 Through clouds] And through a cloud NP, CJC
16 sepulchres ... ones] sepulchre of that sainted one NP, CJC
17 tumuli] tumulus NP, CJC
19 death, in] death and NP, CJC
20–1 kin: / David] kin / Now dust or mould: David NP, CJC
25 *not in* NP, CJC
26 The relicts] And relicts NP, CJC
27 Fevering] Glowing NP, CJC
106 the huge] this huge NP, CJC
113 witnesses] witness CJC
119 sand; –] NP, CJC; sand; NPrev, SS

SONG OF INNOCENCE. 1. the unrevised manuscript for MS1rev (MS1); 2. the unrevised typescript for MS2rev (MS2); 3. the unrevised manuscript for MS3rev (MS3); 4–6. MS 2640 (MS1rev); MS 2642 (MS2rev); MS 2641 (MS3rev); 7. SP 2090*.
SONG OF INNOCENCE is closely related to ELEGY and to Klein's translation of Glatstein's SMOKE, both dated c. 1947/1947.
3/4 – How many on a smokestack top can dance? – MS1, MS2, MS3; *marked for deletion in* MS1rev, MS2rev
4 Bibles] Evangels *rejected revision in* MS2rev
10 Noughts] *all versions except* SP; noughts SP

ANNUAL BANQUET: CHAMBRE DE COMMERCE. RC, p. 49.

DRESS MANUFACTURER: FISHERMAN. 1. *Contemporary Verse* 22 (Fall 1947), 3–4 (CV); 2. RC, pp. 20–1*.
11 *not in* CV
22 curbstones] curbstone CV

FILLING STATION. RC, p. 48.

HORMISDAS ARCAND. 1. MS 2305; 2. RC, p. 46*.

2 manufactures him historic] is manufacturing his *altered to* manufactures him a
  MS
5 blast] paragraph MS
7 Et] And MS
8 say] be said *altered to* say MS
you have] you've *altered to* you have MS

KRIEGHOFF: CALLIGRAMMES. RC, p. 13.

LES FILLES MAJEURES. RC, p. 47.

LIBRAIRIE DELORME. RC, p. 44.

LONE BATHER. RC, pp. 37–8.

LOOKOUT: MOUNT ROYAL. 1. MS 2402–4 (MS); 2. RC, pp. 33–4*.
Some illegible variants in 30–4 of MS have not been noted.
No heading in MS
5 mandarin mustaches] beard and whiskers MS
6 at ... finally] finally, at the look-out MS
8 the better to watch the motion and the sight MS
9 tripod] three-legged stand MS
11 *not in* MS
14 slums and races] races MS
21–3 *successively (a)* laid out in parallels and diamonds *(b)* the parallels, the squares, the diamonds *(c)* the leading parallels, the lingering square, / the a[...] *(d)* the parallels, the lingering square, / topped by stone angles, and the definitive dome *(e)* parallels, square, and dome MS
24 O next year's [...] *altered to* the picture book of the next grade, extended / and read to that last word, his home, ⟨there,⟩ MS
27 its singsong ... curves] its mapmaker curves and parallels *altered to* its singsong bridges, its mapmaker curves MS
29 water-tower'd] shining island MS
30 mountains] distances *altered to* mountains MS

M. LE JUGE DUPRÉ. 1. MS 2305 (MS1); 2. MS 2435, a typescript (MS2)*.
MS1 has been assigned a date of c. 1947/1947, since it is on the same sheet as
  HORMISDAS ARCAND.
3 Exempli] *ed.*; Exempla MS1, MS2
3–5 Exempli ... Mtre.] *successively (a)* Exempla gratia: Mtre. Hamelin [...] *(b)* Exempla gratia: / since Mtre. Hamelin / organizer of electoral victories /

Mtre. *(c)* Exempla gratia: / There are in Dupré's court / since Mtre. Hamelin / organizer of electoral victories / Mtre. MS1

MONSIEUR GASTON. 1. MS 2437–8 (MS); 2. *Contemporary Verse* 22 (Fall 1947), 5; 3. RC, p. 43*; 4. SP 2075.
No heading in MS
5–6 *one line in* MS
5 clinking coinage] coinage MS
8–9 baize? / In] baize – / he's in MS
12 chauffeur] chauffeur, you know MS
21 Gaston; almost] Gaston, since almost MS
23 is very] *And* is MS
24 distinguished approach] approach MS
25 you] and you MS
gets] gets at Christmas MS

THE MOUNTAIN. RC, pp. 35–6.

PARADE OF ST. JEAN BAPTISTE. 1. MS 2504–8, a typescript (MS); 2. CF 27 (Feb. 1948), 258–9; 3. MS 2509–10, revised tearsheets of CF (CFrev); 4. HPC, pp. 14–16*.
PARADE OF ST. JEAN BAPTISTE was included in the original typescript of RC [letter to Frank Flemington, 6 Mar. 1948]; hence the assigned date of composition, c. 1947/1947.
In 95, a comma has been added after '*le peup*'' to conform to the reading in MS. MS originally had 'the mass,'; the words, though not the comma, were x'd out, and '*le peup*'' was typed in above the line. When MS was transcribed, the comma was missed, and it therefore does not appear in the later versions.
15–16 blue, / ... blond,] CFrev; blue / the rose the vert the blond MS; blue / the rose, the vert, the blond, CF, HPC
31 galerie] MS; gallerie CF, CFrev, HPC
33 Here all] All here MS, CF
34 Hébert] *ed.*; Hebert MS, CFrev, HPC; Herbert CF
108 days] MS; day CF, CFrev, HPC

PASTORAL OF THE CITY STREETS. 1. the unrevised typescript for MSrev (MS); 2. RC, pp. 39–40*; 3. MS 2511–12 (MSrev).
19 O] Now, MSrev

SIRE ALEXANDRE GRANDMAISON. 1. MS 2637–8 (MS); 2. RC, p. 45*.
No heading in MS

2–3 placed ... heirloom] which his secretary / who watched such things, placed on his MS
10 Société] ed.; Societe MS, RC
Fiducie] Fiducie, Inc. etc. etc. MS
11 had been duly elected] was MS
13 attaching now] attaching to the family estate MS
16 pious] and pious MS
18 Mais] Ah MS
20 crate custom] crate old custom and MS
21 Certainly His Eminence, Mgr. Desbaillets should hear about it – / the next thing you know these Voltaires would be planning / a blasphemous commutation of the tithe. / Spiritual values were in retreat. This / was a too commercial age. MS

UNIVERSITÉ DE MONTRÉAL. 1. MS 2701–2, a typescript; 2. RC, pp. 8–9*.

WINTER NIGHT: MOUNT ROYAL. RC, p. 32.

O GOD! O MONTREAL! 1. MS 2502, a typescript (MS); 2. *Contemporary Verse* 22 (Fall 1947), 4 (CV)*.
For the date of composition see explanatory note.
Heading Montreal!] MS; Montreal CV
2 Fréchette] ed.; Frechette MS, CV
4 nymphs)] MS; nymphs), CV

CANTABILE. *Northern Review* 2, 3 (Sept.–Oct. 1948), 30–1 (NR).
For the emendation to 51 see explanatory note to 50–1.
51 E.P.: EP] ed.; E.P.: E P NR

BENEDICTIONS. SS, p. 190.

STANCE OF THE AMIDAH. 1. MS 2656–7 [1–56] (MS); 2. SS, pp. 193–5*.
21 bee] newt *altered to* bee MS
39 to labour] in travail MS
40 our] my *altered to* our MS
56 a burnt offering is] is our burnt offering *altered to* a burnt offering is MS

WHO HAST FASHIONED. SS, pp. 189–90.

OF THE MAKING OF GRAGERS. 1. MS 2500, a typescript (MS); 2. CJC, 3 Mar. 1950, p. 7*.
Most of the nonce-words (or first versions of them) in 3–11 were written by Klein

into the end paper of *The Purim Anthology*, ed. Philip Goodman (Jewish Publication Society of America 1949). Lines 12–15, which appear to have been added as an afterthought to MS, are partly based on the following list of names, also in the end paper: 'Pharaoh, Antiochus, Titus, Torquemada, Chmelnitzki, Hitler.'

The layout of MS has been followed, rather than that of CJC, which is garbled.

11 datadiscords] that-and-this-cords *x'd over and replaced by* datadiscords *in* MS
11/12 tin-panic *x'd over in* MS

EPIGRAMS [1]. 1. MS 7325 [nos. 8, 6], 7345 [no. 4] (MS1); 2. MS 7353–61 (MS2)*.
MS1 is contained in a notebook dated 'June 4, 1952'; MS2 in a notebook dated 'January 5, 1954.' The passage in MS1 corresponding to no. 4 is entitled 'Variation on a Theme'; the passages corresponding to nos. 6 and 8 have no titles.

Heading supplied by ed.

13 poet of] poet, with MS1
14–17 What a comrade you would have been to Catullus MS1
15 you ... been] *added in* MS2
25–7 The ... time] *not in* MS1
27/28 And the bambino, knees up, parted, face crumpled / Crying his short cry. MS1
35/36 And saints sundry and designate MS1
36/37 Jewels scattered like breadcrumbs MS1
38 all singing] Singing MS1
40 sanna] Hosanna MS1; Hosanna *altered to* sanna MS2
46–7 callous'd / also.] *successively (a)* callous'd. / Is her clitoris also? *(b)* callous'd, / that is to say, / her thumb also. *(c)* callous'd / also. MS2
68 details] describes *altered to* details MS2
71 winged] ⟨his⟩ winged MS2
81 are] *added in* MS2

SPINOZA: ON MAN, ON THE RAINBOW. 1. HNJrev, flyleaf (HNJrev1); 2. HNJrev, p. 34 (HNJrev2); 3. the unrevised typescript for SPrev (SP); 4. SP 2109 (SPrev)*.

Replaces section VII of OUT OF THE PULVER AND THE POLISHED LENS in HNJrev.

Heading 'On the Rainbow' HNJrev1; 'On Man, on the Rainbow' HNJrev2, SP
1 All flowers that] Blossoms that are HNJrev1
2 *successively (a)* All jewels th[...] *(b)* That dance [...] *(c)* That colour [...] earth *(d)* All flowers [...] *(e)* All the bright flowers of the earth HNJrev1
3 All] And HNJrev1
their tunnelled night] the [...] night HNJrev1
4 Enkindle and] Their hues HNJrev1

5 *successively (a)* All gems [...] *(b)* All [...] *(c)* Now in the sky [...] thrust *(d)* Now up the sky [...] thrust HNJREV1
6 human] all of HNJREV1
7 Do hang but on] Hang but upon HNJREV1

EPIGRAMS [2]. 1. MS 2275–6 [except for 'Ritual,' 'Palmam Qui Meruit'] (MS1)*; 2. MS 2277 ['Ritual,' 'Palmam Qui Meruit'] (MS2); 3. MS 2276 ['Ritual,' 'Palmam Qui Meruit'] (MS3)*.
MS1 is dated 'July 28, 1955.' 'Ritual' and 'Palmam Qui Meruit' were roughed out in MS2, probably the next day, and then added to the bottom of MS 2276, where they are dated 'July 29, 1955.'
Heading supplied by ed.
12/13 Mâ ... You] Mâ Aleyk *altered to* Mâ Aleyk – No Evil Befall You MS1
27/28 no heading in MS2
28–9 The eulogies have been said. The great tycoon is dead. MS2
31/32 Ethics *altered to* Palmam Qui Meruit MS3
34 political success] politics MS1; success in politics *altered to* political success MS3

POETRY TRANSLATIONS

THE KADDISH. 1. MS 2358 [1–11] (MS1); 2. MS 2359 [12–13] (MS2); 3. MS 2361 (MS3)* [version 1]; 4. MS 2360 [10–15, 19] (MS4); 5. CJC, 24 Oct. 1952, p. 4* [version 2].
MS2 consists of lists of words to be used in translating 12–13. The final list contains the words used in MS3.

Version 1
11 for ... forever] forever, eterne, sempiternal, for aye *altered to* forever, eterne, sempiternal, indesinent *and alteration cancelled in* MS1; *successively (a)* forever *(b)* forever, eterne, sempiternal, for aye *(c)* for all time, eterne, sempiternal, forever MS3
12 most] yea, *altered to* most MS3

Version 2
6–7 *repeated in* CJC
8–10 *successively (a)* Be kyriate and aggrandized his numen in the world [...]; *(b)* Be kyriate and aggrandized in the world [...] *(c)* Benedict, lauded [...] *(d)* Benedict and gloriate, lauded, exalted, extolled [...] *(e)* Benedict and hallelujah'd, gloriate, exalted, extolled, formosal magnified and lauded be his sanct name; MS4
13 glorifications ... anywhere] and solations that is MS4
18 May there be abundant peace [...] MS4

O SITE MOST KINGLY, O ROYAL SANCTUM. 1. *CJC*, 7 Oct. 1949, p. 8; 2–3. MS 5979 (MS1); MS 7408 (MS2); 4. *SS*, p. 117*.

MS1 and MS2 are contained in undated notes for lectures Klein gave after returning from his trip to Israel in 1949, and before publishing *SS*.

3 sorrow] sorrows *MS1, MS2*
7 garment] garments *MS1, MS2*
9 Arise! Arouse! Arise] Arise! Arise! Arise *CJC*; Arise, arise, arouse *MS1, MS2*
10 at last] at length *CJC, MS1, MS2*

Chaim Nachman Bialik. An essay by Klein, 'Chaim Nachman Bialik, 1873–1934' [*LER*, pp. 13–19], contains quotations from a number of his Bialik translations (including passages from some translations for which we have no complete versions). The MS of the essay is in the National Archives of the Canadian Jewish Congress, Montreal (photocopy in PAC, Klein Papers, vol. 35), and the essay forms part of a mimeographed pamphlet, *Chaim Nachman Bialik*, issued by the Hadassah Organization of Canada. Although the pamphlet is undated, it can be no later than 1937, when the essay was published in *Canadian Zionist* 5, 3 (June 1937), 35–6, 43. The essay was reprinted in *CJC*, 7 July 1939, pp. 3, 14. The two printed versions differ slightly and were probably set from two different hand-corrected copies of the pamphlet. A related set of lecture notes, dated 4 July 1942, is in the Klein Papers, MS 6888–96.

In addition to the essay on Bialik, the Hadassah pamphlet contains Klein's translations of several complete poems by Bialik. For three of these poems – BENEATH THE BURDEN, GOD GRANT MY PART AND PORTION BE ..., and THE LORD HAS NOT REVEALED – there are published versions dating from 1936, which, on the basis of textual evidence, predate the versions in the pamphlet. (In the case of a fourth poem published in 1936, THE CHASTISEMENT OF GOD, the evidence is unclear.) Therefore, the pamphlet can be no earlier than 1936.

Translations first appearing in the Hadassah pamphlet have been assigned a date of composition of c. 1936/1937.

Four of Klein's translations of Bialik are not represented in the pamphlet: SEER, BEGONE; STARS FLICKER AND FALL IN THE SKY; THY BREATH, O LORD, PASSED OVER AND ENKINDLED ME; and UPON THE SLAUGHTER. The MS for SEER, BEGONE is on the verso of the MS for THE WORD, which is quoted in the pamphlet; it has therefore been assigned the same date of composition, c. 1936/1937. THY BREATH, O LORD appears to be part of the same set of MSS as SEER, BEGONE and THE WORD (the group contains a number of fragmentary translations as well) and has been assigned the more tentative date, c. 1936/c. 1937. There is no MS for UPON THE SLAUGHTER, which appears only in *Efros*, but stylistically it closely resembles the other translations, and the MS for THY BREATH, O LORD contains a reference to its title, in Hebrew; it, too, has been assigned a date of c. 1936/c. 1937.

STARS FLICKER AND FALL IN THE SKY is in a different category. It is represented by a single MS which appears to date from the early fifties, a period when Klein extensively revised or entirely retranslated several earlier Bialik translations: IN THE CITY OF SLAUGHTER (originally THE CITY OF SLAUGHTER); DANCE OF DESPAIR (THE DANCE OF DESPAIR); O THOU SEER, GO FLEE THEE – AWAY (SEER, BEGONE); and A SPIRIT PASSED BEFORE ME (THY BREATH, O LORD). In style, as well as in handwriting (except for DANCE OF DESPAIR, for which there is no MS), these translations are closely related. Since IN THE CITY OF SLAUGHTER and DANCE OF DESPAIR were published in 1953, the others in the group have been assigned a date of composition of c. 1953/c. 1955.

In the notes to the Bialik translations the following abbreviations are used:
B1 – MS version of the Bialik essay
B2 – version of the essay included in the Haddasah pamphlet
B2a – translations of complete poems included in the Haddasah pamphlet
B3 – version of the essay in *Canadian Zionist* 5, 3 (June 1937), 35–6, 43
B4 – version of the essay in CJC, 7 July 1939, pp. 3, 14
B5 – MS 6888–96, lecture notes (4 July 1942)

BENEATH THE BURDEN ... 1. MS 5334, a typescript (MS1); 2. MS 5333, a typescript (MS2); 3. *Judaean* 9, 8 (May 1936), 61; 4. *Opinion* 6, 9 (July 1936), 17; 5. B1, p. 4 [1–8]; 6–7. B2, p. 3 [1–8]; B2a, p. 8; 8. B3, p. 36 [1–8]; 9. B4, p. 3 [1–8]; 10. B5, p. 4 [1–8]; 11. CJC, 10 July 1942, p. 4 [5–6]; 12. *Jewish Frontier* 10, 8 (Aug. 1943), 22*.

3 Ah] Oh MS1
8 humble] simple B1, B2, B3, B4, B5, CJC
15 No ... I] Now is no time MS1

THE CHASTISEMENT OF GOD. 1. MS 5335–6, a typescript (MS); 2. *Canadian Zionist* 3, 4 (Sept. 1936), 7 (CZ); 3–4. MS 5337, a revised tearsheet of CZ (CZrev1); a second revised tearsheet of CZ (CZrev2); 5. B1, p. 7 [1–6]; 6–7. B2, p. 6 [1–6]; B2a, pp. 11–12; 8. B3, p. 43 [1–6]; 9. B4, p. 15 [1–6]; 10. *Jewish Frontier* 9, 5 (May 1942), 12 (JF); 11. B5, pp. 6–7 [1–3, 5–8]; 12. CJC, 10 July 1942, p. 4 [1–8, 21–4]; 13. *Herzl-Bialik Memorial Book*, mimeographed pamphlet issued by Zionist Organization of Canada (June 1945), pp. 36–7*.

7 drips] drip JF
16 Not, not] No, not JF
26 tap upon] tap JF
windowpane.] MS, JF; windowpane, *all other versions*
33 Yea] MS, JF; Yes *all other versions*
37–8 You shall see in your windows the dead flies / The spiders weaving in the desolate cracks, MS
40 Penury] Destitution CZrev1

COME, GIRD YE YOUR LOINS, AND IN MIGHT ROBE YOURSELVES. 1. *B2a*, p. 17;
2. *Canadian Zionist* 5, 1 (Apr. 1937), 5; 3. *CJC*, 18 July 1941, p. 8 (*CJC1*)*;
4. *B5*, p. 7 [1–13]; 5. *CJC*, 10 July 1942, p. 4 [8–13] (*CJC2*).
Heading supplied by ed.
10 pillar and] hope and our *CJC2*

GOD GRANT MY PART AND PORTION BE ... 1. MS 5339–40, a typescript (MS);
2. *Judaean* 9, 8 (May 1936), 61 (*J*); 3. *B1*, p. 5 [36]; 4–5. *B2*, p. 4 [36]; *B2a*,
pp. 7–8; 6. *Opinion* 6, 9 (July 1936), 17 (*O*); 7. *B3*, p. 36 [36]; 8. *B4*, p. 14 [36];
9. *CJC*, 17 Apr. 1942, p. 3 [36, 10–15]; 10. *B5*, p. 5 [36]; 11. *CJC*, 10 July
1942, p. 4 [27–9, 33–6]; 12. *Jewish Frontier* 10, 6 (June 1943), 20–1 (*JF*)*.
No heading in MS
12 O poets] Poets MS
17 crooking,] *all versions except JF*; crooking *JF*
27 Yea] *all versions except JF*; Yes *JF*
32 museums] museum MS, *J*
34 your life] life *O*
53 In ... and] Revealed in the *O*

THE LORD HAS NOT REVEALED. 1. the unrevised typescript for MSrev (MS); 2. MS
5390–2 (MSrev); 3. *Canadian Zionist* 3, 4 (Sept. 1936), 7 (*CZ*); 4. MS 5338,
a revised tearsheet of *CZ* (CZrev); 5. *B1*, pp. 7–8 [26–30, 46–7, 50–1]; 6–7. *B2*,
p. 6 [26–30, 46–7, 50–1]; *B2a*, pp. 10–11; 8. *B3*, p. 43 [26–30, 46–7, 50–1];
9. *B4*, p. 14 [26–30, 46–7, 50–1]; 10. *Jewish Frontier* 9, 4 (Apr. 1942), 10*.
No heading in MS
2 for ... divined] has he divined for me MS; has he divined MSrev
11 of man] Man *B2a*
16 life] soul MS, MSrev
22 the foot] my foot MS, MSrev
26 like a pearl] a pearl *B2, B3, B4*

ON MY RETURNING. 1. *B2a*, p. 9; 2. *Canadian Zionist* 3, 9 (Feb. 1937), 93*.

THE CITY OF SLAUGHTER. 1. MS 5341–53 [except 128–75] (MS1); 2. *B1*, p. 7 [25–6];
3. *B2*, p. 6 [25–6]; 4. *B3*, p. 43 [25–6]; 5. *B4*, p. 14 [25–6]; 6. *CJC*, 2 Oct.
1940, pp. 9–11 [except 128–75] (*CJC1*); 7. MS 5374–86, a typescript [except
128–75] (MS2); 8. *CJC*, 10 July 1942, p. 4 [90–8, 121–6], p. 4 (*CJC2*); 9. *Jewish
Frontier* 9, 8 (Aug. 1942), 16–19 [except 128–75] (*JF*); 10. the unrevised typescript
for MS3rev (MS3); 11. MS 5361–73 [except 128–75] (MS3rev); 12. MS 5387–8,
a typescript [128–75] (MS4); 13. *Efros*, pp. 114–28 (*E*)* [version 1]; 14. *CJC*, 13
July 1951, p. 3 [15–26] (*CJC3*); 15. MS 5354–60, 5326 [1–158] (MS5)* [version

2, 82–158]; 16. *CJC*, 1 May 1953, p. 4 [1–81] (*CJC4*); 17. MS 5389, a revised tearsheet of *CJC4* (*CJC4*rev)* [version 2, 1–81].

MS2 represents a later stage of revision than *CJC1*, which is very close to the earliest version, MS1. However, MS2 is based directly on MS1, rather than on *CJC1*, since it retains a number of accidentals from MS1 which are missing in *CJC1*. Also, MS2 contains one meaningless reading, 'secret shame dooms' [200], which could only have arisen from a misreading of Klein's revision of MS1.

MS3 is a copy of *JF*, differing from it only in a few typographical errors. Evidence for this chronology (rather than the reverse) is certain peculiarities in MS3 which must have resulted from a misunderstanding of the format of *JF*: in *JF* the opening words of several sections are capitalized, and the initial letter is a large capital; to allow for this capital, the line below is indented. MS3 faithfully reproduces the capitalization and the no longer necessary indentation.

MS5 was intended for periodical publication, almost certainly for publication in *CJC*: the section corresponding to *CJC4* ends with the note '(To be continued),' and the next section, which is incomplete and was never published, begins with the note '(continued from last week).' The last page of MS5, MS 5326, is filed separately from the rest in the Klein papers, but it is clearly part of the same manuscript.

The Klein papers contain four sheets of notes (MS 5322–5) concerning individual words and phrases, indicating possible translations and biblical parallels.

The copy-text for version 2 is *CJC4*rev (rather than *CJC4*) for the published section of the poem [1–81], since it corrects the numerous typographical errors in *CJC4*; variants in MS5 for this section are noted under version 2. MS5 is the copy-text for the unpublished section of version 2 [82–158].

In version 1, line spaces omitted in the copy-text (E), presumably for reasons of space, have been restored, following MS1. The reading 'courtyards' [2] in MS1, MS5, *CJC4*, and *CJC4*rev, has been followed, rather than 'courtyard' in all other versions: it makes better sense and is the correct translation of the Hebrew original.

Version 1
Heading The City[In the City MS1, *CJC1*, MS2
2 courtyards] MS1, MS5, *CJC4*, *CJC4rev*; courtyard *all other versions*
wend] MS1, *CJC1*, MS2, *JF*; wind MS3, MS3*rev*, E
17 its blossoms] the blossoms MS1, *CJC1*
18 Whose] Their MS1, *CJC1*
19 And, spiting thee,] Unto thy nostrils this *all other versions*
21 sun] *all versions except* E; sun, E
22 Will bid thy melancholy to be gone; *all other versions*
24 Will bid thy sorrows pass; *all other versions*
27 observe its] and note a MS1, *CJC1*

41 Multitudinous ... will] The multitudinous eyes that MS1, CJC1
42 silences] *all versions except* E; silence E
44 at long last] after agonies *altered to* at long last MS1
47 as with their] and with a *altered to* as with their MS1
49 wraiths] thither *altered to* spirits MS1; ghosts CJC1
and cower there] a silent band *altered to* and cower there MS1
50 Their ... and] It is their silence asks; MS1, CJC1
55–6 brood ... / Question] brooding in the air / Go then, and question MS1, CJC1
65 Of] And MS1, CJC1
an infant's] that infant's MS2, JF, MS3, MS3rev
67 its] his *all other versions*
88 axes] axe MS1, CJC1
90 also,] *all versions except* E; also E
96–8 Watching – these heroes! – / The ignominious rabble tasting flesh, / Morsels for Neros! MS1, CJC1, MS2, CJC2, JF, MS3; Watching / The ignominious rabble portioning their flesh. MS3rev
103 Perhaps ... watcher] Indeed, each wretch then MS1, CJC1, MS2, JF, MS3
109 thanks] their thanks *all other versions*
110 sallied forth,] went forth, and MS1, CJC1
Rabbi's house they] Rabbi's MS1, CJC1
114 lairs,] *all versions except* E; lairs E
131 bloated] swollen MS4
136–7 descends ... flame] will set / Bleeding her clouds, and flaming gore MS4
139 ambient] ambience MS4
158–9 Brief-weary ... nook] Death-weary and forespent, black Immanence, / It is flung down MS4
162 wing outspread] wings outspread MS4
163–4 dead, / ... silence] dead. / Its tears are MS4
172 dream.] MS4; dream, E
177 thy] your MS1
178 sainted ... stone] saintly graves and martyr's stone *all other versions*
183 long to bellow] bellow CJC1
191–2 Hence, if you come to my door to ask for your reward / It shall be opened to you, and you shall see that Lord / Fallen from high estate. *all other versions*
195–6 for ... cause.] nor for whom. / Even as was your life, so reasonless was your doom. *all other versions*
200 secret shame] dreadful dooms *altered to* secret shame MS1; secret shame dooms MS2
201 My] God's MS1, CJC1, MS2, JF, MS3
207 blot] burden *altered to* blot MS1
209 But] And CJC1

214 tombstones] tombstones dost thou see *MS1, CJC1*
225–6 And fear and trembling will take hold of thee: / In such wise does a people cease to be. *MS1, CJC1, MS2, JF, MS3*
233 trials] trial *MS1, CJC1*
235 denials] denial *MS1, CJC1*
238 Crying] Crying *Peccavi MS1, CJC1, MS2; I have sinned JF, MS3, MS3rev*
239 *not in other versions*
249–50 Let their fists beat / The heavens and the heavenly [...] *altered to* Let fists be flung like stone / Against the heavens and the heavenly Throne. *MS1*
255 Bend down from Thy great mansions in the sky *MS1, CJC1, MS2, JF, MS3*; Remember the cloven infants and their cry! *MS3rev*
259 shall] will *JF, MS3, MS3rev*
thee,] and *all other versions*
260 will not] shall not *all other versions*
284 oil is] tallow's *MS1, CJC1, MS2, JF, MS3*
297 And] But *MS1*
301 brows] brow *MS1*
303 pity] greet *MS1, CJC1, MS2, JF, MS3*
307 For] But *MS1, CJC1*
318 then meet] again meet *altered to* then meet *MS1*; meet *CJC1*
339 And] Your customer, and *all other versions*
341 with] in your *MS1, CJC1*
342 nations] stranger *MS1, CJC1, MS2, JF, MS3*; gentile *MS3rev*
343 *their*] his *all other versions*
351 *replaced by 354 in JF, MS3*
Thy] *MS1, CJC1, MS2*; The *MS3rev, E*
353 And feed thou thy heart to rage, as to a worm! *MS1, CJC1, MS2, JF, MS3*
354 Thy] And O thy *MS3rev*

Version 2
no subheading in MS5
3 see – splashed] see it – *MS5*
4 tree ... stone,] hedge, on mortar, and *MS5*
8–9 walls ... these] walls, – and know / These stripped foundations, these burnt bricks *MS5*
14 garnered] treasured *MS5*
15 Breakage and fracture ...] *not in MS5*
29 You will fly] Flying *MS5*
36 this ... one] their mingled blood to single *altered to* their mingled blood to make one *MS5*
37 With feculence] With sewage and with feculence *MS5*
39 earth, will] deep, or *MS5*

44 Here, from] Here in *MS5*
45 murky] sombre *MS5*
47 stare] silent stare *MS5*
50 their] these *MS5*; the *CJC4*
54 here.] *MS5*; here *CJC4rev*
55 beg ... than] implore, there silence is a *MS5*
58 Survey ... eyes] Lift up your eyes to the roof, – *MS5*
59 damp ... cold] droppings have dropped their ultimate *altered to* mildew has dropped its final *MS5*
60 But the] The *MS5*
64 Of nostrils nailed ... smashed skulls ... lives snuffed ... *MS5*
66 spared babe] babe found *MS5*
72 as] they *MS5*
73 Spirit ... both] Your body ... spirit ... soul ... *MS5*
74 Here] Then *MS5*
75 here you will] then will you *MS5*
76 sink down deep] sink, to hide *MS5*
77 Deep in your heart before your heart will burst! *MS5*
78 You ... will] Then will you leave that place, and *MS5*
80 world] earth *MS5*

THE DANCE OF DESPAIR. 1. *B2a*, pp. 15–17; 2. *Canadian Zionist* 5, 3 (June 1937), 38 (*CZ*); 3. *CJC*, 19 Apr. 1940, p. 6 (*CJC1*); 4. *Jewish Frontier* 9, 9 (Sept. 1942), 21 (*JF*); 5. *CJC*, 7 Apr. 1944, p. 6 (*CJC2*); 6. *Efros*, pp. 214–17 (*E*)* [version 1]; 7. *CJC*, 24 Apr. 1953, p. 4 (*CJC3*)* [version 2].

The following notes list variants from *E* in all versions except *CJC3*, which is printed in full.

In all versions except *E*, the eight-line sections are numbered, and there is no refrain between sections.

Heading not translated in B2a, CZ, CJC1

1, 61 Muppim] Cry, Muppim *all other versions*
2, 62 and ... level] to lips set the fife *all other versions*
4, 64 A wedding: your father takes Lilith for wife! *all other versions*
5 there's ... cake] no, nor bread, neither cake *all other versions*
11 that ... to] which will be like the *B2a, CZ, CJC1*; will be like the *JF, CJC2*
13 of ... drop] no trickle of wine *all other versions*
14–16 Console thee, the full cup of gall is still thine! // The arm must not quiver as you cry wassail, / And quaff it until all your limbs almost fail, – *all other versions*
17 Go to,] And then *all other versions*
19 friends] friend *B2a, CZ*
20 Of your] Of our *all other versions*

28 The very last step of the dance is the tomb ... *all other versions*
29 friends] friend B2a, CZ
41 He ... His] is He who built roof, his blue *all other versions*
53 no revenge] and no meed *all other versions*
57–8 enkindling ... pyre!] a dance of your might / To kindle environs, refulgent and bright; *all other versions*

SEER, BEGONE. 1. MS 5393 (MS1)* [version 1]; 2. MS 5395 (MS2)* [version 2].

Version 1
10 rude] few *altered to* rude MS1

Version 2
15 rot ... fruit] O rot and fungus *altered to* rot, fungus, trodden fruit MS2

WHEN THE DAYS SHALL GROW LONG. 1. MS 5402–3, a typescript; 2. B2a, pp. 13–14; 3. *Canadian Zionist* 4, 10 (Mar. 1937), 103 (CZ); 4. CJC, 27 Dec. 1940, p. 13; 5. *Jewish Frontier* 10, 6 (June 1943), 20; 6. *Efros*, pp. 206–8*.
CZ and CJC have the subheading '(From the visions of the last prophets),' translated from the original.
14 hairs] hair CJC
15 And the whiskers of the cat shall grow bald. *all other versions*
17 bole] limbs *all other versions*
26 into] to *all other versions*
29 moan] murmur *all other versions*
37 web] sand *all other versions*
38 brains] brain *all other versions*
43 his] the CZ, CJC
45 low ... peaked] bruised of flesh, sour in breath *all other versions*

THE WORD. 1. MS 5394*; 2. B1, p. 5 [6–8]; 3. B2, p. 4 [6–8]; 4. B3, p. 36 [6–8]; 5. B4, p. 14 [6–8]; 6. B5, p. 5 [6–8].

THY BREATH, O LORD, PASSED OVER AND ENKINDLED ME. 1. the unrevised manuscript for MS1rev (MS1); 2. MS 5396 (MS1rev)* [version 1]; 2. MS 5397–8 (MS2); 3. MS 5399–400 (MS3)* [version 2].
The revisions to MS1 seem to have been added at a later date. MS2 consists of an incomplete rough draft of MS3. In MS3, 19–25 were originally in the past tense. In revising these lines, Klein missed 'were' in 23. This has been emended to 'are' for the sake of consistency.

Version 1
Heading supplied by ed.

1 over] over me MS1
3 the ... heart] *not in* MS1
4 not flowing] unflowing MS1
5 how] and how MS1
7 There] Here MS1
8 besmirched lips] the lips of the foul MS1
13 Loud] The MS1
17 proud-tongued] proud of tongue MS1
22 Whither to] Where shall I MS1
23 fire] flame MS1
26 [...] go] I shall go MS1
their [...]] their speech MS1
27 speech] lips MS1

Version 2
14 had sent] sent *altered to* had sent MS3
17 the rook's cawing] the cawing of rooks *altered to* the rook's cawing MS3
27 get] naturals *altered to* get MS3
27-8 monstrous ... cockled] impudent, arrogant, from the empty cockles of their *altered to* monstrous, arrogant, loathsome, a flux from empty-cockled MS3
36-7 and ... lips] *successively (a)* shall scald my lips with his coal *(b)* shall cauterize my lips with his coal *(c)* and his gleed shall cauterize my lips MS3

UPON THE SLAUGHTER. *Efros*, pp. 112–13.

STARS FLICKER AND FALL IN THE SKY. MS 5401.
Heading supplied by ed.

THE PRESCRIPTION. MS 2987–8.
The date of composition, c. 1953/c. 1955, has been assigned on the basis of handwriting and of the poem's inclusion in material for the unfinished novel *The Golem*, which dates from this period.
24 ailment] patient *altered to* ailment

WINE. *Schwarz*, pp. 598–9.

Yehuda Halevi. Klein's copy of the bilingual edition of *Selected Poems of Jehudah Halevi*, ed. Heinrich Brody, trans. Nina Salaman (Philadelphia: Jewish Publication Society of America 1924), now in the Montreal Jewish Public Library, contains two unpublished translations, BEAR THOU, O WIND, MY LOVE and O DOVE BESIDE THE WATER BROOK, in Klein's hand, and is dated 1936 in the same hand. This edition includes the originals of all the Halevi poems which Klein translated, and it is cited by him in a list of poems by Halevi [MS 5404], including LORD, HELE ME; O HEIGHTE SOVEREIGN; ODE TO ZION; and TO JERUSALEM THE HOLY. On the basis of the date of Klein's copy, and of the dates of publication of TO JERUSALEM THE HOLY (1936) and RUBAIYAT OF YEHUDA HALEVI (1938), a date of composition of c. 1936/ c. 1938 has been assigned to the unpublished translations and to ODE TO ZION, which was first published in 1941 as part of YEHUDA HALEVI, HIS PILGRIMAGE, but which clearly antedates the rest of the poem.

TO JERUSALEM THE HOLY. 1. *Canadian Zionist* 3, 5 (Oct. 1936), 23 (CZ);
    2. *Reconstructionist* 4, 9 (17 June 1938), 16 (R); 3. CJC, 20 Aug. 1948, p. 4*;
    4–6. MS 5842 (MS1); MS 5846–7 (MS2); MS 5980 (MS3); 7. SS, pp. 93–4 [9–12].
MS1, MS2, and MS3 are included in notes for lectures Klein gave after returning from his trip to Israel in 1949, and before publishing SS. MS1 and MS2 are both dated 21 Feb. 1950; MS3 is undated.
No heading in MS1, MS2, MS3, SS
7 thou art] CZ, R, MS3; thou are CJC; I am MS1, MS2
8 I in] in the MS1, MS2
12 thy] your CZ

BEAR THOU, O WIND, MY LOVE. In Klein's copy of *Selected Poems of Jehudah Halevi*, p. 56.
1–6 Bear thou, O wind, my greeting on thy wing, / And bring it, at the cool of dusk, to him / Of whom I ask but his remembering *on the opposite page*
3 bring it] *ed.*; bring
7 The] Of *altered to* The

LORD, HELE ME, Y-WIS I SHAL BE HELED. MS 5405.
Heading supplied by ed.

ODE TO ZION. The copy-text is CJC, 20 Aug. 1948, p. 4. For further details see textual notes to YEHUDA HALEVI, HIS PILGRIMAGE.

O DOVE BESIDE THE WATER BROOK. In Klein's copy of *Selected Poems of Jehudah Halevi*, pp. 66–7.
5 So ... beautiful] So beautiful, so fair *altered to* So fair, so beautiful

O HEIGHTE SOVEREIGN, O WORLDES PRYS. MS 5406–7.
The MS contains numerous rough notes and revisions, especially for 17–20.
Heading supplied by ed.

RUBAIYAT OF YEHUDA HALEVI. 1. *Reconstructionist* 3, 20 (11 Feb. 1938), 10–11 (R);
    2. CJC, 16 Aug. 1946, p. 8*.

935 / Textual Notes pp 773–81

Heading Rubaiyat] The Rubaiyat R
11 kept,] R; kept CJC
16 footsteps] footstep R
30 art] R; are CJC
43 those] these R
44 besprent] *ed.*; bespent R, CJC

UPON THE HIGHWAY. *Jewish Standard*, 11 Sept. 1931, p. 154.

KINGS OF THE EMEK. 1. *Judaean* 4, 4 (Jan. 1931), 6; 2. *CJC*, 6 Feb. 1931, p. 22; 3. *Schwarz*, pp. 642–3; 4. *CJC*, 9 Aug. 1946, p. 7*.

MOTHER JERUSALEM. 1. *Judaean* 4, 6 (Mar. 1931), 8 (J); 2. *Jewish Standard*, 11 Sept. 1931, p. 154 (JS); 3. *CJC*, 11 Oct. 1940, p. 7*.
Lines 45–6, 51–2, and 58–60 are missing in the copy-text. Because the missing passages are necessary to the sense, they have been restored.
Heading 'Jerusalem' J
26 poverty,] J, JS; poverty CJC
31 her ... day] it small; its day J
35 a riddle most] J; a riddle not JS; riddle not CJC
43 dost] J, JS; does CJC
48 yea, and] J; yea. And JS, CJC
50 one] J, JS; in CJC
61 me] me too JS
gates, no] J; gates no JS, CJC

BE THERE NO ALTAR. 1. *Judaean* 4, 4 (Jan. 1931), 6 (J); 2. *CJC*, Feb. 1931, p. 22; 3. *Opinion* 1, 7 (18 Jan. 1932), 10 (O)*.
3 be] J, CJC; by O
8 this city] these stones J, CJC

MAKE BLIND, O SUN OF JERUSALEM. 1. *Judaean* 4, 4 (Jan. 1931), 6; 2. *CJC*, 6 Feb. 1931, p. 22; 3. *Opinion* 1, 7 (18 Jan. 1932), 10*.

WITH EVERY STONE. 1. *Jewish Standard*, 11 Sept. 1931, p. 154 (JS); 2. *Opinion* 1, 11 (15 Feb. 1932), 7 (O); 3. *Judaean* 7, 7 (Apr. 1934), 56 (J)*.
1 stone;] JS, O; stone J
5 with stones] JS, O; with stone J
7 bones] JS, O; bows J
10 lime] JS, O; time J
thereon.] JS; thereon O, J

THE GLORY OF THE HOMELAND. 1. *Jewish Standard*, 11 Sept. 1931, pp. 152, 154 (*JS1*); 2. *Opinion* 1, 24 (16 May 1932), 15 (*O*); 3. *Judaean* 7, 7 (Apr. 1934), 56 (*J*); 4. *Jewish Standard*, Oct. 1935, p. 20 (*JS2*)*.
JS2 lacks line spacing; the line spacing of the other versions has been restored.
2 splendour] splendours *all other versions*
11 that eternity revealed] shall eternity reveal *J*
20 ensorceled] *ed.*; enscorceled *JS1, JS2*; ravished *O*; enscorched *J*
23 lands] land *O, J*
46–7 *reversed in JS2*
51 while] when *J*
52 I felt I knew] I felt, I knew *O*

BEHOLD. 1. *Judaean* 4, 4 (Jan. 1931), 6; 2. *CJC*, 6 Feb. 1931, p. 22 (*CJC1*); 3. *Opinion* 1, 7 (18 Jan. 1932), 13 (*O*); 4. *Schwarz*, pp. 643–4; 5. *CJC*, 9 Aug. 1946, p. 7 (*CJC2*)*.
2 is parchment] is a parchment *O*
14/15 *no line space in CJC2*

SABBATH. *Jewish Standard*, 11 Sept. 1931, p. 152.

UNFAVOURED. *Jewish Standard*, 11 Sept. 1931, p. 152.

NOW SUCH AM I ... 1. *Jewish Standard*, May 1937, p. 4; 2. typescript in the Canadian Jewish Congress archives; 3. *Schwarz*, pp. 644–5; 4. *CJC*, 9 Aug. 1946, p. 7*.

RACHEL. 1. *Jewish Standard*, May 1937, p. 4; 2. typescript in the Canadian Jewish Congress archives; 3. *Schwarz*, p. 645; 4. *CJC*, 9 Aug. 1946, p. 7*.

KINNERETH. 1. *Jewish Standard*, May 1937, p. 4; 2. typescript in the Canadian Jewish Congress archives; 3. *Schwarz*, p. 645; 4. *CJC*, 9 Aug. 1946, p. 7; 5. *SS*, p. 98*.
No heading in SS
4 labour] my labour *all other versions*
11 your] thy *all other versions*

DAWN. 1. *Jewish Standard*, May 1937, p. 4 (*JS*); 2. typescript in the Canadian Jewish Congress archives; 3. *Schwarz*, pp. 645–6; 4. *CJC*, 9 Aug. 1946, p. 7*.
8 road] roads *JS*

THE CHILDLESS ONE. 1. *Jewish Standard*, May 1937, p. 4; 2. typescript in the

Canadian Jewish Congress archives; 3. *Schwarz*, p. 646; 4. *CJC*, 9 Aug. 1946, p. 7*.

THE PRAYER OF A PHYSICIAN. *Canadian Medical Association Journal* 56 (1947), 100–1.

THE ELEVENTH: IN MEMORY OF ISAAC, SON OF THE TAILOR. *CJC*, 7 Feb. 1947, p. 7.

THE GIFTED ONE. *CJC*, 7 Feb. 1947, p. 7.

SMOKE. *CJC*, 7 Feb. 1947, p. 7.
7 art] *ed.*; are *CJC*
8 All of us] *ed.*; All of *CJC*

PORTRAIT OF THE ARTIST. *CJC*, 9 Sept. 1932, p. 5.

CANTICUM CANTICORUM. *CJC*, 9 Sept. 1932, p. 5.
21 head,] *ed.*; head. *CJC*

THE LAST SONG. 1. *CJC*, 9 Sept. 1932, p. 5; 2. *Jewish Observer* 4, 1 (Dec. 1945), 93 (*JO*)*.
2 too,] *CJC*; too *JO*
3 flung] did fling *CJC*
5 sky] *CJC*; sky, *JO*
11 Sat the prophet, on a stone, and lonely, *CJC*

KI-KI. *CJC*, 9 Sept. 1932, p. 5.

THE GOLDEN PARROT. *CJC*, 9 Sept. 1932, p. 5.

CONCEIT CURIOUS. *CJC*, 9 Sept. 1932, p. 5.

LAST WILL AND TESTAMENT. *CJC*, 9 Sept. 1932, p. 5.

WE ARE A GENERATION, HEAVEN-DOOMED. *CJC*, 26 May 1933, p. 8.

YOU WALK UPON YOUR SUNLIT ROADS. *CJC*, 26 May 1933, p. 8.

NO MORE TEARS. *Jewish Observer* 4, 1 (Dec. 1945), 93.

THE WINDOWS ARE GRATED. *Jewish Observer* 4, 1 (Dec. 1945), 93.
Heading supplied by ed.

SUNSET. *Jewish Observer* 1, 3 (Jan. 1944), 21.

AND THIS I KNOW. 1. MS 5431–2 (MS); 2. *Leftwich*, p. 403; 3. *Canadian Jewish Yearbook* (1940–1), p. 145*.
MS is part of a group of manuscripts including KING RUFUS, which was published in 1931; hence the assigned date of composition, c. 1931/1931.

AUTOBIOGRAPHICAL. 1. MS 5429–30 (MS); 2. *Leftwich*, p. 404 (L); 3. *Canadian Jewish Yearbook* (1940–1), p. 144 (CJY)*.
MS is part of a group of manuscripts including KING RUFUS, which was published in 1931; hence the assigned date of composition, c. 1931/1931.
8 weary] wearied MS, L
9 all things] things all MS
12 earth] the earth MS, L
20 I fall in] MS, L; If all is CJY

GOATS. MS 5427 (MS).
MS is part of a group of manuscripts including KING RUFUS, which was published in 1931; hence the assigned date of composition, c. 1931/1931.

A KING. 1. MS 5425–6 (MS); 2. *Leftwich*, pp. 405–6*.
MS is part of a group of manuscripts including KING RUFUS, which was published in 1931; hence the assigned date of composition, c. 1931/1931.

KING RUFUS. 1. MS 5428; 2. YMHA *Beacon* 6, 14 (1 May 1931), 37 (Y); 3. *Leftwich*, pp. 404–5*.
18 journey] journey on Y

CONFESSION. 1. *CJC*, 23 Oct. 1940, p. 4* (CJC1); 2. MS 5433, a revised tearsheet of CJC1 (CJC1rev); 3. *CJC*, 12 Mar. 1954, p. 3 [1–12, 25–36] (CJC2).
3 Who comes] Come now CJC2
7 those] these CJC2
11–12 ones ... from] ones, the connivers, / Lorded it in CJC2
12 from] through CJC1rev
27 while they go] themselves all CJC2
28 golden] gold CJC2
34 change that] small change CJC1rev, CJC2
36 It will be paid, whatever's due. CJC2
Hard] Near CJC1rev

writ] write *CJC1rev*

OLD GOLD. 1. *CJC*, 23 Oct. 1940, p. 4 (*CJC1*)*; 2. MS 5433, a revised tearsheet of *CJC1* (*CJC1*rev); 3. *CJC*, 12 Mar. 1954, p. 3 [1–8, 21–8] (*CJC2*).
2 A ... broken,] And a peaceful tribe is broken, and *CJC2*
4 grandfather's. His] grandfather's, whose *CJC1rev*, *CJC2*
6 bent] cracked *CJC2*
7 I took, then, bag and baggage, warp and woof, *CJC2*
8 the ... fared] the lost exile, went *CJC1rev*; a lost exile, went *CJC2*
21 And] O, *CJC2*
22 little golden] famous little *CJC2*
23 lullaby] melody *CJC2*
25 and did brood] twilight-hooded *CJC2*
27 And on] Upon *CJC2*
27–8 stood; / ... in] brooded ... / Then ... slid into *CJC2*

REB ZORACH. *CJC*, 23 Oct. 1940, p. 4.

SONG. 1. *CJC*, 23 Oct. 1940, p. 4 (*CJC1*)*; 2. MS 5433, a revised tearsheet of *CJC1* (*CJC1*rev); 3. *CJC*, 12 Mar. 1954, p. 6 [1–12, 17–20] (*CJC2*); 4. MS 25168, a revised tearsheet of *CJC2* (*CJC2rev*).
In *CJC1rev* and *CJC2* all second person pronouns are plural.
2 A sheep] You sheep *CJC1rev*; Like a sheep *CJC2*
3 bear] carry *CJC2rev*
6 Lamb fallen to the ground! *CJC2*
7 weary] tired *CJC2rev*
8 And have no water found. *CJC2*
10 The] That *CJC2*
11 laves her bright] washes her *CJC1rev*, *CJC2*
18 A sheep] Sheep *CJC2*
19 bear] carry *CJC2*

WAR. 1. *CJC*, 23 Oct. 1940, p. 4 (*CJC1*)*; 2. MS 5433, a revised tearsheet of *CJC1* (*CJC1*rev); 3. *CJC*, 12 Mar. 1954, p. 3 [7–15] (*CJC2*).
9 The God] And the God *CJC2*
11 And wonders] And, wondering *CJC2*
11–12 day. / ... his] day. / Drinks in the dew with his great *CJC1rev*; day, / Drinks the dew in with his large *CJC2*

SPEAK TO YOUR PEOPLE, THEREFORE, IN THIS WISE. *CJC*, 2 Nov. 1945, p. 16. *Heading supplied by ed.*

Jewish Folk-Songs. The title for this collection of twenty-seven translations has been taken from Klein's essay of that name (see below). The collection is contained in an untitled notebook [MS 5557–94]. Three of the translations (O MY MOTHER SENT ME; COME YOU HERE, PHILOSOPHER; and HUSH! HUSH!) are also in typescript [MS 5551–3]. The second of these was published in the *Judaean* 3, 3 (Dec. 1929), 8; a date of composition of c. 1929/1929 has therefore been assigned to the notebook as a whole. Most of the translations were published, singly or in groups. Some were included in Klein's 'Jewish Folk-Songs' essay; others in the plays *Hershel of Ostropol* and *Worse Visitors We Shouldn't Have*.

In the notes to 'Jewish Folk-Songs' the following abbreviations are used:

JFS1, JFS2, JFS3 – 'Jewish Folk-Songs,' *Judaean* 5, 9 (June 1932), 2, 5–6; and its reprints in *CJC*, 2 Sept. 1932, pp. 6–7; *CJC*, 7 Apr. 1944, pp. 9–10

HO, HOMS – *Hershel of Ostropol*, *CJC*, 31 Mar. 1939, pp. 19–27; 13 Sept. 1939, pp. 19–26; and its typescript [MS 4033–88]

WV1, WV2 – the two typescripts of *Worse Visitors We Shouldn't Have* [MS 4814–907, MS 4908–5007] (early fifties)

Unless otherwise indicated, headings have been supplied by the editor.

SHALL I BE A RABBI? 1. MS 5557 (MS)*; 2. *Canadian Zionist* 3, 4 (Sept. 1936), p. 3 [1–10] (CZ)*; 3. HOMS, p. 44 [1–10]; 4. HO (13 Sept.), p. 23 [1–10]; 5. WV1, p. 72 [1–10]; 6. WV2, p. 71 [1–10].

CZ has been chosen as the copy-text rather than the later HO because the revisions in HO were determined by the dramatic context, and it is unlikely that Klein would have retained them apart from this context. Lines 11–20 have been supplied from MS.

3 merchant] peddler HOMS, HO, WV1, WV2
5 Now] And *all other versions*
fodder] liquor HOMS, HO, WV1, WV2
6 And the horse neighs hungrily, MS; *not in* HO, HOMS, WV1, WV2
7 the ... nasty] wife has a shrewish MS; the wife's a shrewish HOMS, HO; my wife's a bitter WV1, WV2
9 I behold] So I see WV1, WV2
10 moan] groan WV1, WV2

COME YOU HERE, PHILOSOPHER. 1. MS 5558–9 (MS1); 2. MS 5552, a typescript (MS2); 3. *Judaean* 3, 3 (Dec. 1929), 8 (J); 4. *CJC*, 10 Jan. 1930, p. 22*; 5. HOMS, pp. 25–6 [1–12, 17–20]; 6. HO (31 Mar.), p. 26 [1–12, 17–20]; 7. MS 5458–9 (MS3); 8. MS 5497 (MS4); 9. WV1, p. 19 [1–8]; 10. WV2, p. 20 [1–8].

No heading in MS1, MS2, HOMS, HO, WV1, WV2; 'The Philosopher' MS3, MS4, MS5
1 here] nigh *altered to* here MS1
5 steamboat] drawbridge HOMS, HO
5–6 devised ... / And] thought up, and now / You WV1, WV2

941 / Textual Notes pp 817–21

6 the] your WV1, WV2
9 Strange flying kites you fashion, and HOMS, HO fashioned,] MS1, MS2, J, MS3, MS4, MS5; fashioned CJC
19 there] then HOMS, HO

CHARM. 1. MS 5560; 2. CJC, 31 May 1946, p. 8*.
No heading in CJC

TEAR NOT YOUR HAIR, MY SWEETHEART. MS 5561.

AND WHEN ONE BURNS – ONE BURNS BRANDY. 1. MS 5562; 2. *Jewish Standard*, 22 Apr. 1932, p. 127; 3. JFS1, p. 6; 4. JFS2, p. 7; 5. JFS3, p. 10; 6. CJC, 31 May 1946, p. 8*.

ON THE ATTIC SLEEPS A ROOF. 1. the unrevised MS for MSrev (MS); 2. JFS1, p. 2; 3. JFS2, p. 6; 4. JFS3, p. 9; 5. MS 5562–4 (MSrev); 6. CJC, 31 May 1946, p. 8*.
The revisions in MSrev are limited to 8–11.
MS originally had 'roof' in the second line of the refrain. Klein altered it to 'thatch' in the first and second occurrences of the refrain, but neglected to do so in the third, which is on the following page. In JFS1, JFS2, and JFS3 the refrain occurs only once (with 'thatch'), but CJC reproduces the inconsistency of MS. Since the inconsistency is almost certainly unintentional, 'roof' has been emended to 'thatch' in 20.
6, 13 thatch] roof *altered to* thatch MS
9–10 In it swings a spider, who / Draws my life-blood out of me, MS, JFS1, JFS2, JFS3
10 on my blood] at my breast *altered to* on my blood MSrev
11 Leaves me nothing more than rue ... MS; Leaves me bitterness and rue. JFS1, JFS2, JFS3
17 borrow, and] borrow aught, *all other versions*
20 thatch] *ed.*; roof MS, CJC

YOMA, YOMA, PLAY ME A DITTY. 1. MS 5565–6 (MS); 2. CJC, 31 May 1946, p. 8*.
MS has 'this lassie' wherever CJC has 'our young girl' or 'this young girl.'
In CJC, 3 has been accidentally repeated in place of 17. The correct reading has been supplied from MS.

HUSH! HUSH! 1. MS 5567 (MS1); 2. MS 5553, a typescript (MS2); 3. *Jewish Standard*, 22 Apr. 1932, p. 127 (JS)*; 4. MS 5460 (MS3); 5. MS 5498 (MS4); 6. MS 5534, a typescript (MS5).
No heading in MS1, MS2, JS; 'Sha! Shtill' *altered to* 'Hush! Hush!' MS3
7 right good] proper MS4, MS5

WE ASK OUR BOARDING-MISTRESS. 1. MS 5568–9 (MS); 2. *Jewish Standard*, 22 Apr. 1932, p. 127; 3. JFS1, p. 2; 4. JFS2, p. 6; 5. JFS3, p. 10; 6. CJC, 31 May 1946, p. 8*.
4/5 Refrain: / I curse the hour, / I curse the fatal hour, / When I abandoned / My mother's sheltered bower. MS

SONG OF WINE. 1. MS 5571–3 (MS)*; 2. JFS1, p. 5 [33–44]; 3. JFS2, p. 7 [33–44]; 4. JFS3, p. 10 [33–44]*.
MS is the copy-text for 1–32; JFS3 for 33–44.
No heading in JFS1, JFS2, JFS3

THE GOLDEN PARRAKEET. MS 5574–5.

WHEN I KNEAD THE DOUGH. 1. MS 5576 (MS); 2. JFS1, pp. 5–6; 3. JFS2, p. 7; 4. JFS3, p. 10*.
MS has 'I' altered to 'If I' wherever the other versions have 'When I.'
6 far too] too MS

I GO UPON THE BALCONY. 1. MS 5577 (MS); 2. *Jewish Standard*, 15 Apr. 1932, p. 103 (JS); 3. CJC, 31 May 1946, p. 8*.
Heading 'Folk Song' JS
15 sweetheart] girl who has loved a boy *altered to* sweetheart MS

ONCE UPON A TIME; THIS. MS 5578–9.

BETTER A HEBREW TEACHER. 1. MS 5580 (MS); 2. JFS1, p. 2; 3. JFS2, p. 6; 4. JFS3, p. 10; 5. CJC, 31 May 1946, p. 8*.
4 pants half-rotted] clothes all blotted JFS1, JFS2, JFS3
5 bible] private *altered to* bible MS
11 an apothecary] apothecaries MS; wise apothecaries JFS1, JFS2, JFS3
12 fries his] fry their *all other versions*

O MY MOTHER SENT ME. 1. MS 5581; 2. MS 5551, a typescript; 3. *Jewish Standard*, 22 Apr. 1932, p. 127*.

ON THE HILL, OVER THE HILL. MS 5582.
5 harness me,] harness, my *altered to* harness me,
9 fugitive] *ed.*; fugitive's
10 them ... bridge] my youthful years *altered to* them on the bridge
14 Assuredly] Most certainly *altered to* Assuredly

GONE IS THE YESTERDAY. MS 5583.

4 Betray] Assoil *altered to* Betray
6 The while you all are living *altered to* While living and while dancing

AND AT MY PRAYERS I WILL QUIVER. MS 5584.
11 planets] worlds *altered to* planets

ASKS THE WORLD AN OLD, OLD QUESTION. 1. MS 5585 (MS); 2. WV1, p. 1*.
1 Ask the folk an ancient query MS
5 But] And MS
7 old, old question] ancient query MS
10 *not in* MS

AND WHEN MESSIAH WILL COME. 1. MS 5586 (MS); 2. HOMS, pp. 14–15; 3. HO (31 Mar.), p. 22*.
MS has been followed for 5 and 9 since the revisions in HOMS and HO were determined by the dramatic context and it is unlikely that Klein would have retained them apart from this context.
5 And] MS; For HOMS, HO
9 And] MS; Then HOMS, HO

O WHAT DO YOU WISH, MY DEAREST CHILD. 1. MS 5587–8 (MS1)*; 2. *JFS1*, p. 5; 3. *JFS2*, pp. 6–7; 4. *JFS3*, p. 10*.
JFS1, *JFS2*, and *JFS3* lack both the refrain and the couplet dealing with the tailor's apprentice [7–8]; these have been supplied from MS.
12 must declare herself] wishes her very self MS
15 from] of MS

TELL ME, PRETTY MAIDEN, O HEARKEN PRETTY MAIDEN. MS 5589.

WHAT IS LOFTIER THAN A HOUSE? MS 5590.
3 fool] *ed.*; full

WHEN HE HAS FROLICKED FOR A LITTLE. 1. MS 5592 (MS); 2. *JFS1*, p. 2; 3. *JFS2*, p. 6; 4. *JFS3*, p. 9*.
1 he has] we have MS
4 town] world *altered to* town MS
11 The … dwell] And he will live *altered to* The groom will live MS

LOVELY AM I, O LOVELY, AND LOVELY IS MY NAME. 1. MS 5593 (MS1); 2. *JFS1*, p. 5; 3. *JFS2*, p. 7; 4. *JFS3*, p. 10*.
3 no other] no person *altered to* no other person MS

4 to ... dearly-cherished] my mother's cherished *altered to* my mother's dearly-cherished MS
5 Water ... chamber] Water in the chamber *altered to* Water is in the chamber *and* Fish are in the water *added after end of poem in* MS
sticks in the shed] in the house are ⟨sticks⟩ MS
6 he'll ... head] I bid him get him gone *altered to* he'll have these on his head MS

I SIT ME DOWN UPON A STONE. 1. MS 5594 (MS); 2. *JFS1*, p. 5; 3. *JFS2*, p. 7; 4. *JFS3*, p. 10*.
1 me down] *not in JFS2*
5 Alackaday] O, woe is me *altered to* Alackaday MS
7–9 Today [...] MS

Chassidic Folk-Songs. The thirty-two 'Chassidic Folk-Songs' went through four main stages: (1) they were all entered, in various states of completion, in an untitled notebook [MS 5434–85]; (2) some of the entries in the notebook were revised; (3) the revised notebook served as the basis for a set of manuscripts [MS 5486–518]; (4) these, in turn, served as the basis for a set of typescripts [MS 5519–50]. In the comments that follow, and in the notes to individual translations, these four stages are referred to as MS1, MS1rev, MS2, and MS3, respectively.

A number of the items in MS1, especially towards the end of the notebook, consist only of headings or of notes. Some of these are expanded into complete translations in MS1rev, and for all the items in the notebook (with the exception of headings and notes for two, MS 5435 and 5470) there are corresponding complete translations in MS2 and/or MS3.

MS1 has been assigned a date of composition of c. 1946/1946 since Klein's essay 'On Translating the Yiddish Folk-Song' [*CJC*, 30 Aug. 1946, p. 6] refers to several of the unrevised translations in the notebook. There is evidence to suggest that MS1rev, MS2, and MS3 all date from 1951 at the earliest. The evidence is of three sorts: (1) On 18 Apr. 1951, Klein sent his publisher, Alfred A. Knopf, the opening lines of A THOU SONG, to be used as an epigraph for *The Second Scroll*. The version Klein sent is intermediate between MS1 and MS1rev. (2) The version of HUSH! HUSH! in MS2 [MS 5498] is written on the verso of notes for a lecture on the Bible manuscripts [MS 5499]. Klein published an essay on this topic in *CJC*, 28 Sept. 1951, p. 9, and he delivered a lecture on it on 25 Dec. 1951 [MS 7024–7]. (3) The handwriting of MS2 resembles that of other manuscripts which can be assigned to the early fifties. Therefore, all translations which first appear in completed form in MS1rev, MS2, or MS3 are assigned a date of composition of 1951/1955.

In some cases, where revisions to MS1 have been so extensive as to produce what is, in effect, a new translation, two versions have been printed. In one case, Klein translated a poem in both 'Jewish Folk-Songs' and 'Chassidic Folk-Songs,' in versions so different (AND AT MY PRAYERS I WILL QUIVER/OY, VEY, REBBENU) that both have been printed. Two translations, COME YOU HERE, PHILOSOPHER and HUSH! HUSH!, were copied directly from 'Jewish Folk-Songs.' They are printed only in the earlier collection.

L'CHAYIM, REBBE! 1. MS 5434 (MS1); 2. MS 5519 (MS3)*.
5, 6 Through] By MS1

OY, OUR REBBENU. 1. MS 5436–7 (MS1); 2. MS 5521 (MS3)*.
Heading] ed.; 'Oy Du Rebbenu' MS1; 'Oh, Our Rebbenu' MS3
4 *successively* (a) We'll be [...] (b) We will be leaving for his [...] (c) For our Rebbe's court we'll be leaving MS1
7 Then] And MS1
8–12 *not in* MS1

GOD WILLING, AT THE REBBE'S. 1. MS 5438–40 (MS1); 2. MS 5522 (MS3)*.
4, 5 see each other] meet again MS1
7, 11, 20, 24, 33, 37 of God's] God's MS1
8–9, 12–13, 21–2, 25–6, 34–5, 38–9 *successively* (a) And God willing, / We will meet [quaff it, hop it] again. (b) And God willing, / We will meet [quaff it, hop it] at the Rebbe's again. (c) At the Rebbe's court, God willing, / We will meet [quaff it, hop it] again. MS1
17, 18 drink together] drink again *altered to* quaff it again MS1
30, 31 dance together] hop it again MS1

MYERKA, MY SON. 1. MS 5441–2 (MS1); 2. MS 5486–7 (MS2); 3. MS 5523 (MS3)*.
15 For life and for sustenance, for chiiildren [sic] MS1; For life and for sustenance, and for children *altered to* For the daily bread of my house, and for children MS2
24 O, I am the pauper in deeds. MS1

A THOU SONG. 1. MS 5443 (MS1); 2. MS in the Knopf papers, University of Texas at Austin Library [1, 4–6, 8–10] (SSMS); 3. epigraph to SS [1, 4–6, 8–10]; 4. the unrevised MS for MS2rev (MS2); 5. MS 5488 (MS2rev); 6. MS 5527 (MS3)*.
SSMS forms part of a letter to Herbert Weinstock, of Alfred A. Knopf, 18 Apr. 1951.
4 I'll] I will MS1, SSMS, SS, MS2
6 shall] can MS1
where, where] where MS1, SSMS, SS, MS2
8 For where] wherever MS1, SSMS, SS
9 Or here or] Stay here, turn MS1
10 Ever] And still MS1, SSMS, SS, MS2

13 ill –] ill – oy – MS1
18 Above – thou; below, thou – MS1; Up there, Thou! Down here, Thou! MS2; Skyscape, Thou! Landscape, Thou! *added in margin of MS2rev as possible alternative to above; both alternatives in MS3 but the first x'd over*
20–2 Wherever I turn / Wherever I tarry – Thou! / Thou! MS1, MS2

LEVI YITSCHOK'S KADDISH. 1. MS 5444–6 (MS1); 2. MS 5489 (MS2); 3. MS 5525 (MS3)*.
3 Come to] *successively (a)* Appear before *(b)* Do come now to *(c)* Do come to MS1; *(c) altered to* Come to MS2
your people] *successively (a)* thy people *(b)* thy fol[...] *(c)* your people MS1
6 aught ado] something up *altered to* aught ado MS1
7 something up] aught ado *altered to* something up MS1
18 abandon my plea] budge me from my place MS1; *successively (a)* budge from my place *(b)* abandon this stance *(c)* abandon my plea MS2
19 O let there be an end to it, MS1; *successively (a)* O let there be an end to it – *(b)* And an end let there be *(c)* Until an [...] *(d)* Ere an end is decreed MS2
20 wandering fate] long exile MS1; long exile *altered to* wandering fate MS2

M'LAVEH MALKEH. 1. MS 5447 (MS1); 2. MS 5490 (MS2); 3. MS 5526 (MS3)*.
4, 7 The little Jew, the good Jew MS1
6 Deems] Then feels MS1
12–13 Dance, my hearties / Singly, and in parties MS1
14 For] Our MS1
16 As a hair MS1

THOU HAST CHOSEN US. 1. the unrevised MS for MS1rev (MS1); 2. MS 5448–9 (MS1rev); 3. MS 5491 (MS2); 4. MS 5527 (MS3)*.
Heading 'Atoh B'chartonu' MS1, MS1rev
1 O thou, Lord, hast elected us from out all nations *on facing page in MS1rev*
among all] all the MS1
2, 4 lavished favour on] didst favour MS1
6 nations] people MS1
7 blessed and hallowed] hallowed MS1
9 sanctified] *successively (a)* blessed *(b)* hallowed *(c)* sanctified MS1

O THERE, O THERE, WHERE IS OUR HOLY REBBE. 1. the unrevised MS for MS1rev (MS1)* [version 1]; 2. MS 5450–1 (MS1rev); 3. MS 5492 (MS2); 4. MS 5528 (MS3)* [version 2].
The revisions in MS1rev end at 6.
No heading in MS1, MS1rev, MS2

Version 2
2 is found] abounds MS1rev
3 There be the glory, and there the faith enduring! *altered to* There be the glory, and there the faith that mountains moves! MS1rev

THE REBBE, HE WANTED. 1. the unrevised MS for MS1rev (MS1)* [version 1]; 2. MS 5452–4 (MS1rev); 3. MS 5493 (MS2); 4. MS 5529 (MS3)* [version 2]. The revisions in MS1rev end at 9.

Version 1
6 Chassidim along with him *altered to* With him the Chassidim he's got MS1

Version 2
1 Rebbe wished] Rebbe, ⟨he⟩ wished MS2
journey up] make a trip MS1rev
2 And no horse did he have MS1rev; But he had not a [...] *altered to* But he didn't own a horse MS2
4 So horses appeared, in an hour. MS1rev
6 Chassidim, the whole pious lot *altered to* the Chassidim, the whole lot MS1rev; *above altered to* With him, our Chassidim, ho! MS2
7 that ... that] a pleasure that as yet MS1rev
8 surely ... know] surely can not have *altered to* surely can not ever have MS1rev
28 *successively* (a) The Rebbe wanted tobacco for to make snuff of (b) The Rebbe wished tobacco for to make snuff of (c) The Rebbe wished for Turkish tobacco for sniffing MS2

IN GOD'S GOOD TIME. 1. MS 5455 [1–2] (MS1); 2. MS 5530 (MS3)*; 3. MS 4827–8, first typescript of *Worse Visitors We Shouldn't Have*, pp. 14–15 [1–24] (WV1); 4. MS 4922–3, second typescript of *Worse Visitors We Shouldn't Have*, pp. 15–16 [1–24] (WV2).
WV1 and WV2 date from the early fifties.
No heading in MS1, WV1, WV2
1–2 What will be / With our Rebbe the pious / In due time / With Messiah arriving MS1
4 guzzled] drunk down WV1, WV2
9 leafage] leaves WV1, WV2
14 Red] red Red WV1, WV2
15 neat] well WV1, WV2
20 right good] first class WV1, WV2

A BURGLARY. 1. MS 5456 (MS1); 2. MS 5495 (MS2); 3. MS 5531 (MS3)*.

TELL US, REBBENU. 1. MS 5457 [heading] (MS1); 2. MS 5496 (MS2); 3. MS 5532 (MS3)*.
Heading 'When Messiah Will Come' MS1; no heading in MS2
18 Moishe Rebenu] Moses, our Master altered to Moishe Rebenu MS2

YOSHKA, YOSHKA. 1. MS 5461 [heading] (MS1); 2. MS 5500 (MS2); 3. MS 5535 (MS3)*.
Heading 'The Rebbe, He Bade Us Be Jolly' MS1; no heading in MS2
4 We'll] We will altered to We'll MS2
not ever] forever altered to not ever MS2
5 drink and dine] be jolly altered to drink and dine MS2

OY, VEY, REBBENU. 1. MS 5463 [heading] (MS1); 2. MS 5501 (MS2); 3. MS 5536 (MS3)*.
16 O for] Before altered to O for MS2

OUR REBBE, THE MIRACLE-WORKER, ONCE. 1. the unrevised MS for MS1rev (MS1); 2. MS 5465 (MS1rev); 3. MS 5502 (MS2); 4. MS 5537 (MS3)*.
MS1 contains notes, but no text, for 18–22. The revisions in MS1rev end at 13.
Heading 'There Fared upon the Seas' MS1, MS1rev
2–4 Travelled upon the high seas / And the voyage that should have taken long years / He made in one night, with ease. MS1; Travelled on the high seas / The voyage that should have taken long years / He made in a single night, with ease. MS1rev
2 ocean wide] stormy seas altered to ocean wide MS2
5, 6 sails] travels MS1
7 they sail] travel MS1
8 then their eyes] they MS1; their eyes MS1rev
9 What none did ever view. MS1; What noone else had ever seen. MS1rev
11 and blessed] not in MS1
12 The scoffers who don't believe this fact MS1, MS1rev
13 Their names be blotted out. MS1; Their names be erased, blotted out. altered to Their names be erased and rubbed out. MS1rev
20 His holy look he looked – MS1
23–4 originally reversed in MS2
28 So do you still need further proof altered to Although the atheists who scoff MS1
30 ask for] need some MS1
31 That ... is] Our Rebbe's MS1

AND WHEN OUR REBBE WALKS. 1. MS 5467 (MS1); 2. MS 5504 (MS2); 3. MS 5538 (MS3)*.

OUR REBBE. 1. the unrevised MS for MS1rev (MS1)* [version 1]; 2. MS 5468 (MS1rev); 3. MS 5505 (MS2); 4. MS 5539 (MS3)* [version 2].

MY NODDLE IT IS HUMMING. 1. MS 5469–70 [notes] (MS1); 2. MS 5506 [1–6] (MS2); 3. MS 5540 (MS3)*.
Heading 'I Just Came from My Zaddik' *MS1*; 'I Come Now from My Master' *MS2*
1–6 I come now from my Master – / And need a headache plaster / For such rare learning / Did I gather there. / O every single tenet / Of his, I will explain it, / Miracles and wonders / Rendered true and clear. *MS2*

THE TRAIN. 1. the unrevised MS for MS1rev (MS1); 2. MS 5471–2 (MS1rev); 3. MS 5507 (MS2); 4. MS 5541 (MS3)*.
The revisions in MS1rev end at 6.
Heading 'The Railway' *MS1*
3 tell] will tell *MS1*
6 past all choking] beyond choking *MS1*; not to be choked on *altered to* never to be choked on *MS1rev*
9 *not in MS1*
15 kind of trip] vehicle *MS1*
17 Who has no whip at all ... *MS1*
20–1 never ... wheels] always on the Sabbath / His wheels shall not *MS1*

HOW FARES THE KING? 1. MS 5473 [heading] (MS1); 2. MS 5508 (MS2); 3. MS 5542 (MS3)*.
Heading Fares] Does *MS1*
1 Rabosai, Rabosai] Rebono shel Olam *altered to* Rabosai, Rabosai *MS2*

THE REBBELE, THE GABBAI'LE, THE CANTOR'L, THE SHAMASH'L. 1. MS 5474 [heading] (MS1); 2. MS 5509 (MS2); 3. MS 5543 (MS3)*.

TSIG, TSIGITSAPEL. 1. MS 5475 [heading] (MS1); 2. MS 5510 (MS2); 3. the unrevised typescript for MS3rev (MS3); 4. MS 5544 (MS3rev)*.
15 Who] And *MS2, MS3*
there] so *altered to* there *MS2*

MIRACLES AND WONDERS. 1. MS 5476 (MS1); 2. MS 5511 (MS2); 3. MS 5545 (MS3)*.
15 I know whereof I'm talking *MS1*
17 And he, he sets him walking *MS1*; above *altered to* And he sets him a-walking *MS2*

AKAVYAH BEN M'HALALLEL. 1. the unrevised MS for MS1rev [heading] (MS1);
2. MS 5477 (MS1rev); 3. MS 5512 (MS2); 4. MS 5546 (MS3)*.
5 into ... life?] to this *li-i-i-ife* MS1rev
10 of the ... earth's] of Kings of all the MS1rev

OMAR ADOISHEM L'YA-AKOIV! 1. the unrevised MS for MS1rev [heading] (MS1);
2. MS 5478 (MS1rev) [1–4, 6–8]; 3. MS 5513 (MS2); 4. MS 5547 (MS3)*.
5 *not in* MS1rev
6 are ... so] do they beat us MS1rev
7 are ... mine] do they flog us, Father MS1rev
8 it end, end] come the end MS1rev; it finish *altered to* it end, end MS2

BAR YOCHAI. 1. MS 5480 [2–4] (MS1); 2. MS 5514 (MS2); 3. MS 5548 (MS3)*.
2 blessed] happy *altered to* blessed MS1

THE REBBE ELIMELECH. 1. MS 5481 [heading] (MS1); 2. MS 5515–16 (MS2); 3. MS 5549 (MS3)*.

YONDER! YONDER! 1. MS 5483 [1–10] (MS1a); 2. MS 5482 [1–19] (MS1b); 3. MS 5517 [1–22] (MS2); 4. the unrevised typescript for MS3rev [1–22] (MS3);
5. MS 5550 (MS3rev)*.
MS1a and MS1b are very rough drafts with numerous revisions.
Heading 'There, There' MS1a; no heading in MS1b; 'There [...]' *altered to* 'Yonder! Yonder!' MS2
2 nibble] eat the *altered to* nibble MS2
7 covered gaily] decked MS2, MS3
9 dry ... daily] every stick do blossom MS2, MS3
17 his white steed] a white horse *altered to* his white steed MS2
22 Lead his [...] MS2; L[...] MS3

VESOMACHTO. 1. MS 5464 [heading] (MS1a); 2. MS 5484–5 [1–2 and note on metre] (MS1b); 3. MS 5518 (MS2)*.

OF THE ANCIENT HOUSE OF THE CLINII. 1. MS 5416–18 (MS1)* [version 1]; 2. MS 5419–20* [version 2].
For the date of composition see note to TO L. MUNATIUS PLANCUS.
Heading supplied by ed.

Version 1
6 the chariots are] racing is *altered to* the chariots are MS1
14 wheat-king] regratteur *altered to* wheat-king MS1
granary] barns *altered to* granary MS1

16 wet] good *altered to* wet MS1

TO LYDIA. MS 5421.
For the date of composition see note to TO L. MUNATIUS PLANCUS.

TO LEUCONOE. MS 5422.
For the date of composition see note to TO L. MUNATIUS PLANCUS.
12 Be wise, girl] So smarten up *altered to* Be wise, girl

TO L. MUNATIUS PLANCUS. MS 5423–4.
Part of a set of MSS including OF THE ANCIENT HOUSE OF THE CLINII, TO LYDIA, and TO LEUCONOE. Dated 1 Aug. 1955.

Explanatory Notes

ORIGINAL POEMS, 1937–1955

BLUEPRINT FOR A MONUMENT OF WAR

34 *Big Bertha*: nickname for various large cannons used in World War 1, so named after Frau Bertha von Bohlen of the Krupp family, Germany's leading arms manufacturers

40 *Hinc illae lachrymae*: (Lat.) 'hence those tears' [Terence, *Andria* 1.1.126]

41 *hic jacet*: (Lat.) 'here lies'

43–56 *The blueprint's clear ... Exegi monumentum*: These lines form a Shakespearean sonnet; there is probably an ironic allusion to sonnets such as 55, 'Not marble, nor the gilded monuments,' on the power of poetry over mortality. *Exegi monumentum* ('I have built a monument') are the opening words of Horace's Ode 3.30 on this theme.

68 *Horatius ... ran away*: In Ode 2.7.9–12, Horace relates how he ingloriously fled the battle of Philippi.

71 *Dvlce ... mori*: (Lat.) 'Sweet and proper it is to die for one's fatherland' [Horace, *Odes* 3.2.13].

81 *Mors ... virvm*: (Lat.) 'Death pursues even the man who flees' [Horace, *Odes* 3.2.14].

86–7 *Virtvs ... via*: (Lat.) 'Virtue, opening the heavens for those who do not deserve to die, tries her way along forbidden paths [i.e., the path of immortality normally forbidden to mortals]' [Horace, *Odes* 3.2.21–2].

99 *Isaiah, chapter sixty-seven*: There are only sixty-six chapters in Isaiah. Spiro points out the ironic allusion to Isaiah's 'well-known message of universal peace.' The passage as a whole imitates biblical poetry in its imagery and use of parallellism, and it echoes the vocabulary and syntax of the King James version. For specific borrowings, see below.

108 *whetted tongue*: 'Hide me from the secret counsel of the wicked ... who whet their tongue like a sword' [Psalms 64.2–3].

123 *seven fat years*: an allusion to Pharaoh's dream of 'seven kine, fatfleshed and well favoured,' which Joseph interpreted to mean 'seven years of great plenty' [Genesis 41]

132-3 *rain brimstone*: 'Then the Lord rained upon Sodom and upon Gomorrah brimstone and fire' [Genesis 19.24].

138 *because they are few*: 'the grinders cease because they are few' [Ecclesiastes 12.3]. Lines 135–40 as a whole recall the description of 'the evil days' in Ecclesiastes 12.1–7.

146 *son of man*: a very common biblical expression, especially in Ezekiel, where it occurs over ninety times

OF DAUMIERS A PORTFOLIO

Honoré Daumier (1808–79) was a French caricaturist, many of whose caricatures were directed against the legal profession. In Klein's unpublished novel, *That Walks Like a Man*, he describes a scene clearly based on his own experiences as a lawyer at about the time the poem was written: 'I was tired of looking at the wall in front of me, a green like mild poison, with the hanging Daumier where the judge addressed the wretch at the bar: *But, prisoner, look at me! When I'm hungry I don't steal!* I was beginning to find the thing less and less funny. Definitely, my sympathies were with the wretch at the bar ...' [MS 3972].

5-6 *legal fiction ... the Corporation*: A corporation is a legal fiction in the sense that the law considers it a person for many purposes; that is, it is an inanimate entity which has legal personality.

15 *Hogarth*: an allusion to William Hogarth (1697–1764), an English counterpart to Daumier

Section III: a *voir dire*; that is, a trial within a trial, in this case on the issue of the admissibility of a confession. The title of the section is a punning reference to 'third degree,' 'the process of securing a confession or information from a suspect or prisoner by prolonged questioning, the use of threats, or actual violence' [Black's *Law Dictionary*]. The phrase 'A Song of degrees' begins Psalms 120-34.

30 *Holy, holy, holy*: 'Holy, holy, holy is the Lord of hosts: the whole earth is full of his glory' [Isaiah 6.3]. There may be an allusion to 'Oyez! Oyez! Oyez!' the call of a court officer to command attention.

40 *toils and spins*: 'Consider the lilies of the field, how they grow; they toil not, neither do they spin' [Matthew 6.28].

41/42 *La Glorieuse Incertitude*: (Fr.) The phrase 'the glorious incertitude (or uncertainty) of the law' dates back to at least the eighteenth century. Klein uses the phrase in 'Hapaxlegomenon,' a chapter from an unfinished novel [MS 4469]:

If his cases were ... to be subjected ... to one man's arbitrary discretion,

and that man, being human, a weathervane rotated by meteorological
conditions he couldn't even surmise, let alone control – then he might as
well give up, or play the horses, or, relying on the law's glorious incertitude,
take only cases that seemed to him [to] be bad.

Klein's fullest explanation of the phrase is in 'Baedeker for Law' [*CJC*, 29 Dec. 1939, p. 4]:

> ... all law, as litigants have probably suspected ere this, is two-faced: it has
> aspects both substantive and adjectival. The first reveals what are a
> man's rights as he stands before the blind goddess; the second indicates
> what methods must be taken to make Justice see from behind her
> blindfold. In a civilized country, the first can be realized almost by instinct;
> it is with reference to the second that the law has mainly earned its
> reputation for 'glorious incertitude.'

43-4 *Justinian ... Pothier*: The Corpus Juris Civilis, the basis of all modern civil law, was codified under the Byzantine emperor Justinian I. Robert Joseph Pothier (1699-1772) was a jurist whose legal treatises helped to lay the foundation for French civil law.

48-52 *Two ... / The fifth*: A 2-2-1 split by the provincial Court of Appeal ('the higher court') is not, in fact, possible. According to Art. 11 of the Quebec Civil Code all judges are required to reach a decision: 'A judge cannot refuse to adjudicate under pretext of the silence, obscurity or insufficiency of the law.'

61 *The Mystery of the Door Ajar*: 'When is a door not a door?' 'When it is ajar.'

68 *Hochelaga*: Montreal, founded on the site of the Indian village, Hochelaga.

70 *How have you become*: 'she that was great among the nations ... how is she become tributary!' [Lamentations 1.1].

85-96 *And now ... well-bled*: 'For his major paper in political economy he wrote on the history of the Amalgamated Clothing Workers of America in Montreal, drawing partly on his childhood memories of the two-month Amalgamated Workers strike of 1917, in which his father had participated' [*LOTD*, p. 47].

BARRICADE SMITH: HIS SPEECHES

In a letter to Joseph Frank, 8 Jan. 1938, Klein refers to 'some lines of a play in verse that I am writing. – on industrial strife – dubbed "Barricade Smith."' In another letter to Frank, 5 Aug. 1938, he writes: 'The Forum has also accepted a series for publication in future issues, dubbed "Barricade Smith; his speeches" – intended as revolutionary, but remember, I am only a snuff-tobacco bandit armed with tzitzith and tfillin.'

6-7 *sound / Of belching in the land*: 'the voice of the turtle is heard in our land' [Song of Solomon 2.12].

34-44 *Where will you be ... / Where will you be*: Compare 'What will you do, when the phone rings, / and they say to you: What will you do?' [Kenneth Fearing, 'As the Fuse Burns Down,' in *Poems* (New York: Dynamo 1935), p. 39].

55 *create new heaven*: 'For, behold, I create new heavens and a new earth' [Isaiah 65.17].

Section IV: a parody of Psalm 23. Compare the treatment of the movies in DIARY OF ABRAHAM SEGAL, POET, 183–6.

86 *lotiferous*: 'lotus-bearing'; not in the *OED*. In the *Odyssey* the lotus-eaters (*lotophagoi*) live in a state of dreamy forgetfulness induced by the fruit of the lotus.

106/07 *Of Faith, Hope and Charity*: 'And now abideth faith, hope, charity, these three; but the greatest of these is charity' [1 Corinthians 13.13].

124–6 *Descend the winding staircase ... alive upon a floor*: For 'the winding staircase' see W.B. Yeats, *The Winding Stair and Other Poems* (1933). 'Alive upon a floor' may be an allusion to 'the uncontrollable mystery on the bestial floor' [Yeats, 'The Magi,' 8].

127–8 *Keats ... father's stables ... asphodel*: Keats was the son of a livery stable keeper. Asphodel, in poetic usage, is an immortal flower covering the Elysian fields.

129–30 *Wordsworth ... sell*: an allusion to Wordsworth's lyric beginning 'My heart leaps up when I behold / A rainbow in the sky'

131–2 *Tennyson ... Arthur's King Hotel*: an allusion to Tennyson's Arthurian *Idylls of the King*

134 *What's Hecuba to you?*: 'What's Hecuba to him, or he to Hecuba, / That he should weep for her?' [*Hamlet* 2.2.558–9].

165 *A shirt! ... a shirt*: 'A horse! A horse! My kingdom for a horse!' [*Richard III* 5.4.7].

183 *Tillie the Toiler*: ' "Tillie the Toiler," Lily's working class foil in the poem, is the name of a working girl comicstrip heroine popular in the thirties' [S].

183–5 *consider ... spin*: 'Consider the lilies of the field, how they grow; they toil not, neither do they spin' [Matthew 6.28]. Compare DIARY OF ABRAHAM SEGAL, POET, 76–7.

228–9 *brooding, like a spirit, / Over the champagne flood*: Compare 'O Spirit, that ... / Dove-like satst brooding on the vast Abyss' [*Paradise Lost* 1.17–21]. Milton is paraphrasing Genesis 1.2: 'And the Spirit of God moved upon the face of the waters.'

OF CASTLES IN SPAIN

To One Gone to the Wars: an allusion to Richard Lovelace's 'To Lucasta, Going to the Wars'

Dedication: Samuel H. Abramson was a boyhood friend of Klein's who fought in the Spanish Civil War. In a letter to Abramson, 4 June 1938, Klein refers to the poems and their dedication to Abramson, and expresses envy for Abramson's part in the struggle against fascism. In 'The Mac-Pap's Arrive' [*CJC*, 17 Feb. 1939, p. 4], Klein praises the Mackenzie-Papineau Battalion, mentioning Abramson by name, on its return from Spain: 'At a time when many contented themselves with mouthing the empty phrases of democracy, these young men went across an ocean to fight for those ideals which their detractors so lukewarmly profess to admire. Although the battle took place upon foreign terrain, it was directed against foes who threatened the integrity of this continent no less than that of the continent where they are registering their cruel victory.'

1 *Unworthiest crony of my grammar days*: Klein and Abramson went to school together [*Caplan*, p. 11]. Abramson appears to have been a less than enthusiastic student: in 'The Mac-Pap's Arrive' Klein addresses some Latin verses to Abramson, commenting that 'he was never much of a Latin scholar.'
7 *hind and hawker*: peasant and peddler
13–14 *virtues long since rusty ... spouse and son*: 'As for myself, things are running along the even tenor of the bourgeois way; I am *paterfamilias*, *constant reader*, and *citizen* all in one. Until it hurts ... I have a lovely son who thrives in this northern clime, and who probably will become a lumberjack, and true proletarian' [letter to Abramson].
33–46 *Sonnet without Music*: an unrhymed Petrarchan sonnet. See introductory note to SONNET UNRHYMED.

CHILDE HAROLD'S PILGRIMAGE

At the period of composition of CHILDE HAROLD'S PILGRIMAGE Klein was becoming increasingly concerned with the deteriorating position of the Jews of Germany and with the unwillingness of other countries to accept them as refugees. Compare, for example, the editorial occasioned by the *Kristallnacht* outrages of 9–10 Nov. 1938, 'Vandal and Victim' [*BS*, pp. 35–7].

Klein borrowed his title from Byron, but his poem has little in common with Byron's, apart from the motif of the wanderer. Compare Klein's treatment of a similar theme in IN RE SOLOMON WARSHAWER.

Line references are to version 1.

1 *yclept*: (Middle English) 'called'; a common literary archaism, especially among the Elizabethans. In the draft of a letter to Abraham Duker, 26 June 1942 [MS 115], Klein comments on the poem's archaism: '... the archaic language is there with a specific purpose – the same purpose which motivated the same kind of language in the Sixth Chapter of Joyce's Ulysses.'
1–4 *Zvi ... Cerf ... Hirsch ... Harold*: Zvi, a common Hebrew name, means 'hart' or 'stag,' as do Cerf, in French, and Hirsch, in German and Yiddish. Because of their similarity in sound, Harold is the English name frequently given to

someone whose Yiddish name is Hirsch. In a letter to James Laughlin, 18 Oct. 1944, attacking the 'crypto-Jews' who had ignored *The Hitleriad*, Klein refers to Bennett Cerf as 'a gallicized Hirsch.'

3 *Allmany*: 'Almany' is an archaism for Germany, which Klein may have picked up from *Ulysses* [pp. 202, 385]. The spelling 'Allmany,' however, is Klein's own, and a pun ('all,' 'man,' 'many'), emphasizing the extent of Childe Harold's wanderings, may be intended.

6 *caftan*: common garb of east European Jews

15 *consul of the moon*: Spiro refers to the grim joke among Jewish refugees 'that only "the consul of the moon" was left for them to see regarding a visa to his domain!'

21 *Madagascar*: a reference to the Madagascar Plan, first advocated in 1885 and later taken up by the Nazis, that the Jews of Europe be shipped to Madagascar with the financing coming from world Jewry. The plan was eventually abandoned in favour of the 'final solution.'

24–9 *Aye, but thy fell ... Kamenev ... customs house*: Lev Borisovich Kamenev (Rosenfeld) (1883–1936) was a Jewish member of the Bolshevik leadership. He was arrested by Stalin in the 1934 purges, and at the time Klein's poem was written he had 'confessed' to all charges and been executed. Leo Kennedy, who was planning an anthology of Canadian writing (which never materialized), asked Klein to remove these lines; Klein, in a letter dated 15 Mar. 1940, indignantly refused, mocking Kennedy's 'evangelical Marxism' and asking, 'Would you suggest that my lines, anent Soviet Russia should be deleted and substituted by the following immortal stanzas from the pen of Tolstoi's son: "Stalin, you are like the sun and moon – only better, because the sun and moon can't think." ' Klein did, in fact, delete these lines (as well as the following lines on British policy in Palestine) when he revised the poem in the early fifties.

28 *divine impedimenta*: In 'Look on This Picture and on This' [*LER*, pp. 60–1], Klein describes a photograph of a Jew 'poring over what is obviously a sacred volume; behind him is a blank wall, where, suspended from two hooks, are his *tallis*, his coat, and his staff: *impedimenta*.' In 'A Great Talmudist' [*CJC*, 13 Mar. 1942, p. 4], he refers to the Talmud as 'the impedimenta of the wandering scholars.'

29 *household gods*: When Rachel ran away with Jacob, she stole her father's *terafim* ('images' in the King James version) [Genesis 31.19]. In 'The Bible Manuscripts' [*LER*, p. 142], Klein refers to 'Rachel's god-handling of her father's household gods.' There may also be a reference to the Roman *penates*, perhaps more specifically to the passage in Book 2 of the *Aeneid* (the book of the *Aeneid* which Klein cites most frequently) in which the ghost of Hector urges Aeneas to flee the destruction of Troy, taking his household gods with him on all his wanderings [*Aeneid* 2.293–5].

34 *Several thousand pounds*: In 1922 the British imposed restrictions on Jewish immigration to Palestine on the basis of the 'economic absorptive capacity' of the land, thus limiting the number of immigrants without independent means.

36–8 *O mummied Pharaoh ... shrewd proliferous Israelites*: 'And [Pharaoh] said unto his people, Behold, the people of the children of Israel are more and mightier than we' [Exodus 1.9].

39 *Son of Hamdatha ... witless Mede*: Haman, the son of Hamdatha, was the vizier of Ahasuerus, King of Persia and Media. The story of how he sought to destroy the Jews is told in the Book of Esther. Spiro points out that Ahasuerus 'is called "a foolish King" by the Talmud.' Compare FIVE CHARACTERS.

44 *Antiochus*: Antiochus Epiphanes, the Seleucid ruler of Syria (175–63 B.C.), whose repressive measures led to the Hasmonean revolt described in the Book of Maccabees. See note to MATTATHIAS.

45 *Inimitate*: not in the OED

46 *Torquemada*: Tomás de Torquemada (?1420–98), first head of the Spanish Inquisition

52 *Attila's laws*: The parallel between Attila the Hun and Hitler was no doubt suggested by the derisive use of the word *Hun* for German soldiers. The laws in question are the anti-Semitic Nuremberg Laws. See note to BALLAD OF THE NUREMBERG TOWER CLOCK.

66–7 *the ditty ... the pimp Horst Wessel ... strumpet*: Horst Wessel was a storm trooper who lived with a former prostitute and who may have been a pimp. He was killed by communists in 1930 and left behind a song, the Horst Wessel song, which became the official anthem of the Nazi party.

75 *my spattered gaberdine*: 'And spet [sic] upon my Jewish gaberdine' [*Merchant of Venice* 1.3.112].

89 *marrano*: Jews who were forced to convert to Christianity in Spain and Portugal in the fifteenth century and continued to practise Judaism in secret

132–5 *My father ... without a penny's worth of faith*: Compare PETITION FOR THAT MY FATHER'S SOUL SHOULD ENTER INTO HEAVEN, 66–8.

132 *gathered to his fathers*: a combination of the biblical phrases 'gathered to his people' [e.g., Genesis 25.8, 49.33; Numbers 27.13] and 'slept with his fathers' [e.g., 1 Kings 2.10, 11.21; 2 Chronicles 9.31]

134 *a pauper ... piety*: a paraphrase of *hineni he-ani mimaas* (Heb.), recited by the cantor or *baal tefilah* (master of prayer) on the High Holidays, in which he pleads to be considered worthy of his task. In his translation of the Chassidic folk-song MYERKA, MY SON, Klein translates it 'A pauper in deeds, so behold me' [24].

136 *Esau, my kinsman*: Esau, the brother of Jacob, was a hunter, and traditionally seen as a man capable of bloodshed and violence.

145 *sixth thunder of Sinai*: the sixth commandment, 'Thou shalt not kill'

155 *Ur of the Chaldees*: the birthplace of Abraham [Genesis 11.28]
169 *empirics*: Klein clearly intends something like empiricism in the sense of learning from experience, but *empirics* as a singular noun does not occur in the OED. He uses the word in a similar sense in 'A Definition of Poetry?' [*LER*, p. 180].
170 *cauchemar*: (Fr.) 'nightmare'

TO THE CHIEF MUSICIAN, A PSALM OF THE BRATZLAVER, A PARABLE

The Bratzlaver (Rabbi Nachman ben Simchah of Bratizlava) was the great-grandson of the Baal Shem Tov, the founder of Chassidism, and was himself the founder of a Chassidic sect known as the 'Bratzlaver Chassidim.' He expressed his doctrines in mystical tales which were collected and published by one of his disciples. Music also played an important role in his teachings.

As early as 1933, Klein was planning 'to translate into verse the stories of Reb Nachman Bratzlaver' [Leo Kennedy, 'Orpheus in a Caftan,' *Jewish Standard*, 14 Apr. 1933, p. 208]. The Bratzlaver poems which he eventually did write are all based on a single tale, 'The Tale of the Seven Beggars.' In a letter to Joseph Frank, 5 Aug. 1938, Klein reported that he was 'at work on a poetic rendition of Rabbi Nachman Bratzlaver's "Tale of the Seven Beggars," highly metaphysical, deeply religious – which I am, in an unorganized way – and one of the few examples of autochthonous Yiddish short story.' He later described the tale as 'a most mystical piece of Yiddish literature, ... the only piece of literature in Yiddish which can equal the writings of Dr. John Donne or Traherne' [letter to Jewish Publication Society, 7 Aug. 1942].

Klein may have known 'The Tale of the Seven Beggars' in Yiddish, but his Bratzlaver poems are all based on Meyer Levin's translation, first published in 1932 in *The Golden Mountain*, reprinted by Penguin as *Classic Hassidic Tales* in 1975. Page references in the notes to all the Bratzlaver poems are to the Penguin reprint. Klein is much closer in phrasing to Levin's version than to the one in Martin Buber's better-known collection, *The Tales of Rabbi Nachman*, and two of the poems – TO THE CHIEF MUSICIAN, A PSALM OF THE BRATZLAVER, A PARABLE, and TO THE CHIEF MUSICIAN, A PSALM OF THE BRATZLAVER, WHEN HE CONSIDERED HOW THE PIOUS ARE OVERWHELMED – are based on passages in Levin's version which are not in Buber's.

Klein's choice of passages suggests that he may have originally set out methodically to versify the whole tale, for, apart from the two previously mentioned poems which are based on the opening paragraphs of the tale, the three other Bratzlaver poems – OF REMEMBRANCE (originally entitled 'To the Chief Musician, a Psalm of the Bratzlaver, a Psalm of the Beginning of Things'); TO THE CHIEF MUSICIAN: A PSALM OF THE BRATZLAVER, TOUCHING A GOOD GARDENER; and TO THE CHIEF MUSICIAN, A PSALM OF THE BRATZLAVER WHICH HE WROTE DOWN

AS THE STAMMERER SPOKE – are based, respectively, on the tales told by the first three of the seven beggars.

The specific passage on which this poem is based [p. 333] is the first paragraph of the tale:

> There was once a king who had an only son, and while he lived the king decided to give his crown to the prince. He made a great festival to which all the noblemen of the kingdom came, and in the midst of pomp and ceremony the king placed the crown upon the head of his young son, saying, 'I am one who can read the future in the stars, and I see that there will come a time when you will lose your kingdom, but when that time comes you must not be sorrowful; if you can be joyous even when your kingdom is lost, I too will be filled with joy. For you cannot be a true king unless you are a happy man.'

1 *An aged king, his brittle shins in hose*: Compare 'A bitter king in anger to be gone' [A.J.M. Smith, 'Like an Old Proud King in a Parable' (1929), 1].

6 *from his seventh rib*: 'a literal translation of a Yiddish expression which means "deep down" (*in der zibeter rip*)' [s].

7 *four graveyard ells*: For the measurement 'four ells,' see note to PORTRAITS OF A MINYAN, 137–8.

TO THE CHIEF MUSICIAN, A PSALM OF THE BRATZLAVER, WHEN HE CONSIDERED HOW THE PIOUS ARE OVERWHELMED

based on 'The Tale of the Seven Beggars,' by Rabbi Nachman Bratzlaver. For more information on Klein's source see introductory note to TO THE CHIEF MUSICIAN, A PSALM OF THE BRATZLAVER, A PARABLE.

The specific passage on which the poem is based [p. 333] is the second and third paragraphs of the tale:

> The son became king, appointed governors, and ruled. He was a lover of learning, and in order to fill his court with wise men he let it be known that he would give every man whatever he desired, either gold or glory, in return for his wisdom; then all the people in that kingdom began to seek for knowledge, in order to get gold or glory from the king. And thus it was that the simplest fool in the land was wiser than the greatest sage of any other country; and in their search for learning, the people forgot the study of war, so the country was left open to the enemy.
>
> Among the philosophers in the young king's court there were clever men and infidels who soon filled his mind with doubt. He would ask himself, 'Who am I; why am I in the world?' Then he would heave a deep sigh, and fall into melancholy.

OF REMEMBRANCE

based on 'The Tale of the Seven Beggars,' by Rabbi Nachman Bratzlaver. For more information on Klein's source see introductory note to TO THE CHIEF MUSICIAN, A PSALM OF THE BRATZLAVER, A PARABLE.

The specific passage on which the poem is based [pp. 337–40] is the first tale, of nine survivors of a shipwreck who pass the time by relating their earliest memories: (1) 'when the apple was cut from the bough'; (2) 'the candle that burned'; (3) 'when the fruit first began to grow'; (4) 'when the seed was brought that was to be planted in the fruit'; (5) 'the sage who thought of the seed'; (6) 'the taste of the fruit before the taste went into the fruit'; (7) 'the odour of the fruit before the fruit had an odour'; (8) 'the appearance of the fruit before the fruit could be seen'; (9) 'the thing that is Nothing.' An eagle then appears and interprets the memories:

> ... he who remembered when the apple was cut from the bough remembered how at his birth he was cut from his mother; the candle that burned was the babe in the womb, for it is written in *gemara* that while the child is in the womb a candle burns over his head; and he that remembers when the fruit began to grow remembers how his limbs first began to form in his mother's womb; he that recalls the bringing of the seed remembers how he was conceived; and he that knows the wisdom that created the seed remembers when conception was but in the mind; the taste that preceded the fruit is the memory of Being; the scent is Spirit; and vision is the Soul; but the child that remembers Nothing is greater than them all, for he remembers that which existed before Being, Spirit, or Soul; he remembers the life that hovered upon the threshold of eternity. [p. 339]

1 *Go catch ... time*: Compare 'Go, and catch a falling star, ... / Tell me, where all past years are' [John Donne, 'Song,' 1–3].

TO THE CHIEF MUSICIAN: A PSALM OF THE BRATZLAVER, TOUCHING A GOOD GARDENER

based on 'The Tale of the Seven Beggars,' by Rabbi Nachman Bratzlaver. For more information on Klein's source see introductory note to TO THE CHIEF MUSICIAN, A PSALM OF THE BRATZLAVER, A PARABLE.

The specific passage on which the poem is based [pp. 341–3] is the second tale, of the deaf beggar. Hearing the inhabitants of the Land of Luxury boasting of their wealth, he tells them of 'a life of rarer ease and luxury':

> 'I know a land where a garden grows that is filled with trees overladen with marvellous fruits. Once the fruits had every tempting odour and flavor and beauty in the world, and every good thing that grows was in that

garden. A gardener watched over the trees, and pruned them, and cared for their growth; but the gardener has disappeared and cannot be found, there is no one to take care of the trees, and the people live only from the wild growth of the dropped seed. Even of this, they might have lived well; but a tyrant king invaded their land. He did not harm the people, and he did not himself spoil the garden, but he left behind him three companies of soldiers: one company made the taste of the garden into bitterness, the other made the odour into stench, and the third made its beauty into clouded darkness.'

Then I said to the people of the Land of Luxury, 'Help the people of this other kingdom, for the taste, the beauty, and the odour is gone from their fruit, and if you do not help them, the same evil may reach to your land!' So they set out for the spoiled kingdom, but lived in luxury on their journey, until they came close to the garden, and then the beauty, and the taste, and the delectable odour began to go from their own food, and they did not know what to do. So I gave them some of my bread to eat, and my water to drink, and they tasted all the riches of their fine foods, and they breathed all the delectable odours, and they saw all the beauties of the fruits in the bread and water that I gave them.

Then I went into the city and saw people assembled in the street; I listened to them, and heard one whisper to the other, while the other laughed and whispered to a third, and I knew it was filth that they uttered. I went further, and saw people quarrel and go to a court and quarrel again and go to another court, until the whole city was filled with judges and bribery; and the city was also filled with lust. Then I knew that the invading king had left his three battalions in the city to spread the three diseases: of filth that had spoiled the taste in their mouth, and bribery that had made their eyes blind, and lust that was a stench in their nostrils. So I said to them, 'Let us drive out these strangers; and perhaps the gardener will be found again.' Then the men from the Land of Luxury, who ate of my bread and water, and were well of sight and scent and hearing, helped me, and wherever they caught one of the soldiers, they drove him from the land.

There was a madman that wandered in the streets and cried continually that he was a gardener; everyone laughed at him, and some even threw stones at him. Then I said to them, 'Perhaps he is really the gardener; bring him to me.' They brought him, and I saw that he was indeed the gardener, and he was restored to the garden.

The poem is in *terza rima*.

TO THE CHIEF MUSICIAN, A PSALM OF THE BRATZLAVER, WHICH HE WROTE DOWN AS THE STAMMERER SPOKE

based on 'The Tale of the Seven Beggars,' by Rabbi Nachman Bratzlaver. For more information on Klein's source see introductory note to TO THE CHIEF MUSICIAN, A PSALM OF THE BRATZLAVER, A PARABLE.

The specific passage on which the poem is based [p. 344] is the third tale, of the stammerer. All the sages of the world come together to prove who is cleverest. They all boast of what they can create, but the stammerer proves to be the cleverest, for he can create time:

> You must know that time does not exist of itself, and that days are made only of good deeds. It is through men who perform good deeds that days are born, and so time is born; and I am he who goes all about the world to find those men who secretly do good deeds: I bring their deeds to the great man who is known as the Truly Godly Man, and he turns them into time; then time is born, and there are days and years.

In 'Lillian Freiman: A Tribute' [*CJC*, 8 Nov. 1940, p. 3], Klein writes:

> Some people there are who spend the days of their life upon this earth, and never achieve the destiny to which they were created. Their length of years is merely so much passage of time, so much chronology, but no more. It is for that reason that our sages have always taught us the high moral concept of time. It was Rabbi Nachman of Bratzlav who for one, sought thus to grasp its significance. He asks concerning time [quotes 9–14].

IN RE SOLOMON WARSHAWER

> Perhaps the most appalling example of injustice which our generation beheld was that which was witnessed in Europe from the advent of Hitler until his final downfall. [IN RE SOLOMON WARSHAWER], in its form, seeks to combine poetic technique with legal document. In other words, it is a deposition given under oath, presumably by a member of the Nazi forces. It imagines that a Jew is caught up in the city of Warsaw, as the German army ... enters that country.
>
> There is a legend which says that when King Solomon had reigned upon his throne in ancient times for a number of decades, he was one day visited by the demon Asmodeus, with the cloven feet, the demon who knew how to break rocks, the demon who did not speak. The tale goes on to say that this Asmodeus flung King Solomon from his throne four hundred parasangs out of Jerusalem. And King Solomon thereafter went about in exile and everywhere announced that he was the king and nowhere was he believed, for Asmodeus sat upon the throne. And certainly during the short period when Hitler was enraged, rampant over Europe, it did seem as if Asmodeus was

seated upon the throne of the world. For this legend for background, I imagine King Solomon persisting to the present day, and being that anonymous person who was captured by the Nazis in Warsaw in 1939. And it is concerning what took place then that this poem dedicates itself. It is a poem really about the nature of evil, the nature of the beast Asmodeus.
[McGill reading]

Klein's own comments [K] are cited from a letter to A.J.M. Smith, 21 Jan. 1943.

Version 1

Title: In re is Latin for 'in the affair; in the matter of; concerning; regarding. This is the usual method of entitling a judicial proceeding in which there are not adversary parties, but merely some *res* concerning which judicial action is to be taken' [Black's *Law Dictionary*]. Klein probably used the English pronunciation current in legal circles, *in ree* (he omits the poem's name in the McGill reading), and there may be a pun on INRI (Iesus Nazarenus Rex Iudaeorum), emphasizing the parallel between two martyred 'Kings of the Jews.'

2 *Vercingetorix*: leader of the Gauls in a revolt against Rome; captured by Julius Caesar and put to death. In 'The Book of the Year' [*Canadian Zionist*, 3, 5 (Oct. 1936), 25], a review of *The Jews of Germany*, by Marvin Lowenthal, Klein compares 'Vercingetorix, the old barbarian' and 'Hitler, the new one.'

49 *nalewkas*: 'Polish for "streets" – the slum district of Warsaw' [K]

59 *The eldest elder of Zion*: *The Protocols of the Elders of Zion* is a fraudulent document reporting the alleged proceedings of a group of Jews in the nineteenth century planning world dominion. It was used by the Nazis, among others, to justify anti-Semitism.

75–89 *It is not necessary ... Rome*: 'He [i.e., the orthodox Jew] does not fear annihilation; he belongs to a nation of "outlivers." It has outlived the Pharaohs, it has outlived Antiochus; it has seen Haman vanish into thin air; it has watched the Inquisition disappear in smoke; it has beheld the Tsars vanish in a cellar; and no doubt it will be present at the obsequies of all those who to-day bark and bite at the heel of Jewry' ['Of Him Whom We Envy,' BS, p. 48].

82 *Ekaterinoslov*: site of the execution of Tsar Nicholas II and his family by the Bolsheviks

86 *lone star ... Pharaoh's tomb*: 'The architecture of the pyramids is such, that its principal doorway or entrance is so placed, that the light of a star – name forgotten – always falls upon it. cf. Hogben's Mathematics for the Million' [K].

118 *Ani Shlomo*: (Heb.) 'The King in despair wandered over the countryside crying "Ani-Shlomo – I am Solomon!" He was taken for a madman' [K].

121–2 *did fling me from Jerusalem / Four hundred parasangs*: 'Snatching up Solomon, ... [Asmodeus] flung him four hundred parasangs away from Jerusalem, and then palmed himself off as the king' [JE, 'Asmodeus'].

124–5 *beneath whose hem / The feet of the cock extend*: '... the declaration of the king's women that he always wore slippers, strengthened suspicion; for demons proverbially had cocks' feet' [JE, 'Asmodeus']. Compare EXORCISM VAIN, 5.
133 *or birds, or beasts of the wood*: Solomon 'spake also of beasts, and of fowl, and of creeping things, and of fishes' [1 Kings 4.33].
134 *Spread song*: Solomon's 'songs were a thousand and five' [1 Kings 4.32].
137 *To build the temple*: The first Temple was built during Solomon's reign.
142 *Master of the worm, pernicious, that cleaves rocks*: 'According to legend, Asmodeus was the master of the worm called Shani [*sic*; *should be* Shamir]. It could cleave rocks, and was very important in the construction of the Temple, since it was prohibited to put iron to Temple-stone. Hitler in his concentration camps is also such a master' [K].
162 *And further deponent saith not*: a standard legal formula for concluding a deposition

Version 2
86 *Mizraim*: (Heb.) Egypt
126–9 *craved wisdom* ... / *The understanding heart*: 'Give therefore thy servant an understanding heart to judge thy people, that I may discern between good and bad: for who is able to judge this thy so great a people' [1 Kings 3.9].
129 *enthymemes*: 'Enthymeme' comes from a Greek word meaning 'to consider.' It was originally used by Aristotle to refer to 'an argument based on merely probable grounds; a rhetorical argument as distinguished from a demonstrative one' [OED]. Klein probably has this now obsolete sense in mind rather than the current one: 'a syllogism in which one premiss is suppressed' [OED].
147 *vanitatum vanitas*: (Lat.) the Vulgate rendering of 'vanity of vanities,' a phrase occurring in Ecclesiastes, traditionally ascribed to King Solomon
152 *that famous footstool for the Lord*: the Temple. 'Thus saith the Lord, The heaven is my throne, and the earth is my footstool: where is the house that ye build unto me? and where is the place of my rest?' [Isaiah 66.1].
157 *Qoheleth*: Hebrew name for the Book of Ecclesiastes and its author
166 *ten losing tribes*: an allusion to the ten lost tribes, who constituted the northern kingdom of Israel, and who disappeared from history after being exiled by the Assyrians in 722 B.C.
192 *lych-throne*: 'corpse-throne' ('charnel-throne' in version 1); not in the OED, but coined on analogy with 'lych-gate'

FOR THE CHIEF PHYSICIAN

Compare ss, p. 21/29: 'The world, say the old liturgies, is full of "wild beasts that lie in wait"; these, my doctors thought, included not only the ravenous ones of the forest, the traveler's usual terror, but also the minute destroyers of the air: germs, viruses, microbes ...'

The title is a pun on the phrase 'To the Chief Musician,' which precedes a number of Psalms.

GRACE BEFORE POISON

> It is suggested that [GRACE BEFORE POISON] which is a benediction upon the Lord's poisonous chemicals, be deleted. I pray that you see your way clear to preserving it from limbo. It is a good poem; it is a sincere poem, and though it makes the blessing for poisons, believe me it is not a bracha l'vatala [a vain benediction, a false prayer]. I do not know whether the motivation against this poem was due to the fact that in the last four lines, morphine is spoken of in flattering terms, – but note, it is morphine for medicinal purposes. I myself have on several occasions received the blessing of its effects, and they are precisely as described in the last lines of the poem. He would be a churl who would not be grateful for this piece of the Lord's creativeness. I may point out in addition that this poem has appeared in Poetry Magazine, Chicago, and has been considerably anthologized.
>
> Dr. Grayzel speaks of obscurity with reference to certain poems. I do not know whether the poem under consideration falls under this charge – but I am taking no chances.
>
> 'The hemp of India – and paradise!' – cannabis
> 'The monk's hood, cooling against fever,' – aconite
> 'The nightshade: death unpetalled before widened eyes' – belladonna
> 'And blossom of the heart, the purple foxglove.' – digitalis
>
> I note that some one suggests that the line 'To praise thee for the poisons thou hast brayed,' might be 'brewed.' Specifically the word is bray, as in 'bray in a mortar.' [Letter to Jewish Publication Society, 1 July 1943]

For the title compare 'In the midst of our anguish we were regaled with a dialectic which proved that fascism was but a matter of taste. The taste was bitter unto death ... My ideology had been a saying of grace before poison' [ss, pp. 26/31–2].

MASCHIL OF ABRAHAM: A PRAYER WHEN HE WAS IN THE CAVE

'An example of a religious attitude in a non-religious world' [letter to Jewish Publication Society, 7 Aug. 1942]

The title is from Psalm 142, 'Maschil of David; A Prayer when he was in the cave.' The cave referred to in the biblical psalm is either the cave of Adullam where David hid from Saul [1 Samuel 22] or the cave of En-Gedi where David found the sleeping Saul and spared him [1 Samuel 24]. *Maschil* (pronounced *maskil*) is used in the titles of several psalms; its meaning is doubtful, but it has been traditionally understood as 'a didactic poem.' Psalm 142 is a prayer for help at a time of persecution and despair.

9 *in his Zion lay at ease*: 'Woe to them that are at ease in Zion' [Amos 6.1].

36 *I am that I am*: 'And God said unto Moses, I AM THAT I AM' [Exodus 3.14].

40 *Do justify my ways to them*: 'a reversal of Milton's:
   "I may assert eternal Providence
   And justify the way of God to men."
Or Pope: (apparently "derivative")
   "But vindicate the ways of God to man."
In the manuscript, the process is reversed. It is the ways of one man with reference to his God which are to be justified to other men' [letter to Jewish Publication Society, 7 Aug. 1942].

A PSALM OF ABRAHAM CONCERNING THE ARROGANCE OF THE SON OF MAN

Compare LES VESPASIENNES.

A PSALM OF ABRAHAM, TO BE WRITTEN DOWN AND LEFT ON THE TOMB OF RASHI

occasioned by the nine-hundredth anniversary of the birth of Rashi (Rabbi Solomon bar Isaac), commentator on the Bible and the Talmud, born in Troyes in 1040; died there 13 July 1105. Rashi's commentaries are considered especially appropriate for beginning students.

Klein relied heavily on the article on Rashi in *JE*, which contains extensive markings in his hand.

1 *Now*: In the margin of the article in *JE*, near the date of Rashi's birth, Klein has written '*1940.*'

3 *images of god*: men. 'So God created man in his own image, in the image of god created he him' [Genesis 1.27].

6 *Mild pedagogue*: 'Rashi shows sound judgment and much mildness' [*JE*].

8 *spiral splendid staircase*: 'Nothing better describes the form of logic known as "pilpul" than to picture it as a "spiral splendid staircase" on which one rises ever upward, as in the Hegelian dialectic, upon the compatability of contradictions' [letter to Jewish Publication Society, 1 July 1943].

10 *incomparable exegete*: This phrase is used of Rashi in 'In Praise of the Diaspora.' See passage quoted from Klein in note to 18.

12 *drink ... meat*: Rashi 'seems to have depended for support chiefly on his vineyards and the manufacture of wine'; in Troyes 'butcher-shops were ... shown which were built on the site of his dwelling and which flies were said never to enter' [both passages marked in *JE*].

18 *old archaic Frank*: 'Rashi sometimes translates words and entire propositions

into French, these passages, written in Hebrew characters and forming an integral part of the text, being called "la'azim" ... These glosses are of value ... as providing material for the reconstruction of Old French, both phonologically and lexicographically' [*JE*; marked]. Compare:

> Would you seek to discover the earliest examples of French speech, go not to the authors accredited of that mighty literature; go, rather, to the Jewish vintner of Troyes, Rashi, that incomparable exegete, for it is in his annotations to the sacred Scriptures that you will find them, French verbs, French nouns, – those illuminating *la'azim* – so early shaped, so early recorded, that in comparison Villon's are the very neologisms of modernity. ['In Praise of the Diaspora,' *BS*, pp. 473–4]

19 *his Hebraic crypt*: perhaps suggested by the several illustrations of the 'Rashi Chapel' at Worms in the *JE* article

21 *clear*: The 'primary quality [of Rashi's glosses] is perfect clearness ...' [*JE*].

27 *Onkelus ... Jonathan*: Onkelus and Jonathan ben Uzziel translated the Bible into Aramaic.

28–32 *Yours were such days ... war*: 'His last years were saddened by the massacres which took place at the outset of the first Crusade (1095–1096), in which he lost relatives and friends' [*JE*; marked].

33 *Parshandatha of the law*: Rashi 'won ... the epithet of "Parshandatha" (Esth. ix.7), taken by some writers as "parshan data" (= "interpreter of the Law")' [*JE*; marked]. At the top of the page in *JE*, Klein has written, 'Impeccable parshandatha of the law.'

41 *vintner of Troyes*: See note to 12. This phrase is used of Rashi in 'In Praise of the Diaspora.' See passage quoted from Klein in note to 18.

45–8 *left no son ... Kaddish*: The mourner's *Kaddish* is a prayer recited by the nearest male kin, usually a son. Rashi 'had no sons, but three daughters' [*JE*; marked].

50 *doubt-divided*: '... when perplexed he would acknowledge it without hesitation ...' [*JE*; marked].

A PSALM OF ABRAHAM, TOUCHING HIS GREEN PASTURES

Compare Psalm 23.

7–8 *Messerschmidt ... Heinkel*: German World War II fighter planes, named after their inventors, Willy Messerschmitt and Ernst Heinrich Heinkel.

A PSALM OF ABRAHAM, WHICH HE MADE BECAUSE OF FEAR IN THE NIGHT

based on a prayer recited before bedtime in which the four angels Gabriel, Uriel, Raphael, and Michael are called upon to guard the sleeper

A PSALM OF JUSTICE, AND ITS SCALES

'A thought I am certain which has occurred to all ... is the thought which prompted Jeremiah in his twelfth chapter to question the Lord's wisdom and to wonder why the wicked prosper, and why the righteous receive not their reward – that spirit of criticism which enters into all of us at some time or other, when we think that were but the opportunity given to us, we could improve upon the Lord's design. It is out of such a mood that this PSALM OF JUSTICE is written' [McGill reading].

A PSALM TO TEACH HUMILITY

In response to criticism in a review of *Poems* in *Poetry* magazine, Klein wrote:

> That [A PSALM TO TEACH HUMILITY] struck you in this manner is not a cause of complaint; it has illustrated to me how difficult it is to write in one culture while making allusions to another. Here is the background: among the several dozen benedictions which a good Jew is supposed to utter in his matinal prayers – thanksgiving for God's several mercies, praise for His many powers – there is one 'blessing the Lord for that He gave the rooster understanding to distinguish between day and night.' The thing is so incongruous among the other grandiloquent benedictions that it gives everyone pause; but it is sanctioned by the usage of centuries. It is a part of our folkways; and, indeed, there are few comparisons which can better emphasize man's unworthiness than to show him inferior to a rooster. It is this simple benediction which I sought to translate and amplify; however, without the allusion, there is no impact. That's why it struck you as bathetic ... The rooster belongs, not to me, but to Jewish tradition.
> [*Poetry* 66 (July 1945), 229]

SHIGGAION OF ABRAHAM WHICH HE SANG UNTO THE LORD

Title: taken from Psalm 7. The exact meaning of *shiggaion* is unknown. It is sometimes taken to mean a passionate song, irregular in structure.

A SONG OF DEGREES

'The only imitation in the manuscript of the biblic manner. An elaboration of the evolution of weaponry – the sling, the sword, the arrow, the testudo, gas, the plane' [letter to Jewish Publication Society, 7 Aug. 1942].
  Compare 'War: The Evolution of a Menagerie' [BS, p. 45]:
    The knights of the Middle Ages, with their coats of mail, and lances, fought

precisely like elephants, or rhinoceroses, with tusks and pachyderm.
The swifter methods of the bow-and-arrow are a servile imitation of the
porcupine's protective measures ... None but the skunk suggested warfare by
gas ... And the tank owes its existence mainly to the admirable example of
the tortoise, which suggested a method of defence even to the great
Caesar. But the greatest of these, the most destructive, the most annihilating, is the warplane – the hawk of destruction ...

What a commentary upon mankind, which instead of evolving from the
ape, devolves to the beast, instead of clothing itself, as is its religious
destiny, in the pinion of angels, attires itself with the shells of tortoises and
fits itself with the claws of eagles.

Title: Psalms 120–34 begin with the phrase 'A Song of degrees.'

TO THE CHIEF MUSICIAN, AL-TASCHITH, MICHTAM OF ABRAHAM; WHEN ONE
SENT, AND THEY WATCHED THE HOUSE TO KILL HIM

The poem was included in the original manuscript of *Poems* submitted to the Jewish
Publication Society. It was at first provisionally accepted, but when Klein
refused to change the word 'privy,' he was forced to withdraw it. After the initial
acceptance of the poem Klein wrote to the JPS [1 July 1943]:

I am glad that you decided to keep this poem in. It is a right juicy
malediction upon the Fuehrer and has its place in my book. I note two
annotations on that poem. A mark opposite the second line – I still think that
the line is correct, its particular form being born of the Latin way of saying
the same thing, 'multi sunt illi ...' The other note appears to lift an
eyebrow at the use of the word 'privy.' It is not a pleasant word, but in its
context, in association with Hitler, it is as Flaubert would say, 'le mot
juste.' Besides, what other name is there for a 'privy wall' except 'a privy
wall'?

The title is based on Psalm 59, 'To the chief Musician, Al-taschith, Michtam of
David; when Saul sent, and they watched the house to kill him.' In Psalm 59
David prays to be protected against Saul's men who have been sent to kill him, and
curses them. Spiro suggests Psalm 109 as another source for Klein's maledictions.
Al-taschith means 'do not destroy'; *michtam* is related to a Hebrew word for 'fine
gold,' but its precise meaning is obscure.

For other examples of maledictions see DENTIST and ELEGY [c. 1947/1947], 88–109.

TO THE CHIEF MUSICIAN, A PSALM OF ISRAEL, TO BRING TO REMEMBRANCE

'A fluvial view of Jewish history' [note from one of Klein's poetry readings,
MS 6048]

1–2 *By the rivers of Babylon ... Zion*: quoted from Psalm 137.1

4–5 *Nilus ... firstborn*: 'And Pharaoh charged all his people, saying, Every son that is born ye shall cast into the river' [Exodus 1.22].
6 *yellow like our badge*: In 1215 the Lateran Council decreed that Jews were required to wear an identifying badge, generally yellow.
7–8 *bears ... Vistula*: See introductory note to BALLAD OF THE DANCING BEAR.
9–10 *Spain ... fires*: The Spanish Inquisition sentenced many Jews to death by fire.
11–12 *Rhine ... blood*: Jewish communities along the Rhine were massacred during the First Crusade. Compare DESIGN FOR MEDIAEVAL TAPESTRY and MURALS FOR A HOUSE OF GOD.

TO THE PROPHETS, MINOR AND MAJOR, A PSALM OR SONG

The major prophets are Isaiah, Jeremiah, Ezekiel, and Daniel. Twelve other prophets are referred to as minor. The distinction reflects the length of the books that bear their names.
10 *hapaxlegomena*: (Gr., 'said once') words known from only a single occurrence
15 *signs and wonders*: Exodus 7.3, Deuteronomy 7.19
18 *inspired peasant*: 'I was no prophet, neither was I a prophet's son; but I was an herdman, and a gatherer of sycomore fruit' [Amos 7.14].
20 *explicate the folded present*: Explicate 'is an English word used in its Latin connotation, a technique frequently adopted by Tennyson for the purpose of freshening the English tongue. Thus, it means literally, as in Latin, to unfold, and gives full meaning to the phrase which follows it, "the folded present." In other words, "explicate" is here charged with two meanings, (a) to explain (b) to unfold' [letter to Jewish Publication Society, 1 July 1943].

A BENEDICTION FOR THE NEW MOON

For an earlier version, see KALMAN RHAPSODIZES, section I, especially the version in GHP (GHP 1756), into which Klein has written the title, 'Benediction of the New Moon.' Also, compare ESCAPE, 326–414, in which the lunatic lovers 'heap [the moon] with absurds.'
1 *Elder, behold the Shunamite*: When, in his old age, King David could not keep warm, a young maiden, Abishag the Shunammite, was brought to him to share his bed [1 Kings 1.1–4]; sometimes identified with the Shulamite, King Solomon's beloved in the Song of Solomon [6.13].
13 *Lift up your heels*: See note to KALMAN RHAPSODIZES, 1–2.
15 *open writ*: In a letter to the Jewish Publication Society, 1 July 1943, Klein defends the reading 'open writ' against his editor's suggestion, 'holy writ': 'The word "open" is no accident. It is intended as per contrast to a writ specifically addressed. The moon is indicated in the poem as open to all, and to each according to his lights. Certainly the use of the word "holy" would hardly be

applicable, to something which earlier in the poem is described as that "newly minted coin." '

A PRAYER OF ABRAHAM, AGAINST MADNESS

9–12 *the keepers of the house ... the strongmen ... the golden bowl*: 'In the day when the keepers of the house shall tremble, and the strong men shall bow themselves ... or the golden bowl be broken' [Ecclesiastes 12.3, 6]. In 'The Bible as Literature' [*LER*, p. 128], Klein quotes chapter 12 of Ecclesiastes and comments:
> The highly poetic language, the reference to the spinal column as 'the silver cord,' the brain as 'the golden bowl,' the arms as 'the keepers of the house,' the teeth as the grinders which 'cease because they are few,' these, coupled with the deep and sincere feeling of the disillusioned Koheleth, render this section one of the finest expressions of resigned sorrow in all literature.

For 'the golden bowl' compare OUT OF THE PULVER AND THE POLISHED LENS, 74.

21–2 *Behold him scrabbling on the door! / His spittle falls upon his beard*: an allusion to the madness David feigned to escape Saul: 'And he changed his behaviour before them, and feigned himself mad in their hands, and scrabbled on the doors of the gate, and let his spittle fall down upon his beard' [1 Samuel 21.13].

28 *full death-quiver*: 'The point of the poem lies in the use of the phrase "the full death-quiver." All other ailments are single arrows of the quiver of the Lord. The prayer consists in asking, in lieu of madness, the "works" ' [letter to Jewish Publication Society, 1 July 1943].

A PSALM OF ABRAHAM, WHEN HE HEARKENED TO A VOICE, AND THERE WAS NONE

1 *Since prophecy has vanished out of Israel*: 'alluding to the Jewish tradition that prophecy ceased in the fifth century B.C.E. with Hagai, Zechariah, and Malachi, the last of the prophets' [s]

3 *Urim and Thummim*: (Heb.) a priestly device for obtaining oracles, kept in the breastplate of the high priest [Exodus 28.30]

4 *witch ... En-dor*: After Samuel's death Israel was threatened by the Philistines. When God refused to answer King Saul's inquiries 'neither by dreams, nor by Urim, nor by prophets,' Saul had a witch at En-dor call up Samuel's spirit [1 Samuel 28].

7 *scorpions ... whips*: Rehoboam, the son of Solomon, said to the people of Israel when they complained of forced labour, 'My father hath chastised you with whips, but I will chastise you with scorpions' [1 Kings 12.11].

10 *Baal*: Canaanite fertility god, whose worship by the Israelites was frequently condemned by the prophets

A PSALM OF TIME AND THE FIRMAMENT

'See Rilke: "O wie ist alles fern / Und lange vergangen / Ich glaube, der stern / Von welchen ich glanz empfange / Ist seit Jahrtausenden tot" ' [letter to Jewish Publication Society, 7 Aug. 1942]. Klein is quoting from 'Klage,' 1–5.

A SONG FOR WANDERERS

18 *That has no morrow*: When asked by the Jewish Publication Society to alter 'That' to 'For it' Klein refused: 'first, because "for it" definitely states reason, while "that" constitutes apposition, implying reason. In poetry, implication is to be preferred above statement. Secondly, the last line must be short, heavy and final. The words "for it" instead of "that" change the line to a tripping, hastening one' [15 Dec. 1943].

A PSALM OF ABRAHAM, CONCERNING THAT WHICH HE BEHELD UPON THE HEAVENLY SCARP

18 *geniuses unmanned*: 'a reference to the German procedure of sterilization' [letter to Jewish Publication Society, 1 July 1943]
30 *angels of Sodom*: 'angels specially assigned to works of destruction, cf. Genesis, Chapter 19' [letter to A.J.M. Smith, 21 Jan. 1943]

A PSALM OR PRAYER – PRAYING HIS PORTION WITH BEASTS

5–6 *sheep ... sacrifice*: Genesis 22.1–19
7–8 *The dove ... / Sprigless*: Genesis 8.8–9
9–10 *The ass ... inspired minds*: Numbers 22.28–30
11 *David's lost and bleating lamb*: 1 Samuel 17.34–5
12 *Solomon's fleet lovely hinds*: Song of Solomon 2.7, 3.5
15 *food that desert ravens set*: 1 Kings 17.6
16 *the lion's honeyed fells*: ' "Fells" of course, means skins. See Judges, Chapter 15 [sic; should be 14], verse 18' [letter to Jewish Publication Society, 1 July 1943].
18 *Azazel*: On the Day of Atonement the high priest cast lots upon two goats, one 'for the Lord,' and the other 'for Azazel.' The former was slaughtered; the latter was sent out into the wilderness to 'make an atonement with God' [Leviticus 16.5–10]. The exact meaning of *Azazel* is unclear. Klein follows the King James version which translates it as 'scapegoat,' but there is a traditional view

that Azazel was a desert demon to whom the goat was sacrificed. The article on *Azazel* in JE contains numerous markings. In a note for *The Golem* [MS 2989], Klein describes 'the twin symbols of Jewish history,' the lion of Judah and 'the scapegoat Azazel sent fletch'd, ramm'd, and dogg'd into depths inhospitable and up unscaleable heights, the bullying and crabbish gentiles all about it, against its bleatings roaring.'

BALLAD OF THE DAYS OF THE MESSIAH

'Messiah will come when world is all evil or all good' [note from one of Klein's poetry readings, MS 6047].

7–18 *O Leviathan ... for the good*: 'All of us will yet partake of the messianic feast. The signs of it are everywhere. We have reached such darkness that the only change now due is a change to light. Maybe now it's being prepared somewhere – the great leviathan, couched, scaled, gutted, and splayed, ready to be fried and roasted by a redressed Israel, and the wild ox, caught in the branches of some tree, waiting for the true blade, blessed and without flaw, to make him fit food upon Messiah's board. Ah, will that be a banquet! And how it will be quaffed that day, the wine cherished and hidden, from Noah's day throughout the ages aging, just for this great day! If we will have years, and we will have merit, we will yet see it!' ['Adloyada,' a chapter from an unfinished novel, MS 4477–8].

Compare Klein's translation of the Chassidic folk-song TELL US, REBBENU.

10 *piscedo*: not in the OED; formed from *pisces*, Latin for 'fish'
27 *pillared fire*: 'And the Lord went before them ... by night in a pillar of fire, to give them light' [Exodus 13.21].

BALLAD OF THE DREAM THAT WAS NOT DREAMED

14 *Thirty silver pieces*: the thirty pieces of silver for which Judas betrayed Christ

BALLAD OF THE EVIL EYE

18 *lith and limb*: 'Lith' means 'joint.' The OED lists several instances of 'lith and limb.'

BALLAD OF THE NUREMBERG TOWER CLOCK

The first branch of the Nazi party was established in Nuremberg in 1922, and the city was made a national shrine by the Nazis when they came to power. In 1935, at their annual congress in Nuremberg, the Nazis promulgated the anti-Semitic 'Nuremberg Laws.'

BALLAD OF THE THWARTED AXE

Epigraph: Coram is Latin for 'in the presence of.' The German People's Court, the *Volksgerichtshof*, was a court set up by the Nazis and dominated by members of the party. Its sessions were usually held *in camera* and there was no appeal from its decisions.

BALLAD OF THE WEREWOLVES

3 *Hairlip, Ratface, and Medal-on-the-Chest*: 'Hairlip' is Hitler, the reference being to his moustache. 'Ratface' is Goebbels, who is 'rat-faced' in THE HITLERIAD, 311. 'Medal-on-the-Chest' is probably Goering, who is described in THE HITLERIAD [331-45] as delighting in military paraphernalia.
4 *After us the flood*: 'Aprés nous le deluge,' attributed to Madame Pompadour

OF THE FRIENDLY SILENCE OF THE MOON

Title: amica silentia lunae [Aeneid 2.255]. The phrase occurs in the description of the night attack by the Greek army on the Trojans, who have been betrayed by the Trojan horse.

POLISH VILLAGE

12 *Jesus recrucified into a swastika*: Compare 'crooked cross re-crucifying Christ' [THE HITLERIAD, 225].

SENNET FROM GHEEL

one of a number of poems (compare SONG WITHOUT MUSIC, SPRING EXHIBIT, VARIATION OF A THEME) influenced by *Finnegans Wake*. Klein comments in a letter to Robert Laughlin, of *New Directions*, 3 Nov. 1942:
> The wild direction is Joyce's, but the careful walk is mine. I believe that 'Finnegans Wake' has uncovered a marvellous technique, marvellous in that it approaches the virtues of music, not by mere echolalia, but by releasing simultaneously a swarm of concordant melodies. But it is a technique for poetry, and not for prose. Certainly it is not adapted to long narrative or detailed exposition: Poe's poetic principle here receives its best illustration.

A 'sennet' is 'a set of notes on the trumpet or cornet, ordered in the stage-directions of Elizabethan plays, apparently as a signal for the ceremonial entrance or exit of a body of players' [OED]. 'Sennet' also suggests 'sonnet': the

poem is a Petrarchan sonnet with the eighth line missing. See introductory
note to SONNET UNRHYMED.

'Gheel' is a town in Belgium which, since the Middle Ages, has been
a refuge for the insane. Klein's interest in the town may have been aroused
because its name suggests a Joycean combination of 'Gehenna' and 'Hell' ('Gheel'
rhymes with 'Hell'). For an interesting parallel to the title, compare the rhyme
'senna/Gehenna' in FESTIVAL 22, 24.

5 *Bedlam, Bicetre, and hundemonium*: Bedlam and Bicetre were English and
French insane asylums, respectively. Spiro points out that 'hundemonium'
combines pandemonium with both Hun and *Hunde*, German for 'dog.'

7 *frap*: from *frapper* (Fr.) 'to strike'

8 *guerred*: from *guerre* (Fr.) 'war'

13 *Zuruck*: from *zurück* (Ger.) 'back'

YEHUDA HALEVI, HIS PILGRIMAGE

The poem won first prize in a contest sponsored by the Zionist Organization of
America to commemorate the eight-hundredth anniversary of the death of
Yehuda Halevi (c. 1075–1141), philosopher, physician, and greatest poet of the
golden age of medieval Jewish culture in Spain. Halevi, who was especially
famous for his poems expressing a longing for Zion, was born in Toledo and spent
most of his life in Spain, but at the end of his life he set out on a pilgrimage
to Jerusalem from which he never returned.

Stanzas 34–9 of the poem consist of a translation of Halevi's 'Ode to Zion,' which
Klein had probably completed before the poem itself was begun. In an introduction
to one of the published versions of this translation [*CJC*, 20 Aug. 1948, p. 4], he
wrote:

> Ever since the days of Psalm CXXXVI: *By the waters of Babylon*, a psalm
> which must be counted as the first of the Zionides, the songs of Zion
> upon the lips of Hebrew poets never ceased. Whether he was early liturgist,
> or mediaeval *payaton*, or secular bard of the latter days, the Hebrew poet rightly
> considered his work incomplete and unfinished unless it contained the
> necessary poem in praise of the past glories that were Zion's, or the inevitable
> threnody in lamentation for its present sore plight. In this fashion there
> was developed through the centuries an entire literature all harmonious
> of the melody of Zion, sad or glad; the service for the Ninth of Ab is but
> a little anthology made up of the bitterest excerpts from these works.
> Most famous, and certainly most touching of these odes to Zion is that
> penned in the twelfth century by Rabbi Yehuda Halevi, poignant not
> only for the irresistible tragedy of its lines, but also for the pertinent legend
> that surrounds the manner of the great poet's death. Tradition has it
> that Rabbi Yehuda Halevi, after many wanderings, finally arrived at the

shores of the Holy Land; that upon this shore he knelt, in great thankfulness, to kiss the soil he had so longed to reach; and that thus kneeling, he was trodden to death by an Arab horseman.

Klein's translation is slightly abridged (lines 25–30 and 43–6 of the original's 68 lines are left out). When he incorporated it into YEHUDA HALEVI he made two further changes: he rearranged the order of the stanzas, so that the third stanza (stanza 39 in YEHUDA HALEVI) became the last; and he revised the opening lines of this stanza, so that instead of expressing a wish ('God grant,' 'God give'), as they do in the original, they describe a completed action ('God granted,' 'God gave'). The effect of these revisions is to enhance the dramatic force of Klein's narrative: in the revised version, Halevi does not merely *wish* to fling himself down on the soil of Jerusalem; he actually *does* so, in a gesture which brings both his ode and his life to a dramatic end as he is 'trodden to death by an Arab horseman.'

As Klein points out in a letter to the Jewish Publication Society, 1 July 1943 (referred to as K in the notes that follow), the style of the poem is deliberately archaic: 'It is to be noted that archaic medieval words are frequently used in this poem, obviously for the purpose of bringing out the Eleventh [sic; should be Twelfth] Century atmosphere in which it is set.' In fact, the poem is written in an Elizabethan, rather than a medieval, idiom: more specifically, in the idiom of Edmund Spenser, which was itself deliberately archaic. Except for stanzas 34–9, mentioned above, the poem is in Spenserian stanzas, and, unlike Klein's earlier extended narrative in this form, AUTO-DA-FÉ, which is Keatsian in inspiration, it is quite an accurate Spenserian pastiche. Klein's choice of a sixteenth-century idiom, rather than one closer to Halevi's age, is appropriate, since the legend of Halevi's death appears no earlier than the sixteenth century, and the 'learned rabbin' (see note to 3) whom the narrator cites as his authority was, in fact, a contemporary of Spenser's. For an imitation of Halevi in an idiom from a period closer to his own, see Klein's Chaucerian translations of LORD, HELE ME, Y-WIS I SHAL BE HELED; O HEIGHTE SOVEREIGN, O WORLDES PRYS; and TO JERUSALEM THE HOLY.

The poem follows the traditional account of Halevi's pilgrimage and death quite closely: Klein's major source appears to be the article on Halevi in JE, which is marked in his hand. However, the dream of the princess seems to be Klein's own invention. There are many examples of this motif in romance literature, but a more immediate inspiration may have been the allegorical tales of Rabbi Nachman Bratzlaver. When he began YEHUDA HALEVI, Klein had recently completed a series of poems based on the Bratzlaver's 'Tale of the Seven Beggars' (see introductory note to TO THE CHIEF MUSICIAN, A PSALM OF THE BRATZLAVER, A PARABLE), and one of these poems contains a close parallel to the princess's account of the destruction of her father's kingdom (see note to 134–5). Another tale by the Bratzlaver, 'The Lost Princess,' tells of a long and painful journey in search of an imprisoned princess.

Another likely influence on the poem is Heine's 'Jehuda ben Halevy.' Klein owned a copy of Heine's *Works* (New York: Everyman 1934), which includes the poem, as well as a copy of Halevi's *Selected Poems* (Philadelphia: Jewish Publication Society of America 1924), which contains an introduction discussing the poem in some detail. Heine tells essentially the same story as Klein (with many digressions), and, although Heine's version lacks Halevi's dream of the lost princess, it does present Jerusalem as a wretched suffering lady to whom Halevi, troubadour-like, addresses his love-songs.

Title: The construction 'Halevi, His Pilgrimage' is an archaizing form of the possessive, often used by the Elizabethans. Compare 'Solomon his song' [12].

3 *The learned rabbin*: Gedaliah ibn Yaḥya (1522–88). In a passage marked by Klein, *JE* identifies his *Shalshelet ha-Kabbalah* as the source for the legend of Halevi's death.

11 *The harp of David on the willow tree*: 'We hanged our harps upon the willows' [Psalms 137.2].

12–13 *essay ... eke*: 'The word is "essay" meaning to attempt. The word is "eke" used by Chaucer and Coleridge, and easily comprehensible to Jews to whom it means אויך' [K].

13 *The sons of Asaph*: Psalms 73–83 are attributed to Asaph. The sons of Asaph are mentioned in 1 Chronicles 25.1–2 as one of the groups of singers established by David.

15 *The chief musician*: The phrase 'To the chief Musician' precedes a number of psalms.

19 *Levite of degrees*: The Levites, descendants of the tribe of Levi, served in the Temple and performed the roles of musicians and singers. 'Halevi' is Hebrew for 'the levite.' 'Degrees' probably alludes to the 'Songs of degrees' (Psalms 120–34), thought by some to have been sung by the Levites in the Temple.

21 *leet*: ' "Leet" is the medieval word for a medieval court' [K].

22 *Born ... to a pagan night*: No doubt an allusion to Klein's era in general, but there may also be an allusion to Klein's birthday, on St Valentine's Day.

28 *Whilom*: 'once'

28–30 *Toledoth ... Hebrews ... Moor ... great Christian Don*: Klein uses the Hebrew word *toledoth* ('chronicles') to suggest Toledo. Although Toledo was not 'founded by Hebrews,' as Klein claims, it had the most ancient Jewish community in Spain, dating back to the Visigoths and predating the Moorish and Christian conquests. It is not clear who the 'great Christian Don' is. According to *JE*, Halevi's 'birth occurred about the time of the eventful conquest of Toledo (May 24, 1085) by the Christian king Alfonso VI,' and he may be the one intended. But Alfonso was of an earlier generation than Halevi, and the narrator describes the 'great Christian Don' as his own contemporary ('governed now'), and, therefore, much later than Halevi. Perhaps Charles V is intended: he was Holy

Roman Emperor; he made Toledo his residence; and his years, 1500–58, would make him contemporary with the sixteenth-century narrator.
34 *Melodious ibns*: Ibn is Arabic for 'son of.' It forms part of the name of a number of Hebrew poets of medieval Spain. Compare 'the warbling *ibns* of the golden age of Spain' [SS, p. 21/28].
35 *the bubbling wine, the riddle's coats*: 'Drinking-songs and enigmas in rime by Judah have also been preserved' [JE, marked].
38 *Ezra's sons*: '... there gathered about him as friends ... a large number of illustrious men, like ... Moses ibn Ezra and his brothers Judah, Joseph, and Isaac ...' [JE, marked].
40 *The Saracen or Frankish measure*: 'He was well acquainted with the productions of the Arabic and the Castilian poets' [JE].
41 *tallith*: prayershawl
42 *minnesinger of the Lord*: The minnesingers were German medieval love poets, influenced by the troubadours. Compare 'incomparable troubadour' [31]. In 'Jehuda ben Halevy,' Heine describes Halevi as both a troubadour and a minnesinger.
47 *The hooded falcon on the wrist of God*: Compare 'But the true essence, joyous as a lark, / Will settle on God's wrist, devoutly proud!' [SCRIBE, 34–5].
54 *Mantua or Lesbos or Baghdad*: Latin or Greek or Arabic poetry. Mantua is the birthplace of Vergil, Lesbos of Sappho and Alcaeus.
56 *Al-Kazari*: The Khazars were a people of Turkish stock who converted to Judaism in the eighth century. Halevi wrote a philosophical dialogue, commonly known as the *Kuzari*, based on a legendary disputation conducted before the King of the Khazars by a Moslem, a Christian, an Aristotelean philosopher, and a Jew, as a result of which the king adopted the Jewish faith.
70–2 *the bowled brain ... Samson's bees ... Pharaoh's kine*: 'The bowled brain' is probably an allusion to the 'golden bowl' in Ecclesiastes 12.6 (see note to OUT OF THE PULVER AND THE POLISHED LENS, 74). The other references are to the honey which Samson found in a lion's carcass [Judges 14.8–9] and Pharaoh's dream of 'seven well favoured kine and fatfleshed' [Genesis 41.2].
74–5 *that psalter ... gold ... ruby*: 'alluding to the ornamental lettering (red on gold) of verses from Psalms on the walls of the El Transito synagogue in Toledo' [S]. Spiro criticizes Klein for an anachronism, since the synagogue was built in 1366. However, there is, in fact, no anachronism since the narrator is writing from the perspective of the sixteenth century.
81 *Nazarite*: The Hebrew word for Christian is *Noẓri*, Nazarite, i.e., a follower of Jesus of Nazareth.
85 *y-wis*: 'indeed'
89 *Daughter of sound*: a literal translation of the Hebrew phrase *bat kol*, 'daughter of a sound,' meaning 'echo'

981 / Explanatory Notes pp 547–56

94 *the Cushite*: Cush is the biblical name for Ethiopia. A Cushite is, by extension, a Negro.

98 *Baker or cupbearer*: Joseph interpreted dreams of Pharaoh's baker and cupbearer who were imprisoned with him [Genesis 40].

134–5 *the generals, old, now fight / Only with bloodless chessmen*: Compare 'the prince's generals have gout ... and captains play at chess' [TO THE CHIEF MUSICIAN, A PSALM OF THE BRATZLAVER, WHEN HE CONSIDERED HOW THE PIOUS ARE OVERWHELMED, 25–8].

217–43 *It is a ship ... rove*: The account of Halevi's sea voyage recalls the story of Jonah. Halevi wrote a series of poems describing this voyage.

219 *Alnath ... ald'baran*: 'Arabic names for the constellations. Beautiful words for beautiful things' [K].

234 *Iskandahar*: Alexandria, 'Al Iskandariyah' in Arabic

251 *Demieyet*: Damietta, Egypt's chief Mediterranean port at the time of Halevi's pilgrimage

258 *Mizraim*: (Heb.) Egypt

291 *cross-marked arrogant Frankish knight*: Compare 'the cross-marked varlet' [DESIGN FOR MEDIAEVAL TAPESTRY, 99]. Jerusalem was captured by the Crusaders under Godfrey of Bouillon in 1099.

303 *Hermon*: the highest mountain in Israel

308 *Peniel! Bethel! Mahanayim*: Holy places associated with Jacob [Genesis 31.13; 32.2, 31]

309 *the Immanence*: the *shekhinah* (Heb., 'dwelling,' 'abiding'), the numinous immanence of God in the world, often represented as an exiled queen or bride

320 *The chambers of thy cherubim*: the inner sanctum of the Temple. 'And he set the cherubims within the inner house' [1 Kings 6.27].

338 *Shinar and Pathros*: both mentioned in Isaiah 11.11, where Shinar represents Babylon, Pathros Egypt. To Halevi's contemporaries Shinar also represented Baghdad, the chief city of Islam, and Pathros Byzantium, the chief city of Christendom.

339 *Urim and Thummim*: (Heb.) a priestly device for obtaining oracles, kept in the breastplate of the high priest [Exodus 28.30]

369 *the third temple*: There were two Temples, the first destroyed by the Babylonians in 586 B.C., and the second by the Romans in 70 A.D.

370–1 *the bells / Of high-priest*: The high priest had bells of gold on the hem of his robe [Exodus 28.33–4].

381 *Is still for no head but her lovely head*: 'The effect of the line lies in the repetition of the word "head" with change of accent; in the first place, *no* is accented and *head* unaccented. In the second *ly* of lovely is unaccented, and *head* is' [K].

IN MEMORIAM: ARTHUR ELLIS

In 1936, Klein had an interview with Canada's official hangman (known by the traditional pseudonym for hangmen, Arthur Ellis), which resulted in this poem and 'Portrait of an Executioner' [*Stories*, pp. 191–200]. Page references are to the latter.

Line references are to version 2, the only published version.

15–16 *The Man with the Rope ... The Lark at Dawn, / Frock-coated Mister Death*: 'But to over five hundred departed gallows birds he has been The Man with the Rope, The Gentleman at Dawn, Mister Death' [p. 191].

20 *justiciary fingertips*: ' "If the judge is the arm of the law, I am its fingertips" ' [p. 196].

30 *hanged men, shocked, expelling seed*: This detail does not occur in 'Portrait of an Executioner.' However, in the 'Cyclops' episode of *Ulysses* [p. 299] there is a discussion of hanging and of 'the phenomenon which has been denominated by the faculty a morbid upwards and outwards philoprogenitive erection *in articulo mortis per diminutionem capitis*.' For Klein's familiarity with the 'Cyclops' episode, see notes to CANTABILE, 40, 50–1.

33 *docile ... loud with rage*: ' "Usually they are quite docile ... But once I had a tough customer, a husky fellow, who swore he would break me in two when I came" ' [p. 193].

38–40 *your name / kept out of phone-books ... provincial post*: 'I couldn't reach him by the phone; his name is not in the telephone book. I couldn't go to his house; his address is not listed in the city directory, neither under name nor under occupation' [p. 191].

47 *childless*: 'They have no children. "I did not want my children to be born under a cloud of ostracism, I chose to be an executioner. But the son of an executioner has no choice" ' [p. 196].

AUTOBIOGRAPHICAL

Klein's own comments [K] are cited from a letter to A.J.M. Smith, 21 Jan. 1943.

4 *Sabbath-goy*: 'A Gentile employed by Jews to kindle their fires on the Sabbath, such labor being prohibited on that day to the children of Israel. Goy = Gentile' [K].

5 *Torah-escorting band*: 'The Torah is the scroll of the Law, written on parchment. When such a scroll is donated to a synagogue by a rich knave who seeks with his piety to atone for the wretchedness of his soul, the said scroll is customarily carried from the home of the donor through the streets leading to the synagogue, the whole to the accompaniment of music, to wit, a couple of violins and a flute' [K].

9 *sadness sweet of synagogal hum*: '... I cannot ... hear sad music – music of the

minor keys – without remembering the intonations of the synagogue' [*Stranger and Afraid*, MS 3762].

12–15 *Again ... stores*: 'The impression of my childhood days is that the only people who kept groceries were widows, who always had little bells over their doors, so that they might hear the entering customer, even from the remoteness of the back kitchen, the emporium usually being located in the front double-parlor' [K].

14 *Ashkenazi*: a common Jewish surname. Ashkenazi (Heb., 'German') Jews are of central European descent, as opposed to Sephardi (Heb., 'Spanish') Jews who are descended from the Jews of Spain and Portugal.

26 *sisters*: 'Bessie and Dora, then about twenty and seventeen years old respectively' [*Caplan*, p. 9]

28 *My uncle Mayer*: Kalman Klein's brother. 'At the time when Klein was about nine years old [Mayer] was living together with the family on Hôtel de Ville' [*Caplan*, p. 9]. Caplan sees portraits of Mayer in 'And the Man Moses Was Meek' in PORTRAITS OF A MINYAN and in MOURNERS.

29 *Maariv*: 'The evening prayer. I will not say "vespers" ' [K].

30–4 *And the two strangers ... pogrom*: This incident is recalled in more detail in SS, p. 11/22, where Klein writes, 'Somehow my entire childhood is evoked through this incident.'

31 *Volhynia*: a province in the northwest Ukraine 'formerly belonging to Russia, subsequently to Poland, and now [1943] in German hands' [K]

34 *the four-legged aleph*: 'The first letter of the Hebrew alphabet. cf. Alpha. Called "running" because written א with four legs, like a swastika' [K].

35 *angel pennies*: 'If I knew my lesson well, my father would, unseen, drop a penny on my book, and then proclaim it the reward of angels for good study' [K]. Compare SS, pp. 4–5/18.

38 *Warsovian perruque*: 'Jewesses (married and pious) wear perruques. The custom has died out in America; but not for my mother' [K]. Compare 'My mother is a queen in a brown perruque' [HAGGADAH, 9].

40 *Baal Shem Tov*: 'Literally, the Master of the Good Name – a saintly rabbi of the eighteenth century, founder of the movement known as Chassidism; he placed good works above scholarship. He was a simple good man, a St. Francis of Assisi, without birds or flowers' [K].

45 *my brother's*: 'Jack, who had a cattle farm near Ormstown. Klein would have been eleven or twelve at the time of the visit described' [*Caplan*, p. 9].

49 *Dusty, adventurous, sunny days, all seven*: 'The postpositive of emphatic reminiscence' [note from one of Klein's poetry readings, MS 6034]

64 *Hazelnut games*: Games with hazelnuts were traditionally played by children during Passover.

65 *The burrs*: 'The Ninth of Ab (a month of the Jewish calendar) commemorates the destruction of the Temple. It is a day of mourning and fasting. It is

customary on that day for youngsters to gather burrs and thistles, bring them to the synagogue, and throw them – not always with impunity – into the beards of the mourning elders – so as to give a touch of realism to their historic weeping. For the kids, this is a lot of fun' [K].

65 *the Haman rattle*: 'Haman is the villain of the Book of Esther. On Purim, which is the festival commemorating its events, the Book of Esther is read in the synagogue. Every time the name of Haman is uttered by the reader of the scroll, the youngsters, armed with rattles, make a furious noise, so as to drown out those unspeakable syllables. There will be a day when they will be called Hitler-rattles!' [K]. Compare OF THE MAKING OF GRAGERS.

66 *The Torah-dance on Simchas-Torah night*: Simchas Torah (lit. 'the rejoicing of the law') is a celebration marking the conclusion of one annual reading of the Torah and the beginning of the next. The celebrations include dancing with Torah scrolls around the synagogue.

81 *Not tranquil recollection*: an allusion to Wordsworth's statement in the preface to *Lyrical Ballads* that 'poetry ... takes its origin from emotion recollected in tranquility.' 'Wordsworth he hated from the very first' [S. H. Abramson, 'Abe Klein – In Person,' *Jewish Standard*, Sept. 1936, p. 23].

COME TWO, LIKE SHADOWS

In a letter to Peter Devries of *Poetry* magazine, 29 Sept. 1942, Klein defended the 'uglyduckling adjective – pudendal' in the last line, refusing to change it: 'The fact is that the entire poem is built about the contrast between the slick shave of Plato, and the erotic hirsuteness (considering his theories) – of the learned doctor. The facial contrast, moreover, serves as an apt parallel to the intellectual struggle postulated in the previous stanzas; the physiognomic from the gnomic. Obvious, as you say, it may be; so obvious, I find it irresistible.'

8–9 *Plato ... screen*: a reference to Plato's myth of the cave in the seventh book of the *Republic*

DENTIST

33–5 *And may one canine ... livelong ache*: In 'The Yiddish Proverb,' Klein cites 'the oath full-mouthed breathing execration ... "May all his teeth fall out, except one – for toothache!"' [LER, p. 121].

For other examples of maledictions compare ELEGY [c. 1947/1947], 88–109 and TO THE CHIEF MUSICIAN, AL-TASCHITH, MICHTAM OF ABRAHAM: WHEN ONE SENT, AND THEY WATCHED THE HOUSE TO KILL HIM.

DESIDERATUM

'I would prepare a memorandum to be submitted to the Heavenly Throne, with recommendations for the better creation of man.

'1. Divisibility and adjustability of limbs. It is suggested that the human body would be much increased in efficiency, and the human soul (quare) much increased in its happiness if the varied limbs and members of the frame were painlessly removable, and therefore adjustable, at will. Such a consummation would add greatly to our ubiquity – the head from body removable does multiply life by two – dexterity amplified, etc.' [note for *The Golem*, MS 3047].

2–10 *nerves two hundred forty-eight ... six hundred and thirteen / edicts*: The law of Moses traditionally contains 613 commandments (*taryag mizvot* in Hebrew), of which 365 are prohibitions and 248 positive precepts. Their association with the parts of the human body is an ancient one, going back to the Talmud and perhaps even earlier. Compare 'Twelve score and eight the limbs, parts, and members of the body, and eighteen score and five its organs and sinews – the sum all-embracing of commands and forbiddings, the six hundred and thirteen, *curriculum taryag!*' [SS, p. 139/105].

8 *gematria*: (Heb.) a method of disclosing hidden meanings of biblical or other texts by interpreting words according to the numerical value of their letters

15 *Powers, Dominations, Thrones*: three of the nine angelic orders. Compare 'Thrones, Dominations, Princedoms, Virtues, Powers' [*Paradise Lost* 5.601].

ET J'AI LU TOUS LES LIVRES

'La chair est triste, hélas, et j'ai lu tous les livres'; the first line of Mallarmé's sonnet, 'Brise marine'; cited in DIARY OF ABRAHAM SEGAL, POET, 176
6 *minette*: (Fr.) fashionable, sophisticated, young woman

GIRLIE SHOW

The first two lines are a quotation from Keats's 'Ode on a Grecian Urn,' 8–9 (with 'feigning' in place of Keats's 'struggle'). Klein imitates the stanzaic structure of the Ode, though he is more regular than his model.

5 *Pan*: Pan, the son of Hermes, was the goat-footed pastoral god of fertility. He was associated with Dionysus and Dionysian rites.

20 *omphalos*: (Gr.) 'navel'; the navel-shaped stone used in the rites of many Greek and Roman cults. The most famous was at the oracle of Delphi.

21–2 *Here the crippled come / To throw away the crutches*: Compare THE CRIPPLES.

40 *And once more Pan is god, as he was god of yore*: The conclusion of the poem recalls that of A.J.M. Smith's 'The Faithful Heart' (1939): 'we shall know

him [Pan] as lusty as of yore / And bear the vine-tipped thyrsus into the woods once more.'

THE GOLEM

For the golem legend, see TALISMAN IN SEVEN SHREDS. There are notes in the Klein papers [MS 4517–24] for a play entitled *Death of the Golem,* which suggest that Klein intended to use the golem as a Hitler-figure, as he does in this poem.

9 *The rabbi Nubal*: There is no Rabbi Nubal in the golem legend. The reference is to *Neville* Chamberlain, who is condemned for attempting to appease Hitler by yielding Czechoslovakia ('Bohemia's forests') to him, in an effort to outmanoeuvre the Soviet Union ('the bear of the human walk').

LOVE

7 *It moves the sun and all the stars*: a reference to the final line of Dante's *Paradiso*: 'l'amor chi move il sole e l'altre stelle.' Compare MY LITERATI FRIENDS IN RESTAURANTS, 10.
12 *his name be writ in water*: a reference to Keats's epitaph, 'Here lies one whose name was writ in water'
17 *whose luve's a red red rose*: 'O my luve's like a red, red rose' [Robert Burns, 'A Red, Red Rose,' 1].

MY DEAR PLUTOPHILANTHROPIST

The poem occurs in a fictionalized diary in which Klein expresses his disgust at having written a sonnet in support of 'the annual philanthropic campaign.' MY DEAR PLUTOPHILANTHROPIST is the 'campaign poem which was not written' [MS 3475].
6 *baksheesh*: (Persian) 'gratuity'
17 *a maka*: (Heb.) 'a plague'
18 *zdaka*: (Heb.) In the Bible *zdaka* has the meaning 'righteousness,' 'justice.' Later it came to mean 'acts of charity.'

PAWNSHOP

8 *razed it to the salted ground*: After their final victory over Carthage in the third Punic War, the Romans razed the city and sowed its site with salt.
31 *lombard*: 'a native of Lombardy engaged as a banker, money-changer, or pawnbroker; hence applied *gen.* to a person carrying on any of these businesses' [OED]

31 *kapital*: a reference to Marx's *Das Kapital*. An earlier version has 'This is the house built by das Kapital.'
36–40 *Adam ... smith ... wealth ... let-do*: a reference to Adam Smith, whose *An Inquiry into the Nature and Causes of the Wealth of Nations* provides a justification for laissez-faire ('let-do') economics. An earlier version has 'One Adam Smith whose world of wondrous wealth.'
39 *pleasure-dome*: 'In Xanadu did Kubla Khan / A stately pleasure-dome decree' [Coleridge, 'Kubla Khan,' 1–2].
43 *platonic cave*: a reference to Plato's myth of the cave in the seventh book of the *Republic*
49–50 *gomorrah ... sodom ... salt*: After fleeing the destruction of Sodom and Gomorrah, Lot's wife disobeyed God's command not to look back and was transformed into a pillar of salt [Genesis 19.26].

PENULTIMATE CHAPTER

10 *The dry bones quickened*: Ezekiel 37.1–14
18–22 *ichthyosaurus ... / titanothere and tetrabelodon*: Ichthyosauruses were fishlike reptiles; titanotheres were giant herbivores resembling a tapir or rhinoceros; tetrabelodons were a form of elephant with lower as well as upper tusks.

VARIATION OF A THEME

one of Klein's Joycean poems. See note to SENNET FROM GHEEL.
1–3 *Enamort ... breath*: 'I have been half in love with easeful Death, / Called him soft names in many a musèd rhyme, / To take into the air my quiet breath' [Keats, 'Ode to a Nightingale,' 52–4].
7 *Menhir*: 'a tall upright monumental stone, of varying antiquity, found in various parts of Europe, and also in Africa and Asia' [OED]; a punning reference to *Mein Herr*
7 *Barow de Hearse*: Baron de Hirsch, nineteenth-century Jewish philanthropist
8 *C.G.*: *ci-gît* (Fr.), 'here lies'
10 *L.A.G.*: elegy
32 *And ... die*: 'Now more than ever seems it rich to die' [Keats, 'Ode to a Nightingale,' 55].

THE HITLERIAD

In a letter to James Laughlin, 29 Mar. 1944, Klein responded to a request for a blurb for THE HITLERIAD:

The Hitleriad is neither lyrical, nor cerebral, nor pure poetry. It is a latter-

day attempt to revive (and modify) an old technique, and apply it to
the contemporary event. Augustan verse I know, has long been out of
fashion. When lately used, it has almost invariably concerned itself
with the merely literary squabble. Two centuries ago, Pope employed it to
devastate his dunces; a century later, Byron used it to scotch his reviewers. But
to-day, the poetry of wit and wrath finds mightier themes. Systems and
ideologies, not rhyme-schemes and bardlings, fight for survival. Let
the scop X hunt down his rival minstrel Y; I have sweeter quarry.

Baldly, The Hitleriad is intended as a prosecutor's indictment against
'that wicked man.' Of necessity, it indicates the source and origin of his power.
It postulates the moral issues involved. For the rest, it speaks for itself.

I have felt that the best technique suited to this subject was the heroic
couplet – that cat-o-two-tails, and the second knotted. But the heroic
couplet, if persisted in for too many lines, eventually ceases to sting and
becomes an anaesthetic. Accordingly, the meter and rhyme are varied – terza
rima, Hudibrastic tetrameter, blank verse, concealed sonnets; all serve their
several ends to make the prosecutor's case ... In The Hitleriad, I flatter
myself to think that the prophetic indignations of my ancestors and the
typical cerebralities of my co-religionists, stand combined.

The major source for the poem is Konrad Heiden, *One Man against Europe* (London: Penguin Books 1939; rpt. 1940), of which Klein owned a copy. Unless otherwise indicated, all quotations in the following notes are from Heiden. Klein's copy contains numerous markings and some annotations, especially to those sections dealing with Hitler's character and rise to power.

1 *Heil heavenly muse*: 'Sing, Heav'nly Muse' [*Paradise Lost* 1.6].
6 *hippocrene*: a fountain sacred to the Muses. An allusion is probably intended to 'the true, the blushful Hippocrene' in Keats's 'Ode to a Nightingale,' 15.
7 *lager*: A pun may be intended on *Konzentrationslager*, 'concentration camp.'
41–2 *Is this the face ... Rotterdam*: 'Was this the face that launched a thousand ships, / And burnt the topless towers of Ilium?' [Christopher Marlowe, *The Tragical History of Doctor Faustus* 5.1.97–8, in *The Complete Plays*, ed. J.B. Steane (Harmondsworth: Penguin Books 1969), p. 330]. The entire centre of Rotterdam was destroyed by a German air bombardment on 14 May 1940, several hours after the city had capitulated.
46 *vegetarian*: Hitler was a vegetarian.
50–1 *clown ... pranks*: probably an allusion to Charlie Chaplin's satire on Hitler, *The Great Dictator*
64 *the beast not blond*: 'the magnificent blond beast, avidly rampant for spoil and victims' [Nietzsche, *Genealogy of Morals*, essay 1, aphorism 11]
66–7 *His strength ... ten*: 'My strength is as the strength of ten, / Because my heart is pure' [Tennyson, 'Sir Galahad,' 3–4].
76 *Braunau at the Inn*: 'The little town of Braunau, where Adolf Hitler was born

in the humble room of an inn on the 20th April, 1889, is on the river Inn ...' [p. 10].

80–7 *Schicklgruber ... shame*: Hitler's father was illegitimate. 'He bore his mother's surname – Schicklgruber – a name which sounds so peculiar to German ears that it is fairly safe to say that its bearer could never have embarked on a serious political career. Alois Schicklgruber was already a mature man when his father, now almost eighty, yielding to the pressure of relatives, legitimised his son and gave him his name' [p. 9].

89–91 *Rilke ... Hitler*: 'Rainer Maria Rilke though of Bohemian extraction, wrote in German, so considered himself, and indeed was as much a German as Hitler. He was too, one of the most outstanding German poets of modern times, a deeply religious soul, a holy literary figure, more akin to the East than to Europe. We were reading his Journal recently and were struck by the fact that in his numerous travels, he spent several years in Linz. Linz, Linz, where had we heard of that before? Yes, that is Hitler's birthplace. Strange, indeed, that that small town, should, during the same years, have harboured Hitler, then Shicklgruber, and Rilke. It was as if one little hamlet, were the residence of Mazda and Ahriman, as if Beauty and the Beast dwelt together' ['Of National Characteristics,' *CJC*, 23 Feb. 1940, p. 4].

Klein discusses Rilke as 'the direct antithesis of everything for which the Fuehrer stood' in 'Rilke and His Translators' [*LER*, p. 252].

91 *boden ... blut*: (Ger.) *Blut und Boden* ('Blood and Soil'), Nazi slogan

94 *dunce of the corner*: 'His ... school-reports are bad ... He avoided taking his final school examination – perhaps because he was afraid to – for in fact he failed at the few scholastic examinations he ever took' [p. 13].

102–3 *He / Hated his father*: 'Adolf Hitler's youth was overshadowed by one fundamental experience – his bitter struggle against ... his father ...' [p. 12].

Section v: 'It is true that he had had a little instruction in drawing at a private institution in Munich. After his mother's death he twice applied for admission to the Academy of Arts in Vienna. The first time he failed in the examination; the second time, after showing his specimen drawings, he was not even allowed to sit' [p. 13].

130 *Hitler fecit, pinxit Hitler*: (Lat.) 'Hitler made it, Hitler painted it': *Fecit* and *pinxit* are terms used by artists in their signatures.

138–47 *Vienna's derelict ... public aid ... flophouses ... handouts at the door*: '... he led a life of unspeakable wretchedness and poverty in Vienna. For some time he lived in a casual ward among beggars and vagabonds ... he ate the soup supplied to the destitute at the gate of the *Nonnenkloster* in Gumpendorferstrasse ...' [p. 13].

154 *the Kaiser ... shrivelled hand*: Kaiser Wilhelm II had a withered left arm.

161 *I fell on my knees, I wept, I wept for joy*: ' "To me those hours (of the outbreak

of war) were like a deliverance. I am not ashamed to say that, overcome by a storm of enthusiasm, I fell on my knees and thanked heaven from an overflowing heart." Thus he writes in his book, *Mein Kampf*' [p. 20].

163–4 *where is Adolf's braid? / Where are his medals*: Hitler, in fact, was awarded the Iron Cross. An earlier version has: 'It's true that Hitler wears an Iron Cross, / The spoils of war. / He never had it, sirs, until he had / All Germany's iron ore.' See textual note to 175/76.

167–9 *Too often ... to the rear*: 'His duty was to act as a runner for the regimental staff; so he was not constantly in the trenches, but often in the vicinity of officers of higher rank' [p. 20].

171 *stayed a corporal*: 'In spite of his military zeal he remained a lance-corporal. It never occurred to his superiors to promote this eccentric to higher rank and entrust him with the leadership of men' [p. 21; marginal marking].

172–5 *the ... General Staff ... did not ... bestow ... its generalissimo*: 'At regimental headquarters he had been in closest proximity to his superiors, keen and conscientious in his duties, and yet no one had hit upon the idea that somewhere inside him was a gift for leadership' [p. 27; marginal marking].

Section VIII: an account of the unsuccessful 'beer hall *Putsch*,' which began in the Bürgerbraukeller in Munich on 8 Nov. 1923. The *Putsch* ended when Hitler and his companions, including the World War I general Erich Ludendorff, were fired upon by police. 'Ludendorff alone marched with head high towards the smoking muzzles of the guns ... the first man to get up from the ground, run back and drive off in a car, was Adolf Hitler' [p. 37; marginal marking].

193 *The dotard Hindenburg*: Field Marshall Paul von Hindenburg, the hero of World War I, was President of Germany from 1925 to 1934. In 1933, nearly senile, he gave in to advisers and appointed Hitler chancellor.

194–5 *He marched across the Rhine ... back again*: In March 1936 Hitler occupied the Rhineland, which had been declared a de-militarized zone, with a small token force. His generals agreed to the action only on the understanding that they would immediately retreat if the French army resisted.

196–7 *He coveted the Czech-land ... donated*: The Munich pact of 1938 ceded the Sudetenland of Czechoslovakia to Germany.

213 *circuses ... daily bread*: Heiden quotes Hitler: 'The workers – they want nothing but bread and games' [p. 17].

225 *crooked cross re-crucifying Christ*: Compare 'Jesus recrucified into a swastika!' [POLISH VILLAGE, 12].

236 *Indited by his fellow-convict, Hess*: Hitler dictated *Mein Kampf* to Rudolf Hess when they were in prison together after the 'beer hall *Putsch*.'

251 *The lie, if oft repeated, is the truth*: 'The masses ... always need a certain time before they are ready even to notice a thing, and they will lend their memories only to the thousandfold repetition of the most simple ideas' [*Mein Kampf* (New York: Reynal and Hitchcock 1939), p. 239].

253 *Blood, Honour, Soil*: See note to 91.

310–19 *Goebbels*: Paul Joseph Goebbels was Hitler's propaganda chief. He was short and had a club foot, but prided himself on being attractive to women.

316 *lebensraum*: (Ger.) 'living space.' Hitler claimed that Germany had the right to expand its territory, primarily eastward, to ensure adequate space for its people.

320–30 *Rosenberg*: 'Rosenberg, a Russian of German stock, had fled from Moscow to escape the Bolshevists; he held the view common in Russia that the Jews were the cause of all revolutions and other catastrophes, and he brought with him to Germany a "document" forged by the Russian secret police, the so-called "Protocols of the Elders of Zion" ' [p. 24; marginal marking]. Rosenberg wrote *The Myth of the Twentieth Century* and edited the Nazi journal *Völkischer Beobachter*.

331–45 *Goering*: Hermann Goering was one of Hitler's closest associates and held many powerful posts, including head of the Gestapo. He was notorious for his love of high-sounding titles and elaborate uniforms and pageantry. He was also notoriously corrupt: he used his position to extort gifts, including artwork. He was implicated in the Reichstag fire, which served as an excuse for attacks on communists and other opponents of the Nazi regime.

338 *geheimrat ... geheim*: (Ger.) 'privy councillor ... secret'

342 *Addicted to the narcotic*: 'At times he had been a morphia addict' [p. 34; marginal marking].

346–60 *Ribbentrop*: Joachim von Ribbentrop, the Nazi foreign minister, was 'a man of good family ... after the war he was a traveller for a French champagne company' [p. 40]. He had contacts with the pro-appeasement Cliveden set, centring on the Astor estate at Cliveden.

367–72 *Von Papen*: Franz von Papen was expelled from his post as military attaché to the German embassy in Washington because of his espionage activities. Although not originally a member of the Nazi party, he used his position as chancellor to help bring the Nazis to power. He was appointed vice chancellor by Hitler and continued to serve even after many of his close associates were eliminated by Hitler.

373–84 *Himmler*: Heinrich Himmler was head of the SS. He played an important role in the 'night of the long knives,' 30 June 1934, during which hundreds of his and Hitler's opponents were brutally murdered.

385–95 *Streicher*: Julius Streicher was editor of the sadistic and anti-Semitic *Der Stürmer*.

396–9 *Hoffman*: Heinrich Hoffman was Hitler's 'court photographer,' the only man who for years was allowed to photograph Hitler.

400–5 *Haushofer*: Karl Haushofer was a German geographer and theorist of Nazi geopolitics.

406–9 *Ley*: Robert Ley was the alcoholic Cologne party boss. He was in charge of the German Labour Front.

410–11 *Hess*: Rudolf Hess was one of Hitler's earliest followers. In 1941 he stole an airplane and flew to Scotland, supposedly in order to negotiate a separate peace treaty with Great Britain.

Section XIV deals with victims of 'the night of the long knives.' See note to 373–84.

416 *Strasser*: '... Gregor Strasser ... seemed at one time to be wresting the leadership from Hitler; but in 1932, shortly before the movement attained power, he was defeated by a more powerful block consisting of Hitler and his close friends' [p. 41; marginal marking].

417–18 *Roehm*: Ernst Roehm was commander of the Storm Troops. '... as a homosexual, he made of the Storm Troops, and especially of its headquarters staff, a male harem of unnatural vice' [p. 42].

420 *reproachable but without fear*: an allusion to the phrase *sans peur et sans reproche*

421 *Schleicher*: Kurt von Schleicher was a brillant German general, and last chancellor of the Republic before Hitler. Like Hitler, he sought to subvert the Republic, but Hitler considered him a dangerous rival.

422 *Heines*: Lieutenant Edmund Heines was head of the Munich Storm Troops, and a convicted murderer. Hitler used Heines' notorious homosexuality as an excuse to have him murdered.

423 *Where ... yesteryear*: 'Where are the snows of yesteryear?' ['Mais où sont les neiges d'antan?' (François Villon, 'Ballade des dames du temps jadis,' refrain)].

430 *Junker*: The Junkers were the Prussian land-owning class and main source of the Prussian officer corps. They were, on the whole, contemptuous of the Nazis but acquiesced in Nazi rule because of the privileges granted them.

432–3 *Social Democrat; / The Catholic, and concordat*: The Social Democrats were the most popular party in the Weimar Republic but were unable to come to terms with the Nazi threat. The Concordat of June 1933 gave the Catholic Church control over its own educational and communal institutions in return for recognition of the regime.

435 *Thyssen, Hugenberg*: Fritz Thyssen was the head of the German Steel Trust, which contributed substantial sums to the Nazis. Alfred Hugenberg was originally general manager of Krupps armaments; he served in Hitler's first cabinet. 'In the propaganda struggle against his rival, Hitler, he had for years come off second best despite the enormous funds at his disposal. From the day of the formation of the new government he failed to hold his own against Hitler on this decisive question of new elections, and six months later, on 27th June, 1933, Hitler threw him out of the Government' [p. 49; marginal marking].

457 *umbrellas*: Neville Chamberlain was often seen with an umbrella, most notably in a famous photograph taken on his return from signing the Munich Pact on 30 Sept. 1938.

464 *The Volkswagon*: In 1938, the Nazis set up an automobile factory, promising

to provide each German worker with an inexpensive *Volkswagen*, or 'people's car.' When the war began, the factory was turned over to the production of war supplies and no *Volkswagens* were built.

483-5 *As he would yet send forth ... engines*: a reference to the Lend-Lease Act, passed in 1941, which allowed the United States to provide war supplies to nations whose defence was considered vital to the defence of the United States.

489 *The Tiger, ever-burning bright*: Georges Clemenceau, French premier during World War 1 and negotiator of the Versailles Treaty. Klein marked the following passage in Heiden: 'Clemenceau was regarded in Germany at that time as the "sadist of Versailles," and is said to have remarked that twenty million Germans ought to be annihilated' [p. 79]. At the top of the page he wrote, 'Where was the tiger, burning bright.' The allusion is to the opening of William Blake's 'The Tiger': 'Tiger! Tiger! burning bright.'

518 *the sudden lightning thrust*: Blitzkrieg, 'lightning war'

521 *Stuka*: (Ger.) dive bomber

524 *Clausewitz*: Karl von Clausewitz, author of *On War*

527-8 *the peace / That passeth boundaries*: 'the peace of God, which passeth all understanding' [Philippians 4.7]

559 *Culture, here he cocked his gun*: a reference to the statement 'When I hear the word "culture," I reach for my gun,' usually attributed to Goering. The original quotation is 'When I hear "culture" I release the safety-catch of my Browning [*Wenn ich Kultur höre entsichere ich meinen Browning*].' It comes from Hans Johst's play *Schlageter*, about a leader of German resistance to the French occupation of the Rhineland, published in 1930. Johst later became head of Hitler's Chamber of Culture.

Section XXII surveys Nazi aggression. The episodes alluded to are: the *Anschluss* of Austria (Mar. 1938); the dismemberment of Czechoslovakia (Nov. 1938); the invasions of Norway (Apr. 1941), Poland (Sept. 1939), Holland (May 1940), Yugoslavia (Apr. 1941), and Greece (Apr. 1941); the defeat of France (June 1940); the Battle of Britain (Aug.-Oct. 1940); the invasion of Russia (June 1941).

606 *Skoda ... the four smug men*: The Skoda Steel Works in Pilsen, Czechoslovakia, were the Czechs' main source of armaments. The new borders established by the Munich Pact made the Skoda Works much more vulnerable to Germany, and they were soon occupied, along with the rest of Czechoslovakia. The four smug men are the main representatives of England, France, Italy, and Germany, who negotiated the Munich Pact – Neville Chamberlain, Edouard Daladier, Mussolini, and Hitler.

614 *The fascist and his rods*: Fascism takes its name from *fasces*, the ancient Roman symbol of magisterial authority, consisting of cylindrical bundles of wooden rods, tied tightly together, from which an axe projected.

626 *Domrémy*: birthplace of Joan of Arc

627–30 *The lesser corporal ... / Napoleonic stance*: See introductory note to TRIBUTE TO THE BALLET MASTER.

647–50 *Magyarland ... Italy ... Denmark ... Roumanian land*: Hungary (Magyarland), Italy, and Roumania were all technically allies of Nazi Germany, which, in fact, dominated them. Denmark signed a ten year nonaggression pact with Germany in 1939 but was occupied in April 1940.

656 *blood-and-soiled honour*: See note to 91.

Section XXIV: 'In the summer of 1933 the National Socialists began their struggle against the Evangelical Church, and twelve months later against the Catholics also. With the years this struggle has become a persecution so intense that it seriously threatens the very existence of the Catholic Church in Germany, and must result in changing the Evangelical Church from a free religious community into a national paganism' [pp. 61–2; marginal marking].

For the use of terza rima in this section see note to POLITICAL MEETING.

670 *The creed of the Black Forest*: the *Neuheidentum*, 'new heathenism,' promoted by the Nazis as an alternative to Christianity

681 *In hoc vinco*: (Lat.) The Emperor Constantine was said to have been converted to Christianity by a vision he had, before a successful battle, of a cross inscribed with the words *in hoc signo vinces*, 'in this sign you will conquer.'

695–6 *that voice ... brothers' blood*: a reference to Cain's murder of Abel: 'the voice of thy brother's blood crieth unto me from the ground' [Genesis 4.10]

745 *the lightning strokes the ten*: the Ten Commandments, whose proclamation on Mount Sinai was accompanied by thunder and lightning [Exodus 19.16]

749 *the bright freedoms four*: the Four Freedoms proclaimed by Franklin Roosevelt on 6 Jan. 1941 and incorporated into the Atlantic Charter (Aug. 1941): freedom of speech and expression, freedom of worship, freedom from want, freedom from fear

ACTUARIAL REPORT

Compare Kenneth Fearing's 'Statistics' [*Afternoon of a Pawnbroker* (New York: Harcourt Brace 1943), p. 9] with its similar use of actuarial language.

29 *absence from felicity*: 'Absent thee from felicity a while / And in this harsh world draw thy breath in pain' [*Hamlet* 5.2.347–8].

32 *Famine, disease, and other motley personages*: 'And I looked, and behold a pale horse: and his name that sat on him was Death, and Hell followed with him. And Power was given unto them over the fourth part of the earth, to kill with sword, and with hunger, and with death, and with the beasts of the earth' [Revelation 6.8].

39 *A son is born*: 'For unto us a child is born, unto us a son is given' [Isaiah 9.6].

39–41 *born ... dying*: Compare 'Birth or Death? ... this Birth was ... like Death, our death' [T.S. Eliot, 'Journey of the Magi,' 36–9].

AND IN THAT DROWNING INSTANT

7 *Basle print*: The reference is unclear. Klein may be referring to the fact that Basle, Switzerland, was an important centre for the printing of Hebrew books at the end of the sixteenth century. At this time Jews were forbidden to live in the city, with the exception of those who acted as proofreaders. In 1578 the Talmud was published in Basle; in notes to a lecture on the Talmud [MS 6989], Klein refers to it as the standard edition; the edition was, in fact, expurgated by the Christian authorities. There may also be a reference to Basle's historical significance as site of the first international Zionist convention.
11 *Baal Shem Tov*: See Klein's note on AUTOBIOGRAPHICAL, 40.
14 *Amsterdam*: Amsterdam was an important centre of Jewish culture in the seventeenth century. Compare OUT OF THE PULVER AND THE POLISHED LENS.
16 *Abraham*: Abraham Athias was put to death by the Inquisition in Cordoba in 1665.
18 *arch*: the Arch of Titus, commemorating Titus' victory over the Jews and his destruction of the second Temple. Compare ss, pp. 109–11/85–7.

NOT ALL THE PERFUMES OF ARABIA

Line references are to version 1.
Title: 'Here's the smell of the blood still. All the perfumes of Arabia will not sweeten this little hand' [*Macbeth* 5.1.50–1].
3 *As poison ... royal Denmark*: 'in the porches of my ears did pour / The leperous distillment' [*Hamlet* 1.5.63–4]
5 *nefas*: (Lat.) 'wicked deed, crime.' Compare 'the unspeakable nefas' [ss, p. 146/110].
18 *Sevastopol*: Soviet port in the Crimea; captured by the Germans after an eight-month siege in July 1942; recaptured in May 1944
24 *stukas*: (Ger.) dive bombers
33 *fetor judaical*: *fetor judaicus* (Lat.), the offensive smell which the Romans attributed to Jews
34 *herrenvolk*: (Ger.) master-race

ADDRESS TO THE CHOIRBOYS

> R. Amnon [was] a wealthy and respected Jew of Mayence, whom the archbishop of Mayence, at various times, tried to convert to Christianity. On one occasion Amnon evasively asked to be given three days' time for consideration. When he failed to appear on the appointed day, the archbishop had him brought guarded into his presence. Amnon, rebuked for his failure to keep his promise, pleaded guilty, and said that his

tongue should be cut out, because it had expressed a doubt as to the truth of Judaism. The archbishop, however, pronounced the sentence that Amnon's feet, which had refused to come, and his hands should be cut off. This was accordingly done.

Amnon gave orders that he be carried into the synagogue, where New-year's day was being celebrated ... [He] recited the prayer called, from its initial words, 'U-netanneh Tokef,' which is a description of the Day of Judgment. No sooner had he finished the prayer than he expired; and his body immediately disappeared ... The story is a legend without any historical value, based on the reminiscences of the persecutions during the Crusades, and inspired by the veneration for the 'U-netanneh Tokef.' [JE, 'Amnon of Mayence']

'U-netanneh Tokef' is paraphrased in the italicized passages.
4 *two fasts ... ram's horn blown*: customs serving to reinforce the penitential spirit in the month leading up to the High Holidays (New Year and the Day of Atonement)
6 *The tombstone maker*: 'During the month before the New Year, tombstones are traditionally placed on the graves of those who passed away during the year' [s].

BASIC ENGLISH

In his McGill reading of November 1955, Klein said of BASIC ENGLISH that it was written 'at a time when I was disappointed to learn that the great Sir Winston Churchill had endorsed Basic English as a medium of communication. I felt that Basic English, a vocabulary limited to 800 words, while good enough for the purposes of urgent and emergency communication, hardly constituted a language upon which one could build a literature. And therefore ... I submitted with respect to Sir Winston my comments touching Basic English of Mr I.A. Richards.'

MS 2225 contains the following marginal notes, probably intended for the McGill reading:

I.A. Richards
800 words, – Never was so much owed by so many to so *few*
monosyllabic
Do not deny utility
John S. Astbury, love of language

For Astbury see introductory note to TO KEATS.

Klein frequently wrote about Winston Churchill's oratory. Compare, for example, 'Immortal Speech' [BS, pp. 89–91].
1 *trope of testament and Caesar's wars*: 'Here is language that is as if taken out of Holy Writ, the homely parable, the apt quotation, the ironical aside ... His military reports sound as if they were taken out of Caesar, the same

compactness, the same activity, the same marching towards a purpose, full of grandeur, yet business-like' [BS, p. 89].
12 *grunt of Caliban*: Before being taught language by Prospero and Miranda, Caliban 'would ... gabble like / A thing most brutish' [*The Tempest* 1.2.356–7].
22 *Exhausted well of English, and defiled*: Edmund Spenser refers to Chaucer as a 'well of English undefiled' [*The Faerie Queene* 4.2.32.8].
36 *desesperanto*: a pun on *désespoir* and Esperanto
50 *Basic as bread*: Compare BREAD.

BREAD

In his McGill reading of November 1955, Klein said of BREAD:
... humanity is concerned with basic things, with elementary things. Here it is that there is established a democracy that knows not class nor distinction, the democracy of humanity, where common elements are taken as the hearts, the navel cords which bind one to the other. One of these elements is our common weakness. We are not angels. We must subsist upon matter. No one can exist without bread. This is our Achilles heel. Those of us who would like to rise and mount and soar into the high altitudes empyrean and think of ourselves not only as lesser but almost close to the angels, always are brought back by this basic element, the element of our humanity, of our necessity to lean one upon the other. It is of these feelings that the poem called BREAD speaks.
Compare GRAIN ELEVATOR.
17–18 *Bakers most priestly ... / White Levites*: One of the priestly tasks of the Levites was to bake bread used in sacrificial offerings [Leviticus 2]. Compare ELEGY [c. 1947/1947], 86–7.

THE LIBRARY

'A salon, its walls full of exquisite paintings, library, civilization at its highest. A button is pushed – they are really only panels. Behind them a grating whence roar caged beasts' [note from Klein's 'Raw Material' file, MS 3555].

MONTREAL

preceded by the following note in *Preview* 21 (Sept. 1944), 3–5, signed A.M.K.:
Suiting language to theme, the following verse, – as will be noted, is written in a vocabulary which is not exactly orthodox English. It is written so that any Englishman who knows no French, and any Frenchman who knows no English (save prepositions – the pantomime of inflection) can read

it intelligently. It contains not a word, substantive, adjectival, or operative, which is not either similar to, derivative from, or akin to a French word of like import; in short, a bilingual poem.

MONTREAL reflects Klein's interest at this period in the language experiments of *Finnegans Wake* (see introductory note to SENNET FROM GHEEL), and 'riverain' in 1 may be a punning allusion to the first word of *Finnegans Wake*, 'riverrun.'

PARADE OF ST. JEAN BAPTISTE is Klein's only other bilingual poem.

2 *sainted routs*: Many of Montreal's streets are named after saints. St Lawrence Boulevard, 'the Main,' was the centre of the Jewish district, and for many years Klein lived on St Urbain Street. He had law offices on Ste Catherine Street and St James Street.

4 *erablic*: from *érable*, 'maple'

6 *pendent balcon and escalier'd march*: Montreal row-housing architecture, common on the streets of Klein's youth, is characterized by balconies and by iron staircases descending from the second storey.

11 *Ville-Marie*: the mission settlement, founded 1642, out of which Montreal grew

12–13 *calumet / ... peace*: ritual pipe used by Plains Indians; 'peace pipe'

16 *His statue in the square*: The statue of Maisonneuve in Place d'Armes has four figures at its base, including an Iroquois.

30 *Ecossic*: from *écossais*, 'Scottish'

33 *Hochelaga*: the Indian village on whose site Montreal was founded

36–7 *thunder / From foundry issuant*: 'The susurrus of factories – but is "thunder" the proper correlative?' [note from one of Klein's poetry readings, MS 6034].

38 *hebdomad*: 'week.' Compare the French adjective *hebdomadaire*.

NI LA MORT NI LE SOLEIL

'Le soleil ni la mort ne se peuvent regarder fixement' [La Rochefoucauld, Maxim 26].

A PSALM TOUCHING GENEALOGY

2 *the fathers that begat me*: 'their fathers that begat them' [Jeremiah 16.3]. In a note from one of his poetry readings [MS 6056], Klein says, 'Write out of tradition,' and he refers to 'Dr. Jung's doctrine of the racial consciousness.' He cites Marvin Lowenthal's story 'The Fathers That Begat Us: A Genealogical Inquiry,' in *A Golden Treasury of Jewish Literature*, ed. Leo Schwarz (New York: Farrar and Rinehart, Inc. 1937), pp. 76–113.

5 *They circle, as with Torahs*: a reference to the Simchat Torah ritual which includes dancing around the synagogue with the Torah scrolls. Compare

'Circular, too, was the dance, a scriptural gaiety, with wine rejoicing the heart, and Torah exalting it to heights that strong wine could not reach' [ss, p. 8/20].

SPRING EXHIBIT

one of Klein's Joycean poems. See introductory note to SENNET FROM GHEEL.

EPITAPH

1–6 *Good friend ... bones*: 'Good friend, for Jesus' sake forbear / To dig the dust enclosèd here; / Blest be the man that spares these stones, / And curst be he that moves my bones' [Shakespeare's epitaph].
5 *secondbest bed*: Shakespeare's will leaves his second-best bed to his wife.

LES VESPASIENNES

Vespasiennes are public urinals, named after the Emperor Vespasian, who was the first to establish them in Rome. Vespasian was emperor at the time of the destruction of the second Temple, in 70 A.D.

Klein may have had in mind the *vespasiennes* (no longer used as such) in Carré St Louis not far from where he was living at the time the poem was written. The building is in the style of a classical temple and has VESPASIENNES carved in stone over its entrances.
5 *dancing with daffodils*: 'And then my heart with pleasure fills, / And dances with the daffodils' [Wordsworth, 'I Wandered Lonely as a Cloud,' 23–4].
20 *swim up within our ken*: 'When a new planet swims into his ken' [Keats, 'On First Looking into Chapman's Homer,' 10]
29–31 *'valiant ... hope'*: These lines appear to be a pastiche of Romantic poetry, rather than a quotation or a parody of a specific passage.

OF TRADITION

13 *Onan*: Onan was commanded by God to marry his dead brother's wife. But 'Onan knew that the seed should not be his [i.e., any child she bore would take on his brother's name and inherit his property]; and it came to pass, when he went in unto his brother's wife, that he spilled it on the ground, lest that he should give seed to his brother' [Genesis 38.9]. Compare SONNET UNRHYMED.

SAGA THE FIRST

an imitation, in form as well as content, of Old English verse. Compare the deleted section of PORTRAIT OF THE POET AS LANDSCAPE.

SONG WITHOUT MUSIC

one of Klein's Joycean poems. See introductory note to SENNET FROM GHEEL.

TAILPIECE TO AN ANTHOLOGY

'As far as Canadian poetry is concerned, Klein believes that in the past it has been nothing more than an importation from England free of duty, which privilege it enjoyed not so much because of the Empire connection but because the specific poetry came under the category called antique. He believes that he is one of the few persons who can be called a Canadian poet, who has not mentioned a pine tree in one of his poems. He believes also that contemporary Canadian poets model themselves upon American poets, whereas the old-fashioned Canadian Authors' Association brand model themselves on English poets' [S.H. Abramson, 'Abe Klein – In Person,' *Jewish Standard*, Sept. 1936, p. 23]. Compare 'Writing in Canada' [LER, pp. 216–21].

TRIBUTE TO THE BALLET MASTER

perhaps occasioned by 'Hitler's jig,' a dance of victory which Hitler was supposed to have performed after forcing France to sign an armistice agreement at Compiègne on 22 July 1940. The British newsreel in which the episode was recorded was, in fact, doctored for propaganda purposes. Compare 'The lesser corporal / Over prostrated France / Mimics with carpet-fretting feet / Napoleonic stance' [THE HITLERIAD, 627–30].
  The line reference is to version 1.
24 *Tautentanz*: a pun on *Totentanz* (Ger.), 'dance of death,' and Teuton

PORTRAIT OF THE POET AS LANDSCAPE

MS 7594 contains the following outline of PORTRAIT OF THE POET AS LANDSCAPE, obviously written at great speed and difficult to decipher at several points:
  The world diminished by the contents of my lungs – paid back.
    * * *
  Describe being a poet. Who wants him in this age, the day of gasoline and oil.
  Cursed be the day I penned my first pentameter.

> What prompted me. Vanity, mimesis, afflatus
>
> But here it is. That's what I am. I have yet in me to do something. So many things still unpraised (See Natonek) still unlabelled by my words. My inventory has not yet been taken
>
> Moreover I want more than discrete isolated visions, I want yet to see the world as a photographer on Mars, focussing all of the sunlit in the camera glimpse

The 'Natonek' referred to in the outline is Hans Natonek, a Czech-born Jewish writer who fled the Nazis to New York after the fall of France. Klein's 'Raw Material' file [MS 3454–558], a collection of fictional treatments of the poet's role in society, contains a note [MS 3557], dated 5 Dec. 1943, on Natonek's *In Search of Myself* (New York: Putnam 1943). This account of Natonek's experiences as an unknown writer confronting a materialistic and self-satisfied society with no interest in what he has to say has obvious parallels in Klein's own concerns, as expressed throughout 'Raw Material' and in PORTRAIT OF THE POET AS LANDSCAPE.

Klein's note on Natonek's book indicates that he was both intrigued and repelled by it: 'Sickly sentimental European story, broken by shrewd insights. Supercilious manner of second-rate self-pitying has-been. To me useful for suggestions.' The note goes on to list a number of possible subjects, based on episodes in Natonek's book, for a poem entitled 'To Whom It May Concern,' a phrase borrowed from Natonek [p. 46]. Although, as far as can be determined, Klein never wrote a poem of that title based on those particular subjects, his reading of Natonek seems to have been an important catalyst for PORTRAIT.

In addition to the reference to Natonek, various notes on the same sheet as the outline link it to 'Raw Material.' Thematically, the most important link between the outline and 'Raw Material' is the presentation of the poet's relation to the world in terms of lungs – referred to as the 'inverted tree' in 'Raw Material' – and breathing. This theme, which, on the evidence of the outline, was central to the original concept of PORTRAIT, is developed in the final section of the poem. See especially 139–45, 157.

PORTRAIT was reprinted in *Longer Poems for Upper-School, 1955–1956*, ed. Roy Allin and Alan F. Meikeljohn (Toronto: Ryerson Press 1955). Some of the notes for this edition were provided by Klein himself; these are marked [K] in the notes that follow. For the provenance of Klein's notes see D.M.R. Bentley, 'A Nightmare Ordered: A.M. Klein's "Portrait of the Poet as Landscape,"' *Essays on Canadian Writing*, 28 (Spring 1984), 42, note 3.

Title: 'The modern poet is so anonymously sunk into his environment that, in terms of painting, his portrait is merely landscape' [K]. The title echoes Joyce's *Portrait of the Artist as a Young Man*, and the account of the poet's 'ambitions,' in the final section of the poem, recalls Stephen Dedalus' ambition, at the end of *Portrait of the Artist*, 'to forge in the smithy of [his] soul the uncreated conscience of [his] race.'

1 *bereaved with bartlett*: 'Since the editorial writer feels no real sense of loss, he resorts to quotes from Bartlett's *Familiar Quotations*. These quotes are so impersonal that bartlett becomes a common noun' [K].
2 *Lycidas*: Milton's pastoral elegy 'Lycidas' is a lament for the poet Edward King, who drowned at an early age. Through the figure of the shepherd Lycidas, Milton explores the nature of the poetic vocation.
10 *detective story*: '... we delude ourselves for a sweet moment into believing that perhaps some importance is attached to our function. But it is a mirage, sheer and Saharan. The writers of detective yarns command more attention, more respect, and of course, more gratitude palpable' [letter to *Circle* magazine, 14 May 1945, accompanying a submission of PORTRAIT].
25 *the seven-circled air*: 'A reference to Dante's *Inferno*. In Hell, various actions were punished in different circles, the total being seven according to Aristotle' [K]. The total in Dante's *Inferno* is actually nine.
27 *a Mr. Smith in a hotel register*: 'For hotel-registers to the contrary notwithstanding, not everybody is Smith' [letter to A.J.M. Smith, 6 Jan. 1944].
29 *but only ignored*: 'I have not been curtly ignored; I have been nodded at, and then ignored' [letter to *Circle*].
30–1 *like the mirroring lenses ... guilt*: Compare 'His eyes glassed over and congealed with guilt' [Karl Shapiro, 'Poet,' 30]. Shapiro's account of the 'half-forgotten' [6], 'despised' [33] poet influenced both the general tone and specific phrasing of PORTRAIT.
39 *quintuplet senses*: 'This refers to a modern theory that each sense is a duplicate of the other; thus a situation may be "seen" through the sense of taste and "felt" through the sense of sight. Quintuplet also has a special significance in Canada' [K]. 'Special significance in Canada' is a reference to the Dionne quintuplets, born on 24 May 1934 in Corbeil, Ontario.
43 *warm auxiliaries*: 'This includes auxiliary verbs, adjectives, and adverbs which branch from the "torso" to add to the general beauty and understanding of the sentence' [K].
46 *dimple and dip of conjugation*: 'To the poet the inflections of the verb have all the beauty of a face shining and dimpling with laughter' [K].
49 *like shaken tinfoil*: Compare 'like shining from shook foil' [Gerard Manley Hopkins, 'God's Grandeur,' 2]. Klein underlined this phrase and wrote it in the margin of his copy of Hopkins' *Poems* (Oxford: Oxford University Press 1938), p. 26.
52 *the integers of thought; the cube-roots of feeling*: 'The rational is here contrasted with the emotional. The former is referred to as whole numbers while the latter, more subtle, consists of cube roots' [K].
Section III: Compare the section on the false shepherds with their 'lean and flashy songs' in 'Lycidas,' 103–31.

67 *the bevel in the ear*: 'Describe small bodily blessings – Bevel in the ear etc.' ['Raw Material,' MS 3555].

77 *patagonian in their own esteem*: 'The patagonians were a mythical tribe of giants. Seventeenth century travellers claimed to have seen them in South America. Thus some poets, having joined a party, believe themselves to be world-shakers' [K].

85–6 *another courts / angels*: probably Rilke, for whom the angel is a central symbol and whose *Duino Elegies* (a major influence on PORTRAIT) begin: 'Who, if I cried out, would hear me among the angels' / hierarchies?' Compare 'Rilke invoked angels' ['Rilke and His Translators,' LER, p. 252].

87–8 *sick with sex, and rapt, / doodles him symbols convex and concave*: probably Yeats, who underwent an operation to revive his sexual powers, and whose poetry makes use of geometrical figures such as spirals ('gyres') and intersecting cones. Compare 'the Yeats mystical, gyring about some Byzantium that never was on land or sea; and finally, for one short rejuvenated spell, Yeats the gay old blade' ['The Masked Yeats,' LER, p. 282]. Klein comments on 'symbols convex and concave': 'The poet shows his lack of equilibrium even when abstractedly he makes his marks on paper: he does not draw, he doodles; his symbols are not straight lines, but convex and concave' [K].

Section IV: Compare the section on fame in 'Lycidas,' 70–84.

127 *ape mimesis*: 'The mimicry or imitation practiced by the ape. The poet's motivation is not merely the desire to imitate his predecessors' [K].

128 *merkin joy*: 'The mere joy of self-satisfaction' [K]. A merkin is 'counterfeit hair for women's privy parts' [OED].

129–32 *Rather ... gape of gravity*: 'The poet wishes to defy the law of gravity which drags all toward the earth, the grave, and ultimate anonymity. The enormity of the challenge renders him unhappy (stark infelicity), but he is willing, for such an object to do the unusual, such as investigate the modes and covers (window sills and roofs) of human living, and even make complete revelation (undressed) of his own psychic strengths and weaknesses' [K].

134–5 *the nth Adam ... naming*: 'whatsoever Adam called every living creature, that was the name thereof' [Genesis 2.19].

137 *syllabled fur*: ' "Fur" is metonymy for animal. Unlike humans with their rich vocabulary, animals can master but one or two syllables' [K].

139–45 *For to praise ... his own body's chart*: This account of the 'solitary' poet who 'praises' and 'breathes' the world, confounding the distinction between 'the world' and 'his own body,' owes much to Rilke. Compare the *Duino Elegies*, especially the ninth, and the *Sonnets to Orpheus*, especially 2.1. Klein is probably alluding to the latter ('Rilke's poem on air') in a set of notes in 'Raw Material' concerning the 'inverted tree' [MS 3554].

142 *Item by exciting item*: Compare 'fact by fact' [Shapiro, 'Poet,' 26].

144–5 *they are pulsated ... chart*: 'The poet's aim is to feel in himself what all humanity feels. These "items" become a part of him, as if a map of the world were superimposed upon a diagram of the human body' [K].

153 *archaic like the fletcher's*: Compare 'the way of the fletched buffalo' [MEDITATION UPON SURVIVAL, 35].

159–60 *he / makes of his status as zero a rich garland*: 'O, the victims of frustration worshipping their zero!' [diary entry, 10 Apr. 1944, MS 1298].

163 *phosphorus*: In a note on *Surrealism*, by David Gascoyne – on the same sheet as the note on Natonek – Klein writes: 'Baudelaire enamoured of the "phosphorence of putrescence." '

163 *At the bottom of the sea*: Compare 'Where thou perhaps under the whelming tide / Visit'st the bottom of the monstrous world' ['Lycidas,' 157–8]; 'His death shall be by drowning' [Shapiro, 'Poet,' 65].

Deleted section: 'But I don't fool myself. I am simply Kay, kindler of copy, delving at desk, sheepskin for show, hung over hilding, swinking in slogans for mongers and martmen, writing their warwhoops, heiling their heroes tobacco triumphant victorious vests, skop of the sales-force, bard of their booty with zest for zippers, for gussets gusto, shrilling the shoddy, hawking at hest; Kay, kinsman and conman, homey with housewifes, chaffering chattels, pally with paters, buttering buyers, frighting with fable the yokels unyielding, fighting the foeman in safety, for silver' ['Raw Material,' MS 3544].

For the form of this section, which imitates Old English alliterative verse, compare SAGA THE FIRST.

INDIAN RESERVATION: CAUGHNAWAGA

The Iroquois Indian Reservation of Caughnawaga is located on the south shore of the St Lawrence River, near Montreal. In his student years, Klein worked summers as a guide for a bus tour which included the reservation.

18 *alimentary shawls*: In a letter, 12 July 1945, Marion Strobel of *Poetry* magazine inquired about the meaning of the phrase 'alimentary shawls.' Klein replied: 'The payment of the governmental allowance to Indian women upon reservations is made conditional on their wearing of the black shawl. Cf. the yellow badge – grassy ghetto indeed!' In response, 18 July 1945, Strobel argued that ' "alimentary" without a footnote would still be confusing' and requested 'a better adjective.' Klein replied:

No, I am not Eliot nor was meant to be, providing poems to illustrate a footnote. I do see your point, however; also I would not want to give the impression that things are so bad on the reservations that shawls are part of a latter day Indian diet.

How about: 'Beneath the sufferance of their shawls'? The originally intended connotation would still remain, yet would not be necessary for intelligibility. The grassy ghetto notion, too, would be conveniently preluded – sufferance as a badge is an inevitable evocation. And in any event, – associations, evocations, and legal allusions all ignored – nobody looks happy in a black shawl.

THE PROVINCES

Compare Patrick Anderson's 'Poem on Canada,' especially section v, 'Cold Colloquy' [*The White Centre* (Toronto: Ryerson Press 1946), pp. 29–45]. Klein owned and marked a copy of this volume.

1 *the two older ones*: Ontario and Quebec
10 *their fathers*: England and France
13 *the three flat-faced blond-haired husky ones*: the Prairie provinces: Manitoba, Saskatchewan, and Alberta
14 *the little girl*: Prince Edward Island. A reference may be intended to Prince Edward Island's most famous literary heroine, Anne of Green Gables.
17 *her brothers*: Nova Scotia and New Brunswick
22 *the hunchback*: British Columbia, a hunchback because of the Rocky Mountains which form its spine
26 *Nine of them*: At the time the poem was written, there were only nine Canadian provinces, Newfoundland not becoming the tenth until 1949.
27–8 *the adopted boy of the golden complex ... / the proud collateral albino*: the two Territories: the Yukon, site of the Klondike gold rush, and the Northwest Territories
42–3 *the house with towers ... carillon of laws*: the parliamentary buildings in Ottawa, dominated by the Peace Tower, which houses a carillon

THE ROCKING CHAIR

'I seek to find [in the rocking chair] the symbol for French Canada, a symbol which will at once illustrate a continued preoccupation and will also point to the nature of the psychology, as far as I understood it, of the French people, ties to this continent, and nostalgic memories of the old continent' [McGill reading].

Klein's use of the rocking chair as the symbol of a community was influenced by the work of Karl Shapiro, especially by his first collection, *Person, Place and Thing*, which Klein praises as 'a perfect, an impeccable re-creation in words of the very sound and texture of the American scene ... it was left to Shapiro to endow these pedestrian quotidian things with a richness and vividness which one had hitherto associated only with mediaeval pageantry as floridly painted by Keats' ['Those Who Should Have Been Ours,' LER, p. 248]. One of the poems which Klein singles out for praise is 'Drug Store,' and its opening lines are echoed in the opening lines of THE ROCKING CHAIR:

It baffles the foreigner like an idiom,

> And he is right to adopt it as a form
> Less serious than the living-room or bar;
> > For it disestablishes the café,
> > Is a collective, and on basic country.

24 *St. Malo*: the birthplace of Jacques Cartier

29 *like some Anjou ballad*: The French region of Anjou has no very close connection with either ballads or Quebec. Klein revised this passage many times and it is not until the eighth, and final, version that the word 'Anjou' appears; in previous versions the ballad was 'antique.' Klein may have changed 'antique' to 'Anjou' to suggest a pun on the syllable 'jou' and 'Jew.' He pronounced both identically, as can be heard in the recordings of his readings of THE ROCKING CHAIR [Folkways and McGill reading].

SONNET UNRHYMED

This is probably the 'poem on contraceptives' which Klein lists among his works in MS 3455. Spiro notes that 'the Talmud considers wasting semen a destruction of potential lives and tantamount to murder.' However, another inspiration for this poem may be Joyce's *Ulysses*, in which the 'Godpossibled souls that we nightly impossiblize' [p. 383] is a central theme, especially in the 'Oxen of the Sun' chapter on which Klein wrote his most elaborate commentary. In his commentary Klein cites a statement of Joyce's: 'the idea being the crime committed against fecundity by sterilizing the act of coition' ['The Oxen of the Sun,' LER, p. 289]. Compare Klein's own comment in his notes for *The Golem*: 'Our glory swims away in contraceptives' [MS 3171]. For an early anticipation of the theme of the poem compare AUTO-DA-FÉ, 501–4.

The poem is a Petrarchan sonnet, unrhymed to reflect the theme of incompletion. Compare EXORCISM VAIN, SENNET FROM GHEEL, and SONNET WITHOUT MUSIC.

4 *the vague forward and flawed prism of Time*: 'the dark backward and abysm of time' [*The Tempest* 1.2.50]

8 *Abba*: The article on *abba* in Klein's copy of JE is marked. The word *abba* is Hebrew (originally Aramaic) for father; *abba* is also the rhyme scheme of the first quatrain of a Petrarchan sonnet.

13–14 *the entangled branches ... Absaloms*: Absalom was the third son of King David. He rebelled against his father and was defeated. When he was trying to escape, his long hair became entangled in the branches of a tree and he was killed by one of David's followers [2 Samuel 18.9–17]. When David heard of Absalom's death, he mourned for him: 'O my son Absalom, my son, my son Absalom! would God I had died for thee, O Absalom, my son, my son!' [2 Samuel 18.33].

THE CRIPPLES

in *terza rima*, underlining the ritual solemnity of the occasion. Compare POLITICAL MEETING.

Epigraph: St Joseph's Oratory, a massive domed structure, was constructed on the site of a small chapel built by Brother André (Alfred Bessette, 1845–1937), a porter at Notre Dame College, who became known for his piety and healing powers. The Oratory is a centre for pilgrims, especially those seeking miracle cures, many of whom climb the stairs leading up to it on their knees. Klein may have the Oratory in mind in BALLAD FOR UNFORTUNATE ONES, 2–3: 'The pale wan creatures crawling in the sun / Toward heaven upon much bespatted stairs.'

1 *ninetynine*: In a letter to Frank Flemington, his editor at Ryerson Press, 6 Mar. 1948, Klein defends this spelling: 'Ninetynine. Unhyphenated. The word is thus a longer word, and its n's – in my mind – simulate steps: n-i: n-e: n-i: n-e: treads and risers.'

7 *heads, upon the ninetynine trays*: a reference to John the Baptist whose head is presented 'in a charger' to the niece of Herod, after he is beheaded at her request [Matthew 14]. Compare *ss*, pp. 52–3/49, where the narrator has the illusion of seeing his own head lying upon a platter in a shop window.

12 *ransomed crutches*: Crutches abandoned by the miraculously healed are displayed in great numbers at the Oratory.

13 *sanatorial*: not in the *OED*; perhaps a combination of 'sanatory' (i.e., 'healing') and 'janitorial,' with reference to Brother André's role as porter

14 *God mindful of the sparrows*: 'Are not two sparrows sold for a farthing? and one of them shall not fall on the ground without your Father' [Matthew 10.29].

FOR THE SISTERS OF THE HOTEL DIEU

'Another element which entered into my outlook upon life, in addition to the English language, was the French environment in which I found myself in the province of Quebec. I came early in contact with this environment. For it was when I fell ill as a child [Klein broke his leg in a skating accident] that I was taken and nursed back to health by the sisters of the Hôtel Dieu. And it is to thank them that I have penned these few lines' [McGill reading].

9 *me little, afraid, ill, not of your race*: Compare 'Me, old, alone, sick, weak-down, melted-worn with sweat' [Walt Whitman, 'To the Sun-set Breeze,' 4].

FRIGIDAIRE

2 *hill 70*: a ski hill in the Laurentians. The context would seem to exclude an

allusion to the more widely known 'Hill 70,' site of a major battle of World War I (15 Aug. 1917), involving Canadian troops.

GRAIN ELEVATOR

The reference is to the large concrete grain elevators in Montreal harbour.
2 *babylonian*: the Tower of Babel [Genesis 11.1–9]
4 *Leviathan*: Job 41
6 *ark*: Noah's ark [Genesis 6–9]
10 *Josephdream*: 'And [Joseph] said unto [his brothers], Hear, I pray you, this dream which I have dreamed: For, behold, we were binding sheaves in the field, and, lo, my sheaf arose, and also stood upright; and, behold, your sheaves stood round about, and made obeisance to my sheaf' [Genesis 37.6–7]. Compare 'The Bible's Archetypical Poet' [*LER*, pp. 143–8].
11 *scruples of the sun*: A scruple is 'a small unit of weight or measurement' [*OED*].
12–13 *Saskatchewan / is rolled like a rug of a thick and golden thread*: 'The longest-syllabled flat province in monosyllables unfolded' [note from one of Klein's poetry readings, MS 6034]
18–19 *the grain picked up, like tic-tacs out of time: / ... one by one*: Compare *Stranger and Afraid* [MS 3764]: 'Sitting on my bunk, I feel as if the cell were full of time, a granary full of it, and that it is the condemnation of my sentence to pick off the grains one by one, like in the story.'
29 *It's because it's bread*: Compare BREAD.

M. BERTRAND

6 *icitte*: (Fr.) an archaic form of *ici* still current in Quebec popular speech
11 *conférencier*: (Fr.) lecturer

THE SNOWSHOERS

8 *goodlucks*: The prints of the snowshoes in the snow presumably remind Klein of horseshoes, symbols of good luck. There may also be an allusion to *mazel tov*, the Hebrew expression for 'congratulations,' meaning, literally, 'good luck.'
18 *slapdash backdrop*: Compare 'slapdash lattice' [Patrick Anderson, 'Ski Train,' in *The White Centre* (Toronto: Ryerson 1946), p. 55].
26–8 *the water they will walk! ... / World of white wealth! ... Waves*: Compare 'water whitened, spurned by lightshod hurrying feet ... Wavewhite ...' [*Ulysses*, p. 11].

THE SUGARING

Maple trees are generally tapped around Easter, mid-March to mid-April; hence
the Easter imagery of the poem.
Dedication: Guy Sylvestre (b. 1918), critic, anthologist, and librarian, was an early
  admirer of Klein and encouraged interest in him in Quebec.
1 *lenten ... ash*: a reference to Ash Wednesday, which begins Lent
24–5 *the honeyed dies / the sacred hearts, the crowns*: Maple sugar is prepared in
  moulds which, in Quebec, sometimes take the shape of religious symbols.

DOCTOR DRUMMOND

William Henry Drummond (1854–1907) emigrated from Ireland to Montreal as a
child. He became a doctor and a poet, famous for his verse portraying French-
Canadian *habitant* life in a dialect of his own devising.

THE NOTARY

The legal profession in Quebec is divided into *notaires* and *avocats*. Notaries are
particularly involved in drafting documents of various kinds: for example,
wills, marriage contracts, deeds transferring land.
4–5 *redacted ... witnesses, / ... scarlet seal*: Documents put into proper form or
  'redacted' by the notary frequently must be witnessed. The notary generally
  affixes a seal (scarlet or gold) to such documents.
8 *cadastral*: 'an official statement of the quantity and value of realty made for
  purposes of taxation (French law)' [Jowitt's *Dictionary of English Law*]
12 *the imprescriptible word*: 'Imprescriptible' is a term in civil law. 'Prescription
  is a means of acquiring, or of being discharged, by lapse of time and subject to
  conditions established by law' [Quebec Civil Code, Art. 2183]. Among things
  that are 'imprescriptible' are 'the rights of the Crown with respect to sovereignty and
  allegiance' [Art. 2212] and 'sacred things' [Art. 2217]. In 'The Bible Manuscripts'
  Klein speaks of the 'script eterne, text imprescriptible' [*LER*, p. 136].
13 *sacred upon the roll*: an allusion to the fact that deeds, etc., were once rolled
  up and tied with a ribbon affixed to a wax seal. In some jurisdictions, the
  official list of the relevant law society, containing the names of members in good
  standing, is called the 'roll.'
16 *English-measured*: perhaps a reference to the fact that English measure,
  translated into French, is used in Quebec in such documents as deeds (e.g.,
  pieds for 'feet')
17 *the immoveable*: 'real property' – for example, lands and buildings – which is
  'immoveable either by its nature, or by its destination, or by reason of the object to
  which it is attached, or lastly by determination of law' [Art. 375]

18 *the unborn of the unborn*: The notary, by drafting wills, arranges for the disposal of property not only to living legatees but also to those yet unborn. There are rules limiting the power to dispose of property to persons in the future but there are means of arranging dispositions to the unborn (*à naitre*). Art. 932, which deals with one of these means ('substitution'), states that it 'cannot extend to more than two degrees': that is, it cannot extend beyond 'the unborn of the unborn.'

19 *certainties*: a term used in both common and civil law. The 'three certainities' are the essential characteristics of a trust: 'first, the language of the alleged settler must be imperative; second, the subject matter or trust property must be certain; third, the objects of the trust must be certain' [D.W.M. Waters, 'The Three Certainties,' in *Law of Trusts in Canada*, 2nd ed. (Toronto: Carswell 1984), p. 107].

20 *custom*: perhaps an allusion to the old name for the various systems of law in France. Thus, for example, before codification, the law of Quebec developed from the *Coutume de Paris*.

21 *getting*: acquisition of property; procreation. 'Marriage contracts [which generally involved property arrangements] must be established by notarial deed *en minute*, on pain of absolute nullity' [Art. 472].

POLITICAL MEETING

POLITICAL MEETING describes an anti-conscription rally addressed by the mayor of Montreal, Camillien Houde, who was interned during World War II because of his freely expressed views on conscription. Klein mistrusted Houde, but was fascinated by him: there is a description of him in PARADE OF ST. JEAN BAPTISTE, and in the unfinished novel *Stranger and Afraid*, Klein says of Houde: 'He is a brilliant speaker, colorful, witty, histrionic, a character, and I love to hear him talk' [MS 3753]. In relation to POLITICAL MEETING, Klein's most important treatment of Houde is the editorial 'Little Red Riding Houde,' which appeared in the *Canadian Jewish Chronicle* on 24 Feb. 1939 [BS, pp. 46–7]. This account of a speech by Houde on 'the nature and essence of French-Canadian blood' contains some striking parallels to POLITICAL MEETING, in both ideas and phrasing, noted below. Curiously, Klein sent an inscribed copy of *The Rocking Chair* to Houde, and, even more curiously, Houde replied with a warm letter of appreciation [MS 421], singling out POLITICAL MEETING for special praise.

The last four stanzas of the poem, the climax of Houde's performance, are in strict *terza rima*. The previous stanzas are in a very loose *terza rima*: the two rhyming lines within each tercet are in no particular order, and the rhymes between tercets are either nonexistent or very imperfect. Klein may have adopted this loose *terza rima* from Wallace Stevens' 'Sea Surface Full of Clouds,' which was on the modern poetry course which he was teaching at McGill during the period when POLITICAL MEETING was written. Klein's teaching copy of Louis Untermeyer's *Modern American Poetry* contains annotations to the poem in his hand, and, in particular, the rhyme words in its first section are underlined. Klein frequently uses *terza rima* to emphasize the ritual solemnity of an occasion (compare, for example, THE CRIPPLES and, especially, section XXIV of THE HITLERIAD, which closely parallels POLITICAL MEETING), and his use of it here in a garbled form is symbolically appropriate to the occasion he is describing.

1–3 *platform ... the agonized Y*: 'The agonized Y' no doubt refers to the figure of Christ on the cross, but compare the description of Houde 'upon a Y.M.C.A. platform' [BS, p. 46].

9–11 *the ritual bird ... alouette's*: a paraphrase of the traditional French-Canadian song *Alouette*

20 *sunflower seeds in his pockets*: In SS, p. 11/22, the narrator describes the arrival of relatives from the old country who tell of a pogrom: '... they had sunflower seeds in their pockets. They spoke with a great and bitter intensity.' The narrator comments: 'Somehow my entire childhood is evoked through this incident.'

23 *the Grande Allée*: (Fr.) the street in Quebec City where the most prominent Québécois lived; by extension, the elite of French Quebec

27–8 *speaks of himself / in the third person*: Klein quotes Houde referring to himself in the third person as 'that old fool Camillien' and '*le petit gars de Ste. Marie*' [BS, p. 47]. For the latter, see note to PARADE OF ST. JEAN BAPTISTE, 77.

28 *slings ... folklore*: 'Camillien has decided to take a fling at folklore' [BS, p. 46].

33 *his other voice*: '... ventriloquially, the mayor replies ...' [BS, p. 46].

38 *grim*: 'And his fairy tale was Grimm' [BS, p. 46].

39 *the body-odour of race*: '... these racist theories ... are nothing more than a twentieth century version – but not a harmless version – of the fairy tales of Prevost and Grimm. Readers will recall how the ogre in one of these anecdotes of infancy, rushes into his castle and shouts, "Fee-fi-fo-fum, I smell the blood of an Englishman." That, perhaps, is quite proper in the world of imagination, – but how the mayor of a city upon this continent can afford to indulge, despite his sensitive and capacious nostrils, in sniffing at blood theories, is certainly beyond comprehension' [BS, pp. 46–7].

QUEBEC LIQUOR COMMISSION STORE

15 *Ishmael*: son of Abraham by his maidservant Hagar [Genesis 16]; traditional ancestor of the Arabs

THE SPINNING WHEEL

23 *banality*: a pun on *banalités*, taxes on grains, which under the seigneurial system the tenant had to grind at the *seigneur's* mill

25 *corvée*: (Fr.) required labour in the feudal system. There was no *corvée* in the seigneurial system.

THE WHITE OLD LADY

3 *Cote des Neiges*: (Fr.) a street in Montreal

SESTINA ON THE DIALECTIC

In the draft of a letter to the *Kenyon Review*, 7 Feb. 1947, which was intended to accompany the submission of SESTINA ON THE DIALECTIC and PORTRAIT OF THE POET AS LANDSCAPE, Klein wrote:

> Sestina on the Dialectic: It is the form, here, which particularly engaged my attention. Desiring correspondences, I sought that form which would be best suited to the already intended Hegelian content. I came to the conclusion that it was the sestina, and this because its end-word-scheme is the perfect analogue of the dialectical syllogisms.
>
> Thus the first six lines afford the key-words   1 2 3 4 5 6.
> The next stanza arranges the words   6 1 5 2 4 3.
>
> This is not arbitrary. It is the result of a folding pleating accordion process, thus:
>
> $$\begin{matrix} 1\ 2\ 3\ 4\ 5\ 6 \end{matrix}$$
>
> give
>
> 6 1 5 2 4 3
>
> The third stanza repeats the mathematical technique. No. 2 being
>
> 6 1 5 2 4 3, no. 3 becomes
>
> 3 6 4 1 2 5
>
> and so on, and so on. (It is no wonder that Dante placed the inventor of the sestina, Arnaut Daniel – in hell!)
>
> The sestina, however is a very monotonous form. The examples in our literature – Swinburne's, Kipling, Sir Philip Sidney, Ezra Pound – tend, because of the obvious recurrence of the same end-words, to degenerate into a performance (which, of course, it is). The pattern, which should be the submerged basis of the poem springs to the fore, imposes itself as total pattern, the result – the content is lost; the thing is read only for its end-words.
>
> To obviate this difficulty, while still preserving the pattern, I decided to use as end-words, words that were in themselves insignificant: with, a, to,

out, so, still; and to construct the whole, as befitted the exposition of historic law, in paragraph form. Only the title remained to draw attention to the fact that behind these paragraphs, as behind history, there was a pattern.

A lot of trouble for a small point? Perhaps; but so is the sonnet, or the Spenserian stanza, etc. Either form counts, or it doesn't.

Klein's introduction to his McGill reading of SESTINA summarizes these comments, adding a more detailed account of the poem's 'Hegelian content':

Dialectical thinking, the thinking of the dialectics of the Hegelian philosophy ... holds that all life is made up of thesis, antithesis, these resolving into a synthesis and this again breaking up into antithesis, and so the world moves like a pendulum, backward and forward and yet maintaining a kind of equilibrium as the pendulum reaches its central point. This pendulum effect is observable in many of the phenomena of nature, in the ebbing and flowing of human blood, in the ebb and flow of time, and appears also, according to Hegel, to be a mode of general historical and human behaviour.

The above comments on SESTINA ON THE DIALECTIC, as well as the sestina itself, are probably indebted to Ezra Pound. Klein's account of the 'folding' rhyme scheme of the sestina echoes Pound's characterization of the sestina as 'folding and infolding upon itself' in *The Spirit of Romance* (New Directions 1929), p. 27, of which Klein owned a copy; and Klein's erroneous claim that Dante placed Arnaut Daniel in hell (rather than in purgatory, as is the case) may be a confused reminiscence of the statement in the epigraph to Pound's 'Sestina: Altaforte' that 'Dante Alighieri put this man in hell,' a statement which actually refers, not to Arnaut Daniel, but to Bertran de Born, the Provençal troubadour who wrote the poem on which Pound's sestina is based. 'Sestina: Altaforte' is Pound's best-known work in the form and is probably the poem which Klein has in mind when he refers to Pound as a writer of sestinas. The opening words of Klein's sestina, 'Yes yeasts to No,' recall the closing words of Pound's version in *The Spirit of Romance* of the poem on which his sestina is based: 'go speedily to "Yea and Nay," and tell him there's too much peace about' [48].

For Klein's attitude to Pound as a man and artist see notes to CANTABILE.

In one of the versions of the poem [MS 2622], Klein has written above the title, in Hebrew letters, the Talmudic expression *shakla vetarya* (lit., 'take up and throw back'), meaning 'give-and-take,' 'discussion,' 'debate.'

MEDITATION UPON SURVIVAL

1–10 *At times ... flood*: 'At times I feel – so bewildered and burdened is my gratitude – that the numbered dead run through my veins their plasma, that I must live their unexpired six million circuits, and that my body must be the bed of each of their nightmares. Then, sensing their death wish bubbling

the channels of my blood, then do I grow bitter at my false felicity – the spared one! – and would almost add to theirs my own wish for the centigrade furnace and the cyanide flood' [ss, p. 24/30].
  Compare also A PSALM TOUCHING GENEALOGY.
21–30 *Us they have made ... bodiless legs*: Compare DESIDERATUM.
25 *its members' re-membering*: The pun on 'remembering' may have been suggested by 'redismembers' in *Finnegans Wake* (London: Faber and Faber 1939), p. 8. Klein marked the word in his copy. Compare 're-membered bones' [ss, p. 34/37].
35 *the way of the fletched buffalo*: Compare 'archaic like the fletcher's' [PORTRAIT OF THE POET AS LANDSCAPE, 153].

AT HOME

3 *Hjalmar Schacht*: minister of economics in the Nazi government (1934–7). He was acquitted of war crimes at the Nuremberg Trials. In 'The Herrenvolk' [BS, p. 258], Klein writes of the defendants at Nuremberg: 'All, without exception, hide behind the corpse of Hitler ... Hjalmar Schacht, for example – that wing-collared creature – to imitate a cherub in reverse – poses as if he were innocence personified.'

LOWELL LEVI

Lowell Levi is a satirical portrait of Elliott E. Cohen, founding editor of *Commentary* magazine, published by the American Jewish Committee. Klein himself had expressed an interest in the editorship, but he never put in a formal application, probably because he felt the committee was hostile to his Zionism. Klein's disapproval of *Commentary* was probably also fuelled by his resentment of Randall Jarrell's harsh review of *Poems*, which appeared in the first issue, November 1945.
  Line references are to the longer second version, PORTRAIT, AND COMMENTARY.
15–16 *distinguish / The four-shanked aleph from the swastika*: In 'News, Views and Jews' [*Canadian Zionist* 5, 3 (May 1937), 23], Klein describes Elliott Cohen, then editor of the *Menorah Journal*, as one 'of the Menorah type which gleaned its Judaism, second-hand, via translation. Indeed, a good number of Menorahites could talk profoundly on the philosophy of Spinoza, and yet knew not the difference between an aleph and a swastika.' Compare the 'four-legged aleph' in AUTOBIOGRAPHICAL, 34 and Klein's note: 'written א with four legs, like a swastika.'
17 *roosters of bnai-Adam*: Compare 'the rooster on the page of the prayer of Bnai Adam' [ss, p. 8/21]. In his note to the passage in ss, Spiro refers to the custom (described in PLUMAGED PROXY) 'of circling a rooster about the head

prior to the Day of Atonement. The accompanying penitential prayers begin with the words *Benei Adam*, giving rise to a comical Yiddish expression used when someone exhibits bewilderment or confusion owing to elementary ignorance of some aspect of his situation; he is compared to the circling rooster looking at the prayer of *Benei Adam* to discern what is going on (*Er kukt mir uhn vi a huhn oif Benei Adam*).' Klein cites the Yiddish expression in a note to PLUMAGED PROXY from one of his poetry readings [MS 6040].

27-8 *Shake ... palmleaves ... citron*: A palm branch and a citron (along with a willow branch and myrtle branch) are shaken as part of the ritual of the Jewish holiday Sukkot.

29 *marrano*: Marranos were Jews who were forced to convert to Christianity in Spain and Portugal in the fifteenth century and continued to practise Judaism in secret.

33 *skins of goats*: The Torah is written on a parchment scroll.

34-5 *Bermoothes, / Unvexed of Zion, lie at ease*: 'Bermoothes' is an Elizabethan name for Bermuda. The lines combine allusions to *The Tempest* 1.2.229 ('the still-vex'd Bermoothes') and Amos 6.1 ('Woe to them that are at ease in Zion').

37 *undegenerate workers' state*: Trotsky characterized the Soviet Union under Stalin as a degenerate worker's state.

42-6 *the authentic Jewish / Series ... Brooklyn delicatessen*: The series is 'From the American Scene.' 'The Jewish Delicatessen,' by Ruth Glazer, appeared in *Commentary* 4, 5 (Nov. 1946), 58-63.

45 *O sages of Sura and Pumbeditha's wise*: almost identical to AVE ATQUE VALE, 11. See note.

TO THE LADY WHO WROTE ABOUT HERZL

The 'lady' is probably Hannah Arendt, who attacked Herzl as a 'crackpot' and a false Messiah in 'The Jewish State: 50 Years After, Where Have Herzl's Politics Led?' *Commentary* 3, 5 (May 1946), 1-8.

For Klein's hostility to *Commentary*, see introductory note to LOWELL LEVI.

4 *existenz*: (Ger.) In the same year as the Herzl article, Arendt published an article in the *Partisan Review* 13 (Winter 1946), 34-56, entitled 'What is Existenz Philosophy?'

13 *Thou didst survive*: Arendt left Germany in 1933.

WRESTLING RING

'Klein is an ardent wrestling fan. He knows that most wrestling matches are fakes, but he enjoys the excitement, probably as a compensation for a very pacific youth' [S.H. Abramson, 'Abe Klein – In Person,' *Jewish Standard*, Sept. 1936, p. 23].

4 *muscles as big as mice*: 'Muscle' derives from the Latin *musculus*, literally 'little mouse.'

16 *Donnes-y-là! Donnes-y*: (Fr.) 'Give it to him there! Give it to him!'

DOMINION SQUARE

Dominion Square is one of the most imposing squares in Montreal. Built around a formally laid-out green space [6–7], which contains a statue of Robert Burns [13], the Square includes the Sun Life Insurance Building [9–10]; the Basilique Marie-Reine du Monde et Saint Jacques, a reduced replica of St Peter's Basilica in Rome, with copper statues of the apostles on its roof [11]; the Windsor Hotel [16]; and Windsor Station [21].

ELEGY

Several years after it was written and first published, ELEGY was incoporated into SS as 'Gloss Beth,' where it is described as being written by the narrator for his Uncle Melech, who he presumes was murdered by the Nazis.

The following is a note to ELEGY and to SONG OF INNOCENCE from one of Klein's poetry readings [MS 6049]:
> Explain ash.
> picture of world passed by.
> History in terms of architecture
> Curse.
> Petition.

1 *Named for my father's father*: Klein's paternal grandfather was named Moses.

4–10 *ash ... upon the dark winds borne*: Compare 'The air of Europe is freighted with their ash; the winds of Europe blow four ways murder; invisible, uncountable, but ever inescapable, the gifted and scattered *corpus delicti* floats gruesome under the European sky' ['In Praise of the Diaspora,' BS, p. 464].

6 *the cubits of my ambience*: See note to PORTRAITS OF A MINYAN, 137–8.

8 *iotas of God's name*: In prayerbooks, God's name, *adonai*, is represented by two *yods*; *yod* is the Hebrew equivalent of the Greek *iota*. The same phrase occurs in BALLAD OF THE DANCING BEAR, 158.

26–7 *tatoo'd skin / Fevering from lampshade*: See 'A Lady with a Lamp' [BS, pp. 326–8].

46 *angular ecstasy*: 'Jews, especially those of east European extraction, habitually sway back and forth from the hips during prayers, thus making "angles" with the rest of the body. This motion is traditionally considered an indication of the worshipper's intense concentration' [S].

47 *thunderclap*: God spoke to Moses on Mount Sinai in the midst of 'thunders and lightnings' [Exodus 19.16].

49–50 *talmud ... song alternative in exegesis*: The Talmud is often read in a sing-song manner; its exegesis is 'alternative' since it proceeds dialectically.

52 *fruit-full calendar*: 'Most biblical holidays are harvest festivals' [s].

53 *curled and caftan'd*: Curled earlocks (*peot*) and caftans were typical of the orthodox Jews of eastern Europe.

54 *first days and the second star*: 'The first days of biblical festivals are holy days ... and the appearance of the new moon, or "second star"... which begins a new lunar month, is also of special religious significance ... Both events are celebrated by special congregational prayers and ceremonies' [s].

56 *To welcome in the Sabbath Queen*: The Sabbath is traditionally personified as a queen or bride, and is welcomed as such by orthodox Jews at the beginning of each Sabbath.

58 *Rav and Shmuail*: two sages who laid the foundation of the Talmud. Their discussions are frequently cited in the Talmud.

59 *the thirty-six*: the hidden saints on whom depends the existence of the universe. Compare LAMED VAV: A PSALM TO UTTER IN MEMORY OF GREAT GOODNESS and SS, p. 95/76.

60 *tenfold Egypt's generation*: Six hundred thousand Jews left in the exodus from Egypt [Exodus 12.37]; 'tenfold' six hundred thousand equals the six million Jews destroyed by the Nazis.

63–9 *Look down ... Gomorrah*: 'And the Lord said, Because the cry of Sodom and Gomorrah is great, and because their sin is very grievous; I will go down now, and see whether they have done altogether according to the cry of it, which is come unto me' [Genesis 18.20–1].

70–81 *See where the pyramids ... hollow monoliths*: *pyramids* – the enslavement in Egypt; *Greek marble* – the oppression by the Greeks, as recounted in the Book of Maccabees; *arch and triumph* – the destruction of the second Temple, commemorated in the Arch of Titus; *spires ... inquisitorial* – the Spanish Inquisition; *hollow monoliths* – the Holocaust

86–7 *slabs ... ovens ... manshaped loaves of sacrifice*: Klein links the ovens of the extermination camps, which had slabs for sliding bodies in, to the ritual bread baked by the Levites for use in the Temple sacrifices [Leviticus 2]. Compare the very different symbolic use of the bread of the Levites in BREAD, 17–20.

92 *treponeme*: the organism which causes syphilis

95 *double deuteronomy*: Deuteronomy 28.15–68 contains an extensive list of maledictions for those who disobey God. 'Double,' apart from intensifying the maledictions, may also be a reference to the meaning of Deuteronomy in Greek, 'second law.' For other examples of maledictions compare DENTIST and TO THE CHIEF MUSICIAN, AL-TASCHITH, MICHTAM OF ABRAHAM; WHEN ONE SENT, AND THEY WATCHED THE HOUSE TO KILL HIM.

1018 / Explanatory Notes pp 675–8

97 *bodies ... scripture*: There may be an echo here of Kafka's story 'In the Penal Colony,' in which criminals are executed by having the laws they have broken inscribed and reinscribed on their bodies. Klein was deeply affected by this story, which he discussed in his review 'Hemlock and Marijuana' [LER, pp. 275–8]. The review appeared on 17 Dec. 1948, but in it he remarks that he had read the story 'several years ago' [p. 276].

116–22 *The pharaohs ... royalties*: This list of oppressors of the Jews who have passed into history include: Pharaonic Egypt; Spain, where Jews suffered expulsion or forced conversion in the fifteenth century; Persia (with its capital in Shushan), whose grand vizier, Haman, sought the total destruction of the Jews; Assyria, a powerful enemy of the ancient Israelites, responsible for the disappearance of the ten lost tribes; and the Seleucid dynasty, which, under King Antiochus IV Epiphanes, was defeated by the Maccabees.

128 *of thy will our peace*: 'E'n la sua volontade è nostra pace' [Dante, *Paradiso* 3.85].

129 *Vengeance is thine*: 'Vengeance is mine; I will repay, saith the Lord' [Romans 12.19].

135 *The face turned east*: Jews living west of Jerusalem face east when praying.

141 *Ezekiel's prophesying breath*: a reference to Ezekiel's vision of the resurrection of dry bones [Ezekiel 37.1–14]

142 *Isaiah's cry of solacing*: The later chapters of Isaiah, from chapter 40 on, contain messages of consolation for the exiled Jewish people.

143 *Mizraim*: (Heb.) Egypt

144 *Babylonian lair*: Spiro suggests two allusions: to Nebuchadnezzar's transformation to a grass-eating animal (see note to BESTIARY, 36) and to the episode of Daniel in the lions' den [Daniel 6.16–23].

164–70 *renew our days ... as they were of old*: 'Turn thou us unto thee, O Lord, and we shall be turned; renew our days as of old' [Lamentations 5.21]. The verse is part of the Sabbath liturgy.

165 *Carmel's mount*: a mountain range in northern Israel near the Mediterranean coast. Jeremiah 46.18 refers to 'Carmel by the sea.'

166–7 *song ... raised its sweet degrees*: Psalms 120–34 begin with the phrase 'A Song of degrees.'

SONG OF INNOCENCE

closely related in theme and imagery to ELEGY [c. 1947/1947] and to Glatstein's SMOKE, translated by Klein. See introductory note to ELEGY.

ANNUAL BANQUET: CHAMBRE DE COMMERCE

7 *hip and thigh*: Judges 15.8
18 *O love ... factories*: a parody of the final line of Dante's *Divine Comedy*: 'l'amor che move il sole e l'altre stelle.' Compare MY LITERATI FRIENDS IN RESTAURANTS, 10.

DRESS MANUFACTURER: FISHERMAN

10–13 *speckled with trout / ... little wings ... stipple*: Compare 'stipple upon trout ... finches' wings ... freckled' [Gerard Manley Hopkins, 'Pied Beauty,' 3–8]. Klein underlined these and other phrases in his copy of Hopkins' *Poems* (Oxford: Oxford University Press 1938), p. 30.
25 *percer-proud*: a pun on 'purse-proud' – 'proud of wealth; puffed up on account of one's wealth' [OED]. 'Percer' is an obsolete form of 'piercer' – 'an instrument or tool for piercing or boring holes' [OED]. Klein may intend a reference to both a sewing needle and a fish hook.

FILLING STATION

8 *Route 7*: in Klein's day the main highway to the Laurentians

HORMISDAS ARCAND

Adrien Arcand was the leader of the Nazi party in Quebec. It is not clear why Klein uses the first name 'Hormisdas' instead of 'Adrien.' 'Hormisdas' is a slightly ridiculous name; it sounds old-fashioned and rural, but that is probably not the point. Klein may be suggesting a pun on the French *hormis* (hence his addition of the *s* to the usual spelling of the name), meaning 'except for,' and the German *das* (appropriately enough, considering Arcand's political affiliation), meaning 'that.' The point would then be that Arcand can think of nothing to say *except for* 'à bas les maudits juifs.'

KRIEGHOFF: CALLIGRAMMES

Cornelius Krieghoff (1812–72) was a painter of picturesque scenes of Quebec rural life. 'Calligrammes' refers to the volume of poetry of that name by Guillaume Apollinaire, in which the layout of the poems mimics their content. Compare 'Of Hebrew Calligraphy' [LER, pp. 85–7].
15 *crucifix Y*: Compare 'the agonized Y' [POLITICAL MEETING, 3].
23 *red rufous roseate crimson russet red*: Compare Klein's translation of Segal's KING RUFUS, 25–6: 'Scarlet, rufous, / Roseate.' The poem contains numerous other references to red, including 'crimson apples' [9] and 'Russet horse' [20].

LES FILLES MAJEURES

The title means 'daughters who have reached the age of majority' or 'oldest daughters.' Klein may have had in mind the phrase *les vieilles filles*, meaning 'old maids.'

LIBRAIRIE DELORME

6 *epopic*: not in the OED, although the OED has 'epopee' ('an epic poem') and 'epopoean' ('befitting an epic poet'). Klein no doubt intends an allusion to *épopée*, French for 'epic.'
13 *the Intendants' enterprises, and Laval's*: In the government of New France the intendant was second in rank to the governor and controlled the colony's civil adminstration. François de Laval was the first bishop of Quebec.

LONE BATHER

Compare Gerard Manley Hopkins' 'Epithalamion' and Irving Layton's 'The Swimmer.' Klein marked passages in these in his copies of Hopkins' *Poems* (Oxford: Oxford University Press 1938), pp. 89-90 and Layton's *Here and Now* (Montreal: First Statement New Writers Series 1945), n. pag.
11 *as those, is free, who think themselves unseen*: 'I agree that the line in *Lone Bathers* is grammatically awkward. But I think it is psychologically correct. Like the protagonist, the syntax, too, is introverted, preoccupied with self, and where one should expect as those are free, reads, solipsistically as those, is free, who think themselves alone [sic]' [letter to Frank Flemington, 6 Mar. 1948].

M. LE JUGE DUPRÉ

5 *Mtre.*: (Fr.) Maître, honorific term of address for lawyers and notaries

MONSIEUR GASTON

4 *vaurien*: (Fr.) good-for-nothing

THE MOUNTAIN

1 *the famous cross*: the electrically lit cross at the top of Mount Royal commemorating Maisonneuve's vow to erect a cross on the mountain if he and his men survived their first winter in Montreal
11 *pissabed dandelion, the coolie acorn*: 'Pissabed' is a translation of the French

word for dandelion, *pissenlit*. The acorn presumably suggests to the young Klein a head wearing a coolie hat.

18–22 *Cartier's monument ... nude figures ... bronze tits of Justice*: in Fletcher's Field, on the eastern slope of Mount Royal. It has various allegorical figures around its base (none of them actually nude) including a bare-breasted figure of Justice.

PARADE OF ST. JEAN BAPTISTE

On 24 June (St John the Baptist's day in the church calendar) the St Jean Baptiste Society organizes activities, including parades, to celebrate Quebec's national heritage.

In the *Canadian Forum* the poem is preceded by the following note: 'This is one of a series of experimental poems making trial of what I flatter myself to believe is a "bilingual language" since the vocabulary of the poem is mainly of Norman and Latin origin. There is no word in it (with the exception of articles and auxiliary words) which has not a relationship or similarity to a synonymous word in the French language.' There is a similar note, in French, in *Huit poèmes canadiens*. The poem was included in the original typescript for *The Rocking Chair*, but Klein had second thoughts: 'I now think it altogether too long, and one experimental poem: *Montreal* – is enough' [letter to Frank Flemington, 6 Mar. 1948].

2 *enfilade*: (Fr.) 'a group of objects placed one after the other'

5 *ultramontane*: Ultramontanism, the belief in the absolute supremacy of the Catholic Church in all aspects of society, was still a dominant force in Quebec in Klein's day.

7 *puissant*: (Fr.) 'powerful'

8–10 *crouped ... curvetting ... gambade*: 'Croupade,' 'curvet,' and 'gambade' are all terms referring to 'a leap or bound of a horse' [OED]. The OED cites passages in which they are used synonymously.

28 *Cendrillon*: (Fr.) Cinderella

29 *Massicotte*: Edmond-Joseph Massicotte (1875–1929), Quebec artist and illustrator, who depicted popular customs and traditions of Quebec

31 *chasse-galerie*: Quebec legend of hunters condemned to hunt throughout eternity in a canoe propelled through the air with the aid of the devil. The name probably derives from *chasse*, 'hunt,' and Sire de Gallery, one of the condemned hunters.

34 *Hébert*: Louis Hébert, apothecary and colonist (1575–1627). He settled in Quebec in 1617, and his family was the first to cultivate land in Canada.

39 *parish parallelograms*: Under the seigneurial system, *seigneurs* were granted parcels of land which were divided into rectangular river-lots and leased to *habitants*.

48 *gonfalons*: (Fr.) 'banners'
50 *catena*: (Lat.) 'chain'
52 *chrysostomate*: This verb does not occur in the OED. The OED does have the adjectives 'chrysostomatical' and 'chrysostomic,' from the Greek for 'golden mouthed, an epithet applied to favourite orators.' Klein may have in mind St John Chrysostom, the patron saint of preachers.
55 *berceuses*: (Fr.) 'lullabies.' There may also be an allusion to *la revanche des berceaux* ('the revenge of the cradles'), the high birthrate which helped to ensure the survival of 'philoprogenitive Quebec' [56].
61 *blanched age*: Klein may be using 'blanch' as a French form of 'blank,' in the sense of 'a vacant space, place, or period; a void' [OED].
62 *infidelium partes*: (Lat.) The term *episcopi in partibus infidelium* ('bishops in the territories of the infidels') is used of titular bishops whose dioceses are inaccessible because they are under non-Christian control.
68 *Yamachiche*: a Quebec village, whose old church is visited by many pilgrims
75 *Ablute*: derived from the past participle, *ablutus*, of the Latin *abluere*, 'to wash,' and recalling 'ablutions' in both French and English. 'Ablute' is not in the OED, though 'abluted' is, an obsolete word meaning 'washed away, washed clean'; and 'ablute' is used as a verb in Klein's translation of Bialik's DANCE OF DESPAIR [version 2], 52.
75 *the rotund mayor*: Camillien Houde. For more on Houde see notes to POLITICAL MEETING.
77 *Cyrano*: Houde had a very prominent nose, and as a young man he often played the title role of Rostand's *Cyrano de Bergerac* in amateur theatricals. In an editorial, 'Little Red Riding Houde' [BS, p. 47], Klein refers to Houde's 'sensitive and capacious nostrils.'
77 *p'tit gars de Ste. Marie*: (Fr.) Houde was first elected to public office as the provincial member for the working-class riding of Ste Marie in east end Montreal. Throughout his life he continued to be known as the *petit gars de Ste Marie*; Klein cites the phrase in 'Little Red Riding Houde' [BS, p. 47].
108 *annuair*: from 'annuaire' (Fr.), 'year-book'
118 *pères de famille*: (Fr.) See note to UNIVERSITÉ DE MONTRÉAL, 34.

PASTORAL OF THE CITY STREETS

9 *his ears, like pulpit-flowers*: Jack-in-the-pulpit, a plant of the lily family, has a flower spike partly arched over by a hoodlike covering which resembles a horse's ear.

SIRE ALEXANDRE GRANDMAISON

Title: 'Grandmaison' is French for 'great house.'
1 *Seigneur of Biche*: Under the seigneurial system, established in New France in 1627, the *seigneur* was granted land which he leased to tenants, known as *habitants*, in return for the payment of certain dues. The system was abolished in 1854, so that the title in this case is ironic. There was no seigneury of Biche (Fr. for 'hind, doe, roe').
10 *La Société de Fiducie*: (Fr.) 'trust company'
18 *Mais, que voulez-vous*: (Fr.) 'but, what do you expect?'

UNIVERSITÉ DE MONTRÉAL

Klein graduated in law from the Faculté de Droit of the Université de Montréal.
11 *Code Napoléon*: (Fr.) the name given in 1807 to the French Civil Code. Since 1870 it has been referred to in France as simply the Civil Code, but it continues to be known as the *Code Napoléon* in Quebec to distinguish it from the Quebec Civil Code, which derives from it.
15 *Place d'Armes*: a square in old Montreal, site of the old Court House
22 *the numbers and their truths*: Articles in the Quebec Civil Code are numbered.
22–4 *green raw / ... / warp and wrinkle into avocats*: *Avocat* (Fr.) means both 'lawyer' and 'avocado.'
35 *en bon père de famille*: (Fr.) a phrase that occurs frequently in the Civil Code, indicating a standard of care that persons in certain positions (usually entrusted with the property of others) have to observe. In the English text of the Code the phrase occurs as 'the care of prudent administrator(s).' Compare: 'The first duty of a tutor is to care for the estate of his charge like a prudent administrator, *en bon père de famille*' ['The Ottawa Conference,' *CJC*, 15 July 1932, p. 5].

O GOD! O MONTREAL!

occasioned by an incident described in the editorial 'O God! O Montreal!' [*CJC*, 10 Apr. 1947, p. 3]:

> In English letters there is, to our knowledge, but one notorious reference to our city; and it is not complimentary. It is to be found in a poem written by Butler called *O God! O Montreal!* – a cry of ironic distaste evoked from him by the spectacle of Greek statuary standing in a local museum, pantaloon'd or brassiered to spare a possible outraged modesty.
>
> Ourselves, we have not felt happy about this dubious fame. We would have preferred if our city had found its location in literature on worthier ground. Still, we are fortunate that Butler is not alive to-day. For what,

indeed, would he have written had he had occasion to note the schedule
of wages paid by the City of Montreal to its respective employees? Certainly
he would not have overlooked the very significant fact that upon the
payroll of Concordia, a stableman (grade 1) rates higher than a librarian
(assistant)! Would he not have come to conclusions touching the respective
value, in our metropolis, of cattle and culture? Would he not have considered
this the other side of the coin, already embellished with draped statuary?
We shudder to think of the exclamation that would have escaped his lips at
sight of this revealing schedule, O Dobbin! O Pegasus!

The poem by Samuel Butler (1835–1902) is actually entitled 'A Psalm of Montreal.'
The lines Klein is referring to are:

Stowed away in a Montreal lumber room
The Discobolus standeth and turneth his face to the wall;
Dusty, cobweb-covered, maimed and set at naught,
Beauty crieth in an attic and no man regardeth.
O God! O Montreal!

Compare: 'The Art Gallery. Technicon of eocene glyptics and plastics agamic.
Discoboli non-ithyphallic; nymphs only partially ecdysiast. The temple that
apopemptic Butler apotheosized: O Basilicoria' [*Stranger and Afraid* (MS 3778)].

2 *Louis Fréchette*: The French-Canadian poet Louis Honoré Fréchette (1839–1908)
was forced to leave Canada for the United States at one point in his career
because of lack of recognition and attendant financial difficulties. Klein perhaps
identified with Fréchette, who, like Klein, was a lawyer, a journalist, and ran
for public office.

8 *Concordia Salus*: (Lat.) the motto of the City of Montreal ('Harmony is
Prosperity'). Klein frequently cites it, usually with a note of irony, as in 'A
Summer Idyll, or Love in the Mountains' [*Keneder Adler*, 28 July 1939, p. 6],
in which an anti-Semitic incident is described as 'a remarkable example of
goodwill and concordia salus.'

CANTABILE

In 1946, in his modern American poetry course at McGill, Klein had his students
write parodies of Pound's verse [MS 6648]; this may have given him the idea
of a parody/review of *The Cantos of Ezra Pound I–LXXX* (New Directions 1948).
Klein abhorred Pound's anti-Semitic and fascistic views (see 'Old Ez and His
Blankets,' LER, pp. 278–81), but, as is evident from CANTABILE, he knew Pound's
poetry well; his library contained more books by Pound than by any other
writer, with the exception of Joyce.

Epigraph: (Lat.) 'about books, arms, and men of unusual genius' ['Canto XI'].
Pound quotes Platina (Bartolomeo Sacchi, 1421–81), who was imprisoned
for conspiracy against Pope Paul II.

3 *il miglior fabbro*: (Ital.) 'the better maker' [Dante, *Purgatorio* 26.117]. T.S. Eliot uses the phrase in his dedication of *The Waste Land* to Pound.

9–12 *But bye ... St. Mary's Lough*: the concluding stanza of the Scottish ballad 'The Douglas Tragedy.' The Douglas Klein has in mind is Clifford Hugh Douglas (1879–1952), founder of the Social Credit movement, of which Pound was an adherent.

19 *U S U R A*: (Lat.) Pound saw usury as the root of all evil. See in particular the attack on 'USURA' in 'Canto XLV.'

24 χρύσω χρυσοτέρα: (Gr.) 'more golden than gold,' a fragment attributed to Sappho

32 *bearded like the pard*: Jacques' description of the *miles gloriosus* in his speech on the seven ages of man [*As You Like It* 2.7.150]

35–6 *The art of conversation ... / small talk shouted*: a paraphrase of Allen Tate's comment in his essay 'Ezra Pound': 'The secret of [Pound's] form is this: conversation. The *Cantos* are talk, talk, talk; ... they are just rambling talk' [*Collected Essays* (Denver: Alan Swallow 1959), p. 353]. The line from the *Cantos* which Klein uses as an epigraph is quoted in Tate's essay.

39 *traductore – tradittore*: 'a translator is a traitor' (Italian proverb), Klein's point being that Pound was, literally, both

40 *syphilisation*: In the 'Cyclops' episode of *Ulysses*, the anti-Semitic 'citizen' responds to Leopold Bloom's defence of British civilization: 'Their syphilisation, you mean' [p. 319].

43 *Rapallo*: Pound lived in Rapallo, Italy, for many years.

45 *Gradus ad parnassum*: (Lat.) a Latin or Greek dictionary intended as an aid for students of Latin or Greek verse composition; the subtitle of Pound's ABC *of Reading*, of which Klein owned a copy

46 *a compiler of several don'ts*: an allusion to Pound's article 'A Few Don'ts by an Imagiste'

50–1 *Jimmy ... poor Mr. Breen / ... E.P.*: EP: 'Jimmy' is James Joyce. 'Poor Mr. Breen' is Dennis Breen, a pathetic lunatic mentioned in several chapters of *Ulysses*, including 'Cyclops' [p. 315], who is upset at receiving a postcard with the message 'U. p. up,' which he interprets as an attack on his virility. 'E.P.' is, of course, Ezra Pound, with specific reference to 'E.P. Ode pour L'Election de Son Sepulchre,' the first section of Pound's autobiographical *Hugh Selwyn Mauberley*.

52 *'EP. Est Perditus*: a reference to the medieval anti-Semitic taunt HEP (the apostrophe in 'EP marking the elided H). Compare: 'Throughout the Middle Ages the ugly taunt of the persecutors of Israel was *Hep! Hep!* – a notarikon for *Hierosolyma est perdita!* (Jerusalem is lost)' ['Jerusalem the Golden,' *CJC*, 27 Aug. 1948, p. 4]. The true origin of the term is, in fact, obscure.

BENEDICTIONS

part of 'Gloss Hai' of *ss*, which consists of 'drafts for a liturgy' [*ss*, note, p. 119/91] attributed to Uncle Melech; based on five of the fifteen morning blessings, *birkot hashahar*. They all begin with the formula 'Praised be Thou, O Lord our God, King of the universe ...,' and the relevant ones continue: (1) 'who hast endowed the cock with the instinct to distinguish between day and night'; (2) 'who hast not made me a slave'; (3) 'who clothest the naked'; (4) 'who raisest up those who are bowed down'; and (5) 'who removest sleep from mine eyes and slumber from mine eyelids.'

STANCE OF THE AMIDAH

part of 'Gloss Hai' of *ss*, which consists of 'drafts for a liturgy' [*ss*, note, p. 119/91] attributed to Uncle Melech.

The *amidah*, or 'standing up,' is the core of every Jewish worship service. It is so called because the worshipper recites it while standing. It is also known as the *shemoneh esreh*, or 'eighteen,' because it originally consisted of eighteen benedictions. A nineteenth benediction, actually a curse directed at heretics, was added at the time of the destruction of the second Temple, but it has no equivalent in STANCE OF THE AMIDAH, perhaps because, from an orthodox point of view, Uncle Melech would himself be considered a heretic.

The poem follows the structure of the *amidah* very closely. Like the *amidah*, it begins with Psalm 51.15 (italicized passage), and the eighteen verse paragraphs which follow correspond to the eighteen benedictions. In general, Klein elaborates more freely on the earlier benedictions than on the later ones, which are, for the most part, simply paraphrased or abridged.

4–7 *hast made thyself manifest ... the shadows of thy radiance*: no parallel in the *amidah*

8–12 *Who with single word ... almost know thee*: The corresponding benediction in the *amidah* has, 'You are eternally mighty, O Lord, the Resurrector of the dead are you, abundantly able to save.' Compare OUT OF THE PULVER AND THE POLISHED LENS, section VIII.

13–19 *Whom only angels know / ... not know*: Like the corresponding benediction in the *amidah* (the 'sanctification'), this passage is ultimately based on Isaiah 6.3: 'And one cried unto another, and said, Holy, holy, holy, is the LORD of hosts: the whole earth is full of his glory.'

20–5 *who hast given to the bee ... doomsday-good*: no parallel in the *amidah*

26 *such understanding*: The corresponding benediction has 'Thy Torah.'

38–40 *Shelter us behind ... evening dish*: no parallel in the *amidah*

41–4 *the Shma ... the four fringes to kiss them*: The *shema* (so called from its opening words, *shema yisrael*, 'Hear, O Israel') is the central declaration of

1027 / Explanatory Notes pp 706–7

the Jewish faith; Klein imagines God himself reciting it. In the course of reciting the *shema*, the worshipper gathers up the fringes on the four corners of the prayershawl and kisses them.

55–8 *Make us of thy love a sanctuary ... incense, rises up*: 'Show Thy favour, O Lord our God, unto Thy people Israel and heed their prayers; cause Thy service to be restored in Thy sanctuary in Zion, and mayest Thou receive therein with favour and with love their offerings and their supplications. And may the worship of Thy people Israel always be worthy of Thy acceptance.'

WHO HAST FASHIONED

part of 'Gloss Hai' of ss, which consists of 'drafts for a liturgy' [ss, note, p. 119/91] attributed to Uncle Melech; an expansion of a benediction in the morning service: 'Praised be Thou, O Lord our God, King of the universe, who hast created man with wisdom and hast fashioned within him numerous orifices and passageways. It is well known, by the Law which Thou hast ordained, that if but one of these were impaired, we could not long continue to exist. Praised be Thou, O Lord, who art a wondrous healer of all Thy creatures.'

9 *nails of the fingers ... demons*: See note to SCRIBE, 21.
10 *eight great gates*: 'the ears (2), nose (1), mouth (1), eyes (2), and lower orifices (2)' [s]

OF THE MAKING OF GRAGERS

Klein owned a copy of *The Purim Anthology*, ed. Philip Goodman (Jewish Publication Society 1949), which reprints his REB ABRAHAM. The end-paper of Klein's copy contains notes for OF THE MAKING OF GRAGERS, perhaps inspired by the chapter 'Origin and Use of the *Grogger*,' pp. 211–13. A *grager* is a noisemaker used to drown out Haman's name when the scroll of Esther is read in the synagogue. For more on Purim see notes to FIVE CHARACTERS.

2 *all of that ilk*: includes notorious persecutors of the Jews throughout history: the Pharaohs ('pharophonics'); Titus, Roman general, later Emperor, who captured Jerusalem and destroyed the second Temple ('titus-taps'); Tomás de Torquemada, the first head of the Spanish Inquisition ('torquemadatumps'); Bogdan Chmelnitzki, who led a revolt against Polish rule in the Ukraine in the seventeenth century, which resulted in the death of many Jews ('chmelnizzicatos'); and Hitler ('nazinoisicans'). Klein's notes in *The Purim Anthology* contain the following list: 'Pharaoh, Antiochus, Titus, Torquemada, Chmelnitzki, Hitler.'
10 *brekekex*: (Gr.) an allusion to the refrain in the chorus of Aristophanes' *The Frogs*, brekekekex-koax-koax

12 *borborigmi*: from the Greek βορβορυγμός ('intestinal rumbling'). There is an entry in the OED under 'borborygm.'

EPIGRAMS [1]

10 *Vidi, vici, veni*: (Lat.) '*Veni, vidi, vici*,' 'I came, I saw, I conquered': Caesar's words to the Senate announcing his victory at Zela over Pharnaces, King of Pontus. Klein's rearrangement of Caesar's words – 'I saw, I conquered, I came' – introduces a double entendre.

12 *alea est jacta*: (Lat.) 'the die is cast': Caesar's words upon crossing the Rubicon

12/13 '*Farcie de Comme*': (Fr.) The meaning of this phrase is obscure. *Comme*, as the word used to introduce a comparison, is much abused by bad poets in French. *Farcie* is literally 'stuffed with' and is a vulgar way of saying 'full of.' The reference could, therefore, be to a bad poem, stuffed with comparisons.

13 *poet of the removeable glass eye*: Perhaps an allusion is intended to F.R. Scott, who had a glass eye. If so, the title of the epigram may also be intended to echo Scott's name.

Epigram 8: '... the imagination ... pictures ... the three patriarchs, the good kings of Israel, and all the saintly who have a portion in Paradise, sitting about the heavenly throne, their crowns tilted rakishly on their heads, holding both their wings, ambrosial tears trickling from their gleeful eyes, enjoying, as a reward for a godly life, the bliss of a continual and uproarious hilarity' ['Of Hebrew Humor,' LER, p. 101].

33 *Avrohom, Yitzchok, and Yaacov*: Abraham, Isaac, and Jacob

35 *prophetaeque majores minoresque*: (Lat.) 'the major and minor prophets' as they are referred to in the Vulgate. The major prophets are Isaiah, Jeremiah, Ezekiel, and Daniel. Twelve other prophets are referred to as minor. The distinction reflects the lengths of the books that bear their names.

48 *Mizraim*: (Heb.) Egypt

54/55 *Cui Bono*: (Lat.) 'for whose benefit'

64 *Eleusinian mysteries*: principal religious mysteries of ancient Greece, performed at Eleusis

83 *Hard to be a Jew*: a common Yiddish phrase often said humorously at a circumcision in response to the baby's cry

86 *hip and thigh*: Judges 15.8

88 *sowed with salt*: After their final victory over Carthage in the third Punic War, the Romans razed the city and sowed its site with salt.

103 *Jean Valjean*: the hero of Victor Hugo's *Les Misérables*, an escaped convict who hid in the sewers of Paris

Epigram 24: a haiku

107 *Quails before manna*: God provided the Jews with quails and manna in their wanderings through the Sinai desert [Exodus 16.13–14].

SPINOZA: ON MAN, ON THE RAINBOW

Compare 'And every sand becomes a Gem / Reflected in the beams divine' [William Blake, 'Mock On, Mock On, Voltaire, Rousseau']. For Spinoza, see notes to OUT OF THE PULVER AND THE POLISHED LENS.

EPIGRAMS [2]

2–3 *Old Noah ... vine*: 'And Noah began to be an husbandman, and he planted a vineyard' [Genesis 9.20].
12/13 *Mâ Aleyk – No Evil Befall You*: Klein's library contained a copy of *Travels in Arabia Deserta*, by Charles M. Doughty, abridged by Edward Garnett (New York: Doubleday 1955). In the glossary of Arabic terms at the end of the volume, *Mâ aleyk* is defined as 'No evil shall befall thee.'
14 *souks*: (Arab.) marketplaces
15 *Wellah*: 'lit. "By God!" but it has come to signify *verily, indeed*' [Doughty].
16 *hamzin ... simum*: Doughty defines *simúm* as 'hot wind.' *Hamzin* is another name for the same phenomenon.
30 *pennies on his eyes*: The ancient Greeks placed pennies on the eyes of their dead to pay the ferryman Charon. Compare BLIND GIRL'S SONG, 12.
31/32 *Palmam Qui Meruit*: (Lat.) 'who has obtained the palm [of victory]'
   MS 2277, which contains drafts for RITUAL and PALMAM QUI MERUIT, ends with the following: 'The Ante-Mortem Notes of Franz Kafka. / Prolegomenon to a Psychoanalysis of the Works of A.M. Klein / The subject.'

POETRY TRANSLATIONS

THE KADDISH

doxology, recited with congregational responses at the close of individual sections of public service and at the conclusion of the service itself. The *Kaddish* exists in four main versions: the whole *Kaddish*; the half *Kaddish*; the scholar's *Kaddish*; and the mourner's *Kaddish*, which Klein refers to as 'this wonderful mourner's Magnificat which does not mention death' [SS, p. 121/92]. Version 1 is a translation of the mourner's *Kaddish*, which lacks the clause beginning 'O acceptable ...' Version 2 is a translation of the full *Kaddish*, although most of the congregational responses included in version 1 are omitted.

The *Kaddish* is in Aramaic, except for its last clause, which is in Hebrew. In 'Only Half the Language of Faith' [LER, p. 64], Klein comments on translating Aramaic prayers: 'A prayer from the Aramaic, we think, ought to be rendered in an idiom different from that which is used to render a psalm; that idiom is usually either a legalistic one, or a mystical one; there should be something in the flavour of the English translation to indicate the tang of this particular poured wine.'

Solomon ben Moses ha-Levi Alkabez (c. 1505–76)

Kabbalistic poet and commentator, born in Turkey, settled in Safed in 1529

O SITE MOST KINGLY, O ROYAL SANCTUM

original: *lekha dodi* ('come, my beloved'). Klein translates stanzas 3–5 of the original nine stanzas.

Lekha dodi, a hymn in praise of the Sabbath, forms part of the Friday evening prayer service. In ss, pp. 116–17/90, the narrator recalls the hymn as he passes through the streets of Safed:
> Suddenly there began to hum through my brain an old and cherished melody – the melody of *L'cho doidi,* the song of Sabbath greeting. It was here, here in Safed, that Rabbi Solomon Halevi Alkabez, in the very darkness of his century, had composed its words of hope and consolation.
> The Sabbath had not yet been ushered in, the memory of this music was anticipatory, an obeisance to both the Holy Day and the Holy City. It was a felicitous memory, for it worked in me yet further recollection of my departed father – a paradise of eternal Zohar, his! – with whom, as a boy, I had every Friday night attended the synagogue and had sung, stanza by stanza, by the cantor echoed, the sweet verses of *L'cho doidi.* Then I thought them to be a poem in praise of the Sabbath, the Sabbath queenly as opposed to the week-days, handmaiden and profane. But now the words regained their original significance; now came to me from the rebuilt places of Israel, its hamlets, its cities, the song of Rabbi Solomon Halevi Alkabez, to a melody of the Moors composed, of triumph and fulfillment.

Chaim Nachman Bialik (1873–1934)

the greatest modern Hebrew poet, 'the personification of the Hebrew Renaissance' ['Chaim Nachman Bialik,' LER, p. 14]. He was born in Volhynia and, as a child, he moved to Zhitomir, where he received an orthodox Jewish education. As a young man he was engaged in the lumber trade, but after the publication of his first Hebrew poem, 'To a Bird' (1891), which expressed his Zionist longings, he occupied himself increasingly with literature and with Jewish nationalism. In 1900 he

moved to Odessa, where he taught at a modern Hebrew school, was literary editor
of the Hebrew literary monthly *Hashiloaḥ*, and continued to write poetry and
essays. His poem IN THE CITY OF SLAUGHTER, occasioned by the Kishinev pogrom
of 1905, played an important role in inspiring Jewish self-defence (see note to
Klein's translation). After the Russian Revolution he moved to Berlin and
then, in 1924, he emigrated to Tel Aviv. He wrote relatively little poetry after
emigrating, but, as a publisher, editor, and translator, became the dominant figure
in the culture of the Jewish community in Palestine.

'Next to Joyce, Bialik was [Klein's] greatest literary hero. Klein saw in him the
ideal model of the Jewish national poet, a twentieth century biblical prophet,
an elevated genius who nevertheless remained a true man of the people' [*LOTD*, p.
71]. In 1943 Klein applied for a Guggenheim fellowship to spend a year on the translation
of Bialik's poetry, but the application (like a later one for a commentary on Joyce's
Ulysses) was unsuccessful.

For the originals see *Shirim* (Tel Aviv: Dvir 1973).

BENEATH THE BURDEN ...

original: *shaḥah nafshi* ('my spirit is bowed down'); p. 230

THE CHASTISEMENT OF GOD

original: *akhen gam zeh musar elohim* ('surely this, too, is the chastisement of
God'); pp. 182–3
9 *Pithom and Rameses*: the two treasure cities which the Israelites were forced to
build for Pharaoh [Exodus 1.11]

COME, GIRD YE YOUR LOINS, AND IN MIGHT ROBE YOURSELVES

original: *lamitnadvim baam* ('to the nation's volunteers'); pp. 102–3. Klein omits
the last stanza.
3 *Maccabees*: the Hasmoneans, who under the leadership of Judah Maccabee,
led a successful revolt against Syria in 167 B.C. The meaning of the name is
uncertain, though one interpretation is 'hammer' (compare 'thundering hammer'
in 11).

GOD GRANT MY PART AND PORTION BE ...

original: *yehi ḥelki imakhem*; pp. 219–20
Klein refers to this poem as 'the Gray's Elegy of the Hebrew language, eloquent
tribute to mute and inglorious Herzls' ['Chaim Nachman Bialik,' *LER*, p. 16].

49 *Haiman and Jeduthun*: two of the musicians in service before the Ark of the Convenant [1 Chron. 16.41–2]
51 *Cholcol and Darda*: two of the wise men surpassed in wisdom by King Solomon [1 Kings 4.31]

THE LORD HAS NOT REVEALED

original: *lo herani elohim*; pp. 212–14
51 *Kaddish*: (Heb.) the mourner's *Kaddish*, a prayer recited by male heirs after a parent's death

ON MY RETURNING

original: *bitshuvati*; p. 14

THE CITY OF SLAUGHTER

original: *be-ir haharegah*; pp. 350–60
  In *CJC*, 2 Oct. 1940, p. 9, Klein introduced his translation as follows:
  Shortly after the pogrom in Kishineff in 1905, the late Chaim Nachman Bialik, the most lyric voice that rose in Jewry since the days of Yehuda Ha-levi, wrote 'In The City of Slaughter,' a burning protest, a searing indictment, not so much against the perpetrators of massacre – the condemnation of murder did not require also Bialik's vote – as of the passivity and non-resistance of its victims. Pouring the phials of his wrath and scorn against his contemporaries, Bialik contributed more than any other person, to the creation of that new psychology of self-defense which, organized in the Haganah, today encompasses all Jewry. It is to be noted that Bialik himself re-wrote this poem in Yiddish, a version, however, which lacks both the technique and the fire of the original Hebrew ...
  Line references are to version 1.
110 *Cohanim*: (Heb., 'priests'), the descendants of the high priest Aaron, required to take special measures to avoid pollution
158 *Shekinah*: (Heb., 'presence'), the numinous immanence of God in the world, often represented as an exiled queen or bride

THE DANCE OF DESPAIR

original: *lamnazeah al hameholot* ('to the chief musician upon Mahalath' [see Psalm 53]); pp. 261–4

Version 1
1 *Muppim and Huppim*: two of Benjamin's sons [Genesis 46.21]
2 *Milalai, Gilalai*: two musicians named in Nehemiah 12.36; term for musicians in general

Version 2
4 *Lilith*: a female demon, symbol of lust and sexual temptation, traditionally Adam's first wife
16 *L'chaim*: (Heb.) 'to life'; a toast

SEER, BEGONE

original: *ḥozeh, lekh beraḥ*; p. 209
The title is from Amos 7.12. The title of version 2 is taken directly from the King James translation.

WHEN THE DAYS SHALL GROW LONG

original: *vehayah ki yaarḥu hayamim*; pp. 201–3

THE WORD

original: *davar*; pp. 172–4. Klein omits the last fifty-one lines.

THY BREATH, O LORD, PASSED OVER AND ENKINDLED ME

original: *ḥalfah al panai* ('there passed over my face'); pp. 228–9

UPON THE SLAUGHTER

original: *al hasheḥitah*; pp. 152–3

STARS FLICKER AND FALL IN THE SKY

original: *kokhavim mezizim vekhavim* ('stars flicker and go out'); p. 130

Immanuel (ben Solomon) of Rome (c. 1261–after 1328)

scholar, physician, and poet, born in Rome. He wrote poetry in Hebrew and Italian (under the name Manoello Giudeo) and was acquainted with many of the leading Italian poets of the day. His work is varied, including a poem inspired by Dante's *Divine Comedy*, but he is best remembered for his humorous, satirical works, such as THE PRESCRIPTION. He introduced the sonnet into Hebrew. Klein refers to him as 'the wonderful Immanuel, Dante's friend, first weaver of the Hebrew sonnet' [ss, p. 38/40].

THE PRESCRIPTION

original: *nedivei am krauni lerapot* ('the princes of the people summoned me to attend'); *Anthologie der Hebräischen Dichtung in Italien*, ed. C.O. Shurman (Berlin: Schocken Verlag 1934), p. 159
26 *Mare Rubrum*: (Lat.) the Red Sea
32 *Hippocrates, Razzi, Avenzohar*: the leading physicians of Greece (Hippocrates), Persia (Rhazes or Rasis), and the Arab world (Avenzoar)

Micah Joseph Lebensohn (1828–52)

born in Vilna, Lithuania. He was one of the leading poets of the Haskalah movement which sought to assimilate the ideals of the Enlightenment to Hebrew culture.

WINE

original: *hayayin*; *Shirim, Agadot* (Berlin: Ajanoth Hebräischer Verlag 1924), pp. 170–1

Yehuda Halevi (c. 1075–1141)

For information on Halevi see the introductory explanatory note to YEHUDA HALEVI, HIS PILGRIMAGE. For the edition of Halevi's poems cited in the notes that follow, see the introductory textual note to the Halevi translations.

TO JERUSALEM THE HOLY

original: *libi bamizrah* ('my heart is in the east'); p. 2
    In *CJC*, 20 Aug. 1948, p. 4, Klein introduced the translation as 'Yehuda Halevi's ... famous lines touching the Holy City, lines here rendered, so as to preserve their archaic flavour, into Chaucerian English.'
2 *sote*: sweet
12 *shende*: disgraced, destroyed

BEAR THOU, O WIND, MY LOVE

original: *alei tapuaḥ* ('beside the apple tree'); p. 56

LORD, HELE ME, Y-WIS I SHAL BE HELED

original: *eli refaeini* ('my Lord, heal me'); p. 113
    For the language of this translation see introductory note to TO JERUSALEM THE HOLY.
2 *brennen ... y-brent*: burn ... burnt
4 *lechecraft*: art of healing

ODE TO ZION

original: *zion halo tisheali* ('Zion, will you not ask'); pp. 3–7
    See the introductory explanatory note to YEHUDA HALEVI, HIS PILGRIMAGE.

O DOVE BESIDE THE WATER BROOK

original: *yonah al afikei mayim*; p. 66. Klein omits the last six quatrains, and the last line of the second quatrain.
6 *Tirzah*: ancient Canaanite capital, later capital of Kings of Israel; praised for its beauty, along with Jerusalem, in Song of Solomon 6.4
11 *Mizraim*: (Heb.) Egypt

O HEIGHTE SOVEREIGN, O WORLDES PRYS

original: *yefei nof meshosh tevel*; p. 19
    For the language of this translation see introductory note to TO JERUSALEM THE HOLY.
4 *mappemounde*: map of the world
5 *whilom*: former
6 *wonnyngen*: dwelling places
7 *Swich*: such
11 *raughten*: reach

RUBAIYAT OF YEHUDA HALEVI

original: *haperidah* ('the parting'); pp. 46–50. The original consists of seventy-six lines. Klein translates 1–24, 37–44, 33–6, 49–52, 65–8, 45–8, in that order.
Title: Klein adopts the stanza of Edward Fitzgerald's translation of *The Rubaiyat of Omar Khayyam*: quatrains in iambic pentameter with the rhyme scheme

aaba. The stanza may have been suggested to him by the first four lines of Halevi's poem, which happen to share the *Rubaiyat* rhyme scheme (the pattern is not repeated elsewhere in the poem).

Poets of the Yishuv

The poets grouped together in this edition under the heading 'Poets of the Yishuv' shared a common historical experience, which is reflected in their poetry. They are all from the generation following Bialik, and they were all influenced by his example. Like Bialik, they were all born in eastern Europe and chose to write in Hebrew rather than (or along with) their native languages. Also like Bialik, they all emigrated to Palestine. Unlike Bialik, however, they all continued to write poetry after settling in Palestine, giving expression to the ideals of the Yishuv, the 'settlement' of Jews in Palestine prior to the establishment of the State of Israel.

Klein's translations of most of these poets were first published in 1931, when he was deeply involved in Zionist activities as educational director of Young Judaea and editor of the *Judaean*. He seems to have been attracted to them as representatives of the pioneering spirit of the Yishuv, rather than as individual voices. This is reflected not only in the kinds of poems he chose to translate, but also in the titles of the two sets in which the translations of 1931 were grouped: 'Palestine Poems' [*Judaean* 4, 4 (Jan. 1931), 6], containing KINGS OF THE EMEK; BEHOLD; MAKE BLIND, O SUN OF JERUSALEM; and BE THERE NO ALTAR; and 'The Authentic Word' [*Jewish Standard*, 11 Sept. 1931, pp. 152, 4], described as 'a collection of poems from the pens of Palestine's foremost young poets' and containing UNFAVOURED; SABBATH; THE GLORY OF THE HOMELAND; WITH EVERY STONE; MOTHER JERUSALEM; and UPON THE HIGHWAY.

In 1937 Klein published a set of translations of five poems by Rachel Bluwstein. These intimate lyrics are very different from the highly rhetorical, didactic poems which Klein had translated in the early thirties. Because of the marked differences that set the Rachel translations apart from the earlier ones, as well as the considerable chronological gap between the two groups, the Rachel translations have been placed at the end of 'Poets of the Yishuv'; Klein's arrangement of them has been followed.

Abraham Broides (1907–)

born in Vilna, Lithuania; emigrated in 1923. He worked as a labourer for several years, and many of his poems, including UPON THE HIGHWAY, grew out of this experience.

1037 / Explanatory Notes pp 776-9

UPON THE HIGHWAY

original: *bedarkhayikh, arzi* ('on your roads, my country'); *Emunim* (Tel Aviv: Davar 1937/8), pp. 13-14. Klein omits the last twelve lines.

Uri Zvi Greenberg (1894-1981)

born in Bialykamien, eastern Galicia; emigrated in 1921. In his early years he wrote in Yiddish and Hebrew, but after emigrating he wrote exclusively in Hebrew, becoming one of the most influential poets of his generation. He became closely associated with the right wing Revisionist faction of Zionism, and his poetry presented a mystical view of Zionism and of the Jewish people's divinely ordained destiny. In *ss*, p. 99/79, the narrator says of Greenberg:

> Fiery, explosive, bar-kochbic, the poet Uri Zvi had captured, during the days of the trouble, the imagination of the young and the daring; his hyperboles had been made into slogans; his lacerating indignation, directed alike against the hostile and the docile, had stirred the hero's courage, reddened the compromiser's shame. Himself he had been an army with banners. Now, the battle won, or at least in cessation, he was a spent brand, an outroared lion, a brand smoldering, a lion obliquely pacing, readying his next spring.

KINGS OF THE EMEK

original not identified
Title: The *Emek* (Heb.; literally 'the valley') is the Valley of Jezreel, a large inland plain in northern Israel, a centre of Jewish settlement from the 1920s.

MOTHER JERUSALEM

original: *yerushalayim shel matah* ('everyday Jerusalem' [i.e., as against 'celestial Jerusalem']); *Emah Gedolah Veyareah* (Tel Aviv: Hozaat Hadim 1924/25), pp. 52-3. Klein translates only selected lines from the second part of this poem, entitled *yerushalayim hamenutakhat* ('lacerated Jerusalem').
1 *four ells*: See note to PORTRAITS OF A MINYAN, 137-8.
12 *The Shekina*: (Heb., 'presence') the numinous immanence of God in the world, often represented as an exiled queen or bride
25 *Gischala*: last Jewish city in Galilee to fall to the Romans
34 *Beth-David*: (Heb.) 'the house of David'

36 *no vineyards*: This is a mistranslation of *Ein Kerem*, the name of a village west of Jerusalem.
44 *valley of Jehoshaphat*: a valley near Jerusalem, traditionally where the Last Judgment will take place
58 *tallis*: (Heb.) prayershawl
63 *menorahs*: (Heb.) seven-branched oil lamps used in the Temple

Judah Karni (Valovelski) (1884–1949)

born in Pinsk, Byelorussia; emigrated in 1921. The three poems translated by Klein are typical of the poems on Jerusalem for which he is particularly noted, in which the Holy City is a symbol of the Jewish people and its destiny.

For the originals of the first two translations see *Shearim* (Berlin-Wilmersdorf: Dwir Verlag 1923) of which Klein owned a copy.

BE THERE NO ALTAR

original: *im ein mizbeaḥ*, p. 216

MAKE BLIND, O SUN OF JERUSALEM

original: *sameini, shemesh*, p. 213

WITH EVERY STONE

original: *simuni bapirẓah* ('set me in the breach'); *Yerushalayim* (Tel Aviv: Doron 1944), p. 59

David Shimoni (Shimonovitz) (1886–1956)

born in Bobruisk, in the Minsk district of Russia; emigrated for a year in 1909 and then permanently in 1921. He worked in orange groves and as a watchman in the various settlements mentioned in THE GLORY OF THE HOMELAND. He celebrated the pioneering life in idyllic verse which was primarily classical in form and which was deeply influenced by Bialik.

THE GLORY OF THE HOMELAND

original not identified

Abraham Shlonsky (1900–73)

born in Karyokov, the Ukraine; emigrated in 1921. He was highly influential as an editor, translator, and poet. He brought literary Hebrew closer to the spoken tongue and initiated a shift to symbolism and expressionism in modern Hebrew poetry.

BEHOLD

original: *hineh*; *Shirim* (Tel Aviv: Poale Hamizrachi 1954), p. 162. Klein omits the last eight of the twenty-three lines in the original.
7 *tallis*: (Heb.) prayershawl
14 *Gilboa*: mountain ridge where Saul and his sons died in battle [1 Samuel 31.1–6]; in modern times the site of settlements and afforestation
15 *Tammuz*: fourth month of the Hebrew calendar, corresponding approximately to July

SABBATH

original not identified
6 *menorah*: (Heb.) seven-branched oil lamp used in the Temple

Mordecai Temkin (1891–1960)

born in Siedlice, Poland; emigrated in 1911. He was a teacher and translator, as well as a poet.

UNFAVOURED

original: *haḥozvim* ('the woodcutters'); *Netafim* (Jerusalem: Hoziat Ketuvim 1927), pp. 24–6. Klein omits the first twenty of the forty-five lines of the original.
25 *fields of Jezreel*: See note to KINGS OF THE EMEK.

Rachel (Rachel Bluwstein) (1890–1931)

born in Saratov, Russia; emigrated in 1909. She began writing poetry in Russian but turned to Hebrew after emigrating. She intended to devote herself to agriculture, but she developed tuberculosis and spent her last years in hospitals and sanitoria. Her simple lyrics, elegiac and nostalgic in tone, are popular, and many have been set to music. KINNERETH, in particular, is widely sung (see below).

In ss, pp. 101–2/80–1, the narrator, soon after quoting KINNERETH, comments on the 'poets of the settlements' in terms reminiscent of Rachel:

> Here there still flourished the lyric of sentiment, tender verses modeled on Jammes, Heine, Pushkin. There was a tentativeness about these rhymes, a playing of minor chords, as if the poet were gently inviting, inducing, summoning some grander utterance that as yet had failed to come. One sensed a groping toward the phrase, the line, the sentence that would gather in its sweep the sky above and the earth below and set new constellations in each. But the word did not come.

For the originals see *Shirat Raḥel* (Tel Aviv: Davar 1952).

NOW SUCH AM I ...

original: *ani* ('I'); p. 37

4 *Francis Jammes*: French poet (1868–1938), author of simple, artless poems on rural themes. Compare the reference of the narrator in ss to 'the lyric of sentiment, tender verses modeled on Jammes' [pp. 101–2/80].

RACHEL

original: *raḥel*; p. 59
See note to THE CHILDLESS ONE, 9.

KINNERETH

original: *veulai lo hayu hadevarim* ('it may be these things never did occur'); p. 79

Rachel joined the kibbutz Kinnereth near the Sea of Galilee (*yam kineret* in Hebrew), where she studied at the young women's training farm. In ss, p. 98/78, the narrator describes himself 'sit[ting] on the terrace facing the blue of Lake Kinnereth, listening to the boatman in the gaily painted boat singing Rahel's song'; he then quotes this translation.

DAWN

original: *im shaḥar* ('with dawn'); p. 136

THE CHILDLESS ONE

original: *akarah*; p. 92
5-7 'Uri' ... *sunbeam*: Ur in Hebrew means 'fire,' 'illumination.'
9 *bitter, like Mother Rachel*: Rachel, daughter of Laban and one of Jacob's wives, was one of the four matriarchs. She was bitter because she was barren for many years [Genesis 30.1].
10 *pray, like Hannah in Shiloh*: After her prayer for a son was granted, Hannah dedicated the son, Samuel, to the service of the Lord at the sanctuary in Shiloh [1 Samuel 1].

Mordecai Etziony

a Montreal physician of Klein's acquaintance. He wrote THE PRAYER OF A PHYSICIAN upon graduating from medical school. The original appears never to have been published.

THE PRAYER OF A PHYSICIAN

Dedication: Moses-ben-Maimon ('Maimonides') was the outstanding Jewish philosopher of the Middle Ages; he was also a physician.

Jacob Glatstein (1876–1971)

born in Lublin, Poland, emigrated to the United States in 1914, spent some time in Montreal. A poet, novelist, and critic, he was one of the founders of the *Inzikhist* movement, which aimed to revitalize Yiddish poetry and make it more contemporary by introducing free verse and emphasizing individual experience. His later poetry is much concerned with the Holocaust.

Glatstein wrote a very favourable review of Klein's *Poems*, which Klein gratefully acknowledged [letter, 15 May 1945]. On 12 Feb. 1947 Klein sent Glatstein translations he had done of some of his poems, probably the three which were published.

For the originals see *Shtralndike Yiden* (New York: Farlag Matones 1946).

THE ELEVENTH: IN MEMORY OF ISAAC, SON OF THE TAILOR

original: *der elfter* ('the eleventh'); p. 96
3 *Rasha*: (Heb.) 'wicked one'

11 *machzor*: (Heb.) prayerbook, containing festival prayers, as opposed to the *siddur*, which contains daily and weekly prayers. Klein translates it as 'prayerbook' in 4.
16 *the ten martyrs*: name given to ten sages put to death by the Romans

THE GIFTED ONE

original: *got hot im gegeben* ('God gave him'); p. 67
7 *palmleaf and citron*: See note to PORTRAIT, AND COMMENTARY, 27–8.
15 *And they read Holy Writ, his roosters solemn*: See note to PORTRAIT, AND COMMENTARY, 17.
16 *myrtle-branch*: See note to PORTRAIT, AND COMMENTARY, 27–8.

SMOKE

original: *roykh*; p. 16
Compare ELEGY [c. 1947/1947] and SONG OF INNOCENCE.

Moyshe Leib Halpern (1886–1932)

born in Galicia, emigrated to the United States in 1908. He was a leading member of *Di Yunge*, a group of poets who turned against what they saw as the rhetoricism and didacticism of Yiddish poetry and sought to enrich their work with contemporary literary techniques, particularly those of symbolism.

All of Klein's translations of Halpern were published, on the occasion of Halpern's death, in a set entitled 'The Golden Parrakeet' [*CJC*, 9 Sept. 1932, p. 5]. They are introduced by the following comment, which may be Klein's own:

> M. L. Halpern brought into Jewish poetry an original tone and a singularly un-Jewish vigour. At once tragic, pathetic, and dramatic, he dedicated his talents to the social and national themes, eventually becoming one of the most distinguished of proletarian poets.

In a letter, 21 Jan. 1941, to the Yiddish literary critic Niger (Samuel Charney), Klein says of Halpern that he 'was not a particularly Yiddish poet; he was essentially European and twentieth century.'

For the original of CANTICUM CANTICORUM see *Di Goldene Pave* (Cleveland: Farlag Yidish 1924). For the others see *In New York* (New York: Farlag Vinkel 1919).

PORTRAIT OF THE ARTIST

original: *meyn portret* ('my portrait'); p. 118
5 *Platyrhine*: 'broad-nosed'

CANTICUM CANTICORUM

original: *shir hashirim* ('song of songs'); pp. 7–8

THE LAST SONG

original: *dos letste lid*; p. 232

KI-KI

original: *khi-khi*; p. 185

THE GOLDEN PARROT

original: *di zon vet aruntergeyn* ('the sun will set'); p. 200

CONCEIT CURIOUS

original: *a modne makhshoveh* ('a strange thought'); p. 159

LAST WILL AND TESTAMENT

original: *a nakht* ('a night'); p. 304. Klein has translated only the final lines of a much longer poem.

Leib Jaffe (1876–1948)

born in Grodno, Lithuania; emigrated in 1920. He was an important Zionist leader and was killed in an Arab bomb attack.

In a review of *I Sang My Song of Zion: Poems by L. Jaffe*, trans. Sylvia Satten (Tel Aviv: Palestine Publishing Co. 1936) in *Canadian Zionist* 3, 7 (Dec. 1936), 54, Klein writes of Jaffe's 'still small voice, the poignant love for Erez Israel, the anguished concern over Jewry, the unequivocal self-dedication to the work of the national renascence. Through every line there breathes the spirit of Palestine; or, to change the western metaphor, and apply the oriental, upon this necklace of poesy the names of Ain Harod, Jerusalem, Tel Hai, hang like pearls.'

Satten includes the two poems Klein translates under the titles 'Our Generation' and 'You Walk along a Sunlit Road.' Satten's version of the second of these, in particular, has some strong similarities to Klein's. It seems likely either that Klein, whose translations appeared in 1933, had come across Satten's versions before they were published in book form, or that Satten knew Klein's translations.

WE ARE A GENERATION, HEAVEN-DOOMED

original not identified
21 *Pisgah*: the mountain from which Moses viewed the Promised Land before his death

YOU WALK UPON YOUR SUNLIT ROADS

original not identified

H. Leivick (Leivick Halpern) (1886–1962)

poet and dramatist, born in Byelorussia; imprisoned in Siberia for left-wing activities; escaped to the United States in 1913. The two poems translated by Klein arose out of Leivick's experience of imprisonment. Klein writes of the prison poems in general that they 'indicated the high results which might be obtained when a man of genius is subjected to soul-purging experiences ... they are the definite and vivid outcry of what the German critics ... used to call *Erlebnis*' ['Welcome to Leivick,' *CJC*, 28 Apr. 1939, p. 4]. For a time Leivick came under the influence of *Di Yunge* (see note on Halpern), but he turned away from the ideals of the movement to devote himself to social themes. Leivick's most important work as a dramatist was *The Golem* (1921), which, according to Klein, foreshadowed 'the Nazi golem treading with heavy boot upon the European scene' ['Welcome to Leivick'] and probably influenced Klein's own treatments of the Golem theme in the poem THE GOLEM, and in the unfinished play *Death of the Golem*.

For the originals see *Ale Verk fon H. Leivick* (New York: Posy-Shoulson Press 1940), volume 1.

NO MORE TEARS

original: *nito mer kayn trenen*; p. 26

THE WINDOWS ARE GRATED

original: *di shoybn farmoyert* ('the windows are walled up'); p. 25

Mani-Leib (Mani-Leib Brahinsky) (1883–1953)

born in Russia, emigrated to the United States in 1905; one of the founders of *Di Yunge* (see note on Halpern). His poetry is essentially neo-romantic, and he was particularly known for his ballads and children's poems.

SUNSET

original: *der tog fargeyt* ('the day dies'); *Lider un Baladen* (Tel Aviv: Y.L. Peretz Publishers 1977), p. 20

Jacob Isaac Segal (1896–1954)

Born in the Ukraine, near Koretz, the subject of many of his poems, he emigrated to Montreal in 1911, remaining there for the rest of his life, except for the years 1923–8, which he spent in New York. While supporting himself as a tailor, Yiddish teacher in the Poale Zion schools, and editor, he produced a very large body of work. His poems are tinged with nostalgia for the vanished world of the *shtetl* and tend to focus on the details of ordinary life and the experiences of simple people.

Klein and Segal were close friends. Klein reviewed several of Segal's books and eulogized him in 'In Memoriam: J.I. Segal' [LER, pp. 87–90]. In 'Poet of a World Passed By,' a review of Segal's *Sefer Yidish*, Klein characterized Segal as

> a sort of inspired last survivor of some vanished tribe, a melancholy bard walking among the ruins of his burned-down village, pausing to recall a former felicity associated with this landmark, an historic incident associated with that other, calling to the empty air, and finally turning aside, determined to fashion in words the monument and image of his destroyed birthplace.
>
> For it is in this volume, so full of contemporary poignancy, and yet so eloquent with timeless statement, that Segal emerges as the devoted elegist of all that was fine and beautiful in the life of Eastern Europe in general, and in particular, in the life of the typically Chassidic hamlet from which he hails. The poems, it is true, are concerned with numerous subjects, yet one is the theme to which they are sung – a threnodic ululation for

a world that once shone with piety and humility, and now beyond humbleness lies in ruin and rubble. [LER, p. 79]

It seems clear that Klein, to a certain extent, identified his own situation as a poet with Segal's, as is suggested by the title of his satirical poem DIARY OF ABRAHAM SEGAL, POET.

AND THIS I KNOW

original not identified

AUTOBIOGRAPHICAL

original not identified

GOATS

original not identified

A KING

original not identified

KING RUFUS

original not identified
25–6 *Scarlet, rufous, / Roseate*: Compare 'red rufous roseate' [KRIEGHOFF: CALLIGRAMMES, 23].

CONFESSION

original: *viduyim*; *Dos Hoyz fon di Pshuta* (Montreal: Keneder Adler 1940), pp. 41–2

OLD GOLD

original: *alt-gold*; *Di Drite Seuda*; *Lider* (Montreal: Keneder Adler 1937), p. 21

REB ZORACH

original: *in der ebiker velt* ('in the eternal world'); *Dos Hoyz fon di P'shuta*, p. 96
Title: *Reb*, Yiddish for 'mister,' is a traditional title prefixed to a man's first name.

1 *Rabbi Joshua ben Chananya*: rabbi of the Talmudic period; worked as a blacksmith
2 *Benedict de Spinoza ... glass*: philosopher; worked as a lens grinder. See introductory note to OUT OF THE PULVER AND THE POLISHED LENS.
3 *Rabbi Jochanan the Cobbler*: rabbi of the Talmudic period, known as ha-Sandlar ('the sandal-maker'); a cobbler by trade
4 *Koretz*: See introductory note.
14 *pilpul*: (Heb.) dialectical logic used in the study of the Talmud. See Klein's note to A PSALM OF ABRAHAM, TO BE WRITTEN DOWN AND LEFT ON THE TOMB OF RASHI, 8.
18 *Gamaliel*: There were six Gamaliels, all descendants of Hillel (see below), who served as head of the Sanhedrin, the supreme political, religious, and judicial body in Israel under Roman rule and until about 425 A.D.
22 *Hillel*: rabbi of the Talmudic period, noted for his compassion and tolerance

SONG

original: *a klang* ('a lament'); *Amerikaner Yidish Poezie*, ed. M.R. Bosin (New York: Varlag Felt 1940), p. 514

WAR

original: *milkhomeh*; *Dos Hoyz fon di Pshuta*, pp. 348–9. Klein abridges the original considerably, especially its opening and closing lines.

SPEAK TO YOUR PEOPLE, THEREFORE, IN THIS WISE

original: *zog azoy* ('speak thus'); *Lider un Loyben* (Montreal: Keneder Adler 1944), p. 188

Jewish Folk-Songs

In his essay 'Jewish Folk-Songs,' Klein writes:
> ... there is hardly a phase of Jewish life which is not echoed or mimicked in the ubiquitous folk-song, written by an unseen hand, and sung by an impersonal voice ... There are the wistful self-commiserating songs of dowerless old maids waiting for belated lovers until, as the proverb has it, their braids grow grey; boisterous carousal-hymns; ditties for teamsters; melodies for the lovelorn; epithalamia, and their logical aftermath in lullabies;

Chassidic ecstasies tunefully rendered; satiric thrusts at the atheist and the heterodox; and pithy graveyard commentaries. [LER, p. 93]

All of these topics are represented in 'Jewish Folk-Songs,' and all of the folk-songs which Klein quotes in the essay are from this collection. Comments from the essay, followed by page references, are cited in the notes to individual translations.

Klein's arrangement of the translations has been preserved.

SHALL I BE A RABBI?

original: *zol ikh zayn a rov.* Klein omits the last two stanzas of the original.

In 'Knight of the Road' [*Canadian Zionist* 3, 4 (Sept. 1936), 3], Klein cites this folk-song as an illustration of the lowly status of 'the ubiquitous teamster of the hamlets of Eastern Europe':

Time was when his was an unfortunate lot; considered as being of the lowest rung of our social ladder, he was an object of despising, the target of wit, the butt of ribaldry. Proverb satirized him, and folk-song quipped at him. Sang the *baal-agolah* upon the lonely highways of the world: [quotes 1–10].

That was his fate in the ghetto days; he sat him down, and moaned. Crass, ignorant, one of the disinherited of the earth, his companion was his nag, his longings pedestrian, and his destiny opprobrium.

COME YOU HERE, PHILOSOPHER

original: *der filozof* ('the philosopher')

Although generally accepted as a genuine Chassidic folk-song, this poem, originally entitled *dos gute kepl*, was written by the Galician poet Zbarazer (Benjamin Wolf Ehrenkranz) (c. 1812–c. 1882) as a satire. See introductory note to 'Chassidic Folk-Songs.'

CHARM

original: *tsigele, migele, kotinke* ('little goat, little colt, pussy-cat')

TEAR NOT YOUR HAIR, MY SWEETHEART

original: *veyn nish, veyn nish kale* ('weep not, bride')

AND WHEN ONE BURNS – ONE BURNS BRANDY

original: *ven men brent*

ON THE ATTIC SLEEPS A ROOF

original: *oyf dem boydem shloft der dakh*
'In the days when the hand that rocked the cradle was the man's, while the wife went a-bargaining, it is thuswise that a father in Israel hums to his cradle-Kaddish: [quotes 1–7].

'Immediately the impression of poverty is made indelible. The child lies in the cradle without even the luxury of diapers; and the goat, unable to find sustenance in fodder, is forced to pull straw from the thatched roof. Then symbolism: [quotes 8–11].

'Follows the refrain in which the hop-hop echoes the to-and-fro action of a cradle pushed by a masculine foot. Then, finally, an ingenious and typical solution of the problem of an empty pantry: [quotes 15–18]' [pp. 94–5].

YOMA, YOMA, PLAY ME A DITTY

original: *yome, yome, shpil mir a lidele*
18 *Shadchan*: matchmaker

HUSH! HUSH!

original: *sha, shtil!*

WE ASK OUR BOARDING-MISTRESS

original: *mir zogen der balebuste*

SONG OF WINE

original: *di mashkeh* ('liquor'). The original has ten stanzas. Klein omits the fifth, ninth, and tenth.
9 *Shadchan*: matchmaker
22 *its odd mission*: Before being circumcised, the baby is given a few drops of
   wine.

THE GOLDEN PARRAKEET

original: *di gildene pave* ('the golden parrot')

WHEN I KNEAD THE DOUGH

original: *knet ikh khaleh*

I GO UPON THE BALCONY

original: *oyfn ganikl* ('on the balcony')

ONCE UPON A TIME; THIS

original: *amol iz geveyn a mayse*

BETTER A HEBREW TEACHER

original: *beser a melamed*

O MY MOTHER SENT ME

original: *di mame hot mikh geshikt*. Klein's translation omits the first stanza of the original.
4 *Shochet*: (Heb.) ritual slaughterer

ON THE HILL, OVER THE HILL

original: *oyfn barg, ibern barg*

GONE IS THE YESTERDAY

original: *siz nito keyn nekhten*

AND AT MY PRAYERS I WILL QUIVER

original: *oy, vey, rebenyu*
9 *mikva*: (Heb.) ritual bath
16 *seventeen*: The original has 'seventy' (*zibetsik*).

ASKS THE WORLD AN OLD, OLD QUESTION

original: *di alte kashe* ('the old question')

AND WHEN MESSIAH WILL COME

original: *un az moshiakh vet kumen*

O WHAT DO YOU WISH, MY DEAREST CHILD

original: *vos zhe vilstu, mayn tayer kind*
'The heroine of this folk-song discusses her suitors with her father, and by a process of elimination in which she spares no opprobrious epithet it is upon a Big Business man that she sets her heart' [p. 96].

TELL ME, PRETTY MAIDEN, O HEARKEN PRETTY MAIDEN

original: *zog mir, du sheyn meydele*. The original has two stanzas.

WHAT IS LOFTIER THAN A HOUSE?

original: *vos iz hekher fon a hoyz*

WHEN HE HAS FROLICKED FOR A LITTLE

original not identified
6 *Responsa*: (Lat.) replies sent by authorities in Jewish law to questioners who address them in writing

LOVELY AM I, O LOVELY, AND LOVELY IS MY NAME

original: *sheyn, bin ikh, sheyn*

I SIT ME DOWN UPON A STONE

original: *zits ikh afn shteyn*

Chassidic Folk-Songs

Chassidism was a popular religious and social movement, founded in the eighteenth century by Israel ben Eliezer, known as the Baal Shem Tov. To the Talmudic learning of the educated elite Chassidism opposed ecstatic forms of worship open to all, with an emphasis on joyful song and dance (see DANCE CHASSIDIC). As Chassidism developed, great importance came to be attached to the role of the charismatic leader – the *zadik* or *rebbe* – whose piety and miraculous powers were often celebrated by his followers in song.

Chassidism had its opponents, the rationalistic *mitnagdim* and the secularist *maskilim*, who often satirized the songs of the credulous Chassidim. A number of the songs Klein translated are, in fact, such satires. It is not always easy to distinguish satire from genuine naïvety, and, in any case, some songs originally intended as satires were adopted, over the years, as genuine folk-songs. Some of the more obvious satires are: MIRACLES AND WONDERS; OUR REBBE; OUR REBBE, THE MIRACLE-WORKER, ONCE; THE REBBE, HE WANTED; THE TRAIN.

Klein was greatly interested in Chassidism throughout his career, but his decision to translate Chassidic folk-songs may have been specifically related to the writing of his play on Chassidic themes, *Worse Visitors We Shouldn't Have*, in the early fifties. The play includes one of the translations, IN GOD'S GOOD TIME, as well as some translations from the earlier collection, 'Jewish Folk-Songs.'

In 'On Translating the Yiddish Folk-Song' [LER, pp. 109–12], Klein discusses the difficulties facing a translator of Yiddish folk-songs. Although no folk-songs are identified in the essay, all the examples are from 'Chassidic Folk-Songs.' Klein's comments, followed by page references, are cited in the notes to individual translations, with two exceptions, his comments on the expressions *Oy veh!* and *Gewald!* Since these expressions both occur in several of the translations, Klein's comments are cited here:

> Or take – may it not harm you! – the exclamation, *Oy veh!* Bold, indeed, would he be who sought to transliterate this *cri du coeur* with a lorryman's 'O, woe!' It is true that the words are essentially onomatopoetic, and, therefore, should be translated by a similar onomatopoeia, but the fact denies the theorem. The personal and historic associations, which vibrate from the phrase, cannot be Englished. The epic memory which is evoked by the two monosyllables is not conjured by any English equivalent. One does not translate a groan. A groan? *Oy veh!* is so to our manner born that not always does its utterance imply connotations of woe. The tragedy which invented the phrase has, indeed, been so constant that *Oy, veh*, as often in the folk-songs, is uttered in the presence of something exciting though not unpleasant, by way of mere reflex. How, then, to show the distinction? It cannot be done. *Oy veh* remains ineluctably *Oy veh*, and only its context shows the nuance.
>
> *Gewald!* That is another one. The exclamation is a cry for help, as when one is beset by thieves; it is also a mere expression of exuberance. Some of the Chassidic folk-songs, it will be noted, do begin with these afflative out-cries; they are made in the very presence of the *rebbe*; they are not intended as cries for help. But neither can they be rendered, when the translator bursts in upon the sacred assembly, by an Englishman's ejaculations, no matter how high-spirited. 'Heigh-ho'? Imagine *Chassidim*

shouting 'heigh-ho!' ... *Gewald*, what is the world coming to! [pp. 110–11]

Klein's arrangement of the translations has been preserved. In this arrangement, COME YOU HERE, PHILOSOPHER and HUSH! HUSH! follow TELL US, REBBENU, but since they originally appeared in 'Jewish Folk-Songs,' they have not been included in 'Chassidic Folk-Songs.'

L'CHAYIM, REBBE!

original: *lekhayim rebbe*

'How, for example, is one to translate *l'chaim, rebbe*? Obviously, the *rebbe*, like all titles and designations, remains unchanged in English, but the *l'chaim*? Is one to acknowledge the Hebrew and translate "To life!" much as one would bid the sedentary *rebbe* – "To horse!"? Even "To your life!" paralleled on "To your health!" will not do, for the word is idiomatic, like *skoal!* and *prosit!* and like them should not be translated. *L'chaim, rebbe* must perforce remain: *l'chaim, rebbe!* Any other version would be a perversion' [p. 110].

OY, OUR REBBENU

original: *oy, der rebenyu*

GOD WILLING, AT THE REBBE'S

original: *im yirtseh hashem, baym reben*

MYERKA, MY SON

original: *mayerke, mayn zun*; by Rabbi Levi Yitschok of Berditchev

The phrases in Hebrew are all translated in the lines which follow them. Klein comments:

> There is yet another peculiarity to these songs which must surely tax the translator. Often they are bilingual, Hebrew and Yiddish, and sometimes, trilingual, with Russian thrown in. Certainly the translator would be unfaithful to the original if his version went English, English all the way, and failed to indicate, in the text itself, that more than one language was involved. Some translators have sought to achieve the necessary authenticity by substituting for the Hebrew, Latin equivalents. This method, we fear, gives an impression altogether too Gregorian. It is safer, we imagine, to leave the Hebrew intact, pure, and by translation undefiled. Certainly, if it is communication that is intended, Latin is a dubious medium; it is, in fact, merely to substitute the unknown for the esoteric.

Moreover, in most of the songs the Yiddish translates the Hebrew, anyway. [p. 111]

4 *Lifnei ... hamlochim*: (Heb.) from the *aleinu*, the prayer that concludes every service

22 *Hineni ... mi-ma-as*: (Heb.) a prayer recited by the cantor or *baal tefilah* (master of prayer) on the High Holidays, in which he pleads to be considered worthy of his task

A THOU SONG

original: *a du-du*; by Rabbi Levi Yitschok of Berditchev

Klein used part of this translation for an epigraph to ss. The Hebrew phrases are translated in the lines which follow them. See introductory note to MYERKA, MY SON.

In 'The Yiddish Proverb' [LER, p. 121], Klein says of A THOU SONG: '[The Jew's] rabbis were more than rabbis, they were cronies of the Lord, familiars in heaven, able to address the *Rebono Shel Olam* in the second person singular: I will sing thee, says Rabbi Levi Yitschok of Berditchev, a *thou*-song. "Le bon Dieu, – ils le tutoyaient." '

5 *Ayeh ... lo emtzoeko*: (Heb.) a paraphrase of the opening line of *kevodkha malei olam* ('the world is full of your glory') by Yehuda Halevi

LEVI YITSCHOK'S KADDISH

original: variously entitled *a din-toireh mit got* ('God on trial') or *kaddish*
Compare REB LEVI YITSCHOK TALKS TO GOD.

16 *Yisgadal ... rabah*: (Aramaic) 'Sanct and exaltate ... be the great name' [THE KADDISH, 1–2]. See introductory note to THE KADDISH.

18 *Lo ozuz mimkomi*: (Heb.) 'I will not move from my place'; the words of Honi ha-Meagel ('the circle-maker'), a miracle-worker in the period of the Second Temple who refused to move from a circle he had drawn until God answered his prayer for rain

M'LAVEH MALKEH

original: *melaveh malkeh*

Title: The title is Hebrew for 'the Queen's escort.' It refers to songs sung at the conclusion of the Sabbath, which was frequently personified as a queen or bride.

THOU HAST CHOSEN US

original: *atoh bekhartonu*; based on a passage in the prayerbook, in the Musaf Amidah for the Three Festivals

O THERE, O THERE, WHERE IS OUR HOLY REBBE

original: *dort un dort vu undser heyliker rebe is do*

THE REBBE, HE WANTED

original: *der rebe hot gevolt*
There are several versions of this satirical song, differing in their lists of absurd miracles.
8 *Mithnagdim*: (Heb). See introductory note to 'Chassidic Folk-Songs.'

IN GOD'S GOOD TIME

original: *vos vet zayn mit dem reben dem frumen* ('what will happen to our pious rabbi')
14 *the Red Heifer*: an animal whose ashes were used in the purification of persons and objects defiled by a corpse [Numbers 19. 1–10]; had to be unblemished and never yoked
21 *gopher*: wood used in Noah's ark [Genesis 6.14]
22 *tzitzis*: (Heb.) fringes of the prayershawl
22 *shofar*: (Heb.) ram's horn
26 *tsholent*: (Yid.) a stew traditionally eaten on the Sabbath
26 *kigel*: A *kigel* or *kugel* (Yid.) is a pudding, usually savoury but sometimes sweet, based on such ingredients as potatoes or noodles. 'And *kugel* ... is, with one exception, always and in all languages, *kugel*. The exception is when it is *kigel*' [p. 111].

A BURGLARY

original: *a ganevah*

TELL US, REBBENU

original: *az moshiakh vet kumen* ('when the Messiah comes')
See introductory note to BALLAD OF THE DAYS OF THE MESSIAH.
18 *Moishe Rebenu*: 'Moishe Rabbeinu is not, certainly not in a folk-song, ever to be rendered as "Moses our Teacher." The latter phrase evokes a pedant, the

former a prophet, a patriarch, a member of our family. Upon the Yiddish tongue, which forgets that the talk is Hebrew, it is as if Rabbeinu were a surname' [p. 111]. Klein initially translated the phrase as 'Moses, our Master' [MS 5496].

YOSHKA, YOSHKA

original: *yoshke, yoshke*

OY, VEY, REBBENU

original: *oy, vey, rebenyu*
13 *mikveh*: (Heb.) ritual bath

OUR REBBE, THE MIRACLE-WORKER, ONCE

original: *amol iz geforen oyfn yam* ('once fared forth on the ocean wide')

AND WHEN OUR REBBE WALKS

based on the refrain of THE REBBE, HE WANTED

OUR REBBE

original: *unser rebenyu*

MY NODDLE IT IS HUMMING

original: *ikh kum yetst fun mayn tsadik* ('I have just come from my tsadik')

THE TRAIN

original: *der ayzenban*. There are numerous versions, some much longer.

HOW FARES THE KING?

original: *vi azoy lebt der keyzer*
   The original has 'Czar' (*keyzer*) rather than 'King.'
6 *a loaf of sugar*: The original has 'a little hat of sugar.' Russian sugar refineries produced blocks of sugar in the form of cylindrical hats.

THE REBBELE, THE GABBAI'LE, THE CANTOR'L, THE SHAMASH'L

original: *der rebele, der gabele, der khazendel, der shamashel*
The *gabbai* is the chief lay official of a synagogue, originally the treasurer. The cantor or *khazen* leads the services. The *shamash* is the caretaker of the synagogue.

TSIG, TSIGITSAPEL

original: *tsig, tsigitsapel.* Klein omits stanzas 4, 8, 10–12. In the original the goat turns out to be possessed by a dybbuk, the soul of a sinner, which is defeated by the rabbi. *Tsig* is Yiddish for 'goat.'
4 *Hoshana Rabah*: (Heb., 'the great *Hoshana*') the seventh day of the festival of
   Sukkot, on which the exclamation *Hoshana* ('save us') is frequently repeated
5 *Gabbai*: (Heb.) the chief lay official of a synagogue, originally the treasurer
7 *mikveh*: (Heb.) ritual bath
14 *Shochet*: (Heb.) ritual slaughterer

MIRACLES AND WONDERS

original: *nisim venifloys*
'A *Mithnagid*, heatedly inveighing against the shams of Chassidism, might regale his cronies in the *Vilna Klaus* with fictitious tales of ludicrous miracles and questionable wonders that befell some mythical *rebbe*; – how, as the folk-song has it, the Master of the Name went dry into the water, and *mirabile dictu* came out a great deal wetter ...' ['Of Hebrew Humor,' LER, p. 106].
Title: Exodus 7.3, Deuteronomy 7.19

AKAVYAH BEN M'HALALLEL

original: *akavyo ben mehalaleyl*
Akavyah ben M'halallel was one of the rabbis of the Talmudic period. He is best known for his saying 'Reflect upon three things and you will not come within the power of sin; know whence you came, whither you are going, and before whom you are destined to give account.'

OMAR ADOISHEM L'YA-AKOIV!

original: *omar adoishem leyaakoiv* ('the Lord said to Jacob')

BAR YOCHAI

original: *bar yokhay*
   This is the refrain of a song written (in Hebrew) by the sixteenth-century Kabbalistic scholar and poet Shimon Labi. Shimon bar Yoḥai was a rabbi of the Talmudic period who was venerated by the Kabbalists, and was wrongly supposed by them to have written the *Zohar*, the central Kabbalistic text. The song is sung on Sabbath in the Sephardic tradition, and on the holiday of Lag Beomer, the supposed anniversary of Bar Yoḥai's death, in the Ashkenazic tradition.

THE REBBE ELIMELECH

original: *der rebe elimelekh*; by Moshe Nadir (1885–1943), Yiddish poet and humorist
16 *Havdala*: (Heb., 'distinction') blessing recited at the end of the Sabbath or a festival to mark the boundary between the sacred and the profane
17 *shamash*: (Heb.) caretaker of a synagogue

YONDER! YONDER!

original: *tsu kent ir den dos land* ('do you know the land')
   The original is inspired by Mignon's song in Goethe's *Wihelm Meister's Apprenticeship*. Goethe's poem begins 'Kennst du das Land, wo die Zitronen blühn' ('Do you know the land where the citrons blossom') and has the refrain 'Dahin! Dahin / Möcht ich mit dir, O mein Geliebter, ziehn' ('Thither! Thither / I would go, O my beloved, with you'). Klein replaces the second stanza of the folk-song with one on a Zionist theme.
2 *bokser*: (Yid.) '*Bokser*, too, is rebellious, like its namesake, against translation. Upon the market-place, it is known as St. John's bread. But that is obviously impossible! *Chassidim* and St. John, *l'havdil*! And even to call it the fruit of the carob is no great aid to digestion' [p. 111]. Klein initially translated *bokser* as 'St. John's bread' [MS 5482].
25 *Yishmoel*: Ishmael, Abraham's son by his concubine, Hagar, is, according to tradition, the ancestor of the Arabs.

VESOMACHTO

original: *vesomakhto* ('do you rejoice'); based on Deuteronomy 16.14

Horace

Klein's acquaintance with the poetry of Horace probably dates from his years at McGill, where he majored in classics (and political economy). The Horace translations, however, are late, Klein's latest dateable work. They are very free, showing the influence of the translations of Ezra Pound.

OF THE ANCIENT HOUSE OF THE CLINII

original: Ode 1.1 ('*Maecenas atavis edite*')

TO LYDIA

original: Ode 1.8 ('*Lydia, dic, per omnes*')

TO LEUCONOE

original: Ode 1.11 ('*Tu ne quaesieris*')

TO L. MUNATIUS PLANCUS

original: Ode 1.7 ('*Laudabunt alii claram Rhodon*'). Klein omits the last eighteen lines.

Appendix A
Contents of Published and Unpublished Collections

PUBLISHED COLLECTIONS

Hath Not a Jew ... (1940)

Ave Atque Vale
Childe Harold's Pilgrimage
Portraits of a Minyan
Greeting on This Day
Sonnet in Time of Affliction
Out of the Pulver and the Polished Lens
Talisman in Seven Shreds
Design for Mediaeval Tapestry
Haggadah
Reb Levi Yitschok Talks to God
Plumaged Proxy
Dance Chassidic
Preacher
Scribe
Sacred Enough You Are

Sonnets Semitic
   Would That Three Centuries Past Had Seen Us Born
   These Northern Stars Are Scarabs in My Eyes
   Upon a Time There Lived a Dwarf, a Jew
   I Shall Not Bear Much Burden When I Cross
   Now We Will Suffer Loss of Memory

For the Leader – with String Music
   Song of Toys and Trinkets
   Song of Exclamations

Song to Be Sung at Dawn
Market Song
Counting-out Rhyme

Of Kith and Kin
Heirloom
Bestiary
Mourners
Gift

Of Sundry Folk
Into the Town of Chelm
Jonah Katz
Bandit
A Deed of Daring
Biography
Doctor Dwarf

Of Kings and Beggars
Ballad of the Dancing Bear
Ballad for Unfortunate Ones
King Elimelech
King Dalfin
Wandering Beggar

Of Holy Vessels
Baal Shem Tov
Elijah
Cantor
Scholar
The Venerable Bee
Rev Owl

Of Nothing at All
Orders

Appendix A

Poems (1944)

1. The Psalter of Avram Haktani

Psalm I: A Psalm of Abraham, When He Hearkened to a Voice, and There Was None
Psalm II: Maschil of Abraham: A Prayer When He Was in the Cave
Psalm III: A Psalm of Abraham, When He Was Sore Pressed
Psalm IV: A Psalm of Abraham, Touching His Green Pastures
Psalm V: A Song of Degrees
Psalm VI: A Psalm of Abraham, concerning That Which He Beheld upon the Heavenly Scarp
Psalm VII: For the Chief Physician
Psalm VIII: Psalm of the Fruitful Field
Psalm IX: A Psalm, to Be Preserved against Two Wicked Words
Psalm X: Lamed Vav: A Psalm to Utter in Memory of Great Goodness
Psalm XI: A Psalm of a Mighty Hunter before the Lord
Psalm XII: To the Chief Musician, Who Played for the Dancers
Psalm XIII: A Song for Wanderers
Psalm XIV: A Psalm for Five Holy Pilgrims, Yea, Six on the King's Highway
Psalm XV: A Psalm of Abraham, Touching the Crown with Which He Was Crowned on the Day of His Espousals
Psalm XVI: To the Chief Scribe, a Psalm of Abraham, in the Day of the Gladness of His Heart
Psalm XVII: For the Bridegroom Coming Out of His Chamber, a Song
Psalm XVIII: For the Bride, a Song, to Be Sung by Virgins
Psalm XIX: A Benediction
Psalm XX: A Psalm of Abraham, Which He Made at the Feast
Psalm XXI: A Benediction for the New Moon
Psalm XXII: A Prayer of Abraham, against Madness
Psalm XXIII: A Psalm of Justice, and Its Scales
Psalm XXIV: Shiggaion of Abraham Which He Sang unto the Lord
Psalm XXV: To the Prophets, Minor and Major, a Psalm or Song
Psalm XXVI: To the Chief Musician, a Psalm of Israel, to Bring to Remembrance
Psalm XXVII: A Psalm to Teach Humility
Psalm XXVIII: A Psalm or Prayer – Praying His Portion with Beasts
Psalm XXIX: To the Chief Musician, a Psalm of the Bratzlaver, a Parable
Psalm XXX: To the Chief Musician, a Psalm of the Bratzlaver, Which He Wrote Down As the Stammerer Spoke
Psalm XXXI: To the Chief Musician, a Psalm of the Bratzlaver, Touching a Good Gardener

Psalm XXXII: A Song That the Ships of Jaffa Did Sing in the Night
Psalm XXXIII: A Psalm, Forbidden to Cohanim
Psalm XXXIV: A Psalm of Abraham, to Be Written Down and Left on the Tomb of Rashi
Psalm XXXV: A Psalm of Abraham, Which He Made Because of Fear in the Night
Psalm XXXVI: A Psalm Touching Genealogy

2. A Voice Was Heard in Ramah

In Re Solomon Warshawer
Rabbi Yom-Tob of Mayence Petitions His God [*from* Murals for a House of God]
Ballad of the Thwarted Axe
Ballad of the Days of the Messiah

3. Yehuda Halevi, His Pilgrimage

The Rocking Chair and Other Poems (1948)

The Rocking Chair
The Provinces
The Cripples
The Snowshoers
For the Sisters of the Hotel Dieu
Grain Elevator
Université de Montréal
The Sugaring
Indian Reservation: Caughnawaga
Krieghoff: Calligrammes
Bread
Political Meeting
The Spinning Wheel
Frigidaire
Air-Map
Dress Manufacturer: Fisherman
Pawnshop
The Green Old Age
The Break-up
Commercial Bank
Quebec Liquor Commission Store
Montreal

Winter Night: Mount Royal
Lookout: Mount Royal
The Mountain
Lone Bather
Pastoral of the City Streets
M. Bertrand
The Notary
Monsieur Gaston
Librairie Delorme
Sire Alexandre Grandmaison
Hormisdas Arcand
Les Filles majeures
Filling Station
Annual Banquet: Chambre de Commerce
Portrait of the Poet as Landscape

UNPUBLISHED COLLECTIONS

Gestures Hebraic and Poems (1932)

SECTION ONE

Greeting on This Day
Holy Bonds
Out of the Pulver and the Polished Lens
Arabian Love Song
Prothalamium [A Psalm of Abraham, Touching the Crown with Which He Was
    Crowned on the Day of His Espousals]
Lost Fame
Invocation to Death
Kalman Rhapsodizes
Design for Mediaeval Tapestry
Portraits of a Minyan
Talisman in Seven Shreds
Preacher
Ballad of the Dancing Bear
Ballad of Signs and Wonders
Dialogue
Kaddish [A Psalm, Forbidden to Cohanim]
Koheleth

Scribe
The Words of Plauni-Ben-Plauni to Job
Gestures Hebraic
Haggadah
Dance Chassidic
Plumaged Proxy
Reply Courteous
Oriental Garden
Nehemiah
Exorcism Vain
Portrait
Saturday Night
Incognito [Lamed Vav: A Psalm to Utter in Memory of Great Goodness]
These Candle Lights
Joseph
Ecclesiastes 13
Cargo [A Song That the Ships of Jaffa Did Sing in the Night]
Soirée of Velvel Kleinburger
Reb Levi Yitschok Talks to God
Diary of Abraham Segal, Poet
Rather Than Have My Brethren Bend the Knee
Ave Atque Vale

SECTION TWO

Sacred Enough You Are
XXII Sonnets
Litany
Homage
This Is No Myth
Gargoyle
Business
Histrionic Sonnet
Dark Cleopatra on a Gilded Couch
Sybarite Though I Be
Five Weapons against Death
Where Shall I Find Choice Words
Coward in Consolation
Prayer [A Prayer against the Witnessing of Grief]
Bounty Royal
A Sequence of Songs
Frankly

Finis
Pathetic Fallacy
Haunted House
Assurance
Funeral in April
Resurrection [Visitation in Elul]
Advice to Young Virgins
Letters to One Absent
Invitation
Last Will and Testament
Words in Their Season
   Spring
   Summer
   Autumn
   Winter
Nocturne
Old Maid's Wedding
Anguish
Fable
Figure
Autumn
Autumn Night
Discord of the Crow
October Heresy
Wood Notes Wild
Fixity
Sleep Walking Scene
Song before Winter
Song
Reveille in Winter
What Winter Has Said, Is Said
February Morning
April Fool
April Disappointments
April Fulfilment
Discovery of Spring
Manuscript: Thirteenth Century
Preface
Christian Poet and Hebrew Maid
Falstaff
Orders
Market Song

Protest
Composition
Momus
Soror Addita Musis
Lothario
Symbols
The Poet to the Big Business Man
Boredom
Divine Titillation
Elegy
Desiderata
Probabilities
An Old Dame Prates in Galilee
Blind Girl's Song
Dissolution
Resurrection [Visitation in Elul]
Advice to the Young
Ecclesiastes 13
Shelley
Fragment on the Death of Shelley
A Coloured Gentleman
Bion in His Old Age
Request
Oracles of the Clock
Astrologer
Out of a Pit of Perpendiculars
Arbiter Bibendi

Note: Section One of GHP corresponds to GH and Section Two to P32, with the following exceptions. In GH, LITANY is added after ARABIAN LOVE SONG; BOUNTY ROYAL is added after LOST FAME; and DIARY OF ABRAHAM SEGAL, POET is deleted. In P32 the order of the three poems following NOCTURNE is altered to ANGUISH, FABLE, OLD MAID'S WEDDING; and WHAT WINTER HAS SAID, IS SAID and FEBRUARY MORNING are reversed. Also, P32 is divided into four sections, beginning with SACRED ENOUGH YOU ARE, WORDS IN THEIR SEASON, MANUSCRIPT: THIRTEENTH CENTURY (a section to itself), and PREFACE.

Appendix A

Poems (1934)

Heirloom
Mourners
Town Fool's Song
Into the Town of Chelm
Scholar
Yossel Letz
Jonah Katz
Doctor Dwarf
Jonah
A Deed of Daring
Baldhead Elisha
Song of Sweet Dishes
Biography
Riddle
Bestiary
Gift
Lullaby for a Hawker's Child
Fairy Tale
Concerning Four Strange Sons
Bandit
Toys [Song of Toys and Trinkets]
Paradise [Psalm of the Fruitful Field]
Song of Exclamations
Elijah
Messiah
Arithmetic
Song [Song to Be Sung at Dawn]
Counting-out Rhyme
On the Road to Palestine
Market Song
Getzel Gelt
Nose Aristocratic
Chatzkel the Hunter [A Psalm of a Mighty Hunter before the Lord]
Calendar [A Psalm, with Trumpets for the Months]
Baal Shem Tov
Sonnet of the Starving One
The Venerable Bee
The Mad Monarch [Concerning a Strange King]
Captain Scuttle

Cantor
King Elimelech
Wandering Beggar
Rev Owl
Madman's Song
Cavalcade [A Psalm of Horses and Their Riders]
Pigeons
Ballad for Unfortunate Ones
King Dalfin
Orders
Ballad of the Dancing Bear

The 1942 Typescript of *Poems* (1944)

THE PSALTER OF AVRAM HAKTANI

Psalm I: A Psalm of Abraham, When He Hearkened to a Voice, and There Was None
Psalm II: Maschil of Abraham: A Prayer When He Was in the Cave
Psalm III: [?]
Psalm IV: A Psalm of Abraham, When He Was Sore Pressed
Psalm V: [?]
Psalm VI: A Psalm of Abraham, Touching His Green Pastures
Psalm VII: A Song of Degrees
Psalm VIII: A Psalm of Abraham, concerning That Which He Beheld upon the Heavenly Scarp
Psalm IX: To the Chief Musician, Al-Taschith, Michtam of Abraham; When One Sent, and They Watched the House to Kill Him
Psalm X: To the Chief Musician upon Shoshannim, a Song of Loves [Grace before Poison]
Psalm XI: For the Chief Physician: A Song for Hunters
Psalm XII: [?]
Psalm XIII: To the Prophets, Minor and Major, a Psalm or Song
Psalm XIV: Psalm of the Fruitful Field
Psalm XV: A Psalm for the Sons of Korah [Rather Than Have My Brethren Bend the Knee]
Psalm XVI: A Psalm, to Be Preserved against Two Wicked Words
Psalm XVII: Lamed Vav: A Psalm to Utter in Memory of Great Goodness
Psalm XVIII: A Psalm of a Mighty Hunter before the Lord
Psalm XIX: To the Chief Musician, Who Played for the Dancers

Psalm xx: A Song for Wanderers
Psalm xxi: A Psalm for Five Holy Pilgrims, Yea, Six on the King's Highway
Psalm xxii: A Psalm of Abraham, Touching the Crown with Which He Was Crowned on the Day of His Espousals
Psalm xxiii: To the Chief Scribe, a Psalm of Abraham, in the Day of the Gladness of His Heart
Psalm xxiv: For the Bridegroom Coming Out of His Chamber, a Song
Psalm xxv: For the Bride, a Song, to Be Sung by Virgins
Psalm xxvi: A Benediction
Psalm xxvii: A Psalm of Abraham, Which He Made at the Feast
Psalm xxviii: A Benediction for the New Moon
Psalm xxix: A Prayer of Abraham, against Madness
Psalm xxx: A Psalm of Justice, and Its Scales
Psalm xxxi: Shiggaion of Abraham Which He Sang unto the Lord
Psalm xxxii: A Psalm, with Trumpets for the Months
Psalm xxxiii: A Psalm of Time and the Firmament
Psalm xxxiv: [?]
Psalm xxxv: A Psalm of Abraham of That Which Was Visited upon Him
Psalm xxxvi: To the Chief Musician, a Psalm of the Bratzlaver, When He Considered How the Pious Are Overwhelmed
Psalm xxxvii: To the Chief Bailiff, a Psalm of the King's Writ
Psalm xxxviii: A Psalm of the Heavenly Minister [Kalman Rhapsodizes]
Psalm xxxix: A Psalm to Teach Humility
Psalm xl: A Psalm or Prayer, Praying His Portion with Beasts
Psalm xli: To the Chief Musician, a Psalm of the Bratzlaver, a Parable
Psalm xlii: To the Chief Musician, a Psalm of the Bratzlaver, Which He Wrote Down As the Stammerer Spoke
Psalm xliii: To the Chief Musician, a Psalm of the Bratzlaver, a Psalm of the Beginning of Things [Of Remembrance]
Psalm xliv: To the Chief Musician, a Psalm of the Bratzlaver, Touching a Good Gardener
Psalm xlv: A Song That the Ships of Jaffa Did Sing in the Night
Psalm xlvi: A Psalm for Them That Utter Dark Sayings [Exorcism Vain]
Psalm xlvii: A Psalm, Forbidden to Cohanim
Psalm xlviii: *possibly* A Psalm of Abraham, Which He Made Because of Fear in the Night
Psalm xlix: A Psalm of Abraham, to Be Written Down and Left on the Tomb of Rashi
Psalm l: A Psalm of Resignation

1072 / Appendix A

LONG POEMS

In Re Solomon Warshawer
Murals for a House of God
Yehuda Halevi, His Pilgrimage

BALLADS AND SONNETS

Ballad of the Thwarted Axe
Of the Friendly Silence of the Moon
Ballad of the Days of the Messiah
Ballad of the Nuremberg Tower Clock
Ballad of the Evil Eye
Assurance
   Age Draws His Fingernail across My Brow
   Speak Me No Deaths. Prevent That Word from Me
   Think Not, My Dear, Because I Do Not Call
   Why Do You Love Me, As You Say You Do
   Without Your Love, without Your Love for Me
   Would That Three Centuries Past Had Seen Us Born

Note: This reconstruction of the original typescript of *Poems* (1944), which no longer exists, is based on *Caplan*, Appendix 3, pp. 280-3. Caplan was not able to identify the six sonnets at the end of the typescript. I have been able to do so through an examination of the typescripts in the Klein papers; however, I have been unable to determine their order. Hence, I have listed them alphabetically. Caplan also does not divide his list into subsections. I do so on the basis of Klein's correspondence with his editors.

Selected Poems (1955)

Portrait of the Poet as Landscape
Bread
Bestiary
Plumaged Proxy
Market Song
A Psalm to Teach Humility
Sophist [*from* Portraits of a Minyan]
Sonnet Semitic [Would That Three Centuries Past Had Seen Us Born]
Benediction

Tetragrammaton [*from* Talisman in Seven Shreds]
Syllogism [*from* Talisman in Seven Shreds]
Against Mammon, a Murmuring [*revised version of* Rather Than Have My Brethren Bend the Knee]
Desideratum
Basic English
Rocking Chair
For the Sisters of the Hotel Dieu
Montreal
Frigidaire
Monsieur Gaston
Snowshoers
Political Meeting
On the Heavenly Scarp [A Psalm of Abraham, concerning That Which He Beheld upon the Heavenly Scarp]
In Re Solomon Warshawer
Song of Innocence
Psalm of Justice [A Psalm of Justice, and Its Scales]
Prowler [A Psalm of Abraham of That Which Was Visited upon Him]
Come Two, like Shadows
Sonnet Unrhymed
Ni la mort ni le soleil
The Library
Penultimate Chapter
In Memoriam: Arthur Ellis
Actuarial Report
Sestina on the Dialectic
Les Vespasiennes
Spinoza: On Man, on the Rainbow
Psalm to Be Left on the Tomb of Rashi [A Psalm of Abraham, to Be Written Down and Left on the Tomb of Rashi]
Psalm [A Psalm of Abraham, When He Hearkened to a Voice, and There Was None]
Autobiographical

Appendix B
Poems Revised in the Early Fifties

ORIGINAL POEMS

Actuarial Report
Address to the Choirboys
Autobiographical
Ave Atque Vale
Baal Shem Tov
Ballad for Unfortunate Ones
Ballad of the Nursery Rhymes
Basic English
Beaver
A Benediction
Bestiary
Bread
Childe Harold's Pilgrimage
Come Two, like Shadows
Dance Chassidic
Dentist
Desideratum
Design for Mediaeval Tapestry
For the Sisters of the Hotel Dieu
Greeting on This Day
Heirloom
I Shall Not Bear Much Burden When I Cross
In Memoriam: Arthur Ellis
In Re Solomon Warshawer
Les Vespasiennes
The Library
Love

Market Song
Maschil of Abraham: A Prayer When He Was in the Cave
Meditation upon Survival
Mourners
Ni la mort ni le soleil
Not All the Perfumes of Arabia
Now We Will Suffer Loss of Memory
Out of the Pulver and the Polished Lens
Pawnshop
Penultimate Chapter
Plumaged Proxy
Political Meeting
Portrait of the Poet as Landscape
Portraits of a Minyan
A Prayer of Abraham, against Madness
A Prayer of the Afflicted, When He Is Overwhelmed
Preacher
A Psalm of Abraham, concerning That Which He Beheld upon the Heavenly Scarp
A Psalm of Abraham of That Which Was Visited upon Him
A Psalm of Abraham, to Be Written Down and Left on the Tomb of Rashi
A Psalm of Abraham, When He Hearkened to a Voice, and There Was None
A Psalm of Abraham, Which He Made Because of Fear in the Night
A Psalm of Justice, and Its Scales
A Psalm, to Be Preserved against Two Wicked Words
Rather Than Have My Brethren Bend the Knee
Reb Levi Yitschok Talks to God
Sestina on the Dialectic
A Song of Degrees
Song of Innocence
Sonnet Unrhymed
Talisman in Seven Shreds
That Legendary Eagle, Death
Variation of a Theme
Would That Three Centuries Past Had Seen Us Born

TRANSLATIONS

Asks the World an Old, Old Question
Come You Here, Philosopher
Confession

Appendix B

The Dance of Despair
Hush! Hush!
In the City of Slaughter
Old Gold
Seer, Begone
Shall I Be a Rabbi?
Song
Thy Breath, O Lord, Passed Over and Enkindled Me
War

Note: For revisions to the Chassidic folk-songs see the introductory textual note.

Appendix C
Pages Which End with the Last Line of a Stanza or Verse Paragraph

5	162	275	534	655	754	836
29	163	284	537	656	755	842
31	165	291	538	657	756	844
37	170	295	542	662	766	845
39	176	303	568	663	772	850
52	181	455	569	666	791	851
65	191	465	573	667	797	852
68	195	470	581	678	800	855
73	196	471	600	680	801	856
85	197	475	602	685	802	857
91	198	476	604	688	804	864
115	199	478	607	689	805	866
116	200	480	608	694	806	868
125	201	488	610	698	807	
130	208	489	613	701	808	
134	209	490	614	702	809	
140	233	493	617	727	812	
144	234	494	624	728	813	
149	237	498	629	730	814	
151	239	499	632	738	815	
155	243	505	635	745	819	
156	247	510	636	746	820	
157	250	513	637	749	822	
158	251	517	641	750	825	
159	266	518	642	751	826	
160	267	531	646	752	827	
161	269	532	647	753	829	

Pages have not been listed in the case of stanzas which are numbered or which come at the end of numbered subsections.

Index of Titles

ORIGINAL POEMS

Italics indicate subsections of long poems or of poetry sequences.

Actuarial Report 2.607
Address to the Choirboys 2.613
Advice to the Young 1.85
Advice to Young Virgins 1.85
Aesthetic Curiosity 1.245
Afterword 1.82
Against Mammon, a Murmuring 1.242
Age Draws His Fingernail across My Brow 1.221
Ahasuerus 1.33
Air-Map 2.646
And in That Drowning Instant 2.608
And the Man Moses Was Meek 1.139
Anguish 1.191
Annual Banquet: Chambre de Commerce 2.678
Aphasia 1.42
Apologia 2.716
April Disappointments 1.86
April Fool 1.87
April Fulfilment 1.87
Arabian Love Song 1.155
Arbiter Bibendi 1.88
Arithmetic 1.249
Arrow of Aloofness 1.79
As to Quantum 2.708
Assurance 1.89
Astrologer 1.89

At Home 2.665
At the Sign of the Spigot 1.265
Autobiographical 2.564
Auto-da-fé 1.6
Autumn [c. 1928/1928] 1.63
Autumn [c. 1926/c. 1928] 1.90
Autumn Night 1.90
Ave Atque Vale [Version 1] 1.191
Ave Atque Vale [Version 2] 1.193
Aye, but a Man's Reach 2.710
Baal Shem Tov 1.311
Babe in the Woods 2.709
Baldhead Elisha 1.280
Ballad for Unfortunate Ones 1.281
Ballad of Quislings 2.532
Ballad of Signs and Wonders 1.64
Ballad of the Dancing Bear 1.156
Ballad of the Days of the Messiah 2.533
Ballad of the Dream That Was Not Dreamed 2.534
Ballad of the Evil Eye 2.536
Ballad of the Hebrew Bride 1.269
Ballad of the Nuremberg Tower Clock 2.537
Ballad of the Nursery Rhymes 2.538
Ballad of the Thwarted Axe 2.539
Ballad of the Werewolves 2.541
Ballade of the Poet 1.44
Bandit 1.230
Barricade Smith: His Speeches 2.463
Basic English 2.615
Beatific Vision 2.710
Beaver 2.671
Benediction, A 1.172
Benediction for the New Moon, A 2.525
Benedictions 2.704
Bestiary 1.282
Betray Me Not. Treat Me As Scurvily 1.220
Biography 1.283
Bion in His Old Age 1.91
Bitter Dish, The 1.129
Black Decalogue 1.129
Blind Girl's Song 1.91
Blueprint for a Monument of War 2.453

1083 / Index of Titles

Boredom 1.40
Bounty Royal 1.92
Bread 2.617
Break-up, The 2.646
Business 1.93
Caesar's Plagiarist 2.708
Calvary 1.195
Canine Felicity 2.711
Cantabile 2.701
Cantor 1.284
Captain Scuttle 1.285
Chad Gadyah 1.130
Childe Harold's Pilgrimage [Version 1] 2.475
Childe Harold's Pilgrimage [Version 2] 2.480
Christian Poet and Hebrew Maid 1.140
Chronicler Continues, The 1.274
Club of Final Pain 1.81
Coloured Gentleman, A 1.93
Come Two, like Shadows 2.567
Commercial Bank 2.618
Composition 1.94
Concerning a Strange King 1.290
Concerning Four Strange Sons 1.291
Conjectures 1.67
Consider, Then, the Miracle You Wrought 1.226
Corrigendum 2.462
Counsel 2.712
Counting-out Rhyme 1.250
Coward in Consolation 1.83
Cripples, The 2.647
Cui Bono? 2.711
Dance Chassidic 1.148
Dark Cleopatra on a Gilded Couch 1.94
Dedication 1.6
Deed of Daring, A 1.292
Déjà vu 2.710
Dentist 2.568
Desiderata 1.230
Desideratum 2.569
Design for Mediaeval Tapestry 1.195
Dial B and L 2.715
Dialogue 1.149

Diary of Abraham Segal, Poet 1.231
Discord of the Crow 1.95
Discovery of Spring 1.25
Dissolution 1.26
Divine Titillation 1.96
Doctor Drummond 2.655
Doctor Dwarf 1.292
Dominion Square 2.672
Doubt 1.75
Dress Manufacturer: Fisherman 2.679
Earthquake 1.239
Ecclesiastes 13 1.167
Elder Counsels Self-killing, An 1.270
Elegy [c. 1926/c. 1928] 1.96
Elegy [c. 1947/1947] 2.673
Elijah 1.202
Embryo of Dusts 1.187
Enigma 1.188
Epigrams [1] 2.708
Epigrams [2] 2.715
Epitaph [c. 1930/1930] 1.150
Epitaph [c. 1942/c. 1944] 2.626
Epitaph Forensic 1.37
Escape 1.44
Esther 1.34
Esther Hears Echoes of His Voice. 1.201
Et j'ai lu tous les livres 2.570
Etching 1.128
Exit 1.73
Exorcism Vain 1.204
Exultation 1.73
Ezekiel the Simple Opines. 1.199
Fable 1.97
Fairy Tale 1.294
Falstaff 1.151
'Farcie de Comme' 2.709
February Morning 1.97
Festival 1.239
Figure 1.98
Filling Station 2.680
Finale 1.76
Finis 1.98

Index of Titles

First Sight 1.74
Five Characters 1.33
Five Weapons against Death 1.79
Fixity 1.128
Fons Vitae 1.188
For the Bride, a Song, to Be Sung by Virgins 1.172
For the Bridegroom Coming Out of His Chamber, a Song 1.171
For the Chief Physician 2.505
For the Sisters of the Hotel Dieu 2.648
Foreword 1.79
Fragment on the Death of Shelley 1.99
Frankly 1.99
Frigidaire 2.649
From Beautiful Dreams I Rise; I Rise from Dreams 1.227
From the Beyond 2.711
From the Chronicles 1.267
From the Japanese 2.713
Funeral in April 1.204
Gargoyle 1.100
Gestures Hebraic 1.168
Getzel Gelt 1.295
Gift 1.297
Girlie Show 2.571
Golem, The 2.572
Grace before Poison 2.505
Grain Elevator 2.650
Green Old Age, The 2.619
Greeting on This Day 1.142
Guardian of the Law 2.461
Guide to the Perplexed 1.189
Haggadah 1.129
Haman 1.35
Haunted House 1.68
He Communes with Nature. 1.238
He Considers the Factory Hands. 1.232
He Contemplates His Contemporaries. 1.237
He Eats at the Family-Board. 1.236
He Reads His Pocket-Edition of Shakespeare; and Luxuriously Thinks. 1.236
He Receives a Visitor. 1.234
He Rises. 1.231
He Travels on the Street-Car, and Reads over a Neighbour's Shoulder. 1.232
He Worships at the North-Eastern. 1.235

He Yawns; and Regards the Slogans on the Office Walls. 1.233
Heart Failure 1.42
Heaven at Last 1.246
Heirloom 1.298
Here They Are – All Those Sunny April Days 1.215
Heroic 1.168
His Lordship 2.458
His Was an Open Heart 1.139
Histrionic Sonnet 1.100
Hitleriad, The 2.581
Holy Bonds 1.170
Homage 1.101
Home 1.75
Hommage 2.716
Hormisdas Arcand 2.681
I Shall Not Bear Much Burden When I Cross 1.228
Image Celestial 1.246
Immortal Yearnings 1.189
In Memoriam: Arthur Ellis [Version 1] 2.557
In Memoriam: Arthur Ellis [Version 2] 2.559
In Memoriam: Arthur Ellis [Version 3] 2.561
In Re Solomon Warshawer [Version 1] 2.493
In Re Solomon Warshawer [Version 2] 2.498
Inarticulate 2.713
Indian Reservation: Caughnawaga 2.641
Indictment 1.245
Initiation 2.709
Into the Town of Chelm 1.250
Invitation 1.101
Invocation to Death 1.174
Irony of Fourteen Blades 1.80
Isaiah Epicure Avers. 1.198
Job Reviles. 1.198
Johannus, Dei Monachus, Loquitur 1.267
Jonah 1.251
Jonah Katz 1.299
Joseph 1.72
Judith Makes Comparisons. 1.199
Junk-Dealer 1.138
Kalman Rhapsodizes 1.174
King Dalfin 1.300
King Elimelech 1.205

Kiss ..., A 1.5
Koheleth 1.132
Krieghoff: Calligrammes 2.682
La Belle Dame sans Merci 1.37
La Glorieuse Incertitude 2.460
Lamed Vav: A Psalm to Utter in Memory of Great Goodness 1.175
Landlord 1.134
Last Will and Testament [Version 1] 1.27
Last Will and Testament [Version 2] 1.27
Lay of the Lady, The 1.39
Legend of Lebanon 1.253
Les Filles majeures 2.683
Les Vespasiennes 2.627
Let Them Pronounce Me Sentimental 1.227
Letters to One Absent 1.102
Librairie Delorme 2.684
Library, The 2.620
Life and Eternity 1.5
Litany 1.103
Lockjaw 1.42
Lone Bather 2.685
Lookout: Mount Royal 2.686
Loosen the Drawbridge, Men! I Am Pursued 1.224
Lost Fame 1.176
Lothario 1.103
Love 2.573
Love Call 1.74
Lowell Levi 2.666
Lullaby for a Hawker's Child 1.301
Lunatic 1.42
M. Bertrand 2.651
M. le juge Dupré 2.687
Mâ Aleyk – No Evil Befall You 2.715
Madman's Song 1.302
Mais, c'est pas de mes oignons, ça! 2.716
Manuscript: Thirteenth Century 1.104
Market Song 1.176
Maschil of Abraham: A Prayer When He Was in the Cave 2.506
Mattathias 1.72
Meditation upon Survival 2.663
Messiah 1.240
Midnight Awakening 1.28

Momus 1.112
Monkey, The 1.36
Monsieur Gaston 2.688
Montreal 2.621
Mordecai 1.35
More's the Pity, The 2.711
Mountain, The 2.689
Mourners 1.264
Murals for a House of God 1.265
Mute Heraldry 1.246
My Dear Plutophilanthropist 2.574
My Literati Friends in Restaurants 1.228
Nahum-this-also-is-for-the-good Ponders. 1.197
Narcosis 1.41
Nehemiah 1.177
New Version 1.75
Ni la mort ni le soleil 2.623
Nocturne 1.113
Nose Aristocratic 1.302
Not All the Perfumes of Arabia [Version 1] 2.610
Not All the Perfumes of Arabia [Version 2] 2.611
Not from a Hermit's Grotto, nor Monk's Cell 1.222
Notary, The 2.656
Now We Will Suffer Loss of Memory [Version 1] 1.168
Now We Will Suffer Loss of Memory [Version 2] 1.169
O God! O Montreal! 2.700
Obituary Notices 1.41
October Heresy 1.113
Of Beauty 2.467
Of Castles in Spain 2.473
Of Daumiers a Portfolio 2.458
Of Dawn and Its Breaking 2.464
Of Faith, Hope and Charity 2.467
Of Poesy 2.468
Of Psalmody in the Temple 2.466
Of Remembrance 2.488
Of Shirts and Policies of State 2.469
Of Soporifics 2.469
Of the Clients of Barnum 2.465
Of the Friendly Silence of the Moon 2.542
Of the Lily Which Toils Not 2.470
Of the Making of Gragers 2.707

Of Tradition 2.628
Of Violence 2.463
Old Dame Prates in Galilee, An 1.114
Old Maids 1.178
Old Maid's Wedding 1.206
On Examining a Bill of Fare 2.713
On the Road to Palestine 1.207
Once in a Year 1.129
Oracles of the Clock 1.29
Orders 1.114
Oriental Garden 1.178
Out of a Pit of Perpendiculars 1.115
Out of the Pulver and the Polished Lens 1.208
Palmam Qui Meruit 2.717
Parade of St. Jean Baptiste 2.691
Pastoral of the City Streets 2.694
Pathetic Fallacy 1.30
Pawnshop 2.575
Penultimate Chapter 2.577
Petition For That My Father's Soul Should Enter into Heaven 1.315
Philosopher's Stone 1.241
Pigeons 1.303
Pintele Yid 1.134
Plumaged Proxy 1.179
Poet to the Big Business Man, The 1.117
Polish Village 2.542
Political Meeting 2.657
Portrait 1.179
Portrait, and Commentary 2.666
Portrait of the Poet as Landscape 2.634
Portrait of the Poet as Landscape [Deleted section] 2.640
Portraits of a Minyan 1.134
Post-War Planning 2.629
Prayer against the Witnessing of Grief, A 1.83
Prayer of Abraham, against Madness, A 2.526
Prayer of Abraham That He Be Forgiven for Blasphemy, A 2.508
Prayer of the Afflicted, When He Is Overwhelmed, A 2.508
Preacher 1.151
Preface 1.118
Pride before Fall 1.246
Prince to the Princess in the Fairy-Tale, The 1.216
Probabilities 1.118

Prosecutor 2.459
Protest 1.62
Provinces, The 2.642
Psalm for Five Holy Pilgrims, Yea, Six on the King's Highway, A 2.509
Psalm, Forbidden to Cohanim, A 1.180
Psalm of a Mighty Hunter before the Lord, A 1.303
Psalm of Abraham, concerning That Which He Beheld upon the Heavenly Scarp, A 2.530
Psalm of Abraham concerning the Arrogance of the Son of Man, A 2.510
Psalm of Abraham of That Which Was Visited upon Him, A 2.510
Psalm of Abraham, Praying a Green Old Age, A 2.511
Psalm of Abraham, to Be Written Down and Left on the Tomb of Rashi, A 2.512
Psalm of Abraham, Touching His Green Pastures, A 2.513
Psalm of Abraham, Touching the Crown with Which He Was Crowned on the Day of His Espousals, A 1.181
Psalm of Abraham, When He Hearkened to a Voice, and There Was None, A 2.527
Psalm of Abraham, When He Was Sore Pressed, A 2.514
Psalm of Abraham, Which He Made at the Feast, A 1.173
Psalm of Abraham, Which He Made Because of Fear in the Night, A 2.515
Psalm of Horses and Their Riders, A 1.305
Psalm of Justice, and Its Scales, A 2.516
Psalm of Resignation, A 2.517
Psalm of the Fruitful Field 1.312
Psalm of Time and the Firmament, A 2.528
Psalm or Prayer – Praying His Portion with Beasts, A 2.531
Psalm, to Be Preserved against Two Wicked Words, A 2.517
Psalm to Teach Humility, A 2.518
Psalm Touching Genealogy, A 2.624
Psalm, with Trumpets for the Months, A 1.305
Public Utility 2.460
Quarrel 1.75
Quebec Liquor Commission Store 2.659
Rabbi Yom-Tob Harangues His God 1.272
Rather Than Have My Brethren Bend the Knee 1.241
Reader of the Scroll 1.137
Reb Abraham 1.134
Reb Daniel Shochet Reflects. 1.197
Reb Levi Yitschok Talks to God 1.243
Reb Zadoc Has Memories. 1.196
Recollection 2.713
Reply Courteous 1.181

1091 / Index of Titles

Request 1.119
Rev Owl 1.306
Reveille in Winter 1.120
Rheumatic 1.41
Riddle 1.307
Ritual 2.716
Rocking Chair, The 2.644
Sacred Enough You Are 1.120
Saga the First 2.629
Saturday Night 1.213
Scatterbrain Singeth a Song 1.265
Scatterbrain's Last Song 1.275
Scholar 1.275
Scribe 1.213
Sennet from Gheel 2.543
Sentence 2.459
Sentimental 1.170
Sequence of Songs, A 1.73
Sestina on the Dialectic 2.662
Seventy Regal Moons, with Clouds as Train 1.218
Shadchan 1.136
Shechinah of Shadows, The 1.3
Shelley 1.120
Shiggaion of Abraham Which He Sang unto the Lord 2.519
Simeon Takes Hints from His Environs. 1.200
Sire Alexandre Grandmaison 2.696
Sleep Walking Scene 1.121
Sleuth 2.461
Sling for Goliath 1.81
Snowfall ... Eiderdown ... Cumulus ... 2.709
Snowshoers, The 2.652
Soirée of Velvel Kleinburger 1.183
Solomon Talmudi Considers His Life. 1.199
Song [c. 1926/c. 1928] 1.122
Song [c. 1929/1929] 1.130
Song before Winter 1.122
Song for Wanderers, A 2.528
Song of Degrees, A 2.520
Song of Exclamations 1.277
Song of Innocence 2.678
Song of Love 1.74
Song of Sweet Dishes 1.313

Song of Three Degrees, A 2.459
Song of Toys and Trinkets 1.278
Song That the Ships of Jaffa Did Sing in the Night, A 1.76
Song to Be Sung at Dawn 1.279
Song without Music 2.630
Sonnet in Time of Affliction 1.147
Sonnet of the Starving One 1.307
Sonnet Unrhymed 2.645
Sonnet without Music 2.474
Sophist 1.137
Soror Addita Musis 1.123
Speak Me No Deaths. Prevent That Word from Me 1.221
Spinning Wheel, The 2.660
Spinoza: On Man, on the Rainbow 2.714
Spring 1.123
Spring Exhibit 2.624
Stance of the Amidah 2.704
Still Small Voice, The 1.131
Strabismus 1.41
Style 1.245
Sugaring, The 2.653
Summer 1.124
Sweet Singer 1.138
Sword of the Righteous 1.80
Sybarite Though I Be 1.125
Syllogism 1.186
Symbols [1926] 1.31
Symbols [c. 1926/c. 1928] 1.125
Tailpiece to an Anthology 2.631
Talisman in Seven Shreds 1.186
Technique 2.711
Tetragrammaton 1.187
That Legendary Eagle, Death 2.578
These Candle Lights 1.77
These Northern Stars Are Scarabs in My Eyes 1.223
Think Not, My Dear, Because I Do Not Call 1.217
This Is No Myth 1.126
This Is Too Terrible a Season! Worms 1.218
Threnody 1.43
'Tis Very Well to Parrot the Nightingale 1.222
To Forgive Divine 2.708
To Keats 1.4

1093 / Index of Titles

To One Gone to the Wars 2.473
To the Chief Bailiff, a Psalm of the King's Writ 2.521
To the Chief Musician, a Psalm of Israel, to Bring to Remembrance 2.522
To the Chief Musician, a Psalm of the Bratzlaver, a Parable 2.486
To the Chief Musician: A Psalm of the Bratzlaver, Touching a Good Gardener 2.489
To the Chief Musician, a Psalm of the Bratzlaver, When He Considered How the Pious Are Overwhelmed 2.487
To the Chief Musician, a Psalm of the Bratzlaver, Which He Wrote Down As the Stammerer Spoke 2.491
To the Chief Musician, Al-Taschith, Michtam of Abraham; When One Sent, and They Watched the House to Kill Him 2.521
To the Chief Musician, Who Played for the Dancers 2.523
To the Chief Scribe, a Psalm of Abraham, in the Day of the Gladness of His Heart 1.170
To the Jewish Poet 1.77
To the Lady Who Wrote about Herzl 2.668
To the Prophets, Minor and Major, a Psalm or Song 2.524
Toreador 2.474
Town Fool's Song 1.308
Tremblement du coeur 1.74
Tribute to the Ballet Master [Version 1] 2.631
Tribute to the Ballet Master [Version 2] 2.632
Université de Montréal 2.697
Unveiling 2.712
Upon a Time There Lived a Dwarf, a Jew 1.224
Variation of a Theme 2.579
Vashti 1.34
Venerable Bee, The 1.314
Visitation in Elul 1.126
Wandering Beggar 1.309
Were I to Talk until the Crack o' Doom 1.229
What Winter Has Said, Is Said 1.127
Where Shall I Find Choice Words 1.82
White Old Lady, The 2.661
Who Hast Fashioned 2.706
Why Do You Love Me, As You Say You Do 1.216
Winter 1.32
Winter Night: Mount Royal 2.698
Wishing to Embarrass Me, but Politely 2.669
Within My Iron Days, My Nights of Stone 1.225
Without Your Love, without Your Love for Me 1.225

1094 / Index of Titles

Wood Notes Wild 1.245
Words of Plauni-Ben-Plauni to Job, The 1.153
Would That Three Centuries Past Had Seen Us Born [Version 1] 1.219
Would That Three Centuries Past Had Seen Us Born [Version 2] 1.219
Wrestling Ring 2.669
XXII Sonnets 1.216
Yehuda Halevi, His Pilgrimage 2.544
Yossel Letz 1.247
Young Man Moans Alarm before the Kiss of Death, A 1.271

TRANSLATIONS

Akavyah ben M'halallel 2.860
And at My Prayers I Will Quiver 2.830
And This I Know 2.804
And When Messiah Will Come 2.831
And When One Burns – One Burns Brandy 2.819
And When Our Rebbe Walks 2.852
Asks the World an Old, Old Question 2.831
Autobiographical 2.805
Bar Yochai 2.862
Be There No Altar 2.780
Bear Thou, O Wind, My Love 2.768
Behold 2.784
Beneath the Burden ... 2.725
Better a Hebrew Teacher 2.827
Burglary, A 2.848
Canticum Canticorum 2.796
Charm 2.818
Chastisement of God, The 2.726
Childless One, The 2.789
City of Slaughter, The 2.733
Come, Gird Ye Your Loins, and in Might Robe Yourselves 2.727
Come You Here, Philosopher 2.817
Conceit Curious 2.799
Confession 2.809
Dance of Despair 2.752
Dance of Despair, The 2.749
Dawn 2.789
Eleventh: In Memory of Isaac, Son of the Tailor, The 2.792
Gifted One, The 2.793

1095 / Index of Titles

Glory of the Homeland, The 2.782
Goats 2.806
God Grant My Part and Portion Be ... 2.728
God Willing, at the Rebbe's 2.836
Golden Parrakeet, The 2.824
Golden Parrot, The 2.798
Gone Is the Yesterday 2.829
How Fares the King? 2.856
Hush! Hush! 2.821
I Go upon the Balcony 2.825
I Sit Me Down upon a Stone 2.835
In God's Good Time 2.847
In the City of Slaughter 2.744
Kaddish, The [Version 1] 2.721
Kaddish, The [Version 2] 2.722
Ki-Ki 2.797
King, A 2.807
King Rufus 2.808
Kings of the Emek 2.777
Kinnereth 2.788
Last Song, The 2.797
Last Will and Testament 2.800
L'chayim, Rebbe! 2.835
Levi Yitschok's Kaddish 2.840
Lord Has Not Revealed, The 2.730
Lord, Hele Me, Y-wis I Shal Be Heled 2.769
Lovely Am I, O Lovely, and Lovely Is My Name 2.834
Make Blind, O Sun of Jerusalem 2.780
Miracles and Wonders 2.859
M'laveh Malkeh 2.841
Mother Jerusalem 2.778
My Noddle It Is Humming 2.854
Myerka, My Son 2.838
No More Tears 2.802
Now Such Am I ... 2.787
O Dove beside the Water Brook 2.771
O Heighte Sovereign, O Worldes Prys 2.772
O My Mother Sent Me 2.828
O Site Most Kingly, O Royal Sanctum 2.724
O There, O There, Where Is Our Holy Rebbe 2.842
O Thou Seer, Go Flee Thee – Away 2.756
O What Do You Wish, My Dearest Child 2.832

Ode to Zion 2.769
Of the Ancient House of the Clinii [Version 1] 2.866
Of the Ancient House of the Clinii [Version 2] 2.868
Old Gold 2.811
Omar Adoishem l'Ya-akoiv! 2.860
On My Returning 2.732
On the Attic Sleeps a Roof 2.819
On the Hill, over the Hill 2.829
Once upon a Time; This 2.826
Our Rebbe [Version 1] 2.853
Our Rebbe [Version 2] 2.854
Our Rebbe, the Miracle-Worker, Once 2.851
Oy, Our Rebbenu 2.836
Oy, Vey, Rebbenu 2.850
Portrait of the Artist 2.795
Prayer of a Physician, The 2.790
Prescription, The 2.765
Rachel 2.787
Reb Zorach 2.812
Rebbe Elimelech, The 2.862
Rebbe, He Wanted, The [Version 1] 2.844
Rebbe, He Wanted, The [Version 2] 2.845
Rebbele, the Gabbai'le, the Cantor'l, the Shamash'l, The 2.857
Rubaiyat of Yehuda Halevi 2.773
Sabbath 2.785
Seer, Begone 2.755
Shall I Be a Rabbi? 2.816
Smoke 2.794
Song 2.813
Song of Wine 2.822
Speak to Your People, Therefore, in This Wise 2.815
Spirit Passed before Me, A 2.761
Stars Flicker and Fall in the Sky 2.764
Sunset 2.804
Tear Not Your Hair, My Sweetheart 2.818
Tell Me, Pretty Maiden, O Hearken Pretty Maiden 2.833
Tell Us, Rebbenu 2.849
Thou Hast Chosen Us 2.842
Thou Song, A 2.839
Thy Breath, O Lord, Passed Over and Enkindled Me 2.760
To Jerusalem the Holy 2.768
To L. Munatius Plancus 2.871

1097 / Index of Titles

To Leuconoe 2.870
To Lydia 2.869
Train, The 2.855
Tsig, Tsigitsapel 2.858
Unfavoured 2.786
Upon the Highway 2.776
Upon the Slaughter 2.763
Vesomachto 2.865
War 2.814
We Are a Generation, Heaven-Doomed 2.800
We Ask Our Boarding-Mistress 2.822
What Is Loftier than a House? 2.833
When He Has Frolicked for a Little 2.834
When I Knead the Dough 2.825
When the Days Shall Grow Long 2.757
Where Our Good Rebbe Is to Be Found 2.843
Windows Are Grated, The 2.803
Wine 2.766
With Every Stone 2.781
Word, The 2.759
Yoma, Yoma, Play Me a Ditty 2.820
Yonder! Yonder! 2.864
Yoshka, Yoshka 2.850
You Walk upon Your Sunlit Roads 2.801

Index of First Lines

ORIGINAL POEMS

A field in sunshine is a field 1.312
A fox 1.97
A goat a scholar, 1.275
A grotesque gargoyle on a grey 1.100
A little Jew lived in a little straw hut; 1.283
A microbe sewed his lips, this monger 1.42
A prowler in the mansion of my blood! 2.510
A shirt! a shirt! a kingdom for a shirt! 2.469
A song for hunters: In that wood, 2.505
A tradesman Getzel Gelt would be. 1.295
A whole long week it rained; and were it not 1.101
About the Crematorium where the Jews 2.678
Across my bed-room window pass 1.120
Age draws his fingernail across my brow. 1.221
Agnostic, he would never tire 1.134
Ah, Solomon, you sage who knew the language 1.176
Aleph, Bais, 1.240
All day the crows cracked sky-clefts with their caws. 1.90
All flowers that in seven ways bright 2.714
All he muttered was the same, 1.42
All honour to the memory of Alexander Graham Bell! 2.715
All week his figure mottles 1.138
All worship is doomed to schisms, heresies, 2.712
Amber opaque are autumn skies – 1.128
Among the penny arcades and the dime shows, 2.684
An aged king, his brittle shins in hose, 2.486
An ant shouldering a light straw; 1.246
And after I have slept for many a year 1.126

And all was void; and Spring sprang in undrest, 1.7
And as the orators, rewarded roars, scored, soared, bored – 2.678
And for the sake of you I am become 1.93
And in that drowning instant as 2.608
And now the smiles fall to the floor 2.712
And on that day, upon the heavenly scarp, 2.530
And these touched thunders, this delyredrum 2.543
And they have torn their garments; and have turned 1.80
And though I do not love you any more 1.99
And when he mentioned showers 1.87
And when they brought him back 2.701
And yet the doubt is hither-thither cast – 1.75
Another moon, and the penitential days 2.613
At length, the peasant, plodding from the woods, 2.542
At times, sensing that the golgotha'd dead 2.663
At unprehensile Time, all fingers clutch. 2.491
Autumn 1.206
Autumn 1.246
Autumn, you dement; you wrench from my throat 1.90
Avaunt the nightingale! Perish the rose! 1.168
Avrohom, Yitzchok, and Yaacov, patriarchs; 2.710
Baldhead! Baldhead! 1.280
Bannered, and ranked, and at its stances fixed 2.691
Bard, paying your rental of the ivory tower, 2.468
Be his memory forever green and rich, 1.311
Because the Lord was good to me, and gave 1.103
Because to Him in prayershawl, he prays, 1.236
'Behold the dreamer cometh!' ... They beheld 1.72
Behold the months each in their season: 1.305
Beneath this fretted roof, the knave, swag-bellied, 1.236
Betray me not. Treat me as scurvily 1.220
Between distorted forests, clapped into geometry, 2.694
Beware, – spiritual humankind, – 2.467
Big-bellied dewlapt grand vacuity ... 1.117
Black crows are pecking at the carrion 1.63
Blasé nihilities encompass me, 1.40
Blessed art thou, O Lord, 2.706
Blessed the men this day, 1.233
Booted and armed, the frontier guard 2.536
Bring on the rich, the golden-dotted soup; 1.173
Brown are your eyes, as brown as the gazelle's, 1.155
Bundled their bones, upon the ninetynine stairs – 2.647

1101 / Index of First Lines

By the rivers of Babylon, there we sat down, we wept 2.522
Chivalric more than knight on charger black; 1.305
Christ is risen from the tomb ... 1.45
City of Toulouse, reign of King Philip: 1.181
Clients of Barnum, yours no even break! 2.465
Communists ask for more bank holidays. 1.232
Compute the plagues, your little finger dip 1.129
Concerning four strange sons, the Torah wrote: 1.291
Consider my speech, O Lord, not too severely; 2.508
Consider the son of man, how he doth get him knowledge and 2.520
Consider, then, the miracle you wrought. 1.226
Consider this creature, its peculiar pride, 2.510
Creation's crust and crumb, breaking of bread, 2.617
Cupid in a caftan 1.136
Dark Cleopatra on a gilded couch 1.94
Dawn! and I feel the light 1.97
Dead heroes ride the chariots of the wind; 1.77
Death, the peddler, came to my door this day. 2.521
Defeated 2.709
Dispose of every sting with some safe gnome 1.85
Divinely he sang the scriptured note; 1.137
Dizzy amidst a whorl of fingerprints; 2.461
Do you but say the word, and I will come, 1.101
Do you go to Venus, Love, 1.91
Does an owl appreciate 1.245
Dropped privily below the crotch of squares – 2.627
Elder, behold the Shunamite, the rumour of her face, 2.525
Elijah in a long beard 1.202
Emmerich, Count, of the stentorious voice 1.265
Enamort have I been of bleaseful Death, 2.579
Erudite, solemn, 1.306
Eternity is caught in this dead room. 1.29
Even if in the gutter you were lying dying of thirst 2.708
Even if your heart were stone, 1.89
Even in July it is our winter corner, 2.649
Evenings, they walk arm in arm, in pairs, – 2.683
Every burgher is a feaster; 1.64
Fat grows Stanislaus, *Pan*, whose 1.156
Fill the silver goblet; 1.130
First, the two older ones, the bunkhouse brawnymen, 2.642
Flaunting their canes, their jaunty berets, the students throng 2.697
Flowering jungle, where all fauna meet 2.618

Footsteps are bringing beauty hither. She 1.74
For him to write a poem was to parse 1.120
For that he gave to the stone understanding to understand direction. 2.704
From beautiful dreams I rise; I rise from dreams 1.227
From crater of heart did there rise up a flame-tongue 1.5
From library to library I go – 2.570
From pastures green, whereon I lie, 2.513
From the fjord faring, striding the stream, 2.629
Geographers may mark Prague on the map 1.187
Go catch the echoes of the ticks of time; 2.488
God breathe a blessing on 1.282
God is grown ancient. He no longer hears. 1.198
Good friend, for Jesu's sake, forbear 2.626
Gown'd in ghostly mistiness, she stalks ... 1.121
Guerdon for wit is lavished in the realm; 2.487
Hard to be a Jew? 2.712
He gayly jaunted down the street, 1.42
He is a learned man, adept 1.134
He jaunted down the busy shopping street in natty style, 1.93
He lifts his middle-aged cabby-face from roots, 2.671
He quoted *midrash* and the psalms; 1.151
He reverenced no idol, nor of gold, 1.35
He stuttered when he spoke, and then 1.39
Heaven is God's grimace at us on high. 1.200
Heigh ho! the rooster crows! 1.279
Heigh-nonny-no! 1.275
Heil heavenly muse, since also thou must be 2.581
Here in a sudden meadow dropped amongst brick 2.672
Here lies a lawyer turbulent 1.37
Here they are – all those sunny April days! 1.215
His greeting is of the faith, like the muezzin's. 2.716
His mother's bribes, 1.247
His pillow knew all that he sigh'd; 1.41
His squinted eyes at strife, 1.41
His voice may tear the sky to shreds, 1.204
His was an open heart, a lavish hand, 1.139
Ho, maskers, fix your noses, strike a posture, 1.239
Holy, holy, holy, 2.459
Hormisdas Arcand, about to found a new party 2.681
How came this spectacled, this little Jew, 1.44
How have you become not that which once you were, 2.461
How is he changed, the scoffers say, 2.506

Index of First Lines

How lividly he looks, obliviously! ... 1.35
How pleasant are the times and their cezannes, 2.624
How private and comfortable it once was, 2.646
How sweetly did he sing grace after meals! 1.201
How was I to know, those months in my mother's womb, 2.716
How will you phrase regret when I depart, 1.170
However, for bread and the occasional show, 2.640
I am no brazen face to hale the Lord 1.272
I am no contradictor of Cabbala: 2.569
I am not of the saints, O Lord, to wear 2.517
I eat; the ladle does not leave the bowl. 1.102
I have seen a lark 1.246
I must write my love a poem ... 1.94
I remember Summer by some symbols: 1.31
I remember the old Coltoon, circumciser, in action. 2.709
I said: Autumn 1.245
I said in my heart: 'I shall not love her more. 1.30
I shall no more complain; I shall not ask 2.517
I shall not bear much burden when I cross 1.228
'I think I hear a trumpet overhead. 1.239
I who have expiated life in cities, 2.511
I will make a song for you, 1.74
I will make him a little red sack 1.297
I would be happy if the Winter thawed, 1.87
I would not tell this to the man met on the street, 2.508
If ever I should love I would not pine 1.62
If golem is the effigy of man, 1.186
If I were Jove, I would gloat humouredly 1.112
If so, 1.75
If we will fast for forty days; if we 1.199
If you are joyous now, omit 1.79
If you would snare your lover, mesh 1.85
Impudent female! salvaged none knows whence; 2.668
In back-room dens of delicatessen stores, 1.183
In his wandered wharf on the brake side of the lake; 2.679
In one-armed restaurants where Cretan floors 1.235
In pairs, 2.648
In the fair summer-time when the ether doth quiver 1.3
In these prosaic days when lovers ask 1.151
Instructions to the stenographer: 2.453
Into his beard he laughs at the 1.292
Is this your Canadian poet, with the foreign name? 2.631

It being no longer Sabbath, angels scrawl 1.213
It is an enchanted palace 1.307
It is to be wondered whether he ever really 2.655
It seconds the crickets of the province. Heard 2.644
It was a green, a many-meadowed county! 2.489
Jonah Katz 1.299
Judith had heard a troubadour 1.199
Kind you may be at least when I am dead, 1.27
Kind you may be at least when I am dead, 1.27
King Dalfin sat on his throne, the size of a thimble, 1.300
King Elimelech – 1.205
Koheleth, on his damasked throne, lets weary exhalation follow 1.132
La chair est triste, hélas, et j'ai lu tous les livres. 1.237
Lead me to the mountain-top. 1.119
Lest grief clean out the sockets of your eyes, 1.142
Let me recall. What was that ancient night 1.100
Let me sink into a southern sea, 1.26
Let the blank whiteness of this page be snow 2.682
Let the storm rage; 1.68
Let them pronounce me sentimental. I 1.227
Liveth the tale, nor ever shall it die! 2.544
Look not askance, O Love, upon these gifts; 1.92
Loosen the drawbridge, men! I am pursued! 1.224
Loosen the tangles of the dark, 2.542
Lord, for the days allotted me, 2.526
Love is an ache 1.76
Love is become a memory, 1.75
Love, love, love, 2.573
M. le juge Dupré has all the qualities. 2.687
Madame, I see that you have indeed considered the ant, 2.716
Magic and strife and crapulence 1.125
Manikin, manikin, in your chair, 2.534
May none be called to visit this grim house, 2.575
May the sun wash your eyes; may you 1.277
Milady Schwartz, beloved of the boss, 1.234
Mr. Lowell Levy, finds it difficult to distinguish 2.666
Mud and mire of Moldau, that was the sperm 1.188
Muffle the wind; 1.114
My blood shouts very joyous news 1.73
My dear plutophilanthropist, 2.574
My father bequeathed me no wide estates; 1.298
My literati friends in restaurants – 1.228

My suite is like a violin, so full 2.630
Named for my father's father, cousin, whose cry 2.673
Neither on death, nor at the blazing sun 2.623
Never let me behold her so again ... 1.81
Next to the *curé*, he is hierarch, 2.656
Nigh Lebanon, nigh lofty Lebanon, 1.253
No churl am I to carp at the goodly feres 1.191
No cock rings matins of the dawn for me; 1.231
No man is there but walks his long last mile; 2.557
No man is there but walks his long last mile; 2.559
No Melchizedek Parchment-Parched am I 1.193
No pulpit talk in ale-houses; no sermons 1.267
Nonetheless Ali Baba had no richer cave, 2.659
Not an editorial-writer, bereaved with bartlett, 2.634
Not from a hermit's grotto, nor monk's cell 1.222
Not sole was I born, but entire genesis: 2.624
Now finally, by way of corrigendum: 2.462
Now, in this terrible tumultuous night, 2.512
Now she awaits me at this time we made – 1.74
Now that the guards, in homage to our Lord, unbarred the 1.274
Now we will suffer loss of memory; 1.168
Now we will suffer loss of memory: 1.169
Nuremberg tower-clock struck one: 2.537
O bridegroom eager for the bride, 1.172
O city metropole, isle riverain! 2.621
O incognito god, anonymous lord, 2.519
O Lord, open thou my lips; and my mouth shall declare 2.704
O, not for furs, 1.303
O poet of the removeable glass eye – 2.709
O rooster, circled over my brother's head, 1.179
O sign and wonder of the barnyard, more 2.518
O the days of the Messiah are at hand, are at hand! 2.533
O think, my Love, of what we two will be 1.174
O tribune, tribune manqué, passed over in favour 2.717
O weep your tears, you crocodiles! the great 1.43
'O what can ail thee, flashy sheik, 1.37
O, what human chaff! 1.96
O what is Helen, what is Guinevere 1.126
O what would David say, 1.138
O, when they laved my uncle's limbs 1.264
Of scabrous heart and of deportment sleek, 1.72
Of trope of testament and Caesar's wars 2.615

Of yore yclept in old Judaea *Zvi*; 2.475
Of yore yclept in old Judaea *Zvi*; 2.480
Oh Autumn will come all too soon this year, 1.99
Oh, but in France they arrange these things much better! 2.651
On a little brown pony, a little boy rides 1.250
On bane big-bellied mothers feed; 1.265
On leather, beneath rafters, beside oak, 2.620
On the school platform, draping the folding seats, 2.657
On Wodin's day, sixth of December, thirty-nine, 2.493
On Wodin's day, sixth of December, thirty-nine, 2.498
Once in a year this comes to pass: 1.129
Once upon a time, in a land far far away, a marvellous 1.294
One comes: – he is a very blossoming tree – 2.509
One day the signal shall be given me; 2.516
Orange, citron, fig and date, 1.250
Orchids of music flutter from the keys. 2.665
Out of a pit of perpendiculars 1.115
Out of the ghetto streets where a Jewboy 2.564
Out of the yesterday, and ages gone 2.567
Pharaoh was plagued with lice and frogs, 1.313
Pity who wear the castoffs of the years, 2.619
Plump pigeons, who will buy? 1.176
Poltroons may fear the foeman, for such are less than cattle, 2.532
Prepare the inks, the red, the green, the black; 1.170
Prince Shlemozzle 1.302
Privy to the Eleusinian mysteries 2.711
Quails before manna? 2.713
Queen Esther is out walking in the garden, 1.34
Rather than have my brethren bend the knee 1.241
Rather than have my brethren bend the knee 1.242
Rather that these blood-thirsty pious vandals, 1.199
Reb Abraham, the jolly, 1.134
Reb Levi Yitschok, crony of the Lord, 1.243
Reb Zadoc's brain is a German town: 1.196
Remembering boyhood, it is always here 2.686
Rich and remote in panelled offices 2.666
Sacred enough you are. 1.120
Scars carved crescents 1.285
Seeing that planets move by dynamos, 2.467
Seeing three on the left side, and on the right three, 2.708
Seek reasons; rifle your theology; 1.198
Set in the jeweled fore-part of his crown 1.33

1107 / Index of First Lines

Seventy regal moons, with clouds as train, 1.218
Shall he be sat on a wired electrical seat 2.629
She has laved her body in living water. She 1.172
Since motion was, there has been no such dance! 2.631
Since prophecy has vanished out of Israel, 2.527
Sleep, hungry child, within your crib. 1.301
Slowly, and flake by flake ... At the drifted frond 2.698
Smile never on the ugly ones; 2.711
'So have I spent a life-time in my search 1.241
Soft pious whisperings are drown'd 1.28
Solve me this riddle: Rumours are bruited 1.188
Somewhere a hungry muzzle rooted. 1.195
Somewhere above the innocent clouds there flies 2.578
Spare me, O Lord, if you will spare 1.83
Speak me no deaths. Prevent that word from me. 1.221
Spit spittle on the rose? fling gravel at 1.271
Starved, scarred, lenten, amidst ash of air, 2.653
Striking the melancholy attitudes 1.80
Strolling the Champs Elysée 2.713
Summer had raised herself 1.246
Sybarite though I be, I shall not rest 1.125
That man is too good: suspect his motives; 2.712
The ants repair to cooler galleries; 1.124
The badge of yellow scorn upon his chest, 1.179
The bat beats uncouth wings on mildewed rafters, 1.113
The beauty that my love wore all the seven 1.74
The benison of health will yet be theirs! 1.281
The better to understand Thy ways, 2.531
The birds twitter, excited, behind their copper wires. 2.713
The black phylacteries about his arm 1.213
The blue sea laps the Lesbian rock; 1.123
The candles splutter; and the kettle hums; 1.131
The carefully-evolved and cultured tribes 2.577
The chamberlain burst on the royal feast 1.34
The coffin-board has now been planed; 1.150
The crow upon the hawthorn bush 1.82
The famished one lies down to sleep, and dreams 1.307
The following are the proper instruments wherewith Haman 2.707
The great tycoon is dead. 2.716
The idealist 2.709
The incense, rising, curls the nostrils with its scent: 1.177
The inverted funnel pouring its light like alcohol 2.669

The jolly icicles ringing in their throats, 2.652
The judges sat in their blood-red robes, 2.539
The law is certain; and the law is clear. 2.460
The leper counts his sores; 1.249
The man said nothing, nothing at all, but sat 2.713
This mirror libels me, and cavils at 1.103
The mole can burrow through the brain, 1.302
The moon 1.191
The moon in his head was a strain. 1.42
The moon is a golden hoop 1.75
The music of what sphere? 2.711
The nightingale proclaims no creed; 1.140
The noble Antony 2.708
The nozzle of the earthworm meets 1.122
The old Jews greet the moon 1.174
The old maids think of couches cold i' the moon; 1.178
The paleface mutters: Lord God is a myth; 1.189
The panic jangles repeated themselves every year. 2.661
The paunchy sons of Abraham 1.208
The pigeons coo among the eaves, 1.303
The pimp, he pays his fine and costs, 2.460
The planetary motion of the blood, 2.568
The prince to the princess in the fairy-tale, 1.216
The prisoner confessed most willingly. 2.459
The royal wrapping of your poem embrace 1.6
The sea clutches her hair in grief, 1.96
The *shamash* of the glade, 1.314
The ship leaves Jaffa, treasure in its hold: 1.76
The sky is dotted like th' unleavened bread, 1.128
The snow-flaked crystal stars fall fast – 1.67
The soul of a squirrel 1.98
The stone slabs of milady's walks 1.122
The street is great festivity; 1.73
The sun goes down, and slowly there appears 1.89
The thin and delicate etching of Jack Frost 1.123
The time has come; the brooks begin to break 1.25
The toad seeks out its mud; the mouse discovers 1.197
The tongue has faltered. Hence, revoked the demons, 1.204
The town fool sat on the top o' the roof, 1.308
The two false coins in my copper pot 1.91
The two shawl-covered grannies, buying fish, 1.149
The word of grace is flung from foreign thrones 1.147

1109 / Index of First Lines

The worm doth make the earth a labyrinth 1.167
The wrath of God is just. His punishment 1.197
The young men with the sparse beards laud the bride; 1.171
There lies a corpse upon your memory, plus 1.81
There was a Jewish bandit who lived in a wood, 1.230
There was a mad monarch 1.290
There was a youth in Nazareth, 1.114
There's not a man but must at last go up 2.561
These be repasts lethean of your kind: 2.469
These northern stars are scarabs in my eyes. 1.223
These robbers filched electricity: 2.459
These were but innuendo: 2.700
These were the ones who thanked their God 2.523
They are upon us, the prophets, minor and major! 2.524
They do lie heavily upon me, these 2.466
They quacked and they cackled, 1.284
They smote us hip and thigh; 2.712
They suck and whisper it in mercury, 2.646
Think not, my dear, because I do not call 1.217
This globe, this world, this onion of humanity! 2.716
This is a curious plot 1.130
This is a tale of a deed of daring: 1.292
This is the bread of our affliction, this 1.129
This is the golem. 2.572
This is the man who brought to me 1.181
This is the seventh time this week 1.86
This is too terrible a season! Worms 1.218
This last July a crazy caterpillar 1.245
This last week I have shunned mortality; 1.79
This little Jew 1.139
This mirror libels me, and cavils at 1.103
This spinster neither spins 2.710
This, then, is over ... I will take each paper 1.98
This wrist 1.5
Thou dost not know thy deeds, O Job, when thou 1.153
Thou settest them about my bed, 2.515
Thou wast not born to live thy life on earth – 1.4
Three things I long to see: 1.230
Three werewolves on a deadman's chest! 2.541
Throwback and atavism of Mizraim: 2.710
'Tis very well to parrot the nightingale, 1.222
To sleep, perchance to dream. Where there is smoke 1.189

To the perfume that the rose dreams of, 2.710
Twilight is about to come. 1.178
Twist each side-curl; form the symbol 1.148
Under a humble name he came to us; 1.175
Undoubtedly terror may through the widened eyes 2.610
Undoubtedly terror may through the widened eyes 2.611
Unfurl the scarlet banner, Toreador, 2.474
Unsheathe the blade; transgress your nail 1.270
Until a wiser method entered my 1.113
Unworthiest crony of my grammar days, 2.473
Unworthy even to utter His slightest name, 1.315
Up from the low-roofed dockyard warehouses 2.650
Upon a day, and after the roar had died, 2.538
Upon a time there lived a dwarf, a Jew. 1.224
Upon the ecstatic diving board the diver, 2.685
Upon the piazza, haemophilic dons 2.474
Upon the road to Palestine 1.207
Upon these trees was Autumn crucified ... 1.195
Was it not kindled a million years ago 2.528
We, the undersigned 2.607
Well may they thank thee, Lord, for drink and food: 2.505
Were I to talk until the crack o' doom, 1.229
What a piece of work is man! the paragon 1.232
What does the word mean: *Violence?* 2.463
What is this seasonal nonentity? 1.32
... *What men or gods are these? What maidens loth?* 2.571
What scrofulous ashes upon sack-cloth, what 1.187
What shall I say to you in that grim hour? 1.83
What toys shall I buy my little lad? 1.278
What was the song the gypsy sang 2.528
'What wit, what wonder, winged words work!' 2.711
When fishes soared, and forests danced, 1.36
When I in prayer beseech thy benison, 2.521
When, on the frustral summit of *extase,* 2.645
When Sire Alexandre Grandmaison, Seigneur of Biche, 2.696
When will there be another such brain? 1.137
When you will read this then-archaic rune 1.118
Whenever he wanted some sleep 1.41
Where are the braves, the faces like autumn fruit, 2.641
Where now that tree is, they say, once a man 1.118
Where once the butterfly was seen 1.95
Where shall I find choice words to mention Sorrow 1.82

1111 / Index of First Lines

Where will you be 2.464
Wherefore, upon the twenty-seventh May, ten hundred 1.267
Who can fail to admire the 2.711
Who coming from the synagogue 1.180
Who envies not this beggar, who 1.309
Who has not heard of Blanche the beautiful, 1.104
Who knows it only by the famous cross which bleeds 2.689
Who remembers not this eminently capable man, 2.458
Why do you love me, as you say you do, 1.216
'Why do you set the candlesticks, 1.269
Winter has said what it has said: 1.127
Wishing to embarrass me, but politely, 2.669
With my own eyes I saw it, I who loved my father 2.628
With snakes of rubber and glass thorax, 2.680
Within my iron days, my nights of stone, 1.225
Within the meadow on the mountain-top 1.238
Within the whale's belly 1.251
Without your love, without your love for me, 1.225
Would that the Lord had made me, in place of man-child, beast! 2.514
Would that three centuries past had seen us born! 1.219
Would that three centuries past had seen us born! 1.219
Yes yeasts to No, and No is numinous with Yes. All is 2.662
You can find it only in attics or in ads, 2.660
You cherished them as ancient gems, those tears 1.77
You fear me; and with good reason. 2.713
You have excelled yourself, cher maitre! 2.632
You remember the big Gaston, for whom everyone predicted 2.688
You, Tillie the Toiler and Winnie the Worker, consider 2.470
You well deserve my complimental gesture 1.88

TRANSLATIONS

A curious thought: As I gaze on my pen, 2.799
A ghost of stubble, a leaf that flutters 2.732
A jug of water in the hand, and on 2.789
A spirit passed before my face, it dazzled me; for an 2.761
Akavyah ben M'halallel sayeth: 2.860
And at my prayers I will quiver, 2.830
And do you rejoice upon your feast-day, 2.865
And it shall come to pass when the days shall grow long 2.757
And this I know: It is a devil's play, 2.804

And when Messiah will come 2.831
And when one burns – one burns brandy, 2.819
And when our Rebbe walks, 2.852
Arise, and go now – go to the city of slaughter! 2.744
Arise and go now to the city of slaughter; 2.733
Asks the world an old, old question: 2.831
At last I tore me from their fetters; 2.805
At my Rebbe's, there did happen, there did happen 2.848
Bar Yochai, Bar Yochai, Bar Yochai, 2.862
Be there no altar, then upon high places 2.780
Bear thou, O wind, my love 2.768
Behold my country – the carcass of a savage, 2.784
Beneath the burden of your love, 2.725
Better a Hebrew teacher 2.827
Beyond the farthest oceans 2.807
Come, gird ye your loins, and in might robe yourselves! 2.727
Come you here, philosopher, 2.817
Cry, Muppim and Huppim! Strike blows on your drums! 2.752
Even as a great country withers, and goes to rot, 2.811
Fling, O prophet, the coal of fire from thine altar; 2.759
'Fly! Run away!' Not such as I do run. 2.756
Flying he comes, the little dwarf Ki-Ki 2.797
For whom am I these things recounting? 2.809
From a foreign land has fluttered hither 2.824
From him whom Love's sweet anguish now destroys, 2.773
Gewald! Gewald! Gewald! Gewald! Gewald! 2.836
God willing, after Sabbath 2.855
Gone is the yesterday 2.829
Good liquor, prized and ever unshent, 2.822
Good morning to you, Reboinoi shel Olam! 2.840
Grieving for them, thy captive sons who are 2.769
Heavenly spheres, beg mercy for me! 2.763
Her blood flows in my blood; 2.787
Hush! Hush! let a silence fall 2.821
I am not favoured with the arms 2.786
I go upon the balcony 2.825
I have left my comrades, and the four ells of my youth I have 2.778
I know the path of camels in the sand; 2.776
I sit me down upon a stone; 2.835
In God's good time, and the Messiah appearing 2.847
In sooth, what savoure hath now food for me? 2.768

It may be these things never did occur. 2.788
L'chayim, Rebbe! A happy week to you! 2.835
Let the Bureaux de Tourisme and Chambers of Commerce 2.871
Like an arrow shot 2.766
Little goat, little colt, pussy-cat, 2.818
Lord, hele me, y-wis I shal be heled! 2.769
Lovely am I, O lovely, and lovely is my name; 2.834
Make blind, O Sun of Jerusalem, and shrivel 2.780
Meek of the earth, humble in wit and works, 2.728
Muppim and Huppim! Strike blows on your drums! 2.749
My noddle it is humming 2.854
Myerka, my son, Myerka, my son, O Myerka, my son – 2.838
Neither in the dreams of my nights has the Lord revealed 2.730
Not Abraham did this altar build; 2.792
Now such am I; as quiet 2.787
O, brother, say, 2.841
O do you know the land where the citron's growing 2.864
O dove beside the water brook 2.771
O heighte sovereign, O worldes prys 2.772
O my mother sent me 2.828
O site most kingly, O royal sanctum, 2.724
O there, O there, where is our holy Rebbe 2.842
O there, O there, where our good Rebbe is to be found, 2.843
O what do you wish, my dearest child, 2.832
Of the ancient house of the Clinii, prince, 2.866
Of the ancient house of the Clinii, prince, 2.868
On the attic sleeps a roof, 2.819
On the hill, over the hill 2.829
Once upon a time; this 2.826
Our Rebbe, he went forth into the desert 2.854
Our Rebbe, the Miracle-Worker, once 2.851
Our Rebbe went into the desert 2.853
Oy, our Rebbenu! *Gewald*, our Rebbenu! 2.836
Oy, vey, Rebbenu 2.850
Rabbi Joshua ben Chananya polishes needles, 2.812
Rabosai, Rabosai, scholars for this task: 2.856
Reboinoi shel Olam 2.839
Said the Lord, the Lord, to Jacob – 2.860
Sanct and exaltate 2.721
Sanct and exaltate in the world which to his will he 2.722
'Seer, begone!' One of my kind flees not! 2.755

Set me in breaches of the wall, with stone; 2.781
Shall I be a rabbi? 2.816
Since men ceased to put their faith in God, 2.797
Small frĕckles constellate my face; 2.795
Speak to your people, therefore, in this wise: 2.815
Stars flicker and fall in the sky, 2.764
Summoned to attend this beautiful lady, eight days ailing, 2.765
Tear not your hair, my sweetheart, 2.818
'Tell me, pretty maiden, O hearken pretty maiden 2.833
Tell us, Rebbenu! 2.849
The chastisement of God, is this His curse: 2.726
The funnels of the ship have ceased to smoke. 2.785
The Lord, He endowed him with herds and with flocks, 2.793
The moon set; the sky darkened; and the stars 2.782
The Rebbe comes, 2.859
The Rebbe, he wanted to go to the city 2.844
The Rebbe wished to journey up to the city, 2.845
The Rebbele, the Gabbai'le, the Cantor'l, the Shamash'l – 2.857
The sun goes down. 2.804
The sun will climb over and under the hill, 2.798
The windows are grated, 2.803
There are no more tears, 2.802
There lie two goats 2.806
They are still full of wrath, the many gods, 2.814
This is the one taboo – to think of to-morrow! 2.870
This song is greater than all others: 2.796
Thou hast chosen us from among all nations, 2.842
Thy breath, O Lord, passed over and enkindled me. 2.760
To a king who had 2.808
To Thee, O great Arcane, 2.790
Up from the chimney of the crematory 2.794
We are a generation, heaven-doomed, 2.800
We ask our boarding-mistress – 2.822
What have you done to the man, Lydia? What kind of love is it 2.869
What is loftier than a house? 2.833
What is the crown of kings, and what the glory 2.777
When he has frolicked for a little 2.834
When I knead the dough 2.825
When I will die, then let my hearse 2.800
When our Rebbe Elimelech 2.862
Who maketh a statement, he, he must prove it! 2.858
World, I would take and lift thee up – 2.813

Would that I had a little boy, 2.789
Yoma, Yoma, play me a ditty, 2.820
Yoshka, Yoshka, harness the horse, and 2.850
You walk upon your sunlit roads 2.801